RAIL VENTURES

SEVENTH EDITION

TRAVIS ILSE
PUBLISHERS

POST OFFICE BOX 583
NIWOT, COLORADO 80544

EDITED BY: Jack Swanson

AUTHORS: Jack Swanson, Jeff Karsh

CONTRIBUTING WRITERS:
Den Adler
Pere Marquette, Lake Cities and portions of Cardinal, Empire Builder,
Lake Shore Limited and Algoma Central
Ted Scull
Portions of Northeast Corridor

COPY EDITOR: Doris Swanson
CARTOGRAPHY: Jim Swanson
COVER PHOTO: Courtesy of Amtrak
PRODUCTION: Argent Associates, Boulder, Colorado
PRINTED BY: Data Reproductions Corp., Rochester Hills, Michigan

Seventh Edition, August 1996

Manufactured in the United States of America

Copyright © 1982, 1985, 1988, 1990, 1992, 1995, and 1996 by Jack Swanson.

ISBN 1-882092-18-X

Printed in the United States of America

A B C D E F 0 5 4 3 2 1

Distributed to the trade by
PUBLISHERS GROUP WEST

Contents

Passenger Train
Routes in the U.S.

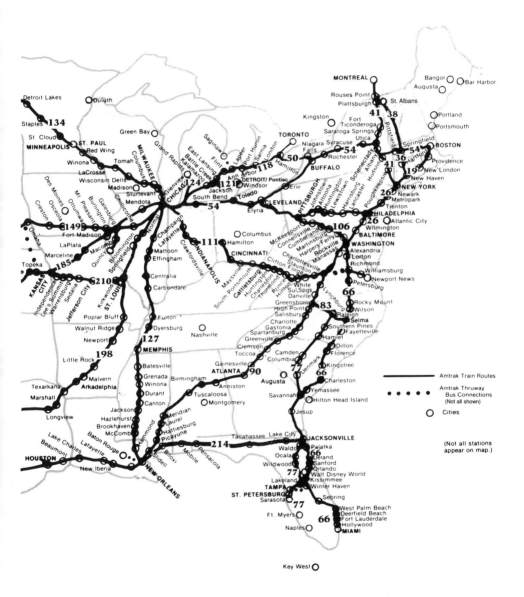

5

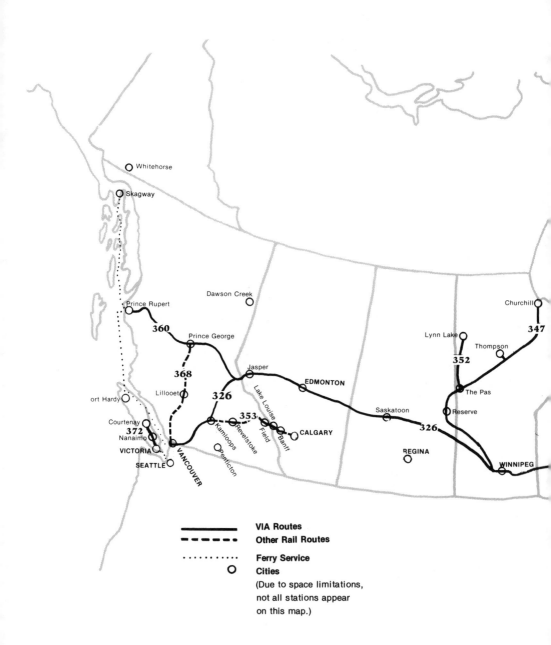

Whitehorse

Skagway

Dawson Creek

Churchill

Prince Rupert

360

Prince George

347

Lynn Lake

Thompson

352

368

Jasper

EDMONTON

The Pas

ort Hardy

Lillooet

326

Lake Louise

Saskatoon

Reserve

Courtenay

353

Revelstoke

Field

326

372

Kamloops

Banff

CALGARY

Nanaimo

VICTORIA

VANCOUVER

Penticton

REGINA

WINNIPEG

SEATTLE

———————— **VIA Routes**

– – – – – – **Other Rail Routes**

· · · · · · · · · · **Ferry Service**

O **Cities**

(Due to space limitations,
not all stations appear
on this map.)

Passenger Train
Routes in Canada

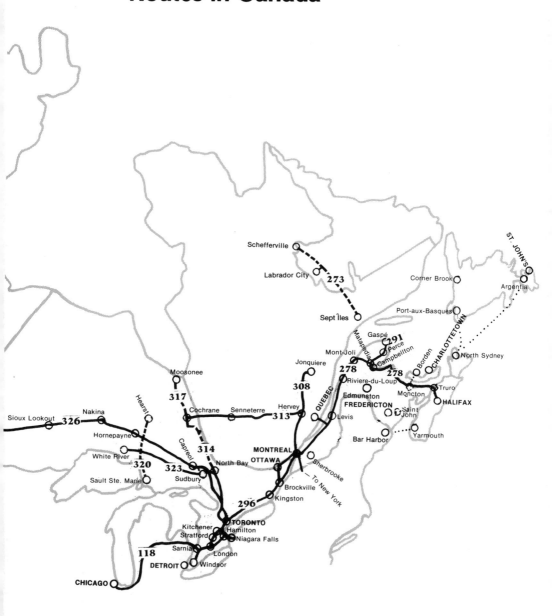

Sunset Ltd. — near Coolidge, AZ
JACK SWANSON

Welcome Aboard

TRAINS HAVE ALWAYS HAD A SPECIAL MYSTIQUE. Their overwhelming size, their sheer brute strength, their thunderous sounds of locomotion—all have contributed to the world's fascination with these mechanical wonders. To ride on a train has been the epitome of romantic adventure. Wonderful names such as *Empire Builder, Sunset Limited* and *California Zephyr* have added to the magic, and being immortalized in both song and legend has further assured a course bound for glory.

Today, it is still these nostalgic intangibles that fuel the modern iron horse. And across the years, one aspect has remained particularly constant, an aspect which this guidebook is specifically designed to enhance—the freedom to savor the sights of our great continent without the concerns or distractions found in all other forms of travel.

A steady stream of panoramas is limited only by our attention. Most certainly there are the soaring monarchs of the Canadian Rockies, the white sand beaches of Southern California and the foliage of a New England autumn to thrill our senses. But also there are the scenes which convey a sense of casual acquaintanceship with so many people and places along one's journey—the fastidiously sculpted woodpile, the backyard heap of time-worn appliances, the elderly couple tending their garden. Then there are the sounds, from the labored growl of a determined ascent ("I think I can..."), to the heroic arrival at the station across the pass ("I knew I could..."). These are joys reserved solely for the train passenger. No other conveyance affords the opportunity to absorb so much in such a relaxed state of mind.

North America's passenger rail network is an extensive one, serving nearly every major metropolis in the United States and Canada. One can board a train in Halifax, Nova Scotia, and traverse the continent to San Diego, California, without having to set foot outside a train station.

To be sure, trains will never whisk anyone from New York to San Francisco in a fraction of a day. They will and do, however, cradle the traveler on an overnight journey between Chicago and New Orleans and then bestow a relaxed and refreshed arrival in the very heart of the city. The ability to simply enjoy the aspect of getting there, the ease of movement in an uncrowded environment, the savoring of a meal while the countryside slips by—these are the experiences reserved exclusively for the rail traveler.

About This Guide

TRAVELING ON A TRAIN CAN BE AN ADVENTURE filled with enjoyment and excitement. Yet as with most pursuits, those who know the ropes can more readily savor such an experience. *Rail Ventures* wants you to have the "inside track," and is designed to better acquaint you with the special nuances inherent in rail travel.

FINDING THINGS IN THIS GUIDE

The guide is divided into two major travel sections: United States Rail Service and Canadian Rail Service. Each of these sections begins with general information about train travel in that particular country. Following this general information, the sections contain very extensive descriptions of the rail routes and the trains that use them. There is also some information for Mexico, limited to the popular Copper Canyon route.

At the front of the book, national rail maps display all routes and major stops. Routes on the maps are keyed to page numbers in the text where all the details for that route will be found. This is the quickest way to locate specific route information. There is also a detailed index at the back of the book for easy reference to any city, train or other subject in this guide. An appendix lists reservation and information phone numbers in the U.S. and Canada.

GETTING THERE

Besides comprehensive route descriptions, information for each long-distance train includes: services and accommodations on board, distance and time it takes to complete the entire route, and approximate arrival and departure times for selected cities. Arrival and departure times are not precise, but are given in general terms, such as: "Early Morning," "Late Afternoon," etc. in condensed schedules.

Obviously, when planning a trip it is important to verify exact times. See the general information section of the appropriate country for how to obtain current timetables.

VIEWING ALONG THE ROUTE

Rail Ventures provides a running description ("route log") of points of interest to be seen along each major route. The description of each point of interest begins with the approximate elapsed time in minutes since departing the last scheduled stop; i.e., 0:25 would be 25 minutes from the last scheduled stop while 1.25 would be one hour and 25 minutes. The name of each stop is shown in boldface and is preceded by a train stop symbol.

In most instances, route logs are presented from east to west or north to south. To use in reverse order, start at the end of the log and read the parenthetical times rather than the boldface. "Right" and "left" would be just the opposite and, of course, "depart" and "arrive" should be interchanged.

These logs are written in a succinct style to allow the reader to quickly determine what is being observed or what to watch for without distracting from the scene. These logs will not only help plan your next train trip but should also be a great travel companion—rather like adding sound to a silent movie.

WHAT TO DO WHEN YOU ARRIVE

Major cities and other destinations are covered in considerable detail. Included are some logical places to stay, some of the more interesting attractions (many within walking distance of the station), how to find other transportation (buses, cabs, rental cars, etc.), where you can obtain tourist information, where the stations are located and station services—redcaps, luggage carts, restaurants, etc. There are maps showing station and hotel locations and points of interest for many of these destinations.

ON-BOARD ACCOMMODATIONS

Since many readers have not traveled by train in recent years (if ever), an equipment chapter is included which describes the various types of passenger equipment (e.g. Amcoaches, Superliner Sleepers, etc.) giving an insight as to what to expect after boarding.

CITY ACCOMMODATIONS

The selection of hotels and motels in *Rail Ventures* is based on location, quality and reasonableness of rates—the latter, of course, being relative to each city. Location is usually within a mile of the station. If no hotels are near the station, then accommodations are included near some of the major attractions, usually in the central business district. Some bed and breakfasts have been shown since there is an increasing number of downtown B&Bs offering reasonable alternatives to high-priced hotels.

Unless otherwise noted, the rate shown for each establishment is the rack (regular) rate for the least expensive (standard) room for two people based on weekday rates recently in effect prior to this guide's publication date. Note that Canadian accommodation rates are shown in Canadian dollars which would translate into lower U.S. dollars.

It is almost always possible to avoid paying a metropolitan hotel's rack rate. Discounts are commonly given for business travel (corporate rates), seniors, AARP members, weekends (in larger cities but not for B&Bs), special promotions, etc. As a hotel manager once stated: "The more questions you ask, the lower the rate." Bear in mind, however, that any discount must be obtained at check-in or earlier. There are also "consolidator" discounts, clubs, discount reservation services, etc. And Amtrak has its own package offerings that include discounted hotel rates for train travelers. To obtain a booklet describing Amtrak package travel, call 1-800-USA-RAIL.

Toll-free reservation numbers (within the continental U.S.) for the following "chains" are not shown in the text and are listed here to avoid repetition:

Best Western	800-528-1234
Choice Hotels	800-228-5151
Days Inn	800-325-2525
Hampton Inn	800-HAMPTON
Hilton Hotels	800-445-8667
Holiday Inns	800-HOLIDAY

11

Hyatt Corp.	800-228-9000
Howard Johnson's	800-654-2000
LaQuinta Motor Inns	800-531-5900
Radisson Hotels	800-333-3333
Ramada Inns	800-272-6232
Sheraton	800-325-3535
Travelodge	800-255-3050

TAXIS

Taxis are generally available at the stations at train times in major cities. Cab phone numbers are given in this guide in case it is necessary to call.

ABOUT MEXICO

Except for the spectacular Copper Canyon, Mexico is no longer covered by this book. Deteriorating service and equipment has led to this discontinuance.

SYMBOLS

 A scheduled train stop.

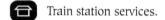 Train station services.

 Visitors information center.

 Other available transportation.

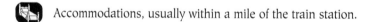 Accommodations, usually within a mile of the train station.

 Some major attractions.

Train enters a different time zone.

A WORD OF CAUTION

The train schedules, fares and routes shown in this guide, as well as accommodation information, are always subject to change at any time. Be sure to ascertain current schedule, fare and accommodation information before starting your trip. City maps are designed to show locations of stations, hotels, attractions, etc. and are not always drawn to scale. Streets may be omitted for simplification.

United States Rail Service

A fter World War II, two events almost spelled the demise of rail service in the United States—the "taking off" of the airlines and the invention of the Interstate Highway. To thwart disaster, Congress in 1970 came up with a legislative solution known as Amtrak (The National Railroad Passenger Corporation). The idea was to relieve the nation's railroads from operating their unprofitable passenger trains and to turn these trains into a viable form of transportation.

After more than two decades of effort, today's trains are modern, comfortable and attractive. On-board personnel are a far cry from those uniformed curmudgeons of postwar days. The food is quite good in full-service dining cars with meals, wake-up coffee and orange juice as well as newspapers included with bedroom fares. And there are even movies and other entertainment on many of the long-distance trains.

Reservations - Reservations can be made at any Amtrak ticket office, travel agent, or by calling Amtrak's toll-free reservation number, 800-USA-RAIL. (Local numbers may sometimes be used and are shown in the Appendix and in the station information for certain cities.) If reservations are made by phone sufficiently in advance Amtrak will mail tickets and bill the customer. If time is short, usually three weeks or less, you will be given a specific time within which you must purchase your tickets, either from a ticket office or authorized travel agent. If tickets are not purchased by that date, your reservations will be canceled. A computer-furnished reservations number is assigned when reservations are made, and it is important to retain this number for future reference in obtaining tickets or changing reservations. If your travel plans change, sleeping car reservations should be canceled at least 24 hours before train time to obtain a refund of accommodation charges. Club Service seating should be canceled at least one hour before departure.

If you are handicapped or aged 62 or older and prefer to sit in the lower level of the Superliner cars, specify this when making reservations for coach travel. There are also separate handicapped bedrooms aboard Superliners (see Equipment section).

Be sure to reserve sleeping-car accommodations early since these are frequently sold out months in advance, particularly on the more popular trains during the summer and holidays. Some trains have unreserved coaches and in this case seating is not guaranteed.

It is possible to upgrade accommodations once on board if such space is available. Passengers wishing to upgrade to sleeping accommodations, Club or Custom Class should see the conductor or the Chief of On Board Services.

Amtrak also offers "Thruway Buses" that make train/bus connections for many off-line cities. Amtrak makes reservations for these as well as some other selected bus routes.

Payment - Tickets may be purchased with most major credit cards. Most cards are also accepted in the dining car and for the purchase of tickets on board. Payment may also be made by personal check, except in California where customers must be over age 62 to use this mode of payment. Purchases must be for at least $25 and some form of photo identification is required along with an acceptable credit card. For a $15 service charge, it is also possible to pay locally for tickets which are to be picked up at another Amtrak ticket office. This can be particularly helpful when a son or daughter calls from college and hasn't funds to get home for Christmas.

Travel Agents - Authorized travel agents will be glad to make train reservations and sell tickets, and since they are paid a commission by the carrier, there is no extra charge to the customer for this service. This certainly simplifies things. The only disadvantage—once the agent issues the tickets, there may be a penalty for changing or canceling reservations.

Timetables - Amtrak publishes system-wide timetables semiannually, coinciding with the nation's changeover to or from daylight saving time. These schedules can be obtained free of charge from any Amtrak ticket office, authorized travel agency or by calling 800-USA-RAIL. Times shown for each stop are the prevailing local times. Bear in mind that if a train is running late, stops at stations may be shorter than those indicated in the timetable. Times and routes are always subject to change, and timetables may not necessarily reflect current schedules.

Fares - All coach travel is one class except for Club Service and Custom Class (available on some trains in the East and Southern California) which, because of the more luxurious seating and service, have a higher price tag. Also, certain service in the Northeast Corridor is designed as Metroliner service. These trains are scheduled for fewer stops and make better time, so a premium is charged for Metroliner tickets. And, quite logically, for sleeping cars you must pay an accommodation charge over and above the basic coach

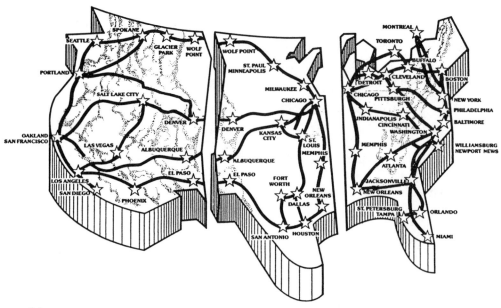

fare. But there's a bonus. Meals are included with the price of sleeping car accommodations (except Slumbercoach, a limited service that may soon be discontinued).

Round-trip excursion fares offer savings and there are also family plans that allow not more than two children (per fare-paying adult), ages two through fifteen, to travel at half-fare if accompanied by a parent. Children under two travel free.

Amtrak's All Aboard America Fare is very attractive, particularly when a round trip is involved. This fare divides the country into three regions—Eastern, Central and Western. The Eastern extends from the Atlantic Seaboard west to Chicago and New Orleans. The Central is that region from those two cities west to a line from Wolf Point, Montana through Denver, Albuquerque and El Paso. The Western region extends from that line to the West Coast. These fares change with the seasons, but as an example, the non-refundable fall fares prior to this publication allowed a round trip within any one of these regions for $158, within two adjoining regions for $198 and anywhere in the U.S. for $278. Rates are higher during the summer months and if refundable. One stopover is allowed each direction as well as the destination point, and you should not be penalized if Amtrak's schedules require that you "overnight" in a city where you must make train connections. Perhaps the best feature is that the return can be on an entirely different route.

Amtrak sells USA Rail Passes which allow unlimited rail travel in the United States for a fixed fare and for a limited period of time. These can be used only by non-residents of the United States, and are only sold outside North America.

Those 62 and older may travel at 15% off the lowest available fare, except during certain holiday periods. Keep in mind that group rates are established from time to time with discounts determined by the size of the group.

Reduced or discounted fares do not normally apply to bedroom charges. Stopovers are permitted at no extra charge unless you are traveling on a special excursion rate.

Amtrak Travel Packages - Amtrak offers a bevy of travel packages that amount to a discounted hotel rate when booked with Amtrak travel. Twice a year, Amtrak publishes a *Travel Planner* that lists these bargains. Amtrak has also introduced some economical train/plane combination packages worth considering.

These package hotel rates apply only to bookings through Amtrak, and there is limited availability. If you must cancel, it should be done through Amtrak. It takes one to three working days for Amtrak to confirm hotel reservations while they check on availability.

For information, check with your travel agent or call Amtrak at 800-USA-RAIL, and ask for the tour desk.

Stations and Connections- Rail stations are frequently located in the heart of town, giving the rail traveler a city-center point of arrival or departure. It may not be advisable to attempt connections between trains having scheduled arrival and departure times within an hour of each other. Amtrak will, however, "guarantee" connections when scheduled arrival and departure times are an hour or more apart. This guarantee means that Amtrak will make other arrangements for you to reach your destination (usually on the next train) if a late train causes a missed connection. Amtrak may also provide overnight hotel accommodations if appropriate.

Metropolitan Lounge - First-class passengers (Club and sleeping car passengers) can use the Metropolitan Lounge located in the stations of New York City, Philadelphia,

Washington, DC and Chicago. These lounges are rather elegant rooms with a quiet and relaxed atmosphere, offering complimentary hot and cold drinks, newspapers and magazines, private conference rooms and other niceties.

Dining - Most long-distance trains carry full-service dining cars that provide complete menus for three meals a day. Lighter fare will be found on other trains in cafe-type or lounge cars. Cafe service includes tray meals, such as light breakfasts, microwave sandwiches and beverages, while sandwiches, beverages and other snacks are available in lounge cars. It is also quite acceptable to bring your own lunch on board, but food should not be taken to the train's dining area.

To reduce the problem of waiting for a dinner table during peak travel periods, on some trains, reservations are now taken early in the day at your seat, and you can select any one of three or four seatings for dinner. Dinner prices range from about eight to thirteen dollars, luncheons five to six dollars and breakfast four to five dollars. A typical dinner menu might include a selection of baked chicken, seafood, roast beef, New York strip steak or lasagna. Lunches may include salads and sandwiches, while breakfast may offer bacon and eggs, pancakes, French toast and hot or dry cereal. Cafe and lounge cars serve simpler fare at lower prices. Always wait to be seated in full-service diners.

Sleeping - As mentioned above, sleeping car accommodations are available for an additional charge. (See the Equipment chapter for a description of these accommodations.) Although a bed is by far more restful for most train travelers and certainly more private, a majority of overnight travelers will prefer the coach, most because of the lower cost, some because they will reach their destination early in the morning and want the convenience of sleeping until the last possible moment.

If you do decide to sleep in your coach seat, pick out a seat near the center of the car to avoid noisy door action that is guaranteed to occur all night at each end of the car. Although Amtrak provides pillows, it might also be a good idea to have a blanket or coat with you just in case the air conditioning becomes too efficient. If two of you are traveling together and only single seats are available, the conductor may ask someone to move so that you can sit together. If not, move to adjoining seats in your coach as soon as some become available, frequently at the next stop, taking the destination slips above your seats to your new location. Be sure to let the conductor know this since a seating chart is sometimes maintained so you can be notified of your stop.

If you should be in a bedroom, plan to pack so that everything you may need at night is handy. Many veteran train riders will take along an extra small suitcase or bag to hold only those items they will need in their bedroom. This is particularly advisable if two people are trying to use small quarters such as an economy bedroom on a Superliner.

Lounge and **Club Cars** - Some trains carry lounge cars where passengers can obtain beverages and light snacks. Superliner lounge cars offer excellent viewing of the passing scenery, with large windows wrapping up over the top of the car. Club cars are on a few Northeastern Corridor trains (between Boston and Washington, DC), and offer more luxurious reserved seats with snack and beverage service at your seat. Fares are higher, of course, for club seating. (See the Equipment chapter for examples of lounge and club cars.) Also, Custom Class, with reserved deluxe coach seating and complimentary coffee, tea or juice and newspaper, is available on many daytime trains.

16

Smoking policy - Amtrak has been moving toward a smoke-free environment. Currently, the following overnight trains permit smoking in lounge cars (during certain times) and in sleeping cars (except where otherwise indicated) and are the only trains that permit smoking: *Auto Train, Crescent, Silver Star, Capitol Ltd.* (except sleepers), *Empire Builder, Southwest Chief, Cardinal* (except sleepers), *Lake Shore Ltd., Sunset Ltd., City of New Orleans, Silver Meteor,* and *Texas Eagle.*

Baggage - Stations at most larger cities handle checked baggage (baggage to be carried in the baggage car) permitting each passenger to check up to three pieces of baggage without charge, not exceeding 50 pounds each. Extra baggage may be checked, but it is subject to a surcharge. Bags should be checked at least 30 minutes prior to departure (even earlier during crowded holiday periods), and will be ready for claiming at your destination within 30 minutes after arrival. Generally, baggage can be checked through to your final destination even when making connections from one train to another at the same station. (But like the airlines, if the connection is tight, there is a risk your checked luggage may arrive the day after you do.)

Personal baggage can also be carried on board, but coach passengers are limited to two pieces of carry-on per passenger. These are stored either in overhead racks or in special storage areas of the car. Sleeping car passengers can carry on as much as can be accommodated in their rooms. But remember, some accommodations are fairly tight such as economy bedrooms on Superliners. Most travelers leave the bulk of their luggage stowed in the luggage bins available near the entrance of the Superliner sleepers (with the disadvantage of lack of security). Amtrak encourages you to check your larger bags.

There should be another luggage consideration when you plan short stopovers. If an overnight visit with a friend in a particular city along the route is planned, pack so the things you don't need for that night can be left in a locker or the baggage check room at the station rather than hauling your entire wardrobe with you. Locker rental rates are for only 24 hours. Many stations have eliminated lockers and will hold luggage in the baggage room for a small fee.

Baggage should always have an I.D. tag with your name and address.

Bicycles - Standard bicycles must be checked and can only be handled between stations with checked baggage service. For most trains, you must box your bicycle before checking it, handlebars turned and pedals removed. There is a handling charge and Amtrak will supply the box (but not the tools). *Vermonter* and some West Coast trains have space for limited number of unboxed bikes.

Pets - Except for certified guide or service animals, pets are not permitted on trains.

Tipping - Tipping dining-car waiters is customary, and the same amount that one would tip in a restaurant is appropriate. Also, many sleeping car passengers tip their car attendant for the extra services they frequently provide; $3 to $5 per night is appropriate— if the service has been good. Some even tip their car attendants in advance believing this will ensure the service they want throughout their trip.

Radios - Earphones must be used when listening to radios, tape players, etc. and volume must be kept low.

Redcaps - Assistance with baggage is furnished at many stations by uniformed redcaps. This service is free, although tipping is appropriate. It is not advisable to accept service from anyone not in a redcap uniform. Redcap service is generally available only in larger cities. The station services shown in this guide for larger cities indicate whether this service is available.

Boarding - If the ticket agent has not told you your car location, ask the gate attendant as you enter the train platform. This can save a walk in the wrong direction in a city like Denver where you have to make a choice—left or right—when reaching the train.

Traveling with the Kids - Small children (and their parents) can get more enjoyment out of a train trip if the kids have some diversions. Drawing paper and crayons can be helpful as well as picture books and games. Older children also enjoy drawing and reading, and also might enjoy writing postcards to their friends. The entire family can enjoy following the train routes using this guide as well as a road atlas.

Unaccompanied Children - Children ages eight through eleven may travel alone under certain conditions (check with Amtrak in advance) but must pay an adult fare.

For **additional information** on enjoying train travel, the book ***Amtraking*** by Mauris L. Emeka is highly recommended.

Important - Train times shown in this section are given only in general terms (such as "Early Morning"), and are for use in planning before making reservations. **Since times are not specific and schedules are always subject to change, actual times should be ascertained from the carrier or a travel agent before setting out on your trip.** Fares and food prices are also subject to change. **Also, routes, fares and stops can be altered without notice.**

Northeast Corridor

The Northeast Corridor, running between Washington and Boston, carries half of Amtrak's annual ridership.

Manicured roadbeds, dedicated exclusively to passenger train service, has resulted in sections rated for speeds up to 125 miles per hour. Between New York and Washington, regular-fare conventional trains now offer the fastest schedules ever, while the premium-fare Metroliner Service trains all have less than three-hour running times making them the fastest regularly scheduled trains in the Western Hemisphere.

Several Northeast Corridor stations have received outstanding restorations, making them worth a special detour to explore. The most notable are Baltimore Penn Station, the Wilmington, Delaware station, Newark Penn Station, Washington Union Station and Philadelphia's venerable Thirtieth Street Station.

New York's Penn Station, Amtrak's busiest, has undergone extensive rebuilding, and Boston's South Station has been in part restored and in part added to, creating an intermodal train, bus and subway station.

The former New Haven's "Scenic Shoreline Route" is one of the finest corridor routes in the country. From spectacular views of the Manhattan skyline while crossing Hell Gate Bridge to mile after mile of New England coastal seascape, the Shore Line route to Boston is a veritable feast for the keenly interested sightseer. All Corridor trains carry coaches with reclining seats, overhead luggage racks, two rest rooms and fold-down, airline-style trays. Most trains carry cafe cars offering sandwiches, snacks and beverages. Club cars with reserved, deluxe seating (eg. two on one side of the aisle, one on the other), complimentary meals, beverages, wine and newspapers are carried on several Corridor trains. Amtrak's reserved, 125-mph Metroliner Service between New York and Washington carry roomier coaches, cafe cars featuring deli fare, telephones and Club Service. Sleeping-car service between New York and Washington is offered by the *Night Owl*.

The route log for the Northeast Corridor is divided into three sections: New York to Boston, New York to Washington, DC, and New Haven to Springfield.

ROUTE LOG

New York to Boston. For route from New York to Washington, DC, see page 26; New Haven to Springfield, see page 36.

To enjoy it all, be sure to sit on the right-hand side of the train when leaving New York, and on the left leaving Boston.

NEW YORK CITY, NY - The first reported real estate transaction in the "Big Apple" was in 1624 when Peter Minuit, the Dutch colonial governor, supposedly purchased Manhattan Island

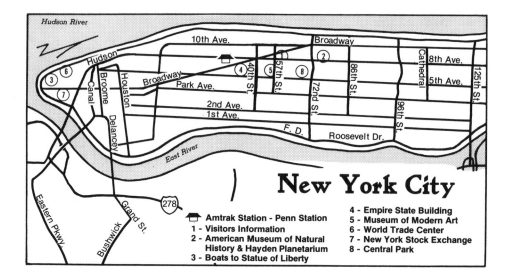

Hudson River

10th Ave.
Broadway
Hudson
Broadway
Park Ave.
2nd Ave.
1st Ave.
8th Ave.
5th Ave.
Cathedral
40th St.
57th St.
72nd St.
86th St.
96th St.
125th St.
Broome
Houston
Canal
Delancey
F. D.
Roosevelt Dr.
East River
Grand St.
Eastern Pkwy.
Bushwick

New York City

Amtrak Station - Penn Station
1 - Visitors Information
2 - American Museum of Natural
    History & Hayden Planetarium
3 - Boats to Statue of Liberty

4 - Empire State Building
5 - Museum of Modern Art
6 - World Trade Center
7 - New York Stock Exchange
8 - Central Park

from the Indians for $24 worth of goods. This set the pattern and tone for the city. Today, New York remains not only a world center for finance and trade, but also for transportation, fashion, the performing arts and many other industries.

The town can be an exhilarating experience. That may be why more tourists come here than any other city in America.

To really enjoy New York, one needs to know how to cope—or maybe better stated, how to get around safely and conveniently in a town with an intimidating subway system, plodding buses, and cabbies that don't speak English. The transportation section below offers some tips that should make your visit more enjoyable.

Pennsylvania Station, bounded by Eighth and Seventh Avenues at 31st and 33rd Streets, is directly beneath Madison Square Garden.

The station is multi-leveled, with all trains arriving at the Platform Level. Immediately above that is Level A which houses the Long Island Rail Road (commuter) station and subway entrance; continuing upward, Level B is the Amtrak station with escalators to the other three levels; and Level C is at street level with entrances and taxis. All levels are handicapped accessible.

There are both video monitors and display boards with arrival and departure information. And besides a refurbished waiting area, surrounded by shops and eateries, first-class ticket holders now have a separate waiting area called Metropolitan Lounge. This plush, club-like room has many niceties, including its own rest rooms, a self-service beverage counter, desks, fax machines, etc. Redcap service is available.

For reservations and information, call (212) 582-6875.

The Island of Manhattan is rather compact and many of its attractions can be reached by walking. When walking is not appropriate, there are several options.

Cabs are what most visitors resort to. There are two kinds of taxis: licensed (yellow medallion) taxis and unlicensed (gypsy) taxis. Use the licensed variety. Those that are available have their roof lights on, and some vigorous waving and shrill whistling should get their attention. Don't expect to catch one in the rush hour or in the rain.

Buses are slow, even slower than the traffic, but they are more civilized than the subway, and you can see the sights as you go. They are easy to use, and route diagrams are posted at many of the stops. You must have the exact change or a token.

The **subway** is usually the fastest way to get around. Statistically, it is safer than the streets in spite of its reputation. Stick to the safer routes, sit toward the center of the train when it isn't full and travel when they're being well used. The daylight hours are the best. On the other hand, avoid the unpleasant rush hours.

Token booths are at each station. If you plan to use the subway more than once, buy enough tokens to avoid waiting in line again. They may also be used on the city buses.

Commuter trains make New York City possible. Metro North has three lines that head north out of Grand Central: The Hudson Line that runs along that river to Poughkeepsie; the Harlem Line that goes farther east, through Scarsdale and north; and the New Haven Line that runs up the coast to that city, with three northerly branches to New Canaan, Danbury and Waterbury. The Long Island Rail Road serves virtually all of Long Island from Penn Station. PATH (Port Authority Trans Hudson) offers excellent service to Hoboken, Jersey City and Newark, with connections to New Jersey Transit. PATH trains run south from 33rd Street along the Avenue of the Americas (Sixth Ave.) and also from the World Trade Center.

Intercity buses operate from the Port Authority Bus Terminal at 8th Ave. and 41st St.

The automobile is not really useful in New York City, but if you must rent one, numerous **rental car** locations are in midtown.

New York Convention and Visitors Bureau, Two Columbus Circle (59th St. and Broadway); (212) 397-8222 or 800-692-8474.

Comfort Inn Murray Hill, 42 West 35th St., 10001; (212) 947-0200. Just across from the Empire State Building. Three blocks from Penn Station. Breakfast. $100.

-**Ramada Hotel Pennsylvania**, 401 Seventh Ave., 10001; (212) 736-5000 or 800-223-8585. Venerable, Stanford White-designed hostelry, formerly the Statler. Its phone number (Pennsylvania 6-5000), made famous by Glenn Miller, is now longest in continuous use in the city. Expect a long wait at check in. Directly across from Penn Station. $130.

-**Herald Square**, 19 West 31st St., 10001; (212) 279-4017 or 800-727-1888. Small, nicely refurbished budget hotel, in rather shabby surroundings. Three blocks from Penn Station. $75.

-**Southgate Tower Suite Hotel**, 371 Seventh Ave., 10001; (212) 563-1800 or 800-637-8483. Just as convenient for train travelers but much less frantic than the Ramada. Diagonally across intersection (31st St. & 7th Ave.) from Penn Station. $150.

An indispensable tool for enjoying New York City is the **Visitors Guide and Map**, available free from the New York Convention and Visitors Bureau. This is a handy, well-designed handout that packs a lot of information on a single sheet of paper.

Circle Line Sightseeing Yacht tours around Manhattan, let you see both the city and harbors. For a bird's-eye view, of course, both the **Empire State Building** and the **World Trade Center** observation decks are magnificent vantage points on a clear day. And boats to the **Statue of Liberty** are boarded at the southern tip of Manhattan.

Museums are in abundance. The **Museum of Modern Art**, 11 W. 53rd St., and the **American Museum of Natural History**, 79th and Central Park West, are national treasures. And, of course, **New York's theaters** offer something for every taste.

0:00 (0:29) Departing New York's Pennsylvania Station, travel eastward under Manhattan streets and East River rising to surface on Long Island in Sunnyside section of Queens.

0:08 (0:26) To left are extensive rail yards for Amtrak and New Jersey Transit trains. All passenger equipment is cleaned, stored, serviced and provisioned here before their next trip. Tracks dropping down to right pass through mechanical washers then loop under main line into Sunnyside Yards.

0:10 (0:19) At Harold Tower interlocking, our elevated Hell Gate Route separates from Long Island Rail Road line that continues on to Jamaica and points east. Route climbs through Astoria, a heavily Greek and Italian community, swinging back over the East River onto Wards and Randalls Islands. On a clear day or night, view of Manhattan skyline to left is nothing less than magical.

0:18 (0:11) Down to left is Manhattan State Hospital, a grim-looking structure built just prior to World War II. To right, small vessels moored at river's edge are New York City sludge boats, popularly referred to as "honey barges." They haul treated waste out to sea for dumping about eight miles beyond Ambrose Channel light tower. Next to sanitation facility, City of New York maintains its Fire Department Training Academy. Four-story windowless brick tenement is used for simulation of real fires and can sometimes be seen erupting in flames for exercise purposes. Often a red fireboat is tied up nearby. Leaving Hell Gate Viaduct, train drops into a cut through South Bronx, a severely depressed area of New York City.

0:25 (0:04) Huge, stark Coop City apartment complex rises to left, as train crosses Pelham Bay drawbridge.

0:28 (0:01) At Shell Tower interlocking, Hell Gate Route joins Metro-North Commuter Railroad Line from Grand Central Terminal.

0:29 (0:00) Arrive New Rochelle.

NEW ROCHELLE, NY - This is the first high-level platform commuter station encountered northbound. High level platforms, a phenomenon of the Northeast, allow for rapid boarding of trains without having to drop the train's steps. The 1848 station was modernized in 1991.

0:00 (0:17) Depart New Rochelle and gather speed on four-track electrified Shore Line Route. First tree-lined suburban streets appear in Connecticut, and brief glimpses of Long Island Sound begin after Greenwich and at Cos Cob.

0:17 (0:00) Arrive Stamford.

STAMFORD, CT - At Stamford, a burgeoning city boasts clusters of international corporate headquarters.

Nearly all Amtrak trains stop here to serve local communities and to allow passengers to make convenient connections with Metro-North's New Haven Line trains.

0:00 (0:25) Depart Stamford.

0:14 (0:11) At Westport, scenery improves substantially, and one of first wooden barn-style stations appears. Through trees, most houses seen are worth small fortunes—some even more. Tidal marshlands open up between Westport and Green's Farms.

0:19 (0:06) Southport may be considered end of intensively used commuting stations, though some daily riders originate even farther east. Approaching Bridgeport, scenes become industrial and urban once again. On right, simple dock serves as landing for Bridgeport and Port Jefferson Steamboat Company's ferry Grand Republic, operating year-round service across Sound to Port Jefferson on Long Island's North Shore. Fanciful Moorish-style building to left houses P.T. Barnum's personal and circus memorabilia collection.

0:25 (0:00) Arrive Bridgeport.

BRIDGEPORT, CT - Passengers for the Metro-North's Waterbury Branch change here for the line up the scenic and historic Housatonic and Naugatuck Valleys.

0:00 (0:24) Departing Bridgeport, line crosses first Pequonnock then Housatonic Rivers and runs through Milford before skirting harbor on approach to New Haven.

0:24 (0:00) Arrive New Haven.

Seconds after coming to a stop in New Haven, the lights will go out and the air circulation will cease for about seven minutes, while the electric locomotive is traded for a diesel engine for the remainder of the trip to Boston. Trains to Hartford, Springfield and other Inland Route stations branch off to the north. Historic New Haven Station is now a major transportation center for Amtrak and commuter trains as well as local and long distance buses.

NEW HAVEN, CT - This is the home of Yale University, where historic personages such as Noah Webster, Nathan Hale and William Howard Taft studied.

AEM-7 power — Northeast Corridor
HOMER R. HILL

0:00 (0:31) Depart New Haven and landscape becomes genuinely rural for first time. It is this 69-mile stretch, as far as Westerly, where Scenic Shore Line earns its name. Rocky hillocks rise out of tidal marshes laced with meandering stream, isolated houses loom large on tiny offshore Thimble Islands, and Long Island Sound is visible for long intervals.

0:31 (0:00) Arrive Old Saybrook.

OLD SAYBROOK, CT - Note the handsome wooden station dating from 1873, one that has changed little in more than 100 years. Passengers leave here for the Connecticut River town of Essex and excursions on the steam-hauled Valley Railroad, a few miles to the north. It is here that the Connecticut River flows into Long Island Sound.

0:00 (0:18) Depart Old Saybrook.

0:03 (0:15) Look both ways while rumbling across drawbridge spanning Connecticut River. Between Old Saybrook and New London, Shore Line parallels sandy beaches at Rocky Neck State Park and along Niantic Bay, at times less than 100 feet from ocean's lapping salt water.

0:18 (0:00) Arrive New London where elegant red-brick 1887 H. H. Richardson railroad station also houses local restaurant.

NEW LONDON, CT - New London, located on the River Thames (rhymes with James), grew up with the whaling industry and other commercial maritime pursuits to become one of the most important ports on the New England coast. Today, the Coast Guard and its Academy, the Navy and the shipyards keep the area humming to a similar salty tune. Nautilus, the world's first nuclear submarine, was launched in nearby Groton. Virtually at station's doorstep, three different ferry operators run boats to Fishers Island, Orient Point and Block Island (summer season only).

0:00 (0:14) Leaving New London, swing right to pass over Thames where a quick look upstream may reveal Coast Guard sail training ship Eagle. Scan both ways for nuclear submarines and other vessels downstream at General Dynamics shipyard.

0:12 (0:02) Approaching Mystic, water laps both sides of embankment. Glance to either side for hundreds of moored sailing and motor yachts.

0:14 (0:00) Arrive Mystic.

MYSTIC, CT - The station built in 1905 has received a complete restoration. The two-tone wooden depot once served as a model for Lionel's Lionelville station. Amtrak and local community groups joined forces to reopen the building as a train information and local community center and gift shop.

Mystic is best known for its 19th-century Seaport Restoration, housing a fine collection of private residences, a noted aquarium, a large fleet of ships and a working shipyard.

0:00 (0:10) Depart Mystic.

0:05 (0:05) At Stonington, one of Connecticut coast's most attractive towns, look for large Victorian structure (a former hotel) next to water on right-hand side.

0:10 (0:00) Arrive Westerly.

WESTERLY, RI - This older Rhode Island city has an industrial background which provides several factory buildings facing Amtrak's brick and granite railroad station.

0:00 (0:14) Depart Westerly and head inland into extensive wooded areas of evergreen and deciduous trees. From here though Davisville train is permitted to run at 110 miles per hour.

0:14 (0:00) Arrive Kingston.

KINGSTON, RI - The town's Victorian-style wooden station is particularly attractive. The nearby University of Rhode Island, the resort towns of Newport, Narragansett and Jamestown are popular destinations for passengers leaving the train here.

0:00 (0:26) Depart Kingston.

0:12 (0:14) At East Greenwich, there are close-up views of Narragansett Bay and numerous yacht marinas.

0:16 (0:10) Cemetery on right seems overgrown with bewildering array of tombstones.

0:24 (0:02) Providence campus of University of Rhode Island is now off to left.

0:26 (0:00) Arrive Providence where State

House, built of white Georgia marble, comes into view. Brown University buildings can be seen on hill above and to right.

PROVIDENCE, RI - Providence is the capital of this smallest state in the nation. Closely associated with the sea during its early years, it has become one of the important commercial and financial centers of the East. Old State House, where the Rhode Island General Assembly renounced allegiance to King George III on May 4, 1776, still stands at 150 Benefit St.

0:00 (0:25) Depart Providence and scenery becomes flat and dull as train runs fast through Attleboro and Canton.

0:25 (0:00) Arrive Route 128.

ROUTE 128, MA - This suburban stop is used mostly by passengers using the Beltway which circles Boston.

0:00 (0:18) Depart Route 128.

The final approach to Boston is slow, finally sinking below grade shortly before Back Bay Station.

0:15 (0:00) Arrive Boston's Back Bay Station.

BOSTON (BACK BAY), MA - This station, just a mile from South Station, serves Boston's rather elegant Back Bay and surroundings. At one time, much of this area was covered by water from the Charles River, forming vast mud flats. Long thought to be a liability, the land was eventually reclaimed to become a very viable part of the city.

0:00 (0:05) Depart Back Bay Station, emerging slowly from below grade.

0:03 (0:02) On right, building signage modestly proclaims "Gillette World Shaving Headquarters." Coachyards appear on right.

0:05 (0:00) Boston's huge central post office facility appears on right upon train's arrival South station.

BOSTON, MA - First settled in 1630, Boston and the nation's history have always been closely intertwined. English Puritans endured early hardships here, including death from disease and cold, but held on through those difficult years. Its location on Boston Bay soon made it the most important port in America, with trading vessels sailing to and

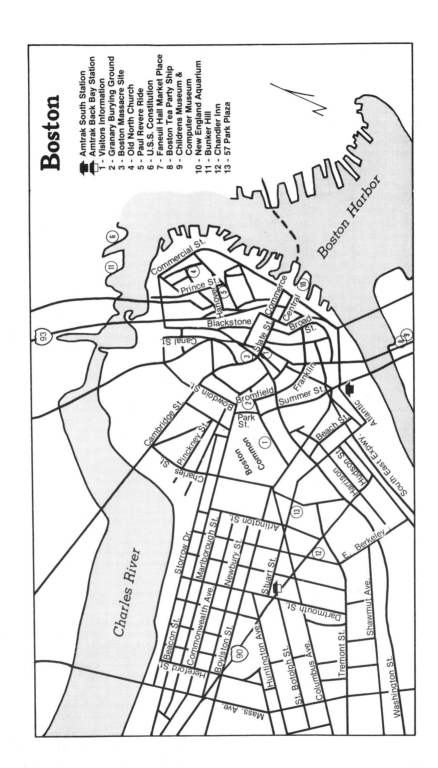

Boston

- 🔊 Amtrak South Station
- 📢 Amtrak Back Bay Station
- 1 - Visitors Information
- 2 - Granary Burying Ground
- 3 - Boston Massacre Site
- 4 - Old North Church
- 5 - Paul Revere Ride
- 6 - U.S.S. Constitution
- 7 - Faneuil Hall Market Place
- 8 - Boston Tea Party Ship
- 9 - Childrens Museum &
      Computer Museum
- 10 - New England Aquarium
- 11 - Bunker Hill
- 12 - Chandler Inn
- 13 - 57 Park Plaza

Boston Harbor

Charles River

Commercial St.
Prince St.
Hanover
Blackstone
Canal St.
Slate St.
Commerce
Central
Broad St.
Bromfield
Bowdoin St.
Franklin
Summer St.
Park St.
Beach St.
Atlantic
Boston Common
Cambridge St.
Pinckney St.
Charles St.
Storrow Dr.
Marlborough St.
Newbury St.
Arlington St.
Hudson St.
South East Expwy.
Harrison
E. Berkeley
Stuart St.
Dartmouth St.
Beacon St.
Commonwealth Ave.
Boylston St.
Hereford St.
Mass. Ave.
Huntington Ave.
St. Botolph St.
Columbus Ave.
Tremont St.
Shawmut Ave.
Washington St.

93
90

from all parts of the world. Its port, yet today, is one of the world's busiest.

The American Revolution had its roots in Boston when British troops fired on a gathering of citizens in 1770, killing several. The Boston Tea Party was held in 1773 and Paul Revere's historic ride started here. It was the early cultural center of the nation having such residents as Hawthorne, Emerson and Longfellow. Historically a leader in education, the city still enjoys the distinction of being a major focal point of scientific and medical research. There are a quarter of a million students attending 50 colleges and universities in the greater metropolitan area.

 South Station, Atlantic Ave. and Summer St., 12210. This glorious old station, constructed largely of pink marble just before the turn of the century, has undergone a massive rehabilitation project. The result is a modern-day gem of a depot.

An enormous canopy encloses a spacious and airy waiting room that houses traditional benches, some very inviting lunch stands, dining tables and slick arrival and departure boards. Redcap service is available. A direct passageway leads to the adjoining MBTA station (Red Line).

Call (617) 482-3660 for Amtrak reservations and other information.

As mentioned above, Amtrak has a second in-town facility, **Back Bay Station**, 145 Dartmouth St.

Checker **Cab**, 536-7000. **Local buses** and **subway** are in front. Also, various **commuter trains** use this station. Commuter trains also use the North Station, 150 Causeway Street. **Greyhound** and other intercity buses now operate out of South Station. Thrifty **rental cars** are one block from the station, 125 Sumner St. and Budget's Long Wharf location is about a mile from the station.

Boston Common Information Booth, Tremont Street at West Street. Also, **Boston National Historical Park Visitor Center**, 15 State Street at Devonshire St. Both of these centers are on the "Freedom Trail." Call (617) 536-4100 or 800-888-5515.

Chandler Inn, 26 Chandler St., 02116; (617) 482-3450 or 800-842-3450. A small, popular hotel, operated as a bed & breakfast. A bit out of the way, but a reasonable walk to the "T" and only three blocks from Back Bay Station. Quiet neighborhood. Twelve blocks from South Station. $90.

-**Howard Johnson**, 57 Park Plaza, 200 Stuart St., 02116; (617) 482-1800. High rise with spacious rooms, all with balconies; in the Theater District. Five blocks from Back Bay Station and ten blocks from South Station. Four blocks from the "T" (Boylston or Arlington on Green Line). $100.

-**Bed and Breakfast Associates Bay Colony, Ltd.**, (617) 449-5302. Boston's oldest B&B reservation service.

 Three of Boston's attractions are within two blocks of the station on Congress Street. The **Boston Tea Party Ship and Museum**, on the Congress Street Bridge, is a replica of the original brig "Beaver" on which the famous act of protest took place in 1773. Just beyond is the **Children's Museum**, with "hands-on" exhibits; it's one of the best such institutions and is extremely popular. Adjacent, is **The Computer Museum**, the only one of its kind, with more "hands-on" exhibits that entertain the kids as well as the grown-ups.

Most of Boston's historic points of interest are along the **Freedom Trail**, a walking route through downtown Boston marked by a red stripe along the sidewalks. Maps of the route and descriptions of the things to visit along the way may be obtained from the visitors center.

NEW YORK TO WASHINGTON, DC

NEW YORK, NY - See page 19. **0:00** (0:14) Depart New York's Penn Station and head westward beneath streets of Manhattan toward Hudson River. Twin tubes, technically known as North River Tunnels, each carry single sets of tracks beneath Hudson. Tunnels were first opened in 1910 when Penn Station was completed, allowing Pennsylvania Railroad to gain com-

Congressional — Delaware River
HOMER R. HILL

petitive presence in New York City. Until then Pennsylvania's passengers had to be ferried across Hudson from New Jersey terminal.

0:05 (0:09) Surface in North Bergen, New Jersey, and curl southward toward wetlands known as Jersey Meadows.

0:08 (0:06) Off to left are familiar silhouettes of 110-story World Trade Center and legendary Empire State Building.

0:09 (0:05) Cross Hackensack River while flood of vehicular traffic streams across same waterway on New Jersey Turnpike.

0:13 (0:01) Cross Passaic River and enter heavily industrialized outskirts of Newark. PATH's shops will be on left.

0:14 (0:00) Arrive Newark's Pennsylvania Station.

NEWARK, NJ - Anchoring the northern end of New Jersey's industrialized core, Newark has the distinction of being one of the world's most important manufacturing communities as well as the largest city in the state.

0:00 (0:33) Upon departing Newark, travel on elevated track through more residential and industrial suburbs.

0:04 (0:29) Pass through Elizabeth, a manufacturing metropolis whose industrial roots date to pre-Revolutionary days—a time when Elizabeth was New Jersey's capital. Both Aaron Burr and Alexander Hamilton lived in this historic city.

0:08 (0:25) Glide into Rahway on elevated track where old brownstones line each side of right-of-way.

0:09 (0:24) Enter Metropark, an impressive, modern business and industrial park on left.

0:16 (0:17) Pass through New Brunswick, home of Rutgers University which was founded in 1776. Although a state university, it took its name from a generous donor in 1825. First intercollegiate football game was played here in 1869 with Rutgers winning over Princeton by a mighty score of 6 to 4.

0:17 (0:16) On right is beautifully landscaped Johnson & Johnson headquarters.

0:26 (0:07) Pass through Princeton Junction where connections are made to trains of New Jersey Transit for Princeton University, just three miles west of here. Branch was originally built in 1865 by Camden & Amboy Rail Road Transportation Company, one of earliest railroads in America. School is nation's fifth oldest institution of higher learning.

TRENTON, NJ - The capital of New Jersey is home to more than 400 industries. British and Hessian troops were housed here during the night General George Washington and his army made their famous Delaware River crossing.

0:00 (0:31) Depart Trenton and cross Delaware. It was on Christmas Eve, 1776, that Washington crossed its icy waters just eight miles northwest of here to attack Trenton's Hessian Garrison. Ensuing Battle of Trenton marked first victory by Washington over German mercenaries. Off to right, beyond bridge with sign "Trenton Makes - The Word Takes," can be seen glistening gold dome of New Jersey's State Capitol, built in 1792 and second oldest continually used statehouse in U.S.

0:05 (0:26) On left, numerous small boats dot picturesque inlet of Delaware River.

0:18 (0:13) On left, note Sterling Paper Company's unique clock tower.

0:19 (0:12) Juniata Terminal Company, easily identified by sign at left, restores antique railroad cars for private car owners. Enormous shops (50,000 square feet) house various railroad artifacts such as Robert Kennedy's funeral car. Company usually has interesting array of rail cars parked outside in view of main line.

0:20 (0:11) North Philadelphia's newly remodeled station is at right.

0:25 (0:06) One of Philadelphia's largest urban gardens is at right, where former rail car now serves as a community room.

0:26 (0:05) Cross Schuylkill River as it meanders through Fairmont Park.

0:27 (0:04) On left is skyline of downtown Philadelphia, while city's popular zoo is in foreground. Two-story brick structure at trackside is called Zoo Tower. Tower oversees Corridor's most complex junction where train traffic is sifted through maze of tracks without a single crossing at grade.

0:28 (0:03) In distance to left is Philadelphia Museum of Art, known for not only fine art but its prominence in movie "Rocky." And in foreground, along far shore

of river and immediately after zoo is Boat House Row, home to numerous racing scull clubs. Crews can frequently be seen practicing their rowing skills along this stretch of Schuylkill.

0:29 (0:02) To left, City Hall can be seen, topped by enduring statue of William Penn—a long-time informal height restriction for buildings in Philadelphia. Barrier was broken, however, with construction of One Liberty Place.

0:31 (0:00) Arrive Philadelphia beneath venerable 30th Street Station.

PHILADELPHIA, PA - William Penn's desire to form a colony for "religious minorities" and the fact the British Crown owed a debt to his father combined to give birth to Philadelphia. King Charles II gave a large parcel of land to Penn to enable him to create such a settlement in the New World, and in 1682 Penn founded the colony of Pennsylvania ("Penn's Woods") in memory of his father. He soon identified a peninsula between the Delaware and Schuylkill Rivers as the site of Philadelphia, Greek for "City of Brotherly Love."

Penn's chief surveyor was asked to lay out the city in a grid pattern with five public squares to provide both sunlight and fresh air for the city's residents—the first recorded effort toward urban planning. These five public squares still exist.

The city's history is tightly interwoven with America's independence. The Second Continental Congress met in what is now called Independence Hall, and it was here the decision was made to prepare the Declaration of Independence. Philadelphia was the nation's capital until the year 1800.

30th Street Station, on the edge of downtown at 30th and Market Streets, is the main passenger train station serving Philadelphia. It is perhaps the best of the grand-style stations with everything done in excellent taste.

There are redcaps, restaurants, snack bars, newsstands, a bookstore and other shops. SEPTA commuter trains also operate from this station. A Metropolitan Lounge serves first-class passengers.

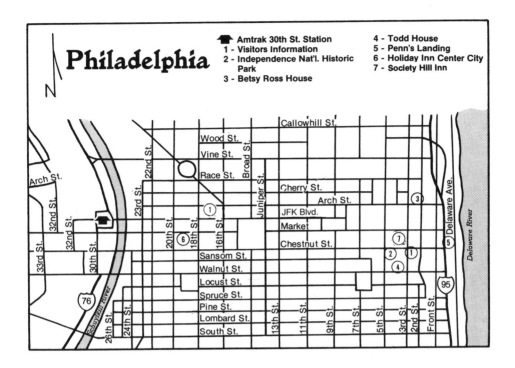

Philadelphia

N

🚂 Amtrak 30th St. Station
1 - Visitors Information
2 - Independence Nat'l. Historic Park
3 - Betsy Ross House
4 - Todd House
5 - Penn's Landing
6 - Holiday Inn Center City
7 - Society Hill Inn

For reservations and other information, call (215) 824-1600.

🚌 Yellow **Cab**, 922-8400. Nearest **local bus** stop at 30th and Market Streets just outside the station. **SEPTA commuter trains** serve both suburbs and downtown from this station's upper level and also provide service to Philadelphia International Airport. New Jersey Transit offers daily commuter train service east to Atlantic City from 30th St. Station. A **subway** station is across the street at the same intersection. **Rental cars** are available at the station, National, Avis and Hertz.

❓ **Philadelphia Visitors Center**, 16th St. and John F. Kennedy Blvd.; (215) 636-1666 or 800-537-7676.

🛏 **Holiday Inn City Center**, 18th and Market Streets, 19103; (215) 561-7500. Nine blocks to the 30th Street Station. $120.

-**Society Hill Inn**, 301 Chestnut St., 19106; (215) 925-1394. A small, homey hostelry, convenient to Independence National Historic Park. Includes continental breakfast. $95.

For downtown bed and breakfast reservations, **All About Town Bed & Breakfast of Philadelphia**, P.O. Box 562, Valley Forge, PA 19481; (610) 783-7838.

⭐ Philadelphia's charm is in its history. Of greatest historic significance is **Independence National Historical Park** in the area of 5th and Chestnut Streets. It can be reached by Transit bus. Among other attractions, the Park includes **Independence Hall** and the **Liberty Bell**.

The **Betsy Ross Flag House**, 239 Arch St., was the home of Betsy Ross who is credited with making the first American flag. The **Todd House**, 4th and Walnut Streets, built in 1775, was the home of Dolly Todd Madison. And **Penn's Landing**, waterfront area in the vicinity of Delaware Avenue and Chestnut Street, is where William Penn first stepped ashore. Old naval ships are anchored here, including a World War II submarine. Also, a trolley runs along the Delaware River.

0:00 (0:21) Depart Philadelphia.

0:01 (0:20) On right stands University of Pennsylvania's Franklin Field.

0:02 (0:19) Pass Philadelphia Convention Center complex, on right.

0:08 (0:13) Tower at trackside named "Baldwin" identifies town of Eddystone where Baldwin Locomotive Works, producer of more than 1,500 locomotives, was once major industry. Former Eddystone facility still stands on left.

0:09 (0:12) Chester, with its ancient brownstones bordering tracks, could easily pass for oldest town in Pennsylvania, which it is.

0:13 (0:08) Leave Pennsylvania and enter Delaware. Unique state boundary was formed in 1681 as section of a circle with center at spire of Old Court House in New Castle, DE. Delaware River comes into view on left. Enormous vessels traverse its wide expanse while a burgeoning maze of machinery and apparatus awaits their arrival at dockside.

0:18 (0:03) Cross Brandywine Creek which flows south to meet Christina River before emptying into Delaware.

0:19 (0:02) Christina River joins on left with drawbridges every mile or so. Immediately thereafter, enter grounds of Fort Christina Park at Wilmington. Here, in 1638, a Swedish expedition, under command of Peter Minuit, came ashore and established first European settlement in Delaware. On right, note "Old Swede's Church," erected in 1698. Maintaining services to this day, church is oldest in North America still standing as originally built. Adjacent log cabin is authentic 200-year-old structure.

0:21 (0:00) Arrive Wilmington. Attractive depot, accented by old brass weather vane atop spire, is an historic 1905 structure which underwent restoration in 1984.

WILMINGTON, DE - In 1802, Eleuthere duPont established a black-powder mill upon the banks of Brandywine Creek. From these humble beginnings, the duPont Corporation has evolved into one of the largest producers of chemicals, plastics, synthetic cloth and dyes

in the U.S. It is still, today, the foundation for Wilmington's claim as "Chemical Capital of the World."

0:00 (0:42) Depart Wilmington. For next several miles, beautiful farmhouses and lush agrarian settings alternate paradoxically with expansive industrial complexes.

0:09 (0:33) On left note large Chrysler Corporation plant.

0:11 (0:31) Once through Newark, DE, cross Delaware state line into Maryland at Mason and Dixon's line, surveyed by those two Englishmen in 1776 to resolve a boundary dispute between Pennsylvania and Maryland. Two small stone markers rest on boundary.

0:16 (0:26) Northeast River appears on left. Northeast, Bush, Gunpowder, and Back Rivers are all inlets of Chesapeake Bay.

0:20 (0:22) Cross Susquehanna River. Large steel bridges span river on right, while multitude of sailboats adorn marinas on both banks.

0:23 (0:20) Pass through Aberdeen where U.S. Army Ordnance Museum exhibits array of historical military hardware, uniforms, and the like.

0:26 (0:16) Cross Bush River.

0:30 (0:12) Cross Gunpowder River. It was here on January 4, 1987 that Amtrak's *Colonial*, just out of Baltimore and traveling in excess of 100 mph, slammed into three Conrail locomotives which, in spite of cautionary and stop signals, had just pulled onto main line. Tragedy resulted in 16 fatalities and 176 injuries.

0:33 (0:09) On left, border facilities of Maryland National Guard. Martin Marietta operation is immediately adjacent.

0:35 (0:07) Back River appears on left.

0:39 (0:03) Enter city limits of Baltimore atop elevated track bed. On right, clusters of high-density brownstones are huddled along hillsides, while on left, beautiful old church presides in foreground of downtown skyline.

BALTIMORE, MD - Started as a harbor town in 1729, Baltimore is now a city of varied nationalities and independent neighborhoods. It has long been one of the more important shipping,

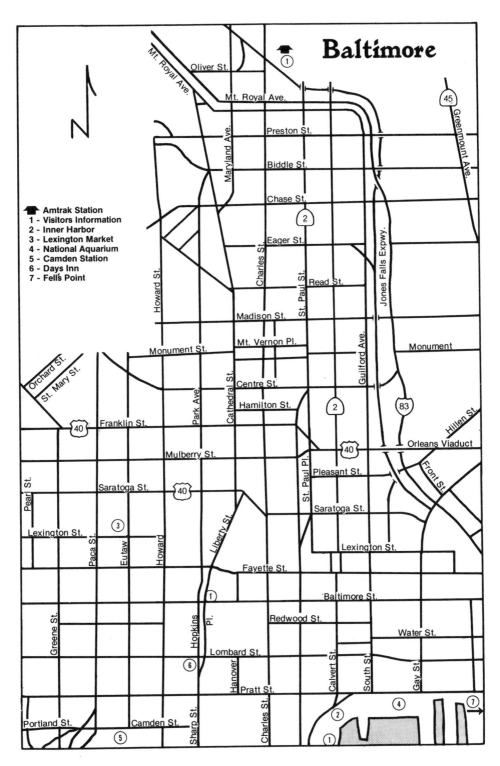

Baltimore

- Amtrak Station
- 1 - Visitors Information
- 2 - Inner Harbor
- 3 - Lexington Market
- 4 - National Aquarium
- 5 - Camden Station
- 6 - Days Inn
- 7 - Fells Point

Oliver St.
Mt. Royal Ave.
Mt. Royal Ave.
Preston St.
Biddle St.
Chase St.
Eager St.
Read St.
Madison St.
Mt. Vernon Pl.
Monument St.
Monument
Centre St.
Hamilton St.
Franklin St.
Orleans Viaduct
Mulberry St.
Pleasant St.
Saratoga St.
Saratoga St.
Lexington St.
Lexington St.
Fayette St.
Baltimore St.
Redwood St.
Water St.
Lombard St.
Pratt St.
Portland St.
Camden St.

Maryland Ave.
Charles St.
St. Paul St.
Jones Falls Expwy.
Guilford Ave.
Howard St.
Park Ave.
Cathedral St.
Pearl St.
Paca St.
Eutaw
Howard
Liberty St.
St. Paul Pl.
Calvert St.
South St.
Gay St.
Front St.
Hillen St.
Greenmount Ave.
Greene St.
Hopkins Pl.
Hanover St.
Sharp St.
Charles St.

Orchard St.
St. Mary St.

45
83
40
40
40

financial and industrial centers for the East. Although many of the older portions of the downtown have been razed and renewed, much of our nation's early history can still be virtually seen and felt amongst the city's retained landmarks.

During the War of 1812, Francis Scott Key penned the words to the *Star Spangled Banner* while witnessing the battle of Ft. McHenry from a ship in the harbor. For a brief period during the American Revolution, Baltimore served as the nation's capital. It is also the birthplace of baseball's Babe Ruth.

Pennsylvania Station, 1515 N. Charles Street, has been finely restored to its original grandeur. The station is about a mile north of downtown, but public buses and rubber-tired "trolleys" provide easy access during the day.

The station has a snack bar, a news-stand and redcap service. An information counter is located in the center of the station with bus schedules and other information. There is an ATM on the premises. Arrival and departure information occurs on electronic display boards and public address announcements are unusually understandable.

Yellow **Cab**, 685-1212; and Sun Cab, 235-0300. There are direct phones to Avis and Hertz for **rental car** pick up at the station. Nearest **bus stop** for southbound buses (to downtown) is one block away on St. Paul Street. Seasonal "**Trolley**" service to downtown is available on Charles Street in front of the station, from 11 am to 7 pm; fare is 25 cents. **Subway-Metrorail** information, call 539-5000. **MARC** commuter trains use Pennsylvania Station and travel south on the Northeast Corridor tracks to Washington, DC, then west to Gaithersburg. MARC trains also use a separate line between the downtown Camden Station and Washington.

Baltimore Convention and Visitors Bureau, 300 W. Pratt St., 21201; (410) 837-4636 or 800-282-6632. A visitor information center is also located at the Inner Harbor. Some information is also available at the station.

Lodging shown below is located in two desirable areas, the beautifully reclaimed Inner Harbor area and historic Fell's Point. Fell's Point and the Inner Harbor are connected during warmer months by the rubber-tired trolleys, and "water taxis." The trolleys also stop at Penn station.

-**Days Inn Baltimore Inner Harbor**, 100 Hopkins Place, 21201; (410) 576-1000. Attractive high rise located downtown on the trolley route, about four blocks from the Inner Harbor and a mile from the station. $90.

-**Inn at Henderson's Wharf**, 1000 Fell St., 21231; (410) 522-7777 or 800-522-2088. Former B&O Railroad tobacco warehouse, now a handsome inn on the harbor at Fell's Point. Breakfast included. $120.

The **Inner Harbor**, at Pratt and Light Streets, is a waterfront showpiece in the heart of the city. Restaurants, shops, harbor tours and harbor activities are delightfully compatible in this urban setting. The **U.S. Frigate Constellation** and the **U.S. Maritime Museum** are here, as well as the outstanding **National Aquarium in Baltimore** with aquatic exhibits, including a coral reef, sharks, eels, jellyfish, whales, dolphin shows, and a rain forest. For a view of the city, an **observation deck** is on the 27th floor of the World Trade Center, also at the Inner Harbor. **Maryland Science Center and Davis Planetarium** is at the southwest corner of the Inner Harbor.

Fell's Point, just a mile east of the Inner Harbor and easily reached by trolley or water taxi in the summer, is Baltimore's old waterfront neighborhood—it's one of the oldest waterfront communities in the country. Once a tough district known for its sailor-filled bars, Fell's Point has become a mixture of Georgetown and Greenwich Village.

Fort McHenry National Monument, at the foot of E. Fort Ave., southeast of the city, is the site of the successful battle against the British during the War of 1812 which inspired Francis Scott Key to write the words of the *Star Spangled Banner*.

And for those interested in trains and

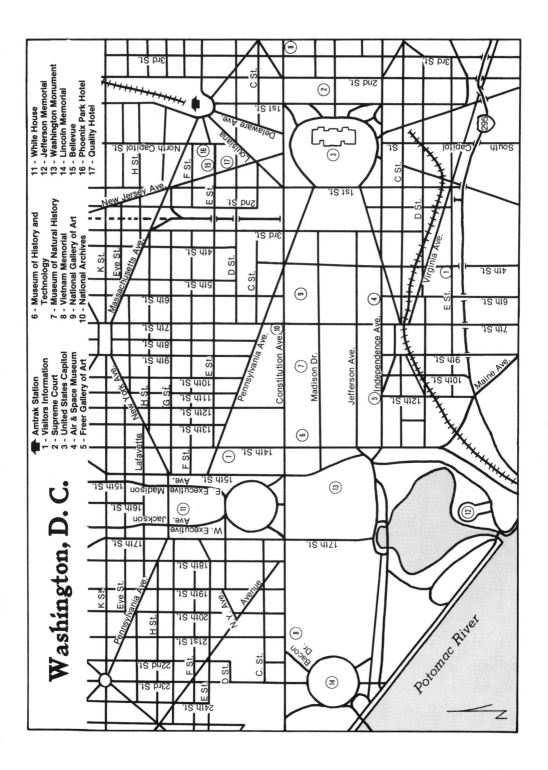

Washington, D. C.

Amtrak Station
1 - Visitors Information
2 - Supreme Court
3 - United States Capitol
4 - Air & Space Museum
5 - Freer Gallery of Art

6 - Museum of History and Technology
7 - Museum of Natural History
8 - Vietnam Memorial
9 - National Gallery of Art
10 - National Archives

11 - White House
12 - Jefferson Memorial
13 - Washington Monument
14 - Lincoln Memorial
15 - Bellevue
16 - Phoenix Park Hotel
17 - Quality Hotel

Potomac River

Washington, DC, Union Station
JACK SWANSON

streetcars: The **Baltimore Streetcar Museum** is at 1901 Falls Road, and the **B. & O. Railroad Museum**, Pratt and Poppleton Streets, the latter in a fine, old circular roundhouse, over 100 years old, with a world famous display of old locomotives and other rail artifacts.

0:00 (0:24) Depart Baltimore, noting old stone bridge on right. Proceed into eerily lit century-old B & P Tunnel—a dark, wet, 7,492-foot bottleneck. Emerge minutes later amidst another covey of old brownstones.

0:10 (0:14) Extensive cemetery lines route on right.

0:12 (0:12) On right pass distilleries of Calvert Whiskey.

0:18 (0:06) Baltimore-Washington International Airport is a stop for some trains where Amtrak passengers are shuttled directly to and from airport's terminal. Guidelights for end of runway are on left.

0:24 (0:00) Arrive New Carrollton.

NEW CARROLLTON, MD - This very modern station serves the northern suburbs of Washington, DC. There is a Metro station here with subway and bus service to DC, Virginia and Maryland.

0:00 (0:09) Depart New Carrollton and cross Maryland state line into District of Columbia.

0:04 (0:05) Cross Anacostia River. Black Entertainment TV Network facilities are on immediate right. Then watch for blue and gold dome of National Shrine of the Immaculate Conception off to right, largest Roman Catholic Church in U.S. and seventh largest church in world.

0:07 (0:02) Approaching Washington, silhouette of Washington Monument can be discerned in distance on right.

0:09 (0:00) Arrive Washington, DC.

WASHINGTON, DC - The nation's first president played a guiding role in developing what would become the country's capital. Not only did he personally select the men to lay out and plan the city, Pierre Charles L'Enfant and Andrew Ellicott, he chose the sites for both the White House and the Capitol Building.

The result of such presidential involvement is an unusually well laid-out city, with broad streets, many radiating from small parks and circles, lined by imposing marble edifices. It is handsome geometry and one of the reasons Washington is among the most visited towns in the U.S.

The city is easy to see. Many of its attractions line the Mall—a lengthy, broad esplanade, stretching from the Capitol Building on the east to the Lincoln Memorial on the west. An extensive, modern and easy-to-use subway system makes it possible to do more venturesome exploring without a car, a real plus since heavy traffic is constant and parking is scarce.

Union Station, 50 Massachusetts Ave., NE, located on Capitol Hill, is undisputedly the nation's premier train station. Thanks to a heroic renovation effort, Union Station is no longer a national eyesore, but a gleaming showpiece of marble floors, mahogany woodwork and gold-leafed ceilings.

When Daniel Burnham's beaux-arts masterpiece was first opened in 1907, it lived up to his simple creed: "Make no little plans." It was large enough to hold the entire U.S. Army—then 50,000 in number. It reached its zenith of activity during World War II when no less than 5,000 employees worked here. Subsequently, rail travel declined and so did Union Station. Surviving a 1953 runaway train that crashed into its main concourse, a 1960 effort to demolish it, and finally the 1968 National Visitors Center fiasco, it has now undergone a triumphant resuscitation.

The station is laid out on three levels. The street or main level contains Amtrak ticket offices, waiting areas and boarding gates as well as banks, rental cars, shops and cafes. The lower level is a huge food concourse and movie theater, while the upper level has a large collection of "destination" shops and boutiques.

Luggage carts and redcaps are available. There is a special Metropolitan Lounge for first-class ticket holders. A large directory in the waiting area has phone lines to numerous inexpensive hotels. A 1,400-car garage guarantees space for Amtrak passengers. Enter on H Street or Massachusetts Ave. Elevators and escalators take patrons to the station.

For Amtrak reservations and other information, call (202) 484-7540.

Diamond **Cab**, 387-6200. A Metrorail **subway** stop (red line) is at the station, as well as a **local bus** stop; call 637-7000 for information. **Tourmobiles**, a convenient way to see many of the sights, also stop at the station. Both Budget and National have **rental cars** available at the station.

Visitors Information Center, 1455 Pennsylvania Ave. Call (202) 789-7000.

The hotels shown here are within easy walking distance from the station and are also convenient to the Capitol, the Mall and the Metro.

-**Bellevue Hotel**, 15 E Street, NW, 20001; (202) 638-9000 or 800-327-6667. Nicely remodeled older hotel. Two short blocks from the station. Special rates for Amtrak passengers. Buffet breakfast. $110.

-**Phoenix Park Hotel**, 520 North Capitol Street, NW, 20001; (202) 638-6900 or 800-824-5419. Smaller hostelry with deluxe accommodations, only a block from the station. Special rate for Amtrak passengers, $150.

-**Quality Hotel Capitol Hill**, 415 New Jersey Ave., NW, 20001; (202) 638-1616. Four blocks from the station. $100.

For a reasonable fare, the popular **Tourmobile** takes passengers on a narrated tour of 18 historic sites, including Arlington Cemetery, while another route goes to historic Alexandria and Mt. Vernon. Passengers are permitted to re-board throughout the day at no extra charge.

The attractions shown below are along or near the Mall, and a healthy walker (read hiker) theoretically could reach them all on foot from the station.

The **"Smithsonian Museums** are mostly spread out along the Mall. Some of the more popular ones include: The **National Air and Space Museum**, with superb displays of aircraft, from the Wright

Brothers' plane to modern-day space vehicles; the **Freer Gallery of Art** with fine displays of Oriental and other art, the **National Museum of American History**, displaying aspects of the nation's history and development; and the **National Museum of Natural History** with collections including the Hope Diamond.

Some other popular points of interest along or near the Mall include: The **United States Capitol**, the **Supreme Court**, the **National Gallery of Art**, the **National Archives**, (the resting place for the Constitution, the Declaration of Independence and the Bill of Rights), the **Washington Monument** and the **Lincoln Memorial**.

NEW HAVEN TO SPRINGFIELD

NEW HAVEN, CT - See page 22.
0:00 (0:16) Departing New Haven, Inland Route trains swing northward away from shoreline route and angle across Connecticut, directly toward Hartford.
0:01 (0:15) Gaggle of Metro-North commuter train cars repose in rail yards at right.
0:08 (0:08) Incongruously colored (pink) tanks comprise Wyatt Fuel Company tank farm.
0:16 (0:00) Arrive Wallingford.

WALLINGFORD, CT - One of Connecticut's older cities, Wallingford is known for its silver manufacturing. Note classic old brick church with fine spire just after station on right.
0:00 (0:06) Depart Wallingford.
0:06 (0:00) Arrive Meriden.

MERIDEN, CT - This is home to the world's largest producer of silverware—International Silver Company. At its main plant visitors can see Heritage House, furnished to illustrate 18th-century life in America, while silversmiths and pewters demonstrate early methods of production.
0:00 (0:08) Depart Meriden.
0:02 (0:06) Former facilities of International Silver Company make forlorn scene at right.
0:03 (0:05) Idyllic Silver Lake stretches along tracks on right.

0:08 (0:00) Arrive Berlin.

 BERLIN, CT - Here, first tinware in America was produced in early 1700s.

0:00 (0:11) Depart Berlin.

0:11 (0:00) Arriving Hartford, marble capitol building with its gold-leafed dome looms above train on right. One of Hartford's more unusual industries, gold-beating, provided the gild for this elegant structure. Some fine historical exhibits are housed within.

 HARTFORD, CT - Referred to as the "Insurance Capital of the World," more insurance is underwritten in Hartford than in any other city in the United States. Other major employers include Colt Industries, makers of firearms (including the famed Colt "45") and Hueblein Industries of alcoholic beverage renown.

During its development, Hartford fostered some of America's greatest intellectuals. In 1874, Mark Twain built a whimsical brick mansion (it looked more like a Mississippi riverboat), and penned Huck Finn and Tom Sawyer as well as many of his other beloved tales. Noah Webster was born in West Hartford, best known for creating the first comprehensive American dictionary, and Harriet Beecher Stowe ("Uncle Tom's Cabin") also lived here.

0:00 (0:12) Depart Hartford.

0:04 (0:08) First glimpse of Connecticut River, flowing southeastward toward its Atlantic mouth at Old Saybrook, is afforded on right.

0:07 (0:05) Windsor, CT, located in shade-grown tobacco country, is one of Connecticut's earliest settlements, having been founded by Plymouth colonists in 1663.

0:08 (0:04) Farmington River is now crossed. This broad stream follows a 60-mile serpentine course from its Algonquin-State-Forest birthplace, only 20 miles straight west of us, to its Connecticut-River joinder just east of here.

0:12 (0:00) Arrive Windsor Locks.

WINDSOR LOCKS, CT - This New England manufacturing community also serves as the location for Hartford's airport (Bradley International Airport) as well as the Bradley Air Museum which houses a collection of vintage military aircraft.

0:00 (0:19) Depart Windsor Locks and roll under Interstate 91, stretching from New Haven northward to Vermont-Québec border.

0:01 (0:18) Across Windsor Locks Canal, on right, sign on factory reads "Dexter-Nonwovens Division."

Dexter Corp. is an American institution. It is the oldest corporation listed on the New York Stock Exchange and quite possibly the third oldest continually operated company in America. This particular plant has manufactured long-fiber papers for tea bags, oil filters, surgical gowns and other paper products. Although the canal was constructed in the early 1800s to provide a shipping bypass needed to avoid a dam further upstream, later it provided fresh water (critical in paper production) to Dexter.

0:04 (0:15) Having tired of following west bank of Connecticut River, rails now cross to eastern shore.

0:06 (0:13) Rumble past Enfield, on right, where Jonathan Edwards, perhaps Colonial New England's most effective revivalist, delivered one of his greatest sermons—"Sinners in the Hands of an Angry God." Although his voice was weak, and he read from manuscripts held closely to his near-sighted eyes, his logic and power were extraordinary. Edwards eventually became president of College of New Jersey—now known as Princeton University.

0:11 (0:08) After passing through Thompsonville, leave Connecticut and enter Massachusetts.

0:15 (0:04) On right, orange and black building is home to Basketball Hall of Fame.

0:19 (0:00) Arrive Springfield.

SPRINGFIELD, MA - An important manufacturing city of the Northeast, Springfield had its start as a mere trading post in the 1630s. In 1794 the United States opened an important armory here, now the Springfield Armory Museum. The Basketball Hall of Fame is located in Springfield.

Vermonter

Following a portion of the route once traveled by an overnight train to Montréal called the *Montréaler*, the *Vermonter* completes its northward, daylight run from Washington, DC, at the border town of St. Albans, VT. Connecting Amtrak Thruway Bus service now transports Montréal passengers between that city and St. Albans.

The *Vermonter's* path follows the Northeast Corridor between Washington and New Haven, then the Corridor's "Inland Route" to Hartford. From there, the train runs its own unique route through Massachusetts, New Hampshire and Vermont, providing access to some of New England's ski areas and wonderfully pastoral viewing of Vermont's maple syrup country. Covered bridges and forest interspersed with small dairy farms enhance the scene.

NORTHBOUND SCHEDULE (Condensed)

Washington, DC - Early Morning Departure
New York, NY - Late Morning
Springfield, MA - Midafternoon
St. Albans, VT - Late Evening Arrival

SOUTHBOUND SCHEDULE (Condensed)*

St. Albans, VT - Early Morning Departure
Springfield, MA -Early Afternoon
New York, NY - Late Afternoon
Washington, DC - Midevening Arrival

*Four hours later on Sunday.

FREQUENCY - Daily.
SEATING - Reserved coaches.
DINING - Sandwiches, snacks and beverages.
BAGGAGE - Checked baggage handled at most stations.
RESERVATIONS - All-reserved train.
LENGTH OF TRIP - 606 miles in 12 hours.

ROUTE LOG

For route between Washington, DC and Springfield, MA, see portions of Northeast Corridor log, pages 19 and 26.

 SPRINGFIELD, MA - See page 37.
0:00 (1:06) Depart Springfield.
1:06 (0:00) Arrive Amherst.

AMHERST, MA - Education and literature permeate this New England community. Amherst College, University of Massachusetts and Hampshire College are all located here, and three well-known American poets, Dickinson, Frost and Field, all resided here. Noah Webster also lived in Amherst.

Amherst also serves as a stop for nearby Northampton, just a few miles to the west. Northampton was the very heart of the religious revivalist movement during the first half of the 18th century and was home of Jonathan Edwards. Later, Northampton was home to "shy, silent" Calvin Coolidge, the country's 30th president. Smith College is now located there.

0:00 (0:55) Depart Amherst.

0:17 (0:38) Trestle carries tracks over Boston & Maine's east-west main line, then cross Millers River.

0:32 (0:23) Another trestle and train crosses to west shore of Connecticut River. Leave Massachusetts and enter Vermont.

0:55 (0:00) Arrive Brattleboro.

BRATTLEBORO, VT - Rudyard Kipling, whose stories and poetry gave heroic support to the British Empire, lived here for four years near the end of the 19th century. His wife was a Brattleboro girl. An old rail station houses the Brattleboro Museum and Art Center.

0:00 (0:34) Depart Brattleboro.

0:34 (0:00) Arrive Bellows Falls.

BELLOWS FALLS, VT - The town derives its "Falls" name from falls in the adjacent Connecticut River, which, in the early 19th century, forced construction of a canal with nine locks to raise or lower river traffic past the cascades.

0:00 (0:22) Depart Bellows Falls, and immediately cross Connecticut River into New Hampshire.

0:22 (0:00) Arrive Claremont Jct., a stop for adjacent Claremont.

CLAREMONT, NH - This community, located on the Sugar River, has the distinction of being Amtrak's only stop in the state of New Hampshire. It is home to New Hampshire VocTech College.

0:00 (0:30) Depart Claremont Jct.

0:02 (0:28) Span carries train high over Sugar River.

0:10 (0:20) Cross Connecticut River once again and re-enter Vermont, then through town of Windsor, birthplace of Vermont. The "Republic's" constitution was signed here July 9, 1777, and tavern where this historic event took place still stands.

0:30 (0:00) Arrive White River Junction where historic, Colonial-style station serves Amtrak passengers. Restored B&M 4-4-0 steam locomotive stands in square in front of station, while just beyond is Hotel Coolidge, where Calvin once slept.

WHITE RIVER JUNCTION, VT - As you might expect, this is the joinder of the White River with the Connecticut River. Historically a railroad center, this is also the point where the Boston and Maine and Central Vermont meet. While the B&M heads due north, the CV angles northwesterly, the latter being the route of the *Vermonter*. Hanover, NH, home to Dartmouth College, is less than five miles from here.

0:00 (1:12) Depart White River Junction and follow White River northwestward across very heart of Vermont.

0:09 (1:03) At West Hartford, cross hikers' delight—the Appalachian Trail.

0:23 (0:49) This is South Royalton. Three miles east of here is Sharon, the birthplace of Joseph Smith, founder of the Mormon Church. A 38 1/2-foot polished granite shaft (not visible from tracks) marks spot.

0:27 (0:45) Bethel is northern end of trackage where Vermont's first passenger train made its way from White River Falls. Town has unique eight-sided library originally constructed as a school.

0:38 (0:34) Cruise through Randolph. Note unusually wide streets which were designed so that town could become state's capital, located at geographic center of Vermont. It didn't happen, however. The Morgan horse breed, now Vermont's official state animal, started here.

0:40 (0:32) Having left Third Branch of White River, we now follow beside Dog River.

0:54 (0:18) Just before Northfield, Norwich University, nation's oldest private military institution, is on right.

0:57 (0:15) As we rumble through Northfield Falls, watch for covered bridges. Four of these picturesque structures are located within a quarter of a mile from here.

1:12 (0:00) Arrive Montpelier Junction, suburban stop for Montpelier.

MONTPELIER, VT - Vermont's capital city is home to not only the state's government but also a large segment of the life insurance industry. Admiral

George Dewey, hero of Manila Bay, was a Montpelierite, and his father founded the National Life Insurance Company located here. Rock of Ages Granite Quarry, largest in the world, is just southeast of here near Barre (rhymes with Harry). Barre is also home to the Canadian-owned Bombardier plant which builds Superliner cars for Amtrak.

0:00 (0:15) Depart Montpelier and proceed northwestward through Winooski River Valley.

0:14 (0:00) Arrive Waterbury.

WATERBURY, VT - This is the heart of Vermont's ski country with several slopes nearby. Stowe is only ten miles up the road.

0:00 (0:28) Depart Waterbury, continuing to trace course of Winooski and through very heart of Green Mountains.

0:24 (0:04) July 7, 1984, one of Amtrak's worst accidents occurred on this segment of right-of-way when seven of *Montréaler's* thirteen cars plunged into a gully by Winooski River Bridge.

A localized storm had plugged a stone culvert (built around 1850) and washed out the track bed shortly before the train reached this point. Five people were killed and 133 injured.

0:28 (0:00) Arrive Essex Junction, which serves adjacent Burlington.

BURLINGTON, VT - Burlington is Vermont's largest city. Beautifully situated on the eastern shore of Lake Champlain with the Green Mountains just to the east, it is home to the University of Vermont, the oldest such institution in the state. Ethan Allen, who helped organize The Green Mountain Boys, and led them on a raid that captured Ft. Ticonderoga from the British during the American Revolution, is buried here. John Dewey, the celebrated philosopher, was born here. Ferry service operates between Burlington and Port Kent, New York.

0:00 (0:29) Depart Essex Junction, continuing on Central Vermont, following a course due north through Vermont's dairy and sugar maple country.

0:13 (0:16) Pass through Milton at southern tip of Arrowhead Mountain Lake which is on our left. A pre-Columbian Indian flint quarry is located here.

0:15 (0:14) Cross Lamoille River on Georgia High Bridge built with picturesque granite pilings.

0:17 (0:12) Vermont Whey Company plant, on left, serves regional dairy farmers.

0:29 (0:00) Arrive St. Albans, where two-story brick Amtrak station, on right, is just north of Central Vermont's headquarters, a large three-story brick structure built in 1866 to serve as a passenger station.

ST. ALBANS, VT - Hardly a likely setting for a Civil War skirmish, but on October 19, 1864, the northernmost conflict of that war took place when Confederates raided three of the town's banks. During the War of 1812, smugglers used the area as a base of operations.

Today, the most excitement occurs during the Vermont Sugar Maple Festival, held here in early April with parades, fiddling contests, trips to nearby sugar houses and even rolling pin competitions.

Amtrak runs connecting Thruway Bus Service between here and Montréal.

Montreal
Albany
New York City

Adirondack

The *Adirondack*, traveling from Washington, DC, to Montréal, passes through 200 years of history along 600 miles of track. And for fourteen hours, those aboard are treated to a changing scene that grows more spectacular as their journey progresses north of New York City. The old New York Central Route (now Conrail) up the east side of the Hudson River is steeped with riverside beauty, history and New England tradition.

But the thrilling part of this journey takes place farther north as the tracks embrace the western shore of Lake Champlain. Rock cuts, lily ponds, sailboats, Victorian depots, the Adirondacks of New York and Green Mountains of Vermont line the route. And in the fall, the color is sublime. If you think you can almost hear the salvos from the battles of Lake Champlain and Saratoga, it could be the cannons that are still fired at Fort Ticonderoga.

NORTHBOUND SCHEDULE (Condensed)
New York, NY - Midmorning
Albany-Rensselaer, NY - Early Afternoon
Montréal, QC - Midevening Arrival

SOUTHBOUND SCHEDULE (Condensed)*
Montréal, QC - Midmorning Departure
Albany-Rensselaer, NY - Late Afternoon
New York, NY - Midevening

*Two hours later on Sundays

FREQUENCY - Daily.
SEATING - Reserved coaches and Custom Class.
DINING - Sandwiches, snacks and beverages.
BAGGAGE - No checked baggage.
RESERVATIONS - All-reserved train.
LENGTH OF TRIP - 606 miles in 14 hours.

ROUTE LOG

For route between Washington, DC and New York City, see that portion of the Northeast Corridor log, page 26.

 NEW YORK, NY - See page 19.

0:00 (0:41) Depart New York City's Penn Station through newly constructed tunnel that curls up and over Amtrak's North River Tunnels (which bore beneath Hudson to Newark). Then pass beneath city's Jacob Javits Convention Center.

0:06 (0:35) Travel beneath Riverside Park.

0:09 (0:32) West 125th Street leads off to right directly into heart of historic Harlem. Glimpses of Hudson River are afforded on left.

0:13 (0:25) Graceful, elegant superstructure of George Washington Bridge now dominates view to left forward. Completed during the Great Depression in 1931, structure was expanded in 1962 to carry 14 lanes of vehicular traffic. Across Hudson, New Jersey's

Adirondack — Tappan Zee Bridge, Tarrytown, NY
SCOTT HARTLEY

Palisades Interstate Park extends northward along river's shore. Just before bridge, "Little Red Lighthouse" can be seen on left, now designated a National Historic Landmark.

0:17 (0:24) Pass by 62-acre Ft. Tryon Park, a gift from John D. Rockefeller, Jr. Above to right is The Cloisters, a mix of Gothic and Romanesque architecture built to house Metropolitan Museum of Art's Medieval art collection. Legendary Unicorn tapestries are housed here.

0:19 (0:22) Slip through Inwood Hill Park and then encounter Harlem River Ship Canal, technically Spuyten Duyvil (a Dutch term used to describe junction of Harlem and Hudson Rivers) Creek. Spuyten Duyvil Swing Bridge carries tracks over river, while auto traffic of Henry Hudson Parkway is lifted across on right by Henry Hudson Bridge. While crossing Harlem River, leave Manhattan and enter "The Bronx." River was once important barge route, but now mainly accommodates sightseeing tours.

0:22 (0:19) Metro North's commuter lines from Grand Central Terminal, formerly used by Amtrak, now join from right. Tracks now proceed along eastern bank of Hudson River, as barges and freighters traverse waters of this inland passage.

0:24 (0:16) At Yonkers large, stately homes nestled along hillsides only preview what will soon become a premier attraction of this Hudson River run.

0:31 (0:10) On right, fanciful European design highlights station at Ardsley-On-Hudson.

0:33 (0:08) Tappan-Zee Bridge on forward left is first of several dramatic structures that span Hudson River between here and Albany.

0:38 (0:03) At Ossining, track borders legendary Sing Sing state prison. Line from Ossining north borders some of country's most graciously endowed estates. From Roosevelts to Vanderbilts, many of society's elite have chosen to make their homes amidst lush woodlands and verdant hills of this Hudson River Valley.

0:41 (0:00) Arrive Croton-Harmon.

CROTON-HARMON, NY - All trains once paused at this old Dutch community, switching from electric to diesel power. Long-standing regulation still prohibits diesel-powered transport within New York City tunnels.

0:00 (0:38) Depart Croton-Harmon past further array of magnificent dwellings. Frequently, river inlets intrude on estates and provide picturesque playground for ducks and swans.

0:12 (0:26) Train glides beneath soaring Bear Mountain Bridge which carries not only vehicular traffic but hikers following Appalachian Trail.

0:18 (0:20) Across river, scenic Highland Falls tumble down cliffs, while campus of West Point Military Academy presides above. Established in 1802, nation's oldest service academy still resides on site where George Washington once stationed Revolutionary troops to thwart British maneuvers along Hudson River. Grant, Lee, Pershing, MacArthur, Patton, Eisenhower, Westmoreland and Schwarzkopf were some of the Point's more illustrious graduates.

0:20 (0:18) Through Cold Spring, probably best known for its summer theater.

0:23 (0:15) Pass through double-bore Breakneck Ridge Tunnel.

0:24 (0:14) Ensconced in middle of river, Bannerman's Castle is fascinating re-creation of old robber baron's stronghold. It was used by original owner as a storehouse for armaments.

0:31 (0:07) North of Chelsea, cross Wappinger River as it spills into Hudson.

0:38 (0:00) Arrive Poughkeepsie.

POUGHKEEPSIE, NY - Formerly the state's capital during the Revolutionary War, Poughkeepsie has since evolved into a thriving manufacturing center, with a diverse range of products ensuring economic stability. The city at one time became synonymous with the Smith Brothers who made their famous cough drops here.

0:00 (0:14) Departing Poughkeepsie, picturesque waterfalls of Fallkill Creek trickle down by trackside on right. Spanning river on left, old cantilever railroad bridge was largest of its type when constructed in 1889. A fire in early 1970s precluded its further use.

0:04 (0:10) Across river, letters "CIA," inscribed on cliffside, face nearby Culinary Institute of America where many of country's renowned chefs honed formative skills.

0:05 (0:04) Shortly after seeing huge, red-roofed house across Hudson (former estate of Father Vine), Franklin Delano Roosevelt's Hyde Park home will be above tracks on right and Vanderbilt Mansion appears shortly thereafter on left.

0:14 (0:00) Arriving Rhinecliff, fine old lighthouse looms in midst of Hudson, while on opposite bank, castle-like mansions embellish scene seemingly plucked from Bavarian landscape.

RHINECLIFF, NY - Rhinecliff is the Amtrak stop for nearby Rhinebeck, a charming community nestled in the hills of the Hudson River Valley. Boasting one of the largest districts of homes on the National Register, Rhinebeck is also the site of Beekman Arms—the nation's oldest continuously operating hotel. F.D.R. chose to conclude many of his campaigns from this historic inn.

Here, too, is the famed Old Rhinebeck Aerodrome where, on weekends from June to October, vintage aircraft take to the skies for daredevil excitement. Its museum of World War I aircraft is world renowned.

0:00 (0:22) Depart Rhinecliff.

0:10 (0:11) Mountains flanking river are part of Catskill chain and will escort train into town of Hudson.

0:20 (0:02) On left, exquisite old lighthouse still maintains watchful vigil.

0:22 (0:00) Arrive comely station at Hudson.

HUDSON, NY - Beautiful gardens grace the avenues of this picturesque town, named for Henry Hudson whose "Half Moon" docked here in 1609.

0:00 (0:25) Depart Hudson.

0:25 (0:00) Arriving Albany-Rensselaer (station is actually in Rensselaer, just across river from Albany), downtown Albany skyline stands out on left. Prominent 42-story skyscraper is centerpiece of Empire State Plaza. Left of tower, low-slung Cultural Education Center houses State Museum and Library, while on right, dynamic elliptical structure is Center for Performing Arts. Four smaller towers in background are also part of this ambitious billion-dollar project. Once in station, inspiring domed archways of St. John the Baptist Catholic Church can be seen protruding above treetops on right.

ALBANY-RENSSELAER, NY - A small-town atmosphere with big-city prestige is the claim of Albany, New York's state capital. Replete with cosmopolitan amenities, Albany is likewise a stone's throw from the rural splendor depicted in the paintings of America's beloved Grandma Moses.

As well as a bastion of state government, Albany has remained a vital inland port since the completion of the Erie Canal in 1825. Today, private operators conduct excursions along this historic waterway that recapture the spirit and grace of an earlier era. And then, too, this has long been an important railroading town. Fortunately, an important piece of this past was preserved when Albany's decaying Union Station, where New York Central and Delaware & Hudson trains once arrived on different levels, was saved from the wrecking ball and restored to its original elegance by Norstar, a bank holding company.

In the adjacent town of Rensselaer, one can tour Fort Crailo, the nation's oldest fort built in 1642. Legend has it that a British surgeon wrote the famous "Yankee Doodle" tune while visiting this site.

Amtrak Station, East Street, is located in the city of Rensselaer, just across the Hudson River from downtown Albany. The station has a good coffee shop as well as snack vending machines, a newsstand with a selection of international newspapers and free luggage carts.

Yankee Doodle **Taxi**, 465-8188. (Always inquire about fare before leaving station in unmetered cabs.) Thrifty **Rental Car**, 465-7315, with downtown Albany location, will pick up and drop off at station during their business hours; courtesy phone in station.

Fort Crailo Motel, 110 Columbia Turnpike, Rensselaer, NY, 12144; (518) 472-1360 or 800-477-3123. Well managed, reasonably priced motel; restaurants within walking distance. Closest to station; a few minutes cab ride for about a $7 fare. $40.

0:00 (0:22) Depart Albany-Rensselaer.

0:04 (0:19) Cross Hudson River. On left, ornate spires and turrets adorn magnificent State University Administration Headquarters. Originally built in 1916 as corporate offices of Delaware and Hudson Railroad, complex is actually three buildings interconnected, with Flemish facades maintaining delightful continuity throughout. Replica of Henry Hudson's "Half Moon" is highlight of weather vane perched atop main tower.

0:05 (0:17) Intriguing amalgam of modern and classical architecture is a most striking feature of Albany's city center on left.

0:07 (0:15) August 9, 1831, one of North America's earliest steam locomotives made its inaugural run between Albany and Schenectady when Mohawk & Hudson's *De Witt Clinton*, pulling three stagecoach-appearing cars, chugged up this grade—steepest on Water Level Route. Mohawk & Hudson was first railroad chartered in New York.

0:10 (0:10) On outskirts of town, four lonesome high rises comprise State Office Building campus on left.

0:18 (0:04) Approaching Schenectady, attractively landscaped parkways dissect sprawling grounds of General Electric industrial park on left.

0:19 (0:00) Arriving Schenectady, tall, gold-domed City Hall clock tower is prominent fixture on right.

SCHENECTADY, NY - Emerging from the heart of the Industrial

Revolution, Schenectady became known as "the city that lights and hauls the world." The American Locomotive Company's Schenectady Works and Thomas Edison's Machine Works were primarily responsible for this designation, the latter eventually evolving into the colossal General Electric Corporation.

Schenectady's "Stockade District" is a premier historical attraction, representing one of the country's best-preserved enclaves of early American architecture and culture. Its name stems from the original 1661 settlement which was surrounded by a stockade to guard against French and Indian attacks.

From here on the best viewing will generally be found on the right (east) side, particularly along Lake Champlain.

0:00 (0:29) Departing Schenectady, city's historic Stockade Area is off to left.

0:02 (0:27) Gold-domed building off to right is on campus of Union College.

0:04 (0:25) Sprawling, old buildings on left were formerly occupied by American Locomotive Works (Alco), one of America's premier locomotive builders.

0:06 (0:23) Cross Mohawk River.

0:29 (0:00) Arrive Saratoga Springs where modern depot on right will be a disappointment to those anticipating more nostalgia from this historic town.

 SARATOGA SPRINGS, NY - At the turn of the century, few spas rivaled Saratoga's popularity with the East's wealthy and socially elite. Stylish Old World bathhouses offered supposedly curative soaks in naturally carbonated mineral water and elegant hotels lined the town's thoroughfares. Fine gardens and even a spouting geyser added to the charm. For those seeking to try their luck, opulent casinos comparable to any in Europe offered gambling while the Saratoga Race Track presented thoroughbred racing. Notables who frequented Saratoga included the likes of Diamond Jim Brady and Lillian Russell, while the Vanderbilts and Whitneys had homes near the track. Today, society no longer looks upon Saratoga Springs with the same fervor, but the town is still a fascinating summer resort.

History buffs will remember that in 1777 the Revolutionary War Battle of Saratoga (actually fought several miles from here at Bemis Heights and Stillwater) brought defeat to 7,000 British troops, Hessian mercenaries and Indians led by Lt. General John Burgoyne and turned the war's momentum in the Patriot's favor. News of this American victory brought about the Franco-American Alliance.

0:00 (0:20) Depart Saratoga Springs.

0:19 (0:01) Cross back to east side of Hudson River. Scott Paper Company plant, which processes wood pulp into facial and toilet tissue, napkins and waxed paper, is clearly visible upstream, on left.

0:20 (0:00) Arrive Ft. Edward where old relic of a depot still stands at left.

FT. EDWARD, NY - This small upstate town derives its name from the fort constructed on the banks of the Hudson during the French and Indian War. In 1825, locks were constructed here, the highest point on the canal, allowing the Champlain Canal to connect to the Hudson River and creating a continuous trading waterway between the St. Lawrence and the lower Hudson. The canal is still used as a part of the New York State Canal System, frequented now by barges with modern-day cargoes such as jet fuel.

This is Amtrak's access to Glens Falls and Lake George.

0:00 (0:23) Depart Ft. Edward.

0:11 (0:12) Champlain Canal, on right, is encased by spectacularly beautiful rock cliffs as a prelude to what is yet to come as we near Lake Champlain. From here to Canadian border, scenery is spectacular as *Adirondack* hugs west shore of 105-mile-long Lake Champlain.

0:15 (0:08) At Comstock, Great Meadows Correctional Facility can be seen on right.

0:23 (0:00) Arriving Whitehall, brick chimney on right once lifted smoke from Champlain Silk Mill prior to Great Depression.

WHITEHALL, NY - This is the northern terminus of the Champlain

Canal, complete with locks giving barges access to and from South Bay—Lake Champlain's southernmost extension.

0:00 (0:29) Departing Whitehall, note old mansion with clock tower, above town to right on Skene Mountain. Using granite quarried from mountain, structure was built in 1875 by Italian artisans as home for New York State Supreme Court judge. In early 1900s, clock was added to cupola when timepiece was removed from weakened steeple of local Presbyterian Church. Movement is controlled by weights in basement.

0:01 (0:28) Hull of U.S.S. Ticonderoga (War of 1812 veteran) has been carefully preserved under protective roof at right.

0:04 (0:25) Here we cross (and get our first view of) Lake Champlain (South Bay). Also, it is here that we enter Adirondack Park, established in 1885—an enormous acreage, much of which is wilderness. It is largest state park in U.S. Sylvan lily ponds with assorted waterfowl stretch along right side of train.

Birthplace of the Navy

Although the U. S. Navy avoids designating any one place as its official birthplace, Whitehall claims the honor. It was here on May 9, 1775 that Colonists under orders from Benedict Arnold captured Skenesborough (now Whitehall) from a Loyalist, Philip Skene. Two days later, Skene's sailing ship was taken to nearby Crown Point where it was armed for war. The schooner was then used to capture the British naval ship Enterprize. These activities seem to predate other Revolutionary naval beginnings.

0:13 (0:16) Navigational buoys are sprinkled along channel on right to guide water traffic between Lake Champlain proper and South Bay. Small pleasure craft are often in abundance. Main body of Lake Champlain, discovered by Samuel de Champlain in 1609, now comes into view.

0:20 (0:09) Shoreline on opposite side of Lake Champlain is Vermont.

0:25 (0:04) Fine view of Fort Ticonderoga, on bluffs ahead and to right, is now afforded.

0:28 (0:01) Train now slips through tunnel immediately under fortification grounds.

0:29 (0:00) Arrive at station serving nearby town of Ticonderoga.

TICONDEROGA, NY - The nearby restored Colonial fort was originally established in 1755 by the French who sliced off the mountain's top and used the rocks found there for its construction. The fort defended the passage between Lake Champlain and the northern tip of Lake George (which are only about a mile apart) as well as the route between the colonies and Canada, making it one of the most strategic locations of the Revolution. It was first captured by the British, but then continued to change hands.

At the start of the Revolution the fort fell to Ethan Allen, Benedict Arnold and the Green Mountain Boys of Vermont without a shot being fired. They sent its guns to help break the siege of Boston. It was again captured by the British in 1777, a severe blow to the Colonists, only then to be later abandoned and burned after Burgoyne's ultimate defeat at Saratoga.

The fort has been beautifully restored and contains a fine museum with Revolutionary artifacts. During the summer, colorfully uniformed "soldiers" march through the grounds playing traditional fife and drum music, and cannons are periodically fired for added atmosphere.

0:00 (0:20) Depart Ticonderoga.

0:04 (0:16) Enormous International Paper plant is just above tracks on left.

0:17 (0:03) Very fine view of Lake Champlain is afforded on right. Protrusion of land across water is Crown Point State

Adirondack — Fort Ticonderoga, NY
JACK SWANSON

Historic Site, location of ruins of two forts that once secured command of this vital waterway. First fort was built by French in 1734. Later, under British occupation, a three-and-one-half-square-mile stronghold was built—one of Britain's most ambitious military engineering projects in North America.

0:20 (0:00) Arrive at Port Henry's neat but old station, set serenely in Witherbee Park.

PORT HENRY, NY - Several architectural artifacts are worth watching for in this community, Port Henry's train station being but one. On departing, note the two brick buildings sitting above the tracks on the left. The three-story town hall could have easily been used for the movie "Psycho," while the other quaint structure, just to the right of town hall, is a former fire station (now used for a garage).

Not to be outdone by Loch Ness, Lake Champlain boasts its own monster—Champ. Champ's likeness has been captured as a weather vane that adorns the roof of the gazebo in the middle of Witherbee Park on left.

0:00 (0:18) Depart Port Henry. Site of Porter and Lewis Mills, former supplier of lumber to Benedict Arnold's fleet, stood just up draw to left near present brick structure of Niagara Mohawk Power.

0:18 (0:00) Upon arriving Westport, note very attractive geodesic dome on right.

WESTPORT, NY - This scenic little shoreline village is perhaps best known for its bass fishing tournaments. But also popular is a summer theater which occupies the freight room of the 1876 train station. This old depot, perched high above the town, is a grand vignette of the past. Still well maintained, it shelters some wonderful woodwork of yesteryear.

0:00 (0:42) Depart Westport.

0:09 (0:33) On left, former Delaware & Hudson stone depot once served town of Essex.

0:18 (0:24) Cross high over pretty Bouquet River.

0:19 (0:23) Grey facilities, on both sides of train, refine walstonite ore which is mined nearby. Principal uses of walstonite include the manufacture of ceramics, china and paint.

0:20 (0:22) Through Willsboro, situated in region where lake trout, walleye and salmon are in abundance. Between here and Port Kent, a few miles up line, the route is embellished by spectacular rock cuts, many high above Lake Champlain. During one 4 1/2-mile stretch alone, the train must negotiate 128 curves.

PORT KENT, NY - This is a flag stop for Amtrak during the summer months. The dock for the summer ferry to Burlington, Vermont (10 miles directly across the lake) can be seen here.

0:00 (0:14) Depart Port Kent.

0:04 (0:10) Cross Ausable River which has its headwaters southwest of here at the base of 5,344-foot Mt. Marcy, highest point in New York.

0:07 (0:07) Leave Adirondack Park, Valcour Island is on right, site of Battle of Lake Champlain, first major naval battle between Britain and the Colonies.

0:09 (0:02) Huge Plattsburgh Air Force Base, home of 380th Air Refueling Wing, stretches along tracks on left.

0:13 (0:01) Flotillas of pleasure craft occupy marinas on both sides of track, then ruins of four-stall roundhouse are on right.

0:14 (0:00) Arrive Plattsburgh after passing yacht basin on right.

PLATTSBURGH, NY - Military posts have been located in this area continually since colonial times. It was off these shores that the British fought and won the Battle of Lake Champlain in 1777, although the delay inflicted on the British played an important role in America's eventually winning the Revolution. And it was from here that Colonel Zebulon Pike,

the discoverer of the peak by the same name, launched an unsuccessful march against what is now Toronto. Later, during the War of 1812, Plattsburgh was the site of two coordinated American victories, one on land and the other in Plattsburgh Bay where American sailors used anchors and winches to pivot their vessels 180 degrees, giving the surprised British two broadsides from each ship. The air base and paper mills now shape the area's economy.

0:00 (0:23) Departing Plattsburgh, turntable and roundhouse for the old Delaware & Hudson shops is on the left. The eagle-crowned obelisk on left is Macdonough Monument, commemorating naval victory of 1814.

0:15 (0:08) Apples are principal product of Chazy which boasts world's largest McIntosh orchards.

0:23 (0:00) Arrive Rouses Point.

ROUSES POINT, NY - Huddled against the U.S.-Canadian Border, Rouses Point was settled in 1793 by Jacques Rouse, said to have had 26 children. The first pioneer settlement in northern New York now serves as the American Customs checkpoint for southbound passengers.

0:00 (0:15) Depart Rouses Point and in a minute, Canadian flags identify Canadian-U.S. Border.

0:15 (0:00) Arrive Cantic, Québec.

CANTIC, QC - Cantic is where northbound passengers are checked by Canadian Customs. Proof of citizenship is important. Although the ceremonies may sometimes be perfunctory, it is not unusual to be here for an hour while normal inspection procedures are carried out.

0:00 (0:57) Depart Cantic and head across southern Québec's flat countryside toward Montréal.

This is the Richelieu River Valley, where trains on Canada's first railway, the Laprairie and St. Johns, followed the Richelieu as early as 1851. Richelieu is actually Lake Champlain's drainage course into the St. Lawrence River. Small agricultural communities with French-speaking citizenry are scattered throughout the region.

0:13 (0:44) Small village of Saint-Blaise, off to left, with its silver-steepled white church, is typical of towns encountered throughout province of Québec. Pristine but plain, they seem as throwbacks to another era.

0:19 (0:38) Enter good-size town of Saint-Jean. On right is College Militaire Royal and then, on right, note rail artistically bent into several-feet-high railroad spike—it's just before red brick station.

0:43 (0:06) Note almost continuous parade of small swimming pools in backyards of homes on left. It's possible to count more than one hundred in an eight-minute stretch.

0:57 (0:00) Arrive St. Lambert.

 ST. LAMBERT, QC - This is one of Montreal's larger suburbs, located immediately across the river from that city.

0:00 (0:12) Depart St. Lambert and immediately start ascent necessary for crossing St. Lawrence River on Victoria Bridge.

This structure was once known as the Jubilee Bridge when it was opened in 1859, later to be rebuilt in 1898, to handle two sets of rails, an electric interurban line and auto traffic. It is one of the world's longest at 1 1/4 miles. Those two concrete-lined channels below us are the St. Lawrence Seaway and the St. Lambert Lock which is just one of many locks needed to raise or lower shipping using this waterway. The Seaway is narrow and, unfortunately, cannot handle larger ships of today's maritime fleet. Once over the Seaway, we cross the St. Lawrence itself.

0:01 (0:11) Islands to right were home to Canada's very successful 1967 world's fair—Expo 67. Geodesic dome was the U.S. Pavilion. Skyline of Montréal forms a dramatic scene forward on right. Sloping tower of Olympic Stadium can be seen near horizon at right. Stadium is home to Montréal Expo's baseball team and was site of 1976 Summer Olympics.

0:06 (0:06) Leaving Victoria Bridge, we enter Montréal through Canadian National rail yards.

0:08 (0:04) Slip over nicely landscaped Lachine (pronounced luh-SHEEN) Canal, constructed before seaway to avoid Lachine Rapids.

0:10 (0:02) Sink underground as we near station.

0:12 (0:00) Arrive Montréal's Central Station.

MONTRÉAL, QC - See page 288.

Other Northeast Service

During the summer months, there is weekend **Cape Cod** service between Boston and Hyannis, Massachusetts.

Toronto
Buffalo New York

Maple Leaf

The charming Hudson River Valley, an international border crossing at Niagara Falls and the fascinating maritime activities along the western tip of Lake Ontario are just some of the highlights along the route of the *Maple Leaf*. This service, since its inception in 1971, has been the result of a joint U.S.-Canadian endeavor that links New York City and Toronto.

NORTHBOUND SCHEDULE (Condensed)
New York, NY - Early Morning Departure
Albany-Rensselaer, NY - Midmorning
Niagara Falls, NY - Late Afternoon
Toronto, ON - Early Evening Arrival

SOUTHBOUND SCHEDULE (Condensed)
Toronto, ON - Midmorning Departure
Niagara Falls, NY - Early Afternoon
Alabany-Rensselaer, NY - Early Evening
New York, NY - Late Evening Arrival

FREQUENCY - Daily.
SEATING - Reserved coaches.
DINING - Sandwiches, snacks and beverages.
BAGGAGE - No checked baggage.
RESERVATIONS - Reservations required.
LENGTH OF TRIP - 544 miles in 12 hours.

ROUTE LOG

For route between New York City and Schenectady, see that portion of *Adirondack* log, page 41. For route between Schenectady and Buffalo, see that portion of Lake Shore Ltd. log, page 56.

 DEPEW, NY - This is a convenient suburban stop for the Buffalo region.
0:00 (0:10) Depart Depew.
0:05 (0:05) Downtown Buffalo skyline looms on forward right, while immediately right, grand clock tower presides atop stately Romanesque archways of old Buffalo Central Terminal.

The terminal, now on the National Register of Historic Places, had as its architect famed station designer Alfred Fellheimer who also created the elegant Cincinnati Union Terminal. It was completed in 1929, shortly before the Crash and the ensuing depression. Amtrak delivered a fatal blow with its move to Depew Station farther east.
0:10 (0:00) Arrive Buffalo (Exchange Street Station). On right, glistening white tower of city center is Niagara Mohawk's "Electric Building."

 BUFFALO, NY - Situated on the eastern shores of Lake Erie, and across the Niagara River from Canada, Buffalo is New York's second largest city. The metropolitan region represents one of the largest manufacturing centers in the U.S. with steel, chemicals, auto parts and flour production a sampling of its major industries. Railroading is also an important facet of the Buffalo economy.

0:00 (0:34) Depart Buffalo. After traversing short tunnels, Lake Erie appears on left.

0:05 (0:29) Lake waters begin narrowing into Niagara River which flows 35 miles north before spilling into Lake Ontario. Brief interruption of Niagara Falls discourages conventional navigation.

0:06 (0:28) On left, Peace Bridge spans river to Fort Erie, Ontario, a major port of entry into Canada. Water intake is curious spectacle protruding from water just north of bridge.

0:11 (0:23) Old drawbridge connects Squaw Island with mainland on left.

0:18 (0:16) Passing through Tonawanda, train departs river route temporarily. Clock tower of Tonawanda Middle School is distinctive fixture on left.

0:20 (0:14) Cross New York Barge Canal, offspring of historic Erie Canal, now only a few blocks from its western terminus.

0:27 (0:07) At town of Niagara, International Airport is situated on left, as well as adjacent Niagara Falls Air Force Base.

0:32 (0:02) Assemblage of towering power stanchions on right readily conjures up images of Martian invasion. Nearby hydroelectric facilities are some of world's largest, tapping mighty resources of Niagara Falls.

0:33 (0:01) Spindly observation towers on forward left are popular vantage points for viewing Falls.

0:34 (0:00) Arrive Niagara Falls, New York.

 NIAGARA FALLS, NY - The breathtaking falls on the Niagara River continue to be the primary attraction that draws over 12 million tourists to this region annually.

 United **Cab**, 285-9331.

Call **Niagara County Tourism**, (716) 285-2400 or 800-338-7890.

Comfort Inn-The Pointe, One Prospect Pointe, 14303; (716) 284-6835. Excellent location for taking in the American Falls. $98.

0:00 (0:10) Depart Niagara Falls, New York.

0:08 (0:02) Cross into Canada via 1,082-foot bridge spanning Niagara River. From its lofty heights, brief glimpse of Falls is afforded on left while torrent of rampaging Whirlpool Rapids is impressive spectacle on right.

0:10 (0:00) Arrive Niagara Falls, Ontario. Journey is delayed here while customs agents board for round of "customary" inquiries. (New York bound passengers are checked by U.S. customs at Niagara Falls, NY.) Amtrak crews are replaced by VIA personnel at this time.

NIAGARA FALLS, ON - Like its New York counterpart, the Falls are the focal point of this town as well. Observation towers, riverboats, helicopters, cable cars and ground-level catwalks are among the many means available for viewing this natural wonder.

VIA Station is located about five minutes by cab from the Falls and the center of town. There are storage lockers, but no vending machines.

5-0 **Taxi**, 358-3232. During the day, **shuttle buses** to the Falls leave from the transportation center across from the station, 15 minutes before and after each hour, 356-1179. **People Mover buses** run regularly along river, connecting many major attractions; fare good for all day. Intercity **bus terminal**, 357-2133. **Thrifty Rental Car** free pick up and delivery, 356-8529.

Visitor & Convention Bureau, 5543 Victoria Avenue (at Kitchener), 356-6061.

The Oakes Inn, 6546 Buchanan Ave.; (905) 356-4514. Next to Minolta Tower. Some rooms with view of Falls. Hotel has its own observation deck. About two blocks from the Canadian Falls. $75 to $178.

-Skyline Brock and Skyline Foxhead (adjacent hotels under common ownership—Brock is the older), 5705 Falls Ave., L2E 6W7; (905) 374-4444. Deluxe rooms, many with excellent view of American Falls. Located at foot of Rainbow Bridge. Dining room at top of the Brock has superb panorama of both Falls. $105.

Maple Leaf — Bear Mountain Bridge, Manitou, NY
SCOTT HARTLEY

The Falls, of course, are the major attraction. There is also an array of museums (wax, Elvis, French perfume, Ripley's, etc.), fun houses and myriad other rather incongruous attempts at competing with one of nature's most wondrous spectacles.

0:00 (0:20) Depart Niagara Falls through Canadian National rail yards before emerging on rolling farmlands of southern Ontario.

0:06 (0:14) Cross Queenston Chippawa Power Canal.

0:10 (0:10) Winery on right represents a popular enterprise of region. Vineyards are also common sights.

0:16 (0:04) Cross newest (1932) Welland Canal, an important shipping link connecting Lake Erie and Lake Ontario. Eight separate locks, like set seen on left, allow vessels to negotiate 326-foot elevation differential between two lakes.

0:20 (0:00) From atop towering bridge, cross original (1842) Welland Canal before arriving St. Catharines.

ST. CATHARINES, ON - Situated in the heart of the Niagara fruit belt, bountiful harvests support St. Catharines' claim as the "Garden City." Wine production is important here, too, with tours of these facilities a popular attraction.

0:00 (0:16) Departing St. Catharines, rolling hills become more pronounced with streams meandering picturesquely through their midst. Bountiful orchards embellish landscape and provide a basic economic staple of area.

0:04 (0:12) Approaching Jordan, cross Sixteen Mile Creek. On western edge of town, Lake Ontario can be seen on right while crossing Jordan Harbor.

0:16 (0:00) Arrive "doll-house" station at Grimsby. "Railhouse Restaurant" is added attraction of this charming facility.

GRIMSBY, ON - Another hub of fruit and wine production, Grimsby was the site of Canada's first municipal government, established at a town meeting back in 1790.

0:00 (0:30) Depart Grimsby.

0:08 (0:22) Rural environs are soon displaced by industrial sprawl approaching Hamilton. Area that curls around western tip of Lake Ontario is known as The Golden Horseshoe due to its industrial and agricultural productivity.

This is Canada's "Steel Capital." Set atop ledges overlooking scenic Lake Ontario, Hamilton is Canada's third largest port and caters to a flourishing manufacturing trade.

0:16 (0:14) Ivor Wynne Stadium on left is home field for Canadian Football League's Hamilton Tigercats.

0:25 (0:05) Emerge on shoreline of Hamilton Harbor, a scenic inlet of Lake Ontario. Train winds about waterfront, eventually settling on northeastern tack towards Toronto.

0:30 (0:00) Arrive Aldershot.

ALDERSHOT, ON - This stop serves both the industrial city of Hamilton as well as its lakefront residential neighbor Burlington.

For route between Aldershot and Toronto, see that portion of Canadian Corridor Service, page 299.

Lake Shore Limited

The historic "Water Level Route" of the old New York Central System is now the path of the *Lake Shore Limited*, Amtrak's New York-Chicago train. The trip, which traces through some of this country's very beginnings, might well serve as a refresher course in America's struggle for her political and economic independence.

From New York City, the tracks head northward up the eastern shore of the stately Hudson River until reaching Albany where they veer westward across upper New York State following the Mohawk Valley and the Erie Canal. Upon reaching Buffalo, the route borders the south shore of Lake Erie (hence the name *Lake Shore Limited*) before slicing across northern Indiana to reach Chicago. Although Boston passengers (by separate section joining at Albany) miss the Hudson River trip, they have the soft, rolling Berkshires of western Massachusetts as a substitute.

Its 19-hour schedule doesn't equal the 16-hour sprints performed in the late thirties by those *20th Century Limiteds* powered by Henry Dreyfuss-streamlined 4-6-4 Hudson steam locomotives, but, on the other hand, those heroic trains of yore didn't have to contend with as many intermediate stops or regulatory-imposed speed limits. Nor does the *Lake Shore* offer a "Barber, Fresh Salt Baths, Valet, Ladies' Maid, Manicurist and Stenographer" as advertised by the New York Central for its *"Centuries"* as early as 1912 on what was then touted as the "fastest train in the world." Today's *Lake Shore* is no slacker, however, whisking you from a New York City evening to a Chicago lunch in more comfort than that offered by any other mode of public transport.

WESTBOUND SCHEDULE (Condensed)
New York, NY - Early Evening Departure
Boston, MA* - Midafternoon Departure
Albany-Rensselaer, NY - Late Evening
Buffalo, NY - Middle of the Night
Cleveland, OH - Early Morning
Chicago, IL - Early Afternoon Arrival

EASTBOUND SCHEDULE (Condensed)
Chicago, IL - Midevening Departure
Cleveland, OH - Middle of the Night
Buffalo, NY - Early Morning
Albany-Rensselaer, NY -Early Afternoon
Boston, MA* - Early Evening Arrival
New York, NY - Midafternoon Arrival
*By separate section between Boston and Albany-Rensselaer.

FREQUENCY - Daily.
SEATING - Reserved coaches.
DINING - Complete meal and beverage service between New York and Chicago. Tray meals between Boston and Albany. Diner and lounge car.
SLEEPING - Roomettes and bedrooms (Viewliners).
BAGGAGE - Handled at most stations.
RESERVATIONS - Reservations required.
LENGTH OF TRIP - 959 miles in 19 hours (New York to Chicago)

ROUTE LOG

For route between New York City and Albany-Rensselaer, see that portion of *Adirondack* log, page 41.

 BOSTON, MA - See page 24.

0:00 (0:05) Depart Boston's South Station. Huge central post office facility appears on left.
0:02 (0:03) On left, building signage modestly proclaims "Gillette World Shaving Headquarters."
0:05 (0:00) Slowly slip below grade before arriving Boston's Back Bay Station.

BOSTON (BACK BAY), MA - This station, just a mile from South Station, serves Boston's rather elegant Back Bay and surroundings. At one time, much of this area was covered by water from the Charles River, forming vast mud flats. Long thought to be a liability, the land was eventually reclaimed to become a very viable part of the city.

0:00 (0:28) Depart Back Bay Station. Continue below grade for brief time as train continues westward.
0:15 (0:14) Leave last of Boston's sprawling suburbs and enter rural Massachusetts, liberally splotched with pine forests and towns.
0:28 (0:00) Arrive Framingham.

FRAMINGHAM, MA - Long a manufacturing community, a General Motors assembly plant employs a large segment of today's populace.

0:00 (0:28) Depart Framingham.
0:25 (0:03) Approaching Worcester, glimpse of Quinsigamund Lake is afforded on right.
0:28 (0:00) Arrive downtown Worcester.

WORCESTER, MA - One of the larger manufacturing cities in the Northeast, this city rightfully has considerable community pride in both its past and present. Isaiah Thomas, one of the outstanding printers of the 18th century, lived in Worcester.

0:00 (1:15) Depart Worcester and cross gentle, rolling countryside of central Massachusetts.

0:47 (0:28) Train accompanies Quaboag River on right for several miles.
0:55 (0:20) Frothy falls in Chicopee River on right add to countryside charm.
1:15 (0:00) Arrive Springfield's grey brick depot.

SPRINGFIELD, MA - Another important manufacturing city of the Northeast, Springfield had its start as a mere trading post in the 1630s. In 1794 the United States opened an important armory here, now the Springfield Armory Museum. The Basketball Hall of Fame is located in Springfield.

0:00 (1:05) Depart Springfield.
0:01 (1:04) Crossing broad Connecticut River, note grand stone-arched Memorial Bridge paralleling tracks off to left.
0:04 (1:01) Train rattles through Conrail freight yards in West Springfield.
0:39 (0:26) Deciduous trees of Chester Blanford State Forest and Westfield River combine for idyllic western Massachusetts scenery.
0:40 (0:25) Immense, abandoned roundhouse on left is nostalgic glimpse of railroad's former dominant presence in this locale.
0:42 (0:23) "S" curves, rock cuts and abandoned stone bridges continue to embellish scenery.
0:50 (0:15) Cross famous Appalachian Trail as train approaches Pittsfield.
1:05 (0:00) Arrive Pittsfield.

PITTSFIELD, MA - This is the very heart of New England's ski country. More than 40 ski areas, most with floodlights and ski-making equipment, saturate western Massachusetts. In addition to the attraction of skiing—golf courses, lakes, cultural events and spectacular fall colors make Pittsfield a year-round resort area. Herman Melville wrote his monumental novel "Moby Dick" while living here. The Boston Symphony performs during the summer months at beautiful Tanglewood.

0:00 (0:58) Depart Pittsfield.
0:06 (0:52) Richmond Pond, immediately on left, is one of many scenic Berkshire lakes in region.

0:16 (0:42) Enter New York and leave Massachusetts as train winds its way through Taconic Range.

0:17 (0:41) Darkness pervades while passing through State Line Tunnel. Abandoned north bore dates back to 1840, while larger south bore was constructed during line upgrading in 1912. Years ago, watchman was stationed here to keep ice from building up on tracks inside tunnels.

0:27 (0:31) Over attractive Taconic Parkway.

0:34 (0:24) Train now brushes past quaint, old Chatham, on left.

0:58 (0:00) Arriving Albany-Rensselaer (station is actually in Rensselaer across river from Albany), downtown Albany skyline stands out on left. Prominent 42-story skyscraper is centerpiece of Empire State Plaza. Left of tower, low-slung Cultural Education Center houses State Museum and Library, while on right, dynamic elliptical structure is Center for Performing Arts. Four smaller towers in background are also part of this ambitious billion-dollar project. Once in station, inspiring domed archways of St. John the Baptist Catholic Church can be seen protruding above treetops on right.

For route between New York City and Albany, see that portion of *Adirondack* **log, page 41.**

 ALBANY, NY - See page 44.

0:00 (0:22) Departing Albany-Rensselaer, reassume westerly tack that will essentially follow route of historic Erie Canal.

0:04 (0:19) Cross Hudson River. On left, ornate spires and turrets adorn magnificent State University Administration Headquarters. Originally built in 1916 as corporate offices of Delaware & Hudson Railroad, complex is actually three buildings interconnected, with Flemish facades maintaining delightful continuity throughout. Replica of Henry Hudson's "Half Moon" is highlight of weather vane perched atop main tower.

0:05 (0:17) Intriguing amalgam of modern

and classical architecture is a most striking feature of Albany's city center on left.

0:07 (0:15) August 9, 1831, one of North America's earliest steam locomotives made its inaugural run between Albany and Schenectady when Mohawk & Hudson's *De Witt Clinton*, pulling three statecoach-appearing cars, chugged up this grade—steepest on Water Level Route. Mohawk & Hudson was first railroad chartered in United States.

0:10 (0:10) On outskirts of town, four lonesome high rises comprise State Office Building campus on left.

0:18 (0:04) Approaching Schenectady, attractively landscaped parkways dissect sprawling grounds of General Electric industrial park on left.

0:19 (0:00) Arriving Schenectady where tall, gold-domed City Hall clock tower is prominent fixture on right.

SCHENECTADY, NY - Emerging from the heart of the Industrial Revolution, Schenectady became known as "the city that lights and hauls the world." The American Locomotive Company's Schenectady Works and Thomas Edison's Machine Works were primarily responsible for this designation, the latter eventually evolving into the colossal General Electric Corporation.

Schenectady's "Stockade District" is a premier historical attraction, representing one of the country's best-preserved enclaves of early-American architecture and culture. Its name stems from the original 1661 settlement which was surrounded by a stockade to guard against French and Indian attacks.

0:00 (1:11) Departing Schenectady, elevated track bed now affords encompassing view of one of nation's oldest communities.

0:01 (1:10) Cross Mohawk River.

0:08 (1:03) Marker buoys bob conspicuously in midst of Erie Canal which joins on left and follows intermittently to Rochester. In early days, freight and passenger vessels were drawn along this scenic passage by teams of horses, tugging from paths alongside canal.

Most of what can be seen today, how-

Erie Canal

The Erie Canal was once the major trade passage between the Atlantic Ocean and the Great Lakes, handling a continuous stream of staples such as grain, lumber and coal, and the westward migration of thousands of Americans. Many called it the Eighth Wonder of the World. But like most things, the canal has been changed by time. The railroads, the New York State Throughway and the St. Lawrence Seaway have reduced the canal to more of an historic artifact than a vital trade artery. While 120,000 pleasure boats now take advantage of its no-fee-for-use policy each year, only an occasional barge load of molasses, asphalt or gasoline can be seen floating through the locks.

New York State spends 115 million dollars a year to keep its present-day barge canal system going, a system made up of the Erie, Oswego, Champlain and Cayuga Seneca Canals. Critics contend the canals have outlived their usefulness as instruments of commerce, but so far, preservationists and other supporters have prevailed, arguing that their historic value is worth the expense, not to mention the canals' roles in irrigation, flood control, domestic water supply and tourism.

Even in 1817 when the Erie's construction had just begun, it had its detractors. No less than Thomas Jefferson called it "little short of madness" to start such a project in America's infancy. Jefferson was probably right. America had virtually no workers familiar with canal building, and worse, precious few engineers. If it hadn't been for an American engineer by the name of Canvass White, who walked 2,000 miles of British canals and persuaded an Irish construction engineer named J.J.McShane to come to New York to help, the canal might well have failed.

On October 26, 1825, the impossible project was finished. A 353-mile-long ditch, 40 feet wide at the top, 28 feet wide at the bottom, and four feet deep had been dug from Albany on the Hudson to Buffalo on Lake Erie. Eighty-three locks were necessary to raise traffic from Albany's elevation to Lake Erie, some 571 feet higher. A six-week trip from New York to Buffalo had just been shortened to a ten-day excursion by "fast packet boat." The impact would be immense. A trade route had been created that would make New York the financial center of the world and its port the largest on the East Coast. (And Buffalo would quickly grow from a village to a city of 18,000.)

Amidst great ceremony, Governor De Witt Clinton, whose dream was now a reality, opened the canal at Buffalo. Cannons had been placed at 10-mile intervals along the entire route between Buffalo and New York City to relay the good news of completion (telegraphy was still a few years away). At 10 a.m. the first salvo was fired and by 11:30 that same morning the last of the cannons was fired, announcing to New Yorkers that the Erie Canal was complete.

ever, is not the original Erie Canal. The original was enlarged in the mid-1800s, widening it to 70 feet and deepening it to 7 1/2 feet, an improvement that allowed for 240-ton-capacity barges—an eight fold increase. This followed the original route, except at Schoharie Crossing. But the biggest change came between 1905 and 1918 when the canal was modernized as part of the State Barge Canal System. Techniques had been developed to control the currents of the Mohawk River. Its channel was deepened to

12 feet and the river virtually became the canal. This resulted in a near-total abandonment of the first waterway, which generally followed the river's edge. Only remnants of the original Erie can occasionally be spotted from the train.

0:09 (1:02) Pass through Hoffmans where Mohawk River ferry crossing was established in late 1700s.

0:12 (0:59) On left, shipping locks spanning canal are first of several sets seen along route. Across river, grand arched windows highlight old, intriguing Adirondack Power and Light facility.

0:15 (0:55) Passing through Amsterdam, architectural devotees will discover veritable bonanza in variety of classic dwellings, here in another cradle of early Americana. On west edge of town, Guy Park is on left with a mansion built by Sir William Johnson for his daughter Molly. (It was Sir William who organized the Iroquois to fight for the British during the French and Indian War.)

0:17 (0:54) Lock Eleven, adjacent to Guy Park and just beyond Johnson Mansion, lifts and lowers vessels a total of 12 feet. Bridge-like structure is used to lift sections of dam to control water level in summer and prevent freeze damage during canal's winter-month closures. To right of tracks, note red Volkswagen precariously perched atop brick chimney, somehow placed there to tout body shop below.

0:18 (0:53) Just beyond stone fence on right is red-shuttered Georgian-style "Fort Johnson," built in 1749 and first home of Sir William. Although no battles were fought here, thick walls contained 18 gun ports—just in case. Besides serving as a military post, it sheltered important Indian council meetings in late 1750s. Sir Williams's family remained Loyalists, however, and fled to Canada when Revolutionary War threatened their freedom.

0:19 (0:52) Schoharie Creek, which drains into Mohawk from south, once created slackwater that posed problems for early "canalers." Solution, in 1841, was to build a stone aqueduct which carried boats above creek. Roman aqueduct-appearing ruins can

be glimpsed on left.

0:39 (0:32) Passing through Nelliston, impressive row of Italianate homes on right has been enshrined in National Register of Historic Places. Immediately thereafter, stone marker across river commemorates stronghold of Fort Plain, once valley headquarters for Revolutionary Army.

0:41 (0:30) On right, charming Old Palatine Church sits amidst fairy-tale setting along banks of Caroga Creek. Built in 1770, church was spared during Revolutionary raids with Tory parishioners purportedly bearing influence on its survival. Today, Palatine remains only pre-Revolutionary church standing west of Schenectady and is considered "the shrine of Lutheranism in the Mohawk Valley."

0:52 (0:19) Old mill town of Little Falls is location of Lock 17, highest "single locking" on New York's Barge Canal System—a 40-foot lift.

0:53 (0:18) West of Little Falls, industrial operations begin intruding on landscape. Although many beautiful vistas remain, scenery never quite recaptures sublime enchantment of earlier route.

1:07 (0:04) Approaching Utica, cross over Barge Canal and elaborate set of shipping locks.

1:11 (0:00) Arrive Utica. Preservation effort was expended at station in 1988 to maintain the interior of this once-glorious structure. Marble floors and columns enhance one of America's finest depots.

UTICA, NY - A proud respect for history pervades the community, and is reflected in several of Utica's oldest institutions that have been preserved and adapted to modern uses. One such landmark is the Utica Steam Engine and Boiler Works, an 1831 industrial plant that has been converted into a workshop for American and European sculptors. Another example is "The Stanley," a grand old movie palace refurbished to house Utica's Center for the Performing Arts.

0:00 (0:43) Depart Utica.

0:10 (0:33) Obelisk atop hill at left commemorates one of bloodiest Revolutionary

Utica, NY, Amtrak Station
JACK SWANSON

War encounters, the Battle of Oriskany.
0:14 (0:29) Entering Rome, sculpture atop Paul Revere brass factory on right portrays "midnight ride" of this famous patriot.

Not only presently noted for its prolific copperware production, Rome, too, boasts a fascinating historical heritage. Fort Stanwix, reconstructed on its original site in the downtown district, commemorates the Battle of Oriskany. Legend maintains that the "Stars and Stripes" were first unfurled in battle during this critical engagement. Inspired by these events, the "Pledge of Allegiance" was later penned by local resident Francis Bellamy. On July 4, 1817, Rome was assured further recognition when ground was broken here, commencing construction of the Erie Canal.

After leaving Rome, Canal makes another brief appearance on right.
0:37 (0:06) In downtown Canastota, Canal Town Museum on right has most extensive collection of Erie Canal memorabilia. First motion picture machine was developed in Canastota by Harry Marvin and Herman Casler, inventors of Wurtoscope once seen in every penny arcade in America.
0:38 (0:05) Just a mile or so south of here is Chittenango, birthplace of Lyman Frank

Baum, author of "The Wonderful Wizard of Oz." Also, meagre limestone, a cement which hardens under water, was uncovered near here by Erie Canal builder Canvass White. Discovery was important to successful completion of canal.
0:43 (0:00) Arriving Syracuse, nice residential area on left overlooks bustling activity of Conrail yards.

SYRACUSE, NY - Long known as "Salt City," Syracuse traces its industrial roots to one Simon LeMoyne, a French missionary who, in the mid-1600s, noted the peculiar taste in the waters of Onondaga Lake. Although Indians attributed this to evil spirits, it was only a matter of time before the majority of American table salt was produced from this region. Early production techniques are demonstrated at the Salt Museum located here.

Another fascinating attraction is the Canal Museum. Housed in an 1849 "weighlock," the building is equipped with scales that formerly determined tariffs for passage on the Erie Canal.
0:00 (1:24) Depart Syracuse.
0:03 (1:19) Buildings of LeMoyne College are silhouetted atop bluffs on left.

0:09 (1:14) Shores of Onondaga Lake come briefly into view on right.

0:14 (1:09) Race track is most notable feature of New York State Fairgrounds on right.

0:31 (0:52) Just west of Weedsport, canal rejoins on right.

0:33 (0:50) Cross canal, first of several times, as train re-emerges on rolling farmlands. Apple orchards are also seen frequently along this stretch. Area was one of more trying stretches for canal workers who labored in waist-deep, malaria-infested waters of Montezuma Swamp.

1:01 (0:22) Pass through Palmyra. Just four miles south is Hill of Cumorah where, according to Mormon theology, Moroni, last survivor of a great American civilization, buried a set of gold plates recording history of the peoples. As an angel, he delivered these plates to Joseph Smith who, in 1827, translated them into the book of Mormon. Smith's former farmstead is just southeast of town.

1:18 (0:05) Approaching downtown Rochester, verdigris-topped clock tower on left is named in honor of Hiram Sibley, founder of Western Union.

1:23 (0:00) Arrive modernistic Rochester station. Tall, distinguished building on right houses international headquarters of Eastman Kodak.

ROCHESTER, NY - Set on the banks of the lovely Genesee River, Rochester has come to be known as the "Picture City"—a reference to the illustrious Eastman Kodak Company which was founded here in 1880. Kodak still maintains its international headquarters here, and together with associated operations, comprises the mainstay of the local economy.

0:00 (0:54) Depart Rochester across Genesee River. Wing-like protrusions atop Times Square Building on left reflect contemporary trend of recent downtown development.

0:05 (0:49) Endeavors of General Railway Signal Company on left are important facet of safe and timely journeys. Immediately thereafter, cross Erie Canal before skirting atop colossal crater of Limestone Dolomite mining operation on right.

0:37 (0:17) Batavia has two claims to historic fame. One of America's biggest land deals occurred in 1791 when Robert Morris (a signer of the Declaration of Independence) purchased a four-million-acre "farm" (most of what is now western New York) from Massachusetts for $333,333.33. Later six Dutch bankers purchased most of that land with an eye to reselling it to pioneers, a tract that became known as The Holland Purchase. Then, along these tracks in May of 1893, a world speed record was set by a steam-powered passenger train which reached 112.5 miles per hour. Never before had humans traveled in excess of 100 miles per hour.

0:45 (0:09) At Lancaster, prison on left and guard shacks on right comprise facilities of Alden Penitentiary.

0:48 (0:06) Airplane sculpted from old garbage cans is amusing attraction of Lancaster Air Park on right.

0:54 (0:00) Arrive Buffalo (Depew Station).

BUFFALO, NY - Situated on the eastern shores of Lake Erie, and across the Niagara River from Canada, Buffalo is New York's second largest city. The metropolitan region represents one of the largest manufacturing centers in the U.S. with steel, chemicals, auto parts and flour production a sampling of its major industries. Railroading is also an important facet of the Buffalo economy.

0:00 (1:30) Depart Buffalo.

1:00 (0:30) Rumble through Brocton, birthplace of George Pullman whose name is synonymous with sleeping cars. Having made considerable money moving houses when Erie Canal was first widened, he went on to create an enterprise which became world's foremost producer and operator of sleeping cars.

1:15 (0:15) Enter Pennsylvania and leave New York. Darkness usually prevails during passage through Pennsylvania wine country. Out there somewhere lurk thousands of acres of vineyards. Nearby wineries include Penn Shore Winery, Presque Isle Wine

Cellar, Heritage Wine Cellars and Mazza Winery, all located here in Erie County.

1:30 (0:00) Arrive Erie.

ERIE, PA - Located in the narrow neck of northwestern Pennsylvania, Erie is the state's only port on the lake by the same name. Freighters from around the world arrive and depart here daily, providing the city with its most important industry. This port was used by the American Navy as early as the War of 1812. Today, the Flagship Niagara, at the foot of State Street, recalls the stirring victory of Captain Perry over the British in 1813.

0:00 (1:28) Depart Erie.

0:22 (1:06) Enter Ohio and leave Pennsylvania.

0:27 (1:01) Former New York Central depot on left, another structure on National Register of Historic Places, now houses Connaught Historical Railroad Museum. Nickle Plate Road 2-8-4 Steam locomotive, hopper car and caboose repose just east of station.

1:28 (0:00) Arrive Cleveland.

CLEVELAND, OH - It is difficult to envision Cleveland as the capital of "Western Connecticut," but that was the plan in the late 1700s when Moses Cleveland was commissioned to chart the Connecticut Western Reserve, part of a land grant made by King Charles II. Today, Cleveland is the largest city in Ohio, with a large concentration of "Fortune 1,000" corporations headquartered here.

The city has had both the economic ability and the foresight to create a living environment that is to the city's credit. Myriad parks surround the city; the Cleveland Orchestra is one of the finest; and The Cleveland Museum of Art has one of the more outstanding collections of fine art in the world.

Amtrak Lakefront Station, 200 Cleveland Memorial Shoreway, is located on the edge of downtown and next to Cleveland Stadium.

Yellow **Cab**, 623-1500. **Loop bus** to downtown is one block from the station. **Rapid transit lines** (light rail service) extend from Terminal Tower downtown to **Cleveland Hopkins Airport**, Windemere Station in East Cleveland, and Shaker Heights. **Local buses** also serve Greater Cleveland. Call Regional Transit Authority, 621-9500.

Convention and Visitors Bureau of Greater Cleveland, 3100 Terminal Tower, 44113. Call (216) 621-4110 or 800-321-1001.

Holiday Inn Lakeside, 1111 Lakeside Ave., 44114; (216) 241-5100. Three blocks from the station. $79.

0:00 (0:30) Depart Cleveland. Cleveland Stadium looms immediately on right while downtown is on left where pointed, 52-story Terminal Tower is clearly visible.

0:02 (0:28) Cross Cuyahoga River having dubious distinction of catching on fire before America became pollution conscious.

0:13 (0:16) Ford facility, then Goodyear plant are major Cleveland employers, on left. Then Cleveland's busy airport, Hopkins Field, is on right, just before International Exposition Center. Surroundings now become mostly residential before returning to rural Ohio.

0:30 (0:00) Arrive Elyria.

ELYRIA, OH - Named for Herman Ely who founded this city in 1817, Elyria has become one of the many industrially oriented communities of northern Ohio and home to the Easter Seal Society.

0:00 (0:31) Depart Elyria.

0:07 (0:24) Train zips through Amherst, allowing glimpse of two old coaches and caboose on exhibit by station at left. Former New York Central depot is nicely preserved and is also on National Register of Historic Places.

0:13 (0:18) Cross Vermilion River where water tower greets visitors with words "Vermilion Sailors"—the name used by sports teams in this city that still has a commercial fishing fleet. Great Lakes Historical Society Museum is located on lakefront and has fine collection of Great Lakes shipping memorabilia.

0:19 (0:12) Glimpses of Lake Erie are

afforded through trees on right.

0:31 (0:00) Arrive Sandusky.

SANDUSKY, OH - Because of its fine Sandusky Bay, the city is one of Ohio's most important ports. This, too, is wine country where large quantities of grapes are grown locally. But, for at least three million annual visitors, the draw is venerable, old Cedar Point amusement park.

0:00 (0:47) Depart Sandusky and pass through industrial area where such familiar names as Chrysler and Litton appear.

0:07 (0:40) Instead of skirting Sandusky Bay, tracks turn north to cross water before returning to a westward tack.

0:14 (0:33) Lake Erie makes its finale in distance on right.

0:18 (0:29) Davis-Bessie Nuclear Power Plant in far distance on right gives off massive steam plume.

0:28 (0:19) On right, enormous mounds of light grey material almost engulf town of Clay Center. These are mountains of screenings from White Rock Quarry that has been in operation since 1880s. Dolomite limestone is unearthed here and shipped throughout U.S. in sizes ranging from four-ton slabs to mere dust particles.

0:39 (0:08) Cross Maumee River as a myriad of industrial plants mark outer reaches of Toledo. Skyline is silhouetted behind bright blue suspension bridge on right.

0:47 (0:00) Arrive Toledo's Central Union Terminal, on right.

TOLEDO, OH - With a 35-mile-long harbor on Lake Erie, it is easy to understand why Michigan and Ohio both claimed this city in the early 19th century. It took presidential action by Andrew Jackson to finally settle the dispute—in Ohio's favor. (However, Michigan received its Wisconsin-connected Upper Peninsula as recompense.) Today, the city lays easy claim to being the world's leading producer of glass and glass products.

0:00 (0:53) Depart Toledo.

0:13 (0:40) Holland, Ohio marks the end of Toledo's western suburbs. Curveless stretch of track from here to Bryan is known as the "Air Line."

0:53 (0:00) Arrive Bryan.

BRYAN, OH - This northwestern Ohio rural distribution center was at one time known as "The Fountain City" because of an abundance of artesian wells, some of which still flow.

0:00 (0:17) Depart Bryan.

0:04 (0:13) Solar panels mounted on ground, through trees on right, identify site of world's first solar-powered radio station, WQTC, which uses 33,600 photovoltaic cells and storage batteries to maintain a constant supply of power to the station's transmitter.

0:09 (0:08) Cross St. Joseph River.

0:13 (0:04) Enter Indiana and leave Ohio. Terrain soon becomes rolling for first time since leaving New York State.

0:17 (0:00) Arrive Waterloo.

WATERLOO, IN - This small Indiana community is a stop for nearby Ft. Wayne.

0:00 (0:50) Depart Waterloo.

0:27 (0:23) Train crosses, then follows meandering Elkhart River, forming a Currier and Ives setting.

0:50 (0:00) Arrive Elkhart. Note old GG-1 electric and steam locomotives of New York Central, on left, as well as numerous ancient rail cars.

ELKHART, IN - More band instruments and mobile homes have been produced here than anywhere else in the world. Miles Laboratories (Alka-Seltzer) was founded here and the city remains the headquarters for this pharmaceutical giant. Elkhart County contains a large Amish and Mennonite population, and the Mennonite Historical Library at nearby Goshen boasts the world's largest collection of historical books and reference works pertaining to this Christian denomination.

0:00 (0:20) Depart Elkhart.

0:16 (0:04) Gold dome, far distance right, locates campus of University of Notre Dame.

0:17 (0:03) Stretching for blocks on left is former Studebaker automobile plant where subsequent occupants have manufactured such diverse products as toys, postal vehicles, tools, auto bodies and hand-built Avanti motor cars. On right, watch for former Union Station.

0:20 (0:00) Arrive South Bend.

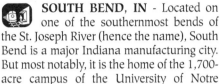 **SOUTH BEND, IN** - Located on one of the southernmost bends of the St. Joseph River (hence the name), South Bend is a major Indiana manufacturing city. But most notably, it is the home of the 1,700-acre campus of the University of Notre Dame.

0:00 (1:03) Depart South Bend. On right large Allied-Signal facility was original Bendix plant where this giant manufacturer of auto and aircraft parts got its start. Bendix was acquired by Allied-Signal in 1981.

 Gain one hour as train passes from Eastern to Central Time. Set your watch back (forward if eastbound) one hour.

0:40 (0:23) Bethlehem Steel Corporation facility appears on right.

0:45 (0:18) Tracks and catenary of legendary Chicago South Shore and South Bend run parallel to our Conrail right-of-way, off to left.

0:47 (0:16) Where Gary began, enormous U.S. Steel Gary Works stretch along tracks at right beyond rail yards.

0:57 (0:06) Inland Steel plants straddle tracks, plant Number One on left and Plant Number Two on right. Then cross drawbridge spanning Indiana Harbor Canal that links Lake Michigan with Calumet River.

0:59 (0:04) Standard Oil Company of Indiana refinery creates apparatus jungle at left. Lake Michigan is now only 100 feet or so to right.

1:03 (0:00) Arrive Hammond-Whiting.

 HAMMOND-WHITING, IN - Most of Amtrak's trains connecting to points east from Chicago make this their eastern metropolitan Chicago stop.

0:00 (0:24) Depart Hammond-Whiting.

0:02 (0:22) Cross massive steel lift bridge over Calumet River. To left, Chicago Skyway reaches its peak over river, as around us huge bridges, grain elevators, and ships and boats of all sizes create a rugged industrial landscape.

0:05 (0:19) Skyway now rises on its steel supports beside us on left.

0:06 (0:18) Pass piggyback yards. Then, on right is foundation of demolished Englewood Station, from which, years ago, Pennsylvania and New York Central engineers raced each other away toward New York in a graphic symbol of their lines' competition.

0:07 (0:17) At right, spectacular view of Chicago skyline is afforded, including Sears Tower, world's tallest building, and John Hancock Building. Now roll across Dan Ryan Expressway (I-90/94) before ducking under Chicago's famous rapid transit—the "El."

0:12 (0:12) To our immediate right is modern replacement for older Comiskey Park, historic home of American Baseball League's Chicago White Sox.

0:14 (0:10) In Conrail piggyback yard at left, it's possible to see large cranes loading semi-trailers from almost every major railroad in America onto flatcars.

0:16 (0:08) Cross South Branch of Chicago River before passing under Dan Ryan Expressway.

0:18 (0:06) To left, it's possible to see an entire train gliding slowly through Amtrak's washer building.

0:20 (0:04) Enter clean, modern Amtrak yards. At right sit examples of nearly every kind of equipment Amtrak owns—coaches and cafes; diners and domes; sleepers and Superliners. To left, Burlington Northern yards are home to double-decker Regional Transportation Authority commuter cars used between Chicago and suburb of Aurora.

0:24 (0:00) Leave daylight as train lumber beneath Chicago's huge post office building just before arrival at Union Station.

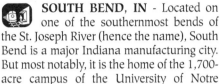 **CHICAGO, IL** - Rail passengers traveling across the U.S. funnel through Chicago like sands through the neck of an hourglass. A quick look at a map of the United States tells why Chicago has grown up to become the nation's major transportation hub, where much of America's east-west traffic has to converge. Lake Michigan, cutting strategically into the heart

Chicago

Lake Michigan

- Amtrak Station
1 - Visitors Information
2 - Chicago Board of Trade
3 - Adler Planetarium
4 - Museum of Science and
    Industry
5 - Sears Tower
6 - Field Museum of Natural
    History
7 - Art Institute of Chicago
8 - John G. Shedd Aquarium
9 - Oxford House
10 - Quality Inn Downtown
11 - Midland Hotel

of the Midwest, provided early-day shipping access to a developing frontier. With the coming of the railroad, tracks soon radiated from The Windy City in almost every direction, a pattern that is still followed today.

Oddly, in spite of heavy volumes of traffic, trains don't go through Chicago—just their passengers do. All through-passengers must change trains. It's always been this way, and it's unlikely to be otherwise in the foreseeable future. So everyone arriving in Chicago on Amtrak gets off here, at least for a little while. This phenomenon, along with 160-or-so commuter trains a day, makes Chicago Union Station a very busy place.

The 1926 depot was the object of a major remodeling project in the early 1990s, greatly improving the interior's efficiency.

Union Station, 210 S. Canal St. (at Adams St.), is in the heart of downtown. Its cavernous, marble-pillared waiting room still contains the original hardwood benches, while a much newer passenger lounge is conveniently located adjacent to the train platform area. There are restaurants and snack bars and a cafeteria in the station, and several restaurants are within easy walking distance. A posh Metropolitan Lounge is available to first-class ticket holders. Luggage carts are obtained by inserting change into cart dispensers. Luggage lockers are available in the southwest corner of the "Great Hall." Parking garages and lots are nearby.

Yellow **Cab**, 829-4222. **Local buses** are just outside the station; for bus and commuter train information, call 836-7000 (suburbs, 800-972-7000). Train to **O'Hare International Airport**, 19 miles northwest of downtown, is two blocks away at Clinton and Congress.

Visitor Information Center, located in the old Water Tower Pumping Station at Pearson and Michigan Ave. Call (312) 744-2400 or 800-487-2446. (State of Illinois including Chicago.)

Oxford House, 225 N. Wabash, 60601; (312) 346-6585 or 800-344-4111. Remodeled older hotel, handy to the Magnificent Mile and The Loop (see below), very nice rooms. $89.
-**Quality Inn Downtown**, One Mid City Plaza (Madison at Halstead); (312) 829-5000. West of downtown, off the Kennedy Expressway. Five blocks from the station, but not a safe walk. $79.
-**Midland Hotel**, 172 W. Adams (at LaSalle), 60603; (312) 332-1200 or 800-621-2360. Excellent hotel, only four blocks from the station. Complimentary full breakfast. $119.

"The Loop," bounded by Van Buren, Wells, Lake and Wabash, has some of the best shopping in the city, particularly along State Street. The **Magnificent Mile** on North Michigan Ave. is home to an assemblage of Rodeo-Drive-class stores, including Saks, Bloomingdales, Neiman-Marcus and Marshall Field's. The **Sears Tower,** Wacker Drive and Jackson, is the world's tallest building at 110 stories. It's just two blocks east of the station and has an observation deck for the best view in town.

Also downtown, but somewhat farther away: the **Field Museum of Natural History,** Roosevelt Rd. and S. Lake Shore Dr., is one of the nation's finest; the adjacent **Shedd Aquarium** has an outstanding collection of marine life; and just east of these two attractions is the **Adler Planetarium** with daily multimedia shows that display much of the heavens.

Two of Chicago's major attractions are out of the downtown area: the **Museum of Science and Industry,** 57th St. and South Lake Shore Dr., with acres of outstanding technological exhibits, one of the best such museums in the world; and the **Brookfield Zoo,** 1st Ave. and 31st St., in Brookfield, one of the largest zoos in the nation.

Other New York State Service

Various unreserved turboliner and Amfleet trains run on segments of the route between New York City and Niagara Falls, NY, with tray meals and snacks available. Checked baggage is not handled on these trains, but hand baggage may be carried on board. Several trains offer Custom Class seating.

Silver Meteor

The Eastern Seaboard, where much of this country's richest heritage will be found, is visited almost from "top to bottom" by the *Silver Meteor*. Philadelphia, Washington, Richmond, Charleston, SC, and Savannah are just some of the historic salients of this trip through eastern America.

As early as 1939, the railroads recognized Florida as a strong market for Easterners wanting to enjoy warmer winters. In February of that year, the *Silver Meteor* was born when Seaboard Air Line commenced its streamliner service between New York and Miami. Now, Florida has become one of Amtrak's best markets.

There is one other daily train between New York and Florida—the *Silver Star* going to both Miami and Tampa, and taking a somewhat different course.

SOUTHBOUND SCHEDULE (Condensed)
New York, NY - Early Afternoon Departure
Washington, DC - Midevening
Richmond, VA - Late Evening
Charleston, SC - Early Morning
Savannah, GA - Early Morning
Jacksonville, FL - Midmorning
Orlando, FL - Early Afternoon
Miami, FL - Early Evening Arrival

NORTHBOUND SCHEDULE (Condensed)
Miami, FL - Early Morning Departure
Orlando, FL - Early Afternoon
Jacksonville, FL - Late Afternoon
Savannah, GA - Early Evening

Charleston, SC - Midevening
Richmond, VA - Middle of the Night
Washington, DC - Early Morning
New York, NY - Midmorning Arrival

FREQUENCY - Daily.
SEATING - Reserved coaches.
DINING - Diner with complete meals and cafe or lounge car with sandwiches, snacks and beverages.
SLEEPING - Roomettes and bedrooms.
BAGGAGE - Checked baggage handled at most stations.
RESERVATIONS - All-reserved train.
LENGTH OF TRIP - 1,424 miles in 27 hours.

ROUTE LOG

For route between New York City and Washington, DC, see that portion of *Northeast Corridor* log, page 26.

 WASHINGTON, DC - See page 35.
0:00 (0:17) Depart Washington.
0:02 (0:15) Emerge from tunnel after passing under Mall. Glimpses of Capitol and oldest Smithsonian structure ("The Castle") can be caught through various federal buildings on right.
0:07 (0:10) Perhaps Washington's most charming monument, Monticello-shaped Jefferson Memorial, resides among cherry trees of Tidal Basin, on right.

0:09 (0:08) Cross Potomac River paralleling 14th Street bridge. Washington National Airport is directly downstream to left. Back on right, Washington Monument, world's tallest masonry structure at 555.5 feet, punctuates horizon. Capitol's dome can still be seen toward rear on left.

0:10 (0:07) The Pentagon, headquarters for America's military establishment, is off to right.

0:12 (0:05) Glass high rises of Crystal City flaunt their starkness on right. Expansive RF&P rail yards are on left.

0:17 (0:00) Arrive Alexandria.

ALEXANDRIA, VA - This historic Washington suburb sits six miles south of the nation's capital, along the west bank of the Potomac River. Most noted for its outstanding examples of early American architecture, the Alexandria area is also replete with numerous national landmarks. Mount Vernon, beloved home and estate of George Washington from 1754 until his death in 1799, is just a few miles down the Potomac.

0:00 (1:34) Depart Alexandria.

0:01 (1:33) George Washington National Masonic Memorial, with museum of Washington memorabilia, dominates skyline on right.

0:09 (1:25) On right, Amtrak's northern Auto Train terminal handles Florida passengers who want to take their cars—but not drive them until they get there.

0:10 (1:24) Cross inlet of Potomac River where barges can frequently be seen on right, and various small boats on left. Numerous Potomac inlets and coves can be seen on left for next 20 minutes.

0:26 (1:08) Virginia Electric Power Company's huge Possum Point generating station stands on far shore at left. Enter facilities of Quantico Marine Base.

0:27 (1:07) Quantico Airfield can be seen on left.

0:29 (1:05) Leave Quantico Marine Base.

0:30 (1:04) Broad expanse of Potomac now stretches into distance to left.

0:31 (1:03) Cross small cove with final look at Potomac before becoming immersed in rolling, wooded interior of Virginia.

0:44 (0:50) Cross Rappahannock River (the one George Washington supposedly threw a silver dollar across) and enter historic Fredericksburg. John Smith visited here in 1608, George Washington grew up on a nearby farm, Thomas Jefferson and Patrick Henry met here with Washington to plan nation's future, and three quarters of a million Civil War soldiers battled here.

0:47 (0:47) Twenty-foot-high stone pyramid on left commemorates "The Federal Breakthrough," one of many Civil War battles fought in this region. In December 1862, Union forces commanded by General Meade broke through Confederate lines, only to be repelled. Formerly known as Meade Pyramid, it is now more appropriately called "A Southern Memorial."

0:58 (0:36) Small white frame house on left with U.S. flag and large grassy area in front is Jackson Shrine, where Stonewall Jackson died on May 10, 1863 after being accidentally wounded by his own troops at Chancellorsville, some 27 miles away. His death would be a devastating blow to Lee's forces.

1:08 (0:26) Cross Mattaponi River.

1:26 (0:08) Enter Ashland and experience charming encounter with an historic Virginia town, originally established by RF&P Railroad as a mineral springs resort. Train seems out of place as it glides past lovely antebellum and Victorian homes, while literally touching doorstep of Randolph-Macon College, on left. College was founded in 1830 in Boydton and moved here in 1868, and is parent of R-M Women's College in Lynchburg. Central business district, rebuilt after 1890s fire (unsuccessfully fought with fire trucks brought in from Richmond on railroad flatcars), contains old Crosses Market on left, while 1922 train station is on right. Just beyond station is reconstructed Henry Clay Inn, original having been built at turn of the century.

1:29 (0:05) Decaying Forest Lodge Hotel, with its four stories of bleached lapboard and ornate balconies, stands on right as forlorn monument to one man's unrealized

Silver Meteor route — Southern Memorial in Virginia
JACK SWANSON

dream. Constructed after Civil War by John Cussons, English adventurer and Confederate scout, this "luxury hotel" failed to capture imagination of rail travelers. Now largely abandoned and half original size, it once featured lakes, gardens and game preserve on 1,000 acres.

1:34 (0:00) Arrive Richmond, where very attractive modern station greets passengers on northern edge of city.

RICHMOND, VA - Overlooking the James River against a backdrop of rolling countryside, Richmond is truly a cradle of Americana infancy. Setting out from the first English settlement at Jamestown in 1607, Captains John Smith and Christopher Newport traveled up river and claimed the site of Richmond in the name of the Crown. The state capital was moved to Richmond in 1779 and remains here today. In 1781, Benedict Arnold turned traitor and attacked the town, forcing Governor Thomas Jefferson to flee to safer environs. In 1861, Richmond was established as the Capital of the Confederacy. Later, after learning of imminent attack, Confederate President Jefferson Davis would evacuate the city and have it

burned, lest it fall intact into enemy hands.

Today, Richmond is said to have more monuments and museums than any other city in the South.

0:00 (0:33) Depart Richmond's station and proceed south through city.

0:08 (0:25) Large Richmond rail yards border main line.

0:14 (0:19) Cross high above James River on venerable Belt Line Bridge.

0:23 (0:10) For next mile or two, acres of brick warehouses and assorted paraphernalia of Defense Central Supply Center line left side of track.

0:33 (0:00) Arrive Petersburg (Ettrick). Note nicely landscaped home made from converted rail car on left.

PETERSBURG, VA - Settled along the banks of the Appomattox River, Petersburg today is a flourishing mecca of tobacco and livestock trade. Yet some 120 years ago, this lush countryside was blighted beneath one of the Civil War's longest and bloodiest sieges. For ten months, Lee and Grant struggled over this strategic rail hub. When Union forces eventually prevailed, Lee's surrender at Appomattox followed within weeks.

0:00 (1:23) Depart Petersburg (Ettrick).

0:01 (1:22) Virginia State University can be seen perched atop hill in far distance to left.

0:02 (1:21) Cross Appomattox River. Waters originate some 75 miles west of here near Appomattox Courthouse, where one of America's most somber dramas occurred on Palm Sunday in 1865—Lee's surrender to Grant, concluding the Civil War. Upon crossing river, enter Petersburg itself. Now cross high over line of Norfolk & Western Railroad.

0:06 (1:17) Clatter through CSX rail yards.

0:14 (1:09) Huge Enfield peanut operations are on right.

0:30 (0:53) Through Emporia and cross Meherrin River. It was along this stretch of track that, in December 1864, Warren's Corps attempted to permanently cut rail service to Confederate forces in Petersburg disassembling miles of track and burning ties.

0:38 (0:45) Leave Virginia and enter North Carolina, America's leading tobacco producer. Plywood plant of Georgia Pacific, on left, marks border.

0:46 (0:37) Cruise high above Roanoke River. Then over an intersecting freight line at Weldon (outskirts of Roanoke Rapids) linking Norfolk with Durham.

0:52 (0:31) One of South's principal products becomes apparent as cotton fields can be spotted along route.

1:22 (0:01) Cross Tar River. During a particularly fierce Civil War battle, Confederate troops from other states retreated, leaving North Carolinians to go it alone. Later, those that had remained to fight allowed that next time they would put tar on the heels of their faltering comrades so they would "stick better." North Carolinians are now known as Tar Heels.

1:23 (0:00) Rumble along Main Street upon arrival at Rocky Mount where old, picturesque three-story brick depot awaits those detraining on right.

ROCKY MOUNT, NC - Established in 1816, Rocky Mount has developed into one of the world's largest bright-leaf tobacco markets. Cotton and peanuts are also important crops.

0:00 (1:25) Depart Rocky Mount.

0:02 (1:23) For next several minutes, pass by sprawling rail yards on left.

0:20 (1:05) Through Wilson, where tobacco warehouses seem to be everywhere. Another bright-leaf tobacco center, its annual auction dubbed "The Greatest Show in Tobaccoland" provides a most unique tourist attraction. It is also one of the country's leading antique markets.

0:35 (0:50) Tall, skinny sheds dotting landscape, some with little chimneys jutting out from their tops, are tobacco curing barns.

0:44 (0:41) Through Selma, another small agricultural center.

1:16 (0:09) Agriculture continues its dominance, as soybean fields now appear on both sides of tracks.

1:25 (0:00) Arrive Fayetteville. Region's tobacco barns apparently influenced architecture of depot on left.

FAYETTEVILLE, NC - Established by Highland Scots in 1739, Fayetteville is now a thriving tobacco, cotton and livestock trade center. Fort Bragg military installation is located here.

0:00 (1:21) Depart Fayetteville.

0:05 (1:16) Pigs are major "crop" of agrarian operation on left.

0:36 (0:45) Just after passing through Rowland, leave North Carolina and enter South Carolina. Watch for enormous, gaily decorated Mexican hat perched on tower of motel complex at "South of the Border." Here, impatient North Carolina couples take advantage of South Carolina's less stringent marital laws allowing them to tie the knot without red tape.

1:06 (0:15) Cross Great Pee Dee River.

1:21 (0:00) Arrive Florence amidst large CSX rail yards.

FLORENCE, SC - Cutting its teeth as a railroad town in the 1850s, Florence developed into a transportation center for goods and troops during the Civil War. It is still an important railroad center, functioning as a division point for the CSX. And teeth are important to Florence. The town claims to be the denture capital of the world, with three clinics offering one-day service for false teeth, turning out 40,000 cut-rate sets a year.

0:00 (0:32) Departing Florence, preserved steam locomotive soon appears on right.

0:08 (0:24) Cross Lynches River.

0:13 (0:19) Tobacco barns continue to checker region.

0:16 (0:16) Prim little church facing tracks on left is nicely adorned by freestanding bell tower.

0:32 (0:00) Arrive Kingstree where well-patronized restaurant occupies portion of train station.

 KINGSTREE, SC - This agricultural center is the hometown of Dr. Joseph Goldstein, winner of the 1987 Nobel Prize for Medicine.

0:00 (0:50) Depart Kingstree, then cross over Black River.

0:14 (0:36) Cross Santee River, which traces northern border of Francis Marion Forest, on left. It was named for an American Revolutionary War general whose quick-striking raids from Carolina's marshes earned him nickname of "Swamp Fox."

0:29 (0:21) Cross broad Cooper River, an outlet for Lake Moultrie. Note coal-fired generating plant on right.

0:50 (0:00) Arrive at Charleston's rail station, some distance from downtown.

 CHARLESTON, SC - Founded in 1670 to offset Spanish intrusions further south, and named for King Charles II, Charleston was once regarded as the richest city in the South, combining an extensive Indian trade with a thriving export business of rice and indigo. Ironically, its post-Civil-War poverty prevented replacement of the city's old buildings which now bestow Charleston with both charm and elegance. In the early 1800s, Charleston stood at the forefront of a pioneering railroad industry. The "Best Friend of Charleston" became the first American steam locomotive in regular service, commencing operations here in 1830. Fort Sumter, located on the city's waterfront, became an historical landmark when it was fired upon in 1861, thus marking the start of the Civil War.

Today the city remains an important manufacturing center for such diverse goods as fertilizer, paint, and clothing. The Citadel, one of the last three state-operated military colleges in the nation, is located here. And Charleston's naval base is the third largest in the United States.

0:00 (0:46) Depart Charleston.

0:02 (0:44) Roll through Charleston's expansive rail yards for two or three minutes, then cross Ashley River. Ashley and Cooper (crossed earlier) discharge into Atlantic at Charleston, forming one of East Coast's finest harbors.

0:13 (0:33) Through Ravenel, where neat, prim white-painted station on right served as temporary town hall after fire destroyed city's headquarters in 1990. Station is typical of those once found throughout the South. It had two waiting rooms—one white and one "colored."

0:26 (0:20) Cross Edisto River.

0:27 (0:19) This small hamlet of Jacksonboro once served as provisional capital of South Carolina while Charleston was under siege during American Revolution.

0:30 (0:16) Cross Ashepoo River.

0:42 (0:04) Cross Combahee River.

0:46 (0:00) Arrive Yemassee.

 YEMASSEE, SC - This small community is named after the Yemassee Indian tribe that once populated this region.

0:00 (0:45) Depart Yemassee.

0:05 (0:40) Under Interstate 95 which traverses entire East Coast, from Houlton, Maine on Canadian border to Miami.

0:06 (0:39) Cross broad Coosawhatchie River.

0:20 (0:25) Particularly charming Southern scene, with magnificent stand of Spanish moss-draped live oaks on left and palmettos with lovely mansion set back from tracks on right.

0:32 (0:13) Pass across very impressive Savannah River and enter Georgia.

0:45 (0:00) Arrive Savannah's rail station, located in western suburbs, about a 15-minute cab ride from downtown.

 SAVANNAH, GA - Richly steeped in its colonial heritage, Savannah remains a city of grandeur and elegance as envisioned by its founding father, General James Edward Oglethorpe. It was established in 1733 by the English as a buffer between the northern colonies and the Spanish in Florida.

Early efforts at raising silk proved a disappointment, but cotton and tobacco soon gave Savannah vitality. Oglethorpe tried to forbid "drinkers, slaves, Catholics and lawyers" from his new community, but it didn't matter—he got them all.

Today, ships from all over the world sail out of the Savannah River, many to retrace the route of the S.S. Savannah which departed here in 1819 to become the first steamship to cross any ocean.

Savannah's attractively remodeled **Amtrak station** is about six miles from downtown at 2611 Seaboard Coastline Drive. There are no nearby hotels, and cabs are the only way to reach downtown.

Yellow **Cab**, 236-1133.

Visitors Center, Martin Luther King, Jr. Blvd., is located in what was once a Georgia Central railroad station on the edge of downtown. Call (912) 944-0456 or 800-444-2427.

Days Inn Downtown, 201 W. Bay St., 31401; (912) 236-4440. Adjacent to the riverfront and historic districts. $74.

-**Best Western Riverfront Inn**, 412 West Bay St., 31401; (912) 233-1011. On the riverfront next to the historic district. $66.

-For information and reservations at several historic inns and guest houses, call 800-262-4667.

The **National Historic Landmark District** has more than 1,200 restored buildings, many of which were grand colonial homes, now renovated to provide lodging. This area comprises much of Savannah's downtown and near-downtown. The **Riverfront Plaza**, composite of restaurants, pubs, and shops imaginatively housed in restored cotton warehouses, is in the heart of downtown.

0:00 (0:50) Depart Savannah southbound

into tall, densely wooded forests of southeastern Georgia.

0:06 (0:44) On left, skirt grounds of Hunter Army Airfield.

0:12 (0:38) Cross Ogeechee River.

0:13 (0:37) Pass through Richmond Hill. Nearby Fort McAllister was key to Savannah's fortifications during Civil war, fending off nine naval assaults before finally succumbing in Sherman's march to the sea.

0:46 (0:04) Cross Altamaha River.

0:50 (0:00) Arrive Jesup.

JESUP, GA - Founded in 1870, the town was named in honor of Morris K. Jessup, a New York financier who personally subsidized the construction of a local railroad. Nearby popular tourist destinations include Brunswick and the Georgia Sea Islands.

0:00 (1:14) Departing Jesup, pass Wayne County Court House on left. Built in 1903, spire-topped clock tower crowns this quaint structure. On outskirts of town, logging and milling operations become frequent sights bordering route into central Florida.

0:18 (0:56) Cross Satilla River.

0:42 (0:32) Pass through Folkston, a point of access to primeval wilderness area known as Okefenokee Swamp.

0:45 (0:29) Crossing St. Mary's River into Florida, Colonial environs of past 1,000 miles are slowly supplanted by Spanish influence of an even earlier period.

1:14 (0:00) Arrive Jacksonville.

JACKSONVILLE, FL - Unlike many other Floridian cities, Jacksonville is not a tourist resort. Rather, it has grown to become the state's leading industrial center. Although lying a few miles west of the Atlantic Ocean, Jacksonville is still an important seaport, with an interconnecting passage along the St. Johns River. Three beautiful beaches, directly east of town, provide a weekend haven for city dwellers. This is a major rail center for CSX, which has an ultra modern $23 million train dispatching operation controlling its entire 20,000-mile system.

0:00 (1:01) Depart Jacksonville.

0:03 (0:53) For five minutes, train slips

Silver Meteor — Orlando, FL
JACK SWANSON

through large Jacksonville rail yards. After a sharp curve to right, downtown skyline will be just to left. Steel bridge on left carries auto traffic over St. Johns River.

0:11 (0:50) Under Interstate 10.

0:18 (0:43) After crossing Ortega River, dramatic view of downtown presents itself on left, just across St. Johns River. Note innumerable fishing and pleasure craft docked on north bank of Ortega.

0:21 (0:40) U.S. Naval Air Station (Jacksonville), with blue WWII PBY and other aircraft at entrance, is on left.

0:40 (0:21) One of Florida's larger dairy farms, with hundreds of black and white Holsteins, appears on right.

0:53 (0:08) Twin cooling towers and giant stack dramatize coal-burning Seminole Cooperative Generating Station on left.

0:56 (0:05) Cross tributary of St. Johns River.

1:01 (0:00) Arrive at Palatka's finely restored depot.

 PALATKA, FL - The town gets its name from a Seminole Indian word

meaning "crossing over" or "cow's crossing." Palatka is one of Florida's older cities, dating back to 1820. An annual Azalea Festival is held in the Ravine Gardens State Park, when more than 100,000 plantings of azaleas burst into springtime splendor the first two weeks in March.

0:00 (0:46) Depart Palatka.

0:06 (0:40) Drawbridge now carries train across a curl of St. Johns River.

0:38 (0:08) Typical citrus packing plant is next to tracks on left.

0:46 (0:00) Arrive DeLand.

DELAND, FL - DeLand has experienced a rather checkered history. First signs of known civilization are the remains of an old sugar mill just north of town, believed to be English or Spanish, and possibly dating back to 1570. Then, in the late 1700s, the British operated plantations here but left when Florida was ceded to Spain. Permanent settlement finally occurred in 1870.

Today, DeLand is the home of Stetson University, named in 1886 in honor of the famous hat-maker. Houseboat tours on the St. Johns River are a popular attraction.

0:00 (0:18) Depart DeLand.

0:12 (0:06) Cross St. Johns River, once again on a drawbridge.

0:18 (0:00) Arrive Sanford, southern terminus of Amtrak's Auto Train. Facilities for loading and unloading autos are on left. Diesel locomotive shops can also be seen.

SANFORD, FL - In 1870, General Henry Sanford, who had been the U.S. minister to Belgium, purchased over 12,000 acres and laid out the town that now bears his name. In 1880, President U.S. Grant was present at ceremonies here, marking the beginning of the construction of the South Florida Railroad which, by 1884, linked Jacksonville with this central Florida community.

Sanford is host to the unique "Golden Age Games" where people age 55 and older from throughout the U.S. and foreign countries compete in a broad spectrum of sporting events.

0:00 (0:21) Depart Sanford.

0:20 (0:01) Area becomes more arid, more urbanized as we enter Orlando's metropolitan area.

0:21 (0:00) Arrive Winter Park beside beautiful downtown park, complete with swaying palms.

WINTER PARK, FL - The first building was erected in Winter Park in 1881—a depot. In 1885, Rollins College offered the first courses of higher learning in Florida. The Cornell Fine Arts Center is one of the finest university museums in the state. This is one of the prettiest towns in Florida, with lush foliage and winding brick streets, many lined with vine-draped oaks.

0:00 (0:13) Depart Winter Park.

0:05 (0:08) Passengers are now "treated" to an unusual trip through a hospital. Buildings of Florida Hospital line both sides of track with a walkway connection directly overhead.

0:08 (0:05) Note Statue of Liberty presiding over small, attractive flower display in street at right.

0:11 (0:02) Just before reaching Orlando's

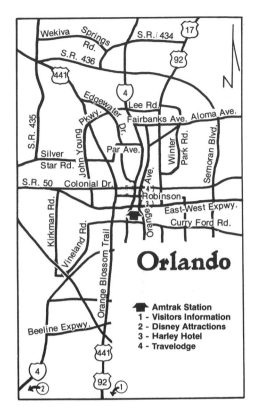

Orlando

- Amtrak Station
- 1 - Visitors Information
- 2 - Disney Attractions
- 3 - Harley Hotel
- 4 - Travelodge

present train station, old Church Street Station, now a popular shopping area and night spot, is on immediate left. Note 0-6-0 steam engine now on permanent display.

0:13 (0:00) Arrive Orlando.

ORLANDO, FL - Originally a sleepy agricultural town dependent on the citrus industry, Orlando has experienced growth in the last three decades that is now legendary. Tourism, due to the area's mild year-round climate, and particularly the proximity to Disney World and its newer offshoots, largely accounts for its recent surge.

It claims to be the world's number one vacation destination. The fact that a half million rental cars cruise central Florida's highways backs this boast.

Amtrak Station, 1400 Sligh Blvd., an attractive Spanish-style depot, is situated just to the south of Orlando's central business district. There are food and beverage vending machines, luggage carts and redcap service. Ample free parking is adjacent to the station.

 Yellow **Cab**, 699-9999. Nearest **local bus** stop is at Orange Ave., three blocks east of the station; call 841-8240. **Rental cars:** Air Rail Rent-A-Car, (407) 649-9283 or 800-228-8024, has cars at the station.

 Visitors Center at 8445 International Drive, (407) 363-5871.

 The hotels listed below are in downtown Orlando, about two miles from the station.

-**Travelodge Orlando Downtown**, 409 North Magnolia (at Livingston), 32801; (407) 423-1671. Well-managed downtown bargain. $50.

-**Harley Hotel of Orlando**, 151 E. Washington St. (at Rosalind), 32801; (407) 841-3220 or 800-321-2323. A Helmsley hotel. Downtown, overlooking Lake Eola. Spacious, attractive rooms. $80.

 Walt Disney World, **Epcot Center** and **Disney MGM Studio** are several miles from Orlando. These are the major reasons people come to Orlando. Unfortunately, there is no bus service between Orlando and these attractions. A car is about the only practical way to see most of Orlando's offerings. (Several hotels near Disney World, however, offer free shuttle service to Disney.)

0:00 (0:20) Depart Orlando. Upon leaving metropolitan area, landscape is still dominated by now familiar citrus groves.

0:20 (0:00) Arrive Kissimmee.

 KISSIMMEE, FL - Kissimmee is the closest rail station to Disney World and Epcot Center.

0:00 (0:45) Departing Kissimmee, Monument of States can be seen on left, a 70-foot-high pyramid comprised of thousands of rocks (and other items) collected from all states and some foreign countries.

0:45 (0:00) Arrive Winter Haven.

 WINTER HAVEN, FL - Nearby is a multitude of family-oriented attractions, including Cypress Gardens, Walt Disney World and Epcot Center.

0:00 (0:38) Departing Winter Haven, cross canal that feeds Lake Ship on right—part of Chain-of-Lakes system surrounding Winter Haven region. Emerge now into heartland of citrus groves, with trees at times within picking distance of train.

0:08 (0:30) In far distance to left, 205-foot Bok Singing Tower is famous for its 57-bell carillon, ranging in weight from 17 pounds to nearly 12 tons. Tower is set in 128-acre Bok Tower Garden and is highest point on Florida's peninsula.

0:38 (0:00) Arrive Sebring.

SEBRING, FL - Founded in 1912, Sebring is situated at the geographical center of Florida. The encompassing fertile terrain has nurtured a thriving agricultural economy.

0:00 (0:34) Depart Sebring.

0:15 (0:19) Lake Istokpoga makes brief appearance on right. Sebring auto track, famous for its course of flat curves laid out on a former World War II airfield, is located off to left.

0:26 (0:08) Cross Kissimmee River.

0:34 (0:00) Arrive Okeechobee.

OKEECHOBEE, FL - This town's name is an Indian word meaning "plenty big water." Lake Okeechobee, largest in southern U.S., lies three miles south and is vital source of fresh water for Miami area.

0:00 (0:51) Depart Okeechobee.

0:23 (0:28) Passing through Indiantown, cross St. Lucie Canal, connecting Lake Okeechobee to Atlantic Ocean.

0:51 (0:00) Arrive West Palm Beach.

WEST PALM BEACH, FL - One of many popular retreats of southern Florida.

0:00 (0:20) Depart West Palm Beach.

0:03 (0:17) Palm Beach airport can be seen on right.

0:07 (0:13) Departure from Palm Beach area is highlighted by scenic canals interweaving throughout attractive residential property.

0:20 (0:00) Arrive Delray Beach.

DELRAY BEACH, FL - Commercial flower growing is a major industry in this tropical resort town.
0:00 (0:12) Depart Delray Beach.
0:05 (0:06) Boca Raton airport borders route on left.
0:12 (0:00) Arrive Deerfield Beach.

DEERFIELD BEACH, FL - Another vacation haven of Florida's southern coast.
0:00 (0:15) Depart Deerfield Beach.
0:07 (0:08) On right, note Pompano Beach Race Track.
0:15 (0:00) Arrive Ft. Lauderdale.

FT. LAUDERDALE, FL - A fort established during the Seminole Wars of 1830s gave its name to this now much-frequented seaside resort.

Days Inn—I-95,1700 W. Broward Blvd., 33312; (305)463-2500 or 800-666-6501. About 1/4th mile from station, not very walkable. $60.
0:00 (0:09) Depart Ft. Lauderdale.
0:04 (0:05) On left, pass Ft. Lauderdale-Hollywood International Airport. Cross numerous navigable canals over the next few miles. This area is often called the Venice of America.
0:09 (0:00) Arrive Hollywood.

HOLLYWOOD, FL - Real estate entrepreneur Joseph Young helped this town blossom in the early 1920s by maintaining a fleet of buses to bring in prospective investors. Since Miami's train station is located in such a poor neighborhood, Hollywood can be a reasonable alternate destination for visiting the Miami area. Hotels, car rentals and Tri-Rail are all here.

Rental cars are available from Springer Car Rental with station delivery and pick up; (305) 921-5530 or 800-327-4127. Tri-Rail into Miami and north to West Palm Beach stops at the station.

Intown Howard Johnson Lodge, I-95 and Hollywood Blvd., 2900 Polk St., 30020; (305) 923 1516. Small, attractive facility, one block east of the station. $56.
0:00 (0:19) Depart Hollywood.

0:04 (0:15) Tall resort hotels of Miami Beach area jut above horizon on left.
0:19 (0:00) Arrive Miami, Amtrak's southernmost destination.

MIAMI, FL - There's always a perceptual reaction at the mere mention of the town's name—cops and cocaine, palms and plush. Miami is a soup that is often brought to a boil, a stew that is often called a modern Casablanca. *Newsweek* described it as "a jazzy, hectic mix of ethnicity, newfangled prosperity and foreign intrigue." But there are still its Miami Beach resorts, particularly the Art Deco District hotels, its weather and its proximity to the mysterious Everglades and that stretch of tropical islands called The Keys.

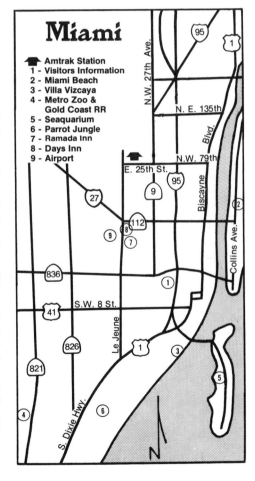

Miami

Amtrak Station
1 - Visitors Information
2 - Miami Beach
3 - Villa Vizcaya
4 - Metro Zoo &
    Gold Coast RR
5 - Seaquarium
6 - Parrot Jungle
7 - Ramada Inn
8 - Days Inn
9 - Airport

These endearments make it a place to visit, and tourism is still a dominant force here.

Miami got its start as a citrus-growing area in the 1890s after killing frosts had ruined much of the orange crops in central Florida. However, its start would not have been possible without Henry Flagler extending his railroad from central Florida into the Miami area. Then in the early 1920s, real estate development began to spur the city's growth. It is now a major international transfer point, having a steady stream of foreign visitors passing through the city each year.

Amtrak Station, 8303 NW 37th Ave., is located a considerable distance north of downtown in a rather grim, industrial area of Hialeah. This is a very modern, attractive facility—incongruous in its environment. There is a large parking lot that is never utilized to any degree, since overnight parking is definitely not recommended. Because of the station's poor location and no rental cars or hotels nearby, rail travelers visiting Miami may consider Hollywood or Ft. Lauderdale as alternate places to detrain.

The station has food and beverage machines, storage lockers, luggage carts and redcap service. The adjacent parking is free. For arrival and departure information only, call 835-1221.

Metro **Taxi**, 888-8888. **Local buses** stop at the station. Route L, which runs to Miami Beach via the 79th St. causeway, makes connections to **Metrorail** and **Tri-Rail** just south of the station at 79th Street. Also, #42 connects the station and bus terminals at Miami International Airport. For local bus, Metrorail and Tri-Rail information, call 638-6700. **Rental cars** are at **Miami International Airport**, six miles southwest of the station.

Convention and Visitors Bureau, 701 Brickell Ave., Suite 2700, 33131; (305) 539-3000 or 800-283-2707.

Logical accommodations for a single overnight are in the airport area where the nearest rental cars will also be found.

-**Ramada Hotel International Airport**, (305) 871-1700. Three-tenths mile to airport. $69.

-**Days Inn Airport**, 3401 NW Le Jeune Rd., 33142; (305) 871-4221. Restaurant and free airport shuttle. $69.

The **Miami Beach** area, with its white sand beaches and handsomely restored Art Deco District, is an enjoyable place for a stroll or a week-long stay. For animal, fish and bird fanciers, consider these: **Metrozoo**, 124th Ave., and SW 152nd St., a newer zoo with unusually realistic environments for the various species on exhibit; **Miami Seaquarium**, southeast of downtown on Rickenbacher Causeway, the world's largest tropical oceanarium; and **Parrot Jungle & Gardens**, 11000 S. Red Road (57th Ave.) with exotic birds in a walk-thru tropical setting.

The **Gold Coast Railroad Museum**, 12450 SW 152nd St., houses a good collection of historic railroad cars, including the Ferdinand Magellan—Franklin D. Roosevelt's private car and later used by Presidents Truman, Eisenhower and Reagan—and the observation lounge, Silver Crescent, from the old *California Zephyr*. Steam train excursions are also available.

New York
Columbia
Tampa
Miami

Silver Star

The *Silver Star* travels the Eastern Seaboard following a trail somewhat similar to the *Silver Meteor*, but keeps farther inland through most of the Carolinas. And just as its sister train does, the *Star* also takes in much of America's most historic environs. After Jacksonville, Florida, the southbound *Silver Star* splits into two separate trains, with the Miami section going by way of Ocala and the Tampa section through Orlando.

SOUTHBOUND SCHEDULE (Condensed)
New York, NY - Midmorning Departure
Washington, DC - Midafternoon
Richmond, VA - Late Afternoon
Raleigh, NC - Midevening
Columbia, SC - Late Night
Savannah, GA - Middle of the Night
Jacksonville, FL - Early Morning
Tampa, FL - Late Morning Arrival*
Miami, FL - Early Afternoon Arrival

NORTHBOUND SCHEDULE (Condensed)
Miami, FL - Early Afternoon Departure
Tampa, FL - Late Afternoon Departure*
Jacksonville, FL - Late Evening
Savannah, GA - Late Night
Columbia, SC - Middle of the Night
Raleigh, NC - Early Morning
Richmond, VA - Late Morning
Washington, DC - Early Afternoon
New York, NY - Early Evening Arrival
*By separate section between Tampa and Jacksonville.

FREQUENCY - Daily.
SEATING - Reserved coaches.
DINING - Tray meals, sandwiches, snacks and beverages.
SLEEPING - Roomettes and bedrooms, New York to Tampa, and Slumbercoach, New York to Miami.
BAGGAGE - Checked baggage handled at most stations.
RESERVATIONS - All-reserved train.
LENGTH OF TRIP - 1,391 miles in 27 ½ hours (New York/Miami).

ROUTE LOG

For route between New York and Rocky Mount, see that portion of the Northeast Corridor log, page 26, and *Silver Meteor* log, page 66.

 ROCKY MOUNT, NC - See page 69.
0:00 (1:20) Depart Rocky Mount.
0:02 (1:18) For next several minutes, pass by sprawling CSX rail yards on left.
0:20 (1:00) Through Wilson, another bright-leaf tobacco center, where tobacco warehouses seem to be everywhere. Its annual auction, dubbed "The Greatest Show in Tobaccoland," provides a most unique tourist attraction.
0:35 (0:45) Tall, skinny sheds dotting landscape, some with little chimneys jutting out from their tops, are tobacco curing barns.

Silver Star — Randolph-Macon College, Ashland, VA
DORIS SWANSON

0:44 (0:36) Through Selma, another small agricultural center, and point where our route now swings back toward Raleigh, departing from southbound CSX tracks followed by *Silver Meteor*.

1:20 (0:00) Arrive at Raleigh's attractive Georgian-style station.

RALEIGH, NC - Capital of North Carolina (named for Sir Walter who never saw the area) and the fastest growing city in North Carolina, Raleigh is a neat-appearing community with over 300 parks, plazas and "green spaces." A heavy emphasis has been placed on education with nine institutions of higher learning located in the metropolitan area, including North Carolina State University.

0:00 (1:06) Depart Raleigh.

0:07 (0:59) Brick fortress-appearing buildings on left comprise North Carolina Central Prison.

0:08 (0:58) Attractive campus of North Carolina State University lies immediately on left.

0:13 (0:53) Leaving Raleigh's suburbs, two barn-like brick buildings on right house vet-

erinarian school of North Carolina State.

0:14 (0:52) North Carolina Fair Grounds are visible off to right.

0:29 (0:37) Cross Haw River.

0:31 (0:35) Train now crosses Deep River. Following battle of Guilford Courthouse, General Cornwallis spent several days constructing a bridge over river about 300 yards upstream to right.

1:06 (0:00) Trundling down "Main Street," train arrives Southern Pines (Pinehurst).

SOUTHERN PINES, NC - This is the heart of the "Sandhills" of North Carolina where rolling green hills forested with pines (having needles up to 16 inches long) make this one of the most popular recreational areas in the U.S. Within a 15-mile radius there are: 27 golf courses (that's 91.03 miles of golf); 131 tennis courts; 6 1/2 miles of race tracks; and 3,460 acres of lakes and ponds. The World Golf Hall of Fame overlooks the fifth tee of the famed Pinehurst No. 2 Course.

0:00 (0:31) Depart Southern Pines.

0:21 (0:10) On right, North Carolina Speedway, ringed with billboards, looks down at tracks.

0:26 (0:05) Seaboard shops appear on left in CSX rail yards.

0:31 (0:00) Arrive Hamlet where, at left, colorful painting of red antique steam locomotive adorns wall of building while marvelous old depot serves as Amtrak station and museum on right at foot of "Main Street."

 **HAMLET, NC** - Founded in the late 1800s when John Shortridge established a woolen mill here, the town soon became an important seaboard rail hub. The rail industry dominates Hamlet's economy with the Southeast's largest electronic rail yard located here. An old opera house still stands where such notable performers as Caruso once brought culture of the highest level to this small town during its early prosperity. The quasi-Victorian rail station is on the National Register of Historic Places and houses a fine collection of Seaboard Airline Railway memorabilia.

0:00 (1:08) Depart Hamlet.

0:08 (1:00) Leave North Carolina and enter South Carolina.

0:20 (0:48) Cross Great Pee Dee River.

0:37 (0:31) On north edge of McBee, impressive-looking plant on left manufactures A. O. Smith water heaters.

0:46 (0:22) Through Bethune, a small agricultural community claiming title of Nation's Egg Capital.

1:08 (0:00) Arrive Camden.

CAMDEN, SC - A major British garrison under General Cornwallis was located here, and some 14 Revolutionary War battles took place in this vicinity. The world-famous "Colonial Cup," one of the nation's richest steeplechase races, is held here each November.

0:00 (0:33) Depart Camden.

0:02 (0:31) Cross broad Wateree River. On right is DuPont's May Plant, producing various synthetic fibers.

Hamlet, NC, Amtrak Station and museum
DORIS SWANSON

0:33 (0:00) Arrive Columbia, where capitol building presides over city at left.

 COLUMBIA, SC - One of the first planned cities, it was established in 1786 to be the state's capital and has held that distinction ever since. Some local attractions include: Woodrow Wilson's boyhood home where the nation's 28th president lived as a youth while his father taught at Columbia Theological Seminary; the State House which still shows scars on its outer walls from cannon fire during one of Sherman's campaigns; and State Farmers Market with tempting fresh produce available daily—largest in the Southeast.

0:00 (0:55) Depart Columbia.

0:02 (0:53) Cross over rock-strewn Congaree River.

0:55 (0:00) Arrive Denmark.

 DENMARK, SC - This community was born out of the intersecting of the Southbound Railroad Company and the South Carolina Railroad in 1891. At one time cotton was Denmark's most important product, but in 1921 the boll weevil appeared, causing such destruction that cotton is no longer grown here. Today, the soybean is king.

Oddly enough, Denmark has played two important roles in man's war against the mosquito. In 1927, a nearby swampy mill pond was the first ever to be sprayed by air in an effort to kill mosquito larvae. In 1901, a resident of Denmark, James Hanberry, served as one of 14 volunteer "guinea pigs" in Dr. Walter Reed's famous experiment in Havana, Cuba, to find the cause of yellow fever. On February 6th of that year, "Mosquito No. 13" that had sucked blood from fever patients stung Hanberry and proved that the female mosquito carried the dreaded germ.

0:00 (1:19) Depart Denmark.

0:55 (0:24) Leave South Carolina and enter Georgia.

1:19 (0:00) Arrive Savannah.

 SAVANNAH, GA - See page 70.

0:00 (2:04) Depart Savannah southbound into tall, densely wooded forests of southeastern Georgia.

0:06 (1:58) On left, skirt grounds of Hunter Army Airfield.

0:12 (1:52) Cross Ogeechee River.

0:13 (1:51) Pass through Richmond Hill. Nearby Fort McAllister was key to Savannah's fortifications during Civil War, fending off nine naval assaults before finally succumbing in Sherman's march to the sea.

0:46 (1:18) Cross Altamaha River.

0:50 (1:14) Through Jesup, an important distribution hub.

1:10 (0:54) Cross Satilla River.

1:35 (0:29) Pass through Folkston, a point of access to primeval wilderness area known as Okefenokee Swamp.

1:37 (0:27) Crossing St. Mary's River into Florida, colonial environs of past 1,000 miles are slowly supplanted by Spanish influence of an even earlier period.

2:04 (0:00) Arrive Jacksonville.

 JACKSONVILLE, FL - Unlike many other Floridian cities, Jacksonville is not a tourist resort. Rather, it has grown to become the state's leading industrial center. Although lying a few miles west of the Atlantic Ocean, Jacksonville is still an important seaport, with an interconnecting passage along the St. Johns River. Three beautiful beaches provide a weekend haven for many city dwellers. This is a major rail center for CSX, which has an ultramodern $23 million train dispatching operation controlling its entire 20,000-mile system.

Here, at Jacksonville, the Miami and Tampa sections of the *Silver Star* split with the Miami section going through Ocala and Wildwood and the Tampa section going through DeLand and Orlando.

TAMPA SECTION (Miami Section begins on page 82.)

For Jacksonville/Kissimmee segment, see *Silver Meteor*, page 71.

 KISSIMMEE, FL - See page 74.

0:00 (1:08) Departing Kissimmee, Monument of States can be seen on left, a 70-foot-high pyramid comprised of thousands of rocks (and other items) collected from all states and some foreign countries.

0:38 (0:30) This is Auburndale, a major intersection for two routes of the historic Seaboard Coast Line. In rail vernacular, this is known as "The Auburn Diamond."

1:08 (0:00) Arrive at Lakeland's immaculate white brick station.

LAKELAND, FL - This is the very heart of citrus country. A fifth of all citrus grown in the United States comes from this immediate area—that's a lot of orange juice. Lakeland is also the marketing center for Florida's entire crop. But one other product is as important as oranges and grapefruit. Most of the world's phosphate is mined nearby, almost all of it going into agricultural fertilizers.

Florida Southern College is located here where students study amidst the largest assemblage of buildings designed by Frank Lloyd Wright. The Detroit Tigers have enjoyed spring training here for years.

0:00 (0:32) Depart Lakeland.

0:07 (0:25) Train slows to 35 mph while coursing through heart of Plant City, spring training camp of Cincinnati Reds.

0:20 (0:12) Cross Tampa By-Pass Canal.

0:32 (0:00) Arrive Tampa, where station is backdropped by Tampa's glassy skyscrapers.

TAMPA, FL - The first adventurers to reach Tampa were Panfilo Narvez in 1528 and DeSoto in 1539. The area was soon abandoned by the white man, however, and it was not until 284 years later in 1823 that the first settler gave Tampa some semblance of permanence.

In 1885, V. M. Ybor was persuaded to bring his cigar-making operations from Key West to the Tampa area, and Ybor City was laid out northeast of Tampa to accommodate this new industry. Tampa's first famous cigars were thus manufactured in 1886. Teddy Roosevelt set up headquarters in the Tampa Bay Hotel in 1892 with 30,000 soldiers camped nearby for training during the Spanish American War, and Tampa became the major embarkation point for troops headed for Cuba. The first regularly scheduled commercial airline flight ever flown

Tampa

- Amtrak Station
1 - Visitors Information
2 - Plant Museum
3 - Harbor Island
4 - Ybor City
5 - Dark Continent - Busch Gardens
6 - Holiday Inn

landed here, arriving from nearby St. Petersburg.

Today, Tampa is the industrial center of western Florida, with fishing and citrus processing being mainstays. Its mild climate has made it not only a major tourist area but also a favorite retirement center.

Tampa Amtrak Station, 601 Nebraska Ave., at Twiggs Street, is a modern, efficient, "temporary" structure immediately behind Union Station. The latter was built in 1912 in Italian Renaissance style, but unfortunately no longer serves as a station.

There are snack vending machines, luggage carts and redcap service. There is limited free parking in front of the station. Pay-parking is at the Twiggs Street Parking Garage.

United **Cab**, 253-2424. **Local bus** information, call 254-HART.

Tampa/Hillsborough Visitor Information Center, 111 Madison St., Suite 1010 (corner of Madison and Ashley), 33602; (813) 223-1111 or 800-826-8358.

Holiday Inn Downtown, 111 W. Fortune, 33602; (813) 223-1351. About a mile from the station, on the edge of the central business district. $76.

 Tampa's downtown is focused on the **Franklin Street Mall**, a pleasant urban stretch of stores, restaurants and services. The south end of the Mall is anchored by the smartly landscaped City Hall Plaza, surrounded by hotels, offices and popular bistros. And on the southern edge of the Plaza, a people mover transports pedestrians to **Harbor Island**, an array of specialty shops, restaurants and quick-service eateries.

Ybor City, just a few blocks east of the station, bounded roughly by 5th and 11th Avenues and 12th and 22nd Streets, is Tampa's Latin Quarter. What was the beginning of Tampa's cigar industry is now filled with many historic sites, as well as **Ybor Square** which is a fine collection of shops and restaurants featuring fine Spanish cuisine.

MIAMI SECTION

0:00 (0:59) Depart Jacksonville. As train embarks on sweeping U-turn, tall bridges spanning St. Johns River are focal point of city scene on left. Soon, pass through Honeymoon Wye, then encounter CSX's huge Baldwin Yard.

0:44 (0:15) On right, Eastern cowpokes show their stuff at Bradford Roping Club Arena.

0:59 (0:00) Arrive Waldo.

 WALDO, FL - This stop affords access to the Gainesville area and University of Florida.

0:00 (0:43) Depart Waldo.

0:20 (0:23) Passing through Lochloosa, Lake Lochloosa can be seen on right.

0:29 (0:14) Thoroughbred horse farm on right features well-kept grounds and "official-size" track.

0:43 (0:00) Arrive Ocala.

 OCALA, FL - As well as an agricultural community, the Ocala region boasts some of the nation's top thoroughbred concerns, with many facilities open to the public.

0:00 (0:25) Depart Ocala.

0:25 (0:00) Arrive Wildwood.

 WILDWOOD, FL - Another small community heavily dependent on the citrus industry.

0:00 (0:34) Depart Wildwood.

0:23 (0:11) Witness more densely wooded terrain over next few miles as train borders fringe of Withlacoochee State Forest.

0:34 (0:00) Arrive Dade City.

 DADE CITY, FL - This stop serves nearby Zephyrhills.

0:00 (0:43) Depart Dade City.

0:32 (0:11) Through Lakeland, then note Minute Maid juicing plant on right.

This is the very heart of citrus country. A fifth of all citrus grown in the United States comes from this immediate area—that's a lot of orange juice. Lakeland is also the marketing center for Florida's entire crop. But one other product is as important as oranges and grapefruit. Most of the world's phosphate is mined nearby, almost all of it going into agricultural fertilizers.

Florida Southern College is located here where students study amidst the largest assemblage of buildings designed by Frank Lloyd Wright. The Detroit Tigers have enjoyed spring training here for years.

0:43 (0:00) Arrive Winter Haven.

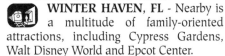 **WINTER HAVEN, FL** - Nearby is a multitude of family-oriented attractions, including Cypress Gardens, Walt Disney World and Epcot Center.

For Winter Haven/Miami segment, see *Silver Meteor*, **page 74.**

New York

Charlotte

Carolinian

The *Carolinian* (perhaps better called the "North Carolinian") offers the people of North Carolina train service that runs during reasonable hours and, traversing the state in an east/west orientation, provides service to such population centers as Charlotte, Greensboro, Durham and Raleigh. At Raleigh, the train then follows the route of the *Silver Star* to New York City. Between Greensboro and Charlotte (its southern terminus) the *Carolinian* follows the route of the *Crescent*.

SOUTHBOUND SCHEDULE (Condensed)
New York, NY - Early Morning Departure
Washington, DC - Late Morning
Raleigh, NC - Late Afternoon
Greensboro, NC - Early Evening
Charlotte, NC - Midevening Arrival

NORTHBOUND SCHEDULE (Condensed)
Charlotte, NC - Early Morning Departure
Greensboro, NC - Midmorning
Raleigh, NC - Late Morning
Washington, DC - Early Evening
New York, NY - Late Evening

FREQUENCY - Daily.
SEATING - Reserved coaches.
DINING - Sandwiches, snacks and beverages with table seating.
BAGGAGE - Checked baggage handled at most stations.
RESERVATIONS - All-reserved train.
LENGTH OF TRIP - 702 miles in 14 hours.

ROUTE LOG

For route between New York and Rocky Mount, NC, see that portion of the Northeast Corridor log, page 26, and *Silver Meteor* log, page 66.

0:00 (0:19) Depart Rocky Mount, NC.
0:02 (0:15) For next several minutes, pass sprawling CSX rail yards on left.
0:19 (0:00) Arrive Wilson.

 WILSON, NC - Another bright-leaf tobacco center; tobacco warehouses seem to be everywhere. Its annual auction, dubbed "The Greatest Show in Tobaccoland" provides a unique tourist attraction. Wilson is also one of the country's leading antique markets.
0:00 (0:21) Depart Wilson.
0:15 (0:06) Tall, skinny sheds dotting landscape, some with little chimneys jutting out from their roofs, are tobacco curing barns.
0:21 (0:00) Arrive Selma.

 SELMA, NC - This small agricultural center is also a major rail junction. From Selma, the *Carolinian* departs the route of the *Silver Meteor* and heads west toward Raleigh.
0:00 (0:52) Depart Selma, heading westward through rolling landscape checked with tobacco farms.
0:52 (0:00) Arrive at Raleigh's attractive Georgian-style station.

RALEIGH, NC - Capital of North Carolina (named for Sir Walter who

Carolinian — Mebane, NC
JACK SWANSON

never saw the area) and the fastest growing city in North Carolina, Raleigh is a neat-appearing community with over 300 parks, plazas and "green spaces." A heavy emphasis has been placed on education with nine institutions of higher learning located in the metropolitan area, including North Carolina State University.

0:00 (0:39) Depart Raleigh on Norfolk Southern line.

0:07 (0:32) Brick fortress-appearing buildings, on left, comprise North Carolina Central Prison.

0:08 (0:30) Attractive campus of North Carolina State University lies immediately on left.

0:20 (0:18) Through Research Triangle Park, a development started in 1959 for industrial and governmental research. It was placed here due to its proximity to numerous institutions of higher learning in Raleigh, Durham and Chapel Hill. Research Triangle area is regarded as being first nationally in number of PhD scientists and engineers per

100,000 population.

0:39 (0:00) Arrive Durham.

DURHAM, NC -The city got its start when Dr. Bartlett Durham provided a gift of land for a railroad station in the 1840s. The city soon developed an economy based on tobacco and textiles. In more recent years, education and medical research have become the city's focus with thousands employed in health care, education and research. Duke University is Durham's largest employer, and the Duke Medical Center is rated in the nation's top five.

0:00 (0:47) Depart Durham and slip past Lucky Strike facility on left.

0:02 (0:45) Liggett and Meyers Tobacco Company operation is on immediate right. East campus of Duke University will also be off to right.

0:04 (0:43) Near this spot is Bennett Place, where Generals Johnson and Sherman met to negotiate a surrender that would soon spell Civil War's end.

0:23 (0:24) Historic town of Hillsborough is to right, a focal point of Revolutionary War activity. General Cornwallis pitched camp here for five days in 1781. Although numerous important state conventions were held here in 1700s, efforts failed to make Hillsborough North Carolina's capital.

0:35 (0:12) Through community of Mebane, home of Kingsdown Mattresses and Dixie Fabrics on right. Colonial trading path dating from 17th century, from Petersburg, Virginia to Carolinas, passed nearby.

0:41 (0:06) At Haw River, disparate conglomerate of Cone Fabrics and Cone Granite Finishing is on right.

0:47 (0:00) Arrive Burlington.

BURLINGTON, NC - Textiles have long been a Burlington mainstay. The textile industry in the South was changed dramatically when a local mill produced the first commercially dyed plaids south of the Mason-Dixon line.

An unusual pre-Revolutionary conflict, the Battle of Alamance, occurred a few miles south of Burlington in 1771. Approximately 2,000 "Regulators," frontiersmen who quit paying taxes because they did not trust Easterners to properly represent them, fought and lost to the colonial militia sent to quell the rebels.

0:00 (0:35) Depart Burlington.

0:02 (0:33) Burlington Industries plant is on right, demonstrating city's textile heritage.

0:07 (0:28) Campus of small Elon College, a United Church of Christ institution founded in 1889, is on right.

0:23 (0:12) On right, Lorillard and Newport cigarette facilities are continued evidence of tobacco industry's regional importance.

0:33 (0:02) On right is University of North Carolina at Greensboro, founded in 1891.

0:35 (0:00) Arrive Greensboro.

For route between Greensboro and Charlotte, see that portion of the *Crescent* log, page 92.

Tidewater Express

New England Express

These trains are Amtrak's access to Newport News, Norfolk, Virginia Beach, and Colonial Williamsburg. Originally, it was thought that this service would carry mostly service personnel to and from the large naval base at Norfolk; however, nearly as many passengers now detrain at Williamsburg as they do at the base. The *Tidewater Express* is the southbound train and has its northern terminus at Boston and follows the route of the *Silver Meteor* between New York and Richmond. It then takes CSX tracks between Richmond and Newport News. The *New England Express* is the northbound train.

Although the route follows the course of the James River, it is generally too far north to allow passengers to see the many magnificent plantations that border the shore of this historic stream. But the history of the region can be felt. McClelland used Berkeley on the James River as his headquarters in the summer of 1862. The trip through Williamsburg, passing within view of the historic section of America's colonial capital, is exciting, even if one does not plan to disembark here. Jamestown, the first English settlement in the New World, is just a few minutes away. Then, still further downline, the route passes near Yorktown, where America literally won her independence on the battlefield.

SOUTHBOUND SCHEDULE (Condensed)
Boston, MA - Early Morning Departure
New York, NY - Late Morning
Washington, DC - Midafternoon
Richmond, VA - Late Afternoon
Newport News, VA - Early Evening Arrival

NORTHBOUND SCHEDULE (Condensed)
Newport News, VA - Early Morning Departure
Richmond, VA - Late Morning
Washington, DC - Early Afternoon
New York, NY - Late Afternoon Arrival
Boston, MA - Late Evening Arrival

FREQUENCY - Daily. (Extra train southbound on Fridays.)
SEATING - Reserved coaches. Club Service available.
DINING - Sandwiches, snacks and beverages.
BAGGAGE - No checked baggage.
RESERVATIONS - All-reserved train.
LENGTH OF TRIP - 644 miles in 12 hours.

ROUTE LOG

For route between Boston and Washington, DC, see *Northeast Corridor* log, page 19, and from Washington to Richmond, the *Silver Meteor* log, page 66.

0:00 (1:05) Departing Richmond's Staples Mills Road station, head south into older section of downtown Richmond.

0:09 (0:56) Off to right a few blocks, granite building with oxidized copper-looking dome is Science Museum of Virginia. This former Seaboard Coast Line station bears a resemblance to Washington, DC's Jefferson Memorial, perhaps because John Russel Pope designed both structures.

0:16 (0:49) Pass through Brown Street rail yards, then 17th Street rail yards.

0:19 (0:46) On right, 1900 French beaux art structure, Main Street Station, is slated for restoration and may see train service in 1997.

0:20 (0:45) Tobacco is important to Richmond's economy, although not as dominant as in years past. Weathered sign on enormous old brick building at left indicates that Lucky Strikes have been produced here.

0:21 (0:44) Just before crossing old drawbridge across S. R. Canal, James River can be seen briefly on right.

0:23 (0:42) Pass through CSX Fulton Yards located in Richmond's eastern industrial suburbs.

0:29 (0:36) Modernistic Nabisco bakery on right churns out tons of cookies, crackers and pretzels. The plant produces "high volume" products, including Ritz Crackers, Oreo Cookies and Premium Saltines. "Almost Home" brand products have also been produced here.

0:31 (0:34) Runways and terminal facilities of Richard Evelyn Byrd International Airport are visible to left. Virginia Army National Guard helicopters are also frequently seen here.

0:37 (0:28) Evidence that we are entering Virginia's low-lying region appears in form of swamplands during next few miles, mostly on right.

0:44 (0:21) Derelict, but picturesque, old Providence Forge station on right is structural clone of beautifully restored depot further downline at Lee Hall.

0:46 (0:19) Symmetrical rows of thousands of pine trees distinguish New Kent Forestry Center on right. Operated by the Virginia Division of Forestry, this is second largest producer of forest tree seedlings in the nation. Up to 60 million pine seedlings are started each year and sold primarily to lumber industry. Loblolly pine is Center's principal product. Watch for deer, quail and other wild creatures since this is also a wildlife preserve.

0:50 (0:15) Sailboats and other small craft can often be seen on broad expanse of Chickanominy River (a tributary of the James further south) which curls up to tracks on right.

1:05 (0:00) Arrive at Williamsburg, where station is just three blocks from this colonial capital's historic area.

WILLIAMSBURG, VA - Williamsburg was the capital of colonial Virginia for 81 years—from 1699 to 1780. Like Washington, DC, it was originally planned and constructed with its governmental role in mind. A carefully planned restoration and preservation effort was started in 1926, and today, Colonial Williamsburg is a marvelous collection of historic structures, gardens and tree-shaded streets. During the day, artisans work their historic crafts dressed in colonial attire for viewing by the public.

Williamsburg Transportation Center, 468 North Boundary St., is only three blocks from the historic district. There are storage lockers, luggage carts, food and beverage machines and free parking.

Colonial **Cab**, 565-1240. There is a **public bus** between the historic area and the Visitors Center.

The Colonial Williamsburg Information Center is on the edge of Williamsburg. Write Colonial Williamsburg Foundation, Box 1776, 23187; (804) 220-7645 or 800-HISTORY. The Information Center should be visited prior to touring Colonial Williamsburg itself.

Governor's Inn, 506 N. Henry St., 23185; (804) 229-1000 or 800-HISTORY. Near the Historic Area and only three blocks from the station. $80.

There are also numerous Holiday Inns, Quality Inns, Best Westerns, etc. in the area. Call 800-446-9244 for reservations.

Colonial Williamsburg is a village full of 18th-century buildings and

Tidewater — Richmond, VA
JACK SWANSON

peopled with actors in attire of that era. Don't miss the Governor's Palace, the Capitol, Burton Parish Church, Raleigh Tavern, the Magazine and Guardhouse to name but a few. Be sure to obtain an Official Guidebook and map when you purchase your ticket.

0:00 (0:10) Departing Williamsburg, a glimpse can be caught of Palace of Governors (topped by small tower and flanked by two chimneys) just beyond brick wall on right which is boundary of historic district. This has served as residence of seven royal governors as well as first two governors of Virginia.

0:06 (0:04) Parking for Busch Gardens is on immediate right—a 360-acre "theme" amusement park.

0:10 (0:00) Arrive at Lee Hall's attractively restored depot, a dolled-up twin to one seen at Providence Forge.

LEE HALL, VA - This is a suburban stop for Newport News and serves nearby Fort Eustis on Mulberry Island, headquarters of the U.S. Army Transportation Center.

0:00 (0:10) Depart Lee Hall.

0:02 (0:08) Cross what appears to be a river but is actually an arm of City Reservoir.

0:12 (0:00) Arrive Newport News station, still some distance from downtown area.

NEWPORT NEWS, VA - Here at the mouth of the James River, four cities cluster around the water's edge and make the absolute most of their coastal status. Newport News, Norfolk, Portsmouth and Hampton share one of the finest harbors in the world. The bay is over 14 miles long and 40 feet deep.

Maritime activities run the gamut from the world's largest shipbuilder, to the world's largest naval base, being the home port for the Atlantic and Mediterranean fleets.

History buffs will definitely want to visit Yorktown where the most decisive battle of the American Revolution was fought. And if naval warfare is of interest, be sure to take in Fort Monroe. Had you been at this site on March 9, 1862 you would have had a front row seat for that mighty but inconclusive battle between the iron clads, Monitor and Merrimack (called the "Virginia" by the South). And, understandably, the finest collection of ship models to be found anywhere is housed in the Mariner's Museum which is located in Newport News.

Other Mid-Atlantic & Florida Service

Additional trains operate along the **Newport News/Richmond/New York/Boston** route. Check with Amtrak for details.

Auto Train is Amtrak's unique service for those who want to travel by train between Washington, DC and central Florida—and take their cars along. The train leaves each end point in the midafternoon and arrives at the other in the early morning the next day. Lorton, VA (south of DC) is the northern terminal, while Sanford, FL (one-half hour from Disney World) is the southern end.

The train provides a "sit-down" dinner with china and linens, and a continental breakfast for sleeping car passengers. The train offers dome cars, lounge service, bedrooms and roomettes, and entertainment consisting of feature-length motion pictures. A complimentary buffet-style dinner and continental breakfast are provided to coach passengers. It is an all-reserved train, and although no checked baggage is handled, extra bags can be stored in your car (with no access during the trip). Only passengers with autos are permitted and should arrive two hours early for boarding. No autos will be accepted less than one hour before departure. Autos must have four inches of ground clearance and cannot be higher than 65 inches. There is limited space for vans which should not exceed 85 inches in height, and specific reservations should be made for these. Superliner equipment is now in use on this train.

In addition to passenger fares, one way for an auto can run in the neighborhood of $175 in season.

Atlantic City/Philadelphia service is offered daily by New Jersey Transit.

Piedmont provides unreserved, daily service between Raleigh, NC, and Charlotte, NC, departing Raleigh early morning and departing Charlotte late afternoon. Tray meals with table service, no checked baggage.

Crescent

The *Crescent* provides direct, no-change service between New York City and New Orleans. The route follows the Northeast Corridor between New York's Pennsylvania Station and Washington, DC, then takes the tracks of the Southern Railway through Atlanta and Birmingham before finally reaching New Orleans.

This train has a distinct case of dual personalities. The northern facet is the bustling, urbanized Northeast Corridor, predominated by New York City, Philadelphia, Baltimore and Washington, DC, while the southern and longest segment leaves one with the relaxed impressions of the rural Deep South. Darkness covers the Carolinas when the *Crescent* crosses these two states.

The most unique aspect of the trip occurs during the approach to New Orleans when the *Crescent* slowly glides for ten minutes or so just above the surface of Lake Pontchartrain. Here the feeling is more of an ocean liner than a passenger train.

SOUTHBOUND SCHEDULE (Condensed)
New York, NY - Early Afternoon Departure
Washington, DC - Early Evening
Charlotte, NC - Middle of the Night
Atlanta, GA - Early Morning
Birmingham, AL - Late Morning
New Orleans, LA - Early Evening Arrival

NORTHBOUND SCHEDULE (Condensed)
New Orleans, LA - Early Morning Departure
Birmingham, AL - Early Afternoon
Atlanta, GA - Early Evening
Charlotte, NC - Middle of the Night
Washington, DC - Midmorning
New York, NY - Early Afternoon Arrival

FREQUENCY - New York-Atlanta: Daily. Atlanta-New Orleans: Wed, Fri, Sat, Sun southbound; Sun, Mon, Thur, Sat northbound.
SEATING - Reserved coaches.
DINING - Complete meal service.
SLEEPING - Roomettes and bedrooms (Viewliners).
BAGGAGE - Checked baggage at most stops.
RESERVATIONS - All-reserved train.
LENGTH OF TRIP - 1,380 miles in 30 hours.

ROUTE LOG

For route between New York City and Washington, DC, see that portion of Northeast Corridor log, page 26.

 WASHINGTON, DC - See page 35.

0:00 (0:17) Depart Washington.
0:02 (0:15) Emerge from tunnel after passing under Mall. Glimpses of Capitol and oldest Smithsonian structure ("The Castle") can be caught through various federal buildings on right.

0:07 (0:10) Perhaps Washington's most charming monument, Monticello-shaped Jefferson Memorial, resides among cherry trees of Tidal Basin on right.

0:09 (0:08) Cross Potomac River paralleling 14th Street bridge. Washington National Airport is directly downstream to left. Back on right, Washington Monument, world's tallest masonry structure at 555.5 feet, punctuates horizon. Capitol's dome can still be seen toward rear on left.

0:10 (0:07) The Pentagon, headquarters for America's military establishment, is off to right.

0:12 (0:05) Glass high rises of Crystal City flaunt their starkness on right. Expansive RF&P rail yards are on left.

0:17 (0:00) Arrive Alexandria.

ALEXANDRIA, VA - This historic Washington suburb sits six miles south of the nation's capital, along the west bank of the Potomac River. Most noted for its outstanding examples of early American architecture, the Alexandria area is also replete with numerous national landmarks. Mount Vernon, beloved home and estate of George Washington from 1754 until his death in 1799, is just a few miles down the Potomac.

0:00 (0:30) Depart Alexandria.

0:01 (0:29) George Washington Masonic National Memorial, with museum of Washington memorabilia, dominates skyline on right. Metro subway station on left provides commuters with quick, easy access to downtown Washington.

0:30 (0:00) Arrive Manassas.

MANASSAS, VA - This was the site of intense fighting during the Civil War. The town was burned several times by both Yankees and Confederates, most often in an effort to cut supply lines to fighting troops. The two Battles of Manassas (Bull Run) were fought in July of 1861 and August of 1862 just northeast of town, and are now commemorated by the 5,000-acre Manassas National Battlefield Park. The quaint rail station was built circa 1915.

0:00 (0:32) Depart Manassa.

0:32 (0:00) Arrive Culpeper, where vast Confederate cemetery is at left.

CULPEPER, VA - The Culpeper Minute Men were the very first to respond in 1775 to Patrick Henry's call-to-arms. Then, during the Civil War, the area saw heavy fighting and the town served as headquarters for both sides. George Washington described this area as a "high and pleasant situation," when he surveyed the county, and the town still prides itself on its fresh water supply and clean air.

0:00 (0:49) Depart Culpeper.

0:16 (0:44) Through town of Orange, home to two U.S. presidents, James Madison and Zachary Taylor. Bloody "Wilderness Campaign" of 1864 was waged just east of here.

0:42 (0:07) Pass through Shadwell, birthplace of Thomas Jefferson.

0:49 (0:00) Arrive Charlottesville.

CHARLOTTESVILLE, VA - "These mountains are the Eden of the United States." Thomas Jefferson wrote these flattering words in describing the area in and around Charlottesville. As the county seat of Albemarle, the town was a veritable treasure trove of talent and wisdom— Jefferson, James Madison and James Monroe were all part of the local scene. In more recent times, William Faulkner, Lady Astor and William McGuffey all called Albemarle County their home during some point in their lives. The University of Virginia is located here, while Jefferson's beautifully designed home (Monticello) and the estate of James Monroe (Ash Lawn) are nearby.

0:00 (1:12) Depart Charlottesville. Campus of University of Virginia will be on right.

0:50 (0:22) Through Sweet Briar, home to Sweet Briar College.

1:12 (0:00) Arrive Lynchburg.

LYNCHBURG, VA - A young Quaker by the name of John Lynch established a ferry here in the 1750s, opening up a trade route to Richmond and beyond. Soon, tobacco warehouses were built which established the town's economic foundation. After the Civil War, however, the tobacco industry began to move south and other endeavors gradually took its place.

0:00 (1:09) Depart Lynchburg.

0:52 (0:17) Community of Chatham is location of Hargrave Military Academy.

1:09 (0:00) Arrive Danville.

 DANVILLE, VA - This colorful tobacco auction center was the last capital of The Confederacy. Near the end of the Civil War, Jefferson Davis and his cabinet settled here for about a week after being forced from Richmond, then fled southward again after the surrender at Appomattox.

0:00 (1:00) Depart Danville.

0:05 (0:55) Leave Virginia and enter North Carolina.

0:32 (0:28) American Brands Tobacco plant proclaims "Lucky Strike" and "Tareyton" on chimney and water tower on right upon entering Reidsville. Town was named for David S. Reid, governor of North Carolina from 1851 to 1854. His former home stands two blocks to left near center of town, the two-story frame buff-colored structure with brown shutters.

1:00 (0:00) Arrive Greensboro.

 GREENSBORO, NC - This is not just golf country—it is the very heart of golf country. No less than eighteen courses in the immediate area offer stiff challenges to any level of player. One of the top PGA tournaments, The Greater Greensboro Open, is held here each April.

0:00 (0:18) Depart Greensboro.

0:18 (0:00) Arrive High Point.

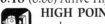 **HIGH POINT, NC** - It was a railroad surveyor, marking this location as the "high point" on the route between Goldsboro and Charlotte, who was responsible for giving the city a name which would stick. High Point can easily lay claim to being the nation's furniture capital with over 80 furniture factories, including several of the largest manufacturers in the world, located near here. And the manufacture of another product is equally as impressive— High Point has the distinction of being the largest hosiery producer in the world.

0:00 (0:38) Depart High Point.

0:38 (0:00) Arrive Salisbury.

 SALISBURY, NC - This attractive community is the center for Rowan County, with a widely diversified manufacturing base as well as agriculture consisting mostly of livestock and small grains. Salisbury was hometown to at least two notables, Daniel Boone and Elizabeth Dole.

0:00 (0:47) Depart Salisbury.

0:47 (0:00) Arrive Charlotte.

 CHARLOTTE, NC - This thriving city is a center for commerce, industry, finance and communications. Charlotte is the home town of evangelist Billy Graham. It also bears the unlikely distinction of being the site of the first authenticated gold discovery in the U.S., and the famous Charlotte Motor Speedway holds stockcar and motorcycle races, drawing thousands each year.

0:00 (0:28) Depart Charlotte.

0:28 (0:00) Arrive Gastonia.

 GASTONIA, NC - The *Crescent* makes a jog in its southerly course to stop at this textile-oriented city, some 28 miles west of Charlotte, before heading into South Carolina.

0:00 (0:57) Depart Gastonia.

0:07 (0:50) Enter South Carolina and leave North Carolina.

0:57 (0:00) Arrive Spartanburg.

 SPARTANBURG, SC - This heavily industrialized community is a major textile producing center, and the county lays claim to being the most prolific peach producer in South Carolina.

0:00 (0:39) Depart Spartanburg.

0:39 (0:00) Arrive Greenville.

 GREENVILLE, SC - The numerous textile manufacturing plants located here give rise to Greenville's title, "Textile Center of the World." Outlet shops of these many factories are favorites of both local and visiting bargain hunters. The city has also been home to some well-known religious figures. Rev. Jesse Jackson was born here, and in 1927 evangelist Dr. Bob Jones chose this location when he founded Bob Jones University.

0:00 (0:35) Depart Greenville.

0:35 (0:00) Arrive Clemson.

CLEMSON, SC - This charming college town was known as Calhoun, named for the political giant John Calhoun. In 1943 the name was changed to that of the university located here. Clemson University allows visitors to tour their unusual greenhouses and gardens, featuring over 2,200 varieties of plants. Also, Clemson's famous ice cream and blue cheese are favorites of dairy product connoisseurs.

0:00 (0:35) Depart Clemson.

0:35 (0:00) Arrive Toccoa.

TOCCOA, GA - Toccoa is the home of Toccoa Falls Bible College which features the spectacular 186-foot Toccoa Falls on its campus. In 1977, an earthen dam above the Falls broke and released a torrent of water engulfing the campus.

0:00 (0:41) Depart Toccoa.

0:41 (0:00) Arrive Gainesville.

GAINESVILLE, GA - This agricultural community of northeastern Georgia is situated near the northern end of Georgia's largest body of water, Lake Sydney Lanier, featuring a 1,200-acre family recreation resort on the Lake Lanier Islands.

0:00 (0:55) Depart Gainesville.

0:35 (0:20) Industrial and commercial developments begin to proliferate near Atlanta.

0:45 (0:10) Medieval-appearing buildings of Oglethorpe University are just to right.

0:47 (0:08) Inviting fairways and greens of Standard Golf Club stretch out on left.

0:51 (0:04) Atlanta's modern skyline is forward on left.

0:55 (0:00) Arrive at Atlanta's Peachtree Station.

ATLANTA, GA - Atlanta grew quickly from its founding as a railhead in the early 1800s to become a major manufacturing center of the South. During the Civil War it served as an arms marshaling point and the intersection of four railroads until General Sherman almost totally destroyed the city during his march-to-the-sea campaign. The city made a quick recovery, however, becoming the center of the Reconstruction process following the war.

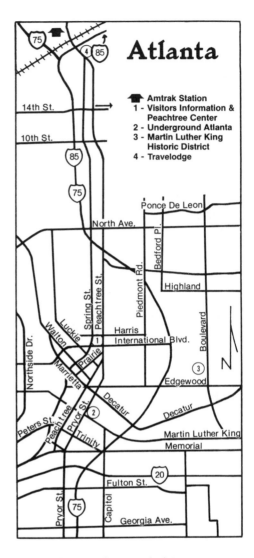

Later, it became the capital of Georgia.

Today, it is the financial, industrial and transportation center of the South. Its MARTA urban rail system is one of the finest transit operations in the country. For many, Atlanta is also a vacation destination, offering numerous options for both fun and leisure. Major league sports, a symphony, numerous historic sites and fine shopping are all found here. The city was the successful bidder for the 1996 Summer Olympic Games.

Crescent — near Birmingham, AL
DORIS SWANSON

 **Brookwood (Peachtree) Station,** 1688 Peachtree St., N.W., is located approximately four miles north of the center of downtown in a bustling neighborhood. The station actually straddles the main line of the Southern. There are food and beverage vending machines. Parking is across the street at the Masonic Temple. Advance arrangements must be made for long-term parking, (404) 874-8514, call weekdays. Redcaps are available.

Yellow **Cab**, 521-0200. **Buses** stop at the station. Take the #23 bus south to the nearest **MARTA** commuter rail station (Arts Center); for MARTA rail and bus information call 848-4711. For **rental cars,** Budget will pick up or pay cab fare from the station to their downtown location; (404) 530-3000.

ACVB Visitor Information center, Peachtree Center Mall; (404) 521-6688. Information centers are also located at Lennox Square (north) and at Underground Atlanta.

Travelodge Atlanta Peachtree, 1641 Peachtree St., N.E.; (404) 873-5731. Reasonably priced and near restaurants. One block from the station. $49.

-**Bed & Breakfast Atlanta**, 1801 Piedmont Ave., N.E., Suite 208, 30324; (404) 875-0525 or 800-967-3224. A reservation service for B&Bs in homes or inns. Dietary needs can often be accommodated and all accommodations have private baths. Several locations are convenient to the Amtrak station. $52 to $120.

On the southern edge of the central business district is **Underground Atlanta.** Rather ominous sounding, it's actually a six-block labyrinth of eclectic shops and restaurants, albeit devoid of sunlight. Nearly abandoned when the city built a system of viaducts that covered the area, a $140 million rejuvenation has turned it into one of Atlanta's "in" places. It is served by MARTA's rail system (Five Points station).

In the heart of downtown, **Peachtree Center** is the focal point of downtown shopping, hotels and restaurants, all in an urban indoor environment. For the professional consumer, the really power shopper, there's Lennox Square, reached by MARTA rail, located in upscale **Buckhead**. Stores include Saks, Neiman-Marcus, Lord and Taylor, Abercrombie and Fitch, and Macy's.

0:00 (2:20) Depart Atlanta.

0:16 (2:04) Cross Chattahoochee River as train proceeds through industrialized area of Atlanta.

0:20 (2:00) What could pass for world's largest hubcap collection is at left in Austell.

0:40 (1:40) Note old trolley on left, now put to some stationary use.

0:45 (1:35) Large-leafed vines that are so prolific along right-of-way are kudzu. Brought here from Japan many years ago to control erosion, plant is now bane of southern agriculture, enveloping everything it encounters. Ramshackle, abandoned house on left is completely covered by the stuff.

1:35 (0:45) Cross Tallapoosa River—just one of many streams between Atlanta and New Orleans.

1:36 (0:44) Leave Georgia and enter Alabama.

Gain one hour as train passes from Eastern to Central Time. Set your watch back (forward if eastbound) one hour.

1:45 (0:35) Train plunges into woods of Talladega National Forest.

2:20 (0:00) Arrive Anniston.

ANNISTON, AL - Anniston is an industrial hub of eastern Alabama. Numerous industries include the enormous Anniston Army Depot just west of the city.

0:00 (1:30) Depart Anniston.

0:07 (1:23) For next four minutes, pass sprawling Anniston Army Depot on right, nation's largest military storage depot. Tanks and other miscellaneous vehicles and equipment can be found here.

0:10 (1:20) Numerous tanks and other armored vehicles on display along highway on right seemingly stand guard over depot complex.

0:27 (1:03) Northern tip of beautiful Logan Martin Lake touches tracks on left.

0:42 (0:48) Pass through only tunnel on today's run, Chula Vista Mountain Tunnel.

1:02 (0:28) Two lofty bridges carry us across Gahaba River.

1:19 (0:11) Industrial suburbs of Birmingham commence, contrasting sharply with miles of forest lands just traversed.

1:25 (0:05) One of Birmingham's former iron-making facilities, Sloss Furnace, is on right. It is now a National Historic Landmark and a museum devoted to early-day iron and steel technology. Concerts and festivals are also held here.

1:27 (0:03) Vulcan, one of the world's largest cast iron statues, keeps watch over city from atop Red Mountain on left. Vulcan was Roman god of fire and patron of metal workers.

1:30 (0:00) Arrive Birmingham. University of Alabama's sprawling Medical Center can be seen to left of station.

BIRMINGHAM, AL - Although no longer the "Pittsburgh of the South," the city has experienced an economic rebirth fostered by biomedical and other high-tech industries. An outstanding downtown shopping area, parks, tree-lined streets, theaters, museums and various festivals all greatly enhance Birmingham's lifestyle. This is the hometown of Nat King Cole, Phil Harris and Willie Mays.

0:00 (1:03) Depart Birmingham.

0:05 (0:58) As we leave through southwestern residential suburbs of Birmingham, take a last look at Vulcan, still visible on horizon to left.

0:12 (0:51) Former Pullman-Standard factory which once produced over 3,000 boxcars a year is on right.

0:45 (0:18) Through Vance, where Mercedes Benz has built their first American automobile plant (not visible from the train) at a cost of $300 million. Plant will employ 1,500 workers.

1:00 (0:03) Campus of perennial football powerhouse University of Alabama (The Crimson Tide) can be seen on right as train nears downtown Tuscaloosa.

1:03 (0:00) Arrive at Tuscaloosa's old but nice-appearing station.

TUSCALOOSA, AL - Once the capital of Alabama, the city is now primarily a vibrant university town, home to the University of Alabama.

0:00 (1:35) Depart Tuscaloosa.

0:12 (1:23) Train slips through swamps of southern Tuscaloosa County.

0:15 (1:20) Prehistoric Indian mounds flash by quickly on right as train passes Mound State Monument.

0:29 (1:06) Cross over muddy, still waters of Black Warrior River.

0:57 (0:38) Cross large Tombigbee River, a link in an ambitious government waterway project (Tenn-Tom) to create an alternative to traditional Mississippi River route between Mississippi's upper tributaries and Gulf of Mexico.

1:19 (0:16) Enter Mississippi and leave Alabama.

1:35 (0:00) Arrive Meridian where passenger rail car, "Miss Alva" is on display.

MERIDIAN, MS - Founded in 1860 at the junction of two railroads, Meridian is now a regional trade center. Jimmy Rogers, father of country music and first name to be entered in Nashville's Country Music Hall of Fame, was born here in 1897. The Jimmy Rogers Museum has exhibits including a steam locomotive that pay tribute to this "Singing Brakeman's" life.

0:00 (0:55) Depart Meridian.

0:07 (0:48) Key Field, on right, has interesting mixture of clientele, including sleek private aircraft close to tracks as well as more pugnacious jets of Mississippi Air National Guard parked on apron in distance.

0:22 (0:33) Neat rows of grave markers grace veterans' cemetery on left.

0:23 (0:32) Large Southern Natural Gas pumping facility is on left.

0:55 (0:00) Arrive Laurel.

LAUREL, MS - This agricultural and trade center boasts an unusually fine art museum, the Lauren Rogers Library and Museum not only has a national reputation for its collection of 19th-century American and European art, but also maintains an excellent collection of Georgian silver and Indian baskets. Laurel was the birthplace of Metropolitan opera star Leontyne Price.

0:00 (0:31) Depart Laurel.

0:30 (0:01) Cross Leaf River.

0:31 (0:00) Arrive at Hattiesburg where two steam engines and baggage cars stand on display adjacent to station.

HATTIESBURG, MS - Referred to as the "Hub City" and "Gateway to the Gulf South," this progressive community was among the first in the state to qualify for the All Merit Community Award. The University of Southern Mississippi is located here, as well as Carey College, with its well-known School of Music.

0:00 (1:02) Depart Hattiesburg.

0:14 (0:48) Facility on right, with tall, stack-like tower, is part of R.D. Morrow Generating Plant using the latest in generating technology. Cooling water is obtained from five nearby wells and coal from southeastern Kentucky to produce 400,000 kilowatts of power with minimal environmental impact.

0:26 (0:36) Complex on right is Purvis Refinery of Amerada Hess.

Mound State Monument

The mounds in this area, several of which are visible from the train, were constructed about 800 years ago by Indians that inhabited this area. Three thousand were estimated to have lived here between 1200 and 1500 A.D. The mounds closest to the tracks originally had homes on them which were used by nobility. The far-distant mounds were ceremonial structures. The tallest mound, farther back in the trees, now has a reconstructed temple at the top and was thought to have been the central ceremonial area.

0:40 (0:22) Through Poplarville, the birthplace of Senator Theodore Gilmore Bilbo, a highly controversial U.S. senator (1934-40) who was also the first to serve two terms as governor of Mississippi.

1:02 (0:00) Arrive Picayune.

 PICAYUNE, MS - This Mississippi border town is our last stop in Mississippi. The terrain now starts to flatten out upon approaching Louisiana.

0:00 (0:17) Depart Picayune.

0:07 (0:10) Enter Louisiana and leave Mississippi as train crosses over Pearl River.

0:15 (0:02) Note Albertson's new 6.2-million-dollar shopping center resembling early-day depot located within easy view of tracks.

0:17 (0:00) Arrive Slidell.

 SLIDELL, LA - Slidell is actually a bedroom community for New Orleans, just across the eastern tip of Lake Pontchartrain.

0:00 (0:53) Depart Slidell.

0:07 (0:46) Now, start an unusual, watery journey as train appears to paddle its way across eastern end of 610-square-mile Lake Pontchartrain on an incredible 6.2-mile-long wooden rail bridge only a few feet above water's surface. Glorious "ocean" sunsets are afforded when sun and train schedules cooperate.

0:17 (0:36) Pick up speed as train reaches terra firma and race past scores of stilted fishing huts along shore.

0:42 (0:28) Pumping stations, like one on left, keep New Orleans above water.

0:45 (0:15) Skyline of downtown New Orleans, our destination, is now clearly visible on left as train takes a roundabout approach in getting there. University of New Orleans Field House drifts by on right, then buildings of University of Tulane Dental School appear on left.

0:51 (—) Stop, and back final few hundred yards to station.

0:56 (0:04) Massive egg-like Superdome is just to right.

1:01 (0:00) Arrive New Orleans.

 NEW ORLEANS, LA - Thoughts of New Orleans stir a swirl of color in

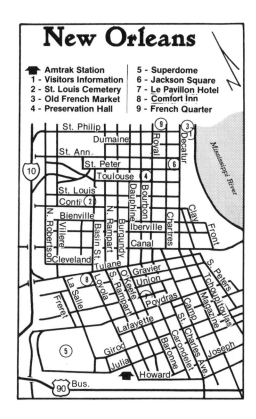

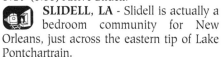

the mind. Excellent restaurants, the French Quarter, jazz, Mardi Gras and, for trolley aficionados, the St. Charles Streetcar line are some of the visions conjured up at the mere mention of this unique city. It is quite understandably one of the nation's more popular places to visit.

New Orleans has existed under four different flags since it was founded in 1723 by Jean Baptiste Le Moyne, Sieur de Bienville. It was first ruled by the French and was the capital of French Louisiana. The Spanish succeeded the French some 40 years later. New Orleans became an American city in 1803 with the Louisiana Purchase, and during the Civil War was a Confederate City. Today, it is Louisiana's largest metropolis and the world's largest (by tonnage) seaport.

 Union Passenger Terminal (also known as the Transit Center), 1001 Loyola Ave., is one of Amtrak's more attractive facilities. Modern and efficient, it not only accommodates Amtrak, but it also serves as the Greyhound bus terminal. There are storage lockers, pay-luggage carts, a restaurant, snack vending machines and a gift shop. Pay-parking is in front of the station.

Yellow **Cab**, 525-3311. Nearest **local bus** stop is across the street, 569-2700. **Greyhound** is at the station. Budget has **rental cars** downtown and will pick up customers at station; 467-2277.

French Quarter Information Center, 916 N. Peters Street. Call (504) 566-5011.

Two hotel choices, about midway between the French Quarter and the station, would be:

-**Le Pavillon Hotel**, 833 Poydras Plaza, 70140; (504) 581-3111 or 800-535-9095. Elderly, elegant and intimate. Seven blocks from the station. $99.

-**Downtown Comfort Inn**, 1315 Gravier St., 70112; (504) 586-0100. Well maintained with larger than average rooms. $85.

For French Quarter accommodations, be sure to reserve well in advance. One possibility is:

-**Le Richelieu**, 1234 Chartres St., 70116; (504) 529-2492 or 800-535-9653. Small, charming hotel. $100.

The **French Quarter** is the core of New Orleans' magnetism; 66 blocks of the old city with restaurants, jazz, shops, small hostelries with ironwork-decorated balconies—and, of course, raucous Bourbon Street. Free tours of the area are offered by the Park Service.

Be sure to take the **St. Charles Streetcar** from the central business district through neighborhoods of fine old homes. This is also a way to reach New Orleans **Audubon Park** and the fine **Zoological Gardens**. The **Riverfront Streetcars**, inaugurated in 1988, now tour 1 1/2 miles of Mississippi waterfront. The **New Orleans Center**, a downtown shopping mall about three blocks from the station, includes Macy's and Lord & Taylor.

Three Rivers

From New York City to Pittsburgh, the *Three Rivers* traces a portion of the route formerly traveled by the *Broadway Limited.* (The *Broadway* went beyond Pittsburgh to Chicago, but was canceled in 1995 due to budgetary restraints.) Today's *Three Rivers* takes a course along the busy Northeast Corridor between New York and Philadelphia before it turns westward. After Philadelphia, the train passes through Pennsylvania's rolling Amish countryside into the Alleghenies where it climbs around the famous Horseshoe Curve and on into Pittsburgh.

WESTBOUND SCHEDULE (Condensed)
New York, NY - Early Afternoon Departure
Philadelphia, PA - Early Afternoon
Harrisburg, PA - Late Afternoon
Pittsburgh, PA - Late Evening

EASTBOUND SCHEDULE (Condensed)
Pittsburgh, PA - Early Morning
Harrisburg, PA - Early Afternoon
Philadelphia, PA - Midafternoon
New York, NY - Late Afternoon Arrival
(The current schedule permits connections at Pittsburgh with the *Capitol Limited* to and from Chicago.)

FREQUENCY - Daily.
SEATING - Unreserved coaches.
DINING - Sandwiches, snacks and beverages.
BAGGAGE - Checked baggage at most stops.

RESERVATIONS - Unreserved train.
LENGTH OF TRIP - 444 miles in 10 hours.

ROUTE LOG

For route between New York and Philadelphia, see that portion of the Northeast Corridor log, page 26.

 PHILADELPHIA, PA - See page 28.

0:00 (0:25) Depart Philadelphia's 30th St. Station with city clearly visible back to right. Course is now due west toward Harrisburg and Pittsburgh. Philadelphia's suburbs dominate for about 30 minutes, on what local commuters have long referred to as the "Main Line," until train departs Paoli where pastoral scenes of central Pennsylvania farmland begin. This nicely engineered section of trackage between Philadelphia and Harrisburg is Amtrak's Keystone Corridor, electrified since 1938.

0:01 (0:24) To right, City Hall can be seen, topped by enduring statue of William Penn—a long-time informal height restriction for buildings in Philadelphia. Barrier was broken, however, with construction of One Liberty Place.

0:15 (0:10) Rosemont College campus is at right.

0:19 (0:06) On left, passing through Strafford, note commuter station which is architectural curiosity. Originally built for

Philadelphia's American Centennial Celebration in 1876, it was later moved to this site.

0:22 (0:03) Legend has it that proprietress of local inn once greased tracks along this portion of line to stall commuter trains which would not have otherwise stopped at her hostelry.

0:25 (0:00) Arrive Paoli.

PAOLI, PA - This stop, named after a revolutionary in Corsica, is the western edge of the densely populated Eastern Seaboard. Historic Valley Forge, where General George Washington and his Revolutionary Army suffered through a trying winter, is just two miles to the north of here.

0:00 (0:43) Depart Paoli.

0:18 (0:25) Long, black buildings of Lukens Steel plant are sprawled on left at Coatesville.

0:20 (0:23) Route now plunges into fascinating "Pennsylvania Dutch" country. Beautiful farms, set in these rolling Pennsylvania hills, have been operated by Amish with little change in lifestyle during last 300 years. Watch for black-attired farmers in their horse-drawn buggies sharing roads with more modern conveyances.

0:27 (0:16) Note unusual gingerbread-adorned three-story home above on left.

0:36 (0:07) Handsome Amish barns dot landscape. Horse-drawn buggies are now common sight through very heart of Pennsylvania Dutch country.

0:37 (0:06) Small airport, on left, has unusually charming setting, with homes actually abutting runway.

0:41 (0:02) Cross Conestoga River.

0:43 (0:00) Arrive Lancaster.

LANCASTER, PA - The train halts briefly in this city which produced arms for the American Revolution and where the first Woolworth store was opened in 1879. The nation's oldest iron mine is but a few miles north at Cornwall, and The Pennsylvania Rifle (misnamed The Kentucky Rifle according to Pennsylvanians) was developed here during the 1700s. The city is now the commercial center and heart of Amish farming country.

At nearby Strasburg is the ever-popular Strasburg Railroad, America's oldest short-line railroad.

0:00 (0:35) Depart Lancaster and roll past Amtrak's Communication and Signal Training Center on left.

0:07 (0:28) Through Mt. Joy, where manufacturing plants of familiar names such as National Standard, NCR and AMP are in evidence.

0:13 (0:22) First commercial telegraph lines in U.S. were strung along this railroad right-of-way between Lancaster and Harrisburg. In 1846 first message was transmitted and logically asked, "Why didn't you write, you rascals?"

0:22 (0:12) Four specter-like cooling towers in distance, to left, each rising 372 feet from its base, belong to infamous Three Mile Island nuclear power plant, which came close to meltdown in March 1979.

0:26 (0:09) Pennsylvania State University's attractive Harrisburg campus lies just beyond highway on right.

0:27 (0:08) On immediate left, runways of Harrisburg International Airport parallel tracks.

0:28 (0:05) Bethlehem Steel's Steelton plant stretches beside tracks on right.

0:32 (0:03) Large bridge on left carries forerunner of interstate highways across Susquehanna River—the Pennsylvania Turnpike.

0:35 (0:00) Arrive Harrisburg's finely remodeled intermodal Amtrak station. Handsome #4859 GG-1 electric locomotive stands on permanent display between train and depot.

HARRISBURG, PA - In 1812, Harrisburg became the state capital and subsequently one of the finest capitol buildings in the nation was built here—just beyond the station. Built in 1906 at a cost of $10 million, the capitol's interior marble was shipped here from Europe. Its exquisite dome was patterned after St. Peter's Basilica in Rome.

0:00 (1:07) Depart Harrisburg and immediately on left is State Capitol Building just described.

Three Rivers route — Rockville Bridge, Harrisburg, PA
DORIS SWANSON

0:04 (1:03) Slip through rail yards of Conrail. Locomotive shops will soon appear at right.

0:11 (0:55) Cross over Susquehanna River on Rockville Bridge, four miles north of Harrisburg. Structure is world's longest and widest stone-arch bridge and contains 48 arches made of Pennsylvania white sandstone. It is 3,820 feet in length, has a 52-foot roadbed and is 42 feet above Susquehanna. Bridge was first crossed in 1902 on Easter Sunday.

0:15 (0:52) Pier for former bridge across Susquehanna now supports mini-Statue of Liberty in midstream on right. Supposedly, some imaginative youngsters sculpted it using old Venetian blinds.

0:24 (0:43) Pass through Duncannon, leave Susquehanna River, and enter easternmost hills of Allegheny Mountains. From here to Altoona, tracks accompany Juniata River. Line was originally built to compete with Erie Canal and is still a busy freight road as will be noted from numerous Conrail freight trains.

0:44 (0:23) Two rather short chairlifts at right would indicate Pennsylvania has, at least, semblance of ski industry.

0:52 (0:15) Large wooden Indian with uplifted arm welcomes clients of campground on right.

0:55 (0:12) Across Juniata River, on right, Empire Poultry, one of largest supplier of poultry to East Coast, is barely visible from train.

1:07 (0:00) Arrive Lewistown.

LEWISTOWN, PA - This industrial town is in the very heart of Pennsylvania. The Frank McCoy House, former home of General Frank Ross McCoy, will be of interest to historians.

0:00 (0:39) Depart Lewistown.

0:23 (0:16) Blue Mountain on left is prominent Allegheny ridge stretching along horizon.

0:31 (0:08) Sand from quarry on right is used in local glass production.

0:39 (0:00) Arrive Huntingdon.

HUNTINGDON, PA - A small industrial town, Huntingdon is

attractively situated along the Juniata River. This is home to Juniata College.

0:00 (0:28) Depart Huntingdon. Immediately on right is large Owens-Corning fiberglass plant.

0:13 (0:15) Cross Spruce Creek, a fine trout fishing stream which at one time provided sport for former president Jimmy Carter. Enter Spruce Creek Tunnel for a sudden but brief period of darkness.

0:14 (0:14) Camp Espy farms, on right, fattens cattle for Eastern markets.

0:43 (0:00) Arrive Tyrone.

TYRONE, PA - A forge was once located near here and iron smelting took place during the 19th century.

0:00 (0:17) Depart Tyrone.

0:12 (0:05) Rumble through short tunnel.

0:17 (0:00) Arriving Altoona, slip through enormous Altoona rail yards.Then pass Railroaders Memorial Museum, on left, where numerous rail cars and locomotives can be seen, including Raymond Loewy-designed GG-1 electric locomotive. Famous K-4, 234-ton steam locomotive, a design that dates back to 1914, is also here. Engine was formerly on display at nearby Horseshoe Curve. At one time, Pennsylvania Railroad had 400 of these, which served as standard passenger engines on this line until World War II. On opposite (right) side of train, predominant structure is Cathedral of Blessed Sacrament. Station is very efficient intermodal transit center.

ALTOONA, PA - A supply point for building the Pennsylvania Railroad, Altoona now has one of the world's largest assemblages of rail maintenance facilities.

0:00 (1:00) Depart Altoona and commence steep climb toward Gallitzin Summit. Ascending grades will now range from 1.75% to 1.85%, forcing most westbound freights to add helper engines at Alto, just west of Altoona.

0:10 (0:50) Reservoirs below on left are part of Altoona's domestic water storage system.

0:12 (0:48) Horseshoe Curve (the Pennsylvania Railroad's rule book spelled horseshoe as two words), a beautiful hairpin turn nearly a half-mile long, is one of railroading's

Horseshoe Curve

Horseshoe Curve permits a tolerable 1.73% grade through this section of mountains which will allow 6 diesels to pull 125 fully loaded freight cars around its perimeter. A shortcut across valley's mouth would have produced a 4.37% grade, but those same diesels would then handle only 43 cars. At one time four sets of track rounded the curve, but one set was removed in 1981 as an economy move. Pennsylvania Railroad GP9 diesel Number 7048 is now displayed on the inside of the Curve. The Curve was designated a National Historic Landmark in 1967. In 1992, the Curve was rededicated with the completion of a new visitors center and funicular that transports visitors from the center to the level of the Curve itself. The two trams were built in the shops of the Durango & Silverton Narrow-Gauge Railroad in Durango, Colorado.

most notable landmarks.

0:24 (0:36) Pass through one of three tunnels, as route handily crests Alleghenies. Allegheny and Gallitzin tunnels, each over a mile in length, usually handle westbound traffic while shorter New Portage Tunnel takes eastbound trains that must descend a 2.27% grade.

At one time, though, it was not so easy. Just three miles to the south, from 1834 to 1855, the Allegheny Portage Railroad, with its system of canals, trains and incline railroads, ingeniously lifted sectionalized canal boats (people, cargo and all) over these mountains on a series of inclined planes and level stretches, allowing continuous transportation between Philadelphia and Pittsburgh. However, construction of the Horseshoe Curve provided a direct rail link and ended operations for one of America's most unique transportation systems.

0:55 (0:05) Cranes using powerful electromagnets can often be seen at work loading scrap onto gondola cars on left.

0:56 (0:01) Johnstown plant of Bethlehem Steel is on left. Also, note church on left with three onion-shaped domes.

1:00 (0:00) Arrive Johnstown.

 JOHNSTOWN, PA - In 1889, the nation's most disastrous flood devastated this city of steel mills. An overly enlarged dam, 14 miles east of here on the Conemaugh River, formed a reservoir some two miles long. The lake was the centerpiece of the South Fork Fishing and Hunting Club, a secretive retreat for many of Pittsburgh's wealthy and socially elite. Two excursion steamers plied the waters in the summer months. On May 31 of that year, after a day of drenching rain, the poorly maintained dam began to give way. Warnings earlier in the day were ignored by the populous—citizens who had heard similar warnings almost every spring. At 3:10 in the afternoon the inhabitants heard a "roar like thunder," then were suddenly engulfed by a 36-foot wall of water. Over 2,200 people died and hundreds more were never accounted for.

Johnstowns's history of flooding has continued. In 1936, 25 lives were lost and in 1977, 85 persons died.

Bethlehem Steel is still the principal employer, but the town's economy has been less than vibrant. In 1983, when the steel market hit bottom, Johnstown had the highest unemployment in the U.S.

0:00 (0:43) Depart Johnstown. Incline on slope behind station is a people conveyor providing unusual access to community atop hill. Seventy-one percent grade may make it world's steepest incline. Bethlehem Steel's bar and rod plant is on right.

0:02 (0:41) Sign painted on brick building, "Conemaugh & Black Lick Railroad Company," touts former Bethlehem Steel operated railroad.

0:43 (0:00) Arrive Latrobe.

 LATROBE, PA - This is the home to past training camps of the formidable Pittsburgh Steelers and also the birthplace of Arnold Palmer. The town was named for Benjamin Henry Latrobe who designed the south wing of the U.S. Capitol, among other notable edifices.

0:00 (0:11) Depart Latrobe.

0:11 (0:00) Arrive Greensburg.

 GREENSBURG, PA - Near this western Pennsylvania town is Bushy Run Battlefield where Colonel Henry Bouquet defeated hostile Indians in 1763.

0:00 (0:44) Depart Greensburg.

0:20 (0:24) Numerous older brick buildings on right are home to historic Westinghouse Air Brake Division.

0:25 (0:18) Elderly Edgar Thomson Works of USX-US Steel are trackside on left.

0:44 (0:00) Arrive Pittsburgh.

 PITTSBURGH, PA - Once known for its steel mills and smoke, Pittsburgh now exemplifies what can be done with urban renewal when the determination (and money) to do so exists. The city now has clean air, shiny skyscrapers and beautiful parks as a result of a massive effort undertaken in recent years.

The downtown is quite compact and more walkable than most cities of comparable size. The city is also unusual in that it still has maintained many ethnic neighborhoods through its years of development and growth. It is located in the "Golden Triangle," where the Allegheny and the Monongahela Rivers join to form the Ohio River, one of the nation's primary industrial centers.

Amtrak Station, Liberty Avenue at Grant Street, is located near the heart of downtown in the remodeled quarters of what was once Penn Central Station. Platforms are at street level, but the station is down one flight by escalator or elevator, beneath exclusive apartments. There are storage lockers and food and beverage vending machines. Pay-parking is in front of the station and also covered parking at the Greyhound terminal across the street.

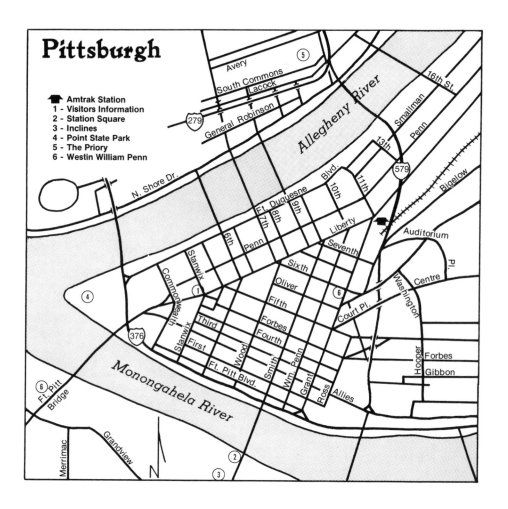

Pittsburgh

- ◤ **Amtrak Station**
- **1 - Visitors Information**
- **2 - Station Square**
- **3 - Inclines**
- **4 - Point State Park**
- **5 - The Priory**
- **6 - Westin William Penn**

Yellow **Cab**, 665-8100. Nearest **local bus** stop, half block from the station. **Light-rail** stop is behind station, free service within downtown area; 442-2000. **Greyhound** is across the street from the station.

Visitor Information Center, Gateway Center, Downtown Pittsburgh, (412) 281-9222.

Hotels in the downtown Golden Triangle area are fairly expensive; two are included since one is close to the station and the other is at Station Square. The other accommodations shown are a few minutes cab ride from downtown and are

logical alternatives.

-**Westin William Penn,** 530 William Penn Place, 15230; (412) 281-7100 and 800-228-3000. Four blocks from the station. $120.

-**Station Square Sheraton Motor Inn,** 7 Station Square, 15219; (412) 261-2000. Next to Station Square, a 300-room resort-conference facility with views of river and downtown Pittsburgh. Few-minute cab ride (light-rail station within two blocks) from station. Station transportation available. $150.

-**The Priory,** 614 Pressley St., 15212; (412) 231-3338. European-style hotel on the transitional North Side about a half mile from the station (but not very walkable). Formerly a rectory for a German Catholic Church, it has been made into a 24-room hostelry. Complimentary breakfast and evening wine. Shuttle service in the morning. $100.

-**Hampton Inn Greentree,** 555 Trumbull Dr., 15205; (412) 922-0100. Continental breakfast included. Between downtown and the airport, about three miles from the station. Can be slow going into town in the rush hour. Continental breakfast. $79.

Point State Park is at the confluence of the Allegheny and Monongahela Rivers, where one will find the only local remnant of the French and Indian War, the Fort Pitt Blockhouse. Also located here are a large fountain, the Fort Pitt Museum with historic exhibits, and military drills held during the summer months.

Station Square, just across the Smithfield Bridge from downtown, includes shops, restaurants, a marina and the Industrial Transportation Museum with antique railroad cars and trolleys. This area also contains the historic buildings of the P&LE Railroad.

Inclines to the top of Mount Washington can be ridden from their lower stations, either at Station Square or west of the Fort Pitt Bridge, both on West Carson Street. Observation platforms are at the top of each, and a restaurant is at the summit of the westernmost incline.

Other Pennsylvania Service

The *Pennsylvanian* links New York City with Pittsburgh by way of Philadelphia. Daily New York departures are early morning with late afternoon arrivals in Pittsburgh.

Pittsburgh departures are midmorning (early afternoon on Sundays) and New York is reached nine hours later.

Capitol Limited

Between Washington, DC and Pittsburgh, the *Capitol Limited* runs on the tracks of CSX Transportation. The stretch, beginning some 40 miles west of Washington at Point of Rocks and continuing to Cumberland, Maryland, is the oldest section of operating railroad in the U.S. This is the original main line of the Baltimore and Ohio Railroad and follows along the equally-as-historic Chesapeake & Ohio Canal. At Cumberland, the *Capitol Limited* swings northward through the scenic hills of southwestern Pennsylvania.

West of Pittsburgh the *Capitol's* route follows Conrail to Cleveland, then continues on Conrail, taking the same route used by the *Lake Shore Limited* across northern Ohio and Indiana into Chicago.

WESTBOUND SCHEDULE (Condensed)
Washington, DC - Early Evening Departure
Cumberland, MD - Early Evening
Pittsburgh, PA - Late Evening
Cleveland, OH - Middle of the Night
Chicago, IL - Early Morning Arrival

EASTBOUND SCHEDULE (Condensed)
Chicago, IL - Late Afternoon Departure
Cleveland, OH - Middle of the Night
Pittsburgh, PA - Early Morning
Cumberland, MD - Midmorning
Washington, DC - Early Afternoon Arrival

FREQUENCY - Daily.
SEATING - Reserved Superliner coaches.

DINING - Complete meal and beverage service in diner. Lounge service, with sandwiches, snacks and beverages.
SLEEPING - Superliner sleepers with deluxe, family, economy and special bedrooms.
BAGGAGE - Checked baggage handled at Washington, DC and most stops Pittsburgh to Chicago.
RESERVATIONS - All-reserved train.
LENGTH OF TRIP - 780 miles in 18 hours.

ROUTE LOG

 WASHINGTON, DC - See page 35.
0:00 (0:20) Depart Washington.
0:02 (0:18) Familiar obelisk of Washington Monument can be seen back on left.
0:03 (0:17) Streamlined "Metros" of Washington's subway stand in storage yard on immediate left. Route now curls to left away from Northeast Corridor.
0:07 (0:13) Beautiful white building on left with dazzling blue and gold tiled dome is National Shrine of the Immaculate Conception—largest Catholic church in United States and seventh largest church in world. Catholic University of America is located here.
0:20 (0:00) Arrive Rockville where curious architecture of church on left resembles hamburger with toothpick stuck in top.

 ROCKVILLE, MD - First settled in the early 1700s, Rockville was fre-

Capitol Ltd. — Harpers Ferry, WV
JACK SWANSON

quented by travelers on a "great road" between Georgetown and Frederick. It is now one of Washington's larger suburbs.

0:00 (0:42) Depart Rockville.

0:04 (0:38) At trackside in Gaithersburg, small charming depot still serves D.C. commuters on right.

0:11 (0:31) Deep red depot on left at Germantown is special trackside adornment.

0:19 (0:23) Cross high over Monocacy River which empties into Potomac half-mile to left.

0:21 (0:21) Through trees on left, broad Potomac River flows placidly toward Washington. Long-since-abandoned Chesapeake and Ohio Canal, now overgrown with shrubs and trees, is still visible between tracks and river.

Quaint rock bridges spanning this historic canal can be seen from time to time. Opened in 1850 shortly after the completion of the B&O Railroad, this 184-mile waterway connected Cumberland with tidewater at Georgetown following the course of the Potomac. It took about a week for freight-laden canal boats to make the entire trip.

Locks, stone aqueducts and the 3,080-foot Paw Paw Tunnel contributed to its hefty $22 million cost. Operations finally ceased in 1924. Today, canoes in its placid waters and bicycles along its towpath are common sights.

0:26 (0:16) On right at Point of Rocks, MD, church-like station, complete with steeple, is another fascinating elderly depot. Designed by Frances E. Baldwin and standing at spot of original B&O main line from Baltimore, station now serves as commuter stop. Place received its name from prominent bulge of granite that once jutted out over tracks.

0:27 (0:12) Through short tunnel. Then in three minutes, through another.

0:35 (0:07) Quaint old roundhouse still stands in rail yards on left.

0:41 (0:01) Into another tunnel, then cross Potomac into West Virginia where Shenandoah River confluence can be seen just to left, and enter Harpers Ferry.

Stonewall's Ploy

During the Civil War, Stonewall Jackson initiated one of his more brilliant strategies near here. For a 44-mile stretch west of Point of Rocks, the B&O main line expanded to two sets of tracks. Jackson convinced the Union-oriented B&O to run their eastbound and westbound trains simultaneously on these two lines and then proceeded to cut them off at each end. The engines were quickly taken apart and shipped overland on wagons, most to Raleigh, North Carolina, where they were reassembled and placed into Confederate service.

0:42 (0:00) Arrive Harpers Ferry. Note unusual signal on roof of rather forlorn-looking station on left.

 HARPERS FERRY, WV - Originally a ferrying point in 1733, the town gained prominence in the 1790s when a national armory was established here. As early as 1836 a railroad bridge linked Maryland with West Virginia by crossing the Potomac at this point.

The first wooden trestle had an unlikely "Y" junction in the middle, branching off to the Shenandoah Valley on the left. This bridge and its many successors were subsequently destroyed by war or flood, and once dismantled by John Brown who hoped to incite a slave uprising with his infamous raid on the armory. Today, Harpers Ferry is a National Historical Park.

0:00 (0:20) Depart Harpers Ferry.

0:01 (0:19) Small hydroelectric plant of an earlier era is on right.

0:20 (0:00) Arrive Martinsburg.

MARTINSBURG, VA - Since 1941, when the B&O Railroad first reached here, Martinsburg has been closely tied to railroading. In 1849, shops and roundhouses were built with extraordinary workmanship and architectural detail, only to be later destroyed by Confederate troops during Stonewall Jackson's 1862 campaign. The present station was the only survivor and is nation's oldest functioning train station. The outstanding roundhouses and most of the other buildings were rebuilt in the 1860s. Then in 1877, workers of the B&O went on strike, one which developed into the largest railroad strike in the nation's history. Unfortunately, two separate fires, both set by vandals, destroyed both roundhouses in recent years.

0:00 (1:25) Depart Martinsburg. Ruins of both West Roundhouse and East Roundhouse are on right.

0:26 (0:59) Small airstrip accompanies tracks at right. This is Hancock, a town built in three states—Maryland, Pennsylvania and West Virginia.

0:37 (0:48) Passengers now are afforded an excellent look up serene Potomac to right.

0:51 (0:34) Enter very short tunnel.

0:53 (0:32) Enter lengthy Graham Tunnel that blots out daylight for about one minute. Both entrance and exit repose in West Virginia, but most of interior is located in Maryland.

0:54 (0:31) Make a quick trip into Maryland and then back into West Virginia as train crosses Potomac twice in rapid succession. More short tunnels are encountered.

1:16 (0:09) Bid final farewell to West Virginia and Potomac as train crosses that stately river for last time and enters Cumberland, Maryland.

1:20 (0:05) Control tower for expansive CSX rail yards loom on left. Then CSX locomotive shops appear on right.

1:25 (0:00) Arrive Cumberland.

CUMBERLAND, MD - At one time, Cumberland was known as "Washington Town" (George Washington's military career started and ended here) and also "Mills Creek," but it was finally christened "Cumberland" for a fort by that name located here during the French and Indian

War (1756-1763). Both Colonel Washington and General Braddock left from here on expeditions against the French.

0:00 (2:20) Depart Cumberland. (From here to Pittsburgh, best viewing will be on left.)

0:03 (2:16) Pass through "The Narrows" where Wills Creek cuts through Allegheny Mountains. Originally a trading route, it was later a military wagon road. Road finally became first federally financed U.S. highway (The National Pike—now U.S. 40). This was also passage for America's first east-west railroad.

0:04 (2:15) Stone quarries are on immediate right.

0:09 (2:11) Leave Maryland and enter Pennsylvania. Large red barn on left marks the approximate boundary.

0:26 (1:54) Wills Creek begins to narrow, and countryside becomes more mountainous as tracks climb toward summit at Sandpatch.

0:28 (1:52) Brief trip through Falls Cut Tunnel.

0:32 (1:48) Pass through village of Glencoe with its colorful array of quaint frame stores and houses.

0:41 (1:39) Rushing waters of Wills Creek, on left, are favorite of trout fishermen in early spring.

0:45 (1:35) Enter Sandpatch Tunnel, nearly a mile long and consuming two minutes before emerging at other end; it is longest of trip.

0:47 (1:34) Crest summit of Alleghenies at Sandpatch. Marker on right places elevation at 2,258 feet.

0:55 (1:26) Pass through Meyersdale which is destination of special trains from Pittsburgh carrying syrup lovers to maple syrup festival held here each spring.

1:01 (1:22) At Blue Lick, pass beneath intriguing, abandoned rail bridge of Western Maryland Railroad.

1:04 (1:19) Those sitting on left should be able to spot two huge stone grain-grinding wheels, long since abandoned in Casselman River next to tracks. Quarry for millstones, with holes in cliff face, is at right.

1:05 (1:18) Serpentine trails etched on hillside across river on left are roads for logging trucks.

1:06 (1:17) Unusual series of "caves," just to right, were once former rock quarry.

1:20 (1:01) Quaint log home across Casselman River on left is one of many locations where deer can frequently be spotted from train.

1:24 (0:58) Pass through Pinkerton Tunnel for 20 seconds and emerge on single set of tracks.

1:25 (0:57) Pass through Shoefly Tunnel and return to luxury of two sets of tracks.

1:29 (0:52) Enter darkness for about one minute as train negotiates Brook Tunnel. Train normally saves three miles by taking "highline" at this point, while "lowline" branches off to left following more leisurely river route.

1:36 (0:45) We are rejoined by "lowline" and Youghiogheny (pronounced yawk-a-haney) River on left. Pass through Confluence and cross sleepy Laurel Creek.

1:43 (0:37) High ridge of Sugar Loaf Mountain can be seen on right, while fallen trees near river below show evidence of hard-working beavers. Watch for canoes which frequent this popular river in summertime.

1:49 (0:31) Enter Ohiopyle, where Ohiopyle Falls are located. Between here and Connellsville, watch for fishermen trying their luck for elusive perch, pike, trout, walleye, and bass, all stocked in the Youghiogheny. Kayaks and rafts can frequently be seen in the summer. Maple trees combine to produce a color spectacular in fall, making this a favorite sightseeing run at that time of year. Evergreens are mostly hemlock.

1:58 (0:21) Road across river on left, zigzagging up through trees, is used to bring rafts up from stream after float trips from Ohiopyle.

2:03 (0:14) Cross Indian Creek spanned by small stone-arch bridge—one of few remaining. Summer youth camp is just across river. Abandoned rail right-of-way, also across river, is now popular hiking trail.

2:15 (0:00) Arrive Connellsville.

CONNELLSVILLE, PA - In the late 1700s, vast coal deposits were discovered in the immediate area but were thought to have no value because of their soft and crumbly character. However, it was later discovered that by roasting this coal in ordinary "beehive" coke ovens for two or three days, it made outstanding metallurgical fuel and became known as the famous pearl-grey Connellsville Coke. Always a railroad town (it is still a division point with a large classification yard), during World War II the "Connellsville Canteen," consisting of 800 women volunteers, served meals to more than 600,000 servicemen that came through on troop trains in a two-year period!

0:00 (1:26) Depart Connellsville, and in a moment, cross under a towering railroad trestle that also spans river on left.

0:06 (1:20) Forsaken structures just to left are ghostly remains of whiskey distillery.

0:23 (1:03) Enormous black slag heaps are first evidence that Pittsburgh is near.

0:28 (0:58) Pass under Interstate 70.

0:58 (0:28) Through McKeesport, a heavily industrialized suburb of Pittsburgh, where the Youghiogheny flows into the Monongahela River. Then pass series of impressive steel mills, mostly belonging to industrial giant U.S. Steel.

1:11 (0:15) Skyline, featuring many new high rises, is discernible forward to left.

1:13 (0:13) University of Pittsburgh's Cathedral of Learning soars majestically skyward on hill to left. Carnegie Mellon University is on right. Enter Schenley Tunnel as train leaves Oakland and enters Pittsburgh.

1:26 (0:00) Arrive Pittsburgh.

PITTSBURGH, PA - See page 103. **0:00** (1:45) Depart Pittsburgh on tracks of Conrail.

0:38 1:07) Through Beaver Falls, birthplace of former football great, Joe Namath.

1:00 (0:45) Leave Pennsylvania and enter Ohio.

1:45 (0:00) Arrive Alliance.

ALLIANCE, OH - This small Ohio industrial town also serves as an Amtrak stop for nearby Canton. Mount Union College is located here.

0:00 (1:18) Depart Alliance.

1:18 (0:00) Arrive Cleveland, where Lakefront Stadium is imposing feature on right.

CLEVELAND, OH - See page 61.

For route between Cleveland and Chicago, see that portion of _Lake Shore_ log, page 61.

Chicago
Cincinnati
Washington, DC

Cardinal

The *Cardinal* makes a thrice-weekly trek between Washington, DC and Chicago by way of Charleston, WV, Cincinnati and Indianapolis. With stops at several small towns, it is perhaps the last of America's full-service locals.

The route is a particular treat through West Virginia's spectacular New River Gorge. In the fall, the color is superb. Eastbound passengers can also view some of the Ohio River scenes during daylight hours across northern Kentucky. Interpretive guides explain points of interest between Charleston, WV, and White Sulphur Springs eastbound during the summer.

WESTBOUND SCHEDULE (Condensed)
Washington, DC - Late Morning Departure (Sun, Wed, Fri)
Charleston, WV - Midevening
Cincinnati, OH - Late Night
Indianapolis, IN - Early Morning
Chicago, IL - Early Morning Arrival (Mon, Thurs, Sat)

EASTBOUND SCHEDULE (Condensed)
Chicago, IL - Midevening Departure (Tues, Thur, Sat)
Indianapolis, IN - Late Night
Cincinnati, OH - Early Morning
Charleston, WV - Midmorning
Washington, DC - Midevening

FREQUENCY - Tri-weekly, see above.
SEATING - Reserved Superliner coaches.

DINING - Lounge car with tray meal service, sandwiches, snacks and beverages.
SLEEPING - Superliner sleepers with deluxe, family, economy and special bedrooms.
BAGGAGE - Checked baggage handled at most larger cities.
RESERVATIONS - All-reserved train.
LENGTH OF TRIP - 925 miles in 23 hours.

ROUTE LOG

For route between Washington and Charlottesville, see that portion of the *Crescent* log, page 90.

 CHARLOTTESVILLE, VA - See page 91.
0:00 (0:58) Depart Charlottesville. Campus of University of Virginia will be on right.
0:05 (0:56) Off to right, ridge of mountains holds beautiful Shenandoah National Park and spectacular Skyline Drive, extending northward from Waynesboro.
0:35 (0:23) Pastoral valley, serene and green, makes great viewing off to left as we ascend renowned Blue Ridge Mountains. Duck into tunnel for full minute before regaining daylight.
0:58 (0:00) Arrive Staunton.

STAUNTON, VA - Located in Augusta County which, when formed in 1738, extended as far as the Mississippi and the Great Lakes, Staunton is distinguished by being the birthplace of both

Woodrow Wilson and the McCormick reaper and home to the Statler Brothers. During the Revolutionary War, the town was pressed into serving as Virginia's capital for a few days. The town is also recognized as having the largest remaining collection of 19th-century architecture in Virginia.

0:00 (1:10) Depart Staunton.

0:17 (0:53) Elliott Knob rises to elevation of 4,458 feet above sea level, back to right.

0:34 (0:36) Through two short tunnels; there will be many more as we progress westward and into West Virginia mountains.

1:06 (0:04) Extensive CSX rail yards begin on approach to Clifton Forge.

1:10 (0:00) Arrive Clifton Forge, also a stop for nearby Hot Springs, site of historic The Homestead resort.

CLIFTON FORGE, VA - This is the very heart of western Virginia's vacationland. The Allegheny Central Railroad, Virginia's only "scenic" railroad, is nearby.

0:00 (0:49) Depart Clifton Forge and continue through CSX yards; locomotive shops are on left.

0:10 (0:39) Pretty Covington, below to right, has idyllic setting beneath mountain backdrop.

0:25 (0:24) Picturesque covered bridge stretches across small stream below on left.

0:38 (0:11) Steep, deep valley to left now provides truly breathtaking view.

0:49 (0:00) Arrive White Sulphur Springs. Four private cars of CSX are permanently moored just to east of station at right, including "Stonewall Jackson" and "Virginia."

WHITE SULPHUR SPRINGS, WV - This is home to one of the world's renowned spas, Greenbrier Resort, just across the road to the right of the train. Well-to-do Southerners began building cottages here in the 1800s, drawn to the area by the natural sulphur springs and cool climate. Many of these summer homes still stand and can be rented for somewhat more than a room in the main hotel, which was constructed in 1913. Just three miles east of here, the first organized golf club in the U.S. was formed in 1884 on the Oakhurst Estate.

Today, golf is the principal attraction at the Greenbrier with no less than three championship courses to be played.

0:00 (1:01) Depart White Sulphur Springs.

0:31 (0:30) Through flag stop of Alderson where gaggle of two-story, light-brick buildings, enclosed by barbed wire to left above, is federal prison for women. Prison stresses vocational rehabilitation and is only federal industrial-oriented prison for women. Both Tokyo Rose and Squeaky Fromme did time here.

0:45 (0:16) Stream that has been following on right is Greenbrier River.

0:49 (0:11) Into Big Bend Tunnel, started in 1870, taking three years to complete.

Mile-long bore now has twin tunnel for two-way traffic. Tradition makes this site of steel driver's ballad "John Henry" and his statue stands above east entrance. He supposedly died from a race with a steam drill while working inside these tunnels.

0:59 (0:03) At juncture of two streams, join New River and start through what is probably highlight of trip—dramatic New River Gorge. Large dam upstream, about a quarter of a mile to left, retains enormous Bluestone Lake, a very popular West Virginia recreational area.

1:01 (0:00) Arrive Hinton where rambling, decrepit brick station is on right.

HINTON, WV - Historically a railroad town, Hinton is now the the county seat.

0:00 (0:30) Depart Hinton.

0:08 (0:22) Small but dazzling Sandstone Falls momentarily interrupt river on left.

0:11 (0:19) New I-64 bridge crosses above.

0:30 (0:00) Arrive Prince.

PRINCE, WV - This small mountain community rests at the east end of the New River Gorge.

0:00 (1:04) As we depart Prince, New River will become increasingly rock-strewn and the scenery more spectacular. Ironically, New River, formed during Mesozoic Period, is one of oldest in world. Gorge has its own ecosystem, supporting over a thousand species of plants and more than 150 species of birds. And during a time now past, as

New River Gorge Bridge

The magnificent New River Gorge Bridge spans the entire valley carrying auto traffic from one rim to the other, some 876 feet above the river! The main span is 1,700 feet long making it the world's longest steel arch span. It is the nation's second highest bridge (only Colorado's Royal Gorge Bridge is higher), and it weighs a total of 88 million pounds.

On "Bridge Day," the second Saturday in October, hundreds of thrill-seekers gather here to go over the railing and parachute to the gorge floor below. This is the only day jumping from the span is legal. The bridge accounts for most of such BASE jumps in the U.S.

many as 14 passenger trains a day thundered along its tracks.

0:15 (0:50) Through community of Thurmond, where coal mining has long dominated town's economy.

0:35 (0:30) Look forward—above and to left. It's the New River Gorge Bridge!

0:46 (0:18) Mouth of three-mile-long Hawk's Nest Tunnel is beyond dam on right. Tunnel, which diverts river water for hydroelectric power, created an awakening for safety in the workplace after several hundred workers died of silicosis.

0:51 (0:13) At Glenn Ferris, on right, beautiful Kanawha Falls interrupt river's smooth flow. Old piers of pre-Civil War bridge can be spotted in Gauley River that flows into New River from north. Bridge was just beyond highway and Conrail bridges and was destroyed by Confederates in 1861. Three crosses on island in New River were placed there by individual "for the glory of God."

1:04 (0:00) Arrive Montgomery.

MONTGOMERY, WV - This stop is home to West Virginia Institute of Technology. School stretches out along left side of tracks, readily visible from station. Salt-making brought early settlers to this valley where chemical industries now predominate. The town was originally called Coal Valley but renamed for James C. Montgomery in 1891.

0:00 (0:30) Depart Montgomery.

0:04 (0:26) London hydroelectric plant and dam are on right.

0:05 (0:25) Through community of Pratt, noted for its residential architecture (ranging from early plantation to Victorian styles) and early labor unrest. Labor organizer "Mother Jones" spent her 84th birthday in prison here.

0:09 (0:21) Another electricity producer, Kanawha Power Plant, is on shores of Kanawha River at right.

0:28 (0:02) As we enter Charleston, state government office complex, with gold-domed capitol building as centerpiece, is off to right.

0:30 (0:00) Arrive Charleston, where downtown is just across river to right. Beautifully landscaped far shore sets off striking skyline.

CHARLESTON, WV - The Kanawha River cuts deeply through the Appalachians at this point, carving out a steep valley setting for Charleston, the state's capital. Designed by internationally recognized architect Cass Gilbert, the capitol building is generally considered to be the most beautiful in the nation, featuring a 300-foot dome supported by Roman porticos and colonnades. Adjacent is the newly built Science and Cultural Center.

0:00 (0:58) Depart Charleston and proceed through a region heavily concentrated with chemical plants and other industrial operations.

0:58 (0:00) Arrive Huntington's modern, white-brick station on left.

HUNTINGTON, WV - Situated on the banks of the Ohio River, where West Virginia, Ohio and Kentucky all converge, Huntington has long been an important railroading town. Today, visitors can experience a bit of earlier times by visiting Heritage Village in a restored B&O rail yard.

0:00 (0:18) Depart Huntington.

0:13 (0:05) Trundle across Big Sandy River Bridge and enter Kentucky.

0:18 (0:00) Arrive Catlettsburg.

 CATLETTSBURG, KY - This stop also serves Kenova, WV, and Ashland, KY.

0:00 (1:00) Depart Catlettsburg. From here to Cincinnati, tracks follow along scenic Kentucky shoreline of Ohio River. Tugs and barges continually ply this stretch of river. Numerous dams and locks make this waterway navigable.

0:08 (0:52) Twin highway bridges span Ohio on right. On left is Ashland, where both steel production and oil refining are important industries. Charcoal furnaces dating back to 1800s can still be found nearby.

0:12 (0:48) Pass by two monstrous, rustbathed Armco steel mills on immediate right.

0:44 (0:12) Off to right is Greenup Dam and Lock. Portion of lock is visible just this side of river. Nineteen navigational locks dot Ohio River between Pittsburgh, PA, and Cairo, IL, with Greenup Lock being number nine upstream.

0:57 (0:00) Arrive South Portsmouth.

 SOUTH PORTSMOUTH, KY - This is a stop for Portsmouth, Ohio, just across the river.

0:00 (0:49) Depart South Portsmouth.

0:42 (0:07) Large conveyor system travels over train and down to river where quarried material is then loaded onto river vessels.

0:47 (0:02) Impressive suspension bridge, on right, carries Highway U.S. 62, between Kentucky and Ohio.

0:49 (0:00) Arrive at Maysville's very attractive small station.

 MAYSVILLE, KY - This charming river gateway was first settled in 1784. Fifteen French-style houses from the 1800s are nicely maintained in an area called "Little New Orleans," while several other colorful frame houses can be seen on the hillside above on the left. Maysville has one of the world's largest burley tobacco auctions and is also the hometown of Rosemary Clooney.

0:00 (1:19) Depart Maysville. Back on right, view is afforded of four-stack, coal-fired power plant. Just to south, between here and Lexington, lies thoroughbred heaven— Kentucky's lush bluegrass country.

0:25 (0:54) Captain Anthony Meldahl Dam with its shipping locks creates brief pause in river's westward flow.

0:29 (0:50) Train literally passes through operating limestone quarry.

0:31 (0:48) Telltale cooling tower of Wm. H. Zimmer Nuclear Power Station rises dramatically from opposite shoreline.

0:49 (0:30) Pass beneath Interstate 275 which spans river on right.

1:04 (0:15) Cross Licking River where Cincinnati's skyline is now visible in distance on right. Saucer-like Riverfront Stadium, home of football's Bengals and baseball's Reds, rests imposingly on far shore.

1:06 (0:13) Leave Covington, Kentucky, and enter Cincinnati, Ohio, as we cross Ohio River. Large bridge to right is aptly named Suspension Bridge, while Brent Spence Bridge, carrying Interstates 75 and 71, is off to left. Fine view of stadium and city's skyline, to right, is afforded from center of river. Lesser structure beyond stadium is Coliseum. Paddlewheeler riverboats are sometimes berthed just below Coliseum.

1:19 (0:00) Arrive at Cincinnati's Union Terminal, located about a half-mile from downtown.

 CINCINNATI, OH - Cincinnati is one of America's most attractively situated midwestern cities. Its business and industrial areas occupy separate terraces above the Ohio River, while these, in turn, are dominated by seven residential-studded hills forming a sweeping arc around the downtown area.

The city's beginning can be traced to its convenient river location, and early days saw a busy river trade carried on by picturesque paddle-wheeler riverboats plying the Ohio. Early-day Cincinnati was marked by a small town appearance with its large population being strung out along the shores of the river; it was, perhaps, this atmosphere that caused many notables to refer to the city as one of the most appealing in America.

 Cincinnati Union Terminal, 1301 Western Ave. (Dalton St. and Ezzard Charles Drive) is a truly magnificent Art Deco structure, completed in 1933. After a hiatus of several years, passenger train service returned to this splendid edifice in the summer of 1991. The building also houses the Cincinnati Museum of Natural History, the Cincinnati Historical Society Museum, an OMNIMAX theater and a visitors information center.

Yellow **Cab**, 241-2100. **Local bus** information, 621-4455.

Visitor Information Center at 5th and Vine at Fountain Square and at the station, (513) 621-2142, or 800-344-3445.

Holiday Inn Queens Gate, 800 West 8th Street (at Linn), 45203; (513) 241-8660. Five blocks from the station. $80.

Downtown attractions include: **Fountain Square**, with an 1871 bronze statue purchased in Munich, Germany; **Fourth Street Art Colony**, at Fourth and Elm, with galleries and shops; **Public Landing**, near the Riverfront Stadium, which is the home port for the Delta Queen and Mississippi Queen; and the **Carew Tower Observation Deck**, Fifth and Vine, offers a 48-story-high view of the city.

0:00 (1:05) Depart Cincinnati, retracing our route out over middle of river, then proceed northward through industrial areas of city.

1:05 (0:00) Arrive at Hamilton's rather ancient brick station.

 HAMILTON, OH - One of southern Ohio's larger cities, Hamilton is located on the northern fringes of Cincinnati.

0:00 (0:55) Depart Hamilton.

0:18 (0:37) Slip through Oxford, home to Miami University founded in 1809.

0:23 (0:32) Through College Corner; leave Ohio and enter Indiana, a state that refuses to recognize daylight saving time.

0:36 (0:19) Huge stone Union County Court

House dominates center of Liberty. Town is birthplace of Ambrose E. Burnside, Union army commander and inventor of breech-loading rifle.

0:55 (0:00) Arrive Connersville.

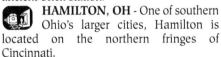 **CONNERSVILLE, IN** - The Whitewater Canal once stretched 101 miles and connected numerous Ohio towns including Connersville and Cincinnati. Just a mile south of here is the Whitewater Valley Rail Road, Indiana's longest scenic railroad. Tour trains run on weekends and holidays, making a 16-mile trek to Metamora with a two-hour sightseeing layover.

0:00 (1:20) Depart Connersville.

0:25 (0:55) Into Rushville, where handsome red-tile-roofed limestone courthouse with central clock tower is centerpiece of town. Wendell L. Wilkie, 1940 Republican nominee for president, sometimes spent his summers here and owned farms in this area. He and other members of his family are buried in East Hill Cemetery at east edge of town off to right of tracks.

1:00 (0:20) Geodesic dome with steeple, on left, is home to Brookville Road Community Church.

1:20 (0:00) Arrive Indianapolis where Union Station has been made focal point of major downtown development.

INDIANAPOLIS, IN - It was in 1820 that Indianapolis was chosen to be the Indiana capital, principally because of its location as the geographic center of the state. Much like Washington, DC, the layout of the city was made after deciding to make it a governmental home using a wheel-and-spoke design for the streets. At the very hub of the city is Monument Circle with the Soldiers and Sailors Monument serving as an axle.

Indianapolis' claim to national fame has to be The Indianapolis 500—that dazzling spectacle of color, motion and sound that takes place every Memorial Day. The city is jammed with people for this renowned event, including the two weeks preceding. If you are planning to attend the big race, or any of the other festivities, make reserva-

Indianapolis Union Station
JACK SWANSON

tions and be sure to make them early.

 **Union Station**, 350 South Illinois. A beautifully restored Romanesque-Revival structure, America's oldest union railway depot (1888), now has over 100 shops, restaurants, nightspots—and a Holiday Inn (without direct access from the station) where guests can elect to stay in actual Pullmans.

Yellow Cab, 487-7777. **Greyhound** terminal is a half mile from the station at 127 N. Capitol. **City buses** at the station, 635-3344.

Indianapolis Convention & Visitors Association, 201 S. Capitol, 237-5206 or 800-323-4639.

Holiday Inn Union Station, 123 W. Louisiana; (317) 631-2221. Adjacent to the station (see station information above). $120.

-**Courtyard by Marriott**, 501 W. Washington (at West), 46204; (317) 635-4443 or 800-321-2211. Seven blocks from the station. $80.

-**Omni-Severin**, 40 W. Jackson Place, 46225; (317) 634-6664 or 800-843-6664. Gracious accommodations, good weekend rates. One block from the station. $99.

Union Station, with its shops and restaurants, has become an attraction itself. The new **Indianapolis Zoo** is located on the west edge of downtown in White River State Park.

Farther out, the **Speedway**, with its 2 1/2-mile oval and museum, can be visited throughout the year. The very fine **Children's Museum**, at 30th and Meridian Streets, is one of best of its kind.

0:00 (0:54) Depart historic Union Station. Immediately, bulbous Hoosier Dome fills our windows to right. Beyond that modern structure, downtown Indianapolis, with attractive capitol as its centerpiece, comes into view.

0:20 (0:35) Pass through Brownsburg and enter more rural surroundings.

0:33 (0:21) I-74 is visible for several miles in midst of typical Indiana flatlands.

0:54 (0:00) Curve sharply to right at Conrail's Ames Tower, now just a modern shack, as train transfers off Conrail onto Seaboard System (former Louisville & Nashville, former Monon Railroad) tracks before arrival at Crawfordsville.

 CRAWFORDSVILLE, IN - A small glass shack serves as the Amtrak station here, next to a red-brick depot bearing the Seaboard System logo. Wabash College, founded in 1832, is located here.

0:00 (0:31) Depart Crawfordsville. Cross high above Sugar Creek as it winds its way prettily through woods, then slide under I-74.

0:31 (0:00) At Lafayette, Tippecanoe County Courthouse, a beautifully ornate-domed building, comes into view.

 LAFAYETTE, IN - Purdue University is located here. Each fall more than 4,500 members of 18th-century reenactment groups—military units, traders, crafts people and merchants, as well as voyagers and most of the midwest's fife and drum corps—gather for two days along the Wabash River southwest of here at Fort Ouiatenon. This is known as the Feast of the Hunters' Moon, commemorating the French and Indian gatherings of the 1700s, when the voyagers arrived from Canada in their 40-foot canoes filled with goods to trade.

0:00 (0:52) Depart LaFayette.

0:03 (0:49) In Seaboard Yards, famous Lafayette Shops are above us on hill to right. In 1888 football game between Wabash College and Purdue University, Wabash, after seeing the immense size of some of their opponents, accused Purdue of adding boilermakers from Monon Shops to their team. The name stuck. Today, Purdue teams are still called the Boilermakers.

0:07 (0:45) Roll under U.S. 52, then cross broad Wabash River a couple minutes later. Shortly thereafter, pass under I-65, main Indianapolis-Chicago freeway.

0:11 (0:41) Tippecanoe Battlefield State Memorial, where General William Henry Harrison defeated Indians led by Prophet, brother of Tecumseh, is marked by 92-foot obelisk on left. Then pass through town of Battle Ground.

0:17 (0:35) Through Brookston where, in 1853, Horace Greeley started a muscle-pow-

ered hand car trip across Kankakee swamps at night after missing train to his next speaking engagement.

0:31 (0:21) Sign, on left, picturing a semi-trailer truck, welcomes us to "Monon, a community built by the transportation industry and Home of the Monon Trailer." It doesn't mention Monon Railroad.

0:35 (0:17) Vulcan Materials Company quarry opens rocky ground to left.

 Pass from Eastern to Central Time. If country is on standard time, set your watch back (forward if eastbound) one hour.

0:40 (0:12) Soon, light blue Monon water tower comes into view and train curves sharply left past red-brick Monon depot on right.

0:52 (0:00) Arrive Rensselaer.

 RENSSELAER, IN - This is home to St. Joseph College.

0:00 (0:40) Depart Rensselaer.

0:20 (0:20) Cross Kankakee River into Shelby.

0:30 (0:10) To right is Cedar Lake, just before city of same name.

1:40 (0:00) Arrive Dyer.

 DYER, IN - Another glass-shack station, functional but without aesthetic value, serves southeastern suburbs here.

0:00 (1:10) Depart Dyer. Amtrak has rerouted the *Cardinal* between Dyer and Chicago from its former Conrail route. Current routing is through Maynard, IN, Thornton Junction and Dolton.

1:04 (0:06) Approaching Chicago's Union Station, it's possible to see an entire train gliding slowly through Amtrak's washer building.

1:06 (0:04) Enter clean, modern Amtrak yards. At right sit examples of nearly every kind of equipment Amtrak owns—coaches and cafes; diners and domes; sleepers, and Superliners.

1:10 (0:00) Leave daylight as we lumber beneath Chicago's huge post office building just before arrival at Union Station.

 CHICAGO, IL - See page 63.

International

As its name implies, the *International* travels in two countries, providing direct passage between Toronto and Chicago. Amtrak and VIA Rail Canada run this train as a joint venture with personnel changes at the border. The path heads west out of Toronto, gliding across southeastern Ontario's flat farmscapes until it crosses into Michigan at Port Huron. From there, it makes a rainbow descent across Michigan to the southern tip of Lake Michigan before proceeding into Chicago. The train is heavily used by Michigan State University students, particularly at school break periods, traveling to and from Lansing.

WESTBOUND SCHEDULE (Condensed)*
Toronto, Ont. - Early Morning Departure
East Lansing, MI - Midafternoon
Chicago, IL - Midevening Arrival

EASTBOUND SCHEDULE (Condensed)*
Chicago, IL - Midmorning Departure
East Lansing, MI - Midafternoon
Toronto, Ont. - Midevening Arrival
*Departures are four hours later on Sundays.

FREQUENCY - Daily (may be reduced).
SEATING - Reserved coaches.
DINING - Sandwiches, snacks and beverages (may be eliminated).
BAGGAGE - No checked baggage.
LENGTH OF TRIP - 501 miles in 12 hours.

ROUTE LOG

For route from Toronto to Sarnia, see Canadian Corridor, page 306.

0:00 (0:10) Depart Sarnia.
0:04 (0:02) Literally sink out of sight for about four minutes as train glides into opening of new (1995), 6,130-foot St. Clair Tunnel, passing beneath St. Clair River. St. Clair River connects Lake Huron (to north) with Lake St. Clair (to south) and is artery for St. Lawrence Seaway. Midway through tube we leave Canada and enter the United States. Customs takes place at our next stop, Port Huron. Although stop can be quite perfunctory, waits up to an hour can occur. Eastbound passengers go through customs at Sarnia.
0:10 (0:00) Arrive Port Huron.
PORT HURON, MI - This city is a significant Great Lakes port and is home to the Fort Gratiot lighthouse, oldest on the lakes.

This is also the eastern terminus of the Grand Trunk Western and the boyhood home of Thomas Edison. Edison worked as a "news butcher" on the Grand Trunk, selling sandwiches and candy on the trains. This job was short-lived, however, when phosphorous he was experimenting with in the baggage car burst into flames and ignited the car. He also printed a paper called the *Weekly Herald* on the train, the first paper printed on a moving train.

0:00 (0:45) Having finished with U.S. customs procedures, depart Port Huron.

0:04 (0:41) Entering Grand Trunk Western's Tunnel Yard, old roundhouse stands on left.

0:30 (0:15) On left, in front of Champion assembly plant, rows of Ford cabs and chassis await transformation into motor homes.

0:45 (0:00) Arrive Lapeer.

 LAPEER, MI - This small Michigan community has an agricultural orientation.

0:00 (0:20) Depart Lapeer.

0:02 (0:18) Brick buildings behind chain link fence on right belong to Oakdale Center, a mental health institution.

0:11 (0:09) Landing strip, complete with assemblage of small planes, parallels tracks on left.

0:16 (0:04) AC Spark Plug factory off to right is easily identified by white and orange initials on silver standpipes.

0:30 (0:00) Arrive Flint.

 FLINT, MI - Second only to Detroit in U.S. auto production, Flint produces Buicks and GM car bodies. General Motors supplies 40% of Grand Trunk railroad's business.

0:00 (0:20) Depart Flint.

0:03 (0:17) GM truck plant on left produces Blazers and GM buses.

0:04 (0:16) Further back on left, grey buildings house another GM plant producing parts and truck assemblies, while hundreds of auto transport cars are parked on sidings awaiting new vehicle shipments.

0:20 (0:00) Arrive At Durand's enormous grey-stone, 1905 depot on left. Train stops on a major intersection of Grand Trunk.

 DURAND, MI - This is the hub of the Grand Trunk's rail operations. Durand is also served by the Ann Arbor Railroad. Although no longer the railroad center of seventy years ago when residents could count an incredible 42 passenger trains, 22 mail trains and 78 freight trains per day, 75% of the Grand Trunk's carloadings still pass through Durand. A fine Railroad History Museum, three blocks from the depot, focuses on train crews, depots, famous train wrecks, track maintenance and workers.

0:00 (0:26) Depart Durand.

0:25 (0:03) High rises of Michigan State University come into view as we enter East Lansing. Stadium, one of college football's largest, is off to right. Now pass directly through campus.

0:28 (0:00) Arrive East Lansing where unusual bell tower can be observed off to right.

EAST LANSING, MI - Adjacent to the capital city of Lansing, East Lansing is home to Michigan State University which is known for its research capabilities—and over 40,000 students. Lansing origins date back to the beginning of the century when R.E. Olds produced and sold one of the first automobiles.

0:00 (0:50) Depart East Lansing.

0:03 (0:43) Cross Grand River and glimpse State Capitol Building at right. Structure has a high rise center with an antenna-like pole on top.

0:06 (0:44) Snake through power plant and then past Oldsmobile plant on right.

0:07 (0:43) Broad Grand River, on left, provides recreational opportunities during summer months, including water-skiing.

0:11 (0:39) Meijer grocery chain's huge automated facility covers several acres on right.

0:12 (0:38) Slip past large Delta Power Plant.

0:28 (0:22) In spring, watch for pails hanging from maple trees to collect syrup throughout this area.

0:35 (0:15) Cross Battle Creek, so named because of an Indian skirmish that took place on its banks in 1825.

0:37 (0:13) At left, built into hillside, are long-abandoned brick ovens.

0:44 (0:04) Now enter Battle Creek through Grand Trunk Western's rail yards where derelict steam locomotive and tenders can be spotted at left. Shops are grey buildings across yards to left. Then past five-story, red-brick Post cereal plant.

0:50 (0:00) Arrive Battle Creek's ultra-modern, intermodal station, on immediate right. Station features unusual seating and imaginative use of brick and glass. Both Greyhound and city buses share this facility with Amtrak.

This is the end of the Grand Trunk tracks. From here to Niles, we will follow Amtrak rails, then Conrail into Chicago.

 BATTLE CREEK, MI - Literally built on the cereal industry, both Kellogg and Post have two enormous facilities here, the largest of their type anywhere.

0:00 (0:28) Depart Battle Creek.

0:05 (0:23) Sprawling complex on left was once operated by Clark Equipment Co., builders of materials handling machinery.

0:21 (0:07) Morrow Hydro Dam and Power Plant are situated off to left.

0:27 (0:02) Cross Kalamazoo River as we enter city of same name. Note some streets are still paved with brick.

0:28 (0:00) Arrive Kalamazoo where lengthy tile-roofed station on left greets passengers with an informative sign that welcomes passengers to Kalamazoo, while announcing Chicago is 138 miles away and Detroit is 142.

 KALAMAZOO, MI - The city with the funny name that everyone has heard of gets its name from the river we just crossed. Kalamazoo is an Indian word roughly translated as "where the water boils in the pot." This town is home to Western Michigan University.

0:00 (0:44) Departing Kalamazoo, note fine collection of older homes with classic, pillared front porches on left.

0:02 (0:41) Slip through campus of aforementioned Western Michigan University.

0:13 (0:29) Watch for vineyards on both sides of tracks. This is wine country.

0:17 (0:27) Grapes are also made into juice and jellies. Note Welch plant on right which processes grapes grown in this area.

0:32 (0:12) Through Dowagiac where steel furnaces were at one time produced. One of those factories is on right.

0:43 (0:01) Large factory of venerable Simplicity Pattern Co., world-wide suppliers of sewing patterns, is on left.

0:44 (0:00) Arrive Niles, with old Michigan Central depot and clock tower on right. This classic 1892 Romanesque station was restored in 1988, and has appeared in several movies, including *Continental Divide* and *Midnight Run*.

 NILES, MI - This railroad and agricultural town is the last stop before leaving Michigan. The Indiana border is just five miles straight south.

0:00 (1:13) Depart Niles.

0:02 (1:11) Cross St. Joseph River which flows northwest and into Lake Michigan.

0:05 (1:08) Vineyards continue, intermixed with fruit orchards.

0:22 (0:51) Lake Michigan's waters come into view. A marina with hundreds of pleasure craft is at right as we near Grand Beach.

0:25 (0:48) Enter Indiana and leave Michigan.

Gain one hour as train passes from Eastern to Central Time. Set your watch back (forward if eastbound) one hour.

0:32 (0:41) Cross a lift bridge at Michigan City, with another marina at right.

0:40 (0:33) Collection of lake-side sand hills, known as Indiana Dunes, is popular destination for weekend recreationalists, at right.

0:44 (0:29) In small town of Porter, join route of *Lake Shore Limited* into Chicago.

0:50 (0:23) Bethlehem Steel Corporation facility appears on right.

0:55 (0:18) Tracks and catenary of legendary Chicago South Shore and South Bend run parallel to our Conrail right-of-way, off to left.

0:57 (0:13) Where Gary began, enormous U.S. Steel Gary Works stretch along tracks at right beyond rail yards.

1:07 (0:06) Inland Steel plants straddle tracks, Plant Number One on left and Plant Number Two on right. Then cross drawbridge spanning Indiana Harbor Canal that links Lake Michigan with Calumet River.

1:09 (0:04) Standard Oil Company of Indiana refinery creates apparatus jungle at left. Lake Michigan is now only 100 feet or so to right.

1:13 (0:00) Arrive Hammond-Whiting.

For route description from here to Chicago, see that portion of *Lake Shore Ltd.* log, page 63.

Lake Cities

The Chicago-Detroit route, Amtrak's "Michigan Corridor," was once the pride of the Michigan Central. Its deterioration began under the New York Central, and became total under the bankrupt Penn Central. The State of Michigan and Amtrak have refurbished old and built new stations, and Conrail and Amtrak have rebuilt the track into a smooth and fast raceway again for the Detroit-Chicago trains.

WESTBOUND SCHEDULE (Condensed)
Pontiac, MI - Early Morning Departure
Detroit, MI - Midmorning
Battle Creek, MI - Early Afternoon
Chicago, IL - Midafternoon Arrival

EASTBOUND SCHEDULE (Condensed)
Chicago, IL - Early Afternoon Departure
Battle Creek, MI - Early Evening
Detroit, MI - Midevening
Pontiac, MI - Late Evening Arrival

FREQUENCY - Daily.
SEATING - Reserved coach seats and Custom Class.
FOOD SERVICE - Sandwiches, snacks, and beverages.
BAGGAGE - No checked baggage service available.
LENGTH OF TRIP - 335 miles in 7 hours.

ROUTE LOG

PONTIAC, MI - Named for the chief of the Ottawa Indians, the city is now home to GM's Pontiac Division. The Pontiac Silverdome, where the Detroit Lions' professional football team plays each fall, is also located here.
0:00 (0:12) Depart Pontiac.
0:12 (0:00) Arrive Birmingham.

BIRMINGHAM, MI - This is one of Detroit's northern suburbs.
0:00 (0:08) Depart Birmingham.
0:08 (0:00) Arrive Royal Oak.

ROYAL OAK, MI - Charles Longhlin, a Catholic priest widely known for his politically oriented national radio broadcasts in the late 1920s and 1930s, served as pastor in Royal Oak from 1926 to 1966.
0:00 (0:12) Depart Royal Oak.
0:12 (0:00) Arrive Detroit.

DETROIT, MI - In 1701, the French colonist Antoine de la Mothe Cadillac landed on what is today's riverfront area of Detroit and established Fort Pontchartrain, later the site of battles during the French and Indian Wars. After the settlement burned to the ground from an accidental fire in 1805, it was rebuilt following, to some extent, the layout of the streets in Washington, D.C. Detroit ultimately became "Motor City" largely because of the imagination and determination of people like Henry Ford, good transportation facilities and an available work force at the time the auto industry was being born.

In the 1970s, Detroit, led by Henry Ford II, made an heroic effort to put a new shine on the city's rusting image in the form of a massive ($350 million) urban development project called the Renaissance Center—"RenCen" for short. Quadruplet 39-story glass office towers surrounding a nearly twice-as-high core hotel were built on the banks of the Detroit River to revitalize the city's downtown. The result was certainly architecturally striking.

Amtrak Station is about three miles north of downtown at Woodward and Baltimore, in the New Center area.

Checker **Cab**, 963-7000. Detroit's **People Mover**, elevated and fully automatic trains, snakes counter-clockwise around the downtown area. Trains are one or two cars in length, arrive at any of the 13 stops every 3 or 4 minutes, and take approximately 15 minutes to make the entire loop.

Visitor Information Center, Tower 100, Suite 126, Renaissance Center; (313) 567-1170 or 800-338-7648.

Hotel St. Regis, 3071 W. Grand Ave., 48202; (313) 873-3000 or 800-848-4810. Nicely refurbished older hotel, across from GM headquarters, about three blocks from the station. $115.

-**Shorecrest Motor Inn**, 1316 E. Jefferson Ave., 48207; (313) 568-3000 or 800-992-9616. Longtime downtown budget favorite. About two blocks from Renaissance Center. $48.

While downtown, be sure to ride the **People Mover** mentioned above. The **Renaissance Center** has numerous shops and is an adventure to explore. **Greektown**, a small downtown enclave, has some great Greek restaurants and numerous small shops anchored by Trapper's Alley, a fashionably converted five-story warehouse with its own collection of boutiques and cafes. Both the Renaissance Center and Greektown are stops for the People Mover.

Detroit's most popular attraction is out in Dearborn. The **Henry Ford Museum** and adjacent **Greenfield Village** are seen by well over a million visitors each year. The Museum has four acres of floor space devoted to displaying the industrialization of America, while Greenfield Village has over 100 buildings on 240 acres, with the likes of the Wright Brothers home and cycle shop, Edison's Menlo Park Laboratory and rides on an 18th-century steam train.

0:00 (0:25) Depart Detroit.

0:20 (0:04) Slip through a large Conrail yard. Off to left, Ford Motor Company's huge River Rouge Plant is an impressive sight.

0:25 (0:00) Arrive at modernistic Dearborn station, built in 1978 to serve Detroit's western suburbs.

DEARBORN, MI - This is the birthplace of Henry Ford. The 12-acre Henry Ford Museum is here, and adjacent is the 240-acre Greenfield Village, a wonderful collection of historical American buildings and artifacts.

0:00 (0:30) Depart Dearborn with Ford Motor's Central Office Building appearing at right. Cross over Southfield Freeway, then over concrete-lined River Rouge for an excellent view on left of Henry Ford Museum and Greenfield Village complex.

0:20 (0:12) Enter Willow Run Yard, and then Ypsilanti, site of Eastern Michigan University.

0:23 (0:07) Make first of innumerable crossings of meandering Huron River as it twists and turns through and between "Ypsi" and western edge of Ann Arbor.

0:30 (0:00) Slip past University of Michigan Hospital high above to left, then follow Huron as it curves right. Pass famous Gandy Dancer Restaurant located in fine Michigan Central depot, on left, as train arrives at new, orange-brick Ann Arbor station on opposite side of Plymouth Road viaduct.

ANN ARBOR, MI - The University of Michigan is located here, making this a major stop on the Corridor. An interesting station feature is the stairway to Plymouth Road with the Amtrak name and logo engraved into the concrete.

0:00 (0:37) Depart Ann Arbor, and immediately resume Huron River crossings.

0:02 (0:35) Dam on immediate right broad-

Lake Cities — Chicago, IL
DEN ADLER

ens river into attractive lake with numerous small boats on far side.

0:10 (0:27) Final crossing of Huron places river on right as it meanders through a wooded park. Then cruise through Dexter, with interesting mill and dam on left.

0:25 (0:12) At Grass Lake, pass small but beautiful stone depot.

0:37 (0:00) After sliding through Conrail's Jackson Yard, arrive at old, red-brick Jackson station on right, oldest of Michigan Corridor's stations, built in 1876 and restored between 1976 and 1978.

JACKSON, MI - Named after Andrew Jackson, the town was founded in 1829 by travelers over the Territorial Road (now roughly paralleled by I-94). It was first called Jacksonopolis and later Jacksonburgh. Several years later, on July 6, 1854, 1,500 Michigan residents assembled here and organized a new political group named the Republican Party. Today, Jackson is home to Michigan's oldest and largest state prison.

0:00 (0:21) Depart Jackson as its downtown rises on left, then past Jackson's airport a few minutes later.

0:18 (0:03) After Parma, Kalamazoo River flows serenely through a farm pasture and marshy area immediately to left, just beyond an abandoned railroad bed.

0:21 (0:00) Arrive at Albion.

ALBION, MI - Albion is home to Albion College, which was passed on our right as we rolled into town.

0:00 (0:30) Depart Albion and, a few minutes later, pass Marengo and continue along Kalamazoo River, wending its way through marshes below to left.

0:25 (0:05) Enter "Cereal City"—Battle Creek—with Kellogg's huge plant and Tony the Tiger (and son) in its front yard on right. A quick succession of Battle Creek sights parade past. Just beyond to left, old GT steam engine sits on silent display. Then General Foods' Post cereals plant looms up suddenly on left. Old Grand Trunk depot comes into view on right, and GT tracks to Lansing and Port Huron, used by Amtrak and VIA's *International*, join from right.

0:30 (0:00) Arrive at New Battle Creek's Transportation Center, built to accommodate all public area transportation systems.

For route between Battle Creek and Chicago, see that portion of *International* Log, page 120.

Pere Marquette

The *Pere Marquette*, named for a French missionary explorer of the Great Lakes, offers service between Grand Rapids, MI, and Chicago, IL, over the tracks of the Chessie System's Chesapeake & Ohio Railroad.

The train provides a daily round trip leaving the Michigan metropolis early in the morning and returning later that evening.

WESTBOUND SCHEDULE (Condensed)
Grand Rapids, MI - Early Morning Departure
Chicago, IL - Midmorning Arrival

EASTBOUND SCHEDULE (Condensed)
Chicago, IL - Late Afternoon Departure
Grand Rapids, MI - Late Evening Arrival

FREQUENCY - Daily. (May be reduced.)
SEATING - Unreserved coaches.
FOOD SERVICE - Snacks, and beverages.
BAGGAGE - No checked baggage service.
LENGTH OF TRIP - 177 miles in 4 hours.

ROUTE LOG

GRAND RAPIDS, MI - After Detroit, this is Michigan's largest city, with well over a half-million people living in the metropolitan area. Although it is famous for its manufacture of home and office furniture since early in its history, the city now has a broad diversity of other industries. The Gerald R. Ford Museum is here in the former president's home town. The town receives its name from the rapids in the Grand River but dredging has virtually eliminated this feature.

Amway Grand Plaza, Pearl St. at Monroe Ave., 49503; (616) 774-2000 or 800-253-3590. Remodeled luxury in downtown's Grand Center. $110.

0:00 (0:38) Depart Grand Rapids' attractive, wood-sided depot south of downtown at the corner of Market and Wealthy. (A depot on a more grandiose scale was demolished some years ago to make way for an interstate highway.) Swing sharply right and roll through Chessie's Lamar Yard.

0:12 (0:26) Pass through mixed residential-industrial suburb of Grandville, then under I-196 and finally gain speed.

0:20 (0:18) Enter Hudsonville, with its fair-grounds and greenhouses, followed by flat, fertile vegetable fields.

0:27 (0:11) Zeeland, where seventy percent of all U.S.-produced grandfather clocks are made, is easily identified by city water tower.

0:38 (0:00) Lake Macatawa lies at right upon arrival at Holland. Depot, surrounded by a tulip-filled park, sits unused as passengers occupy a small adjacent shelter.

HOLLAND, MI - Each May witnesses the famous Tulip Time Festival when this area celebrates its Dutch heritage with parades, dancing and a lavish display of millions of tulips.

0:00 (0:36) Depart Holland past buildings

of Hope College, then re-enter agricultural land while crossing I-196.

0:09 (0:25) Pass quickly through hamlet of East Saugatuck and curve left across pleasant little stream.

0:13 (0:23) Stream again comes into view at left. Sway through New Richmond and soon cross Kalamazoo River on its way to Lake Michigan ten miles west.

0:22 (0:14) Breeze through Fennville, where *Pere Marquette* sometimes makes a special stop in mid-October for town's annual Goose Festival. Now, after scenic areas of rivers, ravines and ridges, terrain once again flattens out.

0:26 (0:10) In next several minutes, roll through towns called Pearl, Bravo and Pullman, and finally reach Grand Junction, where several tracks connect with ours. Orchards are in abundance in this region.

0:36 (0:00) Cross Black River before arrival at Bangor.

BANGOR, MI - The old depot, just outside our window on the right, now houses the "Bangor Train Factory, Manufacturer of the Kalamazoo Toy Train."

0:00 (0:35) Depart Bangor, continuing journey through apple orchards of western Michigan.

0:08 (0:27) Cross Paw Paw River upon reaching Hartford, where Fruit Exchange's wooden skids and boxes lie at left.

0:17 (0:18) After passing grey, wooden Watervliet depot, and crossing Paw Paw River again, ramble through downtown Coloma.

0:25 (0:10) A large electric power station looms at right. At left, Paw Paw appears again as it meanders through trees in search of a march beyond.

0:30 (0:05) Creep across drawbridge over St. Joseph River between Benton Harbor and St. Joseph, where train slows to a mere 15 miles per hour, giving a longer look at Lake Michigan and lighthouse guarding river's mouth.

0:35 (0:00) Arrive at old, grey-stucco depot.

ST. JOSEPH-BENTON HARBOR, MI - Michigan's Twin Cities join numerous other southwestern Michigan communities each spring as sponsors of the Blossomtime Festival in anticipation of the coming fruit harvest. The Benton Harbor Fruit Market is said to be the largest of its kind in the nation.

0:00 (0:28) Depart St. Joseph-Benton Harbor. After gradual ascent to top of bluff, Lake Michigan now spreads out on right until view is obliterated by a clutch of factories as train moves farther inland.

0:11 (0:17) Here, at Bridgman depot on our right, is milepost 100. Cross Galien River.

0:14 (0:14) Paralleling highway on right is I-94. A barn inscribed "Dunes View Farm" is a reminder that distant hills are actually stabilized sand dunes from Lake Michigan and nearby is Warren Dunes State Park.

0:26 (0:02) Cross another stream and follow it for a moment. Then cross handsome set of tracks of Amtrak's Chicago Detroit Corridor.

0:28 (0:00) Arrive at a glass bus shelter that serves as New Buffalo's train station.

NEW BUFFALO, MI - Michigan's largest marina is located here on Lake Michigan.

0:00 (0:48) Depart New Buffalo.

0:08 (0:40) Terrain becomes more urbanized upon approaching Michigan City, IN.

0:24 (0:24) Sign at right proclaims "Indiana Dunes Recreational Area." Pass under I-94 and Chesterton water tower comes into view on left.

0:29 (0:19) Approach white and green Porter Tower, on right, where our Chessie tracks meet Conrail at left and Amtrak's Michigan line at right. Our speed limit is now 79 mph. South Shore Line and its clutter of catenary—overhead wire to power electric locomotives—is on left.

Gain one hour as train passes from Eastern to Central Time. Set your watch back (forward if eastbound) one hour.

0:35 (0:13) Where Gary began, enormous U.S. Steel Gary Works stretch along tracks at right beyond rail yards.

0:42 (0:06) Inland Steel plants straddle tracks, Plant Number One on left and Plant Number Two on right. Then cross drawbridge spanning Indiana Harbor Canal that links Lake Michigan with Calumet River.

Twilight Limited — Chicago, IL
HOMER R. HILL

0:44 (0:04) Standard Oil Company of Indiana refinery creates apparatus jungle at left. Lake Michigan is now only 100 feet or so to right.
0:48 (0:00) Arrive Hammond-Whiting.

For route description from here to Chicago, see that portion of *Lake Shore Ltd.* log, page 63.

Other Michigan Service

The ***Wolverine*** and ***Twilight Ltd.*** provide both morning and evening reserved coach and Custom-Class service between Detroit and Chicago, in addition to the *Lake Cities*.

City of New Orleans

Until 1981, this overnight train between Chicago and New Orleans was called the *Panama Limited*, so named when Midwesterners once set sail for the Orient from New Orleans rather than make the arduous trip across the Rocky Mountains to reach San Francisco. The train was inaugurated at the time the Panama Canal was built.

There was also a *City of New Orleans* but it made a daylight run between these two great towns, carrying some of America's most colorful travelers—gamblers, migrant workers, jazz musicians, to name but a few. "Don't you know me, I'm your native son?" asked Arlo Guthrie.

But one train between Chicago and New Orleans was all Amtrak could afford, and the *Panama Limited* survived. It kept that name until a New Orleans mayor persuaded Amtrak to re-name the train for its southern destination—a much more appropriate appellation.

"The City" travels a direct route between Chicago and New Orleans through Memphis and Jackson. The train passes through eastern Illinois, the western edges of Kentucky and Tennessee, and then through the very heart of Mississippi.

SOUTHBOUND SCHEDULE (Condensed)
Chicago, IL - Early Evening Departure (Daily except Tues)
Champaign-Urbana, IL - Late Evening
Memphis, TN - Early Morning (2nd Day)
Jackson, MS - Late Morning (2nd Day)
New Orleans, LA - Midafternoon Arrival (2nd Day)

NORTHBOUND SCHEDULE (Condensed)
New Orleans, LA - Early Afternoon Departure (Daily except Tues)
Jackson, MS - Late Afternoon
Memphis, TN - Late Evening
Champaign-Urbana, IL - Early Morning (2nd Day)
Chicago, IL - Early Morning Arrival (2nd Day)

FREQUENCY - Five days a week (see above).
SEATING - Reserved Superliner coaches.
DINING - Complete meals in diner. Sandwiches and beverage service in lounge.
SLEEPING - Deluxe, special, family and economy bedrooms.
BAGGAGE - Checked baggage at larger cities.
RESERVATIONS - All-reserved train.
LENGTH OF TRIP - 924 miles in 19 hours.

ROUTE LOG

CHICAGO, IL - See page 63.
0:00 (0:41) Depart Chicago Union Station, backing southbound from beneath Chicago's main post office terminal.
0:03 (0:39) Still in reverse, slip past Amtrak's coach yards and car-washing facility.
0:05 (0:36) Cross South Chicago River.

0:07 (0:34) Train finally ends its backward ways and starts forward, curling slowly right (east) onto Illinois Central tracks, following historic St. Charles Air Line right-of-way. Illinois Central was nation's first major land grant railroad (two-and-a-half-million acres for 7% of its gross revenues) and boasts the likes of Casey Jones, Abraham Lincoln and Mark Twain as employee alumni.

0:09 (0:32) Chinatown's colorful storefronts are just off to right.

0:12 (0:29) Amtrak's best offering of Chicago's spectacular skyline holds forth at left. Dominant building with twin antenna is famous Sears Tower, nation's tallest skyscraper, while slope-sided John Hancock Building (also with two antennae) is also apparent.

0:14 (0:27) Curling south, giant Soldier Field, home of NFL's Chicago Bears, is just off to left, while Field Museum can be seen beyond. Shortly, dome of Adler Planetarium can be discerned back left along lakefront.

0:18 (0:23) Pass beneath entrance to McCormick Place and McCormick Hotel. Black, flat Exposition Center is quite visible back to left after returning to daylight.

0:20 (0:21) Now, waters of Lake Michigan lap against Burnham Park paralleling Lake Shore Drive, on left.

0:22 (0:19) Architecturally interesting collection of older buildings faces tracks, on left. Jackson Park with its world renowned Museum of Science and Industry lies beyond. Campus of University of Chicago stretches off to right.

0:24 (0:17) Rumble beneath Chicago Skyway and tracks of Conrail at aptly named Grand Crossing.

0:27 (0:14) Buildings of Chicago State University border tracks on right.

0:34 (0:07) Cross Little Calumet River.

0:38 (0:03) Expansive Markham Yards of Illinois Central now stretch along route on left. Black IC switchers can be spotted shuffling long consists of freight cars among various tracks.

0:41 (0:00) Arrive at attractive community of Homewood.

 HOMEWOOD, IL - Giant oak and pine trees surround this well-to-do Chicago suburb. Homewood's per capita income places it among 200 most affluent American cities.

0:00 (0:30) Depart Homewood.

0:30 (0:00) Arrive Kankakee.

 KANKAKEE, IL - Set along the banks of the Kankakee River, many vestiges of Kankakee's early French influence still pervade this city. Renowned for its abundant gladiola harvests, unusual rock formations surround the many limestone and sand quarries that are noteworthy here as well. Frank Lloyd Wright once lived here.

0:00 (0:52) Depart Kankakee and cross Kankakee River.

0:26 (0:27) This is Gilman, IL, a stop northbound only. Besides an agrarian focal point for Iroquois County, Gilman has been a modest rail center and division point for the Illinois Central.

0:50 (0:00) Arrive Rantoul.

 RANTOUL, IL - Rantoul affords easy access to Chanute Field, which has been one of the largest technical training centers of the U.S. Air Force.

0:00 (0:14) Depart Rantoul.

0:14 (0:00) Arrive Champaign-Urbana.

CHAMPAIGN-URBANA, IL - Defying consolidation since the mid-19th century, Illinois' "Twin Cities" still maintain separate identities. Champaign has evolved into a commercial and industrial center, while Urbana is more collegiate-oriented with the University of Illinois campus lying primarily within its boundaries.

0:00 (0:38) Depart Champaign-Urbana.

0:38 (0:00) Arrive Mattoon.

MATTOON, IL- An industrial community and service center for the surrounding farmlands, Mattoon is a convenient stop for students attending Eastern Illinois University in Charleston.

0:00 (0:25) Depart Mattoon.

0:25 (0:00) Arrive Effingham.

EFFINGHAM, IL - As well as a service center for smaller agricultural communities, Effingham supports an active manufacturing industry with products spanning the gamut from church furniture to golf clubs.

0:00 (0:44) Depart Effingham.
0:44 (0:00) Arrive Centralia.

 CENTRALIA, IL - Centralia, one of three cities comprising this metropolitan area, is an industrial-oriented community with railroad shops and yards providing major employment for the region. An immense carillon, one of the largest in the world, dominates the town's skyline.

0:00 (0:54) Depart Centralia.
0:54 (0:00) Arrive Carbondale.

 CARBONDALE, IL - As its name implies, Carbondale sits in the midst of extensive coalfields which provide the basic industrial staple of this community. It is home of Southern Illinois University.

0:00 (1:48) Depart Carbondale.
0:58 (0:50) Through the town of Cairo. Situated at confluence of the mighty Ohio and Mississippi Rivers, Cairo was early Civil War headquarters of General Grant, affording him complete command of operations along these waterways. Today, bridges across three rivers connect the states of Missouri, Kentucky and Illinois. (Locals have dubbed this portion of Southern Illinois as "Little Egypt," not to be confused with the dancer but because of its resemblance to the flat silt banks of the Nile River Valley.)
0:59 (0:49) Cross Ohio River and enter Kentucky. Shortly, train crosses a geologic feature known as the New Madrid Fault.
1:48 (0:00) Arrive Fulton.

 FULTON, KY - Some years ago, the majority of banana shipments from Latin America stopped in Fulton while refrigerator cars were re-iced and the fruit was prepared for distribution. The practice has long since been discontinued. The town once concocted a two-ton banana pudding (world's largest, of course) to commemorate this tropical fruit during its annual International Banana Festival.

0:00 (0:51) Depart Fulton.
0:51 (0:00) Arrive Newbern.

NEWBERN, TN - This small town serves as a stop for nearby Dyers-

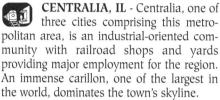

New Madrid Fault

During the winter of 1811-12, the New Madrid Fault caused North America's strongest earthquake, probably an incredible 8.7 on the Richter scale. Nearby, the Mississippi River actually changed direction and as far away as Boston church bells were clanging from the shock. Experts say the fault, more than 500 million years old, is building up pressure and might some day trigger the nation's worst natural disaster.

burg. Dyersburg was founded in 1821 and was named in honor of Colonel William Henry Dyer who served under General Andrew Jackson during the War of 1812. Today, bountiful crops of cotton and fruit are processed by local industry.

0:00 (1:34) Depart Newbern.
1:32 (0:02) Approaching Memphis, Hernando-Desoto Bridge spans Mississippi River, on right, carrying Interstate 40 traffic between Memphis and Little Rock. Pyramid is incongruous sight on right. Mud Island, also at right, is home to park focusing on Mississippi River history and geography and is separated from shore by Wolf River. Once a muddy trap for river vessels, island's reclamation has turned it into a Memphis showplace. Venerable Peabody Hotel, on left, is easily identified by rooftop neon sign. Then historic Beale Street can be seen off to left.
1:34 (0:00) Arrive Memphis.

 MEMPHIS, TN - Memphis was born in 1819 when Andrew Jackson, yet to be elected president, laid out a town on the Chickasaw Bluffs overlooking the Mississippi River. This unusually high location above the Mississippi turned out to be fortuitous, since many towns established along the banks of that great river were ultimately washed away or abandoned due to recurring flooding.

Although severely decimated by several yellow fever epidemics in the 1800s, the city not only came back, it is now the largest city on the Mississippi between St. Louis and New Orleans. Memphis has laid claim to numerous distinctions, including: the world's largest mule-trading market; the "Birthplace of Blues"; the home of W.C. Handy and Elvis Presley; and the first Welcome Wagon.

Central Station, 545 South Main St., has been a terminally (no pun intended) forlorn structure in one of the worst areas of town, an area where passengers should not walk at night. Fortunately, there are plans to improve Amtrak's situation by redeveloping the current site. The present station has storage lockers and adjacent free parking (no security).

 Yellow **Cab**, 577-7777. **Local buses** stop in front of the station; MATA, 274-6282. Main Street Trolley shuttle route is designed to loop around major downtown tourist attractions.

Visitor Information Center, 340 Beale Street, (901) 543-5333.

Ramada Convention Center Hotel, 160 Union Ave., 38103; (901) 525-5491. Attractive downtown hotel, about two miles from the station. $55.

-**Wilson World Graceland**, 3677 Elvis Presley Blvd., 38116; (901) 332-1000 or 800-333-9457. Excellent value. Across from Graceland. $50.

-**The Peabody**, 149 Union, 38103; (901) 529-4000 or 800-833-2548. Venerable landmark, located downtown, about two miles from the station. $145.

Memphis and the Mississippi River are inseparable. Recognizing this, the City of Memphis has spent over $60 million developing **Mud Island** just offshore of the downtown area. This Island is a showcase for all aspects of the River—recreational, educational, cultural, historic and scientific, all set along a five-block river

walk that is actually a flowing model of the entire Mississippi River Basin and the **Memphis Belle**. **Pyramid**, on the edge of downtown, is a 32-story "wonder" housing an entertainment and sports complex.

Nightlife and blues, a Memphis tradition, can be found downtown along **Beale Street** where W.C. Handy lived and wrote much of his beloved music. The best-known tourist attraction in town is still **Graceland**, the showplace home of Elvis Presley, where visitors can get a firsthand look at "The King's" lifestyle. The estate is south of downtown at 3717 Elvis Presley Blvd.

And the legendary **Peabody ducks** are mandatory for anyone visiting Memphis for the first time. At 11 am each day, the hotel's ducks that reside in a rooftop penthouse are herded into an elevator and brought to the lobby for their ritualistic feeding.

0:00 (2:05) Depart Memphis.

0:17 (1:48) Leave Tennessee and enter state of Mississippi.

0:18 (1:47) Waters of Horn Lake appear on right.

0:45 (1:20) Cross Coldwater River just before entering town of Savage.

1:12 (0:53) Cross Coldwater River.

1:16 (0:49) Pass through town of Marks.

1:20 (0:45) Passing through Lambert, wetlands of Okeefe Waterfowl area are off to left.

2:05 (0:00) Arrive Greenwood's 1920s depot.

GREENWOOD, MS - Cotton is king in Greenwood; its prominence dating back to pre-Civil War times. Astride the Yazoo River and located amidst rich cotton productive farmlands, the city grew steadily from a bustling river landing to what is now one of the largest cotton markets in the world.

0:00 (1:00) Depart Greenwood.

1:00 (0:00) Arrive Yazoo City.

YAZOO CITY, MS - Like Greenwood, Yazoo (pronounced Yeah-ZOO) City is located on the Yazoo River and has an economy heavily dependent on agriculture.

Just 22 miles east of here is the small

town of Vaughn, Mississippi, that was the scene of the famous Casey Jones train wreck. Trying to make up lost time, an unsuspecting Casey ran his speeding train into a derailed freight just north of town. He died in the wreck and was supposedly found with one hand on the throttle and the other on the brake. Chronicles of this legendary engineer, as well as other railroad memorabilia, are housed there in a restored depot museum.

0:00 (1:00) Depart Yazoo City.

0:45 (0:15) Entering outskirts of Jackson, cross Interstate 220.

0:48 (0:12) Western arm of large Lake Hico comes up to tracks at left.

0:50 (0:10) Manicured greens and fairways of Grove Park Golf Course are now on immediate right.

0:52 (0:08) On left, Memorial Stadium is scene of fierce gridiron rivalries between "Ole Miss" and Mississippi State University. For rest of season, field is home to Jackson State University and Millsaps College. University of Mississippi Medical Center is situated just south of stadium. Then through classification yards.

0:58 (0:02) Downtown Jackson skyline appears on forward left, with broad dome of "new" Capitol Building predominant. Built in 1903, golden eagle (flying south, of course) is proudly perched atop this grand structure.

1:00 (0:00) Arrive Jackson. Former Hotel King Edward, once an important Jackson landmark, now stands empty and in utter disrepair, forward on left.

 JACKSON, MS - Crossroads of the South, and capital of Mississippi, Jackson had its humble beginnings as a trading settlement on the banks of the Pearl River. This outpost grew to prominence, only to be burned to the ground by General Sherman during the Civil War. The city recovered mightily, and is now the trading and transportation center of the state.

0:00 (0:30) Depart Jackson, with "Old" Capitol Building on left. Mississippi Arts Center and Planetarium are housed within white-domed complex, also on left.

0:25 (0:06) Pass through Crystal Springs whose bountiful tomato harvests of early 1900s prompted its designation as "Tomatopolis of the World."

0:30 (0:00) Arrive Hazelhurst past comely residential district on right.

HAZELHURST, MS - Set deep in the heart of farm country, Hazelhurst serves a region devoted primarily to the production of cotton and livestock

0:00 (0:21) Departing Hazelhurst, on left is Royal Maid Association for the Blind, employing blind workers to manufacture plastic flatware, mops, brooms and other products.

0:14 (0:07) Passing through Wesson, note historic Wesson Hotel on left. During railroad's heyday, a gambling casino was maintained in hotel's attic and proved a popular diversion for awaiting passengers. Building is presently enshrined in National Register. Adjacent to hotel is campus of Copiah-Lincoln Junior College.

0:21 (0:00) Arriving Brookhaven, regal magnolia trees line walkways of station. Small monument on right offers brief account of town's historical highlights.

BROOKHAVEN, MS - A recruiting and hospital center during the Civil War, Brookhaven has likewise flourished since completion of the railroad. Today, industrial development is focused around the region's natural resources of petroleum, wood pulp and clay.

0:00 (0:21) Departing Brookhaven, fanciful Victorian homes enhance neighborhood on left.

0:03 (0:15) Bogue Chitto River makes first of several brief appearances on left.

0:19 (0:02) Outstanding composition of lake and rural homes, on right, produces one of more attractive scenes along route.

0:21 (0:00) Arrive McComb.

MCCOMB, MS - This southern Mississippi town was named in honor of Colonel H.S. McComb who spearheaded reconstruction of the railroad following its destruction during the Civil War.

McComb is presently renowned as the

City of New Orleans — New Orleans, LA
JACK SWANSON

home of the "Lighted Azalea Trail," an enchanting Easter-time spectacle fashioned by local residents who pin tiny lights around the delicate pink and white blossoms of their azalea bushes.

0:00 (0:53) Depart McComb.

0:10 (0:43) At Magnolia, two outstanding Colonial mansions can be seen on right. Splendid magnolia trees grace yard of larger home.

0:13 (0:40) Cross Tangipahoa River which then follows intermittently on left.

0:19 (0:34) At southern edge of Osyka, cross Mississippi state line into Louisiana.

0:28 (0:26) A few miles south of Kentwood, pass Camp Moore Confederate Cemetery on left. Once a major training camp for Confederate Army, museum of Civil War relics now stands amidst graves of over 500 soldiers.

0:31 (0:22) Wetland homes are often elevated a foot or two above ground for obvious reasons. Builder of house at left was expecting the worst.

0:39 (0:14) Early vestiges of French influence can be detected in curlicues and trelliswork adorning homes of Amite. On left, colossal old bell is enshrined in front of fire station. Standpipe on left proclaims Amite as "The Friendly City—500,000 Gallon Capacity."

0:47 (0:06) On southern outskirts of Independence, note intriguing cemetery on right. Tombs are positioned above ground in deference to saturated soil that would otherwise seep into graves. This is a fairly common spectacle throughout pervading wetlands of southern Louisiana.

0:49 (0:04) Copious fields of delectable strawberries line route into Hammond.

0:53 (0:00) Arrive Hammond.

 HAMMOND, LA - Hammond is considered the state's "Strawberry Capital."

0:00 (1:01) Depart Hammond.

0:09 (0:52) Passing through Ponchatoula, old 2-8-0 narrow-gauge steam locomotive of Louisiana Express can be seen on left. Then venture forth amidst haunting beauty of Louisiana swamplands. This primitive wilderness has nurtured the lifeblood and soul around which an entire Acadian culture has evolved.

0:12 (0:50) On right, Interstate 55 sits atop concrete piers, impressively, fixed into forbidding landscape below. Grey-green material hanging from trees is Spanish moss, a harmless non-parasite and one of nature's more attractive embellishments.

0:17 (0:46) Cross Pass-Manchac waterway that connects Lake Maurepas on right with Lake Pontchartrain on left.

0:26 (0:38) Approaching suburbs of New Orleans, train skirts shoreline of Lake Pontchartrain on left.

0:43 (0:22) On left, Moisant Field is New Orleans International Airport.

0:52 (0:13) Famed Huey P. Long Bridge, carrying both automobile and rail traffic across Mississippi River, is visible on horizon at right.

1:00 (0:05) After crossing beneath major highway interchange, campus of Xavier University can be seen on right.

1:03 (0:03) To forward left, Superdome is an imposing structure in foreground of New Orleans skyline. Sports facility is home of National Football League's Saints. Adjacent to east is modernistic Hyatt Regency Hotel.

1:07 (0:02) Engage in U-turn around publishing headquarters of Picayune States-Item Times. Train then backs into New Orleans station past elephantine Superdome.

1:14 (0:00) Arrive New Orleans.

 NEW ORLEANS, LA - See page 97.

New Orleans Union Passenger Terminal
JACK SWANSON

Empire Builder

It was James J. Hill, a rugged empire-building tycoon in the finest sense, who constructed his Great Northern Railway around the turn of the century, creating a transcontinental link between St. Paul and the Pacific Northwest. The railroad brought farmers and ranchers to the prairies of North Dakota and Montana, miners to the mineral rich mountains of western Montana and lumberjacks to Washington's forests. And virtually overnight, an international trade with the Orient developed through Seattle's natural harbor, Puget Sound.

In 1929, Hill's Great Northern inaugurated the passenger train called the *Empire Builder*—a train which became one of the few of that era to have its name live on. Now, the *Empire Builder* makes this same jaunt across the northern tier of states, but starts in Chicago, following the Milwaukee Road to St. Paul before trekking across the old Great Northern route (now the Burlington Northern) to Seattle. This is America's northernmost passage.

Ken Wescott Jones, a British rail travel authority, described today's "Builder" as "the most comfortable, all-class, non-supplementary-fare train in the world." Add to this proclaimed contentment some of this country's most attractive countryside and the trip becomes an enticement that is hard to refuse. America's fruited plains, her purple mountain majesties, her gleaming shores—they are all on display. The pastoral environs of the upper Mississippi River and the vast expanses of the northern plains contrast sharply with the mountains of Glacier National Park and the Cascades of Washington, a contrast that can only be fully absorbed and enjoyed while traveling on a train.

The Portland section breaks off at Spokane and offers its own attractions with a cruise along the northern shore of the majestic Columbia River, including a memorable trip through the verdant-cliffed Columbia Gorge.

WESTBOUND SCHEDULE (Condensed)
Chicago, IL - Midafternoon Departure
Milwaukee, WI - Late Afternoon
St. Paul/Minneapolis, MN - Late Evening
Fargo, ND - Middle of the Night (2nd Day)
Havre, MT - Late Afternoon (2nd Day)
West Glacier, MT - Midevening (2nd Day)
Spokane, WA - Late Night (3rd Day)
Portland, OR* - Midmorning Arrival (3rd Day)
Seattle, WA - Late Morning Arrival (3rd Day)

EASTBOUND SCHEDULE (Condensed)
Seattle, WA - Late Afternoon Departure
Portland, OR* - Late Afternoon Departure
Spokane, WA - Middle of the Night
West Glacier, MT - Early Morning (2nd Day)
Havre, MT - Early Afternoon (2nd Day)
Fargo, ND - Middle of the Night (3rd Day)
St. Paul/Minneapolis, MN - Early Morning (3rd Day)
Milwaukee, WI - Midafternoon (3rd Day)

Chicago, IL - Late Afternoon Arrival (3rd Day)
*By separate section between Spokane and Portland.

FREQUENCY - Daily between Chicago and St. Paul/Minneapolis. West of St. Paul/Minneapolis, quad weekly. Westbound, depart St. Paul/Minneapolis and eastbound, depart Seattle and Portland, Sun, Tues, Thur and Fri.
SEATING - Superliner coaches.
DINING - Complete meal and beverage service, Chicago-Seattle. Lounge service available with sandwiches, snacks and beverages, Chicago-St. Paul/Minneapolis-Spokane-Portland. Cold meal service for sleeping car passengers, Spokane-Portland. Diner/Lounge, sandwiches, snacks and beverages, Spokane-Seattle.
SLEEPING - Superliner sleepers with deluxe, family, economy and special bedrooms, Chicago-Portland-Seattle.
BAGGAGE - Checked baggage handled at most stations.
RESERVATIONS - All-reserved train.
LENGTH OF TRIP - To Seattle: 2,209 miles in 45 hours. To Portland: 2,261 miles in 45 hours.

ROUTE LOG

 CHICAGO, IL - See page 63.

0:00 (0:26) Depart Chicago's Union Station beneath streets of Chicago, emerging amidst some of city's most notable landmarks. On immediate right, Marina City's twin cylindrical towers are an architectural eye-catcher, while on forward right, Merchandise Mart is stoutly entrenched on banks of Chicago River.
0:03 (0:20) Following a quick turn west, smartly tapering design of Hancock Building is readily distinguishable back on right. Multi-tiered Sears Tower, currently world's tallest building at 1,353 feet, dominates skyline back on left.
For the next several miles, elevated track

bed affords encompassing views of Chicago's older north side.
0:23 (0:00) Arrive Glenview.

 GLENVIEW, IL - Glenview is a convenient suburban stop for the northern Chicago region.
0:00 (1:03) Depart Glenview north through a comely residential district. Between here and Milwaukee, landscape bares an interesting mix of older farms and modern industrial complexes. Underwriter's Laboratories, Fiat, Sara Lee, and AC are but a few of the corporate strongholds seen throughout this stretch.
0:02 (1:01) On left, skirt grounds of Glenview Naval Air Station where numerous helicopters, fixed-wing craft and a star-spangled water tower can be observed.
0:03 (1:00) Green berm, on right, hides enormous regional landfill, while just beyond, twin towers (circa 1920) mark beautiful complex of Techny, U.S. headquarters for the Chicago Province of the Society of the Divine Word. Once a Catholic religious seminary, it has served as a religious conference and retreat center since 1978.
0:20 (0:43) Passing through Gurnee, Marriott's popular Great American Amusement Park can be seen on left.
0:23 (0:40) At Wadsworth, Des Plaines River follows infrequently on left. A couple miles hence, cross Illinois state line into Wisconsin.
0:30 (0:33) On right, field serves as storage facility for hundreds of new cars awaiting transport to dealers' showrooms.
0:38 (0:25) Old hotel at Sturtevant, on right, is interesting curiosity with its turret-adorned corners.
0:40 (0:23) Looking almost inviting, one of nation's newest prisons, Racine Correctional Institution, is on right.
0:54 (0:09) On right is General Mitchell Field, Milwaukee's airport.
0:58 (0:05) With Milwaukee's skyline coming into full view, note two architecturally outstanding and historical churches to left. St. Josaphat's Basilica, distinguished by its inspiring verdigris dome (modeled after St. Peter's in Rome), was built at turn of the cen-

tury by poor immigrant parishioners using materials salvaged from Chicago's Federal Building. It was first Polish basilica in North America.

St. Stanislaus Cathedral, readily identified by its twin golden-domed spires, was nation's third Polish church at time of its construction. Colorfully faceted glasswork and sculptured marble bedeck interior of this magnificent structure.

0:59 (0:04) On left, Allen Bradley clock tower is stately landmark in foreground of downtown.

1:03 (0:00) Arrive Milwaukee station, crossing confluence of Menomonee and Milwaukee Rivers.

MILWAUKEE, WI - Milwaukee, an Indian word meaning "beautiful meeting place by the waters," is the largest city in Wisconsin with a metropolitan population of 1,400,000. It is also one of the nation's leading industrial centers, as well as being an important inland seaport on the Great Lakes.

Of course, a major industry is the brewing of beer—so important that Milwaukee is oft referred to as "beer town." The brewery image should not be misleading. Milwaukee, located on a beautiful bay of Lake Michigan, is one of America's most attractive cities. Nor does the city lack for a healthy dose of culture. It has a fine symphony, a ballet company, theater groups, a top-notch zoo and a well-stocked art museum.

Union Station, 433 W. St. Paul Ave., is on the edge of downtown. The station has a large waiting room, redcaps, a restaurant and a newsstand. Pay-parking is across the street.

Yellow **Cab**, 271-1800.

Milwaukee Visitors Bureau, 510 W. Kilbourne Ave., (414) 273-3950 or 800-231-0903.

Ramada Inn Downtown, 633 W. Michigan St., 53203; (414) 272-8410. Attractive and convenient. Three blocks from the station. $66.

-**Marc Plaza Hotel**, 509 W. Wisconsin Ave., 53203; (414) 271-7250 or 800-558-

7708. A Milwaukee landmark. Three blocks from the station. $100.

Milwaukee is one of several cities that has a **Skywalk** system, permitting weatherproof strolling and shopping. Nearest access is W. Michigan and 4th, three blocks from the station. Spirit of Milwaukee Theatre, on Wisconsin Avenue between 1st and 2nd Streets in the Grand Ave. Mall, has a **multimedia show** giving a Milwaukee overview, four blocks from the station. **First Wisconsin Center**, 11 blocks east of the station, is the state's highest building; the 41st floor has a superb view.

0:00 (1:14) Depart Milwaukee.

0:04 (1:10) On left, three unusual glass domes house Mitchell Park Horticultural Conservatory (world's largest curved-glass horticultural structures). Botanical displays representing the world's three climatic conditions—arid, temperate and tropical—are cultivated here in buildings that simulate their native environs.

0:06 (1:08) Milwaukee County Stadium, home of baseball's "Brewers," can be seen on left.

0:07 (1:07) Miller brewery is on right. Immediately thereafter, cross Menomonee River.

0:21 (0:53) Passing through handsome suburb of Elm Grove, campus-like-complex on right is Notre Dame Health Care Center, a facility for elderly nuns.

With the vestiges of urban influence slowly waning, embark across the open spaces that are America's heartland. Thomas Jefferson once exhorted that we be "a nation of yeoman farmers." To that end, the rustic farmsteads set amidst rolling fields of grain are picturesque reminders that this early American ideal still flourishes.

0:39 (0:36) In Okauchee, on right, signage on St. Jerome's Church garage admonishes "Thou Shalt Not Park."

1:13 (0:01) Cross Crawfish River, then wonderfully crafted tree house is cradled next to tracks on right.

1:14 (0:00) Arrive Columbus where, on right, tidy depot is adorned with city's name

Tree house — near Columbus, WI
BRUCE LEMAY COLLECTION

in raised relief above front door and unusually sculpted bricks in platforms each side of tracks.

Note interesting design of 125-year-old Zion Evangelical Lutheran Church on left. Large bell mounted beneath its steeple was gift from Emperor of Germany, cast from pieces of French cannon captured during Franco-Prussian War.

Immediately adjacent to church, fanciful clock tower sits atop 1892 Columbus City Hall.

COLUMBUS, WI - Famed for its springtime regalia of redbud blossoms, Columbus is also a convenient stop for students attending the University of Wisconsin in nearby Madison.

0:00 (0:25) Depart Columbus.

0:16 (0:09) While passing through Wyocena, don't miss "Santa's Super Rocket." Looking capable of interplanetary travel, this cosmic contraption was surely the highlight of many Christmases past. Regrettably, it has since been put out to pasture and today ages gracefully in back lots of a Wyocena salvage yard on right.

0:43 (0:00) Arrive Portage.

PORTAGE, WI - Situated on a narrow strip of land between the Fox and Wisconsin Rivers, Portage is a prosperous commercial hub of the surrounding farmlands. As its name implies, the town was once a popular stopover for traders and settlers who had to "portage" their gear from one river to the other.

0:00 (0:15) Depart Portage through rail yards that boast a small roundhouse and turntable.

0:07 (0:07) Wisconsin River joins on left.

0:15 (0:00) Arrive Wisconsin Dells' 1989 station, built to replace former depot destroyed when a coal train derailed here in

1982. Magnificent canyon cut by river can be seen on left. Area is also highlighted by a host of man-made amusements, several of which surround station site.

WISCONSIN DELLS, WI - From airplane rides to water slides, an amusement-park atmosphere pervades this renowned Midwestern resort. Yet, as previously noted, the natural beauty and drama surrounding "The Dells" is still the mainstay around which the town has flourished.

0:00 (0:42) Depart Wisconsin Dells across Wisconsin River.

0:21 (0:21) Built in 1902, multi-spired St. Patrick's Catholic Church, on right, is prominent feature of "midtown" route through Mauston.

0:30 (0:12) Fascinating rock formations are an unexpected delight of Camp Douglas area. Once in town, Camp Douglas Village Hall is a most impressive structure on left.

0:40 (0:00) Arriving Tomah, well-preserved Pullman car of Milwaukee Road houses Chamber of Commerce on left.

TOMAH, WI - In a tribute to its agricultural roots, Tomah is host each July to the Wisconsin Dairyland Grand National Tractor Pull—a grueling test of skill and equipment, attracting hundreds of farmers from across the Midwest and Canada.

Tomah is also noted as the boyhood home of Frank King, creator of the famed comic strip "Gasoline Alley." Many of King's drawings and cartoons are preserved throughout the town. Walt and Skeezix can be seen holding up the sign in front of the Chamber of Commerce office next to the station.

0:00 (0:41) Depart Tomah.

0:01 (0:40) On left, pass Tomah Lake.

0:05 (0:36) Brief intrusion of alpine-like terrain highlights geography surrounding Tunnel City. Quick trip through tunnel appropriately follows.

0:20 (0:31) Entrance to US Army Ft. McCoy is at left.

0:21 (0:22) On right, pass small Sparta airport. At same time, begin following La

Crosse River on right to its juncture with Mississippi River twenty miles west.

0:41 (0:00) Two beautiful churches on right preview arrival at La Crosse.

LA CROSSE, WI - An old Indian game that the French dubbed "lacrosse" gave its name to this picturesque community, set at the confluence of the Black, La Crosse and Mississippi Rivers. Agricultural, industrial and commercial enterprises all contribute to the town's well-balanced economy.

0:00 (0:33) Departing La Crosse, cross Mississippi River into Minnesota. Islands in middle of this historic waterway divide river into three channels here. Once on western bank, pass through "apple capital" of La Crescent and begin a northerly tack that generally parallels river through Richard J. Dorer Memorial Hardwood State Forest. Oak, birch, maple and walnut are but a sampling of hardwood trees that thrive in these parts.

The ensuing 125 miles is one of the most scenic legs of the *Empire Builder* route. Quaint little townships, elegant in their simplicity, are splendidly well-preserved along these riverbanks. At their doorstep, barges and riverboats leisurely traverse the waters of the mighty Mississippi. To the west, the lush farmlands and forests of this fertile river valley provide a serene backdrop for a setting that has assuredly inspired many an artist or photographer.

0:32 (0:01) Towering 500 feet above the river, Sugar Loaf Mountain is a renowned landmark of Winona on left. According to Indian legend, silhouette of famous Sioux Chief Wa-Pa-Sha was once prominent feature of mountain prior to quarrying operations of late 1800s.

0:33 (0:00) Another "midtown" route into station avails intriguing insights into this hardy Midwestern community upon arriving Winona. Cozy chalet-style depot greets passengers on left.

WINONA, MN - Since construction of the first sawmills here in the early 1850s, Winona has grown from a one-industry town into a bustling manufacturing center. It is also a popular connection for passengers traveling to the famed Mayo Clinic in nearby Rochester.

0:00 (1:01) Depart Winona.

0:03 (0:58) Large cluster of grain elevators, on right, evidences major distribution port.

0:20 (0:41) Numerous fishing camps flourish about Weaver, supporting area's claim as "White Bass Capital of the World." Passing through town, stately structure perched atop bluffs on left was formerly grandiose hotel, recognized in National Register.

0:32 (0:29) Comely Wabasha is home of Anderson House Hotel, Minnesota's oldest operating inn since 1856. As special amenities, complimentary shoeshines are provided, as well as hot bricks to warm the feet in winter. For lonesome travelers, house cats are also available upon request.

0:33 (0:28) Mississippi River widens considerably to accommodate waters of Chippewa River flowing in from east. Waterskiing is said to have originated here in resultant expanse known as Lake Pepin.

0:49 (0:12) Pass through beautiful little town of Frontenac whose roots trace back to original French fort established here in 1723.

0:50 (0:11) On left, T-bar lift ascends slopes of Mt. Frontenac Ski Area.

0:55 (0:06) On right, nostalgic advertisement for Beechnut chewing tobacco weathers picturesquely on side of barn.

0:57 (0:04) Approaching Red Wing, Minnesota State Training School is easily recognized on left by its lofty tower, with Minnesota and U.S. flags fronting properly. Internationally acclaimed for success of its "Positive Peer Group" therapy, facility was originally established in 1891, and modeled after castle on Rhine River.

1:01 (0:00) Arrive Red Wing which is situated at upstream end of Lake Pepin. Just south of station, historic St. James Hotel can be seen on left. Its 41 rooms are adorned in Victorian splendor, and each named for a famous riverboat that once plied waters of Mississippi. Built in 1875, Red Wing Shoe Company saved it from decay in late 1970s with an ambitious restoration program. Prior to invention of dining cars, trains stopped here to feed passengers in hotel's well-regarded restaurant.

 RED WING, MN - This lovely riverside community takes its name from generations of Sioux Chieftains who chose as their emblem a swan's wing dyed scarlet. Long known for its manufacture of shoes and pottery, tourists are presently discovering a wealth of recreational opportunities in the hills, forests and rivers surrounding Red Wing.

0:00 (1:04) Depart Red Wing. Then scores of boat shelters appear at marina on right.

0:07 (0:57) Prairie Island is home to nuclear power plant, with its reactor domes and banks of cooling units, appearing on right.

0:20 (0:44) Cross Mississippi River, its lakes and inlets bordering on left into St. Paul/Minneapolis.

0:43 (0:21) On left, St. Paul Downtown Airport can be seen across river. At same time, city skyline juts imposingly above horizon in distance.

0:49 (0:15) On left, old sternwheelers are frequently moored alongside Harriet Island. St. Paul's former Union Station is expansive brown brick building stretching away from tracks on right.

0:50 (0:14) Modeled after St. Peter's in Rome, magnificent St. Paul Cathedral on right is readily identified by its verdigris domes and outstanding classical architecture.

0:53 (0:11) Whimsical, castle-like facilities on left are home of Landmark Brewery.

1:04 (0:00) Arrive modernistic Minneapolis-St. Paul's Midway Station.

MINNEAPOLIS-ST. PAUL, MN - After Lt. Zebulon M. Pike explored the region, Ft. Snelling was established in 1819 approximately five miles from the current site of St. Paul. Its location as the northernmost navigable portion of the Mississippi River made the region a natural port and trade center. St. Paul received its start as a trading post while Minneapolis was born somewhat later when flour and lumber mills were started on the other side of the river.

Today, those industries are still impor-

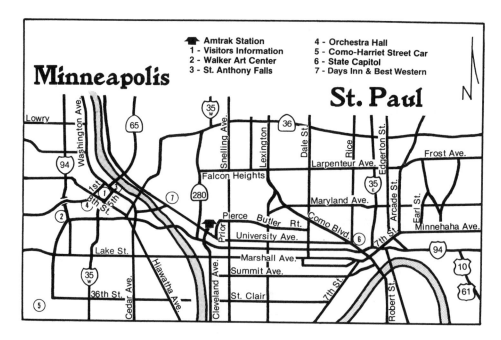

Minneapolis

St. Paul

Amtrak Station
1 - Visitors Information
2 - Walker Art Center
3 - St. Anthony Falls

4 - Orchestra Hall
5 - Como-Harriet Street Car
6 - State Capitol
7 - Days Inn & Best Western

tant to the area's economy, and the "Twin Cities" are the financial, cultural and industrial focal point of the upper Midwest. Their combined population is well over two million and St. Paul is the capital of Minnesota. Companies like General Mills, Control Data and Dayton Hudson are headquartered here. Clean, modern, young and growing are first impressions, and an elaborate pedestrian "skyway" system throughout downtown Minneapolis makes legendary winters more tolerable.

Midway Station, 730 Transfer Road, St. Paul, is literally "midway" between the two downtown areas of Minneapolis and St. Paul, being approximately four miles from each. Storage lockers, luggage carts and food and beverage machines are available at the station. Free parking is adjacent to the station.

Yellow **Cab** (direct line in station), 824-0228. Budget **rental cars** are located downtown Minneapolis, 727-2000. **Local buses** (16A) run along University Ave. (two blocks south of the station at Transfer Rd.) and provide service to both downtowns.

Minneapolis Convention and Visitors Assn., has visitors center at City Center on the Skyway level. Call (612) 661-4700 or 800-445-7412.

Although there are motels closer to the station, those listed below are in a more desirable location. These are conveniently situated in the University area near downtown Minneapolis, and the 16A bus line provides service not only to downtown Minneapolis and downtown St. Paul but also to within two blocks of the station. They are about two miles from the station.

-**Days Inn University of Minnesota**, 2407 University Ave., SE, 55414; (612) 623-3999. Attractive high rise, free continental breakfast, $60.

-**Best Western University Inn**, 2600 University Ave., SE, 55414; (612) 379-2313. $65.

The nation's longest shopping plaza, **Nicollet Mall**, stretches along Nicollet Ave. in downtown Minneapolis. Saks, Dayton's and Neiman Marcus are just some of the stores that anchor this area. **Loring Park** (and lake) is a great place to relax in the heart of the city.

The **Mall of America**, in the suburb of Bloomington, is the largest fully enclosed retail mall and amusement park in the nation. This extravaganza was opened in 1992.

Rail fans will be interested in the **Como-Harriet Streetcar Line and Minnesota Transportation Museum** southwest of downtown.

0:00 (1:25) Departing Minneapolis-St. Paul, in distance left, 57-story I.D.S. Tower is prominent landmark of downtown Minneapolis.

1:25 (0:00) Arrive St. Cloud.

 ST. CLOUD, MN - Set scenically along the banks of the Mississippi River, St. Cloud is noted for its numerous granite quarries which have supplied stone for many venerable structures throughout the country.

0:00 (0:59) Depart St. Cloud.

0:59 (0:00) Arrive Staples.

STAPLES, MN - Once a dying railroad town, Staples' fortunes improved dramatically when its Vocational Training Institute was established in 1960.

0:00 (0:54) Depart Staples.

0:54 (0:00) Arrive Detroit Lakes.

DETROIT LAKES, MN - Surrounded by no fewer than 412 lakes, Detroit Lakes is the hub of a vast recreation haven. Although outdoor adventure is nearly limitless, fishing is still king, with walleye, bass and sunfish the most frequent catches.

0:00 (0:56) Depart Detroit Lakes.

0:56 (0:00) Arrive Fargo.

FARGO, ND - Lying in the heart of the fertile Red River Valley, Fargo is North Dakota's largest city, and is a vital commercial and livestock center for a vast region. Named for the founder of the Wells Fargo Express Company, Fargo is a stop for students attending North Dakota State University located here.

0:00 (1:20) Depart Fargo.

1:20 (0:00) Arrive West Grand Forks, a western suburb of Grand Forks.

GRAND FORKS, ND - As suggested by its name, Grand Forks is situated at the confluence of the Red Lake River and the Red River of the North. Located here, the University of North Dakota lends a collegiate atmosphere to this agriculturally oriented community. A 1980s study named Grand Forks and State College, PA the least stressful cities in America.

0:00 (1:23) Depart West Grand Forks.

1:23 (0:00) Arrive Devils Lake.

DEVILS LAKE, ND - Settled along the shores of North Dakota's largest natural lake, Devils Lake is acclaimed as the goose- and duck-hunting capital of North America. Not always held in such high esteem, Sioux and Chippewa Indians originally named the lake in deference to the evil spirits that once overturned their canoes in the midst of a fierce inter-tribal battle.

0:00 (1:02) Depart Devils Lake.

1:02 (0:00) Arrive Rugby.

RUGBY, ND - As well as an agricultural stronghold, Rugby is noted as the geographical center of North America. Located a half-mile south of town, a towering stone monument pays tribute to this distinction.

0:00 (1:06) Depart Rugby.

1:06 (0:00) Arrive Minot.

MINOT, ND - Once a desolate frontier outpost, Minot has blossomed into a flourishing industrial mecca, due in large part to its abundant natural resources of oil and coal. Set along the House River that frequently floods the town, Minot is also host to numerous military installations that further supplement its economy.

0:00 (0:50) Depart Minot.

0:50 (0:00) Arrive Stanley.

STANLEY, ND - Grain and livestock production are the foremost concerns of this small agricultural community. A prominent focal point of the town is the resplendent Montrail County Courthouse, located just north of the train station.

0:00 (1:05) Depart Stanley.

1:05 (0:00) Arrive Williston.

 WILLISTON, ND - Since completion of the Garrison Dam Project along the adjacent Missouri River, Williston has maintained a dependable agricultural and livestock trade, virtually free from threat of drought that frequently plagued the region. Yet, like Minot, oil discoveries have played an important part in Williston's development.

Just west of Williston are two important historical sites: Fort Union which in its heyday was one of the most active trading posts in the West and Fort Buford where Chief Sitting Bull surrendered following the Battle of Little Bighorn.

0:00 (1:28) Departing Williston, Missouri River joins on left and follows intermittently for next 60 miles.

0:24 (1:04) Cross North Dakota state line into Montana and proceed through one of world's largest grain production belts.

Gain one hour as train passes from Central to Mountain Time. Set your watch back (forward if eastbound) one hour.

0:52 (0:36) Just west of Culbertson, enter grounds of Fort Peck Indian Reservation that extend nearly ninety miles west to Nashua.

1:12 (0:16) Cross Poplar River.

1:28 (0:00) Arrive Wolf Point.

WOLF POINT, MT - Once a popular haunt of wolf trappers, Wolf Point is host each July to the "Wild Horse Stampede," acclaimed statewide as the "granddaddy of Montana rodeos."

0:00 (0:45) Depart Wolf Point.

0:40 (0:04) Approaching Glasgow, beautiful farmstead is nestled amidst wooded glen on left. Bordering property is Milk River which train follows and crosses periodically to Havre.

0:45 (0:00) Letter "G" inscribed on hillside at right denotes arrival at Glasgow.

GLASGOW, MT - Lying in the heart of the Great Northern Wheat Belt, Glasgow has flourished in earnest since construction of the Fort Peck Dam just south of town. Glasgow is also renowned as a haven for fossil hunters. Exhibits at the Fort Peck Museum display the many varieties of dinosaur bones that have been found in the region.

0:00 (0:59) Depart Glasgow.

0:50 (0:08) Cross arm of Lake Bowdoin. Abundance of waterfowl denotes success of nearby Bowdoin National Wildlife Refuge.

0:59 (0:00) Arrive Malta.

MALTA, MT - Once the center of a great cattle empire, the region surrounding Malta was also the inspirational setting for many works of the famous artist Charles Russell whose paintings so vividly captured the unbridled spirit of the Western frontier.

0:00 (1:13) Depart Malta.

0:09 (1:04) Here in Wagner, at turn of the century, Butch Cassidy and The Sundance Kid carried out one of their many successful train robberies, escaping with nearly $70,000.

0:30 (0:43) Passing through Savoy, note quaint old country schoolhouse on right. Built in 1916, drought and crop failures of early '70s precipitated a rapid decline in enrollment. School had only four students left when finally closed in 1974.

0:45 (0:28) In Zurich, another venerable schoolhouse stands proudly on right.

A few miles south of town lies historic Chief Joseph Battleground of the Bear's Paw. In 1877, after a 1,700-mile retreat through some of the most rugged country in the West, a disheartened Chief Joseph surrendered proclaiming, "From where the sun now stands, I will fight no more forever."

1:13 (0:00) Finely preserved S-2 steam locomotive of Great Northern Railway previews arrival at Havre station on left.

HAVRE, MT - Once the commercial hub of a sprawling agricultural region, Havre's attention is more recent times has focused on discoveries of natural gas. Of Havre's many interesting attractions, the H.Earl Clark Museum, with its famous "Buffalo Jump Site," is one of the most popular. Here beneath precipitous cliffs are the skeletal remains of buffalo herds driven to a death plunge by Indian hunters.

0:00 (1:35) Depart Havre.

0:04 (1:31) On right, Milk River departs north for a brief tour of Canada before

Two Medicine River Trestle — near East Glacier, MT
DORIS SWANSON

returning to its source amidst Montana's Glacier National Park.

1:35 (0:00) Arrive Shelby.

 SHELBY, MT - Although oil and farming are the principal concerns here, Shelby is most remembered as the unlikely site of the 1923 world heavyweight championship fight between Jack Dempsey and Tommy Gibbons.

Remembering Dempsey after his death in 1983, a *Time* magazine writer opined that Shelby had a fight "the way Johnstown had a flood." The town of 2,000 constructed a 40,000-seat arena but then had trouble raising the guaranteed purse. While 24,000 attended the Fourth of July bout, only 7,000 bothered to pay; the rest crashed the gates. Dempsey won on points, the promoter skipped town, two banks failed and the town was left insolvent.

0:00 (0:29) Depart Shelby.

0:29 (0:00) Arrive Cut Bank.

CUT BANK, MT - Another bastion of agriculture, livestock and oil production, Cut Bank often has the unglorious distinction of recording the nation's coldest midwinter temperatures.

0:00 (0:32) Depart Cut Bank across high trestle spanning Cut Bank Creek. Dramatic panorama of Rocky Mountain peaks begins to jut above the horizon, becoming more and more dramatic as train approaches Glacier National Park. Enroute, pass through territory of Blackfeet Indian Reservation.

0:22 (0:11) On left, small obelisk alongside highway commemorates northernmost explorations of Lewis and Clark when searching for passage through Rocky Mountains.

0:32 (0:00) Arrive Browning.

BROWNING, MT - A seasonal winter stop, Browning lies in the heart of the Blackfeet Indian Reservation, and is a popular shopping haunt for Native American goods.

0:00 (0:18) Depart Browning.

0:16 (0:02) Cross Two Medicine River atop lofty trestle.

0:18 (0:00) Arrive Glacier Park Station. In early 1900s, Great Northern Railway transported timber in from Washington and Oregon to construct spacious Glacier Park Lodge on right, as well as other hotel facilities within Park. Development not only promoted rail travel along their line, but enlightened tourists to a previously untapped vacation haven.

GLACIER PARK STATION, MT (East Glacier) - This seasonal summer stop is the gateway to untold adventure amidst the breathtaking beauty of Glacier National Park. Established by Congress in 1910, hundreds of miles of hiking trails now lead to the rich forests, shimmering lakes and flower-blanketed meadows of this Rocky Mountain retreat. As reflected in its name, the Park is also home to 50 "living" glaciers, among the few in the U.S. considered relatively accessible.

Jacobson's Cottages, Box 101, East Glacier, MT, 59434; (406) 226-4422. Light and cheerful cabins, about one mile from the station.

-**Glacier Park Lodge**, East Glacier, MT, 59434; (406) 226-5551 or 800-332-9351. Built by Great Northern Railway with huge, timbered lobby. Faces station. $80.

0:00 (1:43) Departing Glacier Park Station, begin ascent of Marias Pass and Continental Divide just south of Glacier National Park. Within minutes, rolling terrain of last 1,500 miles gives way to jagged intrusions of Rocky Mountains. On western slopes of pass, scenery is even more dramatic as train winds past waterfalls, river gorges and other wondrous spectacles of this diverse alpine geography.

0:20 (1:23) Arriving 5,213-foot summit of Marias Pass (lowest Rocky Mountain rail crossing in U.S.), tall monument seen on left is commemorative to Theodore Roosevelt for whom adjacent highway is named. Statue proclaims explorations of John Stevens, civil engineer for Great Northern Railroad. Prior to completion of highway across pass in 1930, autos were loaded onto rail cars and transported from one side to the other.

Although reputedly traversed by Indians during inter-tribal raids, abortive and inaccurate attempts at charting this area gave rise to its original designation as "Mystery Pass." It was only when the railroad hired Stevens in 1889 that this elusive passage was at last established as a permanent route through the northern Rockies.

0:56 (0:47) From high atop dramatic trestle, cross Flathead River which then proceeds to follow on right.

1:03 (0:40) Small village of Essex features impressive Izaak Walton Hotel on right. This Tudor-style structure was originally built to house railroad workers. Helper engines are stationed in Essex to help freights surmount Continental Divide. This is a flag stop for the *Builder*.

Izaak Walton Inn, P.O. Box 653, Essex, MT 59916; (406) 888-5700. Built by Great Northern Railway for train crews. A rustic inn with railroad motif faces the rail yards. Shuttle van to and from nearby station stop. $72. Also, smartly decorated cabooses available as living units, 3-day minimum, $425.

1:43 (0:00) Arrive West Glacier.

WEST GLACIER, MT - This stop affords access to the western reaches of Glacier National Park.

0:00 (0:31) Depart West Glacier.

0:10 (0:20) Cross Flathead River which is soon joined by South Fork approaching from left.

0:17 (0:13) Large Anaconda aluminum plant on right is one industrial stronghold of Columbia Falls. Once in midst of town, note old steam locomotive preserved on left.

0:31 (0:00) Old Bavarian-style station is a handsome sight on left arriving Whitefish.

WHITEFISH, MT - Besides its proximity to Glacier National Park, Whitefish is only 25 miles from Flathead Lake, the largest natural freshwater lake west of the Mississippi. Closer to home, Whitefish Lake borders the town to the north, and is a noteworthy attraction in its own right.

0:00 (1:54) Depart Whitefish.

0:44 (1:05) Penetrate seven-mile-long

Izaak Walton Inn — Essex, MT
DORIS SWANSON

Flathead Tunnel, third longest in North America.

1:45 (0:00) Arrive Libby.

 LIBBY, MT - From its formative development as a gold-mining town, Libby is now the center of an active logging industry, with tours of its sawmills and processing plants an interesting attraction. The region is also rich in vermiculite, mined for its use as a horticultural rooting agent.

0:00 (1:50) Depart Libby.

Gain one hour as train passes from Mountain to Pacific Time. Set your watch back (forward if eastbound) one hour.

1:50 (0:00) Arrive Sandpoint.

SANDPOINT - ID - Set along the shores of beautiful Lake Pend Oreille (a seemingly bottomless lake which produces occasional "sightings" of its own sea monster), Sandpoint is rapidly emerging as one of the most popular vacations resorts of the Northwest.

0:00 (1:13) Depart Sandpoint and cross mouth of Pend Oreille River on ultra-long (8,000-foot) deck bridge.

1:13 (0:00) Arrive Spokane.

SPOKANE, WA - From its humble beginnings as a sawmill town, Spokane has emerged as one of the most vibrant cities of the Northwest, set alongside the thundering falls of the Spokane River. An important rail center as well, the Great Northern Clock Tower (that presided atop what was once one of the nation's finest train stations) remains a cherished landmark of the downtown district.

Spokane was host to the 1974 World's Fair, its facilities built around the site of the town's original sawmill. Several of the Fair's most prominent attractions are now preserved amidst the beautifully landscaped acreage of Riverfront Park.

Also of interest is Spokane's Old Flour Mill, refurbished as a delightful setting for cozy shops and restaurants. Further shopping adventures are also in store along the city's Skywalk, a ten-block enclave of retail merchants, interconnected by glass-enclosed walkways suspended above the downtown streets.

(At Spokane, the Portland and Seattle sections of the *Builder* divide. Spokane to Seattle route appears first below.)

For route from Spokane to Portland, see page 147.

0:00 (2:05) Depart Spokane.

2:05 (0:00) Arrive Ephrata.

EPHRATA, WA - A town of 5,000, it is in the heart of irrigated farmland with water coming from the Columbia River Basin irrigation project.

0:00 (1:00) Depart Ephrata.

0:40 (0:20) Pass Rock Island Dam, stretching across Columbia River, on left.

0:45 (0:15) Cut sharply to left and cross Columbia, then roll high above its west bank into Wenatchee.

1:00 (0:00) Arrive Wenatchee. Note new glass-box depot in place of more traditional one, still standing nearby.

WENATCHEE, WA - Another of the world's "Apple Capitals," Wenatchee is nestled in the scenic foothills of the Cascade Mountains that provide the ideal climes for its abundant orchards.

0:00 (2:55) Depart Wenatchee, rolling past warehouses surrounded by piles of skids and apple crates with Wenatchee River to left.

0:22 (2:33) Curving right, squeeze between rocks and Wenatchee River. Train crosses river three times in next five minutes while approaching Cascades, with mountains beginning to appear at left.

0:30 (2:25) Begin gradual climb out of river valley and pass through Bavarianesque Leavenworth, a 19-century railroad center. Town literally resorted to its alpine-lodging-and-cuckoo-clock appearance in 1962 when town's economy was failing.

0:34 (2:20) Scenic mountains on left offer preview of what is to come.

In the next several minutes, the *Builder* passes through a beautiful valley dotted with houses, barns and horses, and then enters the first of several tunnels built to establish this incredible route through the Cascades.

0:44 (2:10) Soon after first tunnel, again cross Wenatchee River with beautiful scenery to both sides.

0:59 (1:55) At Merritt, old wooden water tower is visible to right as train slows for its charge through mountains.

1:05 (1:48) Roll across trestle over a beautiful canyon, move through another tunnel,

and emerge with tumbling river on right which is followed to Cascade Tunnel, as scenery becomes more dramatic.

1:14 (1:40) Enter Cascade Tunnel, 2,247 feet above sea level, a 7.8-mile bore beneath forbidding Stevens Pass and taking 15 minutes to traverse.

Completed in 1929, it is the second longest railroad tunnel in North America, exceeded only by the 9.1-mile-long Mount MacDonald Tunnel through the Canadian Rockies.

1:29 (1:25) Emerge from Cascade Tunnel, soon passing sign at right correctly indicating that our location is "Scenic."

1:34 (1:20) "Cross roaring South Skykomish River which will be followed to Everett north of Seattle.

1:37 (1:15) Rushing stream and small waterfall appear to left of train. Tall trees, huge granite rocks, ravines and streams dominate our curving route punctuated by crossing of Skykomish River on high steel trestles.

1:47 (1:05) Curve to right across a spectacular steel trestle high above fast-moving Foss River on its way to join Skykomish.

1:55 (0:57) Roll through old railroad town of Skykomish. Skykomish Hotel, on right, has been social hub of community since its completion in 1904. Train crews still park their engines in front and go in for a hearty lunch. On left, multi-storied concrete structure once was power plant for railroad when 71-mile section from here through Cascade Tunnel was electrified. Diesels took over in 1956. Old Great Northern depot also still stands.

2:09 (0:45) Roll past Sunset Falls, actually a steep rapids, on left. Vertical cliffs and spectacular finger-like Mt. Index rise above valley floor beyond river.

2:11 (0:43) Cross river at village of Index, on right. Large boardinghouse-like building at southwest corner of town, partially hidden by trees, is historic Bush House, a 1904 hostelry which once accommodated such notables as Calvin Coolidge, Teddy Roosevelt, William Howard Taft and William Jennings Bryan.

2:33 (0:21) Gradually leave Cascades

behind for flatter terrain, and enter Monroe.
2:55 (0:00) Arrive Everett.

EVERETT, WA - Noted foremost for its lumber production and airplane manufacturing, Everett's location along a natural landlocked harbor is likewise tailor-made for a shipping and fishing industry that continues to flourish.

0:00 (0:23) Depart Everett southbound, skirting shoreline of Puget Sound. Whidbey Island can be seen directly right, while peaks of Olympic Range loom majestically in distance.

0:23 (0:00) Arriving Edmonds, state ferries shuttling to and from Olympic Peninsula can be observed on right.

EDMONDS, WA - Self-proclaimed as the "Gem of the Puget Sound," Edmonds is a gracious residential suburb, only 15 miles north of Seattle's city center.

0:00 (0:31) Depart Edmonds.

0:04 (0:27) Large refinery and dockside facilities are entrenched along waterfront at Point Wells.

0:10 (0:21) Approaching Seattle, colonies of sailboats are a picturesque backyard spectacle for a host of elegant homes, perched atop colorfully foliated sea cliffs on left.

0:14 (0:17) Statue of Leif Ericson maintains vigil over hundreds of boats tethered at Shilshole Bay Moorage on right. Across water lies Bainbridge Island.

0:16 (0:15) Temporarily depart coastline route, crossing Salmon Bay inlet of Puget Sound. In middle of bridge, note elaborate Chittenden Locks on left, affording access to more easterly ports along Lake Washington.

0:21 (0:10) Travel through grounds of U.S. Naval Reservation before emerging amidst Seattle's colorful waterfront district.

0:23 (0:08) On right, Pier 70 is largest wooden building to be restored in America. In its heyday, warehouse was chock full of teas and spices arriving from Orient. Today, imaginative shops and restaurants are tucked within this historic structure.

On left, Seattle's towering "Space Needle" was centerpiece of 1962 World's Fair. In foreground, delicate arches front grounds of Pacific Science Center.

0:30 (0:01) Enter tunnel, then emerge minutes later. White castle-like Smith Tower was tallest building west of Mississippi River when constructed in 1914. Fanciful clock tower to its left rises above King Street Station, western terminus of *Empire Builder* route.

0:31 (0:00) Arrive Seattle.

 SEATTLE, WA - See page 232.

SPOKANE TO PORTLAND ROUTE LOG

0:00 (2:36) Depart Spokane.

2:36 (0:00) Arrive Pasco.

PASCO, WA - The community has been closely linked to transportation, with rail lines radiating in all directions, as well as river freight transfers due to its location at the confluence of the Columbia and Snake Rivers. This is the Columbia's farthest navigable point for sizable ships.

0:00 (1:55) Depart Pasco.

1:12 (0:43) Now, Columbia River makes its dramatic appearance at left. This 1,210-mile giant produces more than one-third of America's hydroelectric power! Bluffs on other side are northern edge of Oregon's landscape. River traffic, mostly tugs pushing barges, will be quite heavy between here and Vancouver.

1:19 (0:36) This is Roosevelt, with grain-loading facilities between tracks and river.

1:25 (0:30) An unusual orchard "oasis," surrounded by slender poplar trees, is above to right.

1:32 (0:23) River begins to look more gorge-like as train moves closer to Pacific.

1:40 (0:15) Impressive John Day Dam backs up Columbia, on left. Navigational lock is on this side of river and handles eight million tons of commercial traffic each year. With 113 feet maximum lift, it is one of world's highest single lift locks. Dam's 16 generating units can produce enough electricity to handle needs of two Seattles.

1:45 (0:10) Bridge spanning Columbia is U.S. 97. Maryhill Museum is located here; originally built as a mansion, it was dedicated as a museum by Queen of Romania in 1920s and now houses an extensive collection of rare art. Above tracks is Stonehenge, built as a memorial to World War I dead by railroad entrepreneur Sam Hill and is a replica of its namesake in England.

1:52 (0:03) Through a brief tunnel, one of thirteen between Pasco and Vancouver.

1:55 (0:00) Arrive at rail yards of Wishram.

 WISHRAM, WA - This is primarily a stop for railroad workers, with one of the last railroad-operated "beaneries" in the country.

0:00 (0:29) Depart Wishram.

0:01 (0:28) Rail bridge crossing Columbia is Burlington Northern line.

0:10 (0:19) The Dalles Dam (pronounced dals) staggers across Columbia, making two-mile-long Z. Powerhouse, located in portion of the dam which runs parallel to the tracks, is half-mile long and contains 22 generators. Town of The Dalles can be seen on the Oregon shore. White building above on bluff is unique electric rectifier, changing AC to DC for transmission to Los Angeles.

0:23 (0:06) Mount Hood, highest peak in Oregon at 11,235 feet and continually snow-capped, rises like a pyramidal specter in distance to left.

0:29 (0:00) Arrive Bingen-White Salmon.

BINGEN-WHITE SALMON, WA - This is orchard country. From here west, foliage will become more abundant due to high annual rainfall.

0:00 (1:13) Depart Bingen-White Salmon.

0:07 (1:06) Venerable Hood River Hotel can be spotted across river with waterfalls higher up.

0:13 (1:00) More falls can be seen across river as train enters Columbia Gorge, once explored by Lewis and Clark.

0:16 (0:57) *Empire Builder* slows to a crawl and now crosses geographic fault that is so active tracks must be realigned almost monthly.

0:23 (0:50) Enter a rain forest, having left near-desert country just minutes ago.

0:30 (0:43) Bridge of the Gods, a magnificent web of steel, crosses Columbia on "exact spot" where legendary natural stone bridge of Indians supposedly fell into river when nearby volcanic peaks argued, causing ground to tremble. Town of Cascade Locks is on far shore.

0:33 (0:40) Bonneville Dam, forming 48-mile-long Lake Bonneville, utilizes two islands in mid-stream to help close off river's flow. This was earliest of Columbia River dams.

0:38 (0:35) Sheer-walled, 800-foot monolith on right is Beacon Rock, proclaimed to be largest such formation in U.S. and second only to Gibraltar.

0:40 (0:33) Most spectacular of waterfalls on far side is 620-foot Multnomah Falls, third highest in nation. Its downward plunge ends in beautiful tree-lined pool.

0:46 (0:27) Longest tunnel of day is 2,369 feet in length and penetrates Cape Horn on western edge of Cascades as we exit Columbia Gorge.

1:13 (0:00) Arrive Vancouver where delightful chalet-style depot greets passengers.

From here to Portland *Empire Builder* **follows route of the** *Coast Starlight.* **See page 235.**

California Zephyr

Named after a gentle west wind, the *California Zephyr* breezes along one of Amtrak's most delightful routes. Not so long ago, in the fifties and sixties, its predecessor by the same name was considered the West's premier train. Today's *Zephyr* unquestionably vies for that same honor, revealing much of America's finest scenery to passengers riding comfortably in state-of-the-art Superliner equipment. The verdant croplands of northern Illinois and southern Iowa, a splendid excursion through the heart of the Colorado Rockies, and finally a trek over magnificent Donner Pass of the Sierra Nevadas are highlights of this two-day adventure.

This trip is also a visit to some very historic moments in U.S. railroading. The first generation of diesel streamliners, the *Pioneer Zephyr*, made much of its inaugural run along these tracks in 1934, blazing a dawn-to-dusk nonstop dash from Denver to Chicago in just over 13 hours—a stellar accomplishment, even by today's standards. And in the Far West, today's train follows much of the route established when the race was on to build America's first transcontinental railroad—the successful construction of which stands as one of the world's greatest railroading achievements.

This blend of beauty and history makes the *California Zephyr* a very special train, and riding it a very special event. American poet Joaquin Miller brought things into perspective when he pointed out there is "more poetry in the rush of a single railroad train across the continent" than there is in all of the "story of burning Troy."

WESTBOUND SCHEDULE (Condensed)
Chicago, IL - Midafternoon Departure
Omaha, NE - Late Evening
Denver, CO - Early Morning (2nd Day)
Salt Lake City, UT - Late Evening (2nd Day)
Reno, NV - Midmorning (3rd Day)
Oakland, CA - Late Afternoon Arrival (3rd Day)*

EASTBOUND SCHEDULE (Condensed)
Oakland, CA - Midmorning Departure*
Reno, NV - Late Afternoon
Salt Lake City, UT - Early Morning (2nd Day)
Denver, CO - Midevening (2nd Day)
Omaha, NE - Early Morning (3rd Day)
Chicago, IL - Late Afternoon Arrival (3rd Day)
*Motorcoach transfer between nearby Emeryville stop and San Francisco.

FREQUENCY - Four times a week. Depart Chicago Sun, Tues, Wed, Fri. Depart Oakland Mon, Wed, Fri, Sat.
SEATING - Superliner coaches.
DINING - Complete meal and beverage service. Sandwiches, snacks and beverages in Sightseer Lounge.
SLEEPING - Superliner sleepers with deluxe, family, economy and special bedrooms.
BAGGAGE - Checked baggage handled at

larger cities.
RESERVATIONS - All-reserved train.
LENGTH OF TRIP - 2,425 miles in 52 hours.
ON-BOARD GUIDE - Weekdays, Reno-Sacramento segment.

ROUTE LOG

 CHICAGO, IL - See page 63.
0:00 (0:35) Depart Chicago.
After emerging from beneath Chicago's huge post office, slowly pull through Amtrak's coach yards, then, picking up speed, take a westward course through lighter industrial areas, with familiar names such as Ryerson Steel, Kroehler, Burlington Northern and Nabisco in evidence. Numerous commuter stops, such as Berwyn, La Grange, Western Springs and Hinsdale, are mere blurs as "Windy City's majestic skyline, dominated by twin-spiked Sears Tower, slowly narrows on eastern horizon.
0:35 (0:00) Arrive Naperville.

NAPERVILLE, IL - This attractive town has replaced Aurora as Chicago's western suburban stop. Connections are made here to commuter trains serving towns along the Burlington Northern between Chicago's Union Station and Aurora.
0:00 (1:06) Depart Naperville.
0:09 (0:57) Upon entering Aurora, note dilapidated stone roundhouse on right. This relic of bygone days is the oldest such structure still standing in U.S. Adjacent buildings are Burlington shops where Vistadome cars and early dining cars were first designed. The Chicago, Burlington and Quincy Railroad got its start here in 1844. Aurora also claims the distinction of being the first city in Illinois to install electric street lights.
0:11 (0:55) Cross Fox River.
0:53 (0:13) Two small "mountains" in distance to left are mine tailings which mark spot of one of nation's worst coal mine disasters. In 1909 a fire ignited, resulting in the deaths of over 200 miners.
1:06 (0:00) Upon arriving at Princeton, note

quaint community picnic shelter, at left.
PRINCETON, IL - Founded in 1833, this fine old town interestingly claims to be the world's pig capital, while at the same time takes on the motto "where tradition meets progress."
0:00 (0:49) Depart Princeton.
0:23 (0:26) Passing through Kewanee, historic Kewanee Boiler Corporation's old brick buildings face tracks on right.
0:30 (0:19) Hog farming is not limited to the Princeton area, but is prevalent throughout Illinois and Iowa. Small A-frame buildings, on left, are typical shelters for porkers.
0:38 (0:11) When passing through Oneida, be sure to look to left at what must be world's smallest high school—it's about five-foot square and not much higher, with "High School" written over the door.
0:49 (0:00) Arrive at Galesburg's handsome new South Seminary Street Station. Gaggle of railroad antiquities can be seen at right.
GALESBURG, IL - Reverend George Washington Gale chose this spot for a ministers' college after searching westward on behalf of a fundamentalist Presbyterian group located in Oneida, New York. Famed American poet Carl Sandburg was raised here, and this was the site of a Lincoln-Douglas Debate in 1858. Olmstead Ferris, a "Galesburgite" (and a relative of George Washington Ferris, inventor of the Ferris wheel), was an important experimenter with popcorn—one of the area's important products. This was such a novelty in those days that Ferris gave a corn-popping command performance before England's Queen Victoria and Prince Albert.
0:00 (0:44) Depart Galesburg through Burlington Northern freight yards, then watch on right for Knox College, site of 1858 Lincoln-Douglas debate, and identified by bell-topped building.
0:09 (0:35) Pass beneath main line of Santa Fe. This is route once used by legendary *Super Chief* between Chicago and Los Angeles, and now traveled by Amtrak's *Southwest Chief.*
0:18 (0:25) Cruise through Monmouth, birthplace of Wyatt Earp—one of West's

Coffeepot water tower, Stanton, IA
JACK SWANSON

most famous lawmen.

0:41 (0:02) *Zephyr* now crosses mighty Mississippi River, where splendid views of river and town of Burlington are afforded from a 2,002-foot-long bridge. At midstream, enter Iowa and leave Illinois. From its source to its Gulf-of-Mexico outlet, this great river travels 2,350 miles and drains an area equal to two-fifths of U.S.

0:44 (0:00) Arrive Burlington, where steam engine #3003 is enclosed by fence just beyond station, on left.

BURLINGTON, IA - The Indians considered this neutral territory since it was one of the few locations in the region where important flint could be acquired for tools and weapons. Burlington holds the distinction of having served as a temporary capital of two territories—Wisconsin in 1837 and Iowa from 1838 to 1841—when its river location gave it considerable prominence. Later, the convergence of three railroads made it a

major rail hub as the river's dominance waned. Much of the research in developing George Westinghouse's air brake occurred on West Burlington Hill—perhaps one of the most significant advancements in railroading technology.

0:00 (0:30) Depart Burlington and slip through older portion of downtown, nearly touching some of buildings that virtually enshroud tracks. Three spires of St. John's Catholic Church are prominent on crest of hill to left.

0:01 (0:29) While passing beneath 6th Avenue Bridge, look up to right for glimpse of "Snake Alley," once dubbed by Ripley as "crookedest street in the world."

0:08 (0:22) Burlington shops are on immediate right.

0:12 (0:18) Facility on left is Iowa Army Ammunition Plant—presumably U.S. Army in Iowa.

0:30 (0:00) Arrive at attractive little town of Mt. Pleasant.

MT. PLEASANT, IA - Originally accessed by three toll roads which were protected from the elements by plank surfaces, Mt. Pleasant was eventually reached by railroad, putting the expensive toll roads out of business (they charged two cents a mile). Today, the Midwest Old Settlers and Threshers Association holds an annual reunion for five days ending each Labor Day. This event has grown to become internationally famous, involving antique farm machinery, autos, crafts, "old thresher meals" and much more.

0:00 (0:39) Depart Mt. Pleasant. Historic Iowa Wesleyan College will be on right in just a moment. School was founded in 1842, making it oldest collegiate institution west of Mississippi River.

0:16 (0:23) Entrance to Fairfield is easily identified by golf course and small lake to right of tracks at east edge of town.

Fairfield has the distinction of being home to Maharishi International University, partially visible off to the right, the only school in the U.S. to make transcendental meditation basic to its curriculum. Started in Santa Barbara in 1973 by Maharishi

Mahesh Yogi, the university moved here in 1974 and occupies the 260-acre campus of now-defunct Parson's College. Two gold domes are twice-daily meditation places for the entire student body.

0:30 (0:09) White stone letters on right, reading "Chief Wapello," commemorate former Fox Indian leader, buried in this park. It was here in 1842 that a treaty was signed purchasing Iowa from Sac and Fox Indians.

0:39 (0:00) Arriving Ottumwa, John Deere plant and Hormel meat-packing facility on left are typical of industries which have been foundation of community's past.

OTTUMWA, IA - Located on the banks of the Des Moines River, the city is a major trading center of southeastern Iowa. The city council proclaimed Ottumwa as the "Video Gaming Capital of the World" when the first American video championships were held here in 1983. The elegantly stark house which served as a backdrop for Grant Wood's classic painting "American Gothic" is at nearby Eldon.

0:00 (1:15) Departing Ottumwa, large brick structure on hill to right is Ottumwa High School.

0:05 (1:10) Cross Des Moines River, a serene tributary of Mississippi River.

0:08 (1:07) In Chillicothe, birdhouses fill front yard of feathered creatures' friend, on left.

0:10 (1:05) Off to right, smokestack and coal conveyors identify one of newer Iowa Southern power plants.

1:00 (0:15) Through Lucas where sign in park at right identifies this as birthplace of John L. Lewis, foremost national labor leader of his time and known for his stern appearance and bushy eyebrows. John L. Lewis Mining-Labor Museum is in town beyond park.

1:15 (0:00) Arrive Osceola.

OSCEOLA, IA - The first settlers arrived here in the mid-1800s and named their settlement in honor of a Seminole Indian chief. Supposedly the first delicious apple tree was discovered 30 miles from here, becoming the ancestor of some eight million fruit trees.

Bust of Osceola — Osceola, IA
JACK SWANSON

0:00 (0:30) Depart Osceola.

0:02 (0:28) Note large carved bust by Peter Toth of Osceola himself, at shopping center on left.

0:16 (0:14) Cross Grand River.

0:30 (0:00) Arrive Creston.

CRESTON, IA - Creston has long been a railroad town and at one time sported large rail yards, a roundhouse and shops. One of the early-day engineers gained renown by noisily roasting two ears of corn for lunch each day using his engine's steam whistle.

0:00 (1:42) Depart Creston.

0:22 (1:20) Community of Corning, on left, is birthplace of comedian Johnny Carson.

0:39 (1:03) Whimsical water tower, on right, is enormous coffeepot (640,000 cups!) in honor of Mrs. Olsen (Virginia Christine), once known for TV coffee commercials and who was born here in Stanton. Not surprisingly, town considers itself "Swedish Capital of Iowa."

0:46 (0:56) In Red Oak, on right, grand old brick Montgomery County Courthouse is centerpiece for town, crowned with a clock tower and flagstaff. Completed in 1891, building is now on National Register.

1:08 (0:33) Above, on right, are buildings of Glenwood State Hospital-School. Originally a home for Civil War orphans, today mentally retarded persons are cared for and trained here. Many patients live in residential-type housing resembling a typical middle-income subdivision.

1:13 (0:29) Intersect Interstate 29, connecting Omaha and Kansas City.

1:17 (0:25) Enter Nebraska and leave Iowa as Missouri River is crossed. Note large natural gas pipeline also spanning waters at right.

Over 100 years ago steamboats plied these waters between Omaha, just 20 miles north of here, and St. Louis, almost 500 miles downstream. Its headwaters are in the mountainous regions of western Montana. The river then starts its long north and east trek through Montana, swings southeastward through North and South Dakota, slips between Iowa and Nebraska, and finally flows eastward across Missouri, joining the Mississippi River at St. Louis.

1:24 (0:18) *Zephyr* bridges Platte River, once described by a James Michener character as "the sorriest river in America." However, its surface waters and underflow provide vital irrigation to large portions of Nebraska, Colorado and Wyoming, and its flat valley floor has been an excellent east-west route for trails, highways and railroads crossing Nebraska.

1:29 (0:13) Nearing Omaha, cruise through Bellevue, oldest continuous settlement in Nebraska. Of greater note, however, is Offutt Air Force Base, partially visible off to left, which is headquarters for nation's Strategic Air Command.

1:42 (0:00) Arrive Omaha.

OMAHA, NE - Located on the mighty, muddy Missouri River at the eastern terminus of the Union Pacific Railroad, Omaha has risen from its pioneer beginning on the plains to become both a transportation hub and the major cattle and grain market of the Prairie States.

Amtrak Station, 1003 South 9th Street, is about a mile south of the downtown shopping area. There are candy bar and beverage vending machines, handcarts and adjacent free parking.

Yellow, Happy and Checker **Cabs** have common dispatch, 341-9000. Avis is closest **rental car** agency (about a mile) and will reimburse cab fare to pick up car; returns can be made at the station; (402) 348-0621.

Greater Omaha Convention & Visitors Bureau, 1819 Farnam St., Suite 1200; (402) 444-4660 or 800-332-1819.

Red Lion Inn, 1616 Dodge St., 68102; (402) 346-7600 or 800-547-8010. Courtesy shuttle. Ten blocks from the station. $120.

-**Holiday Express**, 3001 Chicago Street, 68131; (402) 345-2222. Complimentary continental breakfast. Courtesy shuttle to and from the station. Two miles from the station. $60.

Union Pacific Historical Museum, at 12th and Dodge Streets, has a large collection of railroad memorabilia, housed in the national headquarters of the Union Pacific. **Omaha History Museum** now occupies the old Union Station, 10th and Marcy Streets, three blocks from the present Amtrak station. **Boys Town**, formed by Father Flanagan in 1917 on the west edge of Omaha, is the best-known home and school for underprivileged youths. A good way to spend an evening waiting for the westbound train is to take in a production at the **Omaha Community Playhouse**—nation's largest with 11,000 members. Henry Fonda made his debut here; 69th and Cass, four miles west of downtown.

0:00 (1:00) Depart Omaha.

0:30 (0:30) Incongruous "light house," on left, stands next to Platte River, marking location of once-popular summer beach resort area frequented by both Omahans and Lincolnites.

Built in 1939, structure had no real use other than acting as landmark for Linoma Resort. Train now crosses broad waters of Platte River.

0:33 (0:27) Enter Ashland, located on site of old Ox-Bow Trail. Thousands of emigrants and millions of pounds of freight moved along this route from towns such as Plattsmouth and Nebraska City north to Platte River, then westward to settlements, mining camps and military posts.

1:00 (0:00) Arrive Lincoln, where former Burlington steam locomotive and bevy of colorful boxcars are on exhibit as part of restored eight-block Haymarket area.

LINCOLN, NE - Lincoln's rather subdued skyline is dominated by the State Capitol, a 400-foot "Tower of the Plains" which is an early 20th-century architectural masterpiece. The only unicameral (one house) legislature in the nation occupies this structure.

Lincoln is home of the University of Nebraska, a perennial football powerhouse, and Nebraskans would have you believe the bronze statue atop the capitol dome is of the University's football coach. It is actually "The Sower," casting grain upon the plains.

William Jennings Bryan, the "silver-tongued orator from the Platte" and thrice-defeated presidential candidate, once lived in Lincoln.

0:00 (1:24) Depart Lincoln.

0:17 (1:07) Plant on left produces well-known Alpo pet food. Town is Crete, home to Doane College, a Congregational Church-founded liberal arts institution.

0:40 (0:44) Rumble through town of Exeter started by railroad in 1871. In 1886, Charles C. Smith manufactured his bookkeeping indexing tabs here which were used world-wide.

0:46 (0:38) In March of 1884, Fairmont Creamery Company was incorporated here in town of Fairmont. Company grew to become one of the nation's largest food processors—Fairmont Foods.

1:29 (0:00) Arrive Hastings.

HASTINGS, NE - Hastings, together with its nearby rival cities, Grand Island and Kearney, combine to form the major trade and manufacturing hub for this central Nebraska region.

0:00 (0:51) Depart Hastings.

The rolling-to-flat fertile farmlands that have prevailed since leaving Chicago start to disappear as the more arid plains of the West begin to dominate. Irrigated cropland slowly gives way to more arid cattle country, except for the heavily farmed river valleys. And we start to climb—nearly nine feet per mile between here and Denver.

0:15 (0:36) Pass through Kenesaw and cross historic Oregon Trail that was used by hundreds of westward-bound wagon trains.

This was the most used of the various overland routes. With completion of the Union Pacific Railroad, the trail fell into disuse. Its wagon tracks are still visible in several places across the prairies of the West.

0:30 (0:21) Breeze through Minden where renowned Pioneer Village, recreating early prairie life, can be glimpsed beyond grain elevators on right. Covered wagon is parked on top of entrance.

0:47 (0:00) Arrive Holdrege.

HOLDREGE, NE - Holdrege is an agricultural trading center for this region, with much of its population being of Swedish extraction.

0:00 (1:03) Depart Holdrege.

0:07 (1:01) Pass through Atlanta, a detention center during World War II and located far from more sensitive wartime areas. This POW camp held 3,000 German soldiers captured in North African and Italian campaigns.

0:51 (0:17) Marble monument, just across highway to right, commemorates pioneer women who "drowned in this canyon" enroute to their homestead in May of 1885.

0:59 (0:09) Through Indianola, situated in Republican River Valley, center of major buffalo ranges of Great Plains and favorite hunting grounds of Pawnee, Sioux, Oto and Cheyenne. These tribes, continually at war with one another, spent much time here as late as 1874.

1:05 (0:03) Three miles east of McCook, red-brick walls just above tracks to right are memorial to Harry D. Strunk, a man instrumental in developing region's rivers.

1:13 (0:00) Arrive McCook.

 MCCOOK, NE - Founded as a division point on the railroad in 1882, McCook still enjoys this status. Senator Norris, father of the Tennessee Valley Authority, once lived here.

0:00 (2:27) Depart McCook.

0:23 (2:04) Off to left is Massacre Canyon where last battle between Pawnee and Sioux occurred in 1873. Half-mile distant, rough-hewn granite obelisk, with faces of two Indian Chiefs facing in opposite directions, memorializes battle.

0:31 (1:56) Swanson Reservoir on left, resulting from Trenton Dam on Republican River, furnishes important irrigation water and flood control as well as recreational opportunities.

 Gain one hour as train passes from Central to Mountain Time. Set your watch back (forward if eastbound) one hour.

0:43 (1:44) Benkelman was hometown of Ward Bond of "Wagonmaster" TV series.

1:11 (1:16) Enter Colorado and leave Nebraska. Sign on right marks the spot.

1:15 (1:12) Republican River Valley continues to provide a gentle route for tracks. North Fork of Republican is on right.

1:18 (1:09) It was along these tracks that history-making *Pioneer Zephyr* reached its top speed of 112.5 mph during its Denver to Chicago sprint in 1934. Today's *California Zephyr* cruises closer to 80 mph through here.

1:30 (0:57) Giant irrigation sprinklers seen along route sweep from a center pivot, creating green circles of crops a quarter-mile across. Water is pumped from enormous but vastly over-used Ogallala Aquifer.

1:32 (0:55) Enormous, Monfort feedlots are immediately north of tracks. Monfort is world's largest cattle feeder.

1:38 (0:49) On left, small, neat brick Yuma train depot is adorned with most unusual chrome canopy.

1:52 (0:35) Westbound passengers should now see for miles in all directions as train rumbles through eastern Colorado. This was formerly domain of buffalo, sodbusters and Pony Express riders.

1:56 (0:31) Rocking arms of pumps on right draw oil from one of many isolated "pools" found throughout region.

1:58 (0:29) This is Akron, trading center for an area rich in wheat and ranchland as well as oil production.

2:18 (0:09) Broad valley off to right has been formed by shallow but wide South Platte River.

2:27 (0:00) Arrive Ft. Morgan.

 FT. MORGAN, CO - This city was named for a fort built here in 1864 to protect westbound pioneers from Indian attacks. Later an Overland Stage stop was established, which served the route to Denver. Sugar beets, cattle sorghums and oil all make Ft. Morgan one of eastern Colorado's more prosperous cities.

0:00 (1:25) Depart Ft. Morgan.

0:09 (1:16) Off to right a few miles is Orchard, where much of television's "Centennial" was filmed.

0:23 (1:02) Westbound passengers, weather permitting, receive first glimpse of Front Range of Rockies, on right—some eighty miles distant. Pikes Peak, 14,110 feet high, can be discerned far off to left as a mere bump on horizon—but only on clearest of days.

0:52 (0:33) Vast acreage of U.S. Army's Rocky Mountain Arsenal spreads out on left, where controversial nerve gas was manufactured and stored for many years. Massive, expensive cleanup efforts are now underway.

1:05 (0:20) Industrial sights of aptly named Commerce City, a northeast Denver suburb, now prevail.

1:13 (0:12) Formerly bustling stockyards area is location of National Western Stock Show, held here each January. It is largest event of its kind and draws exhibitors from throughout western U.S. and Canada. On left, with its enormous curved roof, Coliseum is focus of those activities. Pass beneath Interstate 70. Denver's newly shaped skyline now dominates on left.

1:22 (—) Front of train is now clearly visible on right as train makes a giant curl northward while *Zephyr* prepares to back into station. (Train will depart northbound retracing, for a short distance, tracks on which it has just arrived.)

1:30 (0:01) Coors Field, home to major league baseball's Colorado Rockies, is beside tracks.

1:31 (0:00) Arrive Denver's Union Station, built in 1881.

DENVER, CO - Compared to most cities its size, Denver's history is relatively short, having been founded in 1858 during the gold rush to the mountains. The gold played out, but Denver's climate, its proximity to the mountains and its institutions born of those early years assured Denver's destiny as the trading, financial and tourism center of the Rocky Mountain region.

First-time visitors are often surprised to find a mile-high city not in the mountains, just near them, and a ski-oriented community that gets only 16 inches of moisture per year. Its once modest downtown is now a maze of glassy skyscrapers which sprouted in the 80s—largely the result of a brief energy boom.

The Civic Center, presided over by the golden-domed state capitol, is a jewel; Denver's parks are some of the finest anywhere; its tree-lined boulevards in east

Denver

- Amtrak Station
1 - Visitors Information
2 - Civic Center
3 - Larimer Square
4 - Sakura Square
5 - U.S. Mint
6 - State Capitol
7 - Tabor Center
8 - Denver Art Museum
9 - Tivoli
10 - Forney Transportation Museum
11 - Oxford Alexis
12 - Comfort Inn

Denver are delights to drive; and its downtown area is easy to shop with free transit up and down the 16th Street Mall.

Union Station, 17th and Wynkoop Streets, anchors the revitalized end of downtown. When it was completed in 1881, it was said to be the largest single structure in the West. Its classic waiting room still has its old high-back wooden benches. The station has a gift shop, food counter, restaurant, storage lockers, luggage carts and adjacent pay-parking. A parking garage is across from the station on Wynkoop St., between 16th and 17th Streets, with special Amtrak rates. There are direct phone lines to several hotels and rental car companies.

Yellow **Cab**, 777-7777. Direct phones to Hertz and Budget, **rental cars** with limited hours pick up and drop off at the station. Local and regional **buses** stop in front of the station; main terminal is two blocks away; call RTD, 299-6000; schedules and maps available at the station. **Greyhound bus** terminal at 19th and Curtis Streets, seven blocks from the station.

Denver Metro Convention and Visitors Bureau, 225 W. Colfax; (303) 892-1112.

Comfort Inn, 401-17th St., 80202; (303) 296-0400. Small but luxurious rooms at the uptown end of 17th Street in what was once the "new" annex of Denver's Brown Palace Hotel. Breakfast included. Thirteen "short" blocks from the station. $69.

-**Oxford**, 1600-17th St., 80202; (303) 628-5400 or 800-228-5838. Marvelously restored old hotel with some good weekend packages. Half block from the station. $125.

Downtown attractions include: the **U.S. Mint**, across from the visitors center; **Civic Center**, a handsomely landscaped set of state and city buildings, near Colfax and Broadway; **Denver Museum of Natural History**, in City Park; **Denver Art Museum**, 100 West 14th Parkway; **shopping** at Larimer Square, Sakura Square, Tabor Center, The Tivoli (all in lower downtown), and the 16th Street Mall with free shuttle buses. The excellent Tattered Cover Bookstore is diagonally across the street in front of the station. Nearby Coors Field, home of baseball's Rockies, has revitalized the station area which has good eateries and microbreweries.

Near downtown is the **Forney Transportation Museum**, 1416 Platte St., and near Golden is the **Colorado Railroad Museum**, 17155 W. 44th Ave. The **Platte Valley Trolley** provides rides from Confluence Park along the South Platte River.

0:00 (1:57) Depart Denver.

We bid farewell to the Burlington and take to the rails of the highly scenic Denver and Rio Grande Western, along the route of the former Denver and Salt Lake Railroad, exploring the very heart of the Colorado Rockies. The pace is slow. Grinding up laborious grades and negotiating never-ending twists and turns, it takes more than seven hours to reach Grand Junction, 273 rail miles to the west—a less-than-blazing 38 miles per hour.

But this is the Rio Grande. The railroad cut its teeth on narrow-gauge tracks (3 feet between the rails) which allowed it to snake up canyons and cling to cliffs while reaching almost every remote mining camp in the state. This "baby railroad" could "curve around the brim of a sombrero," so it was said. Mark Twain once wondered why the Rio Grande even bothered to use cow-catchers since their trains couldn't outrun the beasts.

Although the Rio Grande converted to standard gauge long ago, trains on this line still take their time. And that's perfect for seeing the Rockies.

0:01 (1:54) Just to right again, is Coors Field, home to baseball's Colorado Rockies.

0:02 (1:55) Cross usually placid South Platte River.

0:05 (1:52) Slip through extensive freight yards of Rio Grande, as sights of Denver's industrial aspects continue.

0:13 (1:39) Angling through Arvada, a large northwestern Denver suburb, Front Range of

California Zephyr — above Rocky Flats, CO
JACK SWANSON

Rockies looms directly ahead. Tallest peak in distance to right (north) is 14,255-foot Longs Peak. Immediately to left is 14,264-foot Mt. Evans.

0:32 (1:19) At Rocky, train reaches formidable foothills and a giant "S" curve (called "Big Ten" in reference to degrees of curvature) is negotiated to gain necessary altitude. On inside of upper curve weathered hopper cars filled with sand are permanently anchored to protect trains from fierce west winds which occasionally reach velocities in excess of 100 miles per hour. Grade is a demanding two percent as route steadily ascends across face of foothills before turning westward directly into mountains.

0:40 (1:12) Rumble through first of 28 tunnels between here and six-mile-long Moffat Tunnel.

0:45 (1:10) This area is referred to as Plainview—understandably, as plains of eastern Colorado seem to stretch out forever. Back on right, Denver's entire metropolitan area is now visible. Industrial complex in foreground is controversial Rocky Flats, once nation's only processor of plutonium. Forward on right is city of Boulder and University of Colorado with its red-tiled roofs.

0:51 (1:06) After having enjoyed sweeping panoramas of plains while train gained altitude along eastern face of Rockies, we now head up South Boulder Canyon into very heart of mountains. This is where eastbound passengers first get one of Amtrak's most breathtaking views—looking down on evening lights of Denver's metroplex.

0:59 (0:58) Gross Reservoir, one of Denver's many important water storage facilities, is below on right.

1:35 (0:23) Fine views are afforded of towering Continental Divide directly ahead as train enters Roosevelt National Forest. Watch for deer and elk on slopes above tracks.

1:42 (0:15) At last, plunge into historic Moffat Tunnel where total darkness prevails for nine minutes as train passes beneath Continental Divide.

1:48 (0:06) We are suddenly awash in brilliant daylight as train pops out of Moffat Tunnel into land where all water now flows westward. Immediately on left is Winter Park ski area.

1:53 (0:00) Arrive Winter Park (Fraser).

WINTER PARK, CO - This popular ski destination, particularly for Denverites, is in a section of the Rockies composed of mountains and meadowlands called Middle Park, where ranching and tourism are of primary importance. A favorite fishing retreat of former president Dwight Eisenhower was in the mountains off to the left. The depot is actually in the small town of Fraser, adjacent to the Winter Park ski area. For years, Fraser often recorded the coldest wintertime temperatures in the nation, but the situation was finally alleviated when the town's weather station was removed.

0:00 (0:22) Depart Winter Park (Fraser).

0:10 (0:05) Sparkling trout-filled Fraser River escorts train through remote canyon.

0:25 (0:00) Arrive Granby.

GRANBY, CO - This is a trading center for Middle Park and popular stopping point for travelers. Beautiful Grand Lake and Rocky Mountain National Park are just to the north (right) of here. Incomparable Trail Ridge Road—highest continuous auto road in the world—traverses the Continental Divide through the center of the Park.

0:00 (2:57) Depart Granby.

0:02 (2:53) Here we join Colorado River near its headwaters, and follow its winding course for next 238 miles.

0:13 (2:44) Small mountain community of Hot Sulphur Springs derives its name from local geothermal springs. Indoor swimming pool, on right, capitalizes on this free source of heated water.

0:14 (2:43) Enter Byers Canyon where invincible rocky-spired cliffs tower high above roadbed. Highway on left is U.S. 40.

0:22 (2:35) Emerge from Byers Canyon and for first time since Denver pick up considerable speed as train heads for Kremmling in heart of some of Colorado's best cattle coun-

Moffat Tunnel

The construction of the Moffat Tunnel was considered a Colorado need. David Moffat's Denver and Salt Lake Railroad had not proven to be the answer. That line's arduous negotiation of Rollins Pass was not only slow, but winters at that elevation turned schedules into shambles. (The original route over the top can still be seen above and to the right before entering the tunnel westbound.)

When it was finished in 1927, the Moffat Tunnel was 6.2 miles long, the longest rail tunnel in North America. (It was subsequently bettered by the 1929 Cascade Tunnel in Washington and a Canadian Pacific tunnel.) The feat was of such moment that President Calvin Coolidge pushed a button from the White House triggering the holing-through blast. It took one thousand men digging from both ends and using 2.5 million pounds of dynamite nearly four years to complete the task.

It is now a mere nine-minute trundle through 13,260-foot-high James Peak instead of a five-hour ordeal over the top. Somewhere in the tunnel's innards the rails reach their apex—9,239 feet above sea level, and the highest point anywhere for Amtrak.

try. Large herds of deer can often be seen along right-of-way, particularly in winter.

0:36 (2:22) Roll through Kremmling. Lofty peaks to left belong to Gore Range and reach elevations in excess of 13,000 feet.

0:41 (2:18) Enter awesome Gore Canyon, where sheer rock sides of this rugged gorge hover menacingly overhead, and where not

California Zephyr — Front Range, Colorado Rockies
JACK SWANSON

even an auto road has dared to invade.

0:52 (2:08) Emerge from Gore Canyon. Small meadows and ranches will continue to fleck landscape as we journey westward through middle of Rockies.

0:57 (2:03) Enter Little Gore Canyon, not as exciting as Gore, but still impressive.

1:00 (2:00) Hole in canyon wall at about water level on left was to be intake of ambitious irrigation tunnel, but project was abandoned circa 1913.

1:02 (1:58) Exit Little Gore Canyon.

1:25 (1:36) Remains of historic State Bridge (it preceded railroad) and its modern replacement are just to left.

1:31 (1:21) Curl through old railroad town of Bond, with its handful of rundown buildings. On right, a Rio Grande branch line can be seen angling above, making its way to Steamboat Springs and Craig, Colorado.

1:36 (1:18) Giant waterwheel on left, looking more like an incongruous Ferris wheel, scoops water from river and empties into irrigation ditch.

1:37 (1:17) Enter Red Canyon, where surprisingly red cliffs offer an almost refreshing change from dramatic scenery behind. Eroded rocks play fanciful tricks on imagination—note pilgrims' "Mayflower" resting at anchor just to right.

2:24 (0:34) Train rolls through Dotsero where Eagle River, from left, now adds to Colorado River's flow. It was from this point that an early Colorado River survey was commenced and marked ".0" or "dot zero." Rails also join Rio Grande's Royal Gorge route which threads its way back through mountains to Pueblo.

2:29 (0:29) Enter Glenwood Canyon where the grandeur of these great cliffs is said to have inspired creation of Vistadomes.

In July of 1944, the general manager of GM's Electro-motive Division was riding through the canyon in the cab of a Rio Grande diesel locomotive when he first visualized glass-canopied rail cars. Five years later they were in service on the *California Zephyr*. The tracks twist and turn, lazily following the river through this truly beautiful gorge for nearly half an hour.

2:32 (0:26) Across river, Interstate 70's rock cuts and concrete structures are stained to blend with canyon walls. Started in 1981, project was not finished until 1993—at a cost of nearly a half billion dollars, one of nation's most expensive stretches of interstate.

2:39 (0:19) Dam diverts water into underground penstocks that carry water to power plant farther downstream.

2:43 (0:15) On right, Public Service Company of Colorado's Shoshone hydroelectric generating plant is outlet for water diverted upstream. Plant is small, producing a relatively modest 15 megawatts. Below this point, river rafters are frequent sight.

2:57 (0:00) Arrive Glenwood Springs at western mouth of Glenwood Canyon. Be sure to note picturesque stone and brick station on left, considered one of most attractive in nation. Its architecture intentionally blends with that of Hot Springs Lodge across Colorado River.

GLENWOOD SPRINGS, CO - Ultra-posh Aspen is just up the Roaring Fork Valley from Glenwood Springs, making this a busy skier stop for the *California Zephyr*. But many who come to Glenwood are not interested in Aspen—they come here because of the world's largest outdoor hot-water swimming pool. This attraction is just to the right and across the river from the station and is always filled with swimmers—even in the dead of winter. Water is supplied by the adjacent Yampa Hot Springs.

Beyond the pool can be seen the venerable Hotel Colorado, opened in 1893. Built of sandstone and trimmed with Roman brick, it was patterned after the Medici Hotel in Florence, Italy. This hostelry has accommodated numerous well-known personages over the years, including Teddy Roosevelt to name but one. One story has it that when Roosevelt came back empty handed from a bear hunt, the hotel staff made a stuffed bear for him, the first "teddy bear."

That famous gunslinger, Doc Holliday, once lived in Glenwood and is buried here.

0:00 (1:40) Departing Glenwood Springs, majestic Mt. Sopris dominates Roaring Fork River Valley on left.

0:08 (1:32) Train wends its way through Colorado River Valley encased by red stratified mountains which typify this region of Rockies. Above and to right is Storm King Mountain, where tragic Canyon Creek fire took the lives of fourteen firefighters July 6, 1994.

0:18 (1:22) Near New Castle, black slash on left identifies former Wheeler coal mine, long ago abandoned due to persistent fires. Two catastrophic explosions, one in late 1800s and one in early 1900s, resulted in 91 deaths.

0:30 (1:10) This is Rifle. Historically a ranching community, some years ago it experienced a rather short-lived boom based on prospects of developing vast Colorado shale oil reserves which lie north and west of here. Some of these deposits are visible high up on cliffs, just to right and forward of train.

0:42 (0:56) Community of Battlement Mesa is on higher ground to left. Originally built to house oil shale workers, it is now a retirement settlement.

1:01 (0:37) Enter Debeque Canyon which easily could have been setting for Zane Grey novel.

1:11 (0:26) Colorado River (until 1921, known as "Grand River" east of juncture with Green River in Utah) is momentarily held back by ornate Grand River Diversion Dam, built by U.S. Bureau of Reclamation for irrigation purposes.

1:15 (0:22) Buffalo in field at left are unusual twentieth-century sight.

1:16 (0:21) Coal mine, across river on left, taps some of region's vast coal reserves to fuel power plant on right. Coal is transported via impressive conveyor spanning river.

1:23 (0:14) Emerge from Debeque Canyon and enter famed fruit-growing region of Colorado's Western Slope. Peaches, harvested here at end of summer, are outstanding. Huge plateau on left is Grand Mesa, reputedly world's largest flat-top mountain. Unusual variegated palisades on right are known as Book Cliffs.

1:40 (0:00) Arrive Grand Junction.

GRAND JUNCTION, CO - This in western Colorado's largest community. Overlooked by white men long after the rest of the state was overrun by fur trappers, it finally saw "civilized" settlement in 1881 when settlers were permitted to stake claims shortly after the Northern Ute Indians were removed to Utah. It was first named Ute, then West Denver, and finally Grand Junction because the Colorado (remember it used to be the Grand) and the Gunnison Rivers joined here.

Of particular interest to visitors are nearby Colorado National Monument with its free-standing rock monoliths, Grand Mesa's beautiful forests and lakes, and a unique museum with life-size dinosaurs that growl and snap at visitors. Region was once heavily populated by dinosaurs, and important skeletal remains have been unearthed nearby.

0:00 (1:18) Departing Grand Junction, broken red cliffs of Colorado National Monument border route on left.

0:20 (0:58) Refinery on left has processed gilsonite, a hard black asphalt rarely found in usable quantity but readily available in this region.

0:22 (0:56) Mack was former eastern terminus of narrow-gauge Uintah Railroad which hauled gilsonite from eastern Utah until line was abandoned in 1939.

0:23 (0:55) West of Mack, emerge from short tunnel and follow Colorado River's graceful meanders through spectacular gorges of Ruby Canyon.

0:36 (0:41) On right, markings inscribed on canyon wall denote Utah-Colorado boundary.

0:38 (0:39) After a 238-mile joint venture, Colorado River now departs tracks at Westwater and heads for Arizona. Now canyonlands are quickly displaced by a vast expanse of desert terrain. Stark mesa tops of Roan Cliffs stand stoically on right as train weaves across this barren landscape. What sometimes appears to be sparkling snow in the heat of summer is only surface alkali.

1:15 (0:00) Arriving Thompson, La Sal Mountains are an imposing sight in distance on left. Henry Mountains are prominent lump on horizon left forward.

THOMPSON, UT - Thompson is a flag stop for nearby Moab, hub of southeastern Utah's vast, scenic wonderlands. Surrounding Moab are such spectacular settings as Canyonlands National Park, Arches National Park, Dead Horse Point and Monument Valley.

0:00 (1:40) Departing Thompson, note intriguing Desert Moon Hotel on left. Sign touts it as also a retirement home and trailer park.

0:25 (1:16) Cross Green River, then through town of same name. At an altitude of 4,080 feet, river crossing lies at lowest point along this section of Rio Grande line. Town is best known for its cantaloupes and watermelons, nurtured by Green's waters.

0:54 (0:49) Cross Price River which will subsequently rejoin in Helper.

1:37 (0:10) Re-emergence of agriculture and ranching spreads around Price signals gradual departure from desert climes.

1:40 (0:00) Arrive Helper.

HELPER, UT - As evidenced by the congestion of this busy rail terminal, Helper is a vital distribution outlet for a region replete with abundant coal resources. So rich are these deposits, it is said they alone could supply the U.S. for 300 years. When founded in 1882, the town was named in deference to "helper" locomotives which were coupled here onto westbound freights for the arduous ascent up Soldier Summit.

0:00 (1:53) Departing Helper, historic Western flavor pervades downtown area on left.

0:03 (1:50) At Martin, on left, substantial brick building ensconced on hillside houses operating headquarters of Utah Railway Company. Railway is a short-line coal hauler.

0:05 (1:48) Balanced Rock, perched high above tracks on right, has seen numerous attempts to top it with Old Glory. As Price River rejoins on left, enter Wasatch Mountains and proceed up 2.4 percent twisting grade to Soldier Summit.

0:08 (1:46) On right, pass entangled maze of machinery and apparatus at Castle Gate

Preparation Plant. Situated in midst of extensive coal beds, this sprawling operation serves as a "washing" facility for loads from nearby Price River Coal Company.

0:10 (1:44) Castle Gate Rock is renowned landmark of this stretch, protruding like prow of ship above trackside on right.

0:40 (1:13) Breaking out onto flat terrain denotes arrival at Soldier Summit—7,440 feet in elevation. Name of pass commemorates Union soldiers buried here in 1860. Train now descends into Spanish Fork River Canyon.

0:49 (0:55) Across next six minutes, train bends around two giant reversing horseshoe curves to resolve dilemma of steep terrain.

1:25 (0:33) On both sides, recesses carved in sandstone cliffs shelter towering rock spires, poised like chess pieces in their midst.

1:32 (0:24) Enter Thistle Tunnel.

1:56 (0:00) Arrive Provo.

 PROVO, UT - Nestled between the Wasatch Mountains to the east, and Utah Lake to the west, Provo has flourished since it was first founded by Mormons in

Thistle Tunnel

During the heavy spring rains and snow runoff of 1983, the town of Thistle met an untimely end. An enormous mud slide permanently dammed the river and submerged the town, the highway and the main line of the Rio Grande under 200 feet of water. The Rio Grande tunneled above and to the east of the resulting lake, creating a 3,100 foot-long bore on a 4-degree curve. The lake was subsequently drained, but the new track and tunnel remain. The slide area is quite apparent to the west.

1849. Of particular importance has been the influx of large industry into the region, attracted in particular by the area's abundant mineral wealth and a labor force whose strong work ethic is a longstanding tradition of Mormon culture. Provo, too, is the home of Brigham Young University, the largest privately owned college in America. Mormons Donnie and Marie Osmond have a recording studio in Provo.

Provo is also a convenient gateway to the highly acclaimed ski resorts of Sundance and Park City. Both lie a short distance up the magnificent Provo Canyon.

0:00 (0:50) Depart Provo.

0:02 (0:48) Cross Provo River.

0:07 (0:43) Mounds of coal surround furnaces of U.S. Steel Geneva complex on right.

0:10 (0:40) Shoreline of fresh-water Utah Lake borders on left, while Tintic Mountains hover in distance. Mount Timpanagos soars to 11,975 feet on right.

0:26 (0:24) Across valley on left, cavities of famed Kennecott open-pit copper mine are just beyond lengthy strand of tailings stretched along hilltops.

0:33 (0:17) Highway turnoff on right at Midvale represents only half-hour trek to ski resorts of Alta and Snowbird.

0:45 (0:05) Approaching Salt Lake City, copper-domed Capitol Building and spires of Salt Lake Temple are both readily distinguishable landmarks of downtown skyline on forward right.

0:50 (0:00) Train now glides to stop beside D&RGW's 1910 station.

SALT LAKE CITY, UT - Although Jim Bridger first discovered the Great Salt Lake in 1824, it was not until 1847 that a group of Mormons, led by Brigham Young, arrived at the current site of Salt Lake City and decided to settle here. An industrious people, they planted crops on the day of their arrival.

Today, Utah is still predominantly Mormon, the name given to members of The Church of Jesus Christ of Latter-day Saints. The church is well known for its stance against consumption of alcohol, but, inter-

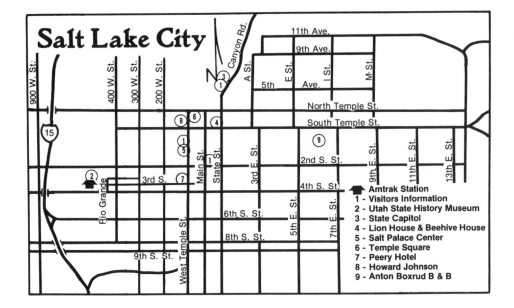

Salt Lake City

Amtrak Station
1 - Visitors Information
2 - Utah State History Museum
3 - State Capitol
4 - Lion House & Beehive House
5 - Salt Palace Center
6 - Temple Square
7 - Peery Hotel
8 - Howard Johnson
9 - Anton Boxrud B & B

estingly, Brigham Young imbibed and Utah voted to repeal prohibition. The state is not dry (but has complex drinking laws) and, even more interestingly, owns and operates (near Temple Square) one of the finest wine stores in the U.S.

The city, which is the capital of Utah, is clean, modern and architecturally both interesting and attractive. Its wide streets have been a trademark.

D&RGW Station, 3rd South & Rio Grande St., is a handsomely remodeled depot of classical architecture, with Amtrak occupying the south wing. A restaurant in the north wing has a unique trackside patio that is a summertime favorite for lunch. There are snack vending machines and a food vending truck at trainside in the mornings. A museum occupies the central portion of the building.

Yellow **Cab**, 521-2100. **Local buses** are approximately four blocks east of the station on West Temple; 287-4636. **Greyhound** bus terminal, 160 West South Temple, is about a mile from the station. **Rental cars** are available downtown and 24 hours at the airport, six miles west of the station.

Salt Lake Valley Convention & Visitors Bureau, 180 South West Temple (next to the Salt Palace), (801) 521-2822.

Peery Hotel, 110 West Broadway (Third South), 84101; (801) 521-4300 or 800-331-0073. An elegantly restored small hotel. Free Amtrak shuttle service. Complimentary newspaper and continental breakfast. Four blocks from the station. $89.

-**Hornes Howard Johnson**, 122 West South Temple, 84101; (801) 521-0130. Nice hotel in an excellent location. Seven blocks from the station. $75.

-**Anton Boxrud Bed and Breakfast**, 57 South 600 East, 84102; (801) 363-8035 or 800-524-5511. Lovely Victorian on a quiet residential street, close to downtown. Shared and private baths. Thirteen blocks from the station. $59-$119.

In the downtown area, **Temple Square**, South Temple and Main, is the heart of The Church of Jesus Christ of Latter-day Saints. A magnificent six-spired Temple and the near-acoustically perfect Tabernacle are the highlights; beautifully landscaped grounds. Free tours of the Tabernacle and Visitor Center are offered daily. The **Mormon Tabernacle Choir** rehearsals on Thursday evenings are open to the public. Also, their broadcasts on Sunday morning are public.

And, of course, the **Great Salt Lake**, with its high salt content, tempts swimmers to try their buoyancy. It lies west of downtown along Interstate 80.

0:00 (4:37) Depart Salt Lake City, skirting southern tip of Great Salt Lake on tracks of Union Pacific, formerly of Western Pacific acquired by UP in 1982.

Amtrak's scheduling is such that darkness usually prevails between Salt Lake City and Winnemucca, Nevada—a desert stretch that, in any event, offers little to see during the daytime.

Gain one hour as train passes from Mountain to Pacific Time. Set your watch back (forward if eastbound) one hour.

4:12 (0:00) Arrive Elko, completing Amtrak's longest run without a scheduled stop.

ELKO, NV - Once an important wagon-train stop along the Humboldt River Overland Trail, Elko has emerged as the commercial hub of a vast ranching and mining domain. Its first boom came when the railroad arrived in 1869, but a far more dramatic explosion occurred in recent years with the development of gold-mining equipment that squeezed millions of minute flecks of the precious metal from heretofore unyielding ore from nearby mines.

0:00 (1:50) Depart Elko.

1:50 (0:00) Arrive Winnemucca.

WINNEMUCCA, NV - Winnemucca traces its roots to an 1850s trading post, eventually named to honor the last great Paiute chief whose people inhabited the region.

Winnemucca was visited by the notorious Butch Cassidy gang who, in 1900, successfully robbed the First National Bank, despite the efforts of a determined posse who tracked them all the way into central Wyoming.

0:00 (2:48) Depart Winnemucca.

0:15 (2:33) Low, soft mountains rise from the desert floor everywhere, presenting a pleasing surrealistic scene to early-morning risers on westbound *Zephyr*.

1:55 (0:53) Alkali-coated dry lake bed on right is typical of region.

Most of Utah and portions of surrounding states lie in what is known as the Great Basin, a large expanse of desert where all lakes and streams stay within the Basin's boundaries. Rivers either disappear beneath the earth's surface or flow into lakes and evaporate. Sinks (depressions that hold water) occur throughout the region, the Great Salt Lake being the largest. The tracks follow the Humboldt River through this portion of Nevada, one of the many streams that are eventually absorbed back into the ground.

2:22 (0:31) At Fernley, Truckee River joins on right. Numerous crossings occur as train traces river to its source atop Sierra Nevadas.

2:41 (0:11) Across river on left, what could pass for just another motel is notorious Mustang Ranch, easily identified by its large parking lot, iron fence and guard tower. In past, world's oldest profession has been legally practiced here.

2:53 (0:00) Arrive Sparks.

SPARKS, NV - Historically a railroad town, Sparks has become a major distribution center for western markets due to Nevada's tax-free warehousing. The *Zephyr* is also serviced at this large Southern Pacific division point.

0:00 (0:09) Departing Sparks, elaborate hotels and casinos can be spotted, while industrial ticky-tacky best describes rest of scene.

0:07 (0:02) Approaching Reno, massive MGM Grand Hotel is a prominent fixture on left, set a short distance east of downtown hub.

0:09 (0:00) Arrive Reno. Arched windows and tile roof highlight Spanish design of station.

RENO, NV - In many respects, Reno has never departed from its illustrious frontier heritage—it's just better lighted than it used to be. Although best known as one of the nation's foremost gambling resorts, Reno is also a gateway to the untold beauty and year-round recreation of nearby Lake Tahoe, nestled in the Sierras only 35 miles southwest of town.

Amtrak Station, 135 E. Commercial Row, is in the heart of downtown.

Yellow **Cab**, 331-7171. Budget **rental cars** will pick and deliver Amtrak passengers during business hours; (702) 325-7590.

Reno-TahoeVisitors Information, call 800-367-7366.

Numerous hotels are within a few blocks of the station. Those shown below are two of the closest. Weekend rates are higher than those shown.

-**Harrahs,** 210 N. Carter St., at 2nd St., 89504; (702) 786-3232 or 800-427-7247. Posh and close. Half block from the station. $85.

-**Eldorado Hotel and Casino**, 4th and Virginia Streets, 89505; (702) 786-5700 or 800-648-5966. Two blocks from the station. $65.

As well as the glitzy hotels and **casinos** for which this city is most renowned, a host of additional attractions enhance Reno's stature as one of the nation's foremost gambling resorts. Headlining a long list is **Harrah's Automobile Collection** with its magnificent array of antique and classic cars, a perennial favorite of nostalgia and auto buffs alike.

0:00 (0:52) Depart Reno. On left, archway spanning breadth of famous Virginia Street welcomes visitors to "The Biggest Little City in the World." At night, street is ablaze in neon psychedelia, as hotels and casinos vie for attention of potential patrons.

0:10 (0:42) Attractive ranching spreads surround handsome River Inn Mineral Spa on left.

As train emerges in Tahoe National Forest, proceed across the Sierra Nevadas, retracing the route of the early "Gold Rush" enthusiasts. Still a marvel of railroad engineering, this magnificent mountain passage remains a lasting tribute to the thousands of Chinese and Irish laborers who miraculously hand-cut much of the current railbed over a century ago—the route of America's first transcontinental railroad.

0:18 (0:32) Small hydroelectric plant at Verdi takes water from flume above on left.

0:21 (0:29) Cross Nevada state line into California. On left, wooden flumes clinging to cliffside are nostalgic remnant of mining era. Troughs would originate upstream and transport water to mill sites that were often much higher than adjacent riverbed.

0:53 (0:00) Arriving Truckee, horses are about only thing missing amidst delightfully preserved Main Street of "Old West."

TRUCKEE, CA - Set along the banks of the lovely Truckee River, this rustic Western town has grown from a small logging concern into a bustling vacation retreat.

0:00 (2:09) Depart Truckee past magnificent grouping of Victorian homes before embarking on ascent of Donner Pass. A scenic wonderland, snow-capped peaks still provide an all-too-vivid reminder of ill-fated "Donner Expedition," many of whose members froze or starved to death during unrelenting winter blizzards of 1846.

The route today still remains one of the snowiest in the world. The small town of Norden, elevation 6,963 feet and near the summit, averages over 34 feet of snowfall each winter. It once took 40 miles of snowsheds to protect this right-of-way, but today, because of better snow removal techniques, less than three miles of track are covered by these structures.

0:16 (1:49) Attractive vacation homes and lodges dot shoreline of Donner Lake on right, flanked by picture-postcard backdrop of Sierra peaks.

0:25 (1:46) Westbound line now passes beneath eastbound, as train enters tunnel that carries westbound traffic under Mt. Judah. Inside, *Zephyr* reaches highest point in Sierra Nevadas—approximately 7,000 feet.

0:29 (1:42) Exiting tunnel, slopes of Sugar Bowl ski area appear, as chairlift passes directly overhead. Start careful descent of what is known as "The Hill."

0:54 (1:17) It was here, near Yuba Gap, that an ill-fated *City of San Francisco*, with its crew and passengers, became snowbound for four harrowing days in January, 1952.

0:56 (1:15) Interstate 80 passes overhead at Emigrant Gap. Strange-looking green cubicle on stilts, off to right, is fire watchtower.

1:01 (1:09) Unbounded alpine beauty surrounds shimmering blue waters of Spaulding Lake on right.

1:18 (0:52) Pass through quaint old mining community of Blue Canon.

1:30 (0:48) Continue tour of this historic region as train winds slowly along cliffs of spectacular American River Canyon.

1:47 (0:21) On left, old frame post office is nostalgic fixture at Gold Run.

2:03 (0:05) High steel trestle, known as Long Ravine Bridge, affords excellent view of encompassing mountainscapes.

2:08 (0:00) Arriving Colfax, clapboard storefronts on right and turn-of-the-century hotel on left are enduring reminders of town's colorful frontier legacy.

COLFAX, CA - Noted today for its bountiful harvests of Bartlett pears, Hungarian prunes and Tokay grapes, Colfax rose to prominence during the Gold Rush era when goods were transferred here by mule train for transport to remote mountain camps.

0:00 (0:45) Departing Colfax, east and westbound lines take separate routes for next 35-mile stretch into Rocklin. Scenery is essentially same for both, except in Auburn where distinctions are made for each train.

Subtle geographic changes can now be detected as train proceeds down western side of Sierra Nevadas.

0:33 (0:23) Emerge upon charming little Gold Rush town of Auburn.

For westbound trains, pass steepled Firehouse #1 on right. This 1888 structure houses a hand-pulled hook-and-ladder truck, and boasts oldest volunteer fire department this side of Boston. Fire bell fixed atop adjacent stanchion still bears 1869 San Francisco inscription.

0:35 (0:21) Still in Auburn, westbound passengers can look to right and spot gold-domed Placer County Courthouse standing on grounds that were once site of public hangings.

Eastbound travelers can also view courthouse on right, as well as adjacent structures of Auburn's "Old Town." Red and white bell tower of Firehouse #2 is a distinctive focal point of this historic district.

As the descent continues, golden hills slowly displace mountainous terrain. Tucked within their midst are some of the most beautiful ranchlands one is likely to find in any part of the country. A little further downline, abundant orchards and agricultural fields reflect the fertile environs of the Sacramento River Valley.

0:48 (0:18) Royal palms and prickly pear cacti on right are assurances we are approaching warmer climes.

0:57 (0:09) East and westbound routes rejoin, and together travel through attractive residential neighborhoods of Rocklin. Bohemia Brewery stands next to tracts at left.

1:06 (0:00) Arrive Roseville.

ROSEVILLE, CA - Roseville started as a railroad town and, as will be noted upon departure, the community still relies heavily on this activity. The *Coast Starlight*, which links Los Angeles to Seattle, joins the route of the *California Zephyr* at this point and uses the same Southern Pacific tracks between here and Oakland.

0:00 (0:24) Depart Roseville and negotiate miles of switches and tracks through vast Southern Pacific classification yards. Shortly, boxcar rehabilitation shops will appear on right and locomotive shops ("Pride of the Sierras") will be on left.

0:11 (0:14) Approaching Sacramento, pass facilities of McClellan Air Force Base on right.

0:16 (0:09) On left, modernistic "Cal Expo" center is September site of lively State Fair. Harness racing is also popular attraction at park throughout summer.

0:18 (0:07) Cross American River.

0:23 (0:02) Travel directly through midst of sprawling Blue Diamond Almond Company.

0:29 (0:00) Arriving Sacramento, gracious Spanish architecture highlights many buildings of downtown district on left. Ornamental domed tower is City Hall.

SACRAMENTO, CA - The famous California "Gold Rush" began here when nuggets were discovered at Sutter's Mill in 1848. Only 12 years later, the Pony Express was welcomed into town at the completion of its first historic run. And in 1863, a group of Sacramento visionaries began charting a route across the Sierra Nevadas that would eventually become the most ambitious link in the nation's first transcontinental railroad. The city now maintains statewide prestige as the capital of California.

Historical highlights are the emphasis of Sacramento's major attractions, from the reconstructed facilities of Sutter's Fort to a splendid array of Victorian homes. Of particular interest to train buffs is the outstanding California State Railroad Museum, located one block from the Amtrak station.

0:00 (0:20) Departing Sacramento, stately capitol building can be seen on left. Built in 1869, gilded globe still remains atop dome, despite protestations of original architect who described it as "simply ridiculous and abominable—a slur on our tastes forever."

On immediate left is aforementioned California State Railroad Museum, while Sacramento Locomotive Works are on right.

0:02 (0:17) Proceed across Sacramento River, noting on left riverboats along shore and interesting drawbridge a few blocks downstream.

0:10 (0:06) At considerable expense, railroad and highway have been elevated for several miles permitting underlying lands to be flooded for rice farming.

0:20 (0:00) Arrive Davis. Spanish motif of this handsome station is popular style of depots throughout Southern California.

DAVIS, CA - Long known for its prolific production of agricultural crops, Davis is noted more recently for its pioneering attitude in the field of energy conservation. Among other achievements, Davis claims that its many miles of scenic bicycle paths account for as much as 25% of the city's total vehicle traffic.

0:00 (0:26) Departing Davis, border University of California at Davis campus on right. Grapevines are part of school's renowned wine research program.

0:24 (0:00) Arriving Suisun-Fairfield, stately, white-pillared Solano County Courthouse stands distinctively on right at terminus of palm-lined Union Avenue.

SUISUN-FAIRFIELD, CA - At once another agricultural stronghold, this "twin-city" stop also affords access to the nearby facilities of Travis Air Force Base.

0:00 (0:20) Depart Suisun-Fairfield, shortly emerging upon waters of Suisun Bay.

0:10 (0:10) On immediate left,unmarked Glomar Explorer, sporting a white heliport platform on its stern, is normally anchored just before rail bridge. This deep-sea research vessel made headlines some years back when it attempted to retrieve a sunken Russian sub from ocean's floor.

0:16 (0:04) Cross drawbridge spanning Suisun Bay. Prior to its construction in 1930, train was broken down into sections and ferried across water. Once on southern shore, entangled maze of refinery apparatus escorts train into Martinez.

0:22 (0:00) Arrive Martinez.

MARTINEZ, CA - This important commercial and military port was also the home of John Muir, one of the nation's earliest and most outspoken conservationists. Joe Dimaggio Drive is on the right side of the train, honoring the renowned "Yankee Clipper" who was raised here.

0:00 (0:30) Depart Martinez along Carquinez Strait, connecting Suisun and San Pablo Bays. Carquinez Bridge looms impressively in foreground right, while on left, famed golden hills are subtly encroaching upon landscape.

0:09 (0:20) With town of Crockett huddled on hillside left, travel directly through midst of C&H sugar refinery. Immediately thereafter, train bears south along shores of San Pablo Bay.

0:29 (0:00) Arrive Richmond.

RICHMOND, CA - Richmond's popularity as a convenient suburban stop is enhanced by its trackside connections with BART, a rapid transit system servicing many outlying regions throughout the Bay Area.

0:00 (0:12) Departure from Richmond affords first view of dramatic San Francisco skyline across bay. Golden Gate Bridge can be seen north of city, while Bay Bridge connects with Oakland to the south. Alcatraz Island is also visible below Golden Gate Bridge.

0:05 (0:03) On right, pass Golden Gate Race Track.

0:12 (0:00) Arrive Emeryville's award-winning station at left.

EMERYVILLE, CA - This is the Bay Area stop for most passengers using connecting buses to and from San Francisco.

0:00 (0:15) Depart Emeryville.

0:05 (0:00) Arrive Oakland's Jack London Square Station, a glass-enclosed jewel at left, while Jack London Square is on right.

OAKLAND, CA - Oakland, California's fifth largest city, is situated across the bay from San Francisco. The *California Zephyr* never actually gets to San Francisco, but terminates in Oakland. Shuttle bus connections to and from San Francisco are at the nearby stop of Emeryville. This is not necessarily a disadvantage, however, since some travelers looking for a San Francisco vacation find Oakland an economic alternative as a base of operations.

 Amtrak Station, at Alice and Embarcadero, was completed in 1995 to replace the former earthquake damaged station at 1701 Wood.

Friendly **Cab**, 536-3000. For bus information, call 839-2881; for BART, call 465-BART; Enterprise **Car Rentals**, 3030 Broadway, (510) 893-7000 or 800-325-8007 offers pick up at the station; open weekdays and Saturday mornings. **Ferry Service** between Jack London Square and San Francisco's Pier 39 and Ferry Building.

Oakland Convention and Visitors Authority, 1000 Broadway, Suite 200, (510) 839-9000 or 800-262-5526.

Best Western Thunderbird Inn, 233 Broadway, 94607; (510) 452-4565. One block from Jack London Square. $74.

-Clarion Suites Lake Merritt, 1800 Madison (at Lakeside Drive), 94612; (510) 832-2300 or 800-933-4683. Wonderfully restored landmark overlooks lake, adjacent to downtown but in quiet setting. About two miles from the station. Complimentary local shuttle service. Few blocks from BART. $89.

Lake Merritt, in the heart of downtown, has boat rentals, a sightseeing launch, parks, a Japanese Garden and a special "Children's Fairyland" (with child-size buildings, animals and puppet show). **Jack London Square**, Broadway and Alice, on the waterfront, has many restaurants, specialty and import shops; Oakland's leading tourist attraction.

 SAN FRANCISCO, CA - See page 240.

Pioneer

The feature of this excursion is *Pioneer's* "cruise" along the dramatic Columbia River, following the same route taken by those earlier pioneers that once braved the Oregon Trail. After traversing southern Idaho in darkness, passengers are treated to all the spectacular grandeur of the Columbia Gorge in broad daylight. After Portland, the train courses northward through western Washington to Seattle, its ultimate destination.

Between Chicago and Denver, the *Pioneer* follows the route of the *California Zephyr*, sometimes as a section of that train. At Denver, the *Pioneer* heads northward toward Cheyenne, then westward through Wyoming to Ogden, UT where connecting buses provide direct service for Salt Lake City passengers. From Ogden, the train angles northwest through Idaho and on to Portland and Seattle.

WESTBOUND SCHEDULE (Condensed)
Chicago, IL - Midafternoon Departure
Denver, CO - Early Morning (2nd Day)
Ogden, UT - Midevening (2nd Day)
Boise, ID - Middle of the Night (2nd Day)
Portland, OR - Early Afternoon (3rd Day)
Seattle, WA - Early Evening Arrival (3rd Day)

EASTBOUND SCHEDULE (Condensed)
Seattle, WA - Early Morning Departure
Portland, OR - Late Morning
Boise, ID - Late Evening
Ogden, UT - Early Morning (2nd Day)
Denver, CO - Early Evening Departure (2nd Day)
Chicago, IL -Late Afternoon Arrival (3rd Day)

FREQUENCY - Three times a week, departing Chicago Sun, Tues and Thur, and Seattle Mon, Wed and Sat.
SEATING - Superliner coaches.
DINING - Complete meals, snacks, sandwiches, beverages and lounge service. Movies, Chicago-Denver.
SLEEPING - Deluxe, economy, family and special bedrooms.
BAGGAGE - Checked baggage handled at larger cities.
Reservations - All-reserved train.
Length of Trip - 2,662 miles in 53 1/2 hours.

ROUTE LOG

See the *California Zephyr* for route log from Chicago to Denver, page 150.

 DENVER, CO - See page 156.

0:00 (1:15) Depart on Union Pacific trackage—which will be followed to Ogden. As train heads northward, good views are afforded of Denver's skyline back on right. Just to right is Coors Stadium, home to major league baseball's Colorado Rockies.

0:11 (1:04) National Western Stock Show is held here each January and is largest of its kind, drawing exhibitors from throughout western U.S. and Canada. Enormous curved roof of coliseum (focus of those activities) can be seen on right.

0:18 (0:57) Pass through heavily industrialized Commerce City. Arapahoe Power plant of Public Service Company of Colorado belches clouds of steam off to left.

0:40 (0:35) Large nondescript building on left once processed sugar beets into Great Western Sugar. Tallest mountain of Rockies' Front Range is directly to left—14,255-foot Longs Peak, which is located amidst other giant peaks of Rocky Mountain National Park.

0:53 (0:22) Ft. Vasquez's walls still stand on left, carefully preserved while divided highway traffic passes nonchalantly on each side.

1:08 (0:07) Cross unimpressive South Platte River.

1:10 (0:05) As train enters Greeley, high rise dorms of University of Northern Colorado are off to left.

1:15 (0:00) Arrive Greeley. Grecian facade of Weld County Courthouse can be seen to left.

GREELEY, CO - Originally a temperance community and named for newspaperman Horace Greeley, the town now is in the heart of an agricultural cornucopia. Weld County, by many measurements, is the most agriculturally productive county in the world! Monfort feedlots east of the city are the world's largest.

0:00 (1:03) Depart Greeley.

0:03 (1:00) On right, one of area's largest cattle auctions, Greeley Producers, can be seen.

0:07 (0:56) Another sugar mill appears on right.

0:36 (0:27) Very unusual rock outcroppings look as though they might have been sculpted from adobe.

0:41 (0:22) Enter Wyoming and leave Colorado. This is a good place to spot pronghorn antelope which populate Wyoming's southern prairies.

1:00 (0:03) Cheyenne can be seen in distance on right. Look now—train does not get much closer.

1:03 (0:00) Arrive Cheyenne's Borie Station. Station is several miles west of Cheyenne to save cost and time of train making side trip into city. Cheyenne passengers are greeted by bus at trackside.

CHEYENNE, WY - It began in 1867 when the Union Pacific, pushing westward to form part of the first transcontinental railroad, selected this site as a terminal and supply point. Originally called "Shey-an-nah," it was named after the largest family of Indians in North America. Eastern capitalists and foreign nobility began to invest heavily in the area's cattle industry, and by the 1800s, Cheyenne was the wealthiest per capita city in the world. This was when the renowned Cheyenne Club was built, which had splendid cuisine and reputedly the finest liquor in the world. Concerts, theatrical performances and art now mark the city's character rather than the 60 saloons which operated back when the town was first nicknamed "Hell On Wheels." But the West is still alive and well here. In July of each year, Cheyenne holds its rip snorting Frontier Days, the granddaddy of all rodeos.

0:00 (0:52) Depart Cheyenne's Borie Station.

0:06 (0:46) On left are seven very symmetrically organized, small concrete footings, which formerly supported a water tank needed when steam locomotives were king. Such towers were placed at approximately 20-mile intervals to supply enough water during arduous climb over Sherman Hill, directly ahead.

0:14 (0:38) Rock fence on right was obviously built when labor was cheap.

0:17 (0:35) Pastoral valley off to left was site of movie *My Friend Flicka*.

0:25 (0:27) It takes sharp eyes to catch it, but several miles off to right, beyond maze of snow fences, is a red pyramidal monument erected to commemorate Ames Brothers, early-day railroad entrepreneurs. Its height belies its great distance from tracks.

0:26 (0:26) Cross 8,018-foot summit of Sherman Hill—highest point on our route. Colorado's mountains are now 60 miles south. Butch Cassidy and his train-robbing Hole-in-the-Wall Gang once greased tracks on western slope of Sherman Hill, stalling eastbound trains and making them easy prey.

0:28 (0:24) Water tower on left was one of many that once served steam locomotives of the Union Pacific.

0:33 (0:19) Pass through quarter-mile-long Hermosa tunnel, first of several between Denver and Ogden.

0:42 (0:10) Fancifully eroded red rocks of Red Buttes area decorate landscape.

0:51 (0:01) Entering Laramie, stadium and field house of University of Wyoming are clearly visible off to right.

0:52 (0:00) Arrive Laramie where, on right, station's unappealing exterior conceals its very attractive interior.

 LARAMIE, WY - Early-day Laramie had a split personality—both wild and civilized. Jack McCall was arrested here for the shooting of Wild Bill Hickok in Deadwood, South Dakota, and Jesse James spent a brief period in the Laramie jail on suspicion of a nearby stagecoach holdup. The University of Wyoming was founded here in 1887, three years before Wyoming's statehood. Women were first called for grand jury duty in Laramie—at that time a very controversial procedure. And in 1870, Wyoming became the first state to grant women the right to vote, an even more controversial step.

0:00 (1:33) Departing Laramie, town's progressive spirit is evident in newly remodeled older buildings on immediate right. Historic Oregon Trail is off to left. Both Pony Express and Overland Stages used trail, giving rise to Union Pacific's nickname *The Overland Route.*

0:12 (1:21) We're crossing the open Laramie Plains, where small herds of antelope can often be spotted. Snowy Range is off to left.

0:25 (1:08) Snow fences lining nearby hill help reduce drifting across tracks which occur during frequent Wyoming blizzards.

0:39 (0:54) Protrusion on horizon off to right is Como Bluff, one of world's most renowned dinosaur graveyards and fossil beds. It was discovered in 1877.

0:42 (0:51) Bright red buildings, just to right of tracks, is famed "Robbers' Roost" where Butch Cassidy and his gang hid from the law.

0:43 (0:50) On right, three-story beige-colored Virginian Hotel is center of Medicine Bow, where Owen Wister lived for a short time before writing his famous novel "The Virginian." Much of story is based on this locale. Log cabin in foreground was once Wister's home.

0:45 (0:48) Gigantic wind generator stands 26-stories tall on left. At one time, two of these experimental contraptions stood here; the largest was designed to generate four megawatts—enough electricity for a community of 1,500 people.

0:57 (0:36) Pass through Hannah, a coal-mining town since turn of century. Large strip mines with enormous dragline can be seen off to right. Note steam-powered red-nosed rotary snowplow off to right.

1:01 (0:32) Elk Mountain of Medicine Bow Range reaches an elevation of 11,162 feet on left, while on right, two domed concrete slabs mark site of coal mine that exploded in 1930s. Innards still smolder, but smoke cannot be seen from surface.

1:16 (0:16) At Walcott, Hole-in-the-Wall Gang pulled off largest Union Pacific train robbery—close to $5 million by today's values. Train was accosted while stopped for water.

1:20 (0:13) At milepost 666, as train rounds Devil's Curve, vertebra-like formation on right is known as Devil's Backbone.

1:21 (0:12) Stone remains of Ft. Steele stand on west bank of North Platte River on right. Buff building on left side of tracks was gun powder shed. Town was on left.

1:26 (0:07) On immediate right, Sinclair refinery "flares off" undesirable gasses.

1:33 (0:00) Arrive Rawlins.

 RAWLINS, WY - A railroad and ranching town, it too had its day with outlaws. In 1878, vigilantes hanged a train robber and at the same time sent notes to 24 other desperados, suggesting they might wish to leave before meeting a similar fate. The next day, 24 one-way train tickets were purchased. Red pigment mined near here was used in paint for the Brooklyn Bridge.

0:00 (1:45) Departing Rawlins, immediately up street to right can be glimpsed old Territorial Prison, now Wyoming State Prison, identified by silver water tower and stone edifice.

0:26 (1:19) About 100 yards west of milepost 705, adjacent to tracks on right, is what Union Pacific calls "Cherokee National Forest" or "Tree of Love on the Range."

The tree was planted by a section gang (it was known as "The Cherokee Gang") worker and his wife after the section hand complained to his spouse of the incessant Wyoming summer heat. She kept it nurtured through the years, taking water from a spring on left side of the tracks, and it grew to the lovely shrub it is today.

0:50 (0:55) Black material that is prominent along the right-of-way is not dust from coal trains, but cinders left from coal-burning steam locomotives from early-day railroading.

0:51 (0:54) Here at Tipton, last train robbery in Wyoming was committed. Again, it was the Hole-in-the-Wall Gang, but this time about all that was taken were cavalry horses after dynamited express car produced little of value.

1:14 (0:31) Pass through strip mining operation where two-mile conveyor belt on left takes coal for loading into 100-ton capacity hopper cars. Coal trains travel continuously at two-tenths mile per hour while receiving their cargoes from overhead bins. Railroad loads two trains per day with most of coal destined for nearby Jim Bridger Power Plant that furnishes electricity to a five-state region. Black Butte Mountain is off to left.

1:22 (0:23) Small one-room log cabin was once homestead of one of Wyoming's more important sheep ranching families.

1:25 (0:20) Well preserved limestone building with adjoining wall at "Point of Rocks," at left, is location of remains of historic Rock Point State Station which served as relay point in 1862 for Ben Hollady Overland Trail Stages.

1:45 (0:00) Arrive Rock Springs.

ROCK SPRINGS, WY - An early stagecoach stop and outfitting point, Rock Springs has maintained a rugged reputation. The boom and bust of minerals has produced all the problems of erratic growth and a fluctuating population.

0:00 (0:20) Depart Rock Springs.

0:14 (0:06) It takes little imagination to spot rock formation on left known as "Old Man's Face."

0:20 (0:00) Arrive in Green River amidst impressive rail yards of Union Pacific.

GREEN RIVER, WY - Located amidst spectacular rock formations on the banks of the Green River, the town was originally an Overland Stage crossing and later an important rail construction point. Before it was torn down, a 32-stall roundhouse provided repairs to the multitude of steam locomotives that once passed through here.

0:00 (1:25) Depart Green River.

0:05 (1:20) Cross over and then climb banks of Green River, whose flow fills rugged Flaming Gorge Reservoir several miles downstream to left.

0:21 (1:04) Albino-looking FMC Chemicals plant, on left, produces soda ash used in soap, glass and other products. World's largest supply is in this area. A typical Wyoming gas field is checkered by green storage tanks and equipment on right.

0:24 (1:01) Mountain Men Rendezvous was held near this spot in 1834.

1:10 (0:15) Darkness pervades while train pierces through a long tunnel.

1:25 (0:00) Arrive Evanston, where turn-of-the-century depot has been beautifully restored. Original baggage scales were constructed then depot built over them. Scales still form portion of station floor. Station was given to city in 1985.

 EVANSTON, WY - At first, Evanston was another railroad town, but

Pioneer — Echo, UT
DORIS SWANSON

this activity soon waned in importance. Now, oil, cattle, sheep and tourism make up Evanston's economy. The town boasts the nation's oldest courthouse still in use.

0:00 (1:10) Departing Evanston, watch for 1912 roundhouse, complete with turntable and 27 bays, on left. Tank-car repair firm now uses this wonderful relic. Structure replaced 15-bay roundhouse torn down in 1911.

0:06 (1:04) Enter Utah and leave Wyoming.

0:13 (0:57) Three short tunnels assist crossing increasingly difficult terrain.

0:30 (0:40) Devils Slide power plant on right belches towering columns of steam from its twin stacks.

0:36 (0:34) More tunnels and frequent river crossings are necessary as train descends toward Ogden.

0:46 (0:24) Train courses through lovely pastoral valley, contrasting sharply with earlier scenes in southern Wyoming. Interstate 80 escorts train on right.

0:55 (0:15) Nestled in Weber (pronounced WEE-ber) Canyon, small hydroelectric plant of Utah Power and Light squeezes valuable energy from Weber River on left.

0:56 (0:14) Emerge from mountains and

look down to left toward next stop—Ogden.
1:10 (0:00) Arrive Ogden Union Station, a 1924 Spanish Colonial style structure. Antique railway cars and steam locomotives are sometimes parked on adjoining track, some undergoing restoration. Salt Lake passengers will be driven to that city by a connecting bus.

Boise, ID, Amtrak Station
JACK SWANSON

OGDEN, UT - Railroading history was made near Ogden when the Union Pacific and Central Pacific Railroads met at Promontory just north of the Great Salt Lake in 1869. This meeting was ceremoniously climaxed on May 10th of that year when a golden spike was driven completing a rail route between both oceans. Immediately after completion of this transcontinental line, Ogden was chosen by the Union Pacific as a major junction point, assuring the city's future growth and prominence.

The Golden Spike National Historic Site, northwest of here, has exact replicas of the engines used in the original ceremonies. A fine railroad museum in the Ogden Amtrak station has audiovisual displays depicting functions of steam locomotives, historic engines and a rail history relief map. Browning Museum, also in the station, has the definitive gun collection of the world's foremost firearms inventor for whom the museum was named.

0:00 (2:25) Depart Ogden.
2:25 (0:00) Arrive Pocatello.

POCATELLO, ID - It was the Portneuf Valley which provided a transportation corridor to the western Montana mines in the 1860s that gave birth to Pocatello. Now this city of nearly 50,000 is a vibrant trade center and home of 5,000-student Idaho State University. Enjoying both a mild climate and a proximity to many rivers and lakes, recreational opportunities abound, including several popular geothermal pools.

0:00 (1:30) Depart Pocatello.
1:30 (0:00) Arrive Shoshone.

SHOSHONE, ID - Shoshone is a small southern Idaho trading center situated in one of the more arid regions of the state, receiving 10.3 inches of precipitation annually. Of interest are nearby Shoshone Ice and Mammoth Caves.

0:00 (2:05) Depart Shoshone.
2:05 (0:00) Arrive Boise. Situated on a pleasantly landscaped hilltop setting, commanding a fine view of the city, station boasts a handsome clock tower and an unusually attractive waiting room, topped by a high beamed ceiling. Some consider station to be most beautiful in U.S. It is also headquarters for Morrison Knudsen.

BOISE, ID - Although the Oregon Trail passed through here, so did most of those using it—that is, until gold was discovered near here in 1861. Then a fort was established by the federal government to thwart Indian raids along the trail which not only assured Boise protection but also eventual economic success. The railroad brought more activity to the region in 1865—but to the disappointment of the citizenry, bypassed Boise in favor of nearby Nampa when a dispute developed between the Oregon Short Line Railroad and the

Boise city fathers. Finally, in 1887 a stub line was completed, giving Boise direct rail access to the rest of the country. Today, Boise boasts capital city status as well as being home to several national corporations, including Morrison Knudsen, Boise Cascade and J R Simplot.

0:00 (0:35) Depart Boise.

0:14 (0:21) Train moves gingerly along "Boise Cutoff" connecting Boise to main line of Union Pacific at Nampa.

0:35 (0:00) Arrive Nampa.

NAMPA, ID - In 1886 several settlers began to build here, naming their new town after a legendary Shoshone Chief—Nampuh (Bigfoot), supposedly being of "huge proportions." The town has had its share of setbacks, most notably in 1903 when an untimely fire burned much of the business district, just when wooden water mains were being replaced that left the town with no water. A "silver-plated" pumper truck was quickly hauled in by special train from Boise, making the harrowing trip in only 20 minutes.

Today, this is the heart of a desert-area-turned-Eden due to the resourceful use of irrigation from deep wells and the Snake River. Of interest is the museum in the restored U.P. Depot and pictographs 20 miles from town, including one of the largest Indian rock drawings on record.

0:00 (0:36) Depart Nampa on main line of Union Pacific.

0:05 (0:31) Mountains on right form a special backdrop for irrigated farmlands.

0:27 (0:09) Enter Oregon and leave Idaho. Metal-superstructured bridge carries us over Snake River on its way toward one of Western Hemisphere's deepest gorges, just 90 miles north of here—Hells Canyon.

0:36 (0:00) Arrive Ontario.

ONTARIO, OR - Located on the beautiful Snake River which divides Oregon and Idaho, Ontario serves as a trade center for eastern Oregon's extensive ranch country.

0:00 (1:50) Depart Ontario and immediately cross twisting course of Snake, as *Pioneer* pays one last visit to state of Idaho.

0:07 (1:43) Cross Payette River where myriad of bird species can often be spotted along its shores.

0:08 (1:42) Through Payette, birthplace of Minnesota Twins' baseball great, Harmon Killebrew.

0:14 (1:39) Cross waters of Snake River which continue northward flow until eventually reaching Columbia River at Pasco, Washington.

0:31 (1:22) On right, unusual sand dunes stretch lazily for almost half mile.

0:32 (1:21) At Farewell Bend, note campground across river. Here, Oregon Trail made its final contact with Snake River after following it, off and on, for 350 miles. Pioneers camped at this site 100 years ago, including explorer John C. Fremont. Train now enters one of many canyons of Snake, as bordering mountains rise to almost 1,000 feet above roadbed.

0:36 (1:17) Exit canyon and recross Snake River, as *Pioneer* enters Oregon and leaves Idaho.

Gain one hour as train passes from Mountain to Pacific Time. Set your watch back (forward if eastbound) one hour.

0:40 (1:13) Through Union Pacific yards at Huntington and enter broadening Burnt River Valley as train slants across northeastern Oregon.

0:48 (1:05) Limestone from mine on right has only short distance to go to reach cement plant, also on right.

0:58 (0:55) Tunnel's darkness interrupts scenery for about half minute.

1:09 (0:44) Another cement plant, on left, takes advantage of area's prevalent limestone.

1:39 (0:14) Having climbed out of Burnt River drainage, crest Encina Pass at 3,998-foot elevation and descend toward Powder River Valley. To left is 5,392-foot Dooley Mountain.

1:53 (0:00) Arrive Baker City.

BAKER CITY, OR - In 1861, Baker experienced its own gold rush when exaggerated stories of fantastic gold-laden streams lured miners here in droves. Now encircled by ghost towns that were once flourishing mining communities, Baker City is the center for wheat farming and ranching. Recreationalists are drawn here by excellent fishing and trips to Snake River country. The dominant white structure in the center of town is the historic Antler Hotel, built in 1912. Of interest is an incredible 80-ounce gold nugget on display in the lobby of a local bank.

0:00 (0:58) Depart Baker City.

0:07 (0:51) Train follows a route bordered by forested Eagle Cap Wilderness Area in Wallowa Mountains on right and Elkhorn Ridge in Wallowa Whitman Forest on left.

0:10 (0:48) After passing through Haines, where steam is rising from a patch of trees, green-roofed building houses town's therapeutic springs.

0:48 (0:10) Hot Lake Resort's overgrown facilities can be seen on left.

0:55 (0:03) Anchoring north end of mountain range on right is 6,725-foot Mt. Prominence.

0:58 (0:00) Arrive LaGrande.

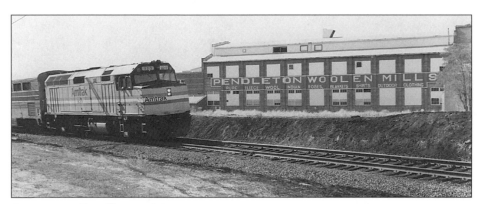 **LAGRANDE, OR** - Farming and ranching, made possible by the fertile lands of the Grande Ronde River Valley, give LaGrande a rich Western flavor. The scenery and outdoor recreational opportunities of the Wallowa and Blue Mountains make this a sportsman's paradise.

0:00 (2:05) Depart LaGrande and start a grinding ascent taking us over ridge of Blue Mountains directly ahead.

0:08 (1:57) Train slips beneath old arched concrete structure which once carried highway traffic prior to Interstate 84.

0:47 (1:18) Train finally crests 4,205-foot summit of lovely forested Blue Mountains at Kamela and starts its downward roll toward Pendleton, a 2.2% grade—steepest of route.

0:58 (1:07) Train follows sweeping reverse curves.

1:47 (0:18) Cross Umatilla River and return to flatter environs of farm and ranch country.

2:04 (0:01) On right, *Pioneer* slips past one of several world-renowned Pendleton Mills. This particular factory specializes in producing blankets.

2:05 (0:00) Arrive Pendleton.

PENDLETON, OR - This historic Western town (ruts of the Oregon Trail can still be seen at the edge of the city) hosts the renowned Pendleton Round-up during the second full week of each September. The main attraction is one of the nation's most important rodeos, including unusual trick riding and stagecoach races, as well as standard rodeo fare. Another highlight is the Happy Canyon Pageant when regional Indian tribes compete in age-old ceremonial dances.

0:00 (0:40) Depart Pendleton, following meandering Umatilla River to Pioneer's next stop, Hinkle.

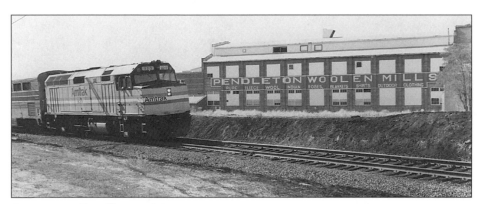

Pioneer — Pendleton, OR
JACK SWANSON

0:02 (0:38) Grandstands for famous Pendleton Round-up appear at right.

0:05 (0:35) Barbed wire and bars do little to enhance Eastern Oregon Psychiatric Center on left.

0:37 (0:03) Enter impressive Hinkle rail yards.

0:40 (0:00) Slip past large Simplot potato processing plant, on left, then arrive Hinkle.

HINKLE, OR - Here, a very small station serves the Hermiston area.

0:00 (1:22) Depart Hinkle, and continue to roll through northeastern Oregon's farm and ranch country as route approaches Columbia River.

0:05 (1:17) Hundreds of earthen mounds on right house ammunition of Umatilla Army Ordnance Depot.

0:15 (1:07) Suddenly, broad waters of Columbia River are off to right. This 1,210-mile giant produces more than a third of nation's hydroelectric power! Bluffs on far side are in state of Washington.

0:57 (0:25) Cross 300-mile-long John Day River, named after former Western scout.

0:59 (0:23) On right, John Day Dam momentarily interrupts Columbia's westward flow. Navigational lock is on far side of river and handles eight million tons of commercial traffic annually. With 113 feet maximum lift, it is one of world's highest single-lift locks. Dam's generating units can produce enough electricity to handle needs of two Seattles.

1:01 (0:21) On far side of river, just to right of bridge supporting U.S. 97, are mysterious-looking ruins of Stonehenge, a memorial to World War I dead, built by railroad entrepreneur Sam Hill.

1:05 (0:17) Just to left of that same bridge, set in a small grove of trees on far side, is Maryhill Museum. Originally built as a mansion, it was dedicated as a museum by Queen of Rumania in 1920s and now houses very diverse collections of art.

1:12 (0:10) Deschutes River crosses beneath tracks just before it flows into Columbia.

1:16 (0:06) Mount Hood, like some pyramidal specter, rises to an elevation of 11,235 feet almost directly ahead, visible now on right.

1:17 (0:05) The Dalles Dam stretches impressively across Columbia on right. Dam's hydroelectric capacity gives it a top-ten ranking in free world. Powerhouse is located in dam and is half-mile long, containing 22 generators. There are two fish ladders and a navigational lock along Washington shore.

1:22 (0:00) Arrive The Dalles' new transportation center, on left, modeled after former UP depot.

THE DALLES, OR - This was the terminus of the Oregon Trail, and a basalt memorial in a city park marks the spot where it actually ended. Now, The Dalles has become a major shipping point, and, in season, wheat-laden barges and other traffic can be seen headed down-river from here. The Dalles Dam, where visitors can see the powerhouse and a fish-counting station, can be reached by a free passenger train leaving Seufert Park. Also of interest, St. Peter's Catholic Church with 36 stained glass windows donated by pioneer families and an old pipe organ built from rare tigerwood.

0:00 (0:26) Depart The Dalles.

0:01 (0:25) Red spire of "Carpenter Gothic" St. Peter's Catholic Church, tallest structure in town, is at left.

0:04 (0:21) On right, water tower depicts principal industries of area—fishing and cherries.

0:14 (0:12) Small monument on island in river marks burial site of frontier trapper who had expressed a longing to be buried with his "Indian friends." His wish was granted.

0:26 (0:00) Cross Hood River and arrive at town of same name.

HOOD RIVER, OR - This area was probably first visited by white men in 1805 when Lewis and Clark camped in this locale. Hood River is the gateway city to Mt. Hood with its year-round recreational opportunities, including one of the continent's longest ski runs. Sailboarding is popular throughout the Columbia Gorge due to its smooth waters and prevalent winds.

Annually, sailboarders from around the world compete in the Gorge Pro-Am. Fruits and berries thrive here, and packing can be observed in October—or perhaps better yet, wine made from these products can be sipped at a local winery.

0:00 (1:13) Depart Hood River and catch glimpse of majestic Mt. Adams on right. Sadly, Mt. St. Helens is no longer viewable from here since its spectacular 1980 eruption.

0:01 (1:12) Columbia Gorge now begins to take on more dramatic proportions as river cuts through a gap in Cascades while foliage of heavy rain forests blankets southern shore. Farming and ranching of western Oregon are now scenes left behind.

0:05 (1:08) Logging flume on far side of Columbia was last one used in U.S.

0:21 (0:52) At Cascade Locks, Columbia River boat docks and river cruise boats can be seen on right.

This is the site of the historic Cascade Locks built in 1896 to bypass what were then the Cascade Rapids. The town is the beginning of several trails in the gorge as well as the beautiful Pacific Crest Trail.

0:22 (0:51) Bridge on right is "Bridge of the Gods" which now crosses river on "exact spot" where legendary natural stone bridge of Indians supposedly fell into river when nearby volcanic peaks caused ground to tremble by arguing amongst themselves.

0:26 (0:47) Venerable Bonneville Dam, first federal hydroelectric dam on Columbia, is on right. Built in 1933 at a cost of $88 million, it is now but one of nine on entire river. Shipping lock is able to raise or lower vessels 70 feet in 15 minutes, a process that uses 40 million gallons of water. Visitors can watch salmon and steelhead trout find their way up giant fish ladders.

0:29 (0:44) Sheer-walled, 800-foot monolith across river is Beacon Rock, proclaimed to be largest such formation in U.S., and second only to Gibraltar.

0:33 (0:40) Appropriately named Horsetail Falls can be glimpsed at left.

0:36 (0:37) Mostly hidden by trees at left is 620-foot Multnomah Falls. It's high, but still dwarfed by California's 1,430-foot Yosemite and 1,612-foot Ribbon Falls.

0:42 (0:31) Rooster Rock, the tall black spire on right, stands watchful guard over river as it makes its way to Pacific Ocean.

0:44 (0:29) Final tunnel before reaching Portland plunges train into momentary darkness for last time.

0:58 (0:10) Interstate 84 (Banfield Freeway) escorts train along a winding course through eastern Portland.

1:10 (0:02) Now in heart of Portland, cross over navigable waters of Willamette River on Steel Bridge. Oceangoing vessels can usually be spotted on either side of train.

1:13 (0:00) Arrive Portland.

 PORTLAND, OR - See page 236.

For route between Portland and Seattle, see the *Coast Starlight* log, page 232.

Desert Wind

Ample portions of desert landscape are served passengers on board the aptly named *Desert Wind* as it crosses some of the most arid regions of Utah, Nevada and California. Darkness usually prevails for much of the time between Salt Lake City and Las Vegas, but beyond, travel is during daylight hours allowing for fine desert viewing. The unusual rock formations of Cajon Pass are particularly intriguing.

Between Chicago and Salt Lake, the *Wind* follows the route of the *California Zephyr*. At Salt Lake City, however, and the *Desert Wind* strikes out on a route to Los Angeles formerly traveled by the *City of Los Angeles*, the once-proud flagship of the Union Pacific.

WESTBOUND SCHEDULE (Condensed)
Chicago, IL - Midafternoon Departure
Omaha, NE - Late Evening
Denver, CO - Early Morning (2nd Day)
Salt Lake City, UT - Late Night (2nd Day)
Las Vegas, NV - Early Morning (3rd Day)
Los Angeles, CA - Midafternoon Arrival (3rd Day)

EASTBOUND SCHEDULE (Condensed)
Los Angeles, CA - Late Morning Departure
Las Vegas, NV - Early Evening
Salt Lake City, UT - Early Morning (2nd Day)
Denver, CO - Midevening (2nd Day)
Omaha, NE - Early Morning (3rd Day)

Chicago, IL - Late Afternoon Arrival (3rd Day)

FREQUENCY - Triweekly departing Chicago Mon, Thur, Sat and departing Los Angeles Sun, Tues, Thur.
SEATING - Superliner coaches.
DINING - Complete meal and beverage service. Movies, except Salt Lake-Los Angeles westbound. Lounge service with sandwiches, snacks and beverages.
SLEEPING - Superliner sleepers with deluxe, family, economy and special bedrooms.
BAGGAGE - Checked baggage handled at larger cities.
RESERVATIONS - All-reserved train.
LENGTH OF TRIP - 2,397 miles in 50 hours.

ROUTE LOG

See the *California Zephyr* for route log from Chicago to Salt Lake City, page 150.

 SALT LAKE CITY, UT - See page 163.
0:00 (3:05) Depart Salt Lake City, following Union Pacific rails until we reach Daggett, California.
2:10 (0:55) Pass through Delta, Utah, a farming community situated in Utah's western desert country.
2:57 (0:05) In distance, off to left, cluster of

lights pinpoints Milford geothermal power plant of Utah Power and Light Company. Electricity is produced from steam generators powered by tapping underground reservoir of 500-degree-Fahrenheit water. Although output is a modest 20,000 kilowatts, it is first sizable facility of its kind outside of California.

3:02 (0:00) Arrive Milford.

MILFORD, UT - Predominantly a railroad town for more than a hundred years, a new thrust has resulted from Milford's geothermal developments. The nearby geothermal power plant has created new employment and lower energy costs.

0:00 (2:05) Depart Milford.

Gain one hour as train passes from Mountain to Pacific Time. Set your watch back (forward if eastbound) one hour.

1:53 (0:00) Arrive Caliente. Old Union Pacific depot houses city offices, police department, an art display and Amtrak's waiting room.

CALIENTE, NV - As reflected in its name, Caliente (Spanish, for "hot") is blessed with an abundance of geothermal energy. Its hot springs and mud baths were a welcome respite for railroad workers who founded the town at the turn of the century. Today, studies are under way directed at encouraging resort development which could capitalize on this valuable resource.

0:00 (2:19) Departing Caliente, enter Meadow Valley Wash. Lovely Rainbow Canyon is contained within but unfortunately *Desert Wind's* schedule calls for traversing this scenic stretch mostly at night.

2:19 (0:00) Arrive Las Vegas. Station is located downtown in Jackie Gaughan's Plaza hotel. Just beyond lies dazzling neon maelstrom of world-renowned Fremont Street.

LAS VEGAS, NV - From its humble beginning, first as a Mormon settlement and then a railroad town, the city has grown to become famous as a world gambling mecca and "Showtown, U.S.A." Casinos and posh hotels line "The Strip" from one end of town to the other.

Las Vegas

🚂 Amtrak Station
1 - Visitors Center
2 - Plaza Hotel & California Hotel

Even the Amtrak station is located in one of the many high-rise hotels. Nevada's legalized gambling, the city's warm and dry desert climate and its proximity to populous Southern California combine to account for Las Vegas' uniqueness.

Amtrak Station, 1 Main St., is located in the Jackie Gaughan's Plaza hotel. The station itself is quite spartan, with limited seating and some snack and drink vending machines. But down the hall is another world, the hotel's lobby, restaurants and casino.

Checker and Yellow **Cabs**, 873-2227. **Local buses** in front of the station at Fremont and Main; 228-7433.

Hoover Dam
JACK SWANSON

Las Vegas Convention and Visitors Authority, Convention Center, 3150 Paradise Rd., 89109; (702) 892-0711.

Because this is Las Vegas, there is an abundance of reasonably priced hotels throughout the city. Weekend rates are higher than those shown.

-**Jackie Gaughan's Plaza**,1 Main St., 89125; (702) 386-2110 or 800-634-6575. Amtrak station is in the hotel. $40.

-**California Hotel and Casino**, 12 Ogden Ave., 89101; (702) 385-1222 or 800-634-6255. Within a block from the station. $40.

Gambling, of course, is the chief attraction for millions of visitors each year. Casinos abound and most will be found along "The Strip" (Las Vegas Boulevard). **Shows and Reviews** at the larger hotels are true spectaculars.

Hoover Dam and the Lake Mead National Recreation Area are located 32 miles southeast on U.S. 93.

0:00 (2:54) Depart Las Vegas past lavish hotels and casinos of city's illustrious "Strip" district on left. Train then proceeds south-west across parched landscape of Mojave Desert.

0:25 (2:29) Back on left, Las Vegas now spreads out across valley floor presenting a spectacular blanket of lights for eastbound evening passengers.

0:51 (2:03) Whiskey Pete's casino, at right, offering Californians their first chance at Nevada gambling, clearly defines California-Nevada border.

2:39 (0:15) At Yermo, travel through expansive Union Pacific yards.

2:41 (0:13) Calico Ghost Town, snuggled against hillside on right, surrounds site of richest silver strike in California history. Of interest is nearby Calico Dig. In 1968, a limestone hearth was unearthed, suggesting evidence of prehistoric man over 50,000 years earlier.

2:42 (0:12) Water-filled tower on left is focus of 1,818 huge mirrors which continually track sun, creating steam for nation's first solar electric facility.

2:43 (0:11) Vast array of military equipment is stockpiled alongside warehouses of Marine Logistics Base Annex on right. Main facilities are located in nearby Barstow.

2:44 (0:10) Passing through Daggett, note two historic structures on right. Venerable 1880s Stone Hotel (built of stone) was home-away-from-home for Death Valley Scotty, who continuously reserved room #7 (with private entrance) for his personal use. On corner two doors to west is Scott's Market, once a popular spot for miners to convert "high grade" into spendable currency. Destroyed by fire in 1908, reconstructed market became first fireproof building in desert, using cement freighted in from the East.

2:48 (0:06) Marine Corps Logistics Base on left is largest of two such facilities in country. It is presently Barstow's largest employer.

2:50 (0:04) On left, McDonald's restaurant and host of shops are imaginatively housed within refurbished railroad cars.

2:54 (0:00) Arrive Barstow.

On the right, "Casa del Desierto" (House of the Desert) is appropriately inscribed across the facade of a grandiose structure next to the station. This old building was originally a Harvey House—just one of a chain of elegant eateries and hotels that once stretched along the Santa Fe. Fred Harvey's restaurants became legendary for good food—many thought it the best in the country—and pretty waitresses, in what was an otherwise wild and woolly West.

 BARSTOW, CA - Originally founded as a way station along the old Santa Fe Trail, Barstow has emerged as an important distribution lifeline, strategically located at the crossroads of two major interstates and railroads. Large military installations and a healthy tourist trade further bolster the city's burgeoning economy.

Barstow, too, enjoys a share in technology. Located here is NASA's Goldstone Tracking Station, a vital communications link for orbiting satellites and deep space probes.

0:00 (0:33) Depart Barstow through awesome sprawl of Santa Fe's classification yards. Over next several miles, onset of hillier terrain previews approach into San Bernardino Mountains.

0:21 (0:12) Just beyond peaks of Kramer Range on right lies Edwards Air Force Base, primary landing site of NASA's space shuttle.

0:29 (0:04) At Oro Grande, well-preserved steam locomotive is enshrined in town park on left.

0:33 (0:00) Arrive Victorville.

VICTORVILLE, CA - Cement production is an important Victorville industry with several such plants located here. The area has also been the setting for numerous Western movies.

0:00 (1:09) Depart Victorville.

0:02 (1:07) Sudden rock outcroppings form scenic little canyon as train crosses Mojave River. Then begin ascent of Cajon Pass which will lift us out of the Mojave Desert. Noble Joshua tree cactus is a prominent feature of northern climb, while spectacular

Cajon Pass

Since 1885 when Santa Fe's predecessor, the California Southern, pushed the first rails over the 3,811-foot top, Cajon Pass has been one of railroading's more fascinating artifacts. Three sets of tracks now descend Cajon. To the right is the Southern Pacific, the left set is Santa Fe's steeper South Track, while in the middle is Santa Fe's gentler but two-mile-longer North Track. Since a third railroad, the Union Pacific, has Cajon trackage rights on the Santa Fe, this can become a very busy place. Westbound traffic on the Santa Fe will normally descend the three percent grade of the South Track (unless weight dictates the more moderate routing), while eastbound Santa Fe traffic will climb the "casual" 2.2% North Track.

rock formations line descent into San Bernardino.

0:20 (0:46) Nearing Cajon summit, San Gabriel Mountains are prominent features to right, with San Bernardino Mountains off to left.

0:22 (0:44) Bid farewell to unconfining spaces of West and start dramatic descent of Cajon Pass into Los Angeles Basin.

0:29 (0:36) White flatiron-like Mormon Rocks are most prominent geographic feature on right. Infamous San Andreas Fault is nearby.

—- (0:31) Eastbound trains now curl through horseshoe turn known as Sullivan's Curve, named after early-day railroad photographer.

0:41 (0:24) Two Santa Fe routes now become one again. Highway on left is Interstate 15, linking Los Angeles and Las Vegas.

0:52 (0:13) Passage beneath I-15 marks finish of Cajon Pass adventure.

1:03 (0:02) Approaching San Bernardino, lush woodlands, colorful shrubbery and majestic palms represent radical departure from environs of last 750 miles.

1:05 (0:00) Arrive San Bernardino. Railroad equipment is maintained within large Santa Fe shops, while nicely landscaped grounds encircle vine-covered station.

 SAN BERNARDINO, CA - Lying in the heart of fertile citrus country, San Bernardino was first settled in the mid-19th century by a group of Mormons who modeled the town after their former home of Salt Lake City.

0:00 (1:03) Depart San Bernardino and traverse Riverside/Fullerton branch of Santa Fe.

0:17 (0:46) Through Riverside, home to March Air Force Base.

0:42 (0:21) Cross northern end of Santa Ana Mountains, and descend into congestion of southeastern Los Angeles. One last glimpse of San Gabriels is afforded to right where 10,064-foot Mt. San Antonio stands above all.

0:56 (0:07) At Orange Growers Association on left, seedling orange trees await transplantation.

1:03 (0:00) Arrive Fullerton. Santa Fe depot is a delight. Its pink stucco facade topped with a dark, red tile roof is further enhanced by unusually large, arch-shaped windows and fine grill work.

 FULLERTON, CA - Although the city has had its roots in the citrus industry, Los Angeles' growth to the south has now made Fullerton virtually indistinguishable from its much larger northern neighbor.

0:00 (0:34) Depart Fullerton.

0:09 (0:23) Pass through refinery operations and active oil wells of Santa Fe Springs. One of area's larger tank farms will soon be seen on right.

0:13 (0:21) Cross San Gabriel River.

0:15 (0:19) Cross Rio Hondo Channel.

0:22 (0:15) Acres of truck trailers used on piggyback freight trains are assembled on right at north end of yards.

0:25 (0:09) Train crosses Los Angeles River, then curls sharply right. Diesel shops, roundhouse and its companion turntable are on left where twenty or so Amtrak diesels can generally be counted.

0:27 (0:07) Amtrak coach yard is on immediate left where gaggle of Superliner cars are stored.

0:29 (0:05) Los Angeles River, encased in concrete on right, has followed our route for several minutes. Take note of old stone bridges that cross over tracks along this section. Their sculpted pilasters are reminiscent of ancient Rome and memorialize an era of Los Angeles long gone. Excellent view of Los Angeles' cityscape is on left where distinctive white-towered City Hall has center stage.

0:33 (0:01) Curl left off of main line of Santa Fe at Mission Tower.

0:34 (0:00) Arriving Los Angeles Union Station, Dodger Stadium rests atop hill off to right, then Los Angeles County Jail looms on left just before coming to stop at Los Angeles Union Passenger Terminal.

 LOS ANGELES, CA - See page 246.

Southwest Chief

When the Atchison, Topeka and Santa Fe ran its *Super Chief* between Chicago and Los Angeles, ladies received boutonnieres of fresh flowers, gentlemen were given alligator wallets and it was possible to have your hair cut in the train's barbershop. In the diner, meals were furnished by the Fred Harvey organization. Movie stars and other important personages were commonplace among the train's passengers. It was the first diesel-powered all-sleeper train in the nation.

The *Southwest Chief*, Amtrak's direct descendant of the *Super Chief*, still travels those same historic rails along the Santa Fe Trail and still provides luxurious accommodations and carries a fascinating clientele. Haircuts are not available and Amtrak doesn't give away wallets, but passengers are treated to the likes of movies in the evening and bingo in the afternoon. There is a Native American guide who travels the segment between Albuquerque and Gallup, describing some of the scenes and historical aspects of that fascinating area.

This is the shortest and quickest route of the three used by Amtrak between Chicago and Los Angeles.

WESTBOUND SCHEDULE (Condensed)
Chicago, IL - Late Afternoon Departure
Kansas City, MO - Late Night
Albuquerque, NM - Late Afternoon (2nd Day)
Flagstaff, AZ (Grand Canyon) - Late Evening (2nd Day)
Los Angeles, CA - Early Morning Arrival (3rd Day)

EASTBOUND SCHEDULE (Condensed)
Los Angeles, CA - Midevening Departure
Flagstaff, AZ (Grand Canyon) - Early Morning (2nd Day)
Albuquerque, NM - Early Afternoon (2nd Day)
Kansas City, MO - Early Morning (3rd Day)
Chicago, IL - Midafternoon Arrival (3rd Day)

FREQUENCY - Daily.
SEATING - Superliner coaches.
DINING - Complete meal and beverage service as well as lighter fare, including sandwiches, snacks and beverages. Lounge service with movies.
SLEEPING - Superliner sleepers with deluxe, family, economy and special bedrooms.
BAGGAGE - Checked baggage handled at most stations.
RESERVATIONS - All-reserved train.
LENGTH OF TRIP - 2,259 miles in 41 hours.

ROUTE LOG

 CHICAGO, IL - See page 63.

0:00 (0:55) Depart Chicago's venerable Union Station and emerge from beneath huge Chicago Post Office.
0:04 (0:51) Amtrak coach yards, on right,

Southwest Chief — Mississippi River, Ft. Madison, IA
SCOTT HARTLEY

offer interesting variety of modern-day Amtrak equipment.

0:12 (0:38) Chicago's dynamic skyline is now clearly visible back on right. Sears Tower, with its twin antennae, is world's tallest skyscraper with 110 stories.

0:15 (0:29) On left, busy Stevenson Expressway briefly accompanies tracks.

0:38 (0:13) Cross Chicago Sanitary and Ship Canal at Lemont where, on right, former flagstone quarry was accessed through tunnel beneath road.

0:47 (0:03) Somber walls of Illinois State Prison can be seen on left.

0:50 (0:00) Arrive Joliet.

JOLIET, IL - Joliet's economy is dominated by manufacturing and refining, largely developed due to its strategic rail and waterways location.

0:00 (0:45) Depart Joliet where industrialization continues with enormous coal-powered generating plants and oil refineries appearing on either side of tracks.

0:14 (0:41) Cross Kankakee River.

0:45 (0:00) Arrive Streator.

STREATOR, IL - Manufacturing of glass containers gives Streator an unusual industrial base. Containers were hand-blown in early days, but mechanization has now supplanted that older art form.

0:00 (0:35) Depart Streator and cross Vermilion River. Typical Illinois farming scenes now prevail throughout this flat, fertile land.

0:34 (0:01) Cross Illinois River whose waters flow 420 miles from Indiana to Mississippi River.

0:35 (0:00) Arrive Chillicothe.

CHILLICOTHE, IL - Just 18 miles upstream from Peoria, this grain-processing community has a delightful setting on the west bank of the Illinois River.

0:00 (0:45) Depart Chillicothe.

0:45 (0:00) Arrive at Galesburg's North Broad Street station.

GALESBURG, IL - Reverend George Washington Gale chose this spot for a ministers' college after searching westward on behalf of a fundamentalist

Presbyterian group in Oneida, New York. Famed American poet Carl Sandburg was raised here, and this was the site of a Lincoln-Douglas Debate in 1858. Olstead Ferris, A "Galesburgite" (and a relative of George Washington Ferris, inventor of the Ferris wheel), was an important experimenter with popcorn—one of the area's important products. This was such a novelty in those days that Ferris gave a corn-popping command performance before England's Queen Victoria and Prince Albert.

0:00 (0:54) Depart Galesburg.

0:38 (0:16) After passing through Lomax, *Southwest Chief* is escorted on right by America's mightiest of rivers—the Mississippi. This 2,350-mile giant drains an area equivalent to two-fifths of U.S.

0:48 (0:06) Just a few miles south of here is historic Nauvoo, a community founded by Latter-day Saints (Mormons) in 1839 after being driven out of Missouri for their religious beliefs. Today, Nauvoo has been beautifully restored and is open to visitors.

0:49 (0:05) Turn westward and cross Mississippi on bridge with world's largest double-track, double-deck swing span, handling both trains and vehicles. At midpoint, cross Illinois state line and enter Iowa.

0:50 (0:01) Upon reaching west end of bridge, Iowa State Prison is at right. Then on immediate right is factory of well-known pen maker, W.A. Shaeffer, long-time important area employer. Then on left, retired Santa Fe 4-8-4 steam locomotive stands on display while old Santa Fe depot with red caboose now serves as museum of local history.

0:54 (0:00) Arrive Fort Madison, only Iowa stop on route.

FORT MADISON, IA - Built on the site of Historic Fort Madison (1808-1813) which protected an early trading post, the city is now a community that is dependent on light manufacturing.

0:00 (1:03) Depart Fort Madison, with final view of Mississippi River Valley afforded back on left.

0:12 (0:51) Traverse Des Moines River, and at midpoint, cross Iowa state line and enter Missouri.

1:03 (0:00) Arrive LaPlata.

LAPLATA, MO - This small farming community of 1,400 also serves as a stop for its much larger northern neighbor, Kirksville. America's oldest school of osteopathic medicine was founded there in 1892.

0:00 (0:34) Depart LaPlata.

0:34 (0:00) Arrive Marceline.

MARCELINE, MO - This pleasant little Missouri community was the boyhood home of the now legendary Walt Disney. Walsworth Press, one of the country's largest book printers, is Marceline's major employer.

0:00 1:39) Depart Marceline.

0:05 (1:34) Swampy environs on right are edge of wetlands comprising Swan Lake Refuge, a way station for hundreds of thousands of migrating waterfowl.

0:11 (1:28) Cross Grand River.

1:39 (0:00) Arrive Kansas City, some 450 miles from Chicago. Santa Fe originally constructed this entire stretch in only nine months.

KANSAS CITY, MO - This second largest city in Missouri has long been one of America's most important rail centers. The city's Union Station, which also served Kansas City, Kansas, was once the third largest rail passenger station in the nation.

Everything is still up to date in Kansas City—with the nation's first and perhaps finest shopping center Country Club Plaza (it's much more a neighborhood than a traditional shopping center), a futuristic airport, and the $500 million Crown Center, about a block from the station, with 85 acres of new office buildings, apartments, and other facilities.

Amtrak Station, 2200 Main St., is located in the downtown area. This is a relatively new station, constructed adjacent to the much older Union Station. Small, but functional, there are storage lockers, redcaps, a newsstand, a gift shop and covered pay-parking.

Yellow **Cab**, 471-5000. Hertz, Avis, National and Budget have downtown **rental-car** locations, some offering station pick up and drop off. **Local buses**, 221-0660.

? Convention and Visitors Bureau, City Center Square, 1100 Main, Suite 2550, 64105. Call (816) 221-5242 or 800-767-7700.

The Westin Crown Center, Kansas City, One Pershing Road, 64108; (816) 474-4400 or 800-228-3000. Luxurious high-rise hotel, 1 1/2 blocks from the station. $160.

-**Raphael Hotel**, 325 Ward Parkway, 64112; (816) 756-3800 or 800-821-5343. Overlooks Country Club Plaza. Small and elegant. Fine location, but considerably south of station. $111.

The following hotels are about 12 blocks from the station and in the heart of downtown:

-**Holiday Inn City Center**, 1215 Wyandotte, 64105; (816) 471-1333. $60.

-**Radisson Suite Hotel**, 106 W. 12th, 64105; (816) 221-7000. A pleasant, popular hotel. $90.

Crown Center, near the station at Grande and Pershing, has retail stores, restaurants and theaters. A good place to spend time between trains.

Country Club Plaza, some distance south of downtown, is a highly attractive shopping area, with tile-roofed buildings modeled after Seville, Spain.

0:00 (0:45) Depart Kansas City, Missouri and cross state line into Kansas City, Kansas.

0:45 (0:00) Arrive Lawrence.

LAWRENCE, KS - In 1854, abolitionists established the town of Lawrence only to have it become a focal point of pro-slavery attacks—Quantrill's raid in 1863 being the bloodiest. Lawrence changed, and the University of Kansas was founded here only three years after that infamous incident.

0:00 (0:28) Depart Lawrence.

0:28 (0:00) Arrive Topeka.

TOPEKA, KS - The capital of Kansas is the location of the world-renowned Menninger Foundation. This institution offers the finest in education, research and treatment of mental illness.

0:00 (1:05) Depart Topeka.

0:32 (0:33) Through Burlingame where in 1863, with most men away fighting as Union soldiers, womenfolk erected a stone fort which they successfully used in defending themselves against Quantrill's Raiders.

1:05 (0:00) Arrive Emporia.

EMPORIA, KS - This is where editor and publisher William Allen White wrote and printed his famed *Emporia Gazette*. Turning down opportunities to write for larger newspapers, White chose to stay in Emporia and wrote some of the most important editorials of his time. A library on the campus of Emporia State University contains many of his mementos.

0:00 (0:12) Depart Emporia.

1:12 (0:00) Arrive Newton.

NEWTON, KS - In 1872, Russian Mennonites immigrated here and brought with them Turkey Red hard winter wheat. Ironically, this Russian wheat import led to Kansas becoming the "Breadbasket of the World." The area is now one of the largest Mennonite settlements in the country.

The Santa Fe intersected the historic Chisholm Trail at this point, a trace that extended as far south as Corpus Christi, Texas.

0:00 (0:34) Depart Newton.

0:34 (0:00) Arrive Hutchinson.

HUTCHINSON, KS - Wheat and salt are Hutchinson's staples. This is the largest prime wheat market in the world, and over 50 elevators handle this commodity, including one structure that holds 18 million bushels and stretches for nearly a half mile! Large salt evaporation plants of Carey, Morton and Barton process rock salt from one of the world's largest salt mines.

0:00 (1:33) Depart Hutchinson.

0:04 (1:29) Forest of white pipes "growing" out of ground on right identifies just one of Kansas' many gas fields.

0:45 (0:48) Profusion of black rocking-arm pumps, on both sides of tracks, pull oil from far beneath ground. These are a common sight throughout oil-productive Kansas.

1:04 (0:29) Passing through Kinsley, note large sign near park on right proclaiming its geographic claim to fame—halfway between New York and San Francisco, 1,561 miles from each. Pioneer sod house and steam locomotive are both restored and on exhibit in park.

1:32 (0:01) *Chief* glides through Santa Fe rail yards on outskirts of Dodge City.

1:33 (0:00) Arriving Dodge City, note two white sundials made of stones on right and next to station, one representing Central Time, the other Mountain. Today, actual time zone boundary is some 60 miles west of here.

DODGE CITY, KS - In 1872 when the Santa Fe Railroad arrived, millions of Texas longhorns were driven here for loading and Dodge City became "Cowboy Capital of the World." The law was slow to arrive, however, and its nickname soon changed to "Wickedest Little City in America."

It is said the term "Red Light District" was first used in Dodge. Headlights on locomotives were fair game for a rowdy citizenry, and train crews departing at night would not light them until the trains were safely out of town. Conditions were once so bad that the Army asked the State to spend money protecting its troops from "the meaner element." Both Bat Masterson and Wyatt Earp served as sheriff here, and Boot Hill became famous as the gunfighter's final resting place.

0:00 (0:42) Departing Dodge City, on right, exterior of First National Bank and Trust Co. sports giant mural depicting a stagecoach being drawn by six horses. Then, town's rebuilt Front Street is on right, catering to tourists anxious to sense part of the Old West.

0:06 (0:36) On hill beyond highway to right, tracks of old Santa Fe Trail are still visible.

0:12 (0:30) Here on right, about five miles east of Cimarron, can be seen snake-like mounds of Soule Canal which are all that

Southwest Chief — Garden City, KS
JACK SWANSON

remain of an early-day attempt at irrigation. A sixty-mile, hand-dug ditch was started to carry water from nearby Arkansas River to Spearville east of Dodge City, but was ultimately abandoned.

0:16 (0:26) Through Cimarron where Santa Fe Trail made its crossing of Arkansas River.

0:21 (0:21) On right, huge Ingalls Feed Yard is positioned on slopes that permit important drainage. Several thousand head are fed here each year.

0:42 (0:00) Arrive Garden City.

GARDEN CITY, KS - A lot of "largests" are in this small Kansas community. One of the world's largest natural gas fields and Kansas' largest buffalo herd are near here. An annual Industry, Irrigation and Implement Show in late June and a concrete municipal swimming pool both claim to be the largest of their kinds in the world.

In 1929, before nighttime flying was commonplace, Garden City played an important role in an imaginative coast-to-coast travel option offered by three transportation companies. Passengers could travel by rail between New York and Cleveland on the New York Central's *Southwestern Ltd.*, by plane from Cleveland to Garden City on Universal Air, and by train between Garden City and Los Angeles aboard the Santa Fe's *California Ltd.* The trip took three nights and two days.

0:00 (1:13) Depart Garden City.

0:06 1:07) Holcomb is easily identified by city standpipe decorated with horns of longhorn steer, an animal that could endure arid southwestern ranges and was foundation of U.S. cattle industry in 1800s. This is also locale for murders Truman Capote described in his book *In Cold Blood*.

Gain one hour as train passes from Central to Mountain Time. Set your watch back (forward if eastbound) one hour.

0:31 (0:42) Watch for fields of sunflowers in this part of The Sunflower State. No longer considered a pesky weed, plants are grown for their seeds and also used as cattle feed.

0:50 (0:23) Leave Kansas and enter Colorado.

The State of Kansas had guaranteed the Santa Fe a grant of three million acres, comprised of all odd-numbered sections ten miles either side of its tracks, if Colorado was reached by March 1, 1873. The Santa Fe almost lost this valuable asset when, in December 1872, construction crews mistakenly stopped four miles east of here thinking they had reached the border. When a government surveyor pointed out the mistake, the crews hurriedly pulled up four miles of sidings for the necessary materials and finished the job.

0:56 (0:17) Cross portion of Arkansas River which once formed the boundary between Mexico and the United States.

1:13 (0:00) Arrive Lamar where statue known as The Madonna of the Trail commemorates pioneer mothers of the covered wagon days, on left.

In the 1920s, a Daughter of the American Revolution and Harry Truman, then a Missouri county judge, jointly petitioned Congress for an endorsement that would commemorate America's well-known pioneer trails. The National Old Trails Road designation was the outcome. Twelve identical statues were commissioned to honor the pioneer women who faced the trails' hardships and were placed at appropriate spots, Lamar being one of those honored places. The mother holds an infant in her left arm, a rifle barrel in her right hand while another child clutches at her skirts.

LAMAR, CO - Ravaged by sand and dust storms in the early thirties, careful conservation efforts have allowed Lamar to become the trading center of southeastern Colorado with cattle and grain important to its economy. Large, shallow lakes nearby make it the "Goose Hunting Capital of America." The major employer in Lamar is Neoplan, a German-owned bus manufacturing firm.

0:00 (0:43) Depart Lamar.

0:09 (0:34) John Martin Dam, on right, backs up Arkansas, creating John Martin Reservoir. Dam was constructed during the 1930s as a flood control and irrigation project by Army Corps of Engineers. Firm that contracted for this work was same one that built Panama Canal's locks. Watch for herons, cranes and other waterfowl.

0:21 (0:22) Brick buildings clustered amidst trees, on right, are Fort Lyon Veterans Administration Hospital and National Cemetery. Old Fort Lyon housed a regiment of soldiers whose job was to protect trappers and traders from Indian attacks. Kit Carson died at Fort Lyon in 1868 due to complications from an arrow wound in his shoulder.

0:22 (0:21) Cross Purgatoire River, so-named by French, but earlier called El Rio de las Animas Perdidas (River of Lost Souls) by Spanish. American frontiersmen, however, cared for neither title and called it Picketwire.

0:32 (0:11) If you look sharply, you may be able to spot Bent's Old Fort just across the river, back to right and through trees. It's hard to see though. Fort controlled mountain fur trade in the early 1800s, and served wagon traffic along Santa Fe Trail. When the fort's owner William Bent tried to sell it to the government, the U.S. wouldn't meet his purchase price of $16,000. Piqued over this rebuff, he leveled it with explosives. Today it is a near-perfect replica of original fort, having been meticulously restored by the National Park Service.

0:43 (0:00) Arrive LaJunta (pronounced LaHunta).

LAJUNTA, CO - Kit Carson once lived in this southern Colorado town that now serves as divisional headquarters for the Santa Fe Railroad. Situated in the fertile Arkansas River Valley, numerous fruit, melon and vegetable crops are grown in the area—perhaps best-known is the famous Rocky Ford cantaloupe.

Highly regarded Koshare Indian dancers, who are really not Indians but local Explorer Scouts, have preserved Koshare dances throughout the years and have given performances from coast to coast.

0:00 (1:15) Depart LaJunta and leave river valley, swinging southwestward through a patchwork of buttes and prairies called Comanche National Grassland.

0:02 (1:13) Another preserved steam locomotive is in park-like setting on left.

1:00 (0:15) Prominent twin summits of West and East Spanish Peaks of Colorado Rockies can be seen on right. Indians once referred to these two mountains as "Breasts of the World."

1:15 (0:00) Arrive Trinidad.

TRINIDAD, CO - Established in 1859 at the base of the Culebra Range and on the Purgatoire River, Trinidad witnessed a period of unrest between Spanish and non-Hispanic settlers which finally reached a climax in the "Battle of Trinidad" on Christmas Day in 1867. After four days of skirmishing, Federal troops arrived and put an end to the open hostilities.

Trinidad has distinguished itself as the "Sex Change Capital of the World." Dr. Stanley Biber, a local physician, has performed well over 3,000 of these operations and has a world-wide clientele.

0:00 (1:04) Depart Trinidad and commence a climb of 1,563 feet within next 10 miles as *Southwest Chief* traverses scenic Raton Pass. Interstate 25 will now accompany train off and on until Albuquerque.

0:15 (0:49) Coal mines on right once fur-

Raton Pass

"Uncle Dick" Wootton settled here and built a hotel and a 27-mile toll road over Raton Pass as part of the Santa Fe Trail, a venture that did quite well. All had to pay except Indians, Mexicans and posses chasing horse thieves. When the railroad came through, he rejected their offer of $50,000 for his operation and asked only for a lifetime pass for his family and $25 per month in groceries.

nished coal to both railroad and steel mills in Pueblo.

0:33 (0:31) Wootton Ranch buildings are on right, as well as portion of original Santa Fe Trail.

0:38 (0:21) Train crests Raton Pass at an elevation of 7,588 feet—highest point on route between Chicago and Los Angeles. Cross Colorado state line and enter New Mexico by way of one-and-a-half-mile tunnel.

1:04 (0:00) Arrive at Raton at southern base of Raton Pass. On right, Spanish-style station greets detraining passengers.

RATON, NM - Raton was founded in the foothills of the Sangre de Cristo (Blood of Christ) Mountains and grew because of coal and the railroad. Livestock is now its mainstay.

0:00 (1:53) Depart Raton, then follow southeast boundary of historic Maxwell Land Grant for 62 miles. This grant from Mexico was huge—roughly three times the size of Rhode Island. It received its name from Lucien Benjamin Maxwell who purchased the property from the original grantees.

0:41 (1:12) At Springer depart from Canadian River and cross Cimarron River. High mountain to right is 12,440-foot Baldy Peak.

1:02 (0:51) Small town of Wagon Mound is named for landmark butte of Santa Fe Trail off to left.

1:31 (0:21) Pass through canyon country where willows and cottonwoods, along with stubby pinon pines, embroider creek bottoms. Just before Watrous, watch for ruins of Fort Union on hillside on left. This historic outpost once guarded old Santa Fe Trail and easier-but-more-Indian-exposed Cimarron cutoff.

1:43 (0:10) Just six miles north of here is Montezuma.

In 1879, Jesse James spent a month there while inquiring about the sheep business and other opportunities. Later the Santa Fe erected a luxurious hostelry called Montezuma Hot Springs Hotel and Sanitarium, a 268-room Queen Anne-style castle pampering to rail travelers. In 1982, no less than England's Prince Charles and financier Armand Hammer transformed the former spa into a unique school, with students from around the world. Known as the United World of the American West, it teaches appreciation and tolerance of cultures and political differences.

1:47 (0:06) Forward on right, at some distance, are higher peaks of Sangre de Cristos.

1:53 (0:00) Arrive Las Vegas. Note Castaneda Hotel just before station on right. This building, with its tiled roof and arched facade, was part of original Harvey House system of hotels and restaurants along the Santa Fe.

Harvey, himself, was dining here one evening in 1883, when a band of drunken cowhands rode their horses into the dining room and began shooting bottles on display behind the bar, swearing loudly and demanding food. Calmly, Harvey stood up and in a cool but authoritarian voice said, "Gentlemen, ladies are dining here. No swearing or foul language is permitted. You must leave quietly at once." They did just that.

In 1899, Colonel Theodore Roosevelt arrived by train to rejoin his Rough Riders for their first reunion which was held in this hostelry.

LAS VEGAS, NM - Although in the 1830s a Mexican land grant gave rise to the first permanent settlement of Las Vegas, Coronado probably first visited this region in 1541. The Santa Fe Trail made Las Vegas important regionally, but with the arrival of the railroad in 1879, the town became the major shipping point for the entire Southwest.

0:00 (1:47) Upon departing Las Vegas, an interesting railroad roundhouse appears momentarily on right.

0:02 (1:45) On left, large "H" etched in hillside is for New Mexico Highlands University.

0:29 (1:18) Off to left and forward, Starvation Peak, appearing like a miniature volcano, is site of a possible tragedy years ago. Supposedly 30 or 40 Spanish settlers, pursued by Navajos, climbed the peak and held off their attackers with rocks. Stories differ whether they then starved to death at the top, or descended because of lack of food, only to be massacred by their Indian foes.

0:38 (1:07) Dramatic double-S curve allows marvelous photo opportunities for those hoping to get shots of entire train, fore and aft.

0:50 (0:57) Cross Pecos River where old Spanish mission of San Miguel can be seen on left.

1:16 (0:31) At Rowe, Pecos National Monument is off to right, containing ruins of one of largest pueblos.

1:25 (0:22) Glorieta is easily identified by Baptist Assembly's huge retreat building on right. One of West's few Civil War conflicts occurred at Glorieta Pass when Colorado Volunteers defeated Texas Confederates March 28, 1862.

1:42 (0:05) *Southwest Chief* seems to miss rocks by only foot or so while snaking through spectacular Apache Canyon, one of trip's highlights.

1:47 (0:00) Arriving Lamy, note Legal Tender saloon and restaurant on right, oldest structure (1881) in Lamy.

Restaurant has had a fine collection of period American paintings and prints, including two works by renowned artist Thomas Moran. Hand-carved cherry wood bar was imported from Germany by first owner who operated premises as a saloon and general store. Building sports National Register of Historic Places plaque—and at least three legendary ghosts.

LAMY, NM (SANTA FE) - Named for the first archbishop of Santa Fe, Lamy serves as Amtrak's stop for Santa Fe, 15 miles to the north. Originally, Santa Fe was supposed to be on the railroad's main line (after all, it was first called the Atchison, Topeka and Santa Fe Rail Road), but by the time the railroad reached New Mexico, Santa Fe had declined in importance as a trade center, and reaching it other than by a spur would pose difficult and expensive construction problems. So only a branch

was built in 1880 to the town that is the railroad's principal appellation. Sante Fe was the western terminus of the Santa Fe Trail and the railroad's arrival meant the trail would soon fade from the scene.

A connecting shuttle van operates between here and Santa Fe, including stops at major hotels. This can be booked when train reservations are made.

0:00 (1:03) Depart Lamy.

0:06 (0:57) Final look at Sangre de Cristo Mountains is afforded, back on right. Former ranch of folk singer Burl Ives is off to left.

0:07 (0:56) Los Cerrillos, freshly painted in 1988 for Hollywoods' film *Young Guns*, passes by.

0:27 (0:36) Note front of Santa Domingo Trading Post, on right, attractively adorned with Indian designs.

0:29 (0:34) Santa Domingo Pueblo, where beehive-shaped ovens are apparent, is at right. Pueblo dates back to 16th century.

0:36 (0:27) Pass by Pueblo of San Filipe Indian Reservation. Here, vivid mural adorning side of church, on right, presents a startling visual contrast with its colorless surroundings.

0:50 (0:13) Sandia Peak, rising to 10,768 feet on left, is eastward buttress of Rio Grande Valley as train approaches Albuquerque.

1:03 (0:00) Arriving Albuquerque, University of New Mexico dormitories can be seen on left.

ALBUQUERQUE, NM - Located in the fertile Rio Grande Valley and protected from severe weather by the Sandia Peaks to the east, Albuquerque enjoys a pleasant year-round climate with an ample quantity of sunshine during the winter months.

Albuquerque rightfully claims to be one of America's oldest inland cities. It was in 1706, seventy years before the American Revolution, that a handful of Spanish settled in what is now called "Old Town." Paradoxically, most of the city's growth has been new. It is the trading and industrial center of New Mexico with industries ranging from nuclear research to the large Santa

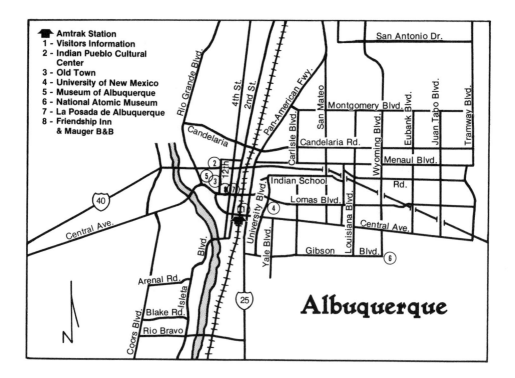

Albuquerque

Map Legend:
▲ Amtrak Station
1 - Visitors Information
2 - Indian Pueblo Cultural Center
3 - Old Town
4 - University of New Mexico
5 - Museum of Albuquerque
6 - National Atomic Museum
7 - La Posada de Albuquerque
8 - Friendship Inn & Mauger B&B

Fe railroad shops.

 Amtrak Station, 314 First St. SW (at First and Lead).

 Yellow **Cab**, 247-8888. Budget **rental cars** are nearby, (505) 768-5900. **Local buses**, call Sun Tran, 843-9200. **Greyhound** is immediately across the street.

 Albuquerque Convention and Visitors Bureau,121 Tijeras NE; (505) 243-3696 or 800-284-2282.

 LaPosada de Albuquerque, 125 2nd St. NW, 87102; (505) 242-9090 or 800-777-5732. Popular, comfortable Southwestern-style hotel. Complimentary full breakfast. Conveniently located on the edge of the central business district, just four blocks from the station. $88.

-**Friendship Inn**, 717 Central Ave. NW, 87102; (505) 247-1501 or 800-424-4777. On the edge of the central business district. About a mile from the station. $40.

-**W.E. Mauger Bed & Breakfast**, 701 Roma Ave., 87102; (505) 242-8755. Three-story restored Queen Anne, on the edge of downtown. Eight rooms, each with private bathroom (showers). About a mile from the station. $70.

 Downtown Albuquerque, with many shops and restaurants, is at the station's doorstep.

An alternative to the standardized stores and restaurants of downtown, **Old Town** is about two miles from the downtown area. This was the first settlement of Albuquerque. Shops and restaurants around a gas-lit plaza offer unique shopping and dining. San Felipe de Neri Church was built in 1793; mass has been held here on an uninterrupted basis since its completion.

Indian Pueblo Cultural Center, 2401 12th NW, is owned and operated by the 19 Indian Pueblos of New Mexico. There are shops with arts and crafts, a museum, a restaurant and dancers. A **visitors center** is also located here.

In early October, Albuquerque is host to its biggest event, the renowned **Inter-**

national Balloon Fiesta. Hot-air balloons from around the world take part for this nine-day extravaganza.

0:00 (2:20) Departing Albuquerque, farmlands of Rio Grande Valley soon give way to arid terrain of Southwestern desert.

0:02 (2:18) On left, pass University of New Mexico's sports stadium.

0:04 (2:16) Grounds of Rio Grande Park and Zoo are visible in distance on right.

0:13 (2:07) Cross Rio Grande River.

0:14 (2:06) Handsome mission stands proudly amidst Isleta Indian Reservation on left.

0:26 (1:54) At railroad junction of Dalies, train intersects with "main line" and proceeds westerly across desert landscape, its mystic beauty now further enhanced by a dramatic intrusion of mesas and buttes.

0:28 (1:52) Peak seen in distance on right is Mt. Taylor, named for President Zachary Taylor and nobly presiding at 11,301 feet.

0:34 (1:46) Cross Rio Puerco which flows into Rio Grande a few miles downstream. Also at this time, embark on a gradual 3,000-foot ascent that culminates atop Continental Divide outside Thoreau.

0:48 (1:32) Pass under wooden trestle that supports historic "Route 66."

0:51 (1:29) "Kneeling Nuns," who appear to be praying before a stone altar, is appropriate title of rock formation on right.

0:54 (1:26) Stark gypsum cliffs border on right as train passes through grounds of Mesita Pueblo. Some primitive buildings seen here on left have been inhabited by as many as five generations of same family.

0:55 (1:25) Join small San Jose River on left

Southwest Chief — near Gallup, NM
DORIS SWANSON

which train crosses several times over next few miles.

0:58 (1:22) Pass through Laguna Pueblo.

1:02 (1:18) Venerable mission of Acoma Indians is most prominent fixture of Acomita Pueblo, on left.

1:08 (1:12) Picturesquely poised atop bluff on left, resplendent two-centuries-old mission at McCartys Pueblo is reputedly built upon foundation of earlier Franciscan mission. Mission is part of Acoma Indian Reservation.

1:11 (1:09) Exposed lava beds lining trackside on left reflect early volcanic nature of aforementioned Mt. Taylor.

1:52 (0:28) Imperceptibly, cross Campbell's "Pass" and Continental Divide where waters behind us flow to Atlantic and waters ahead run to Pacific.

2:12 (0:08) Pyramid Rock and spire-crowned Church Rock appear on right.

2:13 (0:07) Structures and storage mounds of Ft. Wingate Army Depot are on right.

2:14 (0:06) Cliffs on right are part of Red Rock State Park, site of annual Gallup Intertribal Indian Ceremonial where tribes from around the country gather each August for ceremonial dancing and rodeo competition.

2:18 (0:01) Entering confines of Gallup, venerable El Rancho Hotel is on left. Built in 1937 by brother of movie magnate D.W. Griffith to house actors for Westerns (frequently filmed in region), its guests included John Wayne, Humphrey Bogart, Lucille Ball, Tom Mix and Ronald Reagan. After slipping into bankruptcy in 1987, it was restored and reopened the following year.

2:20 (0:00) Arrive Gallup's intermodal train station, remodeled in 1988 at a cost of 1.6 million dollars.

 GALLUP, NM - Hopi, Navajo and Zuni Indians all live in and around Gallup, and these Native Americans comprise more than half of the town's population. Here, visitors can find beautiful silver jewelry, baskets, rugs and pottery in numerous large trading posts, and just east a few miles, the famous Intertribal Ceremonial is held at Red Rock State Park.

0:00 (1:41) Depart Gallup.

0:20 (1:21) Pass beneath I-40, and enter Arizona and southern protrusion of Navajo Indian Reservation.

 Cross Arizona border. Since Arizona does not observe daylight saving time, set your watch back (forward if eastbound) one hour, if rest of country is currently on daylight saving time.

0:32 (1:09) At Sanders, tracks exit Navajo Indian Reservation.

0:56 (0:45) Cross through neck of hour-glass-shaped Petrified Forest National Park. This stark country was heavily wooded 150 million years ago. Now, giant agatized logs and smaller fragments lie scattered throughout area forming world's largest and most colorful concentration of petrified wood. Colorful soils of Painted Desert lend added drama to landscape, particularly when sun is near horizon.

1:14 (0:27) Through Holbrook, one of northern Arizona's larger ranching and trading centers, and former important "gas stop" on legendary Route 66. Little Colorado River follows on left until just before Winslow.

1:22 (0:19) Electric generating station at right consumes about four carloads of coal each hour to keep much of Southwest supplied with energy.

1:41 (0:00) Arrive Winslow.

 WINSLOW, AZ - Another trading center for Navajos and Hopis, Winslow sometimes goes by the nickname "Meteor City." Twenty miles west of town is Meteor Crater, a 4,000-foot-wide, 600-foot-deep hole created when an enormous meteorite, traveling at incredible speed, struck the earth 20,000 years ago.

0:00 (1:02) Depart Winslow.

0:29 (0:33) Cross Canyon Diablo on 560-foot steel bridge, 225 feet above creek's bed. This was one of railroad's major hurdles in its march westward. Original bridge took 15 months to construct and was started on site long before tracks reached this mini-gorge.

0:53 (0:10) San Francisco Peaks, tall mountains right forward, rise to 12,670 feet above sea level.

1:02 (0:00) Arrive Flagstaff.

FLAGSTAFF, AZ - On the nation's 100th birthday, celebrants stripped a pine tree of its branches so that it could serve as a staff for the country's flag. The site was near a spring and frequently served as a camping spot for California-bound travelers—who soon began to refer to it by its present name. This is the stop for Amtrak passengers visiting the Grand Canyon.

0:00 (2:56) Depart Flagstaff.

0:44 (2:12) Rumble across intersection with Grand Canyon Railway, just north of Williams from where steam train excursion service to Grand Canyon is available.

1:37 (1:39) Through Seligman, established in 1882 at the junction of the Santa Fe's main line and a line to Prescott.

2:56 (0:00) Arrive Kingman.

 KINGMAN, AZ - Kingman was established in 1882 along the Santa Fe's main line. Throughout the sparsely settled West, towns had a propensity to sprout along the tracks, quite unlike the East where railroads were built to serve existing population centers.

0:00 (1:01) Depart Kingman.

![clock icon] Pass from Mountain to Pacific Time as train crosses Colorado River and Arizona state line into California. Since Arizona does not observe daylight saving time, set watch back (forward if eastbound) one hour only if rest of country is not currently on daylight saving time.

1:01 (0:00) Arrive Needles.

![icon] **NEEDLES, CA** - California's easternmost city is located in the arid Mojave Desert, where temperatures frequently are the highest in the nation. Named for a group of nearby rock pinnacles, Needles was first a railroad way station, then a mining town, and finally a city of pipeline companies and tourist industries. Fred Harvey once broke with tradition and used male waiters at Needles Harvey House, since he felt town too bawdy for his prim and proper waitresses.

0:00 (2:31) Depart Needles.

2:19 (0:12) Vast array of military equipment is stockpiled alongside warehouses of Marine Logistics Base Annex on right.

2:20 (0:11) Water-filled tower on right is focus of 1,818 huge mirrors which continually track sun, creating steam for nation's first solar electric facility.

2:21 (0:10) Passing through Daggett, note two historic structures on right. Venerable 1880s Stone Hotel (built of stone) was home-away-from-home for Death Valley Scotty, who continuously reserved room #7 (with private entrance) for his personal use. To west on corner, Scott's Market was popular spot for miners to convert "high grade" into spendable currency. Destroyed by fire in 1908, reconstructed market become first fireproof building in desert.

For Barstow to Los Angeles, see log of *Desert Wind*, page 183.

Texas Eagle

From Chicago, the *Texas Eagle* makes its way to St. Louis through Abe Lincoln's central Illinois, on through the Ozarks to Little Rock, across eastern Texas to Dallas and Ft. Worth, then a final southward thrust to San Antonio. Through coaches and sleepers travel to and from Los Angeles, by way of the *Sunset Limited*.

When traveling from Chicago to Los Angeles there is a two-hour layover at San Antonio in the middle of the night. Traveling from Los Angeles to Chicago the layover is one hour in the early morning.

SOUTHBOUND SCHEDULE (Condensed)
Chicago, IL - Early Evening Departure
St. Louis, MO - Late Night
Little Rock, AR - Early Morning (2nd Day)
Dallas, TX - Midafternoon (2nd Day)
San Antonio, TX - Late Night (2nd Day)
Los Angeles, CA - Early Morning Arrival (3rd Day)

NORTHBOUND SCHEDULE (Condensed)
Los Angeles, CA - Late Evening Departure
San Antonio, TX - Early Morning Departure (2nd Day)
Dallas, TX - Midafternoon (2nd Day)
Little Rock, AR - Late Evening (2nd Day)
St. Louis, MO - Early Morning (3rd Day)
Chicago, IL - Early Afternoon Arrival (3rd Day)

FREQUENCY - Three times a week departing Chicago Sun, Tues, Fri and departing Los Angeles Sun, Tues, Fri.

SEATING - Superliner coaches.

DINING - Complete meal and beverage service. Lounge service with sandwiches, snacks, beverages, and movies.

SLEEPING - Superliner sleepers with deluxe, family, economy and special bedrooms.

BAGGAGE - Checked baggage handled at larger cities.

RESERVATIONS - All-reserved train, except coach travel between Chicago and St. Louis.

LENGTH OF TRIP - 2,767 miles in 48 hours.

ROUTE LOG

 CHICAGO, IL - See page 63.

0:00 (0:43) Depart Chicago's venerable Union Station and emerge from beneath huge Chicago Post Office.

0:04 (0:39) Amtrak coach yards on right offer interesting variety of modern-day Amtrak equipment.

For forty minutes the sights of some of Chicago's more industrial environs will pass by as the *Texas Eagle* traverses through rail yards and past power plants, refineries and assorted manufacturing facilities, before finally entering rural Illinois.

0:06 (0:35) Cross South Branch Chicago River, then turn west following Sanitary and Ship Canal out of city. Illinois has more active miles of canals than any other state. Stevenson Expressway briefly accompanies tracks on left.

0:15 (0:28) Chicago's dynamic skyline is now clearly visible back on right.

0:21 (0:22) Illinois Central freight yards stretch along route on left.

0:28 (0:15) Rumble over Calumet Sag Canal connecting Chicago Sanitary and Ship Canal with Lake Michigan—an engineering feat that reversed flow of Chicago River so that it now flows out of Lake Michigan.

0:37 (0:06) Note towpath along banks of Illinois and Michigan Canal, on right.

0:40 (0:03) On left are dreary walls of Joliet Correctional Center.

0:43 (0:00) Arrive Joliet.

JOLIET, IL - Joliet's economy is dominated largely by manufacturing and refining, developed largely due to its strategic rail and waterway location.

0:00 (0:50) Depart Joliet.

0:06 (0:44) Size of cavernous limestone quarry on left is difficult to bring into perspective.

0:13 (0:37) Earthen mounds (in distance through trees) are actually munitions storage bunkers of U.S. Army Arsenal.

0:17 (0:33) Cross Kankakee River.

0:22 (0:28) Large windowless structure with two enormous "silos" is Commonwealth Edison's Briarwood Nuclear Power Station. Golf course on left rests on reclaimed coal strip mine.

0:34 (0:00) As train arrives Dwight, small white church with spire-like steeple is Pioneer Gothic Church where Price of Wales attended services in 1860. Travel down Main Street of Dwight where rambling old depot on right dates back to 1892. Designed by Henry Ives Cobbs, designer of first buildings of University of Illinois, it was considered finest between Chicago and St. Louis.

DWIGHT, IL - Across West Main Street, is a one-story brick structure with a clock on top. This is one of three banks designed by Frank Lloyd Wright, and the only one still standing. Two doors to the right of that is the state hospital, originally a fine hotel. Its lights were first turned on by Teddy Roosevelt while making a brief stop here in 1903.

0:00 (0:18) Departing Dwight, on left, magnificent windmill, built in 1896 to supply water to a private estate, is Dwight's pride. Tower houses an 88-barrel cypress tank, while 3,000-pound fan wheel was constructed in Argentina to replace original which was broken by a 1975 storm.

0:16 (0:00) Arrive Pontiac.

PONTIAC, IL - Pontiac is primarily an agriculturally oriented trading and distribution center.

0:00 (0:31) Depart Pontiac. (Northbound *Texas Eagle* does not stop here.)

0:25 (0:06) Pass under Interstate 55 and enter outskirts of Normal. Archaic buildings off to right once housed Illinois Soldiers' and Sailors' Children's School.

0:27 (0:04) Watterson Towers, impressive twin high rises on right, are dormitories of Illinois State University; campus lies just beyond.

0:31 (0:00) Arrive Bloomington-Normal.

BLOOMINGTON-NORMAL, IL - Nearby Bloomington is the birthplace of former vice president Adlai E. Stevenson and the site of Abraham Lincoln's "Lost Speech" which launched him toward the presidency. Once dependent on coal mining, the Bloomington-Normal area is the corporate headquarters of State Farm Insurance, the home of Illinois State University, the state's first public institution of higher learning, and Illinois Wesleyan University.

0:00 (0:30) Depart Bloomington-Normal.

0:27 (0:00) Arrive Lincoln.

LINCOLN, IL - First town to be named in honor of Abraham Lincoln, an historical marker in the shape of a watermelon on the grounds of Lincoln's old Chicago & Alton Depot, just to the left, marks the spot where he christened the city "Lincoln" in 1853—with watermelon juice. The Amtrak station is glass enclosure just south of the depot. Chamber of Commerce occupies the north end of the depot, utilizing two old cabooses for a most unusual entryway. Domed building, a block to the left, is Logan County Courthouse.

0:00 (0:30) Depart Lincoln.

0:32 (0:00) Arrive Springfield where capitol complex is dominated by awesome State Capitol Building directly to the right. Ground was broken for construction in 1886 where its massive dome and rotunda now rest on bedrock. Multicolumned building midway between train and Capitol is State Supreme Court Building.

SPRINGFIELD, IL - In 1837, the state capital moved to Springfield, and simultaneously a circuit-riding Abraham Lincoln decided to settle here and opened his law office. Also, the only home he ever owned is about five blocks east of the tracks. The Lincoln Depot, where he delivered his famous "Farewell Address" before departing for Washington in 1861, is also a few blocks east of the present Amtrak route.

0:00 (0:37) Depart Springfield.

0:08 (0:29) Cross tip of beautiful Lake Springfield where attractive homes of Springfield's more affluent suburbanites can be seen nestled in trees on left.

0:21 (0:16) Pretty little Virden golf course adjoins tracks on left.

0:37 (0:00) Arrive Carlinville. Note silver-spired Greek Revival county courthouse about three blocks to left.

CARLINVILLE, IL - Coal mining was once prevalent in this area when miners either commuted from Springfield by train, or lived here in Sears mail order houses.

0:00 (0:30) Depart Carlinville.

0:05 (0:25) Terrain becomes momentarily rolling and forested, suggesting the Mississippi River could be near.

0:30 (0:00) Arrive Alton.

ALTON, IL - Located on the mighty Mississippi River across from St. Louis, this historic area was first visited by white men in 1673. Much later, Lewis and Clark built their first camp and spent the winter here before making their great Northwest expedition. In 1858, the seventh and last of the Lincoln-Douglas debates was held in Alton.

0:00 (0:40) Depart Alton.

0:07 (0:33) Cross Cahokia Diversion Canal.

0:18 (0:22) Industrialization, including foundries and other heavy industry, becomes more apparent as we near St. Louis.

0:23 (0:17) Train curls slowly to right as it prepares to cross great Mississippi River on Merchants Bridge.

0:24 (0:16) Now high over Mississippi, an excellent view of St. Louis is afforded on left. Soaring Gateway Arch is clearly visible. At midstream we enter Missouri and leave Illinois.

0:27 (0:13) As train turns southward again, square brick spire of antique water tower stands on hill to right.

0:32 (0:08) Gateway Arch and skyline forward on right create exciting approach to city.

0:34 (0:06) Pass under Martin Luther King Memorial Bridge and then Eads Bridge with fascinating steelwork. Latter was completed in 1874 and designed by a self-educated engineer James Eads. Its spans were largest

---

Mail-Order Homes

Between 1909 and 1937, Sears sold 100,000 precut houses that arrived by train ready for assembly, even including the fixtures. Segments arrived to coincide with construction schedules with the paint arriving last. These "HonorBilt" homes ranged in price from a mere $595 to $5,000, depending on the degree of simplicity or amount of "elegance."

One hundred fifty-six of these were erected in Carlinville's Standard Addition, a subdivision built by Indiana Standard for their coal miners. Today, nearly all are occupied and lovingly maintained.

ever constructed at that time.

0:36 (0:04) Mississippi River sternwheeler can often be seen docked on left.

0:37 (0:03) Imposing Busch Memorial Stadium, home of baseball's Cardinals, is just to right.

0:40 (0:00) Arrive St. Louis.

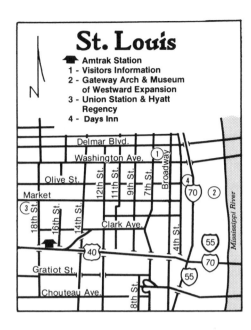

ST. LOUIS, MO - Founded in 1764 by two French fur traders as a trading post, St. Louis grew rapidly into one of the most important cities in the Frontier West. Due to its location at the confluence of the Mississippi and Missouri Rivers, it was readily accessible for river boat travel and farther exploration to the west. Lewis and Clark began their two-year expedition from this point. Railroad construction after the Civil War made St. Louis an even more dominant factor in the nation's development.

Today, the view of this metropolis is dramatized by one of the most striking and imaginative structures to be built in any American city, the Gateway Arch.

Amtrak Station, 550 South 16th Street. A small "temporary" (1978) facility located in an industrial area near downtown and a few blocks from the old Union Station. There are storage lockers and food and beverage vending machines. Free parking is adjacent to the station.

Yellow **Cab**, 361-2345. Both Budget and Hertz have downtown **rental car** locations. **Local bus** and **Metrolink**, the city's new electric light rail system connecting downtown with East St. Louis and the International Airport, 231-2345.

Visitors Center, 803 Washington Ave., (314) 342-5160 or 800-247-9791.

All of the accommodations below are in the downtown or near-downtown area.

-Hyatt Regency St. Louis, St. Louis Union Station, 1820 Market; (314) 231-1234. A luxury hotel located in the original Union Station. Five blocks from the Amtrak station. $119.

-Drury Inn-Union Station, 201 S. 20th St., 63103; (314) 231-3900 or 800-325-8300.

Nicely restored former railroad hotel and YMCA on west side of Union Station, about seven blocks from the Amtrak station. $96.

-Hampton Inn-Downtown, 2211 Market St., 63103; (314) 241-3200. Two blocks west of Union Station, about eight blocks from the Amtrak station. $86.

-Days Inn Downtown at the Arch, 333 Washington Ave., 63102; (314) 621-7900. Directly across from Gateway Arch, in the heart of downtown. About two miles from the station. $69.

Gateway Arch, a magnificent 630-foot-high monument, the nation's highest, has trams at each of the two bases to carry passengers to an observation deck with an incredible view of the metropolitan area.

Museum of Westward Expansion, underground beneath Gateway Arch, portrays early pioneering efforts. **St. Louis Union Station**, 1820 Market St., has been beautifully restored to accommodate shops, restaurants, and the Hyatt Regency Hotel. It's five blocks from the station. The **National Museum of Transport**, 3015 Barret Station Rd., exhibits the history and technology of both transportation and communication. Included are airplanes, autos, locomotives, rail cars, buses and horse-drawn vehicles.

0:00 (3:45) Depart St. Louis.

0:35 (3:10) St. Louis Ship Co. shipyards are on left, as railroad traces Mississippi for several miles.

0:40 (3:05) Through Jefferson Barracks, site of historic 18th-century military post. Pass beneath Jefferson Barracks Bridge.

3:45 (0:00) Arrive Poplar Bluff.

POPLAR BLUFF, MO - This All American City has the undulating Ozarks for recreation while the nearby fertile lands of southeast Missouri produce an abundance of cotton, rice, corn, soybeans, beef and hogs. Local manufacturers turn out such varied products as custom kitchen cabinets, Christmas ornaments, shoes and living room furniture.

0:00 (0:52) Depart Poplar Bluff.

0:18 (0:34) Enter Arkansas and leave Missouri.

0:52 (0:00) Arrive Walnut Ridge.

WALNUT RIDGE, AR - Several points of interest are near this northeastern Arkansas trading center. Old Davidsonville State Park is the site of one of Arkansas' earliest settlements, and Lake Charles State Park has superb camping on the shores of its 645-acre lake.

0:00 (0:34) Depart Walnut Ridge.

0:34 (0:00) Arrive Newport.

NEWPORT, AR - Had it not been for the resistance of steamboat promoters of nearby Jacksonport, the railroad would have gone through that upstream community instead of Newport. Steamboating on the navigable White River faded around the turn of the century and Newport, with its rail service, prospered.

0:00 (1:20) Depart Newport.

1:19 (0:01) Cross Arkansas River separating North Little Rock from Little Rock.

1:20 (0:00) Arrive Little Rock's old multistoried brick station on left, topped by intriguing clock tower.

LITTLE ROCK, AR - The capital of Arkansas and largest city in the state, Little Rock is attractively situated on tree-covered Ozark bluffs overlooking the Arkansas River. Its history runs the gamut from frontier trading post, to a Union-occupied Confederate city, to today's bustling central Arkansas metropolis.

 Union Station, Union Station Square, Markham and Victory Streets, two miles west of downtown.

 Black and White **Cab**, 374-0333.

 Visitors Center, Statehouse Convention Center, Markham and Main, (501) 376-4781.

Little Rock Doubletree, Markham and Broadway, 72201; (501) 372-4371 or 800-937-2789. A mile from the station. $65.

0:00 (0:45) Departing Little Rock, State Capitol Building looms on left. At night, floodlights on its Batesville granite walls produce surrealistic, white brilliance. Massive dome, reaching 230 feet above ground, is clad in 16-carat gold leaf.

0:16 (0:29) *Texas Eagle* seems to have left civilization behind as landscape becomes heavily forested with pines and hardwoods.

0:27 (0:18) Through Benton where bauxite is king. Most of the nation's aluminum ore comes from this region. Town even has a home built with this clay-like substance.

0:28 (0:17) Cross Saline River on southern edge of Benton.

0:45 (0:00) Arrive Malvern.

MALVERN, AR - This stop serves the spa city of Hot Springs and Hot Springs National Park, just 23 miles from here. Nestled in the lovely Ouachita Mountains. The Park is one of the nation's oldest, and its "Bathhouse Row" displays the finest group of historic bathhouses remaining in the U.S.

0:00 (0:22) Depart Malvern.

0:21 (0:01) At left, large plant in distance with silver standpipe is Fafnir Bearing, manufacturer of ball bearings.

0:22 (0:00) Arriving Arkadelphia, cross Ouachita River. Large plant on right with green standpipe is Reynolds Metal aluminum plant.

Texas Eagle — Belt Jct., TX
HOMER R. HILL

ARKADELPHIA, AR - Aluminum is important now, but in earlier times, steamboat traffic once reigned supreme, docking here after steaming up the Ouachita River.

0:00 (1:10) Depart Arkadelphia.

0:18 (0:52) Cross Little Missouri River.

0:24 (0:46) Rather neat depot, on right, with red tile roof is distinguishing feature of downtown Prescott as train chugs along "Main Street."

0:28 (0:42) Some Southern-style ranching is carried on in this part of state with typical herds being Brahma crosses. Watch for rodeo variety bulls on right.

0:36 (0:34) On right, fine old smokestack of brick factory helps pinpoint Hope, President Bill Clinton's home town. Watermelon lovers will be interested to know that world's largest grow here—a record 200-pounder having been harvested in 1979.

0:49 (0:21) Cross 1,300-mile-long Red River which originates in northern Texas, creating a portion of Texas-Oklahoma border. Sometimes tinted red by its high silt content, this stream drains 90,000 square miles of land.

1:02 (0:08) Texarkana Municipal Airport is on immediate left.

1:10 (0:00) Arrive at Texarkana where front of train comes to rest in Texas and rear portion stops in Arkansas.

TEXARKANA, AR/TX - This city lies carefully balanced on the Arkansas-Texas border and even boasts a post office straddling the state line—the only federal building in the U.S. sitting in two states.

0:00 (1:15) Depart Texarkana and enter Texas heading due south along Lone Star State's eastern border.

0:06 (1:09) Enormous rail tie manufacturing and storage operation stretches for almost a mile along right side of tracks.

0:23 (0:52) Through Atlanta. Nearby, over 25 sites of prehistoric Caddo Indian villages have been found.

1:15 (0:00) Arrive Marshall where rail station, looking more like an old brick mansion, greets train's departees on left.

MARSHALL, TX - This northeastern Texas town is located amidst cypress-fringed bayous and pine forests. Both its natural beauty and mild climate make it a popular tourist area. During the Civil War, saddles, harnesses and ammunition were produced here for the Confederacy, and it became the wartime capital of Missouri. This is also the birthplace of Lady Bird Johnson.

0:00 (0:28) Depart Marshall. For some time now, *Eagle* will slip past one industrial operation after another, most turning out the stuff for which Texas is best known. Oil equipment manufacturers and other petroleum-related industries dominate the flat landscape.

0:28 (0:00) Arrive Longview.

LONGVIEW, TX - This industrialized community is heavily oil oriented with refineries, oil equipment manufacturing and the loading end of the famous "Big Inch" pipeline. And another liquid is produced here. Schlitz turns out millions of barrels of beer a year from one of Texas' largest breweries.

0:00 (2:18) Depart Longview.

0:15 (2:03) Through Gladwater and the very heart of famed East Texas oilfield, one of nation's biggest producers.

0:23 (1:55) On right, white board fence looks like it belongs on a Kentucky horse farm, but actually encloses Ambassador College, founded by Garner Ted Armstrong and his brother Herbert.

0:29 (1:49) Jarvis Christian College is just to right.

0:37 (1:41) What looks like world's largest collection of antique merchants is at right.

1:39 (0:30) Enter Dallas' fastest growing suburb, Mesquite (pronounced meskeet), named for that scraggly, thorny shrub that thrives in Southwestern U.S. and northern Mexico.

1:54 (0:24) In far distance to right, top of Ferris wheel identifies location of Texas State Fair Grounds, where Texans hold what they claim is biggest fair in nation.

2:00 (0:18) Dallas cityscape is now clearly visible on right.

2:17 (0:01) Flat-roofed Reunion Arena sports complex, home to Dallas Maverick basketball, is on left.

2:18 (0:00) Arrive Dallas. White marbled Union Station is on right while spectacular glass facades of Hyatt Regency Hotel and spherically domed Reunion Tower rise abruptly above us on left.

DALLAS, TX - Dallas began in 1841 as a trading post which was started by a Tennessee lawyer, John Neely Bryan, who named the post after "his friend Dallas." Although no one today knows who that "Dallas" was, the County of Dallas was eventually named after George Mifflin Dallas, Vice President of the United States under James Polk.

As is true with so many western cities, early growth was due to the arrival of the railroad. In the early 1870s, rail lines extended both to the east and to the north making the city an important distribution center. Today, Dallas is one of the Southwest's leading financial, industrial and transportation centers, and entertains more than two million tourists annually.

Union Station, 400 South Houston St. This beautifully renovated marble structure, included in the National Register of Historic Places, is located on the edge of downtown. There are a variety of restaurants (on the 2nd floor), a gift shop and a florist in this popular setting. Luggage carts and adjacent pay-parking are available. A visitors information counter is also located in the station. An underground walkway connects to the Hyatt Regency Hotel and the Reunion Tower (observation deck and restaurant).

For arrival and departure information only, call (214) 653-1101.

Yellow **Cab**, 426-6262. Hertz **rental cars** are a mile from the station, (214) 979-9494. **Local bus**, 979-1111.

Dallas

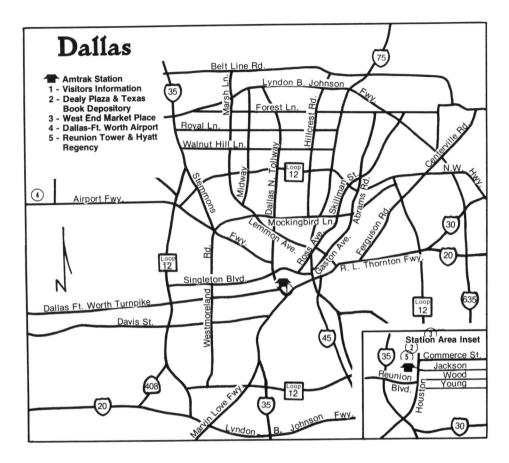

- 🚂 **Amtrak Station**
- 1 - **Visitors Information**
- 2 - **Dealy Plaza & Texas Book Depository**
- 3 - **West End Market Place**
- 4 - **Dallas-Ft. Worth Airport**
- 5 - **Reunion Tower & Hyatt Regency**

Belt Line Rd.
Lyndon B. Johnson Fwy.
Forest Ln.
Royal Ln.
Walnut Hill Ln.
Marsh Ln.
Hillcrest Rd.
Stemmons
Midway
Dallas N. Tollway
Loop 12
Skillman St.
Abrams Rd.
Centerville Rd.
N.W. Hwy.
Airport Fwy.
Lemmon Ave.
Mockingbird Ln.
Ross Ave.
Gaston Ave.
Ferguson Rd.
30
Rd.
Fwy.
Loop 12
Singleton Blvd.
R. L. Thornton Fwy.
20
Loop 12
635
Dallas Ft. Worth Turnpike
Westmoreland
Davis St.
45
Station Area Inset
35
2
5
Commerce St.
Jackson
Reunion Blvd.
Wood
Young
Houston
408
Loop 12
20
35
30
Marvin Love Fwy.
Lyndon B. Johnson Fwy.
N
35
75

Visitor Information Center, in Union Station. Call (214) 746-6679 or 800-752-9222.

Hyatt Regency Dallas, 300 Reunion Blvd., 75207; (214) 651-1234. Dazzling architecture. Connected to the station by a block-long concourse. $180. -**Ramada Inn,** 1011 S. Akard, 75215; (214) 421-1083. Near downtown with downtown transportation, including station. About two miles from station. $80.

Dealey Plaza and the **Texas Book Depository**, site of President Kennedy's assassination, are but three blocks north of the station on Houston St. **Reunion Tower** has an observation deck and a revolving restaurant with commanding views of the city, across tracks from the station and reached by an underground concourse.

0:00 (0:57) Depart Dallas and head westward through solid development which has made Dallas and Ft. Worth almost appear as one city.

0:02 (0:55) Look back on left for a fine view of Hyatt Regency Hotel and Reunion Tower. Texas Book Depository (light brick with green-trimmed windows), which played such an important role in President Kennedy's assassination, is off to right.

0:03 (0:54) Newer Dallas jail facility is just to left.

0:12 (0:45) Top of Dallas Cowboys' Texas Stadium is in far distance to right.

0:15 (0:42) Unique in its neatness, auto junk yard at left displays merchandise in prim rows—each car with hood raised.

0:17 (0:40) Hensley Field and Texas

National Guard aircraft are on left.

0:18 (0:39) Jets and helicopters of Dallas Naval Air Station are parked on left.

0:19 (0:38) Vaught complex, longtime military aircraft manufacturer, is just to left.

0:20 (0:37) Pass through Grand Prairie, a town that boomed with defense plants during World War II.

0:25 (0:32) Unusual tower in distance to right belongs to Six Flags Over Texas, a huge entertainment park—one of Texas' most popular attractions. General Motors assembly plant sprawls at left.

0:27 (0:30) Enter Arlington. University of Texas at Arlington is on right while Arlington Stadium is about a mile in distance.

0:30 (0:27) Perched on hilltop right is "The Home for Aged Masons."

0:52 (0:05) Ft. Worth skyline is now on right as train stops, then backs toward Ft. Worth station.

0:57 (0:00) Arrive Ft. Worth.

 FT. WORTH, TX - This city began as a military camp during the war with Mexico and then became a major shipping point for cattle after the Civil War. Now one of Texas' major cities, it has a wide assortment of industries. A culturally conscious city, Ft. Worth offers musicals, concerts, ballets, theater performances and numerous outstanding museums to satisfy almost any taste.

Ramada Hotel - Ft. Worth Downtown, 1701 Commerce St., 76102; (817) 335-7000. High rise in center of business district, one block from the station. $76.

0:00 (0:40) Depart Ft. Worth.

0:06 (0:34) Last look at downtown Ft. Worth is afforded back on right.

0:38 (0:02) On left, enormous rail shops of Santa Fe Railroad are largest construction and repair shops in Texas.

0:40 (0:00) Arrive Cleburne.

CLEBURNE, TX - Named in honor of Confederate General Pat Cleburne, the city is the trading center for an area featuring farming, dairying and livestock.

0:00 (1:05) Depart Cleburne.

0:08 (0:57) On edge of Rio Vista at right, three large flags help identify "The Cow Pasture Bank" (actually, First State) which provides airstrip in rear for its fly-in customers.

0:15 (0:50) Train now imperceptibly crosses Balcones Fault where flat prairies quickly turn to more hilly terrain.

0:17 (0:48) Cross legendary Brazos River. Off to left is 15,760-acre Lake Whitney, formed by damming Brazos River. This 45-mile-long reservoir is one of nation's most popular water recreation areas with four million visitors annually.

0:42 (0:23) Cross Bosque River which winds its way along our route for next 30 minutes.

1:05 (0:00) Arrive McGregor.

 MCGREGOR, TX - This community serves as a stop for its much larger neighbor 19 miles to the west—Waco.

0:00 (0:25) Depart McGregor.

0:24 (0:01) Santa Fe shops appear at right approaching station in Temple.

0:25 (0:00) Arrive Temple where train is greeted by an attractive brick station whose familiar emblems are a reminder that we have been on Santa Fe tracks since Ft. Worth.

TEMPLE, TX - Since its inception in 1880, Temple has always been closely tied with railroading when it grew along the Gulf, Colorado and Santa Fe Railroad, and the Missouri, Kansas and Texas lines. Railroad shops are still located here. Temple is one of the Southwest's leading medical centers, whose facilities include King's Daughters Hospital, Scott-White Hospital and Clinic, and (quite aptly) the Santa Fe Hospital.

0:00 (0:56) Depart Temple.

0:12 (0:41) Rolling, forested hills provide a most aesthetic backdrop for area's ranches.

0:45 (0:11) Cross San Gabriel River.

0:56 (0:00) Arrive Taylor.

TAYLOR, TX - Having been on the Missouri, Kansas, Texas tracks since Temple, we now change to Missouri Pacific trackage, which leads to San

Alamodome — San Antonio, TX
DORIS SWANSON

Antonio. Taylor is a railroad junction point and retail center for the surrounding farm and ranch country.

0:00 (0:46) Depart Taylor.

0:28 (0:18) Large cement plant on left is just one of many between here and San Antonio.

0:39 (0:07) In Austin suburbs, train passes Camp Mabry, on right, where military aircraft and armored vehicles have been put on display along tracks.

0:46 (0:00) Arrive at Austin's station, somewhat west of downtown.

AUSTIN, TX - In 1839 a site was chosen on the north shore of the Colorado River (not the one of Grand Canyon fame) to become the capital of the Republic of Texas. The site was well-chosen, as Austin has grown to be a hub city of Texas, with healthy industries, numerous colleges and universities, and is still the seat of government. The University of Texas at Austin, the state's largest university, is located here.

0:00 (0:40) Depart Austin. University of Texas Memorial Tower is off to left.

0:04 (0:36) Ornate dome of capitol, con-structed of Texas pink marble, is off to left. Train makes a curve to right and crosses Colorado River.

0:22 (0:18) On right, quaint little storefronts in town of Buda seem to stare at train as it zips past.

0:39 (0:01) On outskirts of San Marcos, train slips through scenic campus of Southwest Texas State University—alma mater of Lyndon B. Johnson, the nation's 36th president.

0:40 (0:00) Arrive San Marcos.

SAN MARCOS, TX - Besides Southwest Texas State University, San Marcos is the site of the Republic of Texas Chilympiad (state chili cooking contest) held each September, with the winner going to the World Chili Cook-off each November at Terlingua, Texas. For several days in June, the Texas Water Safari is celebrated here—the "world's toughest canoe races." Entrants must canoe down hundreds of miles of rivers and saltwater bays, traveling from San Marcos to Seadrift.

0:00 (1:43) Depart San Marcos.

0:02 (1:41) Tower off to right was once used

to train World War II paratroopers.

0:19 (1:23) Cross Guadalupe River.

0:26 (1:16) Enter German community of New Braunfels, famous for sausages, breads and pastries.

0:29 (1:13) Tracks pass through huge limestone quarry supplying raw material for cement plant at right.

0:34 (1:08) (Southbound only.) Swing right while tracks that carry northbound *Texas Eagle* can be observed branching off to left.

0:55 (Southbound only.) San Antonio International Airport is on right.

0:58 (Southbound only.) Enter outskirts of San Antonio with Alamo Cement Plant on left, then pass directly through Olmos Basin Golf Course.

— (0:59) (Northbound only.) Multiple soccer fields are on right, then enormous polo complex amply accommodates this upper-crust diversion.

1:26 (0:11) Lone Star Beer brewery is on immediate right, Skyline is dominated by 750-foot Tower of the Americas, built for HemisFair held in 1968.

1:28 (0:10) Cross San Antonio River. Adjacent to station, huge structure with cable-suspended roof is Alamodome. Completed in 1993, it is city's sport, convention, and concert center.

1:29 (0:00) Arrive San Antonio.

(Note - Trains northbound from San Antonio take a slightly different route on departure, going to Craig Junction where main line is rejoined. This adds 19 miles, but eliminates reversing trains in San Antonio.)

SAN ANTONIO, TX - San Antonio, a city now in excess of one million, was named by Captain Domingo Teran who was exploring the region for Spain in 1691 and arrived in the area on the feast day of Saint Anthony of Padua. However, a permanent settlement was not established until 27 years later when the Mission of San Antonio de Valero was built, later to become known as the Alamo.

San Antonio has the distinction of having been under six different flags since its beginning: French, Spanish, Mexican, Republic of Texas, Confederate and American. It was the scene of one of the most historic and dramatic battles in our nation's history, when 188 Texans defended the Alamo against the Mexican Army led by General Santa Ana, falling on March 6, 1836 after all of its defenders were killed. Later that year, Texas successfully ended Mexican rule and became a Republic.

Today, with its rich past intermixed with the new and modern, San Antonio is clearly one of the more fascinating cities in the United States. The restoration of its charming river-front area is one of the major urban-renewal achievements of our time.

Amtrak Station, 1174 E. Commerce St., is an appealing, Spanish-style structure with an interior that has been restored to its original stateliness. A grand staircase beneath a vivid stained-glass window, and an arched baroque ceiling give the interior a feeling of opulence rarely found in American train stations. The station has storage lockers and food and beverage vending machines.

Yellow **Cab**, 226-4242. **Local bus**, 227-2020.

Visitors Information Center, 317 Alamo Plaza, immediately across from the Alamo; (210) 299-8155.

Menger Hotel and Motor Inn, 204 Alamo Plaza, 78205; (210) 223-4361 or 800-345-9285. This venerable landmark is still an excellent place to absorb San Antonio's relaxed Southwest charm. Five blocks from the station. $118.

-**La Quinta Convention Center**, 1001 E. Commerce, 78205; (210) 222-9181. Closest hotel to the station and convenient to downtown. Three blocks from the station. $82.

-**Best Western Crockett**, 320 Bonham, 78205; (210) 225-6500 or 800-292-1050. Nicely restored 1909 hotel, next to the Alamo and River Center, six blocks from the station. $95.

The Amtrak station is approximately five blocks from the downtown area reached by traveling west on E. Commerce Street. The heart of San Antonio's appeal is Paseo del Rio, nearly two miles of cobblestone walkways with bridges, tropical

foliage, fine shops, restaurants and nightclubs set along the river. Boat rides offer a unique way to see much of this area. **The Alamo**, at Alamo Plaza, is one of the most famous shrines in the country. Tours, a museum, slides and a movie about the battle help re-create the struggle that took the lives of its 188 defenders. **HemisFair Plaza**, which was the site of the 1968 HemisFair, now contains the Convention Center and several attractions including the **Tower of Americas** topped by an observation deck and revolving restaurant. **Alamodome**, next to station, is San Antonio's ultramodern all-purpose arena for concerts, sporting events and conventions.

For route log from San Antonio to Los Angeles, see that portion of *Sunset Ltd*. log, page 222.

Kansas City • Chicago • St. Louis

Ann Rutledge

The *Ann Rutledge* links Chicago and Kansas City through St. Louis. The route of the *Texas Eagle* is followed between Chicago and St. Louis; then the tracks cut across the very heart of Missouri to reach Kansas City, tracing through the undulating farmlands and forests along the Missouri River.

NORTHBOUND SCHEDULE (Condensed)
Kansas City, MO - Early Morning Departure
Jefferson City, MO - Late Morning
St. Louis, MO - Early Afternoon
Chicago, IL - Early Evening Arrival

SOUTHBOUND SCHEDULE (Condensed)
Chicago, IL - Midmorning Departure
St. Louis, MO - Late Afternoon
Jefferson City, MO - Early Evening
Kansas City, MO - Late Evening

FREQUENCY - Daily.
SEATING - Unreserved coaches. Custom Class available with reserved seating including complimentary beverages.
DINING - Sandwiches, snacks and beverages.
BAGGAGE - No checked baggage.
RESERVATIONS - None required except Custom Class.
LENGTH OF TRIP - 563 miles in 11 hours.

ROUTE LOG

 KANSAS CITY, MO - See page 187.

0:00 (0:19) Depart Kansas City, heading due east and somewhat below grade.

0:08 (0:11) Cemetery with tombstone forest on hillside at left obviously has "no vacancies."

0:19 (0:00) Arrive Independence.

INDEPENDENCE, MO - This large Kansas City suburb was the home of former president Harry S. Truman who came into office when Franklin Roosevelt died April 12, 1945. He served until 1953. Not long after becoming president, he made one of the most difficult decisions ever made—the approval to drop an atomic bomb on Japan.

0:00 (0:16) Depart Independence.

0:05 (0:11) On left, Truman High School bears name of town's favorite son.

0:16 (0:00) Arrive Lee's Summit where old red-brick depot is no longer used.

LEE'S SUMMIT, MO - This metropolitan suburb was once the domain of the Osage Indians until they were forced off their land in 1825. Lewis and Clark passed through the county shortly before they spotted their first bison in nearby Kansas. It was the Missouri Pacific Railroad that finally assured the town's future, however, when in 1846 the town became one of the largest shipping points between Kansas City and St. Louis.

0:00 (0:40) Depart Lee's Summit.

0:38 (0:02) Rumble across branch of Blackwater River.

0:40 (0:00) Arriving Warrensburg, about three blocks before station as tracks curve slightly to the right, across street on left was "Warrensburg Brewery Cave" (now boarded up), formerly used to store beer in its cool environs. This use came to a sudden end in 1873, however, when Carrie Nation of Temperance League fame burned it out. Today, only a small house marks the site.

WARRENSBURG, MO - Few towns have had as interesting a past as Warrensburg.

On the south edge of town are Pertle Springs, at one time having its waters shipped to every state in the Union because of their "curative" powers. A renowned resort area surrounded the springs with as many as 10,000 attending camp meetings. The Democratic National Convention was held there in 1895. The land was eventually purchased by Central Missouri State College.

Just a block south of the station was the old Estes Hotel which, in 1899, served as a depot for a small steam train that made eight runs daily to the Pertle Springs Hotel. Carrie Nation attended the State Normal School here, now Central Missouri's State University just three blocks south.

The old courthouse was the site of perhaps the most famous of legal trials involving canines. In 1870, Leonidas Hornsby was found guilty of killing his brother-in-law's dog, but it was the eloquent eulogy given the dog Drum by the plaintiff's lawyer that apparently swayed the jury.

0:00 (0:30) Depart Warrensburg.

0:24 (0:16) Limestone quarry forms large excavation at left.

0:30 (0:00) Arrive Sedalia's modern brick station on left.

SEDALIA, MO - Founded in 1857, Sedalia owes its beginnings to the railroad, serving as a provisioning point and later a military post during the Civil War. One of America's best-known composers, Scott Joplin, composed the "Maple Leaf Rag" in a local saloon known as the Maple Leaf Club. It was this song that first brought him both fame and success. Now, if you're here in mid-August, all the excitement is about the state fair.

0:00 (1:04) Departing Sedalia, note monument to aforementioned Scott Joplin and Maple Leaf Club.

0:02 (1:02) Through Missouri Pacific rail yards.

1:02 (0:02) Entering Jefferson City, broad Missouri River comes into view on left. Highway bridge spanning this great river carries auto traffic north to Columbia, home of University of Missouri, and to Fulton, home of Westminster College. (It was on campus of latter that Winston Churchill delivered his famous "Iron Curtain" speech in 1946.) Then, perched above and to right, is Missouri's sparkling white state capitol. Built in 1917 of Missouri limestone, its Renaissance dome towers 260 feet above ground.

1:04 (0:00) Arrive Jefferson City where Amtrak now occupies first level of former Union Hotel, circa 1855.

JEFFERSON CITY, MO - Named for Thomas Jefferson, the site of this city was chosen as the state capital in 1821. Its location on the Missouri River, halfway between St. Louis and Kansas City, made it a logical choice.

0:00 (0:45) Depart Jefferson City, following Missouri River until just east of Washington, approximately 80 miles downstream.

0:07 (0:38) Neat-appearing buildings with silver water tank on hillside to left are Missouri Department of Corrections minimum security prison.

0:10 (0:35) Train slows as it carefully crosses Osage River.

0:14 (0:31) Note houses on each side of river perched on stilts to avoid Missouri overflows.

0:29 (0:16) Huge form of electric generating facility (reminiscent of Three Mile Island) dominates horizon on left.

0:37 (0:08) Cross Casconade River.

0:45 (0:00) Arrive Hermann.

Ann Rutledge — Gasconade River, MO
JACK SWANSON

 HERMANN, MO - This historic community has several buildings with Bavarian-like architecture, some of which can be spotted here and there, looking uphill to right. This small town, with strong German heritage, is home to two wineries, one of which can be seen at right, just east of the bridge.

0:00 (0:56) Depart Hermann.

0:28 (0:28) Tracks bid farewell to Missouri River and start a gradual ascent towards St. Louis.

0:30 (0:26) Briefly encounter darkness while passing through tunnel for a few seconds.

0:32 (0:24) Turquoise buildings with white roofs comprise Purina Poultry Research Center, a reminder that Ralston Purina makes farm feeds as well as breakfast foods.

0:33 (0:23) Through one more short tunnel.

0:51 (0:05) Three venerable steam locomotives, long since retired from duty, stand in forlorn decay at left.

0:54 (0:02) Over Interstate 270, then past attractive fairways of Greenbriar Country Club on left.

0:56 (0:00) Arrive downtown Kirkwood. Be sure to take note of quaint Kirkwood depot with its swooping roof lines and circular tower.

 KIRKWOOD, MO - This is a western suburb of St. Louis, and the last stop before that city.

0:00 (0:20) Depart Kirkwood.

0:03 (0:16) Two more country clubs pass by on left, first Westborough, then Algonquin.

0:19 (0:01) On left, restored St. Louis Union Station with its marvelous old train shed now houses shops, a beer garden and a luxury hotel. Also, various privately owned rail cars can frequently be seen parked there. In its heyday, Union Station handled as many as 276 trains daily. Unfortunately, Amtrak does not stop here but rolls on to its "temporary" depot opened in 1978.

0:20 (0:00) Arrive St. Louis.

 ST. LOUIS, MO - See page 201.

For route between St. Louis and Chicago, see that portion of *Texas Eagle* route log, page 198.

Other Chicago Area and Missouri Service

The *Illini* provides daily service between Chicago and Carbondale with runs each direction late in the day. Sandwiches, snacks and beverages; no checked baggage. Custom Class available.

The *Illinois Zephyr* carries passengers from Quincy, IL to Chicago early in the day and returns in the evening. Daily. Sandwiches, snacks and beverages; no checked baggage.

The route is the same as the *California Zephyr* between Chicago and Galesburg, but between the latter and Quincy, this train forges its own route through Macomb and Quincy. It is the only Amtrak service to these two communities. Macomb, IL, named in honor of Alexander Macomb, a U.S. general during the War of 1812, is home to Western Illinois University. Quincy is a town of 42,000, and a century ago, was the second largest city in Illinois. Its importance declined along with the steamboat.

The *State House* leaves Chicago midafternoon and takes the route of the *Texas Eagle* to St. Louis, arriving there late evening. St. Louis departures are very early morning with midmorning Chicago arrivals. This daily train is unreserved, has sandwiches and beverages and no checked baggage. Also reserved Custom Class.

The *Loop* links Chicago and Springfield with morning service to Springfield and late afternoon service to Chicago, except Sundays. Snacks and beverages.

Chicago-Milwaukee, in addition to the *Empire Builder*, has several trains connecting these two cities daily.

St. Louis-Kansas City, in addition to the *Ann Rutledge*, has service departing St. Louis for Kansas City early morning, with the return departing Kansas City late afternoon.

Sunset Limited

On April 4, 1993, the route of the New Orleans/Los Angeles *Sunset Limited* was extended eastward from New Orleans to Jacksonville, Florida, and on south to Miami, making the *Sunset* America's first regularly scheduled transcontinental train. This extension filled a significant gap that forced rail travelers between the Southeast and the Southwest to go by way of Washington, DC.

The first through trains between New Orleans and the West Coast were started in February 1883 and were known as the *Atlantic Express* and *Pacific Express* (depending on the direction they were heading). But in 1984, the *Sunset Limited* title was bestowed on this service, appropriate enough since passengers from New Orleans to Los Angeles headed into two sunsets before reaching the end of the line.

Today, the run between Miami and Los Angeles takes nearly three full days, reaching an elevation of nearly a mile high at 5,074-foot Paisano Pass, Texas, and sinking to 202 feet below sea level near Salton, California.

There are through coaches and sleepers between Chicago and Los Angeles by a connection to the *Texas Eagle* at San Antonio.

WESTBOUND SCHEDULE (Condensed)
Miami, FL - Late Morning Departure
New Orleans, LA - Midmorning Arrival, Early Afternoon Departure (2nd Day)

San Antonio, TX - Middle of the Night (3rd Day)
El Paso, TX - Early Afternoon (3rd Day)
Phoenix, AZ - Late Evening (3rd Day)*
Los Angeles, CA - Early Morning Arrival (4th Day)

EASTBOUND SCHEDULE (Condensed)
Los Angeles, CA - Late Evening Departure
Phoenix, AZ - Early Morning (2nd Day)
El Paso, TX - Late Afternoon (2nd Day)
San Antonio, TX - Early Morning (3rd Day)
New Orleans, LA - Midevening Arrival, Late Evening Departure (3rd Day)
Miami, FL - Late Evening Arrival (4th Day)

*Note: Rerouting may eliminate Phoenix as a stop.

FREQUENCY - Tri-weekly. Departs Los Angeles and Miami Sunday, Tuesday and Friday. Arrives Miami and Los Angeles Wednesday, Friday and Monday.
SEATING - Superliner coaches.
DINING - Complete meal and beverage service as well as lighter fare. Lounge service is also available with movies. Dinner is not served upon departure from Los Angeles.
SLEEPING - Superliner sleepers with deluxe, family, economy and special bedrooms.
BAGGAGE - Checked baggage handled at larger cities.
RESERVATIONS - All-reserved train.
LENGTH OF TRIP - 3,066 miles in approximately three days.

Route Log

For route log from Miami to Jacksonville, FL (by way of Orlando) see that portion of *Silver Meteor* log, page 71.

 JACKSONVILLE, FL - See page 71.

0:00 (1:01) Depart Jacksonville. Train will back out of station, unless train was switched through wye at Grand Junction just before arrival.

0:03 (0:58) Back into wye in order to turn train for forward travel.

0:12 (0:49) Final maneuver positioning *Sunset* for its Los Angeles-bound journey occurs at Moncrief Yard where train curls westward.

0:17 (0:44) A gaggle of blue and grey business rail cars of CSX can often be observed parked on siding at left. View of Jacksonville skyline is afforded back to left.

1:01 (0:00) Arrive Lake City.

 LAKE CITY, FL - One of Florida's older towns, today's Lake City has an economy driven by phosphate mining, timber and tobacco.

0:00 (0:53) Depart Lake City.

0:11 (0:42) A sprinkling of blueberry farms now appears along the right-of-way.

0:23 (0:30) Through attractive community of Live Oak, where clock-tower-capped Suwannee County Courthouse is focal point of downtown. Live Oak is home to Florida's oldest and biggest tobacco market.

0:37 (0:16) Cross Suwannee River, made famous by Stephen Foster's *Old Folks at Home*. River drains part of mysterious Okefenokee Swamp into gulf of Mexico and forms boundary for eight of northern Florida's counties.

0:53 (0:00) Arrive Madison.

 MADISON, FL - This community of 3,500 inhabitants serves as the county seat of Madison County on the eastern edge of Florida's panhandle.

0:00 (1:19) Depart Madison and start to traverse virtual length of Florida's panhandle.

0:39 (0:40) At left, older home, with yard containing enormous live oak tree and wicker lawn chairs (and sometimes two dogs), is quintessence of Deep South gentility.

1:07 (0:12) More Deep South atmosphere is encountered when tracks pass through swamp of murky water, cypress trees and Spanish moss.

1:16 (0:03) Entering Tallahassee, look directly up highway to right for quick look at Old Capitol. After new capitol was built, this structure was restored and now serves as Florida's State Building.

1:19 (0:00) Arrive Tallahassee's rambling old station at right.

 TALLAHASSEE, FL - This city has served as the capital of Florida since 1824 and was one of two Confederate capitals not captured by Union troops (Austin, Texas, being the other). Besides state government, Tallahassee is also the center of higher education in northern Florida. Florida State University is here as well as Florida A&M.

0:00 (1:53) Depart Tallahassee. Some Florida State University facilities can be seen off to right.

0:13 (1:40) Cross Ichlockonee River.

1:08 (0:45) Cross impressive Apalachicola River. River traffic can often be seen on these waters.

 Gain one hour as train passes from Eastern to Central Time. Set your watch back (forward if eastbound) one hour.

1:13 (0:40) Near Sneads, Apalachicola Correctional Facility is off to right.

1:29 (0:24) Cross modest-sized Chipola River on eastern edge of Marianna.

1:53 (0:00) Arrive Chipley.

CHIPLEY, FL - A town of 3,300 people, Chipley serves as the trading center for northern Washington County.

0:00 (1:20) Depart through heart of Chipley, rolling along "Main Street" with its collection of depressing old buildings.

1:00 (0:20) Through De Funiak Springs, which claims one of world's two "perfectly round" lakes.

1:20 (0:00) Arrive Crestview's doll-house station, at right.

CRESTVIEW, FL - Crestview is the county seat of Okaloosa County and serves as a stop for nearby Eglin Air Force Base.

0:00 (1:00) Depart Crestview.

0:09 (0:51) Cross good-sized Yellow River.

0:45 (0:15) Train now makes dramatic ascent over Escambia Bay on relatively new two-and-one-half-mile-long CSX trestle, while Interstate 10 is off to left.

0:53 (0:08) Now enjoy a lengthy ride beside Escambia Bay, one of two northerly extensions of Pensacola Bay.

1:00 (0:00) Arrive Pensacola.

 PENSACOLA, FL - Pensacola's history is one of changing rule, a city with a five-flag past. Today, Pensacola is Florida's largest deep-water port.

Because of the area's weather, the U.S. Navy has made Pensacola the home of naval aviation. The choice in 1914 to place the U.S. Naval Air Station there (on the site of old naval shipyard) played a significant part in shaping the town's economy and character.

0:00 (1:20) Depart Pensacola, and head due north to circumvent obstacle known as Mobile Bay.

1:03 (0:17) Leave state of Florida and enter Alabama.

1:20 (0:00) Arrive Atmore.

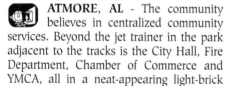 **ATMORE, AL** - The community believes in centralized community services. Beyond the jet trainer in the park adjacent to the tracks is the City Hall, Fire Department, Chamber of Commerce and YMCA, all in a neat-appearing light-brick structure.

0:00 (0:21) Depart Atmore and immediately pass under Burlington Northern Railroad bridge.

0:04 (0:17) Atmore Country Club and golf course are just across highway to left.

0:21 (0:00) Arrive town of Bay Minnette. On right, roof with fencing could hold picnic bench, but actually serves as Amtrak "station."

 BAY MINNETTE, AL - Town is home to the University of South Alabama Baldwin County.

0:00 (0:32) Depart Bay Minnette.

0:10 (0:22) Cross Tensaw River on first of five drawbridges between here and Mobile.

0:15 (0:17) Rumble over Mobile River on second drawbridge.

Amtrak's worst train wreck occurred just west of here at 2:50 in the morning on September 22, 1993, when the eastbound *Sunset Limited* plunged off the bridge over Big Bayou Canot. Just moments before, two barges had broken loose from their tug and struck the bridge (which was barely seven feet above the water) causing a severe misalignment of the tracks. The tragedy resulted in 47 deaths, most from drowning.

0:18 (0:14) Now cross Bayou Sara on third drawbridge.

0:19 (0:13) On left, Mobile River now accompanies train approaching Mobile. Skyline is forward right.

0:20 (0:12) Fourth drawbridge carries train across Chicasaw Bogue.

0:25 (0:07) Roll beneath swooping Bay Bridge carrying vehicular traffic to and from Blakely Island and beyond.

0:26 (0:06) Trundle over Threemile Creek and last drawbridge, and then through freight yards. Alabama state docks, capable of handling 34 oceangoing vessels at one time, are seen on immediate left. Freighters and other maritime vessels are usually prominent sights here. Battleship U.S.S. Alabama, permanently moored in harbor, is just beyond structures at left, but not visible from tracks.

0:28 (0:04) Elaborate, grey structure with red roof, off to right, is former GM&O Terminal, closed in 1957. Tallest structure in downtown Mobile, on right, is 34-story First National Building.

0:31 (0:01) Train now burrows right through Mobile's fancifully designed new Convention Center.

0:32 (0:00) Arrive Mobile's CSX-Amtrak station. In middle of Government Street on right, statue of Admiral Raphael Semmes, who was commander of Confederate States Steamer Alabama, seemingly welcomes Amtrak passengers to Mobile.

Sunset, Ltd. — Mobile, AL Convention Center
JACK SWANSON

MOBILE, AL - A handful of modern skyscrapers alongside Mobile Bay marks the downtown of Alabama's only seaport, in sharp contrast to the collection of handsome Old South neighborhoods that make Mobile a city of charm and grace.

Mobile is at its best in the spring when the city's 35-mile Azalea Trail, comprised of several streets lined with those showy flowers, is in full bloom.

Mobile has lived under six flags: French, British, Spanish, the State of Alabama,

Confederate and U.S. It was the last Southern stronghold to surrender to Union Forces during the Civil War after being completely blockaded by the Union Navy. It was during this blockade that Admiral Farragut supposedly exclaimed: "Damn the torpedoes! Full steam ahead!" The Bay remains important to Mobile, whose maritime trade and shipbuilding are still vital to the city's economy.

Amtrak Station, Government and Water Streets, occupies a portion of the former CSX station, conveniently wedged between the compact central business district and the Mobile River. The station waiting room is small, marginally adequate at best, and parking is very limited. Red caps are available.

Yellow **Cab**, 476-7711. **Local buses**, 344-5656. Enterprise **rental cars**, 432-4476, offer station pick up and delivery during business hours.

Visit the **Information Center** at historic Fort Conde, (334) 434-7304 or 800-666-6282.

Holiday Inn Express, 255 Church St., 36602; (334) 433-6923. Large motel in attractive setting next to central business district and convenient to visitors center. Complimentary continental breakfast. Five blocks from the station. $46.

-**Malaga Inn**, 359 Church St., 36602; (334) 438-4701. Former antebellum townhouses with private balconies and patios create front portion of hotel. Pleasant central courtyard. Six blocks from the station. $75.

-**Adams Mark Mobile**, 64 Water St., 36602; (334) 438-4000 or 800-444-2326. Modern high rise with large, bright rooms. Second floor dining room overlooks station and new convention center. Immediately across intersection from station. $79.

Two blocks from the station is **Fort Conde Historic French Fort**, a reconstruction of the original built circa 1724-36 and serves as the city's information center.

The **Battleship Alabama Memorial Park** is the permanent anchorage for that World War II battle wagon, the submarine USS Drum and a B-52 bomber. The highlight of the Park is the tour of the Alabama herself.

0:00 (0:35) Depart Mobile, and for a short while, pass by numerous docks bustling with maritime activity.

0:06 (0:29) Brookley Airport and industrial complex is now at left.

0:07 (0:25) Cross three creeks in next three minutes, Eslava, Montlimar and Halls Mill, while still in confines of Mobile.

0:26 (0:09) Leave state of Alabama and enter Mississippi.

0:35 (0:00) Arrive Pascagoula.

PASCAGOULA, MS - Situated at the mouth of the Pascagoula River, this port city enjoys a diverse economy based on maritime industries such as shipbuilding and maritime commerce.

0:00 (0:22) Depart Pascagoula.

0:01 (0:19) Cross Pascagoula River and then West Pascagoula River. River is famous for its legendary singing sound, which is subject to numerous scientific theories, but none have been proven. Ships at left are being built for Navy by Ingalls Shipyard.

0:20 (0:02) Cruise directly across mouth of Biloxi Bay, then enter city of Biloxi.

0:22 (0:00) Arrive Biloxi.

BILOXI, MS - Established in 1717, Biloxi was one of the earliest white settlements in the lower Mississippi Valley. It was in Biloxi that Jefferson Davis, president of the Confederacy, spent his retirement years.

0:00 (0:15) Depart Biloxi. Keesler Air Force Base, electronics training center for U.S. Air Force, will be on right.

0:15 (0:00) Arrive downtown Gulfport.

GULFPORT, MS - Planned as a rail/sea terminus, Gulfport is the beneficiary of some of the widest streets of any of the towns along the coast. In 1882, the town became the unlikely setting for the world heavyweight boxing championship when John L. Sullivan beat Paddy Ryan.

0:00 (0:18) Depart Gulfport, with glimpses of Gulf afforded at left.

0:15 (0:01) Train now ventures forth onto two-mile trestle that spans mouth of St. Louis Bay. Highway 90 bridge parallels on right, while waters of Mississippi Sound meet horizon on left.

0:18 (0:00) Arrive Bay Saint Louis' dollhouse station.

 BAY SAINT LOUIS, MS - This city is the location of NASA's National Space Technology Laboratory. Guided tours of its space shuttle complex are available.

0:00 (1:17) Depart Bay Saint Louis.

0:13 (1:04) Creep across Pearl River and enter Louisiana while departing Mississippi. Watch for alligators that can often be spotted in waters below as train progresses through these wetlands.

0:19 (0:58) Offshore oil rigs are visible in Gulf to left.

0:20 (0:57) Cross The Rigolets—grassy lowlands laced with channels that drain Lake Pontchartrain into Lake Borgne and Gulf of Mexico at left.

0:24 (0:53) Ships can sometimes be seen moving through grasses on left, actually plying waters of Intracoastal Waterway.

0:30 (0:47) Cross over major waterway known as Chef Menteur Pass.

0:37 (0:40) Large, multi-storied, blockish building, on left, is NASA's Michoud Space Center.

0:45 (0:32) Cross Inner Harbor Navigation Channel connecting Lake Pontchartrain to Mississippi River. Boats, cranes, barges form interesting maritime scene.

0:47 (0:30) Downtown New Orleans skyline is now left forward.

0:54 (0:23) LSU School of Dentistry makes brief appearance at left.

0:55 (0:22) Just one of several golf courses contained in City Park is on left while Park itself is on both sides of track.

1:00 (0:17) Typical above-ground cemeteries, necessitated by water table that is just below ground's surface, can be seen both sides—Rosedale at left, Metairie across highway at right.

1:08 (0:09) Gigantic golden blister to left is famed Superdome.

1:10 (0:07) Facilities for newspaper publishers *Times Picayune* appear on right.

1:12 (0:05) Cruise beside Amtrak's coach yards and engine shops.

1:17 (0:00) Arrive New Orleans.

 NEW ORLEANS, LA - See page 97.

0:00 (1:25) Departing New Orleans, imposing Superdome structure can be seen directly on right. This multi-purpose sports complex is home of National Football League's Saints.

0:04 (1:15) On left, train winds around publishing facilities of *Picayune States-Item Times*.

0:08 (1:11) Just prior to major highway interchange, campus of Xavier University can be seen on left.

0:14 (1:05) On forward left, magnificent 4.4 mile-long Huey P. Long Bridge comes into view. Within minutes train will ascent its lofty heights, affording "air-liner" view of encompassing sights. Barges and freighters ply waters of mighty Mississippi River at one of nation's busiest ports, and Avondale Shipyards will occupy shoreline at right.

0:30 (0:49) Gradually descend from bridge into swamplands of famous "Bayou Country." Here, amidst haunting imagery of this forbidding wilderness, lies heartland of Cajun culture.

0:40 (0:39) At Harahan, intriguing "above-ground" cemetery on right is typical of many such cemeteries in southern Louisiana where saturated soil discourages conventional burials.

0:46 (0:33) On right, vast grain-loading facilities are entrenched along banks of Mississippi River.

0:48 (0:31) Highway 90 joins on left, and follows for nearly 1,100 miles to El Paso, Texas.

0:50 (0:29) On right, first of many refineries reflects abundant petroleum resources of this area.

0:58 (0:21) Cross Bayou Des Allemands. ("Bayou" is common Southern colloquialism for slow-moving river.)

1:03 (0:16) Sugarcane crop on left represents an important staple of state's agricultural economy.

1:13 (0:06) At town of Lafourche, cross bayou of same name.

1:19 (0:00) Cross Bayou Blue and arrive

Schriever station.

SCHRIEVER, LA - An industrial oriented town of southern Louisiana, Schriever has become home for offshore-drilling related industries.

0:00 (1:23) Depart Schriever.

0:12 (1:11) Slip through watery confines of cypress-imbedded Chacahula Swamp.

0:14 (1:09) Gargantuan equipment of off-shore-drilling rigs is assembled at McDermott plant on left.

0:26 (0:57) Intracoastal Waterway on left affords convenient access to miles of inland industries which line its banks.

0:27 (0:56) At eastern edge of Morgan City, cross Atchafalaya River that, too, is a scene of bustling dockside activity. If Mississippi River had its way, it would flow through this 200-foot-deep channel, but Army Corps of Engineers has built dams diverting Mississippi through New Orleans instead.

0:43 (0:40) At Garden City, some fine plantation estates can be seen on right.

0:52 (0:31) A few miles east of Franklin, cross outlet of Bayou Teche.

1:06 (0:17) Attractive church, on right, and ornate "above-ground" cemetery, on left, highlight journey through Jeanerette.

1:22 (0:01) On right, stately colonial mansions accent gracious neighborhood of New Iberia. Immediately adjacent can be seen lofty domed towers of St. Peter's Catholic Church.

1:23 (0:00) Arrive New Iberia.

NEW IBERIA, LA - A blend of France and Spain in a semi-tropical setting gives New Iberia a special sort of charm. Tabasco Sauce is manufactured on nearby Avery Island.

0:00 (0:22) Depart New Iberia.

0:10 (0:12) Sugarcane, one of state's predominant crops, is grown in field on left.

0:19 (0:03) Lafayette Municipal Airport is immediately across U.S. 90 on right. Cross Vermilion River.

0:22 (0:00) Arrive Lafayette.

LAFAYETTE, LA - This is the very heart of "Cajun" country. Many oil-related firms have located here, and it is home for the University of Southwestern Louisiana. Longfellow described this country as "The Eden of Louisiana" in his poem "Evangeline"—and it is indeed, with soft-flowing bayous, verdant, moss-covered forests and flowers blooming year-round. Each fall, "Festivals Acadiens" is held here, featuring Acadian culture with Cajun food, music and crafts.

0:00 (1:25) Depart Lafayette.

0:22 (1:03) Pool-table-like fields, both sides of train, are often flooded for raising rice, a major regional crop.

0:37 (1:00) Cross Bayou Nezpique which drains into Intracoastal Waterway, a series of connecting bodies of water that extend from Brownsville, Texas to Boston—the world's longest such waterway. Shipyards are at left and sternwheeler is frequently docked here.

0:43 (0:42) Nostalgic Bull Durham ad adorns one of Jennings' buildings at right.

1:25 (0:00) Arrive Lake Charles.

LAKE CHARLES, LA - A deep-water port with access to the Gulf of Mexico has made this the industrial center of southwestern Louisiana. Oil, cement and chemicals are just some of the varied products that are produced or processed here.

0:00 (1:25) Depart Lake Charles.

0:04 (1:21) While crossing Calcasien River, look at railing of adjacent highway bridge for crossed-dueling-pistol decor.

0:38 (0:47) As we cross Sabine River, bid farewell to Louisiana and welcome to Texas, largest of the 48 contiguous states. Don't expect to see the open ranges quite yet, as countryside is still heavily agricultural, with rice fields and sorghums more dominant than Herefords and Angus.

1:18 (0:07) Cross a shipping channel as we near Beaumont; downtown will be off to right. Here, terrain starts to open up a bit, as Texas begins to look a bit more like Texas.

1:25 (0:00) Arrive Beaumont.

BEAUMONT, TX - Although settled much earlier by French and Spanish fur trappers, Beaumont was truly born in 1901 when the world's greatest oil well, the Lucas Gusher of Spindletop fame, blew in and started a new era. Besides being an industrial giant, it is both a major port and an agricultural center. Babe Didrikson Zaharias, perhaps the world's greatest woman athlete, called this her home.

0:00 (1:37) Depart Beaumont.

0:14 (1:23) Small Beaumont Municipal Airport is on right.

0:25 (1:12) On right, some of area's rice fields, which use flood irrigation during growing season, appear just before Nome, TX.

0:47 (0:50) Cross Trinity River about two miles west of Liberty, TX.

1:08 (0:29) Cross large San Jacinto River which flows into Galveston Bay.

1:09 (0:28) Just before Sheldon, St. Regis Paper mill is clearly visible through trees on right.

1:12 (0:25) Far in distance, across enormous pipe storage yard on left, it is possible to pick out 570-foot-high San Jacinto Monument—looking like a small smokestack on the horizon. It was here that Texas finally won its independence from Mexico with Santa Ana's capture by Sam Houston's Texas army in 1836.

1:18 (0:19) Small campus of Southern Bible College is on left as we near Houston.

1:22 (0:15) Sprawling Southern Pacific yards are adjacent on left.

1:37 (0:00) Arrive Houston where, to left and beyond station, America's most dramatic skyline of modern architecture should impress any visitor.

 HOUSTON, TX - Houston, the largest city in Texas, grew for two reasons: its excellent port facilities, enhanced by the construction of a ship canal to Galveston, and the discovery of oil in the immediate area.

In the late 1970s and early 1980s, spurred by a then-booming oil industry, Houston's skyline grew into a compacted maze of geometric patterns and reflections. A resurgence in the American skyscraper occurred here, creating a look that is the epitome of modernism.

 Amtrak Station, 902 Washington Ave., 77002, is a small, efficient structure located on the edge of the

downtown area. There are storage lockers, luggage carts, food and beverage vending machines and ample adjacent free parking.

 United **Cab**, 699-0000. Budget will pick up rental car customers at the station. **Local buses**, 635-4000.

Greater Houston Convention and Visitors Council, 801 Congress, (713) 227-3100 or 800-231-7799.

Allen Park Inn, 2121 Allen Parkway, 77019; (713) 521-9321 or 800-231-6310. Large motor hotel with lots of amenities, just out of the immediate downtown area. Will pick up at station, about two miles. $75.

0:00 (4:08) Depart Houston.

0:26 (3:42) Impressive skyline of Houston's Galleria is off to right.

0:43 (3:25) Plant of Imperial Sugar Company is on right in aptly named Sugar Land, TX.

0:45 (3:23) White and tan buildings, about one-fourth mile distant on right, are facilities of Central State Farm, Department of Corrections.

0:53 (3:15) Cross huge Brazos River just before entering Richmond. Note elegant old frame depot on right.

1:15 (2:53) Cotton and soybeans, growing on both sides of tracks, are typical crops of southern Texas. Rice fields are also prevalent along this stretch.

1:48 (2:20) Cross a Colorado River—not of Grand Canyon fame, but smaller river that drains an enormous section of west-central Texas plains before emptying into Gulf of Mexico.

1:49 (2:19) In Columbus, be sure to note stylish old courthouse on left, complete with clock-embedded dome.

3:35 (0:33) Nearing San Antonio, runways of Randolph Air Force Base are off to left.

4:02 (0:06) East Yards of Southern Pacific are on left.

4:08 (0:00) Arrive San Antonio where nicely renovated station on right is but a stone's throw from heart of downtown. Tower of Americas, constructed for 1968 HemisFair, bolts skyward. Adjacent to station, huge structure with cable-suspended roof is

Alamodome. Completed in 1993, it is city's sports, convention and concert center.

 SAN ANTONIO, TX - See page 208.

0:00 (3:04) Depart San Antonio.

As the train now proceeds across the vast expanse of the west Texas prairie, sage, yucca and cactus periodically punctuate this otherwise arid landscape.

2:56 (0:08) Approaching Del Rio, pass grounds of Laughlin Air Force Base on left. Nice collection of older military aircraft enhances entrance.

3:04 (0:00) Cross series of finely landscaped canals arriving Del Rio.

 DEL RIO, TX - This "Queen City of the Rio Grande" is the largest city between San Antonio and El Paso. Sheep and Angora goat production is the prevalent industry, giving rise to the town's claim of "Wool and Mohair Capital of the World." The Mexican border is just to the south.

0:00 (2:24) Departing Del Rio, Mexican city of Acuna can be seen atop bluffs on left. This is last recognized port of entry until El Paso.

0:11 (2:13) Rio Grande, now on left, represents border between U.S. and Mexico.

0:16 (2:08) Cross waters of Amistad Reservoir which has 850 miles of shoreline. Constructed just below confluence of Rio Grande and Devil's River, Amistad was joint project of U.S. and Mexico, with Spanish word for "friendship" reflected in its name.

0:48 (1:36) Suddenly, train embarks across Pecos High Bridge spanning magnificent canyon cut by Pecos River 321 feet below, one of trip's scenic highlights. High Bridge was completed in 1892. After original was replaced in 1944, it was cut into numbered sections and shipped to Guatemala where it now serves as a highway bridge.

1:04 (1:20) It was near here, on a trestle high over Deadman's Gulch, that a silver spike was driven in January 1888, completing a New Orleans-San Francisco route— nation's second transcontinental rail line. (Actual section of track was abandoned when Pecos High Bridge went into service.)

1:06 (1:18) Pass by Langtry on left where Judge Roy Bean once enforced his own brand of "law west of the Pecos."

A monumental airlift took place here in 1954 when devastating storms, spawned by Hurricane Alice, left an eastbound *Sunset Limited* stranded due to washed out track. Some 200 passengers had to be evacuated by helicopter.

1:26 (0:58) *Sunset* route was especially vulnerable to outlaws who could easily retreat across nearby Mexican border. In 1912, last attempted train robbery in these parts took place at Baxter's Curve. Two desperados, one of whom had ridden with Butch Cassidy, boarded a westbound train from their galloping horses, only to have their villainous effort end in failure when they were shot to death during the incident.

2:24 (0:00) Arrive Sanderson.

 SANDERSON, TX - Now a railroad shipping point for this sparsely settled ranching country, Sanderson was once the lair of renegades, outlaws, cattle rustlers and general ne'er-do-wells. Judge Roy Bean operated a saloon here as well as the one in Langtry.

0:00 (1:40) Depart Sanderson. Sheep pens on right are a time-worn testimonial to an industry that remains a vital economic mainstay of region.

0:05 (1:35) At right, cave and earthen mound were used by Apaches for shelter and cooking, respectively.

0:57 (0:44) On forward right and left, Davis Mountains are now interposed upon horizon.

1:06 (0:34) At right, handsome old Gage Hotel in Marathon faces train, while its newer adobe addition is across street to west. Built with the profits from his nearby 500,000-acre ranch, the original structure was opened by Alfred Gage in 1927 to serve as his headquarters whenever he was on one of his many trips to Marathon. Hotel has been beautifully restored and refurbished with antiques, making it a popular stop for those visiting nearby Big Bend National Park.

1:38 (0:02) Approaching Alpine, large "SR" inscribed on hillside right identifies campus of Sul Ross State University, best known for its rodeo teams.

1:40 (0:00) Handsome Spanish-style station greets passengers arriving Alpine.

ALPINE, TX - This is the trading center and county seat of Brewster County—Texas' biggest county, larger than the state of Connecticut. Its mild winter climate, together with Big Bend National Park 80 miles to the south, have made Alpine a favorite tourist stop.

0:00 (3:33) Small "canyonlands" are a temporary delight departing Alpine.

0:15 (3:18) At Paisano Pas, *Sunset Limited* reaches 5,074 feet, highest point on route.

0:18 (3:15) On forward left, Chinati Peak (7,730 feet) is most prominent member of Cuesto del Burro Range.

0:22 (3:11) At night eastbound be sure to look to south for possible sighting of famous Marfa Ghost Lights.

0:29 (3:04) Passing through Marfa, watch for sailplanes which frequent updrafts above nearby mesas. Palatial domed building seen on right houses Presidio County Courthouse. Although dome was formerly crowned by "Scales of Justice," ornament was displaced by rifle blast from a disgruntled prisoner who apparently felt that justice had not been served. On west side of "Main Street" is landmark El Paisano Hotel. Over 300 members of cast and crew of movie *Giant* stayed here during film's shooting in 1955, while stars Rock Hudson, James Dean and Elizabeth Taylor were housed in some of Marfa's private homes. Hostelry has been one of best in region, complete with indoor swimming pool.

0:31 (3:02) White domes of University of Texas' McDonald Observatory are on southern prominence of Davis Mountains in far distance right. At base, Ft. Davis is highest town in Texas at 5,050 feet. Town's courthouse reputedly has turnstiles to keep stray cattle from appearing in court.

0:47 (2:46) On immediate left, $15 million helium-filled "blimp" is one of several such DEA craft floating over Southwest using radar in an effort to stem drug-carrying aircraft coming up from Mexico. Controversial because of cost and questionable effective-

Marfa Ghost Lights

Mysterious glowings were first spotted near Marfa in 1883 and have been reported sporadically ever since. A subject of TV's *Unsolved Mysteries*, many have speculated but no one is certain what really causes these strange shimmerings. Marfa, nine miles to west, throws a party every Labor Day weekend to celebrate this mystery.

ness, balloons are size of a Boeing 747 and tethered on 10,000-foot cables.

0:49 (2:44) Antelope herds are a frequent sight throughout this particular region.

0:59 (2:34) Re-emergence of agricultural fields outside Valentine reflects gradual descent off high plains. A scene from movie *Giant* was filmed near old windmill on left.

1:27 (2:06) Highway 90, trackside companion of last 24 hours, now departs north.

Gain one hour as train passes from Central to Mountain Time. Set your watch back (forward if eastbound) one hour.

1:57 (1:36) At Sierra Blanca, mountains of same name hover in distance on right, while Quitmans are dwarfed by Mexican Hueso Range on left. Town has only adobe courthouse still in use in Texas.

2:28 (1:05) Remnants of old fort, which once guarded U.S. mail, can be seen on right at Fort Hancock.

2:40 (0:53) Cotton fields and pecan groves are suddenly popular sights of Rio Grande Valley.

3:14 (0:19) Approaching El Paso through industrial district, note marvelous Phelps Dodge brick chimney. Ahead north, Franklin Mountains encircle city. Supposedly, if light is right (and imagination vivid) silhouette of Ben Franklin can be discerned.

3:33 (0:00) Arrive El Paso. Station, styled in early mission architecture, with pieces of Mexican pottery displayed atop surrounding walls, was completed in 1905 and designed by firm of Daniel H. Burnham, designers of Washington, D.C.'s Union Station.

EL PASO, TX - This is the largest U.S. city on the Mexican border, and its southerly neighbor Juarez is likewise the largest Mexican border city. Cradled in an ancient mountain pass (hence the name "El Paso"), it is surrounded by mountains over one mile in elevation. This is Amtrak's gateway to Carlsbad Caverns National Park, 145 miles northeast of here.

0:00 (1:27) Departing El Paso, Mexican sister-city of Juarez can be seen on left atop palisades of Rio Grande. Inscription on mountain above city admonishes "Read the Bible and lead a fuller life."

0:05 (1:22) On right, pass campus of University of Texas at El Paso. Floodlight banks protrude above university's "Sun Bowl" stadium, carved within hillsides on right.

0:06 (1:21) On forward left, massive monument of Christ on cross is ensconced atop Sierra de Cristo Rey. On last Sunday in October, thousands of pilgrims trek four miles to summit to celebrate "Feast of Christ the King." Shrine is at point where Texas, New Mexico and Mexico all meet.

0:10 (1:17) Sprawling Southwestern Portland Cement Company on right, and Asarco refinery on left, greet train as it crosses Rio Grande from Texas into New Mexico.

0:11 (1:16) Sunland Park Race Track can be seen on right.

0:12 (1:15) White post on immediate left identifies international border, only 30 feet away and Amtrak's closest encounter with Mexico. Sprawl of shanties is actually in Mexico.

0:22 (1:05) Mountains now extending both on right and left are Portillos.

0:23 (1:04) In valley off to right, Lee Trevino-designed golf course, lined with homes and condos, is in vivid contrast to surrounding desert.

0:48 (0:39) Ancient lava flows are very visible through this region. Flow now comes within 100 feet of tracks on left.

1:20 (0:07) Florida Peak (7,295 feet) prevails amidst Florida Mountains on left. Mountain with hole through it is Window Peak.

1:21 (0:06) Beyond Floridas, prominent peaks at east end of small range are known as Three Sisters.

1:25 (0:03) On eastern outskirts of Deming, cross Mimbres River.

1:26 (0:01) Note old steam locomotive that now reposes in park off to left.

1:27 (0:00) Arrive Deming.

DEMING, NM - Situated in a beautiful agricultural area, Deming farmers raise cotton, peanuts, pecans, beans and grain sorghums in abundance. This is a rock hound's delight, and a state park has been established just for their needs—appropriately named "Rock Hound State Park." A warm winter climate, with an average snowfall of only 2.7 inches, makes this a popular spot for retirees.

0:00 (0:48) Depart Deming.

0:15 (0:33) Crest Continental Divide at 4,584 feet, Amtrak's lowest crossing of nation's rooftop.

0:48 (0:00) Arrive Lordsburg.

LORDSBURG, NM - As with so many Western towns, Lordsburg was established with the arrival of the railroad. It is situated near the eastern edge of The Gadsden Purchase, a strip of land acquired by the United States from Mexico in 1854 that permitted the railroad to continue its march westward to the Pacific Ocean.

Nestled between the Burro and Pyramid mountain ranges, this area was once controlled by Cochise, greatest of the Apache chiefs. Now a desert community where a mild southern New Mexico climate makes this another appealing retirement area.

0:00 (2:00) Depart Lordsburg.

0:19 (1:41) On left, as *Sunset* crests a ridge, adobe ruins and some live-in shacks mark site of camp where thousands of Chinese laborers were once housed during construc-

Sunset Ltd. — Cochise, AZ
DORIS SWANSON

tion of Southern Pacific.

0:28 (1:32) At left are Chiricahua Mountains which rise to a maximum height of 9,795 feet. Face of Indian warrior Cochise can be clearly distinguished at top of ridge staring skyward as he lies atop "his mountains."

0:30 (1:30) Reddish-brown water tank on right sits in New Mexico while windmill on left is in Arizona as *Sunset* crosses states' boundary.

1:04 (0:56) Breeze through Willcox, AZ, home of former Western movie star Rex Allen, whose museum faces tracks at right. Then, to right, just before enormous old depot, bright red rail car houses Sonora Express Restaurant.

1:11 (0:51) Tracks now stretch across broad flats called Willcox Playa. Although much of surface is covered with brown stagnant water, much more is host to clear imaginary water of one of country's more deceiving mirages. Dragoon Mountains, on left, are clearly reflected in this "non lake." Cochise electric power plant is also off to left.

1:18 (0:42) Two aging establishments at left, Cochise Hotel and Cochise General Store,

comprise entire business district of Cochise. If planning to eat at hotel, it is necessary to call elderly proprietress in advance and make arrangements.

1:59 (0:01) Cross San Pedro River whose waters flow north and west into Gila River, and eventually join Colorado River at Yuma, AZ.

It was along this stretch of the San Pedro in 1540 that Coronado and his expedition, up from Mexico, first entered the present United States in their search for the legendary Seven Cities of Cibola—cities thought to have streets lined with goldsmith shops and doorways studded with emeralds and turquoise.

1:50 (0:00) Arrive Benson where small shelter on left pretends to be a rail station.

BENSON, AZ - As early as 1860, Benson served as a stop for the old Butterfield Stage. Then in 1880, with the arrival of the railroad, it became a shipping point for the mines around Tombstone. In recent times, ranching and explosives manufacturing have become more important.

Sunset Ltd. — near Tucson, AZ
DORIS SWANSON

0:00 (1:07) Departing Benson, Rincon Mountains form desert horizon on right.

0:07 (1:00) Hillside on left has profusion of yucca—those plants with clusters of spear-like leaves out of which tall shafts spurt upwards, culminating in tops of clustered whitish blossoms. Resourceful Indians of Southwest made a variety of products from this decorative bush, including sandals, baskets, edible fruit and even soap.

0:11 (0:56) Coal Tower at left once furnished fuel for steam locomotives from an era past.

0:12 (0:55) Movie set used for TV's *Young Riders* can be glimpsed about a mile off to right. Except during stormy weather, radar surveillance blimp can be seen hovering above Ft. Huachuca in distance to left. Idea is to spot planes bringing in drugs from Mexico.

0:23 (0:45) Precariously perched atop peak on right is "castle" built by one who obviously prefers mountaintop opulence to more mundane flatland setting.

0:25 (0:42) Just ahead lie two overlapping rail bridges, westbound traffic usually taking the higher route and eastbound the lower. Highway bridge also crosses eastbound tracks.

0:35 (0:32) On right, pink Catholic church, with century-plant landscaping, is Shrine of Santa Rita in the Desert.

The church was dedicated in 1935 to the memory of a Japanese scientist, Dr. Jokichi Takamine. Built around stained glass windows of a dismantled Methodist church, the interior contains a black marble font designed in Italy and a hand-carved crucifix from Bavaria. The chapel bell came from a Southern Pacific steam locomotive.

0:45 (0:22) Tall tail fins of mothballed military aircraft can be seen on right at Davis Monthan Air Force Base. Up to 5,000 planes have been stored here for salvage.

0:46 (0:21) Numerous World War II aircraft are huddled together at Pima Air Museum, on right, including presidential plan used by Lyndon B. Johnson.

0:51 (0:16) Last glimpse of Davis Monthan Air Force Base on right. Olive, twin-beamed aircraft are Air Force A-10 attack planes, built with heavy emphasis on survivability. These tank-killing "Warthogs" played prominent role in Gulf War. Their gattling-gun-style 30 mm cannon can spew out two-pound projectiles at rate of 65 per second.

0:52 (0:12) Southern Pacific rail yards extend along route as train enters Tucson.

1:04 (0:03) University of Arizona campus, distinguished by stadium, is off to right, while Santa Rita Mountains hunker down on horizon to left.

1:07 (0:00) Arrive Tucson where stretched-out, mission-style station awaits on left.

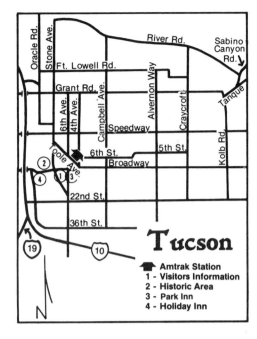

TUCSON, AZ - Very possibly the oldest continually inhabited city in North America, Tucson has lived under four flags in the last 300 years: Spanish, Mexican, Confederate, and American. It was first visited by Father Kino, a Jesuit missionary, in the late 17th century. The Spanish Army later chose the site for a frontier fortress, constructing a walled "Presidio" near what is now the center of Tucson. The site of the original Presidio can still be visited, along with many other old structures in the historic area of the city.

A sunny and dry climate contributes to the popularity of Tucson as both a retirement and a tourist community.

Amtrak Station, 400 E. Toole Ave., 85701. This fine old Spanish-style station is located on the eastern edge of downtown Tucson. There are storage lockers and vending machines and a pay-parking lot is one block away.

Yellow **Cab**, 624-6611. **Local bus** Transit Center is one block west of the station, 792-9222. **Greyhound/Trailways**, two blocks from station. Enterprise **rental cars** offer pick up and drop off for Amtrak passengers, 792-1604.

Tucson Convention & Visitors Bureau, 130 S. Scott Ave., (520) 624-1817.

Holiday Inn Broadway, 181 W. Broadway, 85701; (520) 624-8711. A very popular downtown hotel, five blocks from the station. $65.

-**Park Inn Club & Breakfast**, 88 East Broadway, 85701; (520) 622-4000 or 800-437-7275. Former Santa Rita Hotel, a long-time Tucson landmark. Only three blocks from the station. Breakfast included. $54.

"Historic" Tucson, the original town, is within walking distance,

just west of the station in an area bounded roughly by 6th Ave., Kennedy, Main and Toole. **Old Pueblo Historic Trolley** runs along 4th Avenue and University.

Not in the downtown area, but a must, is the **Arizona-Sonora Desert Museum**, 16 miles west of Tucson, with a fine collection of desert animals and plants.

The **Mission San Xavier Del Bac** (the White Dove of the Desert), nine miles south of Tucson, is perhaps the most beautiful mission in the Southwest. The **Sierra Madre Express of Tucson** offers deluxe passenger train tour service to Mexico's Copper Canyon; (520) 747-0346, or 800-666-0346.

0:00 1:05) Departing Tucson, small but showy downtown skyline appears on immediate left.

0:09 (0:56) Santa Catalina Mountains, off to right, rise to a height of 9,157 feet at summit of Mt. Lemmon and contain Tucson's closest ski area.

0:33 (0:32) Pinal Air Park, in distance to left, has world-wide clientele for restoration of aircraft.

0:34 (0:31) Sprawling pecan orchards pro-

San Xavier del Bac — Tucson, AZ
JACK SWANSON

vide sudden change of scenery on right. Besides pecans and cotton, truck farmers raise the likes of cauliflower, broccoli and cabbage.

0:38 (0:27) On left, Picacho Peak juts dramatically from Arizona desert. Westernmost conflict of Civil War was fought 12 miles south of here. Fine stands of saguaro cactus stud hills on both sides and continue on left for several miles, offering finest stands to be viewed on Amtrak.

0:45 (0:20) Bid farewell to Interstate 10 as tracks curve away to right.

0:46 (0:19) On left, warehouses with adjoining storage yard of yellow cubes are Federal Compress, where bales of cotton are received from nearby gins to have them compressed, stored and then sold. Larger yellow blocks are uncompressed bales while smaller ones are sans air. Crops are harvested in March and October but bales are marketed throughout year.

0:56 (0:08) Facility on left, with enormous piles of scrap metal along tracks, is recycling plant of Proler International Corp., where scrap is shredded and then melted down into ingots of nearly pure tin.

0:57 (0:07) Neatly landscaped, single-story brick buildings, across highway to left, are Arizona Training Center for mentally and physically handicapped.

1:05 (0:00) Arrive Coolidge's glass-box station.

COOLIDGE, AZ - This Arizona community of nearly 7,000 is home of Central Arizona College.

0:00 (0:50) Depart Coolidge.

0:02 (0:40) About a mile or so to left is enormous canopy protecting a smaller structure beneath it. This is Casa Grande Ruins National Monument. The protected building was constructed almost 650 years ago out of unreinforced coursed caliche—a desert soil with a high lime content. Main structure was centerpiece of an Hohokam Indian village, but its exact use and purpose is still unknown. Recent studies, however, suggest possible astrological use.

0:17 (0:33) Note grape vineyard on left—just one more crop raised in this fertile area.

0:20 (0:30) Arizona Boys Ranch, where disadvantaged youth are offered a better chance, is immediately adjacent to route on left.

0:31 (0:19) Agricultural surroundings now

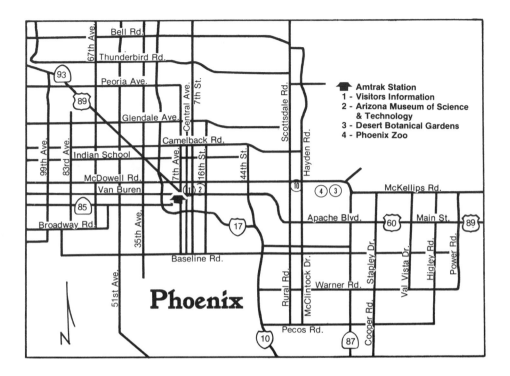

give way to industrialized suburbs of Phoenix.

0:46 (0:04) Arizona State University is on right as we enter Tempe. Sports stadium is site of annual Fiesta Bowl football game, while circular building is school's music hall designed by Frank Lloyd Wright.

0:50 (0:00) Arrive Tempe.

 TEMPE, AZ - A part of the Phoenix metroplex, Tempe is home to Arizona State University, Arizona's largest and oldest institution of higher learning.

0:00 (0:15) Depart Tempe.

0:02 (0:13) *Sunset Limited* crosses Salt River which has its sources in Sierra Anchor and White Mountains to east, providing water for massive irrigation projects throughout south-central Arizona.

0:07 (0:10) Sky Harbor Airport, serving Phoenix, is just to left with major east-west runway paralleling tracks.

0:12 (0:03) Downtown Phoenix stands on right.

0:15 (0:00) Arrive Phoenix.

PHOENIX, AZ - The capital of Arizona and one of America's fastest growing cities, Phoenix began in 1860 as a small settlement on the banks of the Salt River. As with so many other towns, its first real growth came when the railroad arrived in 1887.

The name "Phoenix" comes from the mythical Phoenix bird which supposedly burns itself on its funeral pyre every 500 years, then mysteriously rises from its own ashes. The city was predicted to eventually rise from the ancient Indian ruins found nearby.

Although hot in the summer (air conditioning was invented here), its mild winter climate has accounted for its popularity as a winter destination for tourists from colder climes. Its Southwestern architecture in a desert setting lends further appeal. Besides tourism, manufacturing and agriculture (cotton and citrus) are other leading industries.

While the metropolis seems to enjoy (or suffer) a never-ending expansion, downtown

Phoenix tries to fight off urban shabbiness. The Arizona Center, with shops and dining, the Phoenix Mercado, with Mexican boutiques and cafes, a fine collection of early Phoenix residential architecture in Heritage Square, and Symphony Hall, all gathered around the Civic Plaza, have given the downtown a new heart.

Amtrak Station, 401 West Harrison St., 85003; (on 4th Ave. seven blocks south of Van Buren St.) is a recently renovated structure located in a marginal downtown area. There are storage lockers and very limited free parking.

Yellow **Cab**, 252-5252. **Local buses** are three and four blocks north of the station on Jefferson and Washington Streets; 253-5000. Enterprise offers **rental car** customers station pick-up service, 257-4177.

Phoenix and Valley of the Sun Convention & Visitors Bureau, One Arizona Center, 400 E. Van Buren, (602) 254-6500.

The following hotels are reasonably convenient to the station and are in good downtown locations:
-**Ramada Hotel**, 401 N. 1st St. (at Polk), 85004; (602) 258-3411. Completely renovated in 1988. Eleven blocks from the station. $69.
-**San Carlos**, 202 N. Central Ave. (at Monroe), 85004; (602) 253-4120 or 800-528-5446. Built in 1927, restored and listed on National Register of Historic Places. Ten blocks from the station. $90.

Many of the downtown attractions were mentioned above. Phoenix's major attraction, however, is its winter sun and warmth. To better appreciate this desert environment, you might visit the **Desert Botanical Garden** in Papago Park, with unusual cacti and other desert plants, and the **Phoenix Zoo,** which has over 1,000 animals, many representative of the Arizona-Sonora region.

0:00 (3:20) Depart Phoenix. Darkness usually prevails on stretch between Phoenix and Pomona.

1:30 (1:50) In early morning darkness, October 9, 1995, 59 miles west of Phoenix, Amtrak's *Sunset Limited* struck a sabotaged section of track. An Amtrak employee was killed and about 100 other passengers were injured in ensuing wreck.

3:20 (0:00) Arrive Yuma.

YUMA, AZ - Yuma does quite well in this southwestern Arizona setting. Irrigation from the Colorado River has turned much of its sand into productive farmland and its climate has made it a popular resort center. Just outside of town is the site of the infamous Yuma Territorial Prison which is now a State Historical Park. Built by convicts, it was nearly escape proof and was considered to be the most secure prison in the West.

0:00 (1:45) Depart Yuma.

Pass from Mountain to Pacific Time as train crosses Arizona state line into California. Since Arizona does not observe daylight saving time, set watch back (forward if eastbound) one hour, only if rest of country is not on daylight saving time.

1:10 (0:35) As *Sunset* cruises near California's Salton Sea, lowest point on route is touched—202 feet below sea level.

1:45 (0:00) Arrive Indio.

INDIO, CA - Indio had a typical beginning in 1894 when it was a minor stop on the Southern Pacific, and the depot served as the town's social center. Climate and irrigation, however, led to Indio's eventually becoming "The Date Capital of the World." Just to the south is California's largest inland body of water, the Salton Sea.

0:00 (1:50) Depart Indio.

As the train now emerges upon the Southern California megalopolis, the small farms and dairies which have dotted the landscape since daybreak are suddenly engulfed in the imposing shadows of mammoth industrial operations and the every-encroaching suburban sprawl.

1:26 (0:15) Coming into Colton, cross concrete-lined Santa Ana River. San Gabriel Mountains now border on right into Los Angeles.

1:41 (0:00) Arrive Ontario.

ONTARIO, CA - This Southern California community is now on the southeastern outskirts of the greater Los Angeles metroplex. In earlier times, a fountain near the station was turned on just before trains arrived to entice travelers to stop here and take up farming.

0:00 (0:09) Depart Ontario.

0:01 (0:08) Extensive vineyards surround Brookside Winery on right. Facility is oldest commercial winery in California.

0:02 (0:07) On left, pass Ontario International Airport.

0:09 (0:00) Arrive Pomona Commercial Street station.

POMONA, CA - In 1875, Solomon Gates was awarded a free lot for naming Pomona after the Roman goddess of fruit. The name remains appropriate to this day, reflecting the city's prominence as a mecca of citrus production.

0:00 (0:45) Departing Pomona, St. Joseph's Catholic Church is attractive fixture on left. A short distance downline, St. Paul's Episcopal Church is easily recognized on right by its distinctive mission-style architecture.

0:03 (0:42) On right, skirt campus of California Polytechnic University at Pomona.

0:12 (0:33) At La Puente, massive building complex ensconced atop bluffs on right is Indian Hills Convention and Golf Center.

0:16 (0:28) Between La Puente and El Monte, cross oft-dry San Gabriel River.

0:18 (0:26) Pass El Monte airport on right, then proceed across concrete riverbed of Rio Hondo.

0:23 (0:22) Emerging from brief tunnel at Temple City, train travels briskly down median of Interstate 10 past an envious stream of congestion-bound commuters.

0:30 (0:14) Just prior to departing "freeway route," campus of California State University at Los Angeles can be seen on right.

0:36 (0:09) On right, cluster of tall buildings is Los Angeles County Hospital which operates in conjunction with University of Southern California.

0:39 (0:05) Concrete channel, which sometimes becomes Los Angeles River, joins and follows on left. Perched atop bluffs on forward left is Dodger Stadium, home of one of baseball's powerhouses.

0:44 (0:01) Engage in U-turn across Los Angeles River and slip past County Jail on left. On forward right, City Hall is predominant tower of downtown Los Angeles skyline, while double-domed building in foreground houses Post Office annex.

0:45 (0:00) Arrive Los Angeles.

 LOS ANGELES, CA - See page 246.

Coast Starlight

A cavalcade of aesthetic delights makes this trip worth taking just for the experience of being there. A grand trek through the Cascades of Oregon, a maritime excursion along San Francisco Bay, a delightful amble over Cuesta Grade and a 113-mile daylight traverse along California's frothy shoreline north of Ventura (much of it only accessible by train) are just some of high points of a trip that offers one fascinating glimpse after another.

Although called the *Coast Starlight*, fortunately most of the route is traveled during the daylight, leaving only northern California's scenes obscured in darkness.

Amtrak furnishes train-side motorcoach service from Emeryville and Oakland (depending on direction of travel) to downtown San Francisco.

SOUTHBOUND SCHEDULE (Condensed)
Seattle, WA - Early Morning Departure
Portland, OR - Early Afternoon
Oakland, CA - Early Morning (2nd Day)
San Jose, CA - Early Morning (2nd Day)
Santa Barbara, CA - Late Afternoon
(2nd Day)
Los Angeles, CA - Early Evening Arrival
(2nd Day)

NORTHBOUND SCHEDULE (Condensed)
Los Angeles, CA - Midmorning Departure
Santa Barbara, CA - Early Afternoon
San Jose, CA - Early Evening
Oakland, CA - Midevening

Portland, OR - Late Afternoon (2nd Day)
Seattle, WA - Midevening Arrival (2nd Day)

FREQUENCY - Daily.
SEATING - Superliner coaches.
DINING - Complete meal and beverage service. Lounge service also available, with sandwiches, snacks and beverages, and movies.
SLEEPING - Superliner sleepers with deluxe, family, economy and special bedrooms. Showers available.
PACIFIC PARLOR CAR - Available to first class (sleeping car) passengers only. Complimentary morning and afternoon beverages and snack service, library, games.
BAGGAGE - Checked baggage handled at most stations.
RESERVATIONS - All-reserved train.
LENGTH OF TRIP - 1,389 miles in 35 hours.

ROUTE LOG

SEATTLE, WA - Seattle lies on the eastern shores of Puget Sound and is flanked by two beautiful ranges of mountains, the Olympics to the west and the Cascades to the east. Although situated relatively far north, its proximity to the Pacific Ocean, warmed by the Japan Current, gives it a very temperate climate year-round.

Founded in the mid-nineteenth century, the city grew to importance largely because of its excellent natural harbor—even though it is more than 100 miles from the open sea. It developed rapidly in the 1870s during the Alaska gold rush and more recently as a leader in aircraft and space technology.

King Street Station, 3rd and South Jackson Streets, is located on the south edge of the downtown area next to the Kingdome. The station has vending machines, a snack bar, a newsstand, redcaps, luggage carts, a direct phone for cabs and pay-parking.

Farwest **Taxi**, 622-1717. **Local buses** are one block from station. Buses travel through a unique transit tunnel beneath 3rd Ave. in the heart of downtown. To reach **Tunnel Buses** from the station, take stairs up to Jackson St. then one block east. For **rental cars**, Enterprise and Dollar have station pick up, and Hertz will shuttle in summer. **Monorail** (to the Space Needle) terminal, 5th Ave. and Stewart at Westlake Center. There is a connecting **Amtrak Thruway Bus** between the King Street Station and downtown Vancouver. BC.

The **Waterfront Streetcar** service connects the International District next to King Street Station to Pioneer Square and the waterfront north to Pier 70. Trolley stops close to the station at 5th and Jackson.

Visitors Center, 8th and Pike, Level One, Convention Center. Call (206) 461-5840.

Pacific Plaza Hotel, 4th Ave. at Spring St., 98104; (206) 623-3900 or 800-426-1165. Popular downtown hotel for economy minded. Attractive, small rooms. Short cab ride from the station, two blocks from tunnel bus stop. Free continental breakfast. $80.

-Travelodge by the Space Needle, 200 6th Ave. N., 98109; (206) 441-7878. As the name says, it's near the Space Needle at the Seattle Center. Free continental breakfast. $80.

For those interested in touring sports facilities, the **Kingdome** home to three of Seattle's major league teams, is next to the station. **Iron Horse Restaurant** in Pioneer Square, 311 Third Ave. S., has meals delivered to tables by a model train. **Pioneer Square**, in the area of James St. and First Avenue, features shops, restaurants and "underground tours" of an historic downtown area, much of which was covered over after a fire in 1889; includes underground abandoned stores and store fronts. It's approximately five blocks from the station.

The **Space Needle** has a great observation deck and a nice restaurant (revolving, of

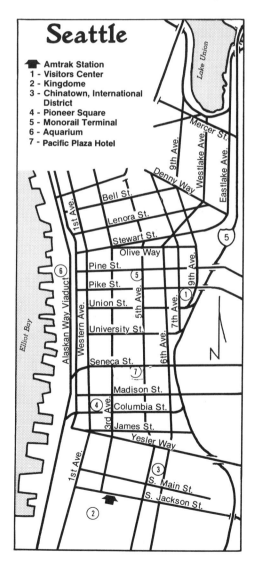

Seattle

🚂 Amtrak Station
1 - Visitors Center
2 - Kingdome
3 - Chinatown, International District
4 - Pioneer Square
5 - Monorail Terminal
6 - Aquarium
7 - Pacific Plaza Hotel

course) at the top. This can be reached from downtown by taking the monorail.

0:00 (0:54) Depart Seattle. Back on right, peaks of Olympic Range hover majestically in distance, while in foreground, castle-like Smith Tower was once tallest building west of Mississippi River. King Street Station's stately clock tower is another impressive fixture of Seattle skyline.

Directly on right is "Kingdome" sports complex, home of baseball's Mariners, basketball's Supersonics and football's Seahawks.

For the next several miles, pass by the grounds of such recognizable corporations as Westinghouse, Sears, Nabisco, Ford and Zellerbach.

0:05 (0:49) Silhouettes of steel superstructures on right evidence major dockside activity at Elliott Bay.

0:13 (0:41) On right is King County International Airport. Boeing's original plant was here.

0:14 (0:40) Green River joins on right as it lazily winds through residential district of Tukwila.

0:16 (0:38) Nicely landscaped grounds of Longacres Race Track can be seen on left.

0:22 (0:32) At tidy community of Kent, quaint old depot is noteworthy on left.

0:25 (0:29) Cross Green River.

0:31 (0:23) Another "modest" Boeing operation can be seen on right.

0:32 (0:22) Cross White River. Soon thereafter, train engages in a broad right turn that eventually settles on a northwesterly tack toward Tacoma.

0:36 (0:18) Cross Puyallup River. Old concrete bridge parallels on right.

0:41 (0:13) Travel directly through downtown streets of Puyallup.

0:43 (0:11) Cross Clark's Creek.

0:47 (0:07) Broad, arching treetops seemingly create tunnel through forest. Splendid covered bridge, crossing overhead, tops off this short but delightful stretch.

0:49 (0:05) Puyallup River joins momentarily on right.

0:51 (0:03) Downtown Tacoma comes into view, perched atop lofty bluff on forward

right.

0:52 (0:02) City Waterway joins on right. This inlet of Commencement Bay is central hub of Tacoma's vast shipping industry.

0:54 (0:00) Arrive Tacoma.

TACOMA, WA - The need for lumber in the 1850s gave birth to Tacoma when the first sawmill was established here. Today, two giants of this industry, Weyerhaeuser and St. Regis Paper, produce thousands of wood products. Shipbuilding is also a major industry, and Tacoma has become the second largest seaport on Puget Sound. The world's largest collection of octopi can be seen here, as well as one of the world's tallest totem poles.

0:00 (0:43) Depart Tacoma, once again traversing banks of City Waterway. Here, shipping, logging and refinery operations share spotlight with bevy of comely shops and restaurants housed in renovated wharf facilities.

0:02 (0:41) Tacoma Dome convention facility bulges up on left.

0:05 (0:38) Looming above cliff walls on left is ornate clock tower of Tacoma's Old City Hall. Originally constructed in 1893, building is enshrined in National Register of Historic Places. Rounded tower, seen immediately adjacent to Old City Hall, presides atop general offices of Northern Pacific Railroad.

0:14 (0:29) Enter tunnel before finally emerging on shoreline of Puget Sound inlet. Impressive suspension bridge connects Tacoma with Olympic Peninsula on right. It was here, in 1940, that the original bridge, known as "Galloping Gertie" due to its erratic heavings during high winds, finally galloped once too often in an unusually strong windstorm. An amateur movie photographer captured the rare event and footage is still shown from time to time on TV or in movies.

0:16 (0:27) Fox Island can be seen directly on right, with McNeil Island lying a short distance south.

0:32 (0:11) Train heads inland now, as farmlands, forests and rolling hills quickly displace nautical environs of last several miles.

0:35 (0:08) Cross Nisqually River.

0:40 (0:03) Cross Lake St. Clair with attractive homes along surrounding shoreline.

0:43 (0:00) Arrive Olympia-Lacy's new intermodal park. On right, Centralia Hotel ad proclaims "Our hack meets all trains," once an enticement for early-day train travelers.

 OLYMPIA-LACY, WA - This is as close as the *Starlight* gets to Washington's capital city, Olympia, just seven miles off to the right and situated at the southern end of Puget Sound.

0:00 (0:20) Depart Olympia-Lacy.

0:03 (0:17) Cross Deschutes River.

0:13 (0:07) Just south of Bucoda, cross Skookumchuck River.

0:20 (0:00) Cobblestone walkways front grounds of handsome brick station as train arrives Centralia. Large white building, situated atop bluffs on left, is Centralia Armory.

 CENTRALIA, WA - Founded in 1875 by a slave named George Washington, Centralia has grown to become a major food-processing and supply area.

0:00 (0:47) Depart Centralia past profusion of logging operations.

0:05 (0:42) Traveling "Main Street" route through Chehalis, another fine old depot stands proudly on left and now serves as Lewis County Historical Museum.

0:12 (0:39) Cross Newaukum River.

0:20 (0:27) Passing through Winlock, note "World's Largest Egg" enshrined in glass monument on right, recalling community's former prominence in poultry industry.

0:30 (0:17) Cross Cowlitz River, which then follows intermittently on right.

0:43 (0:04) After passing through short tunnel, antiquated wooden trestle spans Cowlitz River, on right.

0:44 (0:03) Approach Kelso-Longview with comely neighborhoods clustered along hillsides. A short distance downline, dramatic drawbridge spans Cowlitz River on right.

0:46 (0:01) Early 1900s street scene is subject of colorful building mural on left.

0:47 (0:00) Arriving Kelso-Longview, impressive Cowlitz County Courthouse can be seen across river on right.

 KELSO-LONGVIEW, WA - Lumbering has always been the economic mainstay of the Kelso-Longview area. Located at the confluence of the Cowlitz and Columbia Rivers, deep water port facilities give direct access to the world's markets.

0:00 (0:42) Weather permitting, departure from Kelso-Longview may afford views of truncated Mt. St. Helens (8,365 ft.) and Mt. Adams (12,307 ft.) on left, while further north stands imposing Mt. Rainier at 14,410 feet.

0:05 (0:37) Cross Coweeman River.

0:07 (0:35) Emerge into clearing, affording first view of Columbia River on right. Large stockpiles of timber are corralled out in water awaiting transport. Across river, familiar silhouette of cooling tower readily identifies 460-million-dollar Trojan Nuclear Power Plant.

0:09 (0:33) Cross Kalama River.

0:11 (0:31) While passing through Kalama, note towering totem poles entrenched along river banks on right. Dominant one is world's tallest from a single tree.

0:21 (0:21) Cross Lewis River.

0:25 (0:17) Pass through pleasant little community of Ridgefield.

0:35 (0:07) On right, train borders shoreline of Vancouver Lake.

0:42 (0:00) Delightful chalet-style station greets passengers on left as train arrives Vancouver.

 VANCOUVER, WA - Strategically placed on the Columbia River, where ocean, air, rail and highway transportation converge, Vancouver has become a major shipping hub of the Northwest. Its lengthy history saw the likes of a trading outpost of the Hudson's Bay Company, the construction of Fort Vancouver, and the presence of Ulysses S. Grant when he was but a mere lieutenant in the U.S. Army.

0:00 (0:22) Depart Vancouver, crossing Columbia River (and Washington/Oregon state line) into Portland. In midst of river, traverse Hayden Island, while vessels and dockside facilities of vast shipping industry

Coast Starlight — Portland, OR
JACK SWANSON

abound on both banks.

0:13 (0:08) Cross Willamette River, which then follows on left into Portland station. Willamette is another important shipping channel, as evidenced by heavy concentration of industry along its banks. Dramatic bridges span this waterway, with downtown Portland skyline silhouetted in background.

0:22 (0:00) Arrive Portland beneath stately clock tower of Union Station.

PORTLAND, OR - Portland claims to be "a beautiful, clean, green American City," and indeed it is. An attractively restored downtown is the heart of this community set amongst forested hills along the Columbia River. Its mild climate makes it one of the most desirable cities in which to live in the Pacific Northwest.

And there is energy here. Its seaport ships huge amounts of grain, major electronics firms have located here, there is a snappy light rail system, and the city is still small enough to enjoy.

Union Station, 800 NW 6th Ave., is in an older section of downtown, but handy to Portland's city center. There are redcaps, a newsstand, vending machines, direct phone to Dollar car rental, a snack bar and a restaurant. Pay-parking is in front of the station.

Broadway **Cab**, 227-1234. **Local bus** stop is one block south of the station (chart in station). MAX (Metro Area Express) is Portland's trolley (light rail) system that loops through the downtown core, then crosses Steel Bridge to reach the eastern suburbs. For **rental cars**, Dollar Rent A Car, about five blocks away, will pick up and drop off at the station, 228-3540.

Greater Portland and Visitors Assn., 26 SW Salmon, (503) 275-9750 or 800-962-3700.

Imperial Hotel, 400 SW Broadway (at Stark), 97205; (503) 228-7221 or

800-452-2323. Simple, comfortable accommodations at reasonable rates. Seven blocks from the station. $75.

-**Hotel Vintage Plaza**, 422 SW Broadway, 77205; (503) 228-1212 or 800-243-0555. For a very deluxe stay in downtown. Eight blocks from the station. $150.

Washington Park, 4001 SW Canyon Road, is one of the nation's nicest, has thousands of roses, a zoo with a train, Japanese gardens, a science museum, and an outstanding Western Forestry Center with exhibits of paper mills, lumbering and other unique aspects of this industry. **Gray Line**, 285-9845 or 800-422-7042, with pick up and drop off at hotels, has tours of the city, the northern Oregon coast, the Columbia River and Mt. Hood. The **Annual Rose Festival** is held in early June, with a parade, band and symphonic concerts, sporting events and many other activities throughout the week.

0:00 (1:12) Depart Portland and immediately cross Willamette River. After running on Burlington Northern rails since Seattle, we follow main line of Southern Pacific for remainder of trip to Los Angeles.

0:13 (0:59) On left, pass campus of Reed College.

Proceed for next few miles through attractive suburbs of Milwaukie and Gladstone. On clear days, Mt. Hood may be viewed on left, towering 11,235 feet in midst of Cascade Range. Mountains of Coast Range can be seen on right.

0:27 (0:45) Cross Clackamas River.

0:29 (0:43) Slip through historic Oregon City, end of Oregon Trail and one-time territorial capital.

0:30 (0:42) Large hydroelectric facility harnesses power from Willamette River which rejoins momentarily on right.

0:40 (0:32) Cross Molalla River.

0:45 (0:27) Cross Pudding River.

0:53 (0:19) Passing through Woodburn, old Southern Pacific steam engine in preserved on left.

1:12 (0:00) Arrive Salem, passing directly adjacent to state government offices on right. Very prominent is gold-colored statue

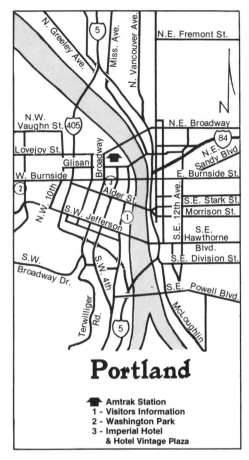

Portland

🚂 **Amtrak Station**
1 - Visitors Information
2 - Washington Park
3 - Imperial Hotel
    & Hotel Vintage Plaza

of early pioneer, standing atop marble tower of State Capitol Building. Immediately thereafter, pass campus of Willamette University, oldest such institution in the West.

SALEM, OR - There is some dispute over just who named this capital city of Oregon, but it does seem certain that it was named after Salem, Massachusetts. The capitol, one of the nation's newest, is constructed of beautiful white marble with fine murals and sculptures.

0:00 (0:27) Depart Salem.

0:04 (0:23) On left, pass Salem's Municipal Airport.

0:15 (0:12) Llama herd can be seen on right. These sure-footed camel cousins are becoming popular with hikers, both as pack animals and as wilderness companions.

0:19 (0:08) At south end of Jefferson, cross Santiam River.

0:27 (0:00) Arrive Albany through well-kept residential district.

ALBANY, OR - The first steamboat reached Albany in 1852, the same year its first industry—a grist mill—was put into production. Finally, in 1870, the railroad reached here, but not until the builder of the then O&C Railroad received a $50,000 "incentive" from the residents so they would not be bypassed by the line. Albany is the home of the World Championship Timber Carnival, featuring tree topping, speed climbing, bucking, log rolling and axe throwing.

0:00 (0:37) Depart Albany.

0:08 (0:30) Cross Calapooia River.

0:25 (0:14) After passing through Harrisburg, cross Willamette River.

0:36 (0:03) Approach Eugene through large Southern Pacific rail yards.

0:40 (0:00) Lane County Jail borders on right as train arrives Eugene, Amtrak's westernmost stop.

EUGENE, OR - Lumbering remains Eugene's economic mainstay, while the University of Oregon lends a college atmosphere to this west-central Oregon community.

0:00 (2:58) Depart Eugene.

0:02 (2:56) Train skirts University of Oregon campus on right before crossing Willamette River into sister-city of Springfield.

0:19 (2:39) Cross Willamette River, and follow to its source atop Cascade Summit. Numerous crossings occur throughout this stretch.

The ensuing 75-mile ascent is one of the most scenic routes in the country, with the jutting peaks of the Cascade Range providing a dramatic backdrop for the dense and colorful vegetation of the Willamette National Forest.

As the train slowly winds through tunnels and snowsheds, quaint little towns, snuggled within the wilderness, offer fascinating glimpses of a robust, pioneer lifestyle. Majestic waterfalls, tumbling down the mountainsides, further embellish this spectacular scenery.

0:34 (2:22) On left, Lookout Point Reservoir dams Willamette River.

0:56 (1:59) Small town of Westfir is highlighted by beautiful covered bridge spanning Willamette River on right.

1:00 (1:55) Begin climbing "The Hill" at Oakridge, an ambitious ascent of over 3,600 feet in 44 miles, that culminates atop Cascade Summit.

1:04 (1:51) Cross Salmon Creek.

1:45 (1:10) Arrive 4,840-foot Cascade Summit. Southern descent is much more gradual, proceeding well into California before losing appreciable altitude.

1:53 (0:54) Deep blue waters of Lake Odell border on left.

2:22 (0:25) Cross Little Deschutes River.

2:47 (0:00) Arrive Chemult.

CHEMULT, OR - Situated between the Deschutes and the Winema National Forests, Chemult is in the very heart of Oregon's mountains and lakes recreational lands.

0:00 (1:13) Depart Chemult through dense woodlands of Winema National Forest. Milling and logging concerns are a most frequent sight throughout this stretch.

0:20 (0:56) Famed Crater Lake is perched high in the mountains, just 15 miles to the right.

0:37 (0:36 Cross Williamson River, which follows periodically on right. A few miles downstream, river plunges unexpectedly into colorful, rocky gorge.

0:49 (0:24) Pass through Chiloquin.

0:59 (0:14) On right, begin skirting shoreline of Upper Klamath Lake, with Mt. McLoughlin (9,495 ft.) towering in distance. Between April and September, large white pelicans are a popular attraction of area.

1:13 (0:00) Arrive Klamath Falls.

KLAMATH FALLS, OR - Klamath Indians once cooked with steam from a vast reservoir of geothermal energy which still lies beneath this area. Thought to be one of the world's largest such stores of energy, it is currently used to heat businesses, schools and homes.

Coast Starlight — Southern Oregon
DORIS SWANSON

0:00 (2:25) Depart Klamath Falls.

0:21 (2:04) Leave Oregon and enter California as border is crossed just before train rumbles through short tunnel.

0:27 (1:58) Through small town of Dorris, where Mount Shasta now looms majestically ahead, left. At 14,162 feet it is a bit shorter than Mt. Rainier, but because of lower surroundings, Shasta is actually the larger.

0:41 (1:44) Prairies now form Butte Valley National Grasslands.

1:15 (1:10) Cresting 5,202-foot Hebron Pass, train is now nearly a mile high.

1:21 (1:04) Mounds on right, between tracks and highway, were actually built by State of California to provide a nesting environment for Canadian geese.

1:22 (1:03) Beyond highway to right is Grass Lake, a wetlands area that in early 1900s was a lake, complete with 32-room resort hotel. Its fate was sealed, however, when dynamite blast created hole in lake bed allowing water to drain into porous rock below. Area is now home to very rare Grass Lake tiger salamander, not discovered until 1969. Another scarce species, the Greater Sandhill Crane, also can be found here.

2:00 (0:25) Through historic lumbering town of Weed, while scenic Mt. Shasta still dominates scene on left.

2:25 (0:00) Arrive Dunsmuir.

DUNSMUIR, CA - Once a major railroad center of the Southern Pacific, Dunsmuir now enjoys an economy dominated by small resorts offering fine fishing in the summer and skiing in the winter.

0:00 (1:49) Depart Dunsmuir. From here, scenery becomes increasingly rugged and mountainous and will remain so until Redding.

1:18 (0:26) Lake Shasta is gemstone of Lake Shasta National Recreation Area.

1:44 (0:00) Arrive Redding.

REDDING, CA - Lumbering and salmon fishing are both important to Redding, but its location at the northern terminus of the Sacramento Valley (the most northern point in California where orange and palm trees grow naturally) provides the weather and geography to attract thousands of vacationers to the area. Beautiful Lake Shasta, with its 370 miles of shoreline, offers boating and fishing, while wild and scenic rivers provide white-water canoeing for the more adventuresome.

0:00 (1:12) Depart Redding.
1:14 (0:00) Arrive Chico.

 CHICO, CA - Gold attracted the earliest settlers to this area, but it was rich agricultural lands that enticed many to stay. Today, ample harvests of rice, almonds, walnuts, peaches, prunes and olives are produced in the area as well as numerous other crops and cattle. Chico is also home of California State University, Chico.

0:00 (0:41) Depart Chico.
0:40 (0:00) Arrive Marysville.

 MARYSVILLE, CA - As in the case of Chico, Marysville got its start when early-day prospectors flocked here to work placer claims in the area's streams. Also, as in Chico's case, the permanence of Marysville has been largely due to agriculture.

0:00 (0:59) Depart Marysville.
0:59 (0:00) Arriving Sacramento, gracious Spanish architecture highlights many buildings of downtown district on left. Ornamental-domed tower is City Hall, whose weighty bronze doors require at least two strong men to open for business each morning.

For log between Sacramento and Oakland, see route of *California Zephyr*, page 168.

 SAN FRANCISCO, CA - It was in 1848, when the "city" had approximately 800 residents, that Sam Shannon discovered gold and started San Francisco's first boom. It has never been the same since. It soon became a bustling, thriving supply center and international port, as people and goods streamed into the area. The city has had its setbacks—the most notable being the devastating earthquake that rocked the area April 18, 1906. The entire business district (as well as many other parts of the city) was completely destroyed. But rebuilding was rapid, and expansion continued. The 1989 quake that registered a hefty 6.9 on the Richter Scale severely damaged two areas of the metroplex, but the city has rebounded from that disaster with style.

Two bridges have been key to San Francisco's development. The Bay Bridge linked the peninsula to Oakland in 1936, and then the Golden Gate Bridge was completed in 1937, giving the city an important direct highway to the north. World War II saw further growth as the area became an important military region. Today the city has a solid based economy and is the financial hub of the West.

Tourism has also boomed in the City by the Bay—and it's no wonder. Superior restaurants, fashionable stores, a sophisticated blend of cultures, all in a perfect setting. It's America's Paris—but perhaps better.

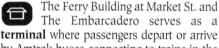 The Ferry Building at Market St. and The Embarcadero serves as a **terminal** where passengers depart or arrive by Amtrak buses connecting to trains in the Oakland area. Buses also take passengers to and from the S.P. 4th Street Station at 4th and Townsend, a station that serves CalTrain commuter trains to San Jose.

 Yellow **Cab**, 626-2345. **BART** (subway) runs through lower downtown beneath Market Street, 788-BART. For **local bus and cable car** information, call 673-6864. Most all major **rental cars** are located downtown.

 Visitors Information Center is at Powell and Market Streets, lower level of Hallidie Plaza, (415) 974-6900.

Cornell Hotel, 715 Bush St., 94104; (415) 421-3154 or 800-232-9698. European flavored, small and unpretentious. Fine restaurant in the basement. Breakfast included. Just off Powell. $90.

-**The Raphael**, 386 Geary St., 94102; (415) 986-2000 or 800-821-5343. One of the nicer affordable boutique hotels. One block from Union Square. $105.

-**Hotel Union Square**, 114 Powell St., 94102; (415) 397-3000 or 800-553-1900. Appealing facility, just a block from Union Square. Complimentary continental breakfast. $100.

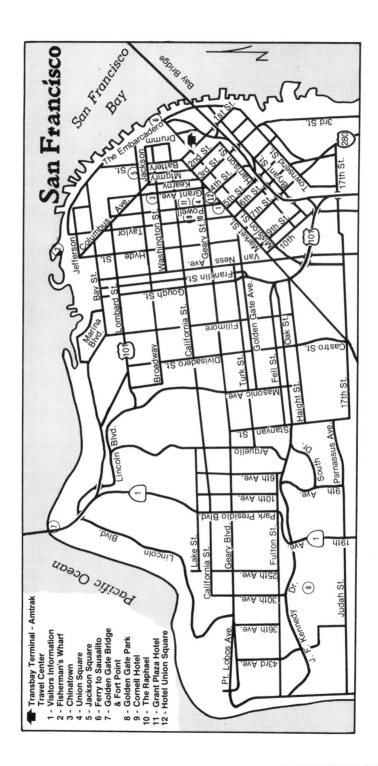

San Francisco

San Francisco Bay

Pacific Ocean

Legend:
- Transbay Terminal - Amtrak
- Travel Center
1 - Visitors Information
2 - Fisherman's Wharf
3 - Chinatown
4 - Union Square
5 - Jackson Square
6 - Ferry to Sausalito
7 - Golden Gate Bridge
    & Fort Point
8 - Golden Gate Park
9 - Cornell Hotel
10 - The Raphael
11 - Grant Plaza Hotel
12 - Hotel Union Square

-**Grant Plaza**, 465 Grant Ave. (at Pine), 94108; (415) 434-3883 or 800-472-6899. Modest accommodations at a budget price. Excellently located at the gateway to Chinatown. $49.

Sightseeing in San Francisco is relatively easy (except for the hill climbing) due to its unusual compaction and good public transportation.

Fisherman's Wharf, in the area of Jefferson and Taylor Streets, is a fine collection of restaurants specializing in seafoods, unusual shops and harbor cruise boats. This is also the location of **Ghiradelli Square** and The **Cannery**.

Chinatown, several blocks in the area of Grant and Washington, has many restaurants and shops and the largest Chinese community outside of the Orient.

Union Square, at Geary and Powell Streets, is the center of the San Francisco shopping and hotel district.

Cable Cars provide transportation and great fun. **Ferries** provide an excellent and inexpensive way to see the Bay and city skyline. Ferries to Sausalito, Larkspur and Tiburon can be boarded at the Ferry Building and Pier 43 1/2 near Fisherman's Wharf. Ferries to Jack London Square leave from Pier 39 and the Ferry Building.

0:00 (1:04) Depart Oakland. Wharfside shops, restaurants and motels of Jack London Square cluster around colony of sailboats and other pleasure craft on right.

0:14 (0:50) Inverted dish, on right, is Alameda County stadium, home of baseball's Athletics and turf of erstwhile Oakland Raiders.

0:30 (0:34) Flower farm presents a spectrum spectacular on left.

0:37 (0:27) White mountains of pure salt extracted from Bay by Morton and Leslie salt companies loom on right.

0:46 (0:18) Small cove provides shelter for multitude of small sailing craft. Larger structures across Bay are blimp hangers of Moffet Field Naval Air Station, built during thirties and now on National Historic Register.

0:48 (0:16) Tops of roller coasters and several other thrill rides are lofty protrusions above Mariotts Great America amusement park on right.

0:57 (0:07) Scores of tank-like vehicles beside FMC plant on left are armored personnel carriers, including Bradley Fighting Vehicles which played an important role in Gulf War.

0:59 (0:05) View of University of Santa Clara, on right, is dominated by athletic stadium and bubble-enclosed sporting facility.

1:01 (0:03) Ancient brick roundhouse with turntable highlights expansive Southern Pacific rail yards at San Jose.

1:04 (0:00) Arrive San Jose.

SAN JOSE, CA - Spanish conquistadors were the first to set eyes on the lush Santa Clara Valley in 1769. Soon thereafter, in 1777, San Jose was founded, making it the oldest incorporated city in California. Orchards and vineyards abound, and familiar names, such as Paul Masson and Almaden, have wineries here. Education also thrives. Stanford University, Santa Clara and San Jose State College are all situated here. Transfer here for peninsula Caltrain service to San Francisco.

0:00 (1:21) Departing San Jose, double-decked Caltrains line tracks on left.

0:32 (0:48) Enter Gilroy, "Garlic Capital of the World." A great festival is held here each year when connoisseurs from around the world come to prepare and savor garlic delicacies during first full weekend in August, when up to ten tons of garlic can be depleted. Although town may occasionally reek a bit, it boasts some points of interest which can be observed on right. First is attractive St. Mary's Church, adorned with its shiny gold bell; a bit further downline is Old City Hall with its highly unusual clock tower; then Spanish-styled depot.

0:37 (0:42) Extensive garlic fields now border each side of track.

0:41 (0:34) *Starlight* now moves one valley westward by traversing through Gabilan Range to reach Salinas River Valley. This pleasant stretch features golden-soft, rolling hills and bare-trunked eucalyptus trees that occasionally line each side of track. Shortly, cross famed San Andreas Fault, milepost 87 at the foot of Chittenden Pass. Tracks must be realigned after quakes that occasionally shake local geography.

0:52 (0:28) Enormous cavern, on left, was once a dolomite quarry, but after being fairly depleted, aggregate became primary product from this huge hole.

0:55 (0:15) Acres and acres of truck farms now spread out across valley.

1:10 (0:12) At Elkhorn Slough, a 2,330-acre wildlife sanctuary, numerous species of waterfowl, including egrets, herons and pelicans, frequent backwater on left.

1:12 (0:10) On right, Moss Landing Power Plant of Pacific Gas and Electric Co. uses natural gas and oil as its power source.

1:14 (0:08) Big, bushy "weeds" in field surrounding Castroville are actually tops of artichoke plants. Forget the garlic, we are now in "The Artichoke Capital of the World."

1:23 (0:00) Arrive Salinas.

SALINAS, CA - Much of the flavor of Salinas' environs has been captured in the writings of Pulitzer Prize winner John Steinbeck, who wrote in glowing prose about his home town's locale. Sometimes referred to as the country's "Salad Bowl," its warm temperatures and abundant sunshine foster an agricultural cornucopia. This is the edge of the Big Sur country, and the Monterey Peninsula is just 12 miles to the west.

0:00 (2:38) Depart Salinas.

0:05 (2:31) Schilling spice operation is on left.

0:22 (2:16) Sprawling "confines" of Soledad Correctional Facilities are just to left.

0:29 (2:09) On right, Salinas River now accompanies train along its course through Salinas River Valley.

0:39 (1:59) Just before 1,305-foot tunnel, colorful single-engine planes parked on right are used for dusting crops with pesticides. Tunnel (number 5 1/2) was constructed in 1923 for curve-reducing line change.

0:46 (1:51) Crates of local produce, including lettuce, grapes, tomatoes, onions and carrots, await shipment on docks of packing companies in King City.

0:50 (1:49) An early bit of Americana appears on side of weather-beaten barn, on right, encouraging populace to "Chew Mail Pouch Tobacco."

1:08 (1:29) Many operating wells can be seen while passing through extensive oil fields of San Ardo.

1:13 (1:24) Train rejoins Salinas River on right, and crosses a few miles downline.

1:26 (1:13) On right, pass Camp Roberts facilities of California National Guard.

1:32 (1:10) Unusual "bell wall" highlights grounds of Mission San Miguel on right. Intriguing adobe structure, built in 1797, boasts best-maintained interior of all California missions.

1:40 (1:02) Glide through Paso Robles, historic stage stop and approximate halfway point between San Francisco and Los Angeles.

1:49 (0:54) On right, at Templeton, billboard for Pesenti Winery entices passersby with "tours and tasting room." Although recently rediscovered in region, wine-making was introduced by Franciscans 200 years earlier, cultivating vineyards on mission grounds to supply needs of church.

1:56 (0:47) For next half hour, ensuing negotiation of Cuesta Grade can be subtly enthralling. Although not what one might describe as spectacular, this small adventure nevertheless seems to capture much of what is romantic and unique to rail travel itself. Monolithic rock formations, protruding suddenly out of nowhere, seem to typify the many curiosities that are encountered "off the beaten path." Frequent tunnels, engineering marvels unto themselves, at once accentuate the myriad of sounds that are as much a part of the rail experience as the vistas that loom outside.

2:32 (0:08) Reversing ten-degree horseshoe curves, named Goldtree and Servano, are fitting finale to Cuesta journey—and also herald a return to "civilization" with fortress-like California Men's Colony dominating scene on right.

2:33 (0:07) Cross splendid old trestle, seen moments earlier during descent of Cuesta Grade.

2:36 (0:02) On left, note athletic field and

campus of California Polytechnic State University.

2:38 (0:00) Arrive at San Luis Obispo's attractive 1934 depot.

SAN LUIS OBISPO, CA - Originally a mission founded in 1772—Mission San Louis Obispo de Tolosa, named for a 13th-century French saint and bishop (because a nearby volcanic peak was thought to resemble a bishop's cap)—this city is now one of the more popular destinations for those wishing to explore the scenic central coast of California. Morro Bay, Pismo Beach, San Simeon and local wineries are some of the area's highlights.

0:00 (2:06) Departing San Luis Obispo, note turntable on right, used to reverse direction of locomotives. Proceed thereafter on slow, winding route through more hills of Santa Lucia Range.

0:17 (1:49) Passing through Grover City, old Amtrak coaches have been converted into

America's Western Spaceport

At Vandenberg, the Strategic Air Command has conducted missile crew training and tested both Peace-keeper and Minuteman ICBMs as well as numerous varieties of smaller missiles. It is the only military installation of its kind.

The base is huge. With 154 square miles of real estate and a working population of several thousand, it is the Air Force's third largest. Although space shots are usually associated with Cape Canaveral, Vandenberg has placed more satellites into orbit than has the Cape. Vandenberg's location is ideal for putting objects into polar orbit which allows surveillance of the entire globe.

restaurant on right.

0:27 (1:39) Cross Santa Maria River on outskirts of Guadalupe. Once in town, note beautiful old mission on left.

0:39 (1:27) Another working oilfield abuts trackside at Casmalia.

After Casmalia, the *Starlight* enters Vandenberg Air Force Base, America's western spaceport. Various launch complexes can be spotted for the next 25 minutes or so.

0:43 (1:23) Vandenberg's Minuteman Area is off to right.

0:51 (1:15) Three-mile-long Vandenberg Airfield is on left. Strip can accommodate space shuttle landings should base become site for future shuttle launches.

0:52 (1:14) Pacific Ocean now comes into full view. For next 113 miles, spectacular vistas abound as train skirts atop seacliffs, overlooking frothy tumult of pounding surf. Because of Vandenberg and two large ranches, public can see much of this country only by train.

0:56 (1:10) Cross Santa Ynez River. Unusually colorful ground cover is most pronounced over next few miles.

1:00 (1:06) Gantries of SLCs (space launch complexes) Four and Five are spread out for next two miles on left.

1:03 (1:03) Pernales (or Honda) Point, on right, has often been confused for Point Arguello a bit further south, causing more than one maritime calamity after ships have mistakenly turned eastward.

1:04 (1:02) SLC Six, nicknamed "Slick Six," lies huddled in hills on left. This 2.5-billion-dollar spacecraft facility is world's most sophisticated. Designed to be first space shuttle launch facility on West Coast, complex was placed on indefinite hold after 1986 "Challenger" disaster.

1:05 (1:01) Lighthouse on right deters oceangoing vessels from jutting cliffs of Pt. Arguello.

1:14 (0:52) Exit southern boundary of Vandenberg Air Force Base at Jalama Beach.

1:18 (0:48) Another lighthouse sits prominently atop bluff of Pt. Concepcion.

1:41 (0:25) Picnic tables and grassy tracts adorn Refugio State Beach on right.

1:48 (0:18) On right, pass El Capitan State Beach.

1:50 (0:16) Small lagoon sits picturesquely below trackside on right. Off-shore drilling rigs and associated facilities at beachside are frequent sights throughout duration of Pacific Coast run.

1:51 (0:15) Late one February evening in 1942, only two months after Pearl Harbor, a Japanese submarine surfaced offshore and lobbed several rounds from its deck cannon into Ellwood oil field off to right. Damage was light, but incident heightened pressures to relocate West Coast Japanese Americans.

1:53 (0:13) Before turning inland toward Santa Barbara station, note San Miguel Island out on right. Three more islands extend south, forming chain that delineates Santa Barbara Channel.

1:57 (0:09) In distance on right, lofty bell tower is landmark of University of California at Santa Barbara campus.

2:04 (0:02) Historic Santa Barbara Mission can be seen on left. Dubbed "Queen of the Missions," distinctive structure is only one in California to employ twin-tower design. Lovely fountain fronting building is fed by aqueduct, built by Indians in 1808.

2:06 (0:00) Arrive Santa Barbara. Immediately left of station is century-old Moreton Bay fig tree, its lengthy branches spreading majestically across four-lane thoroughfare.

SANTA BARBARA, CA - In 1782, the Santa Barbara Presidio Real, which means "Royal Fortress," was constructed, marking the beginning of the city, but the end of Spain's fortress construction in the New World. Then in 1786, the Santa Barbara Mission was founded which was just one of 21 built by Spanish Franciscans. After a devastating earthquake in 1925 destroyed most of the city, rebuilding made liberal use of white adobe and red-tile roofs, using distinctive Spanish-Moorish architecture. Situated on a sweeping palm-lined beach with mountains for a backdrop, Santa Barbara is one of America's jewels.

0:00 (0:44) Depart Santa Barbara southbound through host of well-endowed residential neighborhoods.

0:02 (0:42) Santa Barbara's palm-lined beach lies just beyond Cabrillo Boulevard off to right.

0:04 (0:40) Santa Barbara Zoo can be

Santa Barbara Amtrak Station
DORIS SWANSON

glimpsed at right.

0:05 (0:39) Lagoon, on right, is bird refuge and centerpiece of zoological gardens.

0:07 (0:37) Passing through beautiful little community of Miramar, old station house and passenger cars have been cleverly converted to a restaurant on left.

0:09 (0:35) Overexposed sunbathers are often quite "visible" as train passes by Summerland nude beach on right.

0:22 (0:22) As seacliffs dissipate at Mussel Shoals, remainder of coastline route travels directly along beach into Ventura. Lengthy causeway, seen here on right, extends out to rocky islands where first completely underwater oil well began production in 1964. Tracks follow old state road that was only open while tide was out.

0:33 (0:11) Cross Matilija Creek as it spills into ocean.

0:34 (0:10) Now heading inland, Ventura County Fairgrounds are conspicuous on right, while resplendent San Buenaventura Mission stands proudly on left. San Buenaventura was only California mission to ever use wooden bells, which have subsequently been removed from belfry and now are preserved in Mission Museum.

0:41 (0:03) Cross Santa Clara River.

0:44 (0:00) Arrive Oxnard's modernistic Transportation Center.

OXNARD, CA - A fertile plain makes Oxnard a citrus center and food-processing hub. Sugar was once important, but this has given way to lima beans which make up nearly half of the world's supply.

0:00 (0:33) Depart Oxnard through bountiful farmlands and orchards of Simi Valley.

0:22 (0:01) Scenic Simi Creek crosses beneath tracks several times as it lazily meanders through area of Moorpark.

0:33 (0:00) Arrive Simi Valley.

SIMI VALLEY, CA - This is a northern suburb of Los Angeles.

0:00 (0:40) Depart Simi Valley and continue toward Santa Susana.

0:03 (0:30) At Santa Susana, train suddenly embarks on unlikely adventure across "mini-pass" of Santa Susana hills. Imposing

rock formations, cactus fields and frequent tunnels (a popular setting for older Hollywood Westerns) highlight this delightful, yet seemingly incongruous intrusion. Once at "summit," descend into sprawling expanse of Los Angeles megalopolis.

0:20 (0:19) On right, pass Van Nuys airport.

0:27 (0:12) Good view of Santa Monica Mountains is now afforded on right, while San Gabriels border in background on left.

0:30 (0:10) On left, pass Hollywood-Burbank airport.

0:40 (0:00) Arrive Glendale. This tidy Spanish-style depot, replete with ornamental scroll-work, has been used as a backdrop for many motion pictures.

GLENDALE, CA - Situated on the edge of Hollywood, Glendale is enhanced by many impressive hillside homes.

0:00 (0:14) Departing Glendale, note lush acreage of Forest Lawn Memorial Park on left. Palatial, castle-like building in foreground is "Great Mausoleum." As well as its conventional use, mausoleum boasts a vaunted collection of memorial art, including replicas of Michelangelo's major works, and a glorious stained-glass recreation of da Vinci's "Last Supper."

0:04 (0:10) Metrolink commuter train shops are at right.

0:05 (0:09) Parallel concrete channel on right that sometimes becomes Los Angeles River.

0:06 (0:08) Perched atop bluff on right is Dodger Stadium, home to baseball's Los Angeles Dodgers.

0:11 (0:03) Crossing Los Angeles River avails good view of downtown Los Angeles skyline on forward right. Predominant older tower is Los Angeles City Hall, while double-domed building in foreground houses Post Office annex.

0:13 (0:01) On left, pass Los Angeles County Jail.

0:14 (0:00) Arrive Los Angeles.

LOS ANGELES, CA - Los Angeles is immense, spread out over 460 square miles. The suburb was invented here after World War II, and expansion has

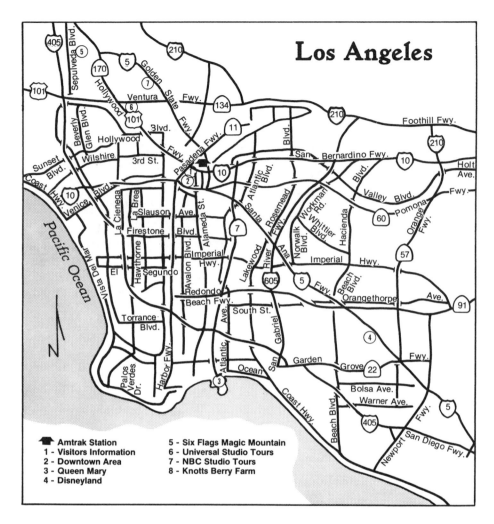

Los Angeles

Amtrak Station
1 - Visitors Information
2 - Downtown Area
3 - Queen Mary
4 - Disneyland
5 - Six Flags Magic Mountain
6 - Universal Studio Tours
7 - NBC Studio Tours
8 - Knotts Berry Farm

never stopped.

Los Angeles' reputation is as mixed as its populace—flaky fads and funky fashions; perpetual sunshine and perpetual smog; freeways free of nothing but tolls; Tinsel Town with a lot of tarnish. But obviously, there is a huge attraction here; it is one of the most visited cities in the world.

All southwestern trains wind up in LA, so it is a city that western rail passengers have come to know, even if for only an "overnight" between trains. Whether you're making connections or have come to see Southern California, it's possible to see some of the sights, contrary to conventional wisdom, without owning or renting a car. Amtrak's service between San Diego and Santa Barbara opens up myriad possibilities.

Los Angeles Union Station, 800 North Alameda St., 90012. One of the nation's most attractive stations, built in California Mission/Moorish style and located in the heart of Los Angeles, has seen extensive renovation to accommodate shops, subway (light rail), commuter trains and a bus terminal. Shuttle buses serve a section of downtown. The station has redcaps, handicap transfer, a restaurant,

Los Angeles Union Passenger Terminal
JACK SWANSON

food and beverage vending machines, newsstand, gift shop, direct phones to some hotels, and adjacent pay-parking.

 Independent **Cab**, 385-8294 and L.A., 627-7000. **Local bus** at the station. Budget **Rental Car** is at the station. Red Line **light rail** service from Union Station to MacArthur Park, where connections are made with Blue Line service to Long Beach can be boarded through subway entrance. Also, Metrolink **commuter trains** to Pomona, Moorpark, Santa Clarita, Riverside and Oceanside can be boarded here. Amtrak has **connecting bus** service to various Southern California towns, including Bakersfield for San Joaquin trains.

Metropolitan Express Van Shuttle service is provided between the Amtrak station (they meet all trains) and any location throughout the Los Angeles area—door to door. For reservations, call (310) 417-5050 or 800-338-3898. Sample fares: Amtrak station (LAUPT) to downtown, $8; LAUPT to LAX. $12.

Visitor Information Center, 685 S. Figueroa St., (213) 624-7300.

 Metro Plaza Hotel, 711 N. Main St., 90012; (213) 680-0200 or 800-223-2223. Completed in 1991, it is the most convenient hotel to Amtrak. Sharp, art-deco rooms, in-room safes, pleasant staff. Next to Olvera Street and two blocks from the station. $69.

-**Miyako Inn**, 328 E. First St., 90012; (213) 617-2000 or 800-228-6596. Japanese speaking staff, next to Japanese Village Plaza. About four blocks from the station. $99.

-**Best Western Dragon Gate Inn**, 818 North Hill St., 90012; (213) 617-3077. In Chinatown, about one mile from the station. $60.

It's possible to breathe in much of the city's beginnings just outside the station. **El Pueblo de Los Angeles State Historic Park**, immediately across from station, is the birthplace of Los Angeles. Many rebuilt structures are around the old plaza. **Avila Adobe** is the oldest existing house in Los Angeles. **Olvera Street** has numerous picturesque Mexican shops and restaurants along one of the first streets in the old city. A great place to spend some time while waiting for a train. Two Mexican restaurants, La Golondrina and El Paseo, are popular lunch spots. La Golondrina (the swallow) is in the first brick edifice in LA, built in 1850.

San Luis Obispo
Los Angeles
San Diego

San Diegans

S everal trains daily scurry both directions between Los Angeles and San Diego to handle the demands of this densely peopled strip of Southern California coast. Some trains have extended runs both to and from Santa Barbara and San Luis Obispo. Although speeds can reach 90 mph at times (an express takes only 2 1/2 hours), a clutter of stops holds the running time for most of the trains to three hours—a time freeway drivers can usually better. However, the train ride hardly compares to the freeway hassle.

Stops along the Santa Fe's "Surf Line" include Anaheim (Disneyland) and San Juan Capistrano (fine beaches and its mission of swallow fame). South of Capistrano the views are particularly good where the tracks hug the shore for several miles, as sunbathers and surfers speckle the beaches on one side and cliffside houses with ocean views are almost as abundant on the other.

The ultimate southbound destination, of course, is San Diego, where the classic mission-style Santa Fe station is located just a stone's throw from the ever-popular harbor area. The San Diego Trolley (formerly known as the "Tijuana Trolley") departs regularly for the Mexican border.

Snacks and sandwiches are available on each train while checked baggage is only available on selected trains. Telephones are available in the food service cars and in Custom Class cars. Reserved Custom Class Service, with roomier seating and free coffee, tea, orange juice and newspapers, is available for a slightly higher fare.

ROUTE LOG

For route between San Luis Obispo and Los Angeles, see page 244.

 LOS ANGELES, CA - See page 246.

0:00 (0:34) Depart Los Angeles. Los Angeles County Jail looms on right and Dodger Stadium rests on hill off to left. Curl south at Mission Tower and roll onto main line of Santa Fe.

0:05 (0:29) Excellent view of Los Angeles cityscape on right where distinctive white-towered City Hall has center stage. Take note of old stone bridges that cross over tracks along this section. Their sculpted pilasters are reminiscent of ancient Rome and memorialize an era of Los Angeles long gone. Los Angeles River, encased in concrete on left, parallels our course for several minutes.

0:07 (0:27) Amtrak coach yard is on immediate right where a gaggle of Superliner cars are stored and await service on trains such as *Desert Wind, Sunset Ltd., Southwest Chief* and *Coast Starlight*.

0:09 (0:25) Diesel shops, roundhouse and its companion turntable are on right where twenty or so Amtrak diesels can generally be counted. Upon passing this facility, train

San Diegan — San Clemente, CA
JACK SWANSON

curves sharply to left and crosses Los Angeles River.

0:12 (0:22) Acres of truck trailers used on piggyback freight trains are assembled on left at north end of Santa Fe rail yards.

0:15 (0:19) Office building of Santa Fe Railroad on left marks southern end of yards.

0:19 (0:15) Cross Rio Hondo Channel.

0:21 (0:13) Cross San Gabriel River.

0:25 (0:09) Pass through refinery operations and active oil wells of Santa Fe Springs. One of area's larger tank farms will soon be seen on left.

0:34 (0:00) Arrive Fullerton.

 FULLERTON, CA - Fullerton has its roots in the citrus industry. Los Angeles' growth to the south has now made Fullerton virtually indistinguishable from its much larger northern neighbor.

0:00 (0:07) Depart Fullerton.

0:05 (0:02) Nearing Anaheim, the obvious question is: "Where's Disneyland?" Look off to the right—a sharp eye can spot The Matterhorn, its white top jutting into the California haze.

0:07 (0:00) Arrive Anaheim's modernistic station immediately below on right. Imposing edifice immediately behind is Anaheim Stadium, home of California Angels.

ANAHEIM, CA - Although best-known for Disneyland, that granddaddy of all theme parks, it may also be thought of as the Valencia orange heartland of California. Even the county's name is Orange. The name is derived from the nearby Santa Ana River and "heim," the German word for home.

0:00 (0:06) Depart Anaheim.

0:06 (0:00) Arrive Santa Ana, where elaborate, mission-style Transportation Center is at right.

 SANTA ANA, CA - We are still in Orange County—as a matter of fact, this is the county seat.

0:00 (0:18) Depart Santa Ana.

0:04 (0:14) On right, two enormous hangars which housed World War II blimps are now part of U.S. Marine helicopter operations at El Toro. These two monstrous blisters are actually constructed of wood. Range of Santa Ana Mountains forms a high horizon on left.

0:08 (0:10) Aircraft of Marine Corps Air Station at El Toro can be seen parked on runways at left.

0:15 (0:03) Cruise through orange orchards which line either side of tracks.

0:18 (0:00) On arrival at San Juan Capistrano, famous mission with its attendant bell tower can be seen on left adjacent to tracks. Depot itself is also on left, complete with a good restaurant. Boxcars surrounding depot provide unusual retail space.

 SAN JUAN CAPISTRANO, CA - The community grew up around the mission which was established in 1776, making the building the oldest in the state. Although this was one of the most beautiful missions built in California, some of its most attractive features were destroyed by an earthquake in 1812. It is world-renowned for its large swallow population that departs about October 23 and returns about March 19 of each year.

0:00 (0:28) Depart San Juan Capistrano.

0:04 (0:24) Suddenly, after having traveled without a hint of ocean, the *San Diegan* spurts out onto beaches of Capistrano, with Pacific Ocean spreading out before us.

For the next 45 minutes, passengers on the right will be treated with seaside vistas.

Those on the left will be able to look up to catch sights of homes perched precipitously on clifftops with stunning ocean views.

0:10 (0:18) This is San Clemente, identified by a lovely little park rising above the tracks on left and a popular wharf restaurant on pier jutting out over ocean on right.

0:17 (0:11) Two gigantic concrete beehives contain reactors of San Onofre Nuclear Generating Station sandwiched between tracks and beach on right.

0:23 (0:05) *San Diegan* now slips through confines of Camp Pendleton Marine base.

0:27 (0:01) Dozens of small sailing vessels clustered in yacht basin on right create a highly appealing maritime scene. Over 800 pleasure craft can be berthed here at any given time.

0:28 (0:00) Arrive Oceanside. At left is ultra-modern, both in design and function, transit center with structures housing Amtrak and Greyhound terminals, while local transit buses are just to its left. Santa Fe rail yards are on right.

 OCEANSIDE, CA - This community, which has a reputation for being "lean and mean," is closely tied to Camp Pendleton U.S. Marine Base that stretches for more than 20 miles northward from the city.

0:00 (0:16) Depart Oceanside.

0:05 (0:11) Monolithic concrete structure on beach at right is San Diego Gas and Electric's first power plant.

0:15 (0:00) Arrive Solana Beach.

 SOLANA BEACH, CA - This stop also serves nearby Del Mar, a pleasant oceanside village with mostly upscale residents.

0:00 (0:36) Depart Solana Beach.

0:01 (0:35) Del Mar's horse racing track, one of the finest in Southern California, is just to left.

0:03 (0:34) *San Diegan* makes a swing inland while last view of ocean is afforded back to right.

0:08 (0:29) While snaking through very rugged terrain, note novel red sculpture in front of nine-story glass building on left—rather like a rocket coming out of an egg

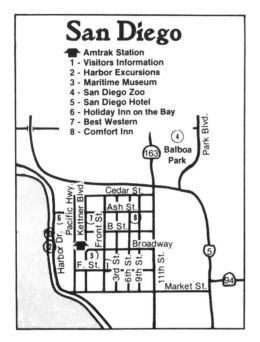

San Diego

🚂 Amtrak Station
1 - Visitors Information
2 - Harbor Excursions
3 - Maritime Museum
4 - San Diego Zoo
5 - San Diego Hotel
6 - Holiday Inn on the Bay
7 - Best Western
8 - Comfort Inn

harbor that now serves as home to one of the nation's largest naval bases.

A mild Mediterranean-like climate, together with the Pacific Ocean and the town's proximity to the Mexican border, have combined to make San Diego one of the country's favorite vacation spots. There are 70 miles of beaches and easily as many miles of golf courses. Electronics, aerospace, medical research and tourism fuel the area's economy.

🚉 **San Diego Station**, 1050 Kettner Blvd., built by the Santa Fe and located on the west edge of the older downtown area, is one of the most attractive depots in use today. Its scale, its Spanish motif, the palm-lined landscape, all blend perfectly in this Southern California setting. There are redcaps, nearby restaurants, a snack cart, espresso bar, food and beverage vending machines and a newsstand. Pay-parking is adjacent to the station.

🚕 Yellow **Cab**, 234-6161. There are direct phone lines to **rental cars;** Enterprise will pick up at the station, 696-5000. The **"San Diego Trolley,"** was completed in 1981 and connects downtown San Diego with San Ysidro, CA adjacent to Tijuana, Mexico 16 miles to the south. These trolleys can be boarded next to the station.

❓ **San Diego Convention and Visitors Bureau Visitor Information Center**, 11 Horton Plaza, 1st Ave. and F; (619) 236-1212.

🏨 **Hotel San Diego**, 339 W. Broadway, 92101; (619) 234-0221; toll free, 800-621-5380. A refurbished older hotel. Four blocks from the station; courtesy station shuttle sometimes available. $60.

-**Best Western Bayside Inn**, 555 West Ash St., 92101; (619) 233-7500. Courtesy Amtrak shuttle. Five blocks from the station. $70.

-**Comfort Inn**, 719 Ash, 92101; (619) 232-2525. Courtesy Amtrak shuttle. Complimentary continental breakfast. About a mile from the station. $55.

-**Holiday Inn on the Bay**, 1355 North Harbor Dr., 92101; (619) 232-3861. High rise with balconies, on the bay. Five blocks

beater.

0:22 (0:14) Tropical palm setting of Hilton resort is on right.

0:23 (0:13) Mission-style tower of University of San Diego can be seen atop bluffs on left.

0:25 (0:06) Convair Division of General Dynamics Corp. is just to right of tracks.

0:31 (0:05) San Diego's Lindbergh Field, unique because of its location near very heart of city it serves, is off to right.

0:36 (0:00) Arrive at San Diego's eye-catching mission-style Santa Fe station. Downtown skyline is just beyond on left and maritime scenes of San Diego Harbor are just a block away on right.

📷 **SAN DIEGO, CA** - It was in 1769 that Gaspar de Portola, Junipero Serra (a Franciscan priest) and several Spanish soldiers ventured north from Mexico to establish a mission here on Presidio Hill. This first European settlement gave birth to what is now California. However, this was not the first discovery of the area. More than 200 years earlier, Juan Cabrillo sailed into a splendid natural

San Diego Trolley — San Diego, CA
DORIS SWANSON

from the station; courtesy Amtrak shuttle. $110.

⊕ **Horton Plaza**, bounded by Broadway, G St., 1st and 4th Avenues, one of the most architecturally bizarre shopping malls anywhere, is located in the heart of downtown. It's a delight just to walk through this post-modernism maze of levels and balconies. The **Museum of Contemporary Art** is directly across the street from the station.

Also, next to downtown is the harbor and its **Maritime Museum**, 1306 Harbor Dr., with three ships including the 100-year-old merchant sailing ship, the Star of India. **Cruises of San Diego Harbor** are available at the foot of Broadway. **Tijuana**, 16 miles south, can be reached by the "**San Diego Trolley**" which starts at the station and runs east along "C" Street.

The **San Diego Zoo**, considered by many as the nation's finest, is in **Balboa Park** where there are also numerous museums and lush tropical gardens. **Sea World of San Diego**, at 1720 South Shores Rd., is one of the world's largest marine-life parks.

San Joaquins

These trains, combined with connecting bus service at each end, join San Francisco and Los Angeles through California's San Joaquin Valley. With major stops consisting of Emeryville, Martinez, Fresno and Bakersfield, it would be easy to assume the *San Joaquins* might someday be renamed the San Ho Hums. The route, however, has its interesting aspects.

In petroleum-rich Kern County the tracks pass through an oil field with more working wells per square mile than will be seen on any other passenger train route in North America. Then the heart of the Valley—one of America's most fertile and productive—has a seemingly unending procession of almond, plum, pistachio and fig groves as well as wine and raisin-grape vineyards, and even occasional cotton fields. These checker the flattened landscape for miles on end. At the north end of the Valley, there is a dramatic change when the terrain becomes rolling and the Bay Area's maritime scenes suddenly grab one's attention. San Francisco itself is an ideal ending point (or starting point) for this journey.

There are several departures daily from both Emeryville and Bakersfield. The 300-mile trip takes six hours, with connecting bus service between Bakersfield and Los Angeles Amtrak stations adding 2 1/2 more hours and the bus between Emeryville and San Francisco another half hour—making a total of nine hours. This is somewhat faster than the *Coast Starlight* following the coast

route. Several bus connections to numerous central California towns are offered along the route.

These trains offer tray meal service, sandwiches, snacks and beverages. Amtrak has been experimenting with Starbuck's coffee, fresh fruit, local wines and a designated car for families and couples. Checked baggage is handled only on the first train of the day southbound and the last train northbound.

ROUTE LOG

BAKERSFIELD, CA - Although agriculture is important (as it has been since the town's humble birth in 1869), oil is king in this community of 100,000. Except for a short bit of excitement in 1885 with the discovery of gold in the area, Bakersfield's real blossoming occurred when oil was discovered at the close of the last century.

Motor coach service connects to Los Angeles and its various suburbs, as well as Barstow.

0:00 (0:24) Depart Bakersfield and slip through Santa Fe rail yards. Rail fans will want to watch for roundhouse which will be on left shortly after departure.

0:05 (0:19) At end of yards, cross large irrigation canal and swing northward which will be our course until we depart Stockton four hours from now. *San Joaquins* now pass through that massive oil field mentioned above.

0:19 (0:05) Through Shafter, then almond groves line both sides of tracks. In late winter, these trees will be covered with millions of pinkish-white blossoms. Groves will appear off and on until we reach Stockton.

0:21 (0:03) Note staked grapevines, which will also be evident for miles to come. Grapes grown in this region are mostly dried into those "California Raisins," while those north of Fresno will become fine California wine.

0:24 (0:00) Arrive Wasco.

 WASCO, CA - This is one of several farming communities that dot the valley.

0:00 (0:27) Depart Wasco and resume ramblings through formal orchards and vineyards.

0:14 (0:13) Sign on left identifies Colonel Allensworth Park named in honor of U.S. Army's first black colonel.

0:27 (0:00) Arrive Corcoran.

 CORCORAN, CA - Cotton is king in Corcoran. Note huge ginning operation to the left of the tracks.

0:00 (0:17) Depart Corcoran.

0:17 (0:00) Arrive Hanford.

 HANFORD, CA - Oddly enough, Hanford boasts one of the best Chinese restaurants in the United States—the Imperial Dynasty. Customers have included presidents, foreign dignitaries and other notables.

0:00 (0:32) Depart Hanford.

0:10 (0:22) Cross Kings River.

0:18 (0:14) Impressive expanse of grape vineyards spills across thousands of acres, stretching for miles along both sides of tracks.

0:27 (0:05) Cribari Winery is just to right as train slows for Fresno.

0:32 (0:00) Arrive Fresno.

 FRESNO, CA - This is the heart of the San Joaquin Valley and the raisin center of the world. Sunmaid has the world's largest dried fruit packing plant here, and the largest fig orchards are in the immediate area. The county claims to be the most farm-productive in the country. Wineries and winery equipment production are also important.

0:00 (0:29) Depart Fresno's rather bedraggled depot and immediately pass by attractive Santa Fe offices on left. Crossing Fresno Street, note historic water tower in downtown a block to left, looking like an extremely squat rocket.

0:08 (0:21) Still in suburbs, campus of Fresno State College is on left.

0:19 (0:10) After appealing golf course on left, cross high over waters of San Joaquin River.

0:28 (0:00) Arrive Madera.

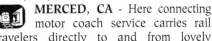 **MADERA, CA** - This is one of the large agricultural communities in the area.

0:00 (0:30) Depart Madera and cross Fresno River.

0:06 (0:24) To right and forward of train, Cathedral Range of Sierra Nevada Mountains, rising to over 13,000 feet above sea level, contains spectacularly beautiful Yosemite National Park which Horace Greeley once called "the greatest marvel of the continent."

0:09 (0:21) Grove of pistachio trees stands just to left of tracks.

0:24 (0:07) As we slowly swing to left at Planada, large grove of scraggly trees on right, short and stubby, are kadota figs.

0:31 (0:00) Arrive Merced.

MERCED, CA - Here connecting motor coach service carries rail travelers directly to and from lovely Yosemite National Park, some 75 miles to the east.

0:00 (0:21) Depart Merced and note picturesque courthouse two blocks away on left and facing tracks.

0:07 (0:14) Castle Air Force Base is on right at Atwater, where assorted World War II aircraft, tethered next to tracks, are on public display and include B-29 flown in by General Jimmy Doolittle—his last military flight.

0:11 (0:10) Magnificent stands of almond trees spread out on each side of right-of-way.

0:12 (0:09) Over Merced River, most

impressive stream seen on trip so far, which joins San Joaquin River west (left) of here.

0:18 (0:03) Low-lying mountains on distant horizon to left comprise Diablo Range.

0:21 (0:00) Arrive Turlock.

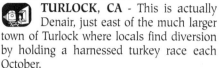 **TURLOCK, CA** - This is actually Denair, just east of the much larger town of Turlock where locals find diversion by holding a harnessed turkey race each October.

0:00 (0:14) Depart Turlock.

0:07 (0:06) Cross Tuolumne River.

0:11 (0:02) Pass over concrete-lined Hetch Hetchy Aqueduct cutting cleanly across valley and built to transport water from Sierra Nevadas to Bay Area. A Reagan Administration official once proposed that the Hetch Hetchy Reservoir be permanently drained and its valley turned into another Yosemite. San Franciscans, however, voiced some objections to idea.

0:13 (0:00) Arrive Riverbank where its attractive station offers pleasant change for depot-watchers.

RIVERBANK, CA - Riverbank began as a ferrying point on the Stanislaus River during the gold rush of the 1880s. Later the Santa Fe Railroad came through the valley and the settlement soon sprouted into a railroad town. This is Amtrak's stop for nearby Modesto, where Gallo operates the world's largest winery.

0:00 (0:25) Depart Riverbank.

0:01 (0:24) Cross Stanislaus River.

0:12 (0:13) Grape vineyards are virtually everywhere along this portion of route. Franzia Wineries contract to buy most of crop grown throughout immediate area.

0:25 (0:00) Arrive Stockton.

STOCKTON, CA - This is California's only inland seaport, with a deep-water channel connecting the city to the Bay Area some 78 miles to the west.

0:00 (0:36) Depart Stockton.

0:26 (0:10) Pacific Gas and Electric power plant is on right.

0:28 (0:08) Enter Antioch, then first evidence of Bay Area's presence will be seen on right where shipping channel of San Joaquin River is just visible. Seagoing vessels are able to navigate into this area via San Francisco Bay. Although hard to spot, San Joaquin and Sacramento Rivers join on right as they continue toward San Francisco Bay and Pacific Ocean.

0:36 (0:00) Arrive Antioch-Pittsburg.

ANTIOCH-PITTSBURG, CA - This is one of the Bay Area's most industrialized areas.

0:00 (0:23) Depart Antioch-Pittsburg.

0:07 (0:16) This is Port Chicago, once a small lumber town called Bay Point. It had a city-owned saloon that was profitable enough to finance the community's water, street lights, sewer and other public services.

0:10 (0:13) Concord Naval Weapons facility is here, with acres and acres of ammunition storage. U.S. Government relocated it a few years back to prevent recurrence of a catastrophe that leveled Port Chicago's buildings when two munitions ships blew up during World War II.

0:11 (0:12) Lift-span rail bridge of Southern Pacific, directly ahead and to right, carries *California Zephyr* and *Coast Starlight* across narrows of Carquinez Strait. Second bridge carries Interstate 680 auto traffic, which is major north-south bypass of Bay Area.

0:14 (0:09) Just before reaching bridge, look directly across strait where grey, unmarked Glomar Explorer, sporting a white heliport platform on its stern, is anchored. It's normally the last ship just before rail bridge. This deep-sea research vessel made headlines some years back when it attempted to retrieve a sunken Russian sub from ocean's floor.

0:16 (0:07) At left, expansive Shell refinery and tank farm snuggle against hillside.

0:23 (0:00) On arrival at Martinez, note semaphore that landscapes station on left.

MARTINEZ, CA - This important commercial and military port was also the home of John Muir, one of the nation's earliest and most outspoken conservationists. His house is now preserved as a National Historic Site. Joe Dimaggio Drive is on the right side of the train, honoring the renowned "Yankee

Clipper" who was raised here.

0:00 (0:29) Depart Martinez along Carquinez Strait, connecting Suisun and San Pablo Bays. Carquinez Bridge looms impressively in foreground right, while on left, famed golden hills are subtly encroaching upon landscape.

0:09 (0:20) With town of Crockett huddled on hillside left, travel directly through midst of C&H sugar refinery. Immediately thereafter, train bears south along shores of San Pablo Bay and passes beneath Carquinez Bridge.

0:12 (0:17) Dart into momentary darkness while passing through trip's first (and last) tunnel.

0:13 (0:16) Union Oil refinery, on left, truly "graces" hillside with its pastel storage tanks set off by ecologically inspired landscaping.

0:27 (0:02) Huge Standard Oil of California refinery stretches across face of slopes across Bay just before Richmond.

0:29 (0:00) Arrive Richmond.

RICHMOND, CA - Richmond's popularity as a convenient suburban stop is enhanced by its trackside connections with BART, a rapid transit system servicing many outlying regions throughout the Bay Area.

0:00 (0:07) Departure from Richmond affords first view of dramatic San Francisco skyline across bay. Golden Gate Bridge can be seen north of city, while Bay Bridge connects with Oakland to the south.

0:05 (0:02) On right, pass Golden Gate Field Race Track.

0:07 (0:00) Arrive Berkeley.

BERKELEY, CA - This stop provides service for the main campus of the University of California. Students study in buildings of striking beauty; most notable architecture is the acclaimed University Art Museum.

0:00 (0:06) Depart Berkeley.

0:02 (0:04) Last, grand view of San Francisco can be captured, again off to right, where Alcatraz Island can now be seen directly below Golden Gate Bridge.

0:06 (0:00) Arrive Emeryville.

EMERYVILLE, CA - This is Amtrak's stop for those using connecting buses to and from San Francisco.

SAN FRANCISCO, CA - See page 240.

Other West Coast Service

The **Cascadia** and **Mount Adams** are reserved daily trains, the former between Seattle and Eugene and the latter between Seattle and Portland. Food service consists of sandwiches, snacks and beverages. Checked baggage is not handled.

Caltrain/SP provides train service between the Southern Pacific station in San Francisco (4th & Townsend) and Amtrak's station in San Jose. Sandwiches, snacks and beverages.

The **Capitols** provide daily service between Roseville and San Jose with numerous bay-area stops, including Sacramento, Martinez, Emeryville and Oakland. Several trains daily (but not all make the entire run).

The **Mount Baker International** is the West's only international train, connecting Seattle and Vancouver, BC. Seattle departures are early morning, and Vancouver arrivals are late morning. Vancouver departures are early evening, and Seattle arrivals are late evening. This service was started in 1995 using Spanish Talgo cars. Reserved seating; sandwiches, snacks and beverages.

Alaska Railroad

They say Alaska is different. Winters can get so cold that locals sometimes leave their cars running all night; then summers can be so warm that weekends are spent waterskiing. Alaska stretches farther west than Hawaii—and farther east than Maine (since the Aleutians actually cross the International Date Line). Vertically, the state juts from sea level to over 20,000 feet— the highest point in North America. And there is no state income tax; it works the other way around in that Alaska pays its residents an annual allotment out of a fund created from pipeline revenues. Alaskans can continue to tick off such contrasts almost indefinitely.

The principal railroad in Alaska is owned by the state, and one may rightfully conclude that it, too, is a different breed. Passenger trains are immaculately maintained, inside and out. Windows throughout are clear and clean, even in the dome cars, while white linen tablecloths and real china grace the diner, where the bill of fare runs from simple sandwiches to Alaskan Seafood Saute. Almost an overabundance of leg room exists in the coaches. Attractive and enthusiastic tour guides are in each coach to keep passengers informed about interesting points along the route and to answer any questions passengers may have. It is the only U.S. railroad that makes unlimited flag stops and it's the railroad that was originally constructed to haul gold from the gold fields around Fairbanks and is now one of the state's top tourist attractions.

For those wanting to go really deluxe, both Gray Line of Alaska (a Holland America-Westours subsidiary) and Princess Tours are operating their own full-length dome cars between Anchorage and Fairbanks. Grayline's operation is called McKinley Explorer, while Princess goes by Midnight Sun Express. These cars are attached to the rear of the regularly scheduled trains and provide upper-level viewing for every passenger. Private dining facilities are on the lower level. Gray Line has cars, each with surprisingly minimal upper-level sway. Princess runs two cars of equal elegance and offers a large viewing platform on the end-car. To book either tour, see your travel agent, or you may contact Princess directly, 800-835-8907 or Gray Line, 800-544-2206.

Most all passengers on the Anchorage-Fairbanks run stop over at Denali National Park to at least take the wildlife tour (and try, weather permitting, to get some more views of Mt. McKinley).

More and more travelers are discovering the route between Anchorage and Seward. Although the Denali experience on the Anchorage-Fairbanks trip is incomparable, the run down to Seward is one of the most spectacular in the world. Not only are the mountains more Swiss-like, the train passes within one-half mile of three magnificent glaciers.

A one-day, round-trip excursion leaves

plenty of time to explore Seward (a delight) or take a half-day cruise on Resurrection Bay.

Schedule for Anchorage-Fairbanks: An "Express" run, from late May through mid-September, making intermediate stops only at Wasilla, Talkeetna, Denali National Park and Nenana, is made seven days per week in each direction. A "Local" train, making numerous stops, operates during the summer on a thrice-weekly schedule.

The Express takes approximately twelve hours between the two cities, departing each city early morning. The Local operates only between Anchorage and Hurricane Gulch, making a round trip each of the three days it operates. During the non-summer months there is only one train per week, departing early morning, leaving Anchorage on Saturdays and leaving Fairbanks on Sundays. Viewing in the winter, of course, is minimal due to the limited amount of daylight. The Express trains carry standard coaches and dome cars and offer complete meal and beverage service. Other trains use rail diesel car equipment and have vending-machine snacks only.

Schedule for Anchorage-Seward: This daily round trip departs Anchorage early morning and arrives back in Anchorage late evening. The trip takes four hours each way, and trains operate from Memorial Day weekend through Labor Day. There is a dining car with complete meal service.

Schedule for Portage-Whittier Shuttle: From late May to mid-September the railroad provides daily, unreserved shuttle service between Portage (a stop on the Anchorage-Seward line) and Whittier, where there is ferry service to and from Valdez (limited service off-season). This unique transport, offering not only coaches but flatcars carrying motor vehicles with their passengers, is Whittier's only land connection to the rest of Alaska. Call (907) 265-2607 for recorded shuttle train schedule. Call 800-642-0066 for State Ferry reservations; these tickets are sold separately.

Reservations: Except for the Whittier Shuttle, reservations are required on all trains operated by the Alaska Railroad and should be made as early as possible. For information, write or call: Passenger Services Department, The Alaska Railroad, P.O. Box 107500, Anchorage, AK 99510; (907) 265-2494 or 800-544-0552 for reservations.

The Railroad also offers several tour packages that offer worthwhile savings.

ANCHORAGE-FAIRBANKS ROUTE LOG

Anchorage-Seward log, see page 267.

ANCHORAGE, AK - Anchorage is the largest city (geographically) in the U.S., having incorporated huge amounts of real estate within its boundaries. In spite of this, the downtown is fairly easily managed on foot. About a day or two will allow you to take in most things Alaska's largest city has to offer; the town is really more of a base for seeing the south central part of the state. (Non-Anchorage residents like to say: When you're in Anchorage, you're only 30 minutes from Alaska.)

Anchorage is located on Knik Arm of Cook Inlet and shielded from heavy rainfall by the Kenai Mountains to the south. Having a moderate climate, its mild summers are comparable to those of Seattle. Very little evidence is left of the earthquake that registered 8.6 on the Richter Scale and devastated the city in 1964, nor were Anchorage's shores fouled by the 1989 oil spill.

Alaska Railroad Station, 421 W. First Ave., Pouch 107500, 99501, is on the edge of the downtown area. There is a covered walkway leading up the hill to town, and parking is available in front of the station. Long-term parking needs a permit, available at the ticket window.

If you wish to sit with someone, keep in mind that people line up early for boarding. One day there may be plenty of seating but the next may be full. Reservations are important. Call 800-544-0552, or (907) 265-2494.

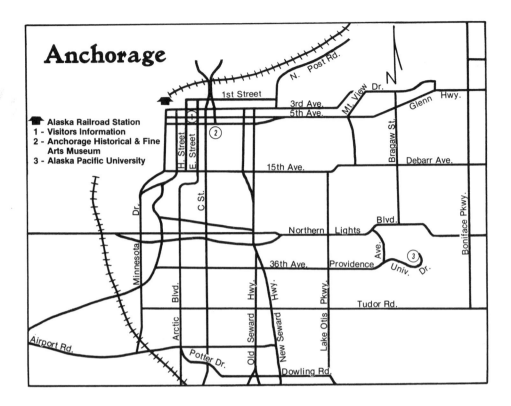

Anchorage

- Alaska Railroad Station
1 - Visitors Information
2 - Anchorage Historical & Fine
    Arts Museum
3 - Alaska Pacific University

N. Post Rd.
1st Street
3rd Ave.
5th Ave.
Mt. View Dr.
Glenn Hwy.
Bragaw St.
Debarr Ave.
15th Ave.
H. Street
E. Street
C. St.
Dr.
Minnesota
Blvd.
Northern Lights Blvd.
36th Ave. Providence Ave.
Univ. Dr.
Boniface Pkwy.
Tudor Rd.
Arctic Blvd.
Hwy.
Hwy.
Lake Otis Pkwy.
New Seward
Old Seward
Airport Rd.
Potter Dr.
Dowling Rd.

Yellow **Cab**, 272-2422. Two blocks to **local buses**, main transit center at 6th Ave. and G St. Avis has **rental cars** near the station, 277-4567.

Log Cabin Visitor Information Center, W. 4th Ave. and F Street. Call (907) 274-3531 or write Anchorage Convention & Visitors Bureau, 1600 A Street, Ste. 200, 99501.

Accommodations in Anchorage are expensive, particularly in the downtown area. There are a few Bed and Breakfasts in the downtown area which are somewhat more economical. Anchorage reservations in the summer should be made well in advance.

-**Voyager Hotel**, 501 K Street, 99501; (907) 277-9501 or 800-247-9070. A small, tastefully decorated hotel in a good location; well managed and one of Anchorage's best hotels. Ten blocks from the station. $149.

-**8th Ave. Hotel**, 630 W. 8th Ave., 99501;

(907) 274-6213, 800-478-4837 (AK only) or 800-825-7287 (lower 48). A converted small apartment building, in a good location, with spacious (suite) accommodations. Nine blocks from the station. $120.

-**Holiday Inn**, 239 W. 4th Ave., 99501; (907) 279-8671. Popular with tour groups. Downtown, four blocks from the station. $140.

-**Bed and Breakfast-Alaska Private Lodgings**, P.O. Box 200047, Anchorage, AK 99520; (907) 258-1717. A bed and breakfast information and reservation service, offering downtown B&Bs and private accommodations ranging from $65 to $110.

Some downtown highlights include: The **Log Cabin Visitors Center**; a walk down 4th Ave., Anchorage's "**Main Street**"; the **Anchorage Historical and Fine Arts Museum**, 121 West 7th Ave., depicting Anchorage and Alaska native cultures; **Resolution Park** at the west end of 3rd Ave., with a view of Knik Arm and Mt. McKinley (on a clear day); and the **Alaska Zoo** on the southwest edge of town.

0:00 (1:23) Depart Anchorage with front range of Alaska Mountains looming in distance. A grand spectacle unto themselves, natives regard these mountains as mere "foothills" in respect to monumental peaks that will soon border route a few miles north.

0:04 (1:19) Cross Ship Creek. A mile west, waters widen before flowing into sea, availing several inland docks to oceangoing vessels.

0:08 (1:15) Train skirts fringe of Elmendorf Air Force Base on left, and Fort Richardson Army Installation on right. Elmendorf is Alaska's largest air base.

0:13 (1:10) On left, myriad of military aircraft are poised alongside Elmendorf runways.

0:14 1:09) Proceed through birch-lined gullies, keeping eyes peeled for great Alaskan moose; 125-mile stretch between here and Curry is favorite haunt of this curious beast.

0:20 (1:03) Brief clearing on forward left provides first breathtaking glimpse of Mt. McKinley. Jutting 20,320 feet skyward, peak is tallest in North America and actually highest in world if measured from base to crest.

Along the route, "mileposts" are conspicuously tacked on trees and telephone poles and represent the distance from the line's southern terminus at Seward. Many subsequent entries will be prefaced by milepost designations (MP) as a further aid in identification.

0:29 (0:54) Cross Eagle River, its waters moving swiftly through small canyon.

0:45 (0:38) MP 136. At Birchwood, small airport seen through trees on left is but one of countless such facilities throughout Alaska. Vast distances of forbidding wilderness make airplane most popular and practical means of transportation.

0:48 (0:35) MP 138. On left, begin bordering Knik Arm, an inlet of Pacific Ocean. Tides here can reach 40 feet—third highest in world. In distance, Mt. Foraker (17,400

Alaska Railroad — Anchorage, AK
BILL COGHILL

ft.), Mt. Hunter (14,573 ft.), Mt. Russell (11,670 ft.) and Mt. Dall (8,756 ft.) are a formidable supporting cast surrounding mighty Mt. McKinley.

0:54 (0:29) MP 141. Eklutna Village is home of Russian Orthodox Church established in 1835. Its adjacent cemetery is most unusual, with colorful "spirit houses" built atop gravesites to preserve souls of those buried here.

1:01 (0:22) MP 146. Traverse series of bridges across Knik River. Prior to 1964 earthquake, river was outlet for ice-flows and floodwaters descending from Lake George. Barren trees dot sunken landscape that became tidal flats after quake.

1:08 (0:15) MP 151. At Matanuska, begin travel through scenic agricultural valley, with surrounding peaks an added embellishment. In 1930s, poverty-striken farmers from Minnesota, Wisconsin and Michigan were allowed to homestead here in a federally sponsored socialistic experiment. Although the effort failed, many stayed, and numerous attractive spreads can still be seen scattered throughout the region.

Despite a brief growing season (100-120 days), long hours of daylight compensate for this shortcoming. A record-size, 76-pound cabbage grown in this region evidences potential of these northern farmlands.

1:12 (0:11) Nearby Pioneer Peak of Alaska Range dominates skyline. To immediate right of Pioneer are East Peak, Middle Peak (with two points) and Goat Mountain (looking somewhat truncated).

1:23 (0:00) MP 159. Recreational lakes border town on arrival Wasilla.

WASILLA, AK - This is a service hub of the Matanuska Valley. On the right, perched on "temporary" cribbing, Teeland's Country Store is the oldest business in Matanuska and Anchorage area. As well as retail merchant, Teeland's was once a veritable museum with old photos, antiques and native artifacts on display. Off to right is a McDonalds with its own caboose. Establishment reportedly had longest line of any McDonalds on opening day.

0:00 (1:29) Departing Wasilla, note towering totem pole fronting property of Kashim Inn.

0:21 (1:08) MP 174. Cross Little Susitna River.

0:30 (0:59) MP 181. On left, clusters of cozy cabins encircle shoreline of Nancy Lake, a popular recreational resort.

0:39 (0:50) MP 185. Pass through Willow, once deemed by voters as future site of state capital. Electorate later nixed move by failing to approve necessary funding. Town's centrality was prime consideration for proposed move from Juneau.

0:55 (0:34) Cross Kashwitna River. Four next 45 miles, enjoy spectacular views of Mt. McKinley on left if skies cooperate. (There's a seven-in-ten chance they won't.) Service personnel will generally open vestibule doors to accommodate photographers, while engineer purposefully slows train where vistas are most dynamic. Enthusiasm that pervades crew adds immensely to this delightful adventure.

1:16 (0:13) MP 224. Susitna River joins and follows on left. It will accompany train for next 40 miles.

1:29 (0:00) MP 226. Arrive Talkeetna.

TALKEETNA, AK - A robust frontier atmosphere is well preserved at Talkeetna, a popular staging ground for Mt. McKinley expeditions.

The white building over to the left is Fairview Inn which housed and fed President and Mrs. Warren G. Harding in 1923 when the president was in Alaska to drive the golden spike at Nenana. Harding died about two weeks later in San Francisco, supposedly from food poisoning.

The town has both spirit and a sense of humor. One of its annual celebrations includes a "moose-nugget-throwing" contest.

0:00 (4:25) Depart Talkeetna and cross Talkeetna River.

Over the next immediate stretch, the train begins a gradual ascent of the Continental Divide that culminates 85 miles north at the summit of Broad Pass. Subtle geographic changes can be detected

McKinley Range and Chulitna River
JEFF KARSH

enroute, with the terrain and vegetation reflecting more alpine-like environs. Brilliant pink flowers, growing profusely along right-of-way in July, are fireweed. The large, white flowery plants in moist areas are cow parsnips—sometimes called wild celery.

0:34 (3:51) MP 248. Pass through Curry, halfway between Seward and Fairbanks. Because of this strategic position, a resort hotel was built here in 1923, off to right. Hostelry sported tennis courts and even an undersized golf course. Years took their toll until, finally, a fire in 1957 ended its colorful career.

0:50 (3:35) MP 258. Sole resident of Sherman has proudly pronounced his home "City Hall," on right.

0:58 (3:27) MP 264. Cross Susitna River as it departs to east.

1:01 (3:24) MP 266. Cross Indian River first of several times as train traces its course through colorful canyon. When train makes its third crossing (in a few minutes) watch

for salmon in pool below on left. Just before that, also on left, will be a small cross above river, erected by two mountaineers in remembrance of a friend killed in a climbing accident.

1:19 (3:06) Emergence from canyon affords another fabulous panorama of Mt. McKinley grouping on left. Range is now only 46 miles away—its closest proximity to rail line.

1:42 (2:43) MP 284. A few anxious moments are in store as train crosses Hurricane Gulch from dizzying height of near 300 feet. Chulitna River joins on left and follows route intermittently to its source atop Broad Pass. This 918-foot trestle was most expensive and difficult to build on entire line. View to left is particularly stunning.

1:47 (2:38) MP 287. Footbridge, relic of prospecting times, stretches ladder-like across river on left.

1:51 (2:34) MP 289. Honolulu (without palm trees) is situated halfway between

Anchorage and Fairbanks.

1:56 (2:29) MP 292. Cross east fork of Chulitna River.

2:01 (2:24) MP 295. Approaching summit of Broad Pass, journey through midst of wide alpine valley, with jagged peaks flanking this treeless expanse.

2:05 (1:36) MP 297. Frequently, siding called Colorado is where northbound and southbound express trains meet. Tour guides swap trains here, enabling them to return home (Anchorage or Fairbanks) on same day as departure. (Train may wait here for some time. Log times are adjusted for an approximate 40-minute delay each direction.)

3:00 (1:25) MP 304. On right, imaginative design highlights log house at town of Broad Pass. Adjacent "storage cache," perched atop tower, keeps provisions beyond reach of foraging "guests."

3:09 (1:16) MP 309. Summit Lake borders on right, while imposing peaks of Mt. Deborah (12,399 ft.) and Mt. Hayes (13,832 ft.) hover in background.

3:10 (1:15) MP 310. Marker on right designates summit of Broad Pass. Elevation of 2,363 feet is highest point along Alaska Railroad, yet pass is still lowest crossing of Continental Divide in entire Rocky Mountain chain.

3:25 (1:00) MP 319. Return to hillier terrain as train passes through Cantwell, marked by airstrip on left. On outskirts of town, note overgrown cemetery along hillside on left. Several gravesites are adorned with spirit houses similar to those found in Eklutna.

3:31 (0:54) MP 323. Cross Windy Creek into southeastern region of Denali National Park. Train then climbs atop bluffs overlooking Nenana River Valley on right. River generally parallels route for next 90 miles.

4:18 (0:07) MP 345. Approaching park station, Nenana River Valley is now totally encircled by towering peaks of Alaska Range. Setting is one of most inspiring along entire run.

4:25 (0:00) MP 347. Traverse lofty bridge across Riley Creek as train arrives Denali. Denali is Indian word for "the great one,"

with obvious reference to nearby Mt. McKinley. Note airpark beside tracks on right.

DENALI NATIONAL PARK, AK - Mt. McKinley is the central fixture of this alpine wonderland, presiding majestically over 3,000 square miles of pristine wilderness. Although a worthy draw in its own right, many other attractions add to the magic of this enchanting tourist haven.

Abundant wildlife roam freely throughout the park, with caribou, fox, grizzly bear and Dall mountain sheep only a few of the many species to behold. Over 100 varieties of birds have been identified and represent migrations from six different continents. Free shuttle buses take visitors deep into the park, with early-morning departures generally offering the best viewing. Wildlife tours (also by bus) offer guided sojourns along the park's one road. Rangers offer dog sled demonstrations daily, just a short bus ride from the Riley Creek Information Center.

Accommodations at Denali are rather expensive, and tour packages generally offer savings.

The spacious Denali National Park Hotel, (907) 683-2215 or 800-276-7234, is the "base camp" for many of the park's activities and the only easy walk from the station. Shuttle buses serve most other nearby hostelries. Nearby McKinley Chalets, (907) 683-2215, is another logical choice for staying overnight. Denali Crows Nest Log Cabins (907-683-2723) are somewhat less expensive. Perhaps the most economical are McKinley/Denali Bed and Breakfast cabins, (907) 683-2733. If you want the newest, try the Denali Princess Lodge, (907) 683-2282.

0:00 (1:44) Departing Denali, note cluster of old Pullman cars on left that once provided lodging following fire at McKinley Hotel, and remain as hotel's calling card.

0:10 (1:34) MP 351. Dall sheep are frequently seen between here and milepost 354. On forward right, impressive highway bridge spans Nenana River.

0:17 (1:27) MP 353. Cross northeastern boundary of Denali National Park, passing

Alaska Railroad dining car
JACK SWANSON

under previously cited bridge before entering short tunnel. Emerge amidst beautiful Nenana River canyon, winding precariously atop colorful rock ledges while river rages through gorge below.

0:30 (1:14) MP 357. Approaching Healy, note coal seams exposed in rock strata on right. Branch line of railroad extends up valley to east, servicing extensive coal-mining operations.

0:42 (1:02) MP 362. North of Healy, coal crushing and loading occurs here at "Usibelli Tipple," Alaska's only coal mine camp. Coal itself is mined at nearby Suntrana. Watch for coal seams along right-of-way.

0:44 (1:00) MP 363. Beyond Healy, rugged terrain is gradually displaced by more gentle, rolling landscape with birch and aspen groves and scrub brush reminiscent of earlier stretches. On right, old railroad cars are positioned in midst of Nenana River as flood control measure. Such sightings are common over next several miles.

0:53 (0:51) MP 370. Cross Nenana River which then follows on left.

1:20 (0:24) MP 391. Train borders grounds of Clear Military Installation. On left, massive radar apparatus is part of "early warning" defense monitor.

1:43 (0:01) MP 411. Nenana River flows into Tanana River on left approaching community of Nenana. Here, railroad operates barge system that services rural outposts nearly 800 miles to west and over 500 miles to east. On forward right, Mears Memorial Bridge stretches dramatically across Tanana River. Structure is one of longest single-span bridges in world. Turning east into town, note visitors center on right, housed in quaint log cabin with sod roof.

1:44 (0:00) Arrive Nenana's restored station, which now houses Alaska State Railroad Museum.

NENANA, AK - Originally one of Alaska's historic roadhouses was located here; then when the railroad arrived, the town flourished as a construction base. President Warren G. Harding drove a golden spike here in 1923, which concluded the Alaska Railroad's construction. But Nenana has a greater claim to fame—the annual "Ice Classic" lottery. Annually, entrants try to guess the time of the spring ice breakup in the Tanana River, and those with the right time share over $100,000 in prize money.

0:00 (1:50) Depart Nenana, and immediately pass wooden tower on left which is placed on ice to act as a giant trigger to stop official time clock for aforementioned lottery.

On outskirts of town, train heads south into U-turn prior to traversing Mears Bridge. While crossing river, note Indian fish wheels positioned along banks. Paddles are propelled by river current and capture salmon swimming upstream to spawn; catch is then deposited into containers on shore. Once across river, monument on left commemorates site where golden spike was driven.

1:27 (0:33) MP 460. Forested hills surrounding Fairbanks provide scenic setting for many outstanding homes secluded in their midst.

1:39 (0:11) MP 465. Picturesque farmstead on left operates in conjunction with University of Alaska, supplying school with fresh produce and meat. Other campus facilities stand immediately to east.

1:46 (0:04) Proceed through industrial district as Chena River joins on right.

1:50 (0:00) Arriving Fairbanks, elegant steeple of Immaculate Conception Catholic Church protrudes above treetops on forward right. Formerly ensconced across river, hierarchy subsequently wanted it moved closer to Catholic hospital. Thus, in 1911, church was jacked up and dragged across ice to its present site.

FAIRBANKS, AK - They count the winters here—not the years. This is the northernmost city in the U.S., only 130 miles south of the Arctic Circle. Temperatures can easily drop to 65 below. It's a hearty lot that live here, but even then, there

are limits. It has been policy to close the schools when the thermometer dips to a frigid minus 50.

In spite of its ice-box image, summers can be spectacularly beautiful, with shorts almost as common as in Los Angeles. Annual average precipitation in Fairbanks is a mere 11 inches, but the area's brief growing season somehow produces unusually lush foliage on the hills that surround the town.

A mixture of old and new, rugged and civilized, Fairbanks got its start in 1902 as a gold-mining settlement when Felix Pedro (pronounced Pee-dro) discovered gold sixteen miles north of here. Fairbanks still maintains a frontier atmosphere, most evident when you walk through downtown. It is Alaska's second largest town and is supported by pipeline-related industries, mining, aviation, government and tourism.

Alaska Railroad Passenger Depot, 280 N. Cushman, Fairbanks, AK 99701. Located on the edge of downtown, just across the Chena River. The station has food and beverage machines and adjacent free parking.

For reservations and other information, call (907) 456-4155.

North Pole **Taxi**, 488-7900. Hertz has **rental cars** in the downtown area; 452-4444 or 800-654-3131.

Fairbanks Convention and Visitors Bureau, 550 First Ave., 99701; (907) 456-5774 or 800-327-5774.

During the middle of the summer, Fairbanks' accommodations are under siege and rather expensive. Reservations should be made several months in advance, particularly if you plan to be here during "Golden Days" in the latter part of July. Since many of Fairbanks' attractions are west of downtown, many visitors prefer to stay out along Airport Way, a newer part of town, albeit strip-like.

-**Super 8**, 1909 Airport Way, 99701; (907) 451-8888 or 800-800-8000. Nicely maintained, a short drive from downtown. They will pick up and deliver train passengers. $85.

-Captain Bartlett Inn, 1411 Airport Way, 99701; (907) 452-1888 or 800-544-7528. A long-time popular motel, a short drive from downtown. They offer train station pick up and drop off. $120.

-Fairbanks Downtown Bed & Breakfast, 1461 Gillam Way, 99701; (907) 452-7700. A nicely run B&B in an older home on the fringe of downtown. Quiet neighborhood. $85.

Downtown Fairbanks is interesting to poke around. Unusual shops without a lot of glitz are in the heart of downtown. Be sure to pick up a walking tour brochure at the visitors center.

-University of Alaska Museum, on University of Alaska-Fairbanks campus, has 10,000 feet of display space divided into six sections. Five are devoted to geographic features of the state while the sixth is devoted to traveling shows. A good place to begin a tour of Fairbanks and the surrounding area.

-Alaskaland is a 44-acre city "theme park" which is the site of many attractions providing visitors with a good look at Fairbanks' past and present. Located between downtown and the airport along Airport Way at Peger Rd.

ANCHORAGE-SEWARD ROUTE LOG

ANCHORAGE, AK - See page 259.

0:00 (3:57) Depart Anchorage, briefly following Knik Arm on right.

0:05 (3:52) If residents of suburbs near tracks are not yet awake, they soon will be, as engineer sounds air horn at several crossings. Jogging trail beside tracks will be quite busy during evening on return.

0:19 (3:34) Alaska's largest shopping mall, Diamond Center, is on left. Suburban mall had typical negative impact on downtown area when it opened a few years ago.

0:21 (3:32) Huge car-squashing operation on right is rather fascinating eyesore.

0:26 (3:26) Airstrip creates common backyard for long row of fine homes and parked aircraft bordering track on right. Some

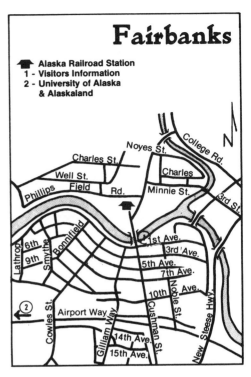

Fairbanks

- Alaska Railroad Station
- 1 - Visitors Information
- 2 - University of Alaska & Alaskaland

homes have been designed to also act as hangars.

0:29 (3:23) Marsh with viewing boardwalks is Potter State Game Refuge where numerous waterfowl find sanctuary. Water on right is Turnagain Arm—supposedly receiving its name when Captain James Cook explored region, having to continually adjust his vessel's course.

0:38 (3:14) Scenery becomes more dramatic as Hawaii-like mountains with thick vegetation rise steeply from water's edge across bay. Cascading waterfalls enhance this Alaskan setting. Watch for Dall sheep above tracks.

1:16 (2:35) At Girdwood, one of five chairlifts of Alyeska Ski Resort is visible on ridge to left. Alyeska is state's largest ski area.

1:32 (2:19) Very attractive waterfall displays its plumage to left of tracks.

1:36 (2:15) Twentymile Glacier rests at top of valley to left.

1:39 (2:06) Train pauses for a few moments at Portage. Road to left leads to Portage

Glacier viewing. Tracks curling off to left are Whittier Cutoff—Alaska Railroad's connection to Whittier-Valdez ferry service. Motor vehicles can board flatcars to be transported to Whittier and ferry connection. (Whittier has no road link to rest of state.) Note vehicle loading lanes on immediate right. This area was hard hit by 1964 earthquake, sinking nearly 12 feet. High tides covered tracks, and trains could only pass while tides were out. Soon, rails and highway separate and won't meet again until Moose Pass.

1:58 (1:55) Spencer Glacier looms, almost menacingly, on left. Engineer usually stops train here to accommodate photographers.

2:05 (1:50) Enter a tunnel and 30 seconds later emerge clinging to Placer River Gorge, where river, full of glacial silt, has carved deeply into earth. Segments of movie *Runaway Train* were filmed along this stretch of track.

2:11 (1:45) Superb waterfall gushes down mountainside across valley to right.

2:16 (1:40) Dirty-faced Bartlett Glacier dominates scene on left. Famous "Loop," a trestle that crossed over itself, once allowed tracks to negotiate rugged terrain. Loop has been replaced by some exceptional hairpin curves—and more powerful locomotion.

2:25 (1:32) Up to left is one more snowy monolith—spectacular Trail Glacier. Over one-half of world's glaciers are in Alaska.

2:52 (1:02) Waters of Upper Trail Lake spread along tracks on right.

2:56 (0:58) Village of Moose Pass is on right, where Seward Highway connects with road to fishing port of Homer. Town was originally construction camp for Alaska Railroad. Middle Trail Lake can be spotted through trees to left.

3:01 (0:53) Lower Trail Lake now accompanies tracks on right.

3:08 (0:51) On right, 24-mile-long Kenai Lake is fed by Snow River to east and is drained by Kenai River at west end.

3:42 (0:12) Nearing Seward, cross Salmon Creek, where fishing for sea-run Dolly Varden is popular.

3:48 (0:06) Seward's airport now appears on left where assorted helicopter and fixed-wing

craft can be seen. Resurrection Bay is just beyond. Bay was named by explorer Alexander Baranoff when, in 1791 on Resurrection Sunday, he found shelter from a ferocious storm.

3:49 (0:05) Railroad's Seward yards swing off to left. On return run, train will back into these yards before heading north toward Anchorage.

3:50 (0:04) Huge piles of coal have been brought here from Interior Alaska coal mines, and will soon be loaded by elaborate equipment onto freighters, mostly bound for Korea.

3:51 (0:03) Cruise ships and freighters can often be spotted in harbor on left.

3:54 (0:00) Arrive Seward adjacent to town's colorful Small Boat Harbor at town's northern edge.

SEWARD, AK - Situated on beautiful Resurrection Bay and ringed by snow-capped mountains, Seward is one of Alaska's more appealing locales. It was further blessed when the 1989 oil spill avoided its shores. Although it rains a lot in Seward, its temperate climate makes it a popular visitor destination.

Named for Lincoln's Secretary of State, William H. Seward, who negotiated Alaska's acquisition from Russia in 1867, the town was established in 1903 by railroad surveyors as an ocean terminal. Tourism and fishing industries are now as important as its shipping activity.

March 27, 1964, Alaska's Good Friday earthquake hit Seward with a vengeance. All of the docks that ring the city were destroyed, and nearly all of the Alaska Railroad yards were lost when a huge wedge of waterfront disappeared into the bay. Tank farms at each end of town burst into flames and created an image of total devastation. Little evidence remains of this enormous disaster.

Daily **bus** service to Anchorage. **Ferry** service to Valdez and Kodiak. Hertz **rental cars**, 224-6097, at the airport.

The **Visitor Information Center** is located in the center of town at 3rd and Jefferson Streets, in a vintage rail car.

Alaska Railroad — Seward, AK
DEBBIE WORDEN

Write Box 749, Seward, AK 99664. Call (907) 224-3094.

Best Western Hotel Seward, Box 670, 99664; (907) 224-2378. Overlooks Resurrection Bay, Seward's most luxurious hotel. $178.

-**Marina Motel**, near Small Boat Harbor, Box 1134, 99664; phone (907) 224-5518. $105.

-**Seward Waterfront Lodging**, P.O. Box 618, 550 Railway Ave., 99664; (907) 224-5563. Small (four rooms) downtown hotel. With shared bath, $70; with private bath, $85.

The entire town of Seward is within walking distance of the train. Head south and you'll see it all. The **Kenai Fiords Visitor Center** in the Small Boat Harbor has several short films about the Seward area and is worth a stop. Seward has a very fine **museum** located downtown at 3rd and Jefferson, across from the Visitor Center, with earthquake displays, railroad memorabilia and other well-presented historic displays. The **University of Alaska's Marine Education Center**, at the south end of Third Street, has some modest but interesting exhibits on local sea life.

Canadian Rail Service

W hether one is in search of breathtaking mountain scenery, spectacular and rugged coastlines, North America's only walled city, or simply a remote Indian village—it can be found using Canada's rail system. The *Canadian*, the country's western transcontinental train, traces a twisting route of trestles and tunnels through the majestic Rockies, including Jasper National Park, while the *Skeena* traverses the beautiful wilderness of central British Columbia. The British Columbia Railway snakes along fiord-like Howe Sound, then takes on the direct challenge of the Coastal Range. A northland adventure is offered by the Hudson Bay which makes an excursion to that immense body of water, where Churchill hunkers down on its desolate and polar-bear-populated shoreline. And in the East, the *Ocean*, after departing Montréal, makes a swing through the Maritime Provinces of New Brunswick and Nova Scotia, before making a triumphant entrance into Halifax along one of the world's most attractive inner harbors—Bedford Basin.

VIA has accomplished a rather spectacular remodeling effort, completely refurbishing their stainless steel transcontinental trains to an elegance not found on any other publicly operated North American trains. Also, modern LRC equipment (Light, Rapid, Comfortable) serves the heavily populated areas in and around Toronto and Montréal, allowing higher speeds with unique automatic tilting capability on curves. Domes are included on transcontinental trains affording great roof-top views of the passing scenes.

As in the U.S., Canada has relegated the operation of most of its passenger train service to a government-owned corporation—VIA Rail Canada. Unfortunately, in 1990 the Canadian government severely curtailed VIA's operations. The legendary *Canadian* no longer runs on CP rail tracks, leaving transcontinental passengers with only one choice of routes, through Edmonton rather than Calgary. Long-distance trains have been relegated to only triweekly service. On the brighter side, most of the former system's routes still see service, albeit less frequently.

In the East, logical access between VIA and Amtrak occurs with direct trains from New York to either Montréal or Toronto. A train connects Chicago and Toronto, crossing the border at Sarnia. VIA can also be found at the border town of Windsor, Ontario across from the Amtrak-served city of Detroit. In the West, direct train service is available between Vancouver, British Columbia, and Seattle.

Reservations - Reservations are required for VIA 1 service and sleeping car accommodations. It's a good idea to make reservations as early as possible, although VIA will not confirm reservations earlier than six months prior to travel. Coach seats are guaranteed when tickets are purchased. For coach, be sure to specify smoking or non-smoking. Reservations can be made through a travel agent or by calling any of the toll-free numbers in the Appendix.

Tickets - Normally, tickets are purchased through a travel agent or directly from a VIA sales office. VIA will accept American Express, Diner's Club, MasterCard and Visa credit cards. Personal checks, if drawn on a U.S. bank or Canadian banking institution, may be used with two acceptable forms of identification. It is possible to buy tickets on board, however, and only with cash and only to destinations served by that train. Tickets can also be ordered by phone using a credit card (see Appendix).

VIA 1 Service - In the Québec City/Windsor corridor, it is possible to ride in first-class seating called VIA 1. Hot meals are included (served at your seat in LRC trains), as well as complimentary beverages. An on-board breakfast might include fruit, juice, muffin or sweet roll, shortbread, cereal, omelette or crepe and coffee, with newspaper and hot towel, while lunch could include an entree selection of steak, Cornish hen or salmon, with shrimp and rice salad along with fruit and cheese. There are special pre-boarding privileges, and in Montréal, Toronto and Ottawa there are handsomely appointed special waiting areas called Panorama Lounge, with complimentary coffee, juice, soft drinks and newspapers. If you want to be pampered, this service is worth the extra fare.

Fares - Fares are generally comparable to those in the U.S. However, several special discounts are available, and it is important to give each consideration in trying to arrive at the lowest fare. These specials can make Canadian rail travel very economical—particularly during off-peak times. For example, in the past VIA has discounted their transcontinental Canadian 25% off between early October and early June, and 40% off early November through mid-December and early January through late April. A travel agent or VIA sales office will be able to help in making these determinations. Seniors, age 60 and older, and youths, 12 to 24, and students over 24 can save 10% off basic transportation, which can be combined with discounted dates for a savings up to 50%. Children ages two through eleven travel at half fare. Those under age two travel free (one child per adult) if not occupying a seat. Children eight through eleven may travel unaccompanied under certain conditions.

And perhaps the greatest bargain, if one plans to travel extensively, is the CANRAIL-PASS. Here, a travel card is purchased allowing unlimited travel for one fixed price. The price varies, depending on the territory in which travel is permitted, the length of time the pass can be used, and the time of year that travel will take place. A ticket agent (travel agent) can calculate your best price.

Baggage - Up to 100 pounds of baggage may be checked per adult fare. Unusually bulky items, such as canoes, might not travel on the train on which you're riding, however. Bicycles may be checked, but as required on Amtrak, must be boxed (VIA has them) and the handlebars must be turned and the pedals removed. Bring your own tools. Pets, except seeing-eye dogs, are not allowed in passenger cars and must travel in baggage cars. Cages can be purchased at most stations.

Smoking - Cigarette smoking is permitted only in specially designated cars or in designated areas of cars. Smoking is not permitted on Corridor (Québec City-Windsor) trains.

Overnight Travel - VIA will furnish pillows or blankets to coach passengers on the *Ocean* and the *Chaluer*. All bedding, of course, is furnished in sleepers.

Flag Stops - Myriad flag stops exist on Canadian routes—so numerous, no effort has been made to include all of them in *Rail Ventures* logs.

Customs - For citizens of the U.S., entry into Canada requires either a passport or at least two other forms of identification, including a certified birth certificate, driver's license, voter registration or baptismal certificate.If you have a passport, it would be advisable to have it with you. Naturalized U.S. citizens should carry their naturalization documents. Persons under 18, not accompanied by an adult, should have a letter from a parent or guardian giving them permission to travel in Canada.

Persons not citizens or legal residents of the U.S. generally will need a passport or some other acceptable travel document. These persons who wish to return to the U.S. should check with a U.S. Immigration Office to make sure they have the necessary papers.

Timetables - To order a VIA timetable, call one of the VIA phone numbers listed in the Appendix.

Important - Train times shown in this section are given only in general terms (such as "Early Morning"), and are for use in planning before making reservations. **Since times are not specific and schedules are always subject to change, actual times should be ascertained from the carrier or a travel agent before setting out on your trip.** Fares and food prices are also subject to change. **Also, routes, fares and stops can be altered without notice.**

Schefferville

Labrador City

Sept Îles

Québec North Shore & Labrador Railway

his is a train reserved for the adventurous. Its amenities are spartan; its destination (Labrador City) is perhaps the coldest city in North America, and just getting to the Québec North Shore & Labrador Ry. (QNS&L) is a bit of a hassle. But if this doesn't sound discouraging, there is a good chance you will find the trip a rewarding sojourn.

The scenery, particularly the first 100 miles out of Sept Îles, a Québec city on the north shore of the St. Lawrence River and the train's southern terminus, is a composite of turbulent rivers, imposing mountains, deep gorges and cascading waterfalls. Farther north into Labrador, the country is virtually uninhabited rolling, forested hills. Only occasional railroad settlements and a handful of Indian camps give evidence of civilization—these and the incredibly long iron ore trains rolling south to the port of Sept Îles.

It was to accommodate these immense serpents that the railroad was built in the early 1950s. The enormous iron ore mines that were developed at Labrador City and Schefferville would not have happened without a means of transporting their ore to world markets.

The railroad was built by flying in men and material to a series of airstrips along its path, a project considered to be the largest civilian airlift in history. Topography, logistics problems, severe cold, black flies and mosquitoes made this one of Canada's most difficult construction projects.

The mines at Schefferville, the northern end of the line, have now been depleted and closed, and the town is not really worth a visit. But the mines are still alive and well at Labrador City, which is at the end of a 37-mile leg of track that veers westward from the line to Schefferville at Ross Bay Jct., milepost 224. Tours of the Iron Ore of Canada Labrador City mine are interesting and can easily be arranged upon arrival during the summer months.

Unfortunately, you can't reach the QNS&L by train. You can fly, drive or be bused to Sept Îles; or you can fly or drive on a new wilderness road to Labrador City. But undoubtedly the most unusual and interesting way to reach Sept Îles is by a freight-and-passenger ship that sails weekly from Rimouski, Québec, a town with VIA Rail service on the south shore of the St. Lawrence River. (See below.)

SCHEDULE - SEPT ÎLES/LABRADOR CITY

Year-round: Northbound to Labrador City departs Sept Îsle Tuesday early evening and Thursday early morning. Southbound to Sept Îles departs Labrador City the next day, Wednesday midday and Friday midmorning. Trip takes about ten hours.

Summer time: Same as above with an additional train departing Sept Îles Monday early morning, departing Labrador City Tuesday midmorning.

Be sure to check scheduling with the railroad in Sept Îles before finalizing your plans for any trip that includes travel on this train.

FREQUENCY - See above.
SEATING - Rail diesel cars. (Dome car available for groups in summer.)
DINING - Sandwiches, snacks and beverages are available.
LENGTH OF TRIP - 261 miles in 9 to 10 hours.

ROUTE LOG

 SEPT ÎLES, QC - A surprisingly modern city, it developed from just a small fishing village into a major seaport with the construction of the Québec North Shore & Labrador Railway in the 1950s. A large natural harbor, attractively accented with seven islands (hence the town's name), Sept Îles is a logical shipping point. The processing and exporting of iron ore is now the community's economic mainstay. And be sure to bring your French/English dictionary.

QNS&L Station, 100 rue Retty, near the edge of the city; (418) 968-7803 (general information). Tickets are purchased, not at the station but at a travel agency in Sept Îles: Write, visit or call Cacances Inter, 451 Ave. Arnaud, Sept Îles, QC G4R 3B3; (418) 962-9411. Station is a modest facility, with a rather cramped waiting room, filled mostly with Montagnais and other Indians that live in the region, most of whom will be traveling between Sept Îles and Schefferville. Two antique steam locomotives decorate the grounds.

Taxi Carillon, 962-9444. For **boat reservations** on the Nordik Express from Rimouski, Québec, sailing from there Tuesday afternoons, arriving in Sept Îles Wednesday mornings, contact Relais Nordik, 205 Ave. Léonidas, Rimouski, QC G5L 2T5; (418) 723-8787.

Tourisme Sept Îles, 1401 Boul. Laure, G4R 4K1; (418) 962-1238, provides city **visitor information**.

Hôtel des Gouverneurs, 666 Boul. Laure, G4R 1X9; (418) 962-7071 or 800-463-2820. Sept Îles' nicest hostelry, in a newer shopping area. Excellent dining room. About three miles from the station. $59.

-**Hotel/Motel Mingan**, 665 Boul. Laure, G4R 1X8; (418) 968-2121 or 800-223-5720. Attractive facility, across the street from Hôtel des Gouverneurs. $55.

Museum of Sept Îles, 500 Boul. Laure, one block from the hotels listed above, has both permanent and traveling exhibits (with all explanations in French).

(Note: Best viewing will be on left. Since train schedule varies during any particular trip, milepost references have been included in this log. Certain sidings where stops are generally made are arbitrarily shown as ending and beginning points for times given in the route log.)

0:00 (1:42) MP 0. Depart Sept Îles and trundle past collection of QNS&L passenger cars on right.

0:05 (1:37) Mountains of stockpiled iron ore stand beside tracks at right. Reddish ore is either hematite ore or concentrated pellets, while grey mounds are specular hematite.

0:12 (1:30) Sept Îles' beautiful harbor is off to right. Trees begin to line tracks. Those along route will consist mostly of black spruce, poplar, birch and aspen.

0:28 1:14) MP 12. Rumble through crudely illuminated (a string of light bulbs tacked to wall) tunnel, 4/10 of a mile long. Tunnel was difficult to construct, not only due to rock but also mud. Once during construction, tunnel's silty roof gave way, flushing a worker out of tunnel's south portal. Miraculously, he was unharmed.

0:29 (1:13) Out of tunnel and cross high over Moise River, which follows on left. Bridge is most impressive of numerous trestles along route; it's 700 feet long and 155 feet over Moise. Crossing Moise was a political as well as tactical problem, since Moise Salmon Club was here, boasting prestigious American members with names such as Rockefeller and Eisenhower. Scenery now becomes more spectacular.

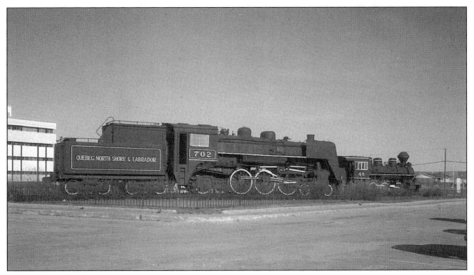

Display locomotives at QNS&L station — Sept Îles, QC
JACK SWANSON

0:49 (0:53) MP 21. Transmission lines carry electricity generated by renowned Churchill Falls hydroelectric plant. Plant is one of largest underground electric generating facilities in the world.

0:50 (0:52) MP 22. Worst accident during railroad's construction occurred here when runaway work train smashed into a caboose, killing five men who were sleeping inside.

0:57 (0:45) MP 27. Moise River branches to left, while tracks keep a northward tack along Wacouna River.

0:59 (0:43) MP 28. Compound of neat cabins, below on left, once served as fishing retreat for Johnson & Johnson corporate executives and their guests.

1:03 (0:39) Spectacular rapids are created by churning Wacouna on left.

1:09 (0:33) MP 35. At Nicnam siding, note waterfalls at very top of rock monoliths on left.

1:25 (0:17) More lovely waterfalls above to left. Then radio communication tower of Iron Ore Company of Canada is on right, one of several that appear along route.

1:33 (0:09) MP 53. Above to left, marvelous set of ribbon falls stream down rocky cliff.

These falls are most evident during heavy springtime runoffs.

1:42 (0:00) Arrive Tika's collection of small white buildings.

 TIKA, QC.

0:00 (0:33) MP 57. Depart Tika.

0:15 (0:18) MP 64. Pierce second illuminated tunnel.

0:20 (0:13) MP 68. Many feel this is best sight of trip! Tumultuous Tonkas Falls, on left, are created by spectacular 200-foot plunge of Wacouna River.

0:33 (0:00) Arrive siding at milepost 73.

 SIDING MP 73.

0:00 (1:20) Depart siding, MP 73.

0:02 (1:18) MP 74. Colorful Indian camp is nestled next to railroad right-of-way.

0:14 (1:06) MP 82. Terrain has become less mountainous.

0:20 (1:00) MP 84. Gravel pit at left furnished highest quality ballast for railroad.

1:08 (1:12) MP 120. Mountains have long since disappeared, having been replaced by soft, rolling, forested hills. Trees are nearly all black spruce now.

1:20 (0:00) Arrive siding at milepost 129. Collection of white buildings on left belongs to railroad, and crew sometimes stops for lunch while southbound ore train passes. These are extremely long trains, sometimes having 260 cars and stretching for nearly two miles. Pelletized ore is hauled in open gondola cars, while concentrate, an extremely fine, sparkling particulate, is transported in special tank cars. Wheels that stick up from top of tank cars aid in automatic unloading at Sept Îles. Loading is also automated, taking about four hours to load a single train.

 SIDING MP 129.

0:00 (0:41) Depart siding, MP 129.
0:31 (0:10) Just before MP 149, cross watershed that is border between Québec and Labrador (actually, mainland portion of province of Newfoundland). South of here, waters flow into St. Lawrence, while north of here, all streams flow toward Labrador's Atlantic Coast. This was called "the height of the land" at 2,066 feet of elevation.

 Having now entered Labrador, adjust your watch to Atlantic time by setting it forward one hour.
0:41 (0:00) MP 155. Arrive Seahorse, named for nearby lake.

 SEAHORSE, NF.

0:00 (0:44) Depart Seahorse.
0:14 (0:30) MP 166. That faded green ground cover is caribou moss. During survey of railroad, one party reported they virtually lived off of this plant, but said stuff "didn't stick to their ribs." Trees have become stunted and muskeg is now prevalent in this northern clime. While great herds of caribou are north of here, moose (many unexplainably and fatefully drawn to the train) are prevalent in this area.
0:36 (0:08) MP 182. Large lake on left is Ashuanipi and will appear off and on for nearly 35 miles. During construction of the railway, five bulldozers were lost when they fell through the ice on this body of water.
0:44 (0:00) MP 186. Arrive Oreway. Large, modern building on right has served as overnight stop for ore train crews. Muskeg between here and Ross Bay Jct. caused some of worst railway construction headaches. A unique solution eventually evolved. Dynamite was placed in mud, then covered with fill. When blasted, muskeg could only go outward and was displaced by the new material.

 OREWAY, NF.

0:00 (0:49) Depart Oreway.
0:38 (0:11) MP 215. Water on left is Ross Bay, an extension of Lake Ashuanipi.
0:49 (0:00) MP 224. Pull into huge culvert-like train shed upon arrival Ross Bay Jct. Red-roofed, two-story structure to left is railroad bunk house.

 ROSS BAY JCT. - This is the main QNS&L junction, where one set of tracks proceeds straight north to Schefferville, while the line to Labrador City curls west (left).
0:00 (0:27) MP 0. Depart Ross Bay Jct.
0:19 (0:08) Road beside tracks is major Labrador highway. Road comes up from Baie-Comeau, Québec, through wilderness to reach Fermont, QC, (across-the-border neighbor to twin cities of Wabush and Labrador City) then on to Ross Bay Jct. Until recently, vehicle traffic wishing to continue on to Goose Bay on Atlantic Coast had to be placed aboard trains at Ross Bay Jct., transported several miles north to Esker, then unloaded where road continued on to Goose Bay. Road was completed in early 1990s to make rail link unnecessary and is now called Trans Labrador Highway.
0:27 (0:00) Arrive Menistouc.

 MENISTOUC, NF.

0:00 (0:46) Depart Menistouc.
0:20 (0:26) MP 23. Neat little frame house, on left, has fenced walkway across marshes to allow occupants to reach navigable water.
0:21 (0:25) Cross Trans Labrador Highway.
0:37 (0:09) Immense plants of Iron Ore Company of Canada, known locally as IOC, are off to left. Beyond plant, Smokey Mountain Ski Area is on side of mountain that also contains vast iron ore reserves.

0:39 (0:07) Area's second huge iron ore operation is Wabush Mine. Its plant can now be seen off to left. Town of Wabush is only three miles from Labrador City.

0:46 (0:00) MP 37. Arrive Labrador City.

 LABRADOR CITY, NF - Although it was known in the early 1900s that there were commercial deposits of iron ore in this region, because of their inaccessibility, these deposits were left undeveloped until the 1950s when the Iron Ore Company of Canada (IOC) constructed the Québec North Shore & Labrador Railway to what is now Labrador City and Knob Lake (now Schefferville). The IOC mine is considered to be the world's largest open pit iron ore mine. Labrador City and its neighboring communities of Wabush (only three miles distant) and Fermont (just to the west across the Québec border) probably produce more iron ore concentrate than any other region in North America. Some 20,000 people live in the tri-city area.

Winters are long and cold here, frequently reaching 60 degrees (or more) below zero. But winters are mostly sunny and humidity is below that of the Sahara, all of which helps make the weather almost bearable. Summers can be mild, but it rains a lot in this "second" season and black flies are an ever-present curse. Understandably, the people here are the best paid in Canada.

 QNS&L Station is on the edge of Labrador City and only a five-minute taxi ride to neighboring Wabush. Station phone, (709) 944-2745.

 Target **Taxi**, 944-2624. Avis **rental cars**, (709) 282-6233, offer shuttle service to and from their airport office. **Airport** is conveniently situated between Labrador City and Wabush.

 Labrador West Tourism, (709) 282-3337. Office is located downstairs in the Wabush Hotel.

 Wabush Hotel, P.O. Box 700, Wabush, A0R 1B0; (709) 282-3221. Large, comfortable hotel with distinctive architecture. Dining rooms and cafe. In Wabush, about an $8 cab ride from the station. $90.

-Two Seasons Inn, Box 572, Labrador City, A2V 2L3; (709) 944-2661. On Avalon Drive in Labrador City. This is the area's newest hotel. Short cab ride from the station. $84.

 Both IOC and Wabush offer **mine tours.** You may arrange for a tour by calling Labrador West Tourism (see above).

Ocean

The *Ocean* is VIA's connection to the Atlantic provinces. This is an overnight trip between Halifax and Montréal, skirting above the topside of Maine along the St. Lawrence River during the western leg of the journey, with the segment between Lévis, QC, and Campbellton, NB, normally traveled in darkness.

The *Ocean* has been given a beautiful facelift. Refurbished stainless steel cars with electric heat provide a most stylish ride.

WESTBOUND SCHEDULE (Condensed)
Halifax, NB - Early Afternoon Departure
Moncton, NB - Early Evening
Campbellton, NB - Late Evening
Lévis, QC - Early Morning (Ferry Service to Québec City) (2nd Day)
Montréal, QC - Early Morning Arrival (2nd Day)

EASTBOUND SCHEDULE (Condensed)
Montréal, QC - Early Evening Departure
Lévis, QC - Late Evening (Ferry Service to Québec City)
Campbellton, NB - Early Morning (2nd Day)
Moncton, NB - Late Morning (2nd Day)
Halifax, NB - Midafternoon Arrival (2nd Day)

FREQUENCY - Departing both Halifax and Montréal daily except Tuesday.
SEATING - Standard coaches, Skyline dome car and Park observation dome (for sleeping car passengers).

DINING - Complete meal and beverage service as well as lighter fare. (Meals are included with price of bedroom.)
SLEEPING - Berths, single, double and triple bedrooms. Overnight coach passengers are provided with blankets and pillows. Sleeping cars have a shower in each car.
BAGGAGE - Checked baggage at larger towns.
RESERVATIONS - All-reserved train.
LENGTH OF TRIP - 840 miles in 19 hours.

ROUTE LOG

HALIFAX, NS - Halifax was founded by Edward Cornwallis in 1749 as an army and naval base for the English after the French established an imposing fortress at nearby Louisbourg. The deep harbor, protected by both islands and bluff, made it an ideal naval base, particularly after the Citadel Hill Fortress was constructed as protection. Halifax has remained a military center to this date.

Because of its excellent harbor, Halifax has always been oriented toward ocean industries with ship-repair facilities, containerization docks and various other shipyards still dominating its waterfront. It's a remarkably clean city and attracts thousands of visitors every year, many using this provincial capital as a base for touring the rest of the province. The shores, particularly to the south, are noted for their ruggedness.

Halifax, Nova Scotia
HALIFAX CONVENTION & VISITORS BUREAU

 **VIA Station**, 1161 Hollis St., is a nicely remodeled station on the edge of downtown. There is a snack bar, a newsstand, free luggage carts and redcaps. Thirty-minute free parking is in front of the station. Pay-parking is at the rear of the station. Call 429-8421 for reservations and other information.

Yellow **Cab**, 422-1551. **Local buses** at the station; Metro Transit, 421-6600. Tilden **rental cars** are close to the station, (902) 422-4439.

Tourism Halifax and the Province of Nova Scotia have a combined office at the corner of Sackville and Barrington. Call (902) 424-4247/8.

Waverly Inn, 1266 Barrington, B3J 1Y5; (902) 423-9346. An 1876 inn with spacious and comfortable rooms, many furnished with fine antiques. Whirlpools available. Complimentary breakfast. Two blocks from the station. $77.

-**Halliburton House Inn**, 5184 Morris Street, B3J 1B3; (902) 420-0658. Elegant smaller hotel occupying a Registered Heritage Property. Excellent dining room. Complimentary breakfast. Only two blocks from the station. $110.

(Note: The Halifax Hilton which adjoins the station was closed for remodeling at press time and it is not known when it will reopen.)

Many attractions are within walking distance. A map of Halifax describing a **walking tour** may be obtained from the Visitors Bureau which is about a 15-minute walk north of the VIA station. Points of interest include: the old waterfront where the "**Bluenose II**," a replica of the famous racing schooner and used for pleasure cruises, is often berthed (the original Bluenose, built in 1921, kept the International Fisherman's Trophy in Canada for 20 years); **Historic Properties**, which is made of nicely restored buildings along the waterfront; and the **Maritime Museum of**

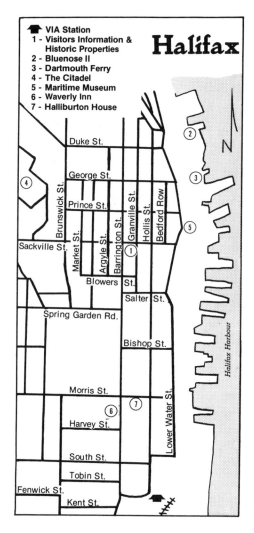

Halifax

- ⬛ VIA Station
- 1 - Visitors Information & Historic Properties
- 2 - Bluenose II
- 3 - Dartmouth Ferry
- 4 - The Citadel
- 5 - Maritime Museum
- 6 - Waverly Inn
- 7 - Halliburton House

Duke St.
George St.
Prince St.
Brunswick St.
Granville St.
Hollis St.
Bedford Row
Market St.
Argyle St.
Barrington St.
Sackville St.
Blowers St.
Salter St.
Spring Garden Rd.
Bishop St.
Morris St.
Harvey St.
South St.
Tobin St.
Fenwick St.
Kent St.
Lower Water St.
Halifax Harbour

---

on left, while on right, equally as impressive storage elevators use overhead conveyors to transport grain to loading docks.

0:04 (1:15) Four orange and white gantries handle loading and unloading of oceangoing freighters off to left.

0:12 (1:07) Tracks now make an encompassing arc along westerly shore of beautiful Bedford Basin, on right. Everything from giant oceangoing freighters to smallest pleasure craft speckle harbor, creating a scene that captures very essence of Canada's Maritime Provinces. Two suspension bridges in distance span harbor entrance and connect twin cities of Dartmouth (on left) and Halifax. It was in that general area that munitions ship Mont Blanc exploded in 1917, the largest man-made explosion prior to the atom bomb, devastating large portions of Halifax and Dartmouth.

0:16 (1:03) Small gazebo-like house on right was built years ago by a British nobleman as solitary retreat.

0:17 (1:02) Wooden hull of half-submerged tug, on right, marks long-ago maritime misadventure.

0:39 (0:38) Elongated waters of Shubenacadie Grand Lake form inviting scene on left as train cuts through rolling Nova Scotian countryside. Many other small lakes can be observed through here.

0:55 (0:24) Cross Shubenacadie River and slip through nice-appearing town with same unusual name (an Indian Word meaning "where the potato grows").

1:15 (0:04) Newer brick building on right is home to Nova Scotia Teachers College.

1:19 (0:00) Arrive Truro.

TRURO, NS - Located at the tip of Cobequid Bay, actually an extension of the high-tidal-action Bay of Fundy, Truro is one of the largest of the early-Acadian settlements. Here, railroading and manufacturing play important economic roles, while higher education is also prominent. It is the home for Nova Scotia Agricultural College and Nova Scotia Teachers College just mentioned.

0:00 (1:20) Depart Truro and start a twisting trek across upper thumb of Nova Scotia.

---

the **Atlantic**, which includes exhibits of such nautical subjects as a "skinned" torpedo and flotsam from the Titanic.

The Citadel, located on a hill overlooking the harbor, is a large star-shaped fortress that replaced the earlier wooden one built by Cornwallis. It also has Maritime and Historic Museums.

Musquodoboit Railway Museum, the largest in eastern Canada, is located at Musquodoboit Harbor north of Halifax.

0:00 (1:19) Depart Halifax.

0:02 (1:17) Enormous docking facilities are

0:16 (0:52) Cross Canada Highway 104 and then travel 87 feet above small, but lovely, Folly River.

0:38 (0:41) Train grinds over summit where Folly Lake lies nestled just to right of tracks, a glacier-formed pond several thousand years old.

0:45 (0:35) Wentworth Valley Ski Area, below on right, provides wintertime sport for skiers from across central Nova Scotia.

1:05 (0:15) Cross River Phillip coursing through pine-laden forests.

1:20 (0:00) Arrive Springhill Jct. where delightfully tiny one-roomer station serves local VIA passengers.

 SPRINGHILL JUNCTION, NS - This very small town was named for springs found in the nearby hills. Its once-active coal mines are no longer being operated and perhaps just as well. Numerous tragic explosions plagued the mines, almost from their beginning in the late 19th century.

0:00 (0:22) Depart Springhill Jct.

0:17 (0:05) On immediate right, Sifto Salt plant rests above mine that is source of its product.

0:22 (0:00) Arrive Amherst.

 AMHERST, NS - Geography buffs will be happy to learn that this is the geographical center of the Maritime Provinces. It is also a manufacturing center, producing such varied products as clothing, structural steel, dairy goods and tanning oils.

0:00 (0:17) Depart Amherst.

0:02 (0:15) Orange-colored rail car on right now serves as Amherst visitor center.

0:07 (0:10) Enter New Brunswick and leave Nova Scotia while crossing Missaguash River.

0:08 (0:09) Historic Fort Beausejour, perched atop knoll on right, stands silent guard over Tantramar Marshes which stretch across 84 square miles on left. These marshes were once tidal flats until French Acadians, more than 200 years ago, resourcefully constructed elaborate dike systems, turning what was once muddy bogs into fertile farmlands. Dikes are still visible today.

0:13 (0:04) Forest of antennae of Radio Canada International (Canada's shortwave radio service) sprout from ground on right.

0:17 (0:00) Arrive Sackville.

 SACKVILLE, NB - This city is the location of Mount Allison University, which, in 1875, awarded the first degree given to a woman in the British Empire. Sackville was a seaport until a landslide changed the course of the Tantramar River in 1920.

0:00 (0:51) Depart Sackville.

0:16 (0:35) Perched atop hill on right is Dorchester Penitentiary, maximum security prison holding felons from all of eastern Canada.

0:51 (0:00) Arriving Moncton, needle-like communications tower, which juts above town, is one of tallest such structures in Canada.

 MONCTON, NB - The present location of the city was first occupied for a short while in the mid-1700s by French Acadians who reclaimed the surrounding marshes by constructing dikes along the river. However, the site was ultimately abandoned when the British forced the Acadians to leave and totally destroyed the settlement. Later, in 1766, several German families from Pennsylvania moved to what is now Moncton, a simplification of the name of Lieutenant General Robert Monckton, who served under Wolfe's command and captured nearby Fort Beausejour in 1755.

Although shipbuilding was once an important industry in Moncton, it gradually declined and the town with it. Finally, new life came with the railroad, and Moncton became a major rail and trade center for eastern Canada. The tides, here in the Bay of Fundy, are some of the highest in the world.

0:00 (1:00) Depart Moncton. From Moncton to Rogersville, tracks will follow eastern margin of interior New Brunswick wilderness, occasionally touching small villages, many of which sprung up when the railroad was first completed.

0:26 (0:34) Cross Richibucto River.

0:54 (0:06) Cross Kouchibouguacis River.

0:58 (0:02) Boat permanently berthed in midst of trees on right creates rather unusual scene.

1:00 (0:00) Arrive Rogersville.

 ROGERSVILLE, NB - This small trading center is named in honor of James Rogers, former Bishop of Chaltham.

0:00 (0:29) Depart Rogersville.

0:07 (0:19) On left, steps lead up to crude hunting platform in tree. Several such contraptions can be spotted along this portion of route.

0:20 (0:06) First, cross glassy smooth, broad waters of Southwest Miramichi River then, moments later, cross equally as impressive Miramichi River, both burgeoning with waters originating from much of central New Brunswick and which finally empty into Miramichi Bay in Gulf of St. Lawrence.

0:23 (0:02) Large pulp mill on right is important regional employer. Another such mill will appear on right in four more minutes.

0:29 (0:00) Arrive Newcastle.

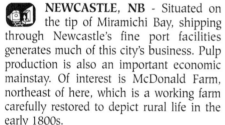 **NEWCASTLE, NB** - Situated on the tip of Miramichi Bay, shipping through Newcastle's fine port facilities generates much of this city's business. Pulp production is also an important economic mainstay. Of interest is McDonald Farm, northeast of here, which is a working farm carefully restored to depict rural life in the early 1800s.

0:00 (0:50) Depart Newcastle and continue through forested lands of eastern New Brunswick.

0:03 (0:47) For eastbound passengers, having just traveled through miles of forest land, view forward left (back to right westbound) of Newcastle will provide dramatic change of scene.

0:44 (0:06) Cross large Nepisiguit River just before it flows into Nepisiguit Bay.

0:50 (0:00) Arrive Bathurst.

 BATHURST, NB - This is the urban focal point for mining and other industry in northeastern New Brunswick. Tourists have also found this area with its many scenic waterfalls and beaches. A pretty drive leads to nearby

Caraquet where Acadian Historical Village is located—a re-created settlement depicting Acadian lifestyle of the early 1800s.

0:00 (1:20) Depart Bathurst and trace course along Chaleur Bay, on right, until Campbellton. Large brick facility on hill to left is New Brunswick Community College.

0:04 (1:16) Cross Tetagouche River.

0:34 (0:46) Pass through small coastal community of Jacquet River (flag stop) where good crab and lobster fishing is afforded along shoreline, and then cross Jacquet River.

0:49 (0:31) Apparent narrowness of bay is caused by Heron Island about five miles off shore to right. Across Chaleur Bay is Québec's famed Gaspé Peninsula with Mount Saint Joseph rising above town of Carleton.

1:07 (0:13) This is Dalhousie Jct., with newsprint mills and popular public beaches nearby.

1:20 (0:00) Arrival at Campbellton is marked by lovely view of bay. Green steel bridge crosses tip of Chaleur Bay, connecting Campbellton and Point-à-la-Croix, Québec.

 CAMPBELLTON, NB - Superb fishing is found throughout this region of New Brunswick, and nearby Sugarloaf Provincial Park provides not only fishing but camping and winter sports as well. In 1760, the bay serving this port city provided the setting for the last naval engagement of The Seven Years War.

 Caspian Motel, 26 Duke Street, E3N 3G9; (506) 753-7606. Large downtown motel, just one block from the VIA station. $59.

0:00 (0:24) When departing Campbellton, impressive bridge can be seen on right, spanning tip of Chaleur Bay, fed at this point by salmon-filled Restigouche River.

0:13 (0:11) Through only tunnel on route.

0:23 (0:01) Cross Restigouche River and, at midpoint, enter Québec and leave New Brunswick.

 Gain one hour as train passes from Atlantic to Eastern Time. Set your watch back (forward if eastbound one hour.

0:24 (0:00) Arrive Matapédia.

MATAPÉDIA, NB - The name Matapédia stems from a similar Indian word meaning "river breaks into branches." Technically speaking, rather than separating, Matapédia and Restigouche Rivers join here, just before rushing into the bay. This is also where the rail line to Gaspé departs our route. The *Chaleur*, a direct link between the lovely Gaspé Peninsula and Montréal, joins the westbound *Ocean* (or splits off of the eastbound) at this point.

0:00 (0:46) Depart Matapédia.

0:28 (0:18) One of region's longer covered bridges (they are sometimes referred to as settlers' bridges) is off to right at Routherville.

0:43 (0:03) Another covered bridge can be seen on left at Heppel.

0:46 (0:00) Arriving Causapscal, sawdust-burning inverted cone (they're called "hells") identifies sawmill on right.

 CAUSAPSCAL, QC - The Matapédia River runs directly through this attractive small community, originally settled by Acadians. Farming, logging and, of course, fishing are important to Causapscal's economy.

0:00 (0:18) Depart Causapscal.

0:10 (0:08) At right, large body of water beyond town of Lac-au-Saumon is lake by same name.

0:16 (0:02) Cross Indian Brook.

0:18 (0:00) Arriving Amqui, cross Amqui River.

 AMQUI, QC - This small commercial center is situated at the southern tip of 16-mile-long, 5-mile-wide Lake Matapédia.

0:00 (0:18) Depart Amqui.

0:04 (0:14) Note covered bridge off to right, situated between two lakes. Glimpses are afforded on right of Lake Matapédia.

0:10 (0:08) At Val Brillant, "called Queen of the Valley," handsome twin-spired church of "flamboyant Gothic" architecture is on immediate left. Statue of Christ and four old-style street lights grace foreground.

0:18 (0:00) Arrive Sayabec. Church on hill, to right, overlooks Lake Matapédia.

SAYABEC, QC - The only particle board plant in the region is located here at Sayabec (pronounced say-beck), an operation which is fed by an abundant local forest.

0:00 (0:38) Depart Sayabec.

0:26 (0:08) Descending toward Mont Joli, St. Lawrence River, once called "road which walks" by Amerindians, comes into view forward right. At this point, waterway has more characteristics of an ocean than a river.

0:34 (0:04) Soar 63 feet above Mitis River on trestle which is more than 400 feet long.

0:38 (0:00) Arrive Mont Joli.

 MONT JOLI, QC - Once called Sainte Flavie Station, this industrial center's newer name ("attractive mountain") refers to the beautiful views afforded from the nearby mountain top.

0:00 (0:23) Depart Mont Joli.

0:05 (0:18) Pass through town of Saint-Anaclet.

0:20 (0:03) Fine view of Rimouski's large harbor is now afforded on right.

0:23 (0:00) Arrive Rimouski, where downtown is on lower terrace to right.

RIMOUSKI, QC - This is the largest city in the province east of Québec City. Established in 1696, the city has become important because of its fine harbor that remains open year-round. Although a fire destroyed nearly a fourth of the city in 1950, no evidence of the disaster is visible today.

A regional museum with historic and scientific exhibits is housed downtown in what was once the 3rd Catholic Church of Rimouski, built in 1824. Nearby, a seamen's school trains sailors to become St. Lawrence River pilots who must steer oceangoing ships once such vessels reach the narrower waters of the St. Lawrence. There is also a Museum of the Sea, with exhibits of marine life.

There are weekly **freighter/passenger ship** sailings (Nordik Express) from here to Sept Îles (terminus of the Québec North Shore & Labrador Railway) each Tuesday, arrive in Sept Îles early the next morning. Contact Relais Nordik, 205

Empress of Ireland

In May of 1914, just two or three miles off shore from Rimouski, the ocean liner *Empress of Ireland* went to the bottom of the St. Lawrence after being struck by a Norwegian freighter. Of the 1,400 persons on board, 1,100 perished.

It was a clear night, and the *Empress* had just departed Québec City bound for Liverpool, England. But as the two ships approached one another, a fog bank apparently reduced visibility. The freighter's bow penetrated deep into the side of the passenger liner, and for a brief moment the two ships remained locked together in the middle of the river. Then the freighter backed up, exposing the *Empress of Ireland*'s gaping hole to a sea of water, and she sank in only fourteen minutes.

The loss of life nearly equaled that of the *Titanic*'s sinking, when 1,500 people drowned only two years earlier. But the *Empress* was more of a "working man's ship" that carried few, if any, notables, and the vessel itself lacked the publicity given the *Titanic*'s "unsinkable" construction. The catastrophe soon faded into obscurity.

Ave. Léonidas, Rimouski, QC, G5L 2T5, for information and cabin reservations; (418) 723-8787.

Auberge Universel, 130 Ave. Belzile, G5L 3E4; (418) 724-6944 or 800-463-4495. Small, nice. A few blocks from the station. $70.

0:00 (1:07) Depart Rimouski and soon cross Rimouski River on 436-foot-long bridge.

0:18 (0:49) Cross Bic River and enter town of Bic situated in a particularly attractive region. Supposedly, angel in charge of mountain and island allocation emptied remainder of her basket here at Bic. River is 25 miles wide at this point, narrowing as we continue westward.

0:34 (0:33) Extensive peat bogs through here are commercially "mined" for their soil-conditioning peat moss.

0:35 (0:32) Saint-Fabian has unusual eight-sided barn, only one in region.

1:07 (0:00) Arriving Trois Pistoles, huge three-spired Notre Dame Church, built in 1857, is city centerpiece.

TROIS PISTOLES, QC - According to legend, the town's unusual name came about when a sailor's silver cup, valued at three pistoles (a French coin of the day), fell into the river. The town is now a major tourist resort.

Three offshore islands are bird sanctuaries, home to double-crested cormorants (their exclusive diet is fish), eider ducks, blue herons and numerous other marine birds. The largest island, Île-aux-Basques, was supposedly used by Basque fishermen prior to Cartier's local explorations. Their furnaces used to extract whale oil have been restored and can be seen here.

0:00 (0:33) Depart Trois Pistoles.

0:04 (0:29) Cross high over Trois Pistoles River on 541-foot trestle.

0:13 (0:20) Île Verte, that long, narrow island off to right, is only place where salt-meadow lambs are raised. Creatures derive their name since they graze on grass salted by river spray. Island's lighthouse, built in 1809, is oldest on St. Lawrence. This stretch of river is known for its beluga and other species of whales.

0:32 (0:01) Entering Rivière-du-Loup, cross river by same name. Largest of eight successive waterfalls that embellish stream can be seen at right. It drops 125 feet.

RIVIÈRE-DU-LOUP, QC - In 1680, there was a French trading post located here, a spot where large wolf packs once roamed. Today it is not only a vibrant commercial center but a popular summer resort as well. The town derives its name from the loup seals that live along the shore.

Although the St. Lawrence is considerably narrower here than it is farther east, it is still 14 miles across. There is regular ferry service from Rivière-du-Loup to the north shore.

0:00 (0:39) Depart Rivière-du-Loup.

0:15 (0:24) Through Saint-André, where Saint-André's church, built in 1806, is oldest in region.

0:28 (0:11) Here at Kamouraska, eel trapping is an industry made possible by shallow, flat riverbed. Many homes seen along the lower St. Lawrence River are graced with uniquely curved eaves somewhat resembling a ship's hull. Feature has been given the name "Kamouraska roof."

0:32 (0:07) More peat bogs can be seen in immediate area.

0:39 (0:00) Arrive La Pocatière.

LA POCATIÈRE, QC - An important agricultural school is located here, started back in 1859. Bombardier, which is building Superliner rail cars in New England, has a plant in La Pocatière.

0:00 (0:38) Depart La Pocatière.

0:19 (0:19) Cross Trois Saumons River.

0:33 (0:05) Mont Ste. Anne Ski Area can be spotted in distance across St. Lawrence.

0:38 (0:00) Cross River du Sud on 584-foot bridge upon arrival Montmagny.

MONTMAGNY, QC - This community was named after a 17th-century governor of New France.

0:00 (0:47) Departing Montmagny, note unusual ten-sided church on right.

0:42 (0:05) Train slowly descends into Lévis, directly across from Québec City. On right, outstanding views of city, shipyards, river activity and Île d'Orléans (large St. Lawrence centerpiece back to right) are now afforded.

0:47 (0:00) Arrive Lévis, where ferry service to Québec City is available. Québec City is immediately across St. Lawrence River on right. Montréal corridor trains go directly into Québec City, but the *Ocean* gets no closer than Levis.

QUÉBEC CITY, QC - Champlain founded Québec City in 1608 as a fur-trading post, and in 1620 he established a fort on the higher plateau portion of the city. Québec soon developed as a city on two levels with the upper portion, 305 feet above sea level, being a natural defensive fortification and becoming a military and administrative area. A stone wall was constructed surrounding a portion of this upper city with an entrance through three large gates. The lower city was primarily trade-oriented. Today, an unusual tubular elevator, "Funiculaire," connects these two levels.

Québec City's strategic location made it the focal point of two major battles. In 1759 an attack across the Plains of Abraham occurred when the British, led by Wolfe, scaled the cliffs of the city and defeated the French commanded by Montcalm. Then in 1775, American Patriots made an effort to siege Québec City, and a force led by Richard Montgomery and Benedict Arnold mounted an unsuccessful attempt to capture it.

Today, Québec City is the provincial capital of Québec. Its strong French-European flavor (over 90% of the population speaks French) and uniquely quaint appearance (it is the only walled city north of Mexico) have made this a popular tourist destination.

VIA Station, Gare du Palais, 450 rue de la gare du Palais. This grand old station was built by the Canadian Pacific Railway in 1916 and served Québec City as a rail station until its closure in 1976, forcing downtown passengers to use the suburban Sainte-Foy station. The early 1980s saw a remarkable renovation ($28 million) and service once again restored to the heart of the city starting in late 1985. (The suburban VIA station in Sainte-Foy is still operational.)

There are storage lockers, luggage carts, a restaurant, a snack bar, a newsstand and underground pay-parking. There are direct phone lines to taxis and several downtown hotels, including some of those listed below. For reservations, call 692-3940.

Taxi Co-op, 525-5191. Tilden has **rental cars**, 295 St-Paul, within walking distance, (418) 964-1727. There is **ferry** service from Québec City to and from Lèvis across the St. Lawrence River for VIA train service to the Atlantic provinces. This ferry service is operated on a 24-hour basis, departing every half hour from 6 am to midnight—less frequently from midnight to 6 am.

Tourisme Québec, 12 rue Sainte-Anne; 800-363-7777.

The following hotels are within the walls of the city:

-LeChâteau Frontenac, 1 rue des Carrières, G1R 4P5; (418) 692-3861 or 800-828-7447. Québec's most famous landmark. A mile from the station. $160.

-Auberge du Trésor, 20 rue Ste-Anne (at du Fort), G1R 3X2; (418) 694-1876. Small, moderately priced hotel, excellently located across from LeChâteau Frontenac, next to the tourism office. Oldest inn in North America. One mile from the station. $85.

-Château de la Terrasse, 6 Place Terrasse-Dufferin, G1R 4N5; (418) 694-9472. 18-room hotel overlooking the St. Lawrence. Two blocks from Le Château Frontenac, one mile from the station. Back rooms, $70; front rooms overlooking the St. Lawrence, $90.

A few In-Town Attractions: The Citadel, with its enormous walls overlooking the entire city, is the largest fortification in North America still garrisoned by regular troops. This British-built fortress can best be seen by guided tours.

If you do nothing else, be sure to stroll along **Dufferin Terrace**, a boardwalk in front of the Château Frontenac Hotel that connects to the **Promenade des Gouverneurs** following the cliffside with sweeping view of the St. Lawrence River and its maritime activity.

Place Royale, in the lower town along the St. Lawrence River, is the birthplace of Québec City, and several of the 18th-century houses are open to the public.

The Notre-Dame-des-Victoires Church

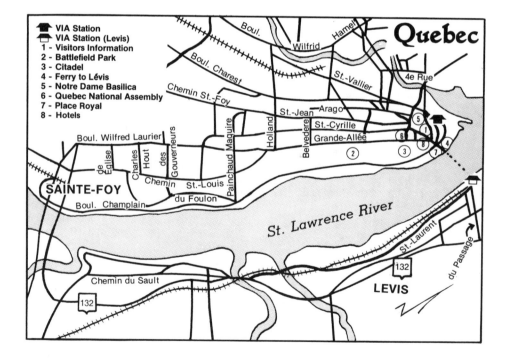

VIA station, Gare du Palais — Québec City, QC
JACKS SWANSON

is one of the oldest in North America. Also, the **Québec Fortifications,** 2 rue d'Auteuil, C.P. 2474, built due to the city's strategic location. Covering a large portion of the city, pathways allow easy viewing.

The Cite Parlementaire, which houses Québec's National Assembly, is located just outside of the walls of the city.

0:00 (0:22) Depart Lévis, and soon begin climb from water level to slightly higher plain for remainder of run into Montréal. Some marvelous views of Québec City and St. Lawrence River with its oceangoing traffic will be afforded on the right as we make this climb.

0:22 (0:00) Arrive Charney.

CHARNEY, QC - At this juncture, trains traveling from Montréal to Québec City depart from this line and curl northward to make a spectacular crossing of the river before entering Québec City.

0:00 (1:46) Depart Charney.

0:03 (1:43) Cross a river named Chaudiere, a French translation of an Indian word meaning "boiling kettle."

0:23 (1:23) Through Laurier, a small town named after Wilfred Laurier, an early Prime Minister of Canada.

0:31 (1:15) Cross swift-moving Henri River.

1:02 (0:44) Note rows of rocks in field on right, waste product of a farmer's effort to

make his field more productive.

1:07 (0:39) Cross Bécancour River at milepost 66.8.

1:21 (0:25) At St. Léonard, cruise high above Nicolet River.

1:32 (0:14) Under Trans-Canada and Québec Autoroute 20, stretching from Victoria, British Columbia, to St. John's, Newfoundland.

1:38 (0:08) Passing through St. Cyrille where St. Cyrille's Church, with a large silver dome and two lesser domes gracing its greystone walls, is centerpiece of town on right.

1:44 (0:02) Note attractive rapids below as tracks span St. Francois River.

1:46 (0:00) Arrive At Drummondville's rather tired-looking depot.

DRUMMONDVILLE, QC - Le Village Québécois d'Antan is located here, a fine collection of restored buildings with a costumed staff depicting typical activities in 19th-century Québec, one of the major historical attractions of the province.

0:00 (0:40) Depart Drummondville.

0:38 (0:02) Cross Yamaska River.

0:40 (0:00) Arrive St. Hyacinthe.

ST. HYACINTHE, QC - This town serves as a trade center for local farming activities and also is home for many who don't mind commuting to Montréal, some 33 miles to the west. The town was not named for lily-like flower but a local landowner.

0:00 (0:33) Depart St. Hyacinthe, then pass town's golf course on outskirts at left.

0:10 (0:23) Royal Hills, those unusual mountains on left, are of volcanic origin dating back millions of years. A quarry can be seen on the slopes of St. Hilaire, two miles away, which is a source of rare minerals, many being found only in this locale. Rougemont Mountain is eight miles distant, while 1,350-foot Yamaska Mountain is 12 miles from here.

0:15 (0:18) Trundle over impressive Richelieu River which drains Lake Champlain, directly south of us in New York State, into the St. Lawrence.

 ST. LAMBERT, QC - We are now immediately across the St. Lawrence from our destination, Montréal. St. Lambert Lock, a lift station for the St. Lawrence Seaway traffic, is here.

0:00 (0:12) Depart St. Lambert and start ascent necessary for crossing St. Lawrence River on Victoria Bridge.

This structure was once known as the Jubilee Bridge when it was opened in 1859 (later rebuilt in 1898). It handled two sets of rails, an electric interurban line and auto traffic, and was one of the world's longest bridges at 1 1/4 miles. Those two concrete-lined channels below us are the St. Lawrence Seaway and the St. Lambert Lock which is just one of many locks needed to raise or lower shipping using this waterway. The Seaway is narrow and unfortunately cannot handle many larger ships of today's maritime fleet. The islands to the right were home to Canada's very successful 1967 world's fair—Expo 67. The geodesic dome was the U.S. Pavilion. The skyline of Montréal is a dramatic scene on the right.

0:06 (0:06) Leaving Victoria Bridge, we enter Montréal through Canadian National rail yards.

0:08 (0:04) Slip over nicely landscaped Canal Lachine (pronounced luh-sheen), built years ago to circumvent Lachine Rapids but discontinued operations when Seaway was opened.

0:10 (0:02) Sink underground as we near end of line.

0:12 (0:00) Arrive Montréal's Central Station.

 MONTRÉAL, QC - Montréal is one of North America's oldest cities. In 1535 Jacques Cartier discovered this location which was already inhabited by 4,000 Iroquois Amerindians. However, it wasn't until 1642 that a permanent settlement was established by some devout French laymen.

Although the British captured the town in 1760 during the Battle of the Plains of Abraham (which ultimately led to all of Canada becoming British), Montréal, to this day, remains a city of charming French character. Three-fourths of its populace still speak that language, and the city has a distinct European look and feel.

Located on a collection of islands in the St. Lawrence River, and only 117 feet above sea level, it is dominated by 765-foot Mount Royal from which the city derives its name. Winters here can be hard, but miles of underground shopping and a good subway system make it a town to be visited during any season.

Central Station, 895 la Gauchetiere W. (at University), is located in the very heart of downtown. This is one of VIA's busiest and best stations. Escalators leading down to train platforms stretch across its central plaza while stores and services are ensconced along the perimeter. There are numerous snack bars, restaurants and shops that line the underground arcades leading to other buildings in downtown Montréal. There are redcaps, and pay-parking is adjacent to the station. Panorama Lounge is available to VIA-1 customers. For reservations and other information, call (514) 989-2626.

Diamond **Cab,** 273-6331. Budget **rental cars** are at the station. **Local buses** stop at the station. **Intercity bus** terminal, Voyageur, (514) 842-2281.

Visitor Information Center, 1001 Square Dorchester (at Metcalf);

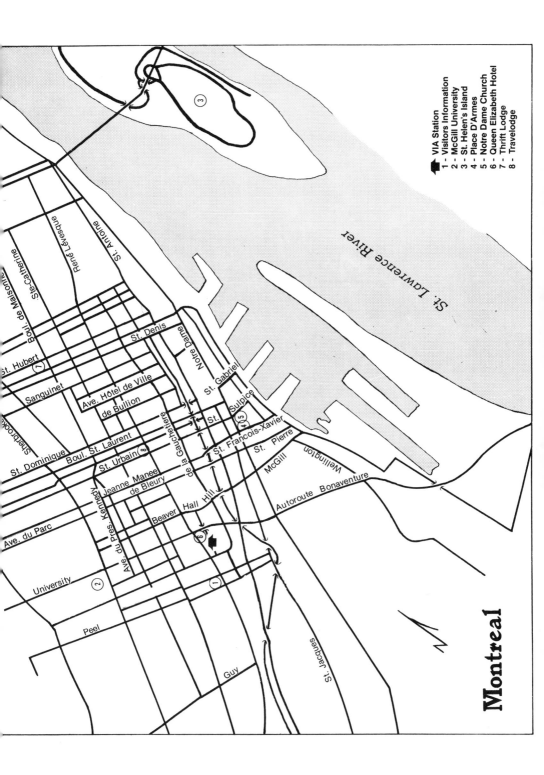

Montréal

Legend:

- VIA Station
- 1 - Visitors Information
- 2 - McGill University
- 3 - St. Helen's Island
- 4 - Place D'Armes
- 5 - Notre Dame Church
- 6 - Queen Elizabeth Hotel
- 7 - Thrift Lodge
- 8 - Travelodge

St. Lawrence River

Street labels: Ste-Catherine, Boul. de Maisonneuve, René Lévesque, St. Antoine, St. Denis, Notre Dame, St. Hubert, Sanguinet, Ave. Hôtel de Ville, de Bullion, St. Gabriel, St. Sulpice, St. François-Xavier, St. Pierre, Sherbrooke, St. Dominique, Boul. St. Laurent, St. Urbain, de la Gauchetière, McGill, Wellington, Jeanne Manee, de Bleury, Ave. du Parc, Ave. du Pres. Kennedy, Beaver Hall Hill, Autoroute Bonaventure, University, Peel, Guy, St. Jacques

(514) 873-2015 or 800-363-7777.

 The Queen Elizabeth Hotel, 900 René-Lévesque Blvd. W. (at Mansfield), H3B 4A5; (514) 861-3511 or 800-828-7447. One of Montréal's best. Located above Central Station. $145.

-**Thrift Lodge Montréal**, 1610 rue St. Hubert, H2L 3Z3; (514) 849-3214. Attractive accommodations, one of downtown Montréal's best values. Easily reached by subway; get off at Berri-de-Montigny Station (Boul. de Maisonneuve). About a mile north of VIA's Central Station, in a quiet neighborhood. $70.

-**Travelodge Downtown**, 50 René-Lévesque Blvd. West, H27 1A2; (514) 874-0906 or 800-363-6535. Small but spiffy rooms. Eight blocks from the station. $80.

Two Bed and Breakfast reservation services include:

-**A Downtown Bed & Breakfast Network**, 3458 Laval Ave. (at Sherbrooke St.), H2X 3C8; (514) 289-9749 or 800-267-5180. A reservation service for numerous B&Bs in the downtown area, including this location.

Much of Montréal is **underground**, with shops, restaurants and services lining miles of walkways underneath portions of the city. A **walking tour** of the old city, roughly defined by McGill, Notre-Dame, Berri Streets and the St. Lawrence River, can be taken starting at Place D'Armes (at St. Sulpice and Notre Dame St.). Here one can see Notre Dame Church, Saint-Sulpice Seminary and the Bank of Montréal Museum. From this point, walk east along cobblestone streets to see Place de la Justice and artists exhibiting works. Upon reaching the church and Bonsecours Market, head west and pass by Place Royale, the d'Youville Stables and the Old General Hospital. The old city also has many galleries, charming shops and cafes.

St. Helen's Island has several attractions including: **The Montréal Aquarium** with fine displays of marine life; **St. Helen's Island Museum** at the Old Fort, Montréal's Military and Maritime Museum, with various military and naval artifacts dating from the 15th century; and **LaRonde**, a spectac-

ular amusement park, resulting from the world's fair (Expo '67) held here in 1967.

The **Montréal Museum of Fine Arts**, 1379 rue Sherbrooke W., has excellent permanent art collections as well as traveling exhibits.

Mount Royal Overlook has a great view and a steep climb—206 steps up a stairway with only two landings. Go up Peel Street, through McGill University to Mount Royal Park to the base of the stairs, then climb!

Some distance northeast of downtown, but reached by subway, is the **Botanical Gardens**, 4101 rue Sherbrooke E. Get off the subway at Pie IX Station (the stop for the **Montréal Expos** stadium). There are over 25,000 species and plant varieties, 30 outdoor gardens and nine greenhouses. This is one of the most outstanding botanical gardens in the world.

Gaspé

Montreal

Chaleur

The *Chaleur* has literally carried you to "Land's end" when it reaches the town of Gaspé on the tip of Québec's scenic Gaspé Peninsula. From Montréal, the *Chaleur* makes an overnight journey down the southern shore of the St. Lawrence River, leaving the excitement of the rocky Gaspé shoreline for daytime passage. The run along the craggy coastal scenery, that many believe to be Eastern Canada's most visually inspiring, is a train ride which in and of itself would justify making the trip. But there are lots of bonuses to be found, such as the towns of Gaspé, with nearby Forillon National Park, Percé in a delightful seaside setting overlooking monolithic Percé Rock jutting up from the surface of the sea and Bonaventure Island, famous for its large and accessible colonies of gannets.

If you love fall colors, you might consider an early October visit to the peninsula. VIA, recognizing the uniqueness of the Gaspésie, has put some of its finely restored cars into service on this route, including a dome car for serious scenery watchers.

EASTBOUND SCHEDULE (Condensed)
Montréal, QC - Early Evening Departure
Matapedia, QC - Middle of the Night (2nd Day)
Carleton, QC - Early Morning (2nd Day)
Percé, QC - Midmorning (2nd Day)
Gaspé, QC - Late Morning Arrival (2nd Day)

WESTBOUND SCHEDULE (Condensed)

Gaspé, QC - Midafternoon Departure
Percé, QC - Late Afternoon
Carleton, QC - Late Evening
Matapedia, QC - Late Evening
Montréal, QC - Early Morning Arrival (2nd Day)

FREQUENCY - Triweekly, departing Montréal on Wednesday, Friday and Sunday, and departing Gaspé on Monday, Thursday and Saturday.
SEATING - Coaches and dome car.
DINING - Complete meal, snack and beverage service.
SLEEPING - Sections (berths), single and double bedrooms.
BAGGAGE - Checked baggage handled.
LENGTH OF TRIP - 840 miles in 17 hours.

ROUTE LOG

(Note that this route log is laid out eastbound, rather than the normal westbound format, since most first-time riders on the *Chaleur* ride toward Gaspé.)

For route between Montréal and Matapedia, see that portion of the *Ocean* log, page 283.

 MATAPEDIA, QC - See page 283.

0:00 (0:57) Depart Matapedia.
0:15 (0:42) Town of Point-â-la-Croix (Cross

Point) is passed where green steel bridge crosses narrows of Restigouche River to Campbellton, NB off to right. Near here, last naval battle between English and French in North America occurred in July 1760, when a small supply fleet, hoping to salvage New France, was met by the British in what would later be called the Battle of the Restigouche.

0:57 (0:00) Arrive Nouvelle.

 NOUVELLE, QC - Just south of this town is Miguasha Park, with its world renowned fossil-imbedded cliffs. The Park is also where the Restigouche River broadens to become Chaleur Bay.

0:00 (0:16) Depart Nouvelle.

0:08 (0:08) Cross Stewart Brook on 175-foot trestle.

0:13 (0:03) Now, tracks hug waters of Chaleur Bay.

0:16 (0:00) Arrive Carleton's neat frame station on right.

 CARLETON, QC - The proximity to both the ocean and mountains has made Carleton a popular tourist spot. Its beaches are particularly appealing because of the unusually warm waters of Chaleur Bay (a name meaning bay of warmth, so named by Cartier).

Although Carleton received its name from British Loyalists who ultimately forced the Acadian residents to leave, the community is still predominantly French speaking.

0:00 (0:39) Depart Carleton through gorgeous rolling forested hills and idyllic fields. Note shrine to Virgin Mary on side of Mt. Saint-Joseph to left.

0:11 (0:28) Through Maria, which boasts tepee-shaped church. Located on Micmac reservation, village was named for wife of third governor of Canada, Sir Guy Carleton.

0:22 (0:17) Make first of two successive crossings of Cascapedia River.

0:24 (0:15) Cross Cascapedia one more time, this time on 604-foot bridge.

0:35 (0:04) Stands of tamarack trees, those lacy-looking "evergreens," line tracks. Needles actually turn yellow in fall before dropping.

0:37 (0:02) Cross Little Cascapedia River.

0:39 (0:00) Arrive New Richmond.

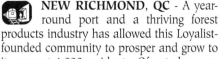 **NEW RICHMOND, QC** - A year-round port and a thriving forest products industry has allowed this Loyalist-founded community to prosper and grow to its current 4,000 residents. Of note here are its many handsome homes of Anglo-Saxon architecture.

0:00 (0:15) Depart New Richmond.

0:02 (0:13) Large plant, steaming profusely on left, uses those large piles of woodchips to produce cardboard.

0:04 (0:11) Dramatic view of Chaleur Bay shoreline now comes into view on right forward.

0:15 (0:00) Arrive Caplan.

 CAPLAN, QC - In 1893, this fishing village was once the eastern end of the rail line on the Gaspé. Although some say the town gets its name from the large number of small fish known as "capelin" that spawn here every spring; there is also reason to believe it was named for an early settler, Jean Caplan.

0:00 (0:15) Depart Caplan.

0:06 (0:09) Note small boat harbor on right protected by hook-shaped breakwater.

0:15 (0:00) Arrive Bonaventure where typical Gaspésie station is on right.

 BONAVENTURE, QC - This French-founded community was destroyed by the British during the battle of Restigouche Estuary, but then was resettled by the French Acadians forced from Nova Scotia. It is probably this Acadian heritage that makes this port town as much farming oriented as it is fishing. The town boasts a modest canoe-building industry and a zoo harboring an eclectic assemblage of animals from around the world.

0:00 (0:13) Depart Bonaventure.

0:02 (0:11) Cross Bonaventure River.

0:13 (0:00) Arrive New Carlisle.

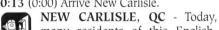 **NEW CARLISLE, QC** - Today, many residents of this English-speaking administrative center are descendants of British Loyalists, and several of the town's large, attractive homes are from the Loyalist era. René Lévesque, Premier of Québec from 1976 to 1985, was born here.

Percé, QC
DORIS SWANSON

0:00 (0:35) Depart New Carlisle.

0:19 (0:16) Sail high over valley floor on Shigiwake Viaduct.

0:28 (0:07) Off to right, enticing-looking town in distance is our next stop, Port Daniel.

0:34 (0:01) Now cruise across steel frame bridge which spans Little River on Port Daniel's outskirts, with glistening little bay at right.

0:35 (0:00) Arrive at Port Daniel's station immediately adjacent to harbor.

PORT DANIEL, QC - This village was named for Captain Daniel (a contemporary of Champlain) who once visited this area.

0:00 (0:43) Depart Port Daniel.

0:02 (0:41) Church on left seems almost overwhelmed by enormous frame rectory.

0:04 (0:39) Now, at milepost 23.7, curl to left through Cap a L'Enfer Tunnel, 630 feet long and peninsula's only rail tunnel.

0:09 (0:34) *Chaleur* virtually hangs to side of rocky cliffs. Seals can often be spotted on rocky shore of ocean straight below, as train continues to trace a course above coast.

0:19 (0:24) Train slows as it ventures out over deep draw on Chouinard Gully Viaduct—506 feet long and 106 feet high. It is highest of today's journey.

0:33 (0:10) Through town of Newport which boasts one of world's most modern fish processing plants. Area also produces huge crops of Christmas trees.

0:35 (0:08) Leaving Newport, continue to follow bay's shoreline with occasional excursions inland through forested hills.

0:40 (0:03) Evidence of maritime disaster is quite visible to right, where Peruvian freighter became grounded and split in two in 1983. Derelict still lies on its side not far offshore.

0:42 (0:01) Pulp mill at left dates back to 1915.

0:43 (0:00) Arrive Chandler.

CHANDLER, QC - The economic mainstay here is the substantial pulp and paper mill operation by Abitibi-Price. The pulp mill was the first on the peninsula. A good natural harbor facilitates the exporting of newsprint to various parts of the world. Named for a Philadelphian, it should not be too surprising that the town is largely English-speaking.

Percé

Percé's two natural attractions, Percé Rock, a skinny rock mesa rising from the ocean but accessible by foot during low tide, and Bonaventure Island, home to nearly a quarter-million birds, reachable by boat during the warmer months, are coastal jewels. Percé Rock, with its small natural window near one end, gives the town the name Percé—French for pierced. Bonaventure Island is a birder's wonderland, with a gannet colony (one of the world's largest and most accessible gannet rookeries) of 50,000 of these interesting birds. There also are puffins, razor-billed auks, gulls and numerous other species. Boat trips to the island for birding and hiking are available from June until October. Both the Rock and Island have been designated conservation parks.

0:00 (0:18) Depart Chandler.
0:09 (0:09) Slip across brief causeway at milepost 49.
0:16 (0:02) Tracks now make lengthy crossing of Grand River on 686-foot-long trestle.
0:18 (0:00) Arrive Grand Rivière.

GRAND RIVIÈRE, QC - Named for the river that flows through it, Grand Rivière is heavily dependent on fishing, particularly crab fishing.

0:00 (0:19) Depart Grand Rivière.
0:13 (0:06) Handsome brick church on right offers relief from region's typical frame architecture.
0:17 (0:02) Suddenly, looming in far distance to right, is Bonaventure Island, home to nearly a quarter-million birds of various species.
0:19 (0:00) Arrive Percé's small station, lit-erally in middle of nowhere. Town is quite distant from here, and tracks go no closer than this.

PERCÉ, QC - This renowned resort is the chief tourist destination on the Gaspésie. Perched on a spectacular bit of shoreline, with mountains ringing three sides of town, Percé has one of Eastern Canada's most stunning settings. French cuisine, live theater and art galleries give it additional appeal.

On the edge of town, a wildlife interpretation center has exhibits and films which describe not only the area's wildlife, but also its natural features.

Cabs usually meet trains. Thrifty has **rental cars** and will pick up and drop off at the station, (418) 689-3739.

Hotel-Motel Le Bonaventure sur Mer. Call year-round (418) 782-2166. Station shuttle if arranged in advance. $58.

0:00 (0:25) Depart Percé and head inland away from sea.
0:10 (0:15) Percé Mountains off to left are more rugged than those encountered earlier on route. In fall, colors through here are outstanding.
0:19 (0:06) Slip beneath highway at curiously named town of Coin-du-Banc. Originally settled by Irish, town is still English speaking. Look back for marvelous view of rugged coast and Percé Rock. We have just started across a three-mile-long causeway, where nearby beaches provide excellent agate hunting.
0:24 (0:01) Leaving causeway, one of better views of Percé Rock is now back to right.
0:25 (0:00) Arrive Barachois.

BARACHOIS, QC - This coastal village probably derives its name from the East Indian French word for pond.
0:00 (0:44) Depart Barachois.
0:10 (0:34) Body of water at right is Bay of Gaspé while land mass on horizon is Cape Gaspé, location of magnificent Forillon National Park.
0:17 (0:27) At milepost 89, sign announces "Prevel." Here, during World War II, heavy artillery aimed toward sea provided impor-

Chaleur — Gaspé, QC
JACK SWANSON

tant coastal defense. Now, area has become a popular resort with former army barracks now serving as a fine provincial inn. After Prevel, train will venture across L'Anse-a-Brillant Viaduct.

0:32 (0:12) Encounter one more causeway. Town of Gaspé lies ahead.

0:42 (0:02) Approaching end of line, Gaspé, laid out above its harbor, provides interesting scene straight ahead. Large red brick facility at top of hill overlooking city is former tuberculosis sanatorium, now serving as regional nursing home.

0:44 (0:00) Arrive Gaspé.

GASPÉ, QC - Gaspé, from the Micmac word "gaspeg" meaning land's end, is a city serving the area's administrative center. This is where Jacques Cartier took possession of the country for France. The bay, around which the town is situated, provides a deep water port complimenting Gaspé's rail-head status.

VIA Station is on the edge of town, just a short taxi ride to downtown. Inside is a small waiting room and ticket office. Call 800-361-5390.

Thrifty Car Rental, (418) 368-1610, offers pick-up and drop-off service at the station. **Bus station** is next to Adams Motel.

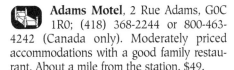

Adams Motel, 2 Rue Adams, G0C 1R0; (418) 368-2244 or 800-463-4242 (Canada only). Moderately priced accommodations with a good family restaurant. About a mile from the station. $49.

-**Auberge des Commandants**, 178 Rue de la Reine, G0C 1R0; (418) 368-3355 or 800-462-3555. Best accommodation in Gaspé, if not the entire peninsula. $80.

Gaspé Cathedral, the only wooden cathedral in North America, was built of cedar to help bring it into harmony with its surroundings. Its stained glass windows were a gift from France in 1934 to commemorate the 400th anniversary of the arrival of Cartier. An adjacent, enormous granite cross also honors that historic event. **Pisciculture de Gaspé**, a century-old fish hatchery, where two million salmon and trout are produced annually, is open to visitors. The **Gaspé Museum** reflects the history of the area. Nearby **Forillon National Park** occupies its own small peninsula. This is some of the region's most beautiful wilderness, with seals, bears, moose and other wildlife living in an environment dominated by 500-foot cliffs overlooking the sea. Canada's tallest lighthouse, where visitors can climb to the top, is also here.

Corridor Service

The very heart of VIA's network is the so-called "Corridor," stretching from Québec City to Windsor, Ontario, with branches to Sarnia, Ottawa, Niagara Falls and Kitchener. And the heaviest used portion is that high-speed track connecting Canada's two largest cities, Montréal and Toronto. LRC trains (light, rapid, comfortable) operate throughout the Corridor.

A multitude of VIA's express trains with VIA 1 service (early boarding privileges, meals served at your seat, complimentary newspapers and magazines) make the trip between Montréal and Toronto on any given weekday. Several more connect Ottawa and Toronto by way of Kingston. Additional VIA 1 trains make runs between Toronto and the border city of Windsor.

ROUTE LOG

Montréal-Ottawa-Toronto is at page 304 and Toronto-Kitchener-Sarnia is at page 306. Québec City-Montréal is at page 285.

MONTRÉAL-TORONTO-WINDSOR

 MONTRÉAL, QC - See page 288.

0:00 (0:18) Depart Montréal's Central Station on CN tracks. In about 60 seconds emerge from underground, heading southeast, and soon parallel St. Lawrence River.

0:04 (0:14) Cross Lachine (pronounced "luh-sheen") Canal, with its very attractive landscaping. Canal was constructed prior to St. Lawrence Seaway providing bypass around treacherous Lachine Rapids of St. Lawrence River. Nine miles in length, it ceased operations in 1965.

Unfortunately, the Seaway no longer serves as it was originally intended. Many of today's freighters cannot be accommodated by the waterway's rather narrow channel, and ice blocks traffic west of Montréal three months or more each winter.

0:05 (0:13) Several tracks now depart to left to cross Victoria Bridge over St. Lawrence and then on to either Maritime Provinces or New York City.

0:09 (0:09) Re-cross Lachine Canal.

0:10 (0:08) Now slip beneath enormous pile of spaghetti called an interchange, which scrambles and then unscrambles traffic carried by Trans-Canada 20 and Autoroute 15.

0:15 (0:03) Sets of CN and CP tracks branch to right toward huge marshaling yards for both lines.

0:18 (0:00) Arrive Dorval.

DORVAL, QC - This is a western suburb of Montréal, home to Dorval International Airport just off to the right.

0:00 (0:23) Depart Dorval.

0:08 (0:15) Stone buildings and round barn on right are part of Macdonald College's experimental farm.

0:09 (0:14) Cross smaller of two tongues of Ottawa River to reach L'Île de Perrot. River is

St. Anne Street — Québec City, QC
JACK SWANSON

principal branch of St. Lawrence. Its origin is in central Québec, some 160 miles above Ottawa, and forms partial boundary between Québec and Ontario. Rapids and falls make most of it unnavigable, but significant elevation change makes stream ideal for hydroelectric power.

0:12 (0:11) Now cross larger segment of river and upon reaching Québec's mainland, enter Vandreuil, named for early-day governor of Canada.

0:23 (0:00) Arrive Coteau.

COTEAU, QC - This is the final stop in the province of Québec and the outer fringe of Montréal's populous suburbs.

0:00 (0:30) Depart Coteau.

0:07 (0:23) Enter Ontario and leave Québec.

0:30 (0:00) Arrive Cornwall.

CORNWALL, ON - Cotton, oddly enough, was once an important product of this most easterly Ontario city,

and it was in one of Cornwall's cotton mills that Thomas Edison installed equipment to achieve the first electric illumination of a factory. Today, the city is headquarters for the St. Lawrence Seaway Authority.

0:00 (0:36) Depart Cornwall.

0:34 (0:02) Spanning St. Lawrence, on left, is International Bridge reaching across to Ogdensburg, New York.

0:36 (0:00) Arrive Prescott.

PRESCOTT, ON - As the only deep-water port between Montréal and Toronto, shipping has become an important aspect of the city's economy. Of particular interest is Fort Wellington; it occupied a strategic point on the St. Lawrence and saw action during the War of 1812.

0:00 (0:13) Depart Prescott.

0:13 (0:00) Arriving in Brockville, somber brick structure of Brockville Psychiatric Hospital dominates scene off to left. Also, to left, can be glimpsed a portal of an abandoned rail tunnel that burrowed beneath the town and had doors on each end (a rarity) to prevent ice from forming on its roof.

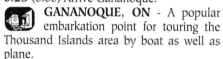 **BROCKVILLE, ON** - Named after a War of 1812 hero, General Sir Isaac Brock, the city is situated at the eastern end of the popular Thousand Islands resort and vacation area. Oscar of the Waldorf once served as a personal chef for George C. Boldt (who lived in this area) and concocted a salad dressing in honor of these St. Lawrence River jewels.

0:00 (0:23) Depart Brockville.

0:23 (0:00) Arrive Gananoque.

GANANOQUE, ON - A popular embarkation point for touring the Thousand Islands area by boat as well as plane.

0:00 (0:18) Depart Gananoque.

0:01 (0:17) Cross Ganonoque River.

0:12 (0:06) Cross Cataraqui River and historic Rideau Canal.

0:18 (0:00) Arrive Kingston.

KINGSTON, ON - At one point, during its evolution from a fur-trading post to a vibrant industrial center, Kingston was actually the nation's capital. With its location at the point where Lake Ontario empties into the St. Lawrence, this was a logical choice. It is also at the southern terminus of the Rideau Canal which connects the St. Lawrence with Ottawa to the north.

0:00 (0:20) Depart Kingston.

0:05 (0:15) Several small pleasure craft can be spotted at Woods Marina on left.

0:20 (0:00) Arrive Napanee.

NAPANEE, ON - During its water power heyday, Napanee boasted tanneries and mills that produced flour, oatmeal, paper, woolen and leather goods, tools and furniture.

0:00 (0:17) Depart Napanee and span Napanee River on 222-foot viaduct, while falls can be seen to left.

0:12 (0:05) Some interesting aircraft are sometimes parked on apron at Belleville Flying Club at left.

0:17 (0:00) Upon arriving Belleville, note quaint two-story, dormer-embellished sta-

tion on left.

BELLEVILLE, ON - This is the gateway to Quinte's Island in the St. Lawrence, where vacationers find long, sandy beaches alluring. The city also offers splendid recreational pursuits with golf, swimming and an excellent yacht harbor.

0:00 (0:12) Depart Belleville.

0:11 (0:01) Cross historic Trent-Severn Canal. Connecting Trenton on Lake Ontario to Georgian Bay (a portion of upper Lake Huron) at 240 miles in length it is longest of province's 540 miles of canals. It contains nearly half of the 100-plus locks found in Ontario.

0:12 (0:00) Arrive Trenton Jct.

TRENTON JCT., ON - This stop serves the attractive community of Trenton which has much the same recreational opportunities as does Belleville. Trenton is also the entrance to the elaborate Trent-Severn Canal.

0:00 (0:25) Depart Trenton Jct.

0:25 (0:00) Arrive Cobourg's handsome stone and brick station on left.

COBOURG, ON - In earlier times, this quaint community served as a lake port for steamers and a staging point on the road connecting Toronto, Kingston and Montréal.

0:00 (0:07) Depart Cobourg.

0:05 (0:02) Lake Ontario finally comes into view, about a mile south (left) of us.

0:06 (0:01) Trundle out on 1,232-foot-long Port Hope Viaduct which spans Ganaraska River. To left, harbor basin is filled with pleasure craft during summer months; large facility at right is uranium processing plant.

0:07 (0:00) Arrive Port Hope's restored 1856 grey stone station, on left.

PORT HOPE, ON - Once called Toronto, in 1819 the town was renamed in honor of Harry Hope, an 18th-century lieutenant governor of Canada.

0:00 (0:27) Depart Port Hope.

0:18 (0:09) Cement plants are fed raw limestone from cavernous quarry on left.

0:19 (0:08) Numerous sets of transmission lines disappear behind earthen berm shielding Darlington Nuclear Power Plant on left.

Plant itself can be glimpsed after passing beneath (west of) power lines.

0:33 (0:00) Arrive Oshawa where auto carriers in rail yards attest to one of town's industries.

 OSHAWA, ON - Originally a lake port, this city has become a major auto manufacturing center for Canada.

0:00 (0:17) Depart Oshawa.

0:02 (0:15) Large blue buildings, on left, are Lasco Steel Plant.

0:10 (0:07) Pickering Nuclear Generating Plant is off to left, the origination of several transmission lines.

0:13 (0:04) Frenchman's Bay is on left.

0:17 (0:00) Arrive Guildwood.

 GUILDWOOD, ON - This is the eastern edge of Metropolitan Toronto, just 13 miles from the heart of the city.

0:00 (0:15) Depart Guildwood.

0:11 (0:04) Distinctive building of Gooderham & Worts ("since 1832") distillery is on right.

0:12 (0:03) Toronto's modernistic skyline now appears ahead of us with tall, spectacular spindle of CN Tower rising 1,821 feet, world's tallest freestanding structure.

0:15 (0:00) Arrive Toronto's Union Station.

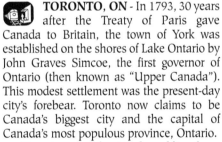 **TORONTO, ON** - In 1793, 30 years after the Treaty of Paris gave Canada to Britain, the town of York was established on the shores of Lake Ontario by John Graves Simcoe, the first governor of Ontario (then known as "Upper Canada"). This modest settlement was the present-day city's forebear. Toronto now claims to be Canada's biggest city and the capital of Canada's most populous province, Ontario.

Downtown is robust and sparkling, busy with theaters, fine restaurants, major sporting events and cosmopolitan shopping. People are attracted here, both day and night, in a way that would make any city planner envious. Actor and noted traveler Peter Ustinov once referred to the town as "New York run by the Swiss."

Getting around Toronto is both relatively easy and inexpensive, making the city all the more appealing. There are trolleys, buses, GO Trains (commuter rail) and perhaps the world's cleanest and safest subway (a reflection of the city itself) that provide Toronto with one of the best urban transit systems found anywhere.

 Union Station, Front Street West, between Bay and York Streets, is a bustling, attractive station nicely located in the downtown area. Its grand facade is adorned with 22 pillars of Bedford limestone. There are storage lockers, restaurants, snack bars, newsstand, miscellaneous shops and redcaps. A Panorama Lounge is provided for VIA 1 passengers.

The station was opened by the Prince of Wales in 1927 and has been changed little throughout the years. Some modern appurtenances include an electronic arrival and departure board and the Panorama Lounge mentioned above. Pay-parking is adjacent to the station. An underground arcade leads to many shops and stores beneath downtown Toronto.

Call 366-8411 for reservations and information.

 Cabs; 366-6868. Nearest **local bus** stop is in front of the station; call 393-4636. Tilden, Avis and Budget **rental cars** are available at the station. Both **GO-Trains** and the **subway** serve this station. **Greyhound** and **Voyageur** buses (and others) are at 610 Bay St. at Dundas, about a mile from the station.

 Metropolitan Toronto Convention & Visitors Association, Queen's Quay Terminal at Harbourfront, 207 Queen's Quay West, (416) 203-2500.

Strathcona Hotel, 60 York St., M5J 1S8; (416) 363-3321 or 800-268-8304. Small accommodations at reasonable rates. Only a block from the station. $80.

-**Bond Place Hotel**, 65 Dundas St., M5J 1E3; (416) 362-6061. Well managed, comfortable hotel; near good shopping (Eaton Center). About a mile and a half from the station, but easily reached by subway (Dundas station is within two blocks). $80.

-**Royal York Hotel**, 100 Front St. W, M5J 1E3; (416) 368-2511 or 800-828-7447. Elderly, dignified Toronto landmark, directly across from the station and can be reached

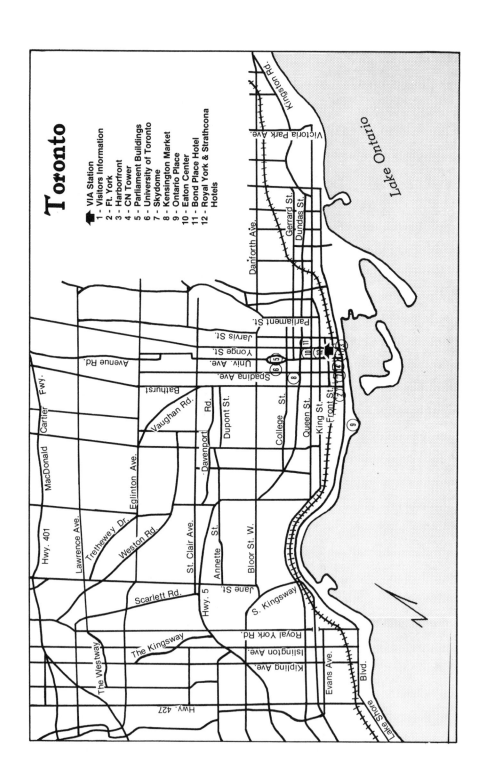

Toronto

- VIA Station
- 1 - Visitors Information
- 2 - Ft. York
- 3 - Harborfront
- 4 - CN Tower
- 5 - Parliament Buildings
- 6 - University of Toronto
- 7 - Skydome
- 8 - Kensington Market
- 9 - Ontario Place
- 10 - Eaton Center
- 11 - Bond Place Hotel
- 12 - Royal York & Strathcona Hotels

by an underground arcade. Was once largest hotel in British Empire. $140.

For shopping there is the stunning **Eaton Centre**, which houses 300 shops and restaurants and 18 movie theaters under a cavernous arched glass arcade, anchored by two of Toronto's department stores. Close to the station, and visible for miles, is the **CN Tower**, the world's tallest (1,821 feet) freestanding structure. On top, of course, is a revolving restaurant and an observation gallery. And vying for "8th Wonder" status is Toronto's new **SkyDome** sports complex, with its retractable roof, North America's largest McDonald's and the SkyDome Hotel. It's the house of the Blue Jays as well as the Canadian Football League's Toronto Argonauts. And on the lake is **Harbourfront**, with its marina, shops and ferryboats to the Toronto Islands.

0:00 (0:23) Depart Toronto's Union Station on CN trackage. In about 60 seconds, emerge from beneath terminal's canopy and CN Tower soars skyward directly in front of us on left.

0:02 (0:21) After passing CN Tower, $400-million SkyDome, on left, overshadows all else. This bulbous edifice, completed in 1989, was built to house baseball's Toronto Blue Jays, shops, restaurants and a 350-room hotel. On nicer days, roof can be shifted from a closed to an open position in 30 minutes to put 90% of its spectators in sunshine. While passing this structure, be sure to look up to see whimsical groupings of spectators protruding from building like modern-day gargoyles.

0:04 (0:19) Tops of brick buildings and sign on grassy knoll are all that can be seen of Historic Fort York Park on left. Park features restored British garrison from War of 1812.

0:06 (0:17) Elaborate facilities on left are annual home of Canadian National Exhibition, Canadian equivalent of American state fairs.

0:07 (0:16) Lake Ontario comes into clear view off to left. Amphitheater poised on lake's edge is handsome attraction of Ontario Place—a cultural, recreational and entertainment complex built atop three man-made islands.

0:10 (0:13) Through rail yards where, on left, VIA Rail has shops and various equipment standing ready for use. Sleek-looking yellow trains are LRCs (light, rapid, comfortable, with tilting capabilities for rounding curves at high speeds) and newer LRC-1s. "GO Trains" (Government of Ontario) are green and white, double-decked equipment parked on right awaiting call for Toronto commuter service and which can be seen along our route until Oakville.

0:12 (0:11) Cross Etobicoke Creek.

0:15 (0:08) At Port Credit, cross Credit River.

0:20 (0:02) On right is sprawling Ontario Ford truck plant.

0:22 (0:01) Observation car of former Florida East Coast Railway has undoubtedly been rescued by rail buff and stands on siding at left.

0:23 (0:00) Arrive Oakville's very attractive, modernistic station.

 OAKVILLE, ON - In the mid-19th century, a host of city-dwellers chose this scenic locale as the site of their summer homes. Most of these lavish retreats have been immaculately preserved, and today are the focal point of a well-documented walking tour. For golfing enthusiasts, the Glen Abbey links, designed by Jack Nicklaus, is of true championship caliber. Its clubhouse was once a monastery, and now is home to the Canadian Golf Hall of Fame.

0:00 (0:12) Depart Oakville.

0:04 (0:08) Industrial area surrounding Oakville bears profusion of refineries and other petroleum-related operations.

0:05 (0:07) Cross Bronte Creek at Bronte.

0:12 (0:00) Arrive Aldershot.

 ALDERSHOT, ON - This stop serves the industrial city of Hamilton as well as its lakefront, residential neighbor Burlington.

0:00 (0:11) Depart Aldershot.

0:03 (0:09) On left, brick-domed structure is Halton Ceramics, Ltd.

0:05 (0:07) At Bay View, quick but startling

view of Hamilton Harbour is offered with its profusion of both commercial and pleasure boats. Momentarily, note tracks that cut off to left; these carry rail traffic to Niagara Falls and ultimately to New York City.

0:13 (0:00) Arrive Dundas, with town proper lying far below grade on left.

DUNDAS, ON - This is a suburb of Hamilton, Canada's steel capital and third largest port. The magnificent Dundurn Castle with splendid furnishings and appointments reflecting the opulent lifestyle of its mid-19th-century inhabitants is located here.

0:00 (0:18) Depart Dundas.

0:02 (0:17) Note fairways of Dundas' Golf Course below on left.

0:16 (0:03) Tall, spindly structure off tower.

0:17 (0:02) On eastern edge of Brantford, huge building complex, immediately left of tracks, is former Massey Ferguson farm equipment plant which ceased operations in 1980s. Brantford has been considered "Combine Capital of Canada" and factory's closure was severe blow to city.

0:19 (0:00) Arriving Brantford, glimpses of downtown and town hall's tower can be had to left. Fine old station on the left, a brick beauty adorned with a stately square tower, is further enhanced by a semaphore at trackside. Station dates back to 1904.

BRANTFORD, ON - The city was named for the Indian chief Joseph Brant who brought his group known as Six Nations Indians from Upper New York State to this site.

This is where Alexander Graham Bell invented the telephone and "placed" the first long distance call which was to Paris, Ontario, a distance of ten miles. Brantford has constructed a museum which displays some of the world's most sophisticated telecommunications equipment, including a NORAD control system.

0:00 (0:24) Depart Brantford.

0:01 (0:23) Fine old three-story brick home sports elegant white gingerbread trim on right. Home and grounds known as Glenhurst Gardens are on left.

0:06 (0:18) Trestle carries train high over Grand River at Paris where three attractive churches predominate cityscape. After crossing river, note wonderful old stone mansion, now converted to retirement facility, on right.

0:24 (0:00) Arrive Woodstock where 1853, almost Victorian-in-style, station greets us on left.

WOODSTOCK, ON - This charming, well preserved town, with many residences dating to the mid-1800s, was named for Woodstock in Oxfordshire, England, in honor of the Duke of Marlborough whose estate was near there.

0:00 (0:10) Depart Woodstock.

0:07 (0:03) Huge excavation on left is result of extensive quarrying operations. Kilns and other paraphernalia are part of operation.

0:10 (0:00) Arrive Ingersoll.

INGERSOLL, ON - This was the birthplace of Canada's cheese industry, with the first factory built in 1864, and still is famous for the manufacture of this dairy product.

0:00 (0:18) Depart Ingersoll.

0:02 (0:16) Be sure to note palatial Landfair Stables horse farm, just to right, with its colonial-style home, handsome landscaping and neatly painted fences and outbuildings.

0:07 (0:11) Focal point of Dorchester is ornate single-spired church on left at milepost 68.

0:13 (0:03) Pass through sprawling CN rail yards with shops on left as we enter London's eastern suburbs.

0:18 (0:00) Arrive at London's very busy VIA station, where two major VIA routes intersect and connections can be made for Windsor to the southwest and Stratford to the northeast.

LONDON, ON - Located on the River Thames, many of London's streets are named for those of its English namesake. This is one of southeastern Ontario's busier industrial centers.

0:00 (0:30) Departing London, many of town's earliest three- and four-story buildings, one block to right, are in vivid contrast with London's newer downtown.

0:02 (0:28) Cross Thames River.

0:03 (0:27) Cross Thames River one more time.

0:13 (0:17) Tobacco kilns, those skinny barns with multiple doors, dot field on left.

0:30 (0:00) Arrive Glencoe's dilapidated 1890s station. Adjacent phone-booth-looking structure now serves VIA customers.

 GLENCOE, ON - This town is VIA's stop for the agricultural area to the west of London. Glencoe was once the end of the line for the Canada Air Line Railway.

0:00 (0:31) Depart Glencoe.

0:11 (0:19) Seven more tobacco barns appear in fields at left, attesting to hot and lengthy growing season and soil well-suited to that crop.

0:25 (0:06) Asparagus can frequently be seen growing in field on left. Cabbages, tomatoes and soybeans are also grown by area farmers.

0:31 (0:00) Arrive Chatham, where older, red-brick station greets arriving passengers.

 CHATHAM, ON - Just as its namesake in England, Chatham rests near the mouth of the Thames River. The city has played an important role in shaping American history, acting as a northern terminus for the American Civil War's underground railway (a clandestine routing of slaves to the North and freedom), scene of a major battle during the War of 1812, and where John Brown hatched his plot to attack the federal armory at Harper's Ferry.

0:00 (0:44) Depart Chatham.

0:15 (0:39) Canals with myriad pleasure craft create surprising contrast to agricultural scenes which have dominated trip.

0:16 (0:38) Lake St. Clair now appears on right. Marinescapes continue; boats, lakefront homes, ducks and geese line water's edge for several miles.

0:28 (0:16) Train now cuts directly through very attractive marina.

0:44 (0:00) Arrive Windsor.

WINDSOR, ON - Windsor lies just across the Detroit River (one of the busiest shipping channels in the world) from the city of Detroit, making it a major port of entry to Canada. Because of the bend in the Detroit River (and hence in the U.S.-Canada border), Windsor is actually south of its American cousin.

The French first settled the area in the early 1700s with British locating nearby in the late 1700s. Agriculture and distilling were important aspects of Windsor's economy in the late 1800s, which saw the founding of the Hiram Walker distillery in 1858. Today, Windsor is a busy manufacturing city, with General Motors, Ford and Chrysler having plants and supply industries here.

VIA Station, 298 Walker Rd., just south of Riverside Drive E., is about 1 1/2 miles from downtown, about a four-minute cab ride. There are storage lockers, food and beverage vending machines, a snack bar and pay-parking a block away.

For information, reservations and tickets by mail, call 256-5511. For arrival and departure information, 254-5252.

Canadian Veteran **Cab**, 256-2621. **Local bus** service is one block from the station. **Tunnel bus** between Windsor and Detroit stops just east of 500 Ouellette in downtown Windsor and at the Renaissance Center in Detroit.

Convention and Visitors Bureau, 333 Riverside Dr., W., Suite 103; (519) 255-6530 or 800-265-3633.

Travelodge Downtown Windsor, 33 Riverside Dr. E., N9A 2S4; (519) 258-7774. By the river, many rooms with view of river, Detroit skyline and Dieppe Gardens. Two miles from the station. $75.

-**Ramada Windsor**, 480 Riverside Dr. W., N9A 5K6; (519) 253-4411. On the river, 2 1/2 miles from the station. $75.

Windsor has an outstanding collection of parks and gardens. Some of the best floral displays will be found at **Jackson Park Sunken Garden**, Tecumseh Rd. at Ouellette Ave. There are fountains as well as a World War II Lancaster bomber on display. The **Dieppe Gardens**, located on Riverside Drive at the foot of Ouellette Ave., overlooks the Detroit River, and offers an outstanding view of the Detroit skyline. There is also a 1911 Pacific-type steam locomotive on display. **Coventry**

Gardens and Peace Fountain, Riverside Dr. E. at Pillette Rd., are a six-acre riverfront park with a 75-foot floating fountain in the Detroit River.

MONTRÉAL-OTTAWA-KINGSTON-TORONTO

For route log between Montréal and Coteau, see page 296.

0:00 (0:24) Depart Coteau.
0:05 (0:19) Note quaint, silver church in St. Polycarpe, to left.
0:15 (0:09) Leave province of Québec and enter Ontario.
0:20 (0:02) Interesting remains of several stone fences are on right.
0:23 (0:01) Delightful appearing golf course is on right, accented with ponds and pedestrian bridges.
0:24 (0:00) Arrive Alexandria, where neat brick station awaits on left.

ALEXANDRIA, ON - This is but one of many small agrarian centers in eastern Ontario.

0:00 (0:11) Depart Alexandria.
0:11 (0:00) Arrive Maxville.

MAXVILLE, ON - Maxville is "Home of the Glengary Highland Games," as proclaimed on building to right. This most important Highland gathering in North America takes place here in August when pipe bands and dancers show their talents.

0:00 (0:40) Depart Maxville.
0:08 (0:32) Very attractive silver-spired church punctuates Moose Creek's modest skyline on right.
0:14 (0:26) At Casselman, just 29 miles east of Ottawa, note very unusual architecture of church one block to right.
0:15 (0:25) Cross South Nation River.
0:27 (0:13) Carlsbad Springs and Caldonia Springs, both north (right) of here, were once frequented for their supposedly therapeutic waters.
0:39 (0:01) Ottawa's skyline now dominates right forward.

0:40 (0:00) Arrive at Ottawa's very slick and airy station.

OTTAWA, ON - As the capital of Canada, Ottawa is a governmental oriented city with very little industry. It is handsomely situated on rounded promontories that are set amongst three rivers and a canal.

Although Champlain used this spot as a base for exploring along the Ottawa River, there was no settlement here until the early 1800s. It was first called Bytown (after Colonel By who constructed the Rideau Canal as a waterway for British gunboats) and was only a small lumbering community when it was designated the capital of Canada by Queen Victoria in 1857. Shortly thereafter, it was renamed Ottawa and subsequently developed into a very carefully planned community.

Today, it is marked by very "British"-looking buildings, several national museums, beautiful parks and abundant flower gardens with showy displays of brilliant colors—particularly the thousands of tulips that bloom in late May.

Ottawa Station, 200 Tremblay Road, is a modernistic steel and glass structure completed in 1966, located about two miles from the downtown area. There are storage lockers, luggage carts, a newsstand, gifts and a coffee shop, and a barbershop. Free parking is adjacent to the station. There is a Panorama Lounge for VIA 1 passengers. For reservations and information, call (613) 244-8289.

Blue Line Cabs, 238-1111. Frequent **buses** to downtown stop at the station, 741-4390; system maps and schedules are posted at stops. Budget and Hertz have direct phone lines for **rental cars**.

Visitor Information, National Arts Center (Elgin Street entrance); (613) 237-5158.

Capital Hill Hotel, 88 Albert St., K1P 5E9; (613) 235-1413 or 800-463-7705. Recently renovated small downtown hotel; one of Ottawa's better values with large rooms. Good location, near

VIA Station — Ottawa, ON
JACK SWANSON

Parliament Hill. Two miles from the station. $72.

-**Lord Elgin Hotel**, 100 Elgin St. at Laurier, K1P 5K8; (613) 235-3333 or 800-267-4298. Original structure has been remodeled to create larger (but fewer) rooms, all very attractive. Good location, near Parliament Hill, across from National Arts Center. Two miles from the station. $109.

In the downtown area, the **Canadian Parliament Buildings** are set on Parliament Hill overlooking the Ottawa River. Changing of the Guard takes place at 10 am in the summer. Various stage productions appear regularly at the **National Arts Center.**

Two of the more outstanding museums are the new **Canadian Museum of Civilization**, in Hull directly across from Parliament Hill, which has 750,000 artifacts on display, History Hall with life-size historic structures, including a prairie depot, an IMAX/OMNIMAX theatre, and much more, and **National Museum of Science and Technology**, 1867 St. Laurent Blvd., about

a mile or so southeast of the station, is great for the entire family. Exhibits include such things as autos, buggies and trains. The **National Aviation Museum** is at Rockcliffe Airport.

0:00 (0:39) Depart Ottawa.

0:02 (0:37) Large blockish building on left houses Ottawa's postal central distribution operation.

0:05 (0:34) Canada Revenue Center, on right, is some evidence that we are in nation's capital.

0:09 (0:30) Small pleasure craft are docked below on left as we cross Rideau River.

0:20 (0:19) Stream which follows briefly on right is Jack River.

0:36 (0:03) Trees continue to dominate route between Ottawa and Brockville, with spruce and aspen most prevalent.

0:39 (0:00) Arrive Smiths Falls.

SMITHS FALLS, ON - This progressive little city has been highly successful in attracting various light industries to the immediate region. Several such enterprises are evident along the route, particularly south of the city.

0:00 (0:26) Depart Smiths Falls.

0:02 (0:24) Planters and Stanley Tools are major local employers, with plants at left.

0:03 (0:23) Cross Rideau River once again.

0:19 (0:07) A gaggle of handsome old-time street lights graces farm yard off to right.

0:26 (0:00) Arrive Brockville.

For route from Brockville to Toronto, see Brockville, page 298.

TORONTO-KITCHENER-LONDON-SARNIA

TORONTO, ON - See page 299.

0:00 (0:28) Depart Toronto's Union Station. In a moment, CN Tower will soar skyward on left, then $400-million SkyDome, home to Toronto Blue Jays, will dominate all else on left.

0:15 (0:13) Industrial confines of western Toronto are momentarily interrupted as train crosses high above Humber River and angles through Weston Golf Course.

0:16 (0:12) Labatts Metro Brewery, on right, is producer of one of Canada's popular brews.

0:23 (0:05) Another producer of a popular beverage is at right, Lipton Tea.

0:28 (0:00) Arrive Brampton.

BRAMPTON, ON - A plethora of nurseries and greenhouses give Brampton the nickname "Flower City." Nearby, the Great War Flying Museum has a fine collection of World War I memorabilia.

0:00 (0:11) Depart Brampton.

0:10 (0:01) Cross over Credit River.

0:11 (0:00) Arrive Georgetown.

GEORGETOWN, ON - This town serves the extreme western edge of the Toronto metropolitan area.

0:00 (0:24) Depart Georgetown.

0:09 (0:15) Gaping excavation on left is result of limestone quarrying operation.

0:23 (0:01) Cross Speed River, then note former CN 4-8-4 steam locomotive on exhibit at right.

0:24 (0:00) Arrive Guelph where an active armory sits off to left, while 1911 station greets passengers on right.

GUELPH, ON - This community has a fine assemblage of architectural styles utilizing locally quarried limestone.

0:00 (0:22) Depart Guelph.

0:01 (0:21) Massive stone edifice above to right with twin towers is Lady of Mercy Church.

0:04 (0:18) At right, faded lettering between windows of sprawling brick structure once advertised everything for barns and stables.

0:16 (0:06) Trundle over Grand River.

0:22 (0:00) Arrive Kitchener's attractive brick station.

KITCHENER, ON - Kitchener and its twin, Waterloo, were originally founded by Pennsylvania Mennonites. Later an influx of German immigrants gave the area an Old Country flavor that persists today.

0:00 (0:27) Depart Kitchener and soon enter some of world's most productive dairy country.

0:04 (0:23) Large complex of brick buildings on immediate right is Uniroyal Tire plant.

0:15 (0:12) Cross Nith River.

0:27 (0:00) Arrive Stratford.

STRATFORD, ON - The Stratford Festival was born here in 1953. From a humble beginning of Shakespearean plays, the event has become world renowned. The annual celebration now runs from May through October.

0:00 (0:15) Depart Stratford.

0:09 (0:06) Numerous ponies can be be seen galavanting around farm on right.

0:15 (0:00) Arrive St. Marys.

ST. MARYS, ON - This small agrarian stronghold boasts one of the more attractive small rail stations, which stands on the north side of the tracks.

0:00 (0:27) Depart St. Marys.

0:03 (0:24) Large cement plant is at right.

0:08 (0:19) Appropriately nomenclatured dairy operation, on right, is named "Railroad View Farms."

0:15 (0:12) London's municipal airport is off

to left, while attractive golf course embellishes scene.

0:27 (0:00) Arrive London.

LONDON, ON - Located on the River Thames, many of London's streets are named for those of its English namesake. This is one of southeastern Ontario's busier industrial centers.

0:00 (0:30) Departing London, many of town's earliest three- and four-story buildings, one block to right, are in vivid contrast with London's newer downtown.

0:02 (0:28) Cross Thames River.

0:03 (0:27) Cross Thames River one more time.

0:17 (0:02) Tobacco curing kilns, those skinny barns with multiple doors, dot fields on either side of tracks.

0:19 (0:00) Arrive Strathroy.

STRATHROY, ON - This community boasts a lovely Victorian mansion built in 1871, known as "Murray House." The home now houses the Strathroy Middlesex Museum with some rare pioneer artifacts.

0:00 (0:36) Depart Strathroy.

0:20 (0:16) Through small town of Wyoming, an Indian word meaning "on the great plain."

0:31 (0:05) Entering Sarnia, industrial sights dominate, with numerous manufacturing and refinery complexes surrounding this seaport at the mouth of Lake Huron.

0:36 (0:00) Arrive Sarnia.

SARNIA, ON - As you may have already inferred from the numerous refineries in evidence, this is Ontario's major oil-refining and petro-chemical center. It is also a Canadian port-of-entry, where auto traffic is carried over the St. Clair River to and from Port Huron, WI, by the Blue Water Bridge. Trains, however, will pass beneath the river.

Jonquière

Montréal

Saguenay

The *Saguenay* slices through the undulating, forested Laurentians, laced with meandering rivers and liberally sprinkled with glossy-surfaced lakes. This is some of Canada's most attractive wilderness. Sparkling waterfalls, spectacular rock cuts and airy trestles add to the excitement. During the fall, the foliage is exquisite, and there is always a chance of spotting some moose or bear. Numerous hunting and fishing clubs, with names such as Jacques Cartier, Iroquois and Orleans, are strung along the route causing the train to make frequent but interesting unscheduled stops.

The tracks were actually built by four different railroads, the earliest construction occurring a century ago. That first section was only a three-mile stretch between L'Assomption and L'Epiphanie, built by the rather obscure L'Assomption Railway.

The service is thrice-weekly, the pace unhurried, and the atmosphere on board is relaxed and friendly. If you can only take the train one way, the return run from Jonquière would be recommended since the more scenic portions will be traversed during full daylight. (There is direct bus service between Jonquière and Québec City.)

NORTHBOUND SCHEDULE (Condensed)
Montréal, QC - Early Afternoon Departure
Hervey, QC - Late Afternoon
Jonquiére, QC - Late Evening Arrival

SOUTHBOUND SCHEDULE (Condensed)*
Jonquière, QC - Late Morning Departure
Hervey, QC - Late Afternoon
Montréal, QC - Midevening
*Approximately two hours later on Sunday.

FREQUENCY - Triweekly. Departs Montréal Monday, Wednesday and Friday. Departs Jonquière Tuesday, Thursday and Sunday.
SEATING - Coaches.
DINING - Sandwiches, snacks and beverages.
BAGGAGE - Checked baggage at larger towns.
RESERVATIONS - Unreserved train.
LENGTH OF TRIP - 308 miles in 9 hours.

ROUTE LOG

(Note that the route described below, between Montréal and Ahuntsic, is for the southbound train. The northbound train circles around through the Côte de Liesse freight yard west of downtown before arriving in Ahuntsic.)

 MONTRÉAL, QC - See page 288.
0:00 (0:20) Depart Montréal's Central Station in complete darkness for eight minutes while encased by Mount Royal Tunnel. This shaft burrows through Mt. Royal, then emerges three miles northwest of its downtown starting point.
0:09 (0:11) Although you can't tell by looking out the window (the train is below grade

Saguenay route
JACK SWANSON

here), we are passing through a citified portion of Montréal called Mount Royal.

0:15 (0:05) After curving to right for a north-easterly course out of Montréal, look back to right where beehive-domed Saint Joseph Oratory Museum, known for its beautiful stained-glass windows and mosaics, is at Mt. Royal's base, one of the world's most unusual Catholic shrines.

0:20 (0:00) Arrive Ahuntsic.

 AHUNTSIC, QC - This stop is in a section of Montréal with intermixed modest income housing, newer apartments and industrial operations.

0:00 (0:15) Depart Ahuntsic.

0:04 (0:11) Enormous expanse of stone quarry is just to right of tracks.

0:13 (0:02) Cross multi-laned Route 40, which is major artery between Montréal and Québec City.

0:15 (0:00) Arrive Pointe-aux-Trembles where waters of St. Lawrence River are visible about three blocks distant on right.

 POINTE-AUX-TREMBLES, QC - This is the easternmost suburban

stop before escaping the metropolitan confines of Montréal and shifting to the pastoral scenes of rural Québec.

0:00 (0:26) Depart Pointe-aux-Trembles.

From here, the landscape becomes dotted with farmsteads and dairy silos, mild-eyed cattle graze contentedly everywhere and small communities make intermittent appearances, each seeming to have a grey stone church topped with a silver-spired steeple. In spite of its northern location, the area is ideal for tobacco, and fields of this crop, as well as curing barns, can soon be spotted along the route.

0:05 (0:21) Cross River des Prairies, actually an offshoot of Ottawa River, just west of its joinder with St. Lawrence. It takes two tries for us to get across. This river and St. Lawrence encircle Montréal, giving it an island status.

0:12 (0:14) Oldest portion of rail line to Jonquière is along this stretch between mile-post 117 and 114, originally built by the L'Assomption Railway in 1885-86.

0:18 (0:08) Cross LacOuareau River.

0:23 (0:00) Arrive Joliette.

JOLIETTE, QC - This city has long been an important rail head and trade center serving the Lanaudière region of Québec, the only Québec region named after a woman. The town was founded in 1832 by her husband, Barthelemy Joliette, a local deputy, notary and businessman. This is tobacco country, with picking occurring in August. Archery range used during 1976 Olympic Games is still located here.

0:00 (1:04) Depart Joliette and cross L'Assomption River.

0:05 (0:59) Typical tobacco curing barns stand in field on right.

0:27 (0:37) Small village of St. Justin, at milepost 78, is demarcation point between plains just visited and wooded, rolling terrain yet to come. Route becomes more and more scenic.

0:29 (0:35) Suddenly, at milepost 76.3, we seem to soar through space as train crosses 175 feet above Maskinonge River, breathtaking because of its abruptness. Don't miss views of surrounding countryside, particularly to right.

0:43 (0:22) Another airy crossing occurs at milepost 65.1, where train traverses 1,071-foot-long bridge over Rivière-du-Loup; again, nice views are afforded.

0:49 (0:16) At milepost 61, cross 165 feet above West Yamachiche River.

0:53 (0:12) Cross East Yamachiche River at milepost 58..

1:02 (0:02) Momentary darkness prevails as train chugs through 610-foot tunnel— second of only two tunnels on route, first being Mount Royal Tunnel at beginning of our trip. Upon exiting, cross Shawinigan River at milepost 50.

1:04 (0:00) Arrive Shawinigan.

SHAWINIGAN, QC - Located on the St. Maurice River, Shawinigan is the birthplace of Québec's chemical industry. Cheap hydroelectric power (totaling a whopping 400,000 horsepower) produced at the falls on the river has accounted for aluminum, paper and chemical industries locating here. The town's Indian name means "angular portage."

0:00 (0:30) Depart Shawinigan.

0:03 (0:27) Huge electric transformers on left identify aluminum smelting operation which requires enormous amounts of electric power.

0:06 (0:24) Fine view of Saint Maurice River is afforded on right.

0:10 (0:20) Now, cross high above Saint Maurice River on a 722-foot-long trestle at milepost 43.5.

0:11 (0:19) One of Shawinigan's major industries is on left. Logs are floated down St. Maurice River to damsite where Canadian International Paper's operation turns them into pulp for paper products. Much of pulp is exported south to U.S.

0:15 (0:15) Stop at CN rail yards of Garneau at milepost zero. Milepost numbers, which have been growing smaller, now get progressively larger as we move farther toward Jonquière.

0:20 (0:10) Depart Garneau.

0:24 (0:06) Three-spired church, about one block from tracks on right, identifies village of Herouxville at milepost 3.

0:30 (0:00) Arriving St. Tite, take note of attractive three-story house on right that has unusual outside spiral staircase between second and third floors.

ST. TITE, QC - This small town calls itself "The City of Leather," for the gloves and boots manufactured here.

0:00 (0:20) Depart St. Tite.

0:05 (0:15) Sylvan setting on right features small lake with cottages nestled along its idyllic shoreline.

0:10 (0:10) Twin spires grace unusually attractive church of Ste-Thecle on left.

0:20 (0:00) Arrive Hervey Jct. at milepost 18.7.

HERVEY JCT., QC - This rather unimpressive-looking small town is a division point for the railroad. Tracks seen taking off to the left at this junction lead north and then west across a vast lakeland wilderness. The cities of Senneterre and Cochrane, the latter being some 495 rail miles from here, are both reached by this line.

0:00 (0:41) Depart Hervey Jct.

0:13 (0:28) At milepost 23, narrow landing strip on right leads directly into pretty little town of Lac-aux-Sables, testing pilot's skill and townsfolk's nerves.

0:15 (0:26) Expansive waters of very scenic Lac-aux-Sables are on left. Forest now becomes almost continuous while small lakes become more abundant.

0:23 (0:18) Just beyond milepost 30, bridge 323 feet in length carries us over Batiscan River which then follows along left side of train. During autumn, foliage is quite spectacular from here on to Jonquière.

0:44 (0:00) Arrive Rivière-à-Pierre at milepost 40.

RIVIÈRE-À-PIERRE, QC - Numerous two-story buildings with a variety of architectural styles pervade Rivière-à-Pierre. From this quaint village, the tracks now turn left 45 degrees and head due north (we've been going northeast) until reaching Chambord, some 120 miles away.

0:00 (1:40) Depart Rivière-à-Pierre.

0:14 (1:26) Lovely Batiscan River, which is flowing south to the St. Lawrence, joins our route again and becomes a familiar scene during the next 50 miles.

0:23 (1:17) White, frothy rapids of Batiscan are particularly appealing for short stretches in either direction from milepost 57.

0:28 (1:12) On left, impressive rocky cliffs of Linton add special flavor to route at milepost 62.

0:30 (1:10) Near milepost 64, on left, three collections of stone piers poking out of river are remains of bridge that carried tracks some fifty years ago.

0:45 (0:55) Note fire lookout tower at tip of mountain on left.

1:35 (0:05) Cross over rapids and bid farewell to Batiscan River which has been our companion since leaving Rivière-à-Pierre.

1:40 (0:00) Arrive Lac Édouard at milepost 95.

LAC ÉDOUARD, QC - This remote village is situated on a lake by the same name, one of the region's larger bodies of water. Cottages mark the shoreline and also huddle here and there throughout the nearby woods. Note the old rail station to the left of the tracks.

0:00 (2:02) Depart Lac Édouard. While following lake's edge for a few moments, it is understandable, upon seeing such pristine beauty, why the area has become inhabited.

0:26 (1:36) On right, near milepost 105 and just before reaching Summit Club, watch for pretty Summit Lake with inviting cabins along its shoreline.

0:51 (1:11) From mileposts 115 to 117, excellent views of northern tip of Kiskissink Lake are afforded. Small boats are evidence that lake is popular with fishermen.

1:10 (0:52) One of area's larger lakes, Mirage, is just to left, between mileposts 128 and 130. Pontoon planes can often be spotted here.

1:11 (0:51) Cross Wip River at milepost 129.

1:34 (0:28) Cross Noisy River as it tumbles toward Lake Bouchette to left.

Civilization is found once again upon arrival at Lac Bouchette, one of the larger settlements in the surrounding region and located on paved Highway 155 leading to Chambord. As a matter of fact, the train straddles the highway as it stops here at milepost 143. On right, rather bizarre colors were selected for house exterior—red, black and green.

1:37 (0:25) On left is Lake Quiatchouan at milepost 144, situated at northern tip of Lake Bouchette.

2:02 (0:00) At milepost 159.5, arrive Chambord (Jct.) where most of remaining passengers usually detrain. Town of Chambord is off to left.

CHAMBORD, QC - This charming town on a cove of Lac St. Jean is a popular resort for those seeking recreational opportunities afforded by the lake. Here, fishing for the ouananiche, an aggressive freshwater salmon, is a major attraction, while rivers of the region offer walleye, pike and speckled trout. The lake itself is huge, sometimes being referred to as an inland sea, having a circumference of 140 miles. Note crucifixion scene on the right.

VIA station — Jonquière, QC
JACK SWANSON

0:00 (0:29) Depart Chambord past CN locomotive shops on left.

0:03 (0:26) Lac Saint Jean now comes into view to left.

0:14 (0:15) At milepost 169, train slips through town of Metabetchouan, where well-known musicians' camp is located. Note outstanding Gothic-style church on right which is constructed of pink granite quarried nearby.

0:25 (0:04) Last view of Lac Saint Jean is afforded on left before train twists to east on its final leg.

0:29 (0:00) Arrive Hébertville.

HÉBERTVILLE, QC - This small town also serves as a stop for nearby Alma.

0:00 (0:33) Depart Hébertville.

0:03 (0:30) Modest ski hill is visible on horizon off to right.

0:12 (0:21) Church on left, with its modern sweeping lines, is centerpiece of town of Larouche.

0:32 (0:01) Cross Sables River on 231-foot bridge.

0:33 (0:00) Arrive Jonquière.

JONQUIÈRE, QC - This city exemplifies what all industrial cities should be. Owing its robustness to the free world's largest aluminum manufacturing complex, Jonquière is modern, clean and attractive. A super-abundance of hydroelectric power has caused Alcan to locate its largest aluminum plant here, even though bauxite (aluminum ore) must be brought in by ship from such faraway places as South America and Africa.

The area was first settled in the early 1800s when Peter McLeod and 21 other men (a collection of Indians and Scotsmen) arrived here to construct and operate a sawmill, its lumber to be sold to Great Britain for her Merchant Marine. Soon, however, interests turned to farming the land that had been cleared, and, in spite of the sometimes bitter winters, the 120-day growing season fostered both vegetable and dairy farming.

Today, paper and aluminum dominate the region's economy, with 75% of the population afforded employment by these two industries. Oceangoing vessels find their way along the St. Lawrence and then up the Saguenay River (meaning "where we set sail") to the port at nearby La Baie. Here, bauxite is offloaded and shipped by rail to aluminum plants in Jonquière and in nearby Chicoutimi and Alma.

VIA Station, at Pierre and Dominique, is a new, attractive station, about a mile west of the former VIA station. There is a small restaurant in the station itself. Call 800-361-5390 for reservations.

Taxi Jonquière, 542-4569. Budget **rental cars** in nearby Chicoutimi will pick up and drop off at station with advance arrangements., (418) 545-8320. City **buses** use station as a terminal.

Holiday Inn Saguenay, 2675 boul. du Royaume, G7S 5B8; (418) 548-3124 or 800-363-3124. Large, attractive high-rise hotel, about four miles from the station. $89.

-**Hotel Jean Dequen**, 2841 boul. du Royaume, G7S 4K6; (418) 548-7173. Small 12-room hotel, about three miles from the station. Ask for a room that does not front on highway. $35.

There is much to do in this remote but fascinating area, although you might consider brushing up on your French. Ninety-eight percent of the populace speak that language, and bilingualism is even less of a trait here than in Québec City and Montréal. This is part of the region's appeal and adds to the adventure. Highlights include: breathtaking **scenic cruises** on North America's longest fiord; tours of the **Alcan aluminum plant**, the Free World's largest; tours of **Shipshaw**, an Alcan dam and enormous power plant; and, in nearby Chicoutimi, the excellent **Saugenay-Lac St. John Museum** with regional artifacts.

Other Québec Service

The *Abitibi* provides triweekly overnight service from **Montréal to Hervey and Senneterre,** departing Montréal in the evening Monday, Wednesday and Friday, and departing Senneterre late in the day Sunday, Tuesday and Thursday. Service is extended to Taschereau from Senneterre Tuesday and Thursday and to Cochrane on from Senneterre on Saturday. These extended trains return, departing late afternoon from Taschereau Tuesday and Thursday and departing late morning from Cochrane on Sunday. There are sleeping cars and snack and beverage service to Senneterre. Coach seats are unreserved.

Cochrane
North Bay
Toronto

Northlander

eading north (as its name implies) from Toronto, the *Northlander's* principal destinations are North Bay and Cochrane. The North Bay area is particularly appealing to the outdoorsman, with nearby Lake Nipissing being a major draw. Cochrane, farther to the north, is the southern terminus of the popular *Polar Bear Express* that takes the adventurous to Moosonee on the lower tip of James Bay. Here, Ontario's oldest permanent English-speaking settlement—Moose Factory—holds forth. To continue on to Moosonee, an overnight stay is required in Cochrane.

Unfortunately, the *Northlander* is no longer comprised of unique sets of European built, articulated streamliner equipment. These jewels, which once were the reason many rode the *Northlander*, literally reached the point of no return and became too expensive to maintain. The Ontario Northland Railway, which operates the *Northlander*, has replaced the streamliner with more conventional equipment.

NORTHBOUND SCHEDULE (Condensed)
Toronto, ON - Early Afternoon Departure
North Bay, ON - Late Afternoon
Cochrane, ON - Late Evening Arrival

SOUTHBOUND SCHEDULE (Condensed)
Cochrane, ON - Early Morning Departure
North Bay, ON - Early Afternoon
Toronto, ON - Early Evening Arrival

FREQUENCY - Daily, except Saturday.
SEATING - Standard coaches.
DINING - Full meal service.
BAGGAGE - Carry-on only.
RESERVATIONS - Reservation of coach seats on purchase of tickets.
LENGTH OF TRIP - 482 miles in 9 1/2 hours.

ROUTE LOG

For route description between Toronto and Washago, see that portion of *Canadian* log, page 327.

0:00 (0:19) Depart Washago, and terrain immediately begins to shift from rich farming countryside to rugged, forested lakelands called Muskoka. Last ice age carved granite base rock into dramatic shapes making numerous rock cuts necessary along route.
0:04 (0:15) Cross one of region's numerous canals where pleasure craft create colorful scene, on right.
0:19 (0:00) Arrive Gravenhurst.

GRAVENHURST, ON - Long popular with the rich and famous, this serene Victorian town is still a tourist center for those wanting to visit the Muskoka Lakes region.
0:00 (0:33) Depart Gravenhurst.
0:01 (0:32) Aforementioned Gull Lake is just through trees on right.
0:12 (0:21) Pass high over south branch of Muskoka River where falls can be seen at

right and boats can occasionally be spotted on left, as train enters Bracebridge.

0:29 (0:04) Siding Lake appears at left.

0:33 (0:00) Arrive Huntsville.

 HUNTSVILLE, ON - This is another lake-country resort town and offers boat cruises along the Muskoka River to Peninsula Lake. Also, Algonquin Provincial Park, a popular canoeing and fishing area, is just east of here.

0:00 (1:01) Departing Huntsville, Lake Vernon is off to left.

0:01 (1:00) Cross very scenic Hunters Bay.

0:04 (0:57) Lumber mill, a frequent sight throughout Canada's forest lands, is on right.

0:24 (0:37) Golf course, on left, is very inviting scene. North branch of Magnetawan flows nearby, a stream we must cross several times.

0:33 (0:28) Through Burk's Falls where old station once served those boarding popular Magnetawan River steamer.

0:54 (0:07) Through attractive Sundridge, which caters to fishermen hoping to land deep-water trout found in waters of Lake Bernard, on right.

1:01 (0:00) Arrive South River.

 SOUTH RIVER, ON - Here, canoeists find ready access to Algonquin Provincial Park.

0:00 (0:56) Depart South River.

0:01 (0:55) Cross South River where waterfalls can be seen off to left.

0:07 (0:49) High trestle carries tracks over small Viaduct Creek.

0:15 (0:41) Through town of Trout Creek, where small white church on right seems to wear an ice cream cone for a steeple top.

0:51 (0:05) Entering outskirts of North Bay, our CN tracks intersect those of CP Rail.

0:56 (0:00) Arrive North Bay's new ONR Station.

 NORTH BAY, ON - Rail buffs will recognize North Bay as home base for the Ontario Northland Railway. Chartered in 1902 as the Timiskaming and Northern Ontario Railway, it started out to serve the farming country north of here but ultimately found its way to Moosonee, its

northern terminus on James Bay, in 1932.

North Bay is a popular destination for fishermen, particularly those wanting to try their luck on adjacent Lake Nipissing. Hunting is also an important North Bay recreational activity.

0:00 (1:29) Depart North Bay.

0:05 (0:24) Numerous small boats are docked at Trout Lake Marina on immediate right.

1:30 (0:02) Arm of Temagami Lake, at left, reaches to edge of town. Note nicely manicured park, boat docks and walkways along shore, a project of Ontario's Development Program.

1:32 (0:00) Arrive Temagami, a Cree Indian word for "deep water."

 TEMAGAMI, ON - This logging community (mostly harvesting white pine) is also a hunting and fishing center.

0:00 (0:41) Depart Temagami.

0:06 (0:35) Lakes are everywhere; one of area's large bodies of water now appears at right.

0:20 (0:21) Note unusual approach to supporting telephone poles which are propped upright with an abundance of rocks.

0:30 (0:11) Dam on left holds back Montréal River.

0:41 (0:00) Arrive Cobalt.

 COBALT, ON - Mining was Cobalt's reason for being. It started in 1903 when, legend has it, a blacksmith heaved his hammer at a fox and missed. The heavy tool chipped into a rock and disclosed what turned out to be the world's richest silver vein. The community still bears the imprint of its early helter-skelter construction. Today, Cobalt's Northern Ontario Mining Museum has perhaps the best display anywhere of native silver.

0:00 (0:14) Depart Cobalt.

0:06 (0:08) Looking right, Lake Timiskaming is beautiful setting for Haileybury. Land on far side of lake is province of Québec.

0:10 (0:04) Plant at right processes some of Ontario's trees into particle board.

0:14 (0:00) Arrive New Liskeard.

NEW LISKEARD, ON - This is a farming and dairying center. Northbound passengers may question this, but once the *Northlander* departs, there can be no doubt. The Little Clay Belt, as it is called, starts just north of town. This fertile farming area can produce many crops grown in more southern climes in spite of a shorter growing season.

0:00 (0:24) Departing New Liskeard, note hundreds of canoes stacked on end in lot of manufacturer on left.

0:02 (0:22) Now, enter upon fertile farmlands of Little Clay Belt, just described. If Iowa were flat, it would look like this.

0:23 (0:01) Cross High over Englehart River.

0:24 (0:00) Arriving Englehart, note 1921 steam locomotive (a 4-6-2, #701), built for the Timiskaming and Northern Ontario Railway, nicely maintained in its green and gold colors, on left.

 ENGLEHART, ON - This town has its roots in both lumbering and railroading.

0:00 (0:30) Depart Englehart's nicely renovated station. Large pulp mill can be seen off to left.

0:08 (0:22) High trestle carries *Northlander* above Blanche River.

0:30 (0:00) Arrive Swastika.

 SWASTIKA, ON - Gold was discovered just south of here after the turn of the century. Swastika was born and soon found itself at the center of one of Canada's richest mineral finds.

0:00 (0:45) Depart Swastika.

0:05 (0:40) Cross arctic divide beyond which all streams flow north to James Bay. Numerous rivers and creeks are crossed before reaching Matheson.

0:45 (0:00) Arrive Matheson.

 MATHESON, ON - Matheson, entrenched in Ontario's northern mining region, still maintains itself as an agricultural trade center.

0:00 (0:20) Depart Matheson.

0:12 (0:08) Crossing Driftwood River, look to left to see Monteith Correctional Centre. Just west of here, two famous gold mines, the Dome and the Hollinger, were discovered in the early 1900s.

0:20 (0:00) Arrive Porquis.

 PORQUIS, ON - At one time, those continuing to Cochrane transferred to an awaiting motorcoach at this community. Now, however, the *Northlander* continues into Cochrane.

0:00 (0:25) Depart Porquis.

0:25 (0:00) Arrive Cochrane.

 COCHRANE, ON - Cochrane has all the appearances of a modern-day frontier town, a bustling little city thriving on a blend of tourism, hunting, fishing, mining, lumbering and railroading. This is the southern terminus of the *Polar Bear Express*, Ontario Northland's popular train to Moosonee on James Bay.

 ONR Station is situated on the edge of Cochrane's small downtown area. This facility, completed in 1991, includes a hotel occupying space directly above. Call 272-4228.

 The inter-city **bus terminal** is at the train station.

 Cochrane Chamber of Commerce, (705) 272-4926.

 Reservations should be made well in advance, particularly during Cochrane's busy summer season.

-**Cochrane Station Inn**, P.O. Box 1926, P0L 1C0; (705) 272-3500. New in 1991, above the ONR Station, 23 rooms. Reception disk is located in the station lobby. $73.

-The **Northern Lites Motel**, Highway 11, Box 1720, P0L 1C0; (705) 272-4281. A short cab ride, or a healthy mile walk, from the station and downtown. Rooms are nice and large, and a good restaurant is open throughout the day. $50.

Polar Bear Express

The *Polar Bear Express* heads north from Cochrane, Ontario, into a land of muskegs, wilderness rivers, moose and bears—but, sorry, no polar bears. The end of the line is James Bay, the southernmost extension of Hudson Bay where Moosonee and its sister outpost, island-ensconsed Moose Factory, live an isolated existence. (Sorry again, there is no moose factory at Moose Factory.)

The draw is the uniqueness of the region and the opportunity to visit Ontario's oldest permanent English-speaking settlement—Moose Factory. That settlement of 1,600 Cree Indians and whites is reached from Moosonee by boat in the summer, by road across the frozen Moosonee River in the winter, and by helicopter during the ice-breakup season. Much of its pioneer past has been maintained, and touring historic buildings and other artifacts gives visitors a strong sense of "the way it was."

A Hudson's Bay Company fort was established on what was then called Hayes Island in 1673, but within 13 years the French captured the installation that had been defended by only 16 men. The English regained it by treaty in 1732. This remote trading post remained virtually unreachable by land until 1923, when the Temiskaming Northern Ontario Railway, now the Ontario Northland, reached Moosonee. These two largest isolated communities in Ontario still remain relatively unknown.

SCHEDULES AND EQUIPMENT - The Ontario Northland Railway, owned and operated by the Province of Ontario, runs round-trip excursion trains (The **Polar Bear Express**) daily, except Friday, from late June through early September. Departures from Cochrane are early morning and from Moosonee late afternoon. The trip takes just over four hours in each direction.

In addition to these summertime excursions, there is a **local** that runs twice a week in the summer and three times a week the remainder of the year. The local is another experience, carrying Indians and hunters from flag stop to flag stop as well as tourists to Moosonee. The local leaves Cochrane midmorning on Tuesday and Thursday in the summer and Monday, Wednesday and Friday the rest of the year. It leaves Moosonee midafternoon on Friday and midmorning on Wednesday in the summer and midafternoon Tuesday, Thursday and Saturday the rest of the year.

Passengers are transported in nicely refurbished rail cars that contrast sharply with the surrounding countryside.

FOOD SERVICE is provided by a full service diner and snack bar on both trains.

RESERVATIONS are required for the *Polar Bear Express* excursions trains. For reservations and information, including tour packages, write Ontario Northland Transportation Commission, 65 Front St. W., Toronto, ON, M5J 1E6; or phone (416) 314-3750 (Toronto) or (705) 472-4500 (North Bay).

Route Log

 COCHRANE, ON - See page 316.

0:00 (4:20) Depart Cochrane as polar bear on town's water tower, on right, watches over all.

(Note: Mileposts are quite visible on this line and are included as additional reference points.)

0:10 (4:10) MP 5. Cockrane's airport handles normal variety of wheeled aircraft on runways as well as seaplanes on waters of Lillabelle Lake on right.

0:13 (4:07) MP 7. Farms interspersed with wooded hills will prevail for several miles as train crosses northern rim of Ontario's Clay Belt.

0:19 (4:01) MP 11. Abitibi River is on right. Stream will be followed off and on as it drifts toward James Bay.

0:28 (3:52) MP 18. Large sawmill of Ontario Paper Company is on right at Gardiner.

1:01 (3:19) MP 43. At Island Falls, cabin on right has own little rail conveyance parked on walkway of cross ties on right.

1:02 (3:18) MP 44. One of numerous Ontario Northland communication towers is on right. Company has several million dollars invested in system that handles radio, telephone and television transmissions to and from remote Northlands.

1:04 (3:16) MP 45. Cross broad waters of Abitibi River where Abitibi River Island Falls Power Plant and Dam can be glimpsed upriver on right.

1:05 (3:15) MP 46. Skip beneath power line leading from power station, then pass another lumber operation of Ontario Paper Company.

1:09 (3:11) MP 49. Expanse of dead trees was caused by June 1976 forest fire.

1:16 (3:04) MP 55. Green wooden boxes at trackside hold shims of wood used for leveling tracks affected by springtime frost heaves. This phenomenon is typical wherever muskeg or permafrost is prevalent.

1:33 (2:47) MP 69. Fraserdale is the northernmost point for road service in this region.

1:39 (2:41) MP 74. Terrain grows more rugged with aspen and black spruce everywhere.

1:48 (2:32) MP 80. Cross 50th Parallel.

2:06 (2:14) MP 93. Huge Otter Rapids generating facility is on right, one of four highly automated hydroelectric stations in region, operated by microwave signals from central location.

2:10 (2:10) MP 96. Note "stuffed folks" standing in yard of Miller's cabin, on right, at Coral Rapids. Diamonds have actually been found in this vicinity. We are now halfway to our destination.

2:47 (1:33) MP 126. Lignite, a very low grade of coal, lies just beneath the surface. Mining these deposits has been considered, but development has yet to occur due to low quality and cost of removal.

3:01 (1:19) MP 131. Cross Onakawana River.

3:09 (1:11) MP 138. Cross first of several "upside-down bridges" on route, designed to permit ice flows and other floating objects to clear structure. Supporting girders are above instead of below bridge.

3:15 (1:05) MP 142. Cross Moose River on 1,800-foot-long trestle, longest on route. Crossing here during ice breakup in spring can be spectacular as tons of ice drift downstream toward James Bay.

3:37 (0:43) MP 158. Cross Otakwahegan River.

3:39 (0:41) MP 159. Cross 51st Parallel.

3:40 (0:40) MP 160. Occasional temporary goose-hunting camps might be spotted through trees. Indians are permitted to hunt year round by aboriginal right.

3:44 (0:36) MP 162. Cross Cheepash River. Extensive Gypsum deposits are nearby.

4:02 (0:18) MP 174. Cross Kwataboahegan River on second upside-down bridge. Others will be at mileposts 176 and 180.

4:20 (0:00) MP 186. Arrive Moosonee, where "Sons of Martha" monument on right commemorates workers who built the Abitibi generating station and extension of railroad to Moosonee. Handsome church, farther to right, is Cathedral of the Oblates Mission.

MOOSONEE, ON - This is the northern terminus of the ONR. First impressions are not great, as the town has never fully entered the 20th century. Streets are either muddy, dusty or frozen, depending on the season. But the town has spirit and has been doing a lot to make things more attractive—new sidewalks, boardwalk at the docks, etc. Except for some fast-food outlets, buildings range from neo-government to early ramshackle, but there is still a certain fascination. Perhaps it's the frontier.

Cree Indians are the major inhabitants, whose lifestyle reflects their long adaptation to living in this remote region. Government and tourism are the major economic mainstays, with the latter holding forth during a very limited season. It is a jumping-off point for hunters and others needing to head farther north toward the Arctic.

In the fall, the town bustles with goose hunters heading to various hunting camps, many such outposts being surprisingly posh and expensive. But Moose Factory Island is where most "tourists" go.

During the winter, the scene changes. This is when the ground (and the river) is frozen, making it possible to travel virtually anywhere by snowmobile. Indian villages north of here, inaccessible by land during the summer months, are reached by "The Winter Road" that consists of packed snow from hundreds of snowmobiles and ATVs. Instead of a time of confinement, it's a time of release.

If you plan to stay overnight,be sure to make reservations well in advance during the summer. Two of the newer accommodations are:

-**Osprey Country Inn**, Box 116, 69 Ferguson St., P0L 1Y0; (705) 336-2226. Restaurant, fully licensed bar. $75 (including taxes).

-**Trappers Lodge**, P.O. Box 220, Moose Cree Complex, Moose Factory, P0L 1W0; (705) 658-4440. On the island. Restaurant. $85 (plus tax).

Before starting out to explore the area, be sure to obtain an ONR walking-tour booklet that describes the area.

Polar Bear Express —
Moosonee, ON
JACK SWANSON

A visit to the **Museum Car**, which stands across from the station, is easy to work into one's schedule. From there, it's about a half mile down First Street (which curves to the left) where the **boats dock**. Just beyond the docks, on the town side of the road, is **Revillon Fréres Museum** with artifacts and photos of early Moosonee days.

At the docks, large Rupert House canoes offer an interesting adventure in reaching **Moose Factory**, situated in the Moosonee River. (ONR suggests buying a one-way fare, since there are many boats, and your return, therefore, can be at any time. They also suggest being at the dock for the return at least an hour before train time.) Guided tour boats are also available.

Once on the Moose Factory Island, there are numerous sights to explore. Highlights include: the **Centennial Park Museum**, operated by Ontario Northland Transportation Commission, which has displays explaining how the area was developed from the formation of the Hudson's Bay Company; **St. Thomas Church**, with its unique floor holes to allow floodwaters to enter, thus avoiding a recurrence of an episode when the church floated away; **Anglican Church Parish Hall** where local crafts can be purchased as well as light lunches and refreshments; and the **cemetery** with tombstones dating back to early traders and missionaries.

Hearst

Sault Ste. Marie

Algoma Central

To "ride in the tracks of the black bear," you have to get up early. At the Algoma Central Railway's Sault Ste. Marie ("The Soo") depot, boarding for the exceedingly popular Agawa Canyon Tour Train begins at 7:00 am, and it's wise to board as soon as possible. Departures are at 8:00 am.

Incorporated in 1899, the ACR's route winds through dense forests and rugged hills and crosses many rivers and deep ravines. Its name at that time, the Algoma Central Hudson Bay Railway, or AC & HB, led some wags to call it the "All Curves and High Bridges."

Besides its most popular Agawa Canyon Tour Train, the ACR operates a Snow Train and its regular Soo-Hearst passenger trains.

Agawa Canyon Tour trains usually arrive back at The Soo on time at 5:00 pm with passengers so enthused about their "ride in the tracks of the black bear" (the logo for this train) that they crowd shoulder-to-shoulder into the depot's interesting gift shop. Veterans of the trip advise shopping the day before when picking up tickets, preferably before that day's train arrives back at The Soo.

FREQUENCY - Varies by train. Canyon Tours run from early June through mid-October. The Snow Train runs Saturdays and Sundays only from January through mid-March. The regular Hearst passenger trains #1 and #2 operate six days a week (no Monday service) from mid-May to mid-

October, and weekends only the rest of the year (northbound Fri., Sat., Sun.; southbound Sat., Sun., Mon.).

SEATING - Coaches only. ACR recommends picking up tickets a day in advance for all trains, even though reservations are available and required for the Canyon Tour and Snow Trains.

DINING - Dining cars, operated by E.J. Merini Catering, stay with the Canyon Tour and Snow Trains the entire trip, and provide hot breakfasts and lunches, as well as snacks and box lunches. Lunch may not be available on board Trains #1 and #2.

BAGGAGE - No service on Canyon Tour or Snow Trains. Regular trains provide baggage cars that carry an unbelievable variety of articles from fishing poles to snowmobiles.

RESERVATIONS - Write to: Algoma Central Railway, Passenger Sales, P.O. Box 130, Sault Ste. Marie, ON, Canada, P6A 6Y2. Call (705) 946-7300 or 800-242-9287.

LENGTH OF TRIP - 296 miles in 10 hours (Soo-Hearst).

ROUTE LOG

(A more detailed log of the route between Sault Ste. Marie and Canyon is furnished by ACR in its "Guide to Agawa Canyon Tour." Since mileposts are quite visible on this route, they are shown below after the passing times. Since Trains #1 and #2 stop almost anywhere and everywhere, no attempt has been made to list all stops and times are approximate.)

SAULT STE. MARIE, ON - The ACR was heavily involved in the development of The Soo waterfront, including the Station Mall shopping center and the Holiday Inn overlooking the river, both near the depot. Boat tours of the Soo Locks are available nearby.

Algoma Central Railway Station, 129 Bay Street. An attractive, modern station near the Station Mall shopping center. Call 946-7300.

Two good hotels are close to the station: The **Quality Inn** (705) 945-9264, $95, is across from the station; and the **Holiday Inn**, (705) 949-0611, $95, is about four blocks away. Both are near the Station Mall with shopping, restaurants and theaters.

0:00 (3:30) Milepost 0. Depart The Soo. Some of The Soo's more interesting sights appear in rapid succession on left: Canadian Lock, St. Mary Paper Mill with its Gothic-like structures, mile-long International Bridge and Algoma Steel Corporation.

0:39 (2:51) MP 19. Cross 810-foot-long, 100-foot-high trestle with a sweeping view of Bellevue Valley to left. Lake Superior can be glimpsed in far distance.

1:30 (2:00) MP 57. Idyllic Trout Lake is at right, with cabins and canoes adding woodland charm.

1:38 (1:52) MP 62. On right, boulder-strewn Pine Lake is one of trip's prettiest scenes.

2:20 (1:20) MP 81. Cross Batchewana River.

2:44 (0:46) MP 92. Curve right across Montréal River on this railroad's most famous trestle, 130 feet high and 1,550 feet long. Below us to left, ground level drops another 100 feet below base of trestle where one of three dams generating electricity for The Soo is located.

2:52 (0:38) MP 97. Crest highest point on line, 1,589 feet above sea level.

3:06 (0:24) MP 102. Begin our descent to canyon floor: 500 feet in 12 miles. Outstanding view to left, all the way to Lake Superior. Deep within canyon, Agawa River

meanders prettily.

3:20 (0:10) MP 112. At canyon level, cross Agawa. Bridal Veil Falls appears to right, Black Beaver Falls to left.

3:30 (0:00) MP 114. Arrive at Canyon.

 CANYON - This is the destination of the Agawa Canyon Tour Train. Here the crew switches the locomotives to the opposite end of that train in preparation for the return trip. (Trains #1 and #2 pause here, but not long enough for through passengers to detrain and see any of the sights.)

Things to do here include:
Picnic in the developed park near the train or farther away in a more rustic area; if you have the required license, fish the river for speckled trout; view the waterfalls; walk up to the lookout points—the intermediate one is fairly easy to reach, the upper point requires a long climb up wooden stairs, the round trip taking considerable time.

0:00 (1:24) MP 114. Depart Canyon.

0:06 (1:18) MP 117. River's descent is punctuated by series of lovely cascades and waterfalls, on right.

0:11 (1:13) MP 120. Cross notorious "Chinese Bridge," built by a Canadian manufacturer for Nationalist China. Firm had contract nullified by Chairman Mao when he came into power, so bridge was sold at a reduced price to an opportunistic Algoma Central.

0:16 (1:08) MP 123. Sign for Windy Lake Lodge identifies flag stop for fishermen in summertime and skiers in winter. Many backcountry hostelries are sprinkled along this stretch to accommodate sportsmen who prefer their wilderness liberally laced with comfort.

0:31 (0:53) MP 132. At Millwood, large lumbering operation is on left.

1:00 (0:24) MP 149. Woods present nice stand of birch trees, at right. Similar in appearance to aspens, which are also found along route, birches are distinguished by their whiter-than-snow trunks. Spruce is a prevalent evergreen, while maple is a common hardwood.

1:10 (0:14) MP 157. Train experiences brief encounter with "outside" world as tracks cross Canada's Highway 101.

1:24 (0:00) MP 165. Arrive Hawk Junction.

 HAWK JUNCTION, ON - There should be enough time to stretch for a few minutes at this Algoma Central division point. The rail yards provide an interesting array of equipment—snowplows, cabooses, diesel locomotives—and long strings of red-painted baggage carts at trackside. This is a jumping-off point for the old trappers' canoe route.

0:00 (3.24) MP 165. Depart Hawk Junction and head deeper into wilderness of Canadian Shield. Watch for moose, bear and white-tailed deer.

0:28 (2:56) MP 184. Dubreuilville is scene of bustling lumber operation, with conveyors, cranes, tracks and a wood burner all laboring at left.

0:45 (2:39) MP 195. At Franz, cross main line of CP Rail.

0:59 (2:25) MP 206. At Wabatong, note "Petticoat Junction" cottage by Lake Wabatongushi, on right.

1:05 (2:19) MP 210. Finger-like Oba Lake extends along tracks at left. Until now, waters have flowed to south. North of here, streams drain across Arctic Watershed north to Hudson Bay.

1:09 (2:15) MP 212. Cross portion of Lake Oba on quarter-mile-long bridge constructed not on a firm foundation, but on buoyant footings that literally float tracks on lake's surface.

1:14 (2:10) MP 215. Expansive body of water on left is Lake Tatnall.

1:49 (1:35) MP 245. Briefly merge with CN main line and yards while crossing that line at Oba. "The Last Resort" stands at right, presumably final home of retired wag. CN tracks carry VIA's *Canadian*.

2:10 (1:14) MP 254. Moose rack over door of hunter's cabin, on left, is most appropriate decoration.

2:40 (0:44) MP 275. Mead is first town since Hawk Junction that has luxury of paved highway access.

3:23 (0:01) MP 295. Pass one of Hearst's

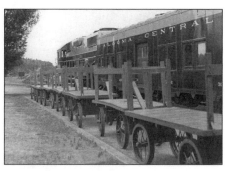

Baggage carts —
Hawk Junction, ON
JACK SWANSON

numerous lumber mills, on left. Plywood industry has long been a Hearst mainstay.

3:24 (0:00) MP 296. Arrive Hearst.

 HEARST, ON - If you visit Hearst in the summer or fall, it's a good idea to have reservations. This is a sportsman's haven with thousands of nearby lakes supplying outstanding fishing as well as excellent goose hunting. Just as important is big game hunting, particularly for moose that abound in this region. Snowmobiling on miles of trails is also popular in the winter months.

Lumbering is the principal industry in this largely French-speaking community. Several large sawmills operate here, some offering tours.

The **station** is located directly behind two of the town's nicer motels and two blocks from George (Main) Street. The waiting room is closed, but tickets may be purchased on board.

Bus service is available to and from Cochrane, connecting to VIA's *Northlander.*

The **Queen's Motel**, (705) 362-4361, is directly in front of the station and has large, comfortable rooms, a sauna and whirlpool, and an indoor pool. $66. The adjacent **Companion Motel**, (705) 362-4304, also has nice accommodations. It has a good restaurant and an interesting lounge filled with local color. $63.

White River   Sudbury

Sudbury to White River

W hite River is still served by VIA, but just barely. The *Canadian* was removed from the CP line through White River in January of 1990, but VIA received a mandate to continue service to that town. As a result, rail diesel cars still make triweekly runs between Sudbury and White River. Trains depart Sudbury midmorning, Tuesday, Thursday and Saturday, and depart White River midmorning, Sunday, Wednesday and Friday. The trip takes approximately nine hours. There are numerous flag stops besides the scheduled stops shown.

ROUTE LOG

SUDBURY, ON - The town was founded in 1823 during the construction of the Canadian Pacific Railway, and it was during this activity that sufficient ore discoveries were made in order to induce serious mining. Today, Sudbury is the largest nickel-producing area in the world. The "Sudbury Basin" is a depression in the earth approximately 17 miles wide and 35 miles in length around which most of the mining activity is carried on by Inco Metals and Falconbridge.

There are three **VIA stations** in the Sudbury area. The CP station at 233 Elgin Street is on the edge of downtown, and now only serves the RDC service to White River. VIA's transcontinental train uses the CN stations in nearby Capreol and Sudbury Junction.

For reservations and other information, call 800-361-1235 (from Sudbury).

Metro **Cab**, 673-6000. **Greyhound**, on Falconbridge Highway, is about three miles from downtown.

Howard Johnson Hotel, 390 Elgin St., P3B 1B1; (705) 675-1273. Nice rooms and a very good restaurant. Some rooms overlook rail yards and station. Two blocks from the CP station. Includes continental breakfast. $60.

One of Sudbury's principal attractions is the **Big Nickel Mine** tours. Also, smelter slag pourings at night are both eerie and beautiful. **Science North** is the region's most popular place to visit, containing hands-on science exhibits.

0:00 (0:53) Departing Sudbury, Community Arena stands in forefront of downtown hub on right, while attractive residential district overlooks activity from atop bluffs on left.

0:04 (0:50) Multi-domed St. Volodymyr Ukrainian Greek Orthodox Church on right is impressive example of Ukrainian Baroque architecture.

0:06 (0:48) On outskirts of town, train winds through small mini-canyons carved within rocky terrain. Nickel open-pit mines are a frequent observation throughout this stretch. Watch for molten slag being dumped.

0:17 (0:35) Typical of most small Ontario communities, elegant church on left at

Chelmsford is prominent centerpiece of town.

0:27 (0:27) Cross aptly named Vermilion River.

0:32 (0:23) Beautiful Onaping Falls tumble down by trackside on right.

0:35 (0:20) Route wends its way past myriad lakes, so numerous that individual identification would be impractical. A scenic wonderland of shimmering beauty, wetlands of Ontario are a recreation haven, with hunting and fishing camps nestled picturesquely along many shorelines. Famous Canadian moose is also a frequent visitor to these parts, often seen lumbering through neighboring marshes.

0:39 (0:16) More waterfalls embellish scenery on right.

0:47 (0:09) Beaver colonies, like those entrenched on right, are perhaps most intriguing architectural structures seen throughout lakelands.

0:55 (0:00) Arrive Cartier.

 CARTIER, ON - A small settlement named for Sir Etienne Cartier.

0:00 (3:16) Depart Cartier.

0:36 (2:37) Just past Sheahan, cross Spanish River which then follows on right.

0:55 (2:21) Names of many towns along route are derived from Indian geographic descriptions. One such example is found here at Metagama, which, when translated, means "river flows out of lake." Name refers to Spanish River which finds its source a few miles north in Biscotasi Lake.

1:20 (1:56) Ducks and geese are sometimes amusing attraction at Biscotasing, waddling about well-kept grounds of station house on right. Resort community is set atop hillside on left, overlooking arm of Biscotasi Lake. Weathered church is particularly picturesque.

1:44 (1:33) Large timber mill operation, on right at Ramsey, is one of first to be observed in countless succession of such facilities seen throughout Canada. While some enterprises harvest woodlands for lumber, pulping operations are much more prevalent.

2:25 (0:56) On left, follow then cross Wakamagasing River, approaching quaint little town of Sultan.

3:00 (0:21) Cross Nemegosenda River just before passing through Nemegos.

3:14 (0:11) Apparently not designed for sleepwalkers, note island cabin, curiously isolated in midst of Lake Poulin on right.

3:15 (0:10) At Devon, freight chutes on right facilitate loading of wood chips—an important byproduct of milling process, used in manufacture of particle board and paper pulp.

3:25 (0:00) Arriving Chapleau, finely preserved CPR steam locomotive, number 5453, is proud fixture of park on left.

CHAPLEAU, ON - Although logging is now Chapleau's main thrust, at one time this was the most important railroad town between Sudbury and Lake Superior. Solid bedrock of the Canadian Shield, when not protruding, is frequently only a foot or so below the surface, and construction of the Canadian Pacific through this area was extremely difficult. Cuts were stubborn and lack of soil for fills was just as troublesome, with soil being shipped in for embankments. Furthermore, there were treacherous sink holes which would sometimes not make themselves known until after several trains had rumbled over them.

Next to the steam locomotive is Centennial Museum with natural history and pioneer exhibits, as well as the Rotary International Friendship Table which has wood inlays from around the world. On the station lawn is a monument to Louis Hemon, well known Canadian author, who died near here when struck by a train.

0:00 (3:07) Departing Chapleau, beautiful homes border edge of Kebsquasheshing Lake, both right and left.

0:14 (2:53) Sign at right indicates location of Chapleau Crown Game Preserve. Tracks form southern boundary of this park for several miles.

0:50 (2:17) Small red shack at right was once depot for Bolkow.

1:27 (1:40) Approaching Missanabie, cross arm of Dog Lake, one of region's largest. Once in town, note general store and old hotel huddled scenically along lake shore on left.

2:00 (1:10) Pass through picturesque community of Franz, tucked neatly in cove alongside Hobon Lake. Here, tracks of CP Rail cross those of legendary Algoma Central. Latter is known for spectacular autumn leaf excursions.

2:15 (0:57) Note dam on left as train crosses Magpie River. Structure was one of earlier hydropower facilities in region.

3:09 (0:06) Join White River on left, then cross several times subsequently. As name might imply, surging falls and foamy rapids are common throughout its course.

3:15 (0:00) Arrive White River.

WHITE RIVER, ON - This small village is situated at one of the few highway intersections in this region, making it a popular base for hunters and fishermen. Its weather station records some of the coldest temperatures in North America. The mercury once dipped to minus 72 degrees Fahrenheit—just 6 degrees above the Canadian record.

Continental Motel, 217 Hwy. 17; (807) 822-2500. Clean and inexpensive. About one and half miles from the station. $49.

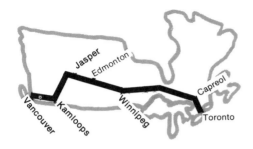

Canadian

A train trip that spans the dominion of Canada is a remarkable visual experience. Nearly every shape and form of Canada's interior beauty sweeps by on one of the longest train rides anywhere. (The longest ride of all shows you a lot of Siberia.) It's almost as though mountains, plains, lakes, rivers and forests were carefully positioned in dramatic sequence just to please those cruising on the *Canadian*.

Heading westward from Toronto, the *Canadian* encounters the lake-studded forests of Ontario's Canadian Shield country before a brief pause at Winnipeg. The route then angles across the ultra-flat expanses of Canada's wheatlands before reaching Edmonton, where soon thereafter, passengers get their first look at the Canadian Rockies—dead ahead. The ensuing trip through these giant bastions of western Canada is the crowning touch to a journey still ranked as one of the best of all travel experiences.

But it's more than just scenery. VIA has performed a near-miracle in the restoration of the rail cars used on the *Canadian*. The service and accommodations are the finest of any regularly scheduled train in North America.

WESTBOUND SCHEDULE (Condensed)
Toronto, ON - Early Afternoon Departure (Tuesday, Thursday, Saturday)
Capreol (Sudbury), ON - Midevening
Winnipeg, MB - Late Afternoon Arrival and

Early Evening Departure (2nd Day)
Edmonton, AB - Early Morning (3rd Day)
Jasper, AB - Early Afternoon (3rd Day)
Kamloops, BC - Late Evening (3rd Day)
Vancouver, BC - Early Morning Arrival (4th Day) (Friday, Sunday and Tuesday)

EASTBOUND SCHEDULE (Condensed)
Vancouver, BC - Midevening Departure (Thursday, Saturday, Monday)
Kamloops, BC - Early Morning (2nd Day)
Jasper, AB - Early Afternoon (2nd Day)
Edmonton, AB - Midevening (2nd Day)
Winnipeg, MB - Early Afternoon (3rd Day)
Capreol (Sudbury), ON - Early Afternoon (4th Day)
Toronto, ON - Midevening Arrival (5th Day) (Thursday, Sunday, Tuesday)

FREQUENCY - Three times each week (see above).
SEATING - Standard coaches, Skyline dome cars and Park observation/dome (for sleeping car passengers).
DINING - Dining car with complete meal and beverage service. (Meals are included with price of bedroom.)
SLEEPING - Sleeping cars with berths (sections), single, double and triple bedrooms. Sleeping cars have a shower in each car.
BAGGAGE - Checked baggage handled at most stops.
RESERVATIONS - All-reserved train.
LENGTH OF TRIP - 2,765 miles, taking approximately three days.

ROUTE LOG

 TORONTO, ON - See page 299.
0:00 (0:46) Depart Toronto.
0:01 (0:45) CN Tower, world's tallest free-standing structure at 1,821 feet, soars skyward on left.
0:02 (0:44) $400-million SkyDome, on left, overshadows lower downtown Toronto. This bulbous edifice, completed in 1989, was built to house baseball's Blue Jays, shops, restaurants and a 350-room hotel. On nicer days, roof can be retracted to an open position in 30 minutes to put 90% of its spectators in sunshine. While passing this stupendous coliseum, be sure to look up to see whimsical groupings of "spectators" protruding from building like modern-day gargoyles.
0:04 (0:42) Tops of brick buildings and sign on grassy knoll are all that can be seen of Historic Fort York Park, on left. Park features restored British garrison from War of 1812.
0:23 (0:23) Haviland aircraft plant appears on right.
0:45 (0:00) Arrive Newmarket.

 NEWMARKET, ON - Its proximity to Toronto and the rich agricultural lands that surround it make Newmarket an important regional trading center. Of particular interest is the town's historic Quaker Meeting House.
0:00 (0:31) Departing Newmarket, former leather works has been elegantly transformed into The Old Davis Tannery Centre shopping mall, adorned with purple awnings and a wonderful four-faced clock tower, on right.
0:01 (0:30) In early 1900s Canadian Government planned to make Newmarket a Great Lakes port by converting Little Holland River into a canal connecting with Lake Simcoe. Although plan was ultimately aborted, locks on right still survive.
0:31 (0:00) Arrive Barrie with Kempenfelt Bay, an arm of Lake Simcoe, at right.

 BARRIE, ON - This commercial center is situated on the shores of Kempenfelt Bay, the western arm of giant Lake Simcoe. Barrie is home to the Base Borden Military Museum with its unusually large collection of military memorabilia.
0:00 (0:25) Depart Barrie.
0:01 (0:24) In small park at right, 4-6-0 CN steam locomotive 1531 has been lovingly preserved.
0:02 (0:23) Modernistic work of metal art, on right, appears to be contemplating flight.
0:03 (0:22) Unusual archway spans city street in downtown Barrie, on left.
0:22 (0:03) Large complex of brick buildings attractively ensconced on hillside left, is Huronia Regional Centre, an institution that houses and works with the handicapped.
0:25 (0:00) Arrive Orillia.

ORILLIA, ON - Orillia is situated on the Trent-Severn Canal System, and has an economy maintained by light industrial activities. Stephen Leacock, Canada's foremost humorist, wrote many of his works while living here, and his home, a 19-room lakeshore mansion, can be toured by the public.
0:00 (0:16) Depart Orillia.
0:04 (0:12) Train creeps across swing bridge spanning Trent-Severn Waterway. This elaborate marine system, comprised of rivers, canals and lakes, snakes across Ontario's countryside linking Lake Ontario with Georgian Bay. Like Erie Canal, commercial traffic has all but disappeared from its waters while recreational use has blossomed and now dominates.
0:16 (0:00) Arrive Washago.

WASHAGO, ON - Nicely situated at the very northern tip of Lake Couchiching, an adjunct to larger Lake Simcoe, Washago comes from a similar Indian word meaning "sparkling waters."
0:00 (1:42) Depart Washago.
0:14 (1:28) Lakeside resort on right often has seaplanes parked in easy view of tracks.
1:00 (0:42) Expansive waters of Lake Joseph are now on right.
1:32 (0:08) Train now switches from CP line to tracks of CN.
1:41 (0:01) *Canadian* rumbles high above Seguin River on lengthy trestle (1,695 feet). Parry Sound is off to left while town of same name comes into view on right.

1:42 (0:00) Arrive Parry Sound.

PARRY SOUND, ON - Excellent fishing, swimming, hunting and boating have made this Georgian Bay community a very popular destination resort area. This is the main access to that area known as 30,000 Islands, the world's largest concentration of islands, which are situated along the shore of the Bay—an eastern satellite of Lake Huron.

0:00 (3:07) Depart Parry Sound.

0:40 (2:30) Cross Shawanaga River.

1:00 (2:10) Cross Magnetawan River.

2:00 (1:10) Cross French River, once a major canoe route between Lake Superior and Montréal.

3:00 (0:10) Black rock outcroppings and white-barked birch trees create bizarre landscape on approach to Sudbury Junction.

3:10 (0:00) Arrive Sudbury Junction.

SUDBURY JCT., ON - This is a brief stop in Sudbury's outskirts.

0:00 (0:32) Depart Sudbury Junction, and skim past eastern edge of greater Sudbury.

0:30 (0:00) Arrive Capreol.

CAPREOL, ON - This is another station used for Sudbury area passengers. Capreol is just a few miles north of downtown Sudbury.

0:00 (0:54) Depart Capreol.

0:01 (0:53) Cross very pretty Vermilion River which will accompany route beyond Laforest.

0:54 (0:00) Arrive Laforest.

Sudbury Basin

Millions of years ago, an enormous meteorite slammed into the earth's crust, forming a gouge some 35 miles in length and exposing rich deposits of nickel and other ores. During the construction of the railroad in the 1800s, these deposits were finally discovered in what is now known as the Sudbury Basin. Sudbury is now the world's largest producer of nickel; the large stack visible in the distance belongs to Inco's smelter and is the world's tallest at 1,250 feet.

Over the years, acid rain from the smoke of Sudbury's mining operations has largely denuded the immediate landscape, but more recent environmental technologies have improved the local scene. As a matter of fact, Sudbury boasts some of the region's finest flower gardens.

West of here the geography becomes increasingly alpine in nature. Rolling hills assume more rugged, angular features, while clusters of evergreens stand tall amidst a thicketed ground cover. Various species of pine, oak and ash, as well as tamarack, balsam, fir, white spruce, birch and hemlock are found in the Great Lakes Forest Region.

Geographic features encountered are characteristic of the Canadian Shield, with extensive lake systems and dense forests nurtured by soil that thinly covers bedrock. This bedrock is 500 million to 5 billion years old and covers one half of Canada as well as portions of the northern U.S. Muskegs (peat bogs) are abundant. Minerals are found throughout the region and mining is still prominent. Many ancient glacial lakes have gradually filled in with clay, creating rich agricultural areas. Approximately one sixth of Ontario (an Iroquois word which could mean "beautiful lake") is covered by fresh water lakes—nearly a half million of them.

LAFOREST, ON - This settlement is typical of many found along the railroads through this section of Ontario—small, isolated (no road access) and devoted to a frontier existence. At one time, schooling for children living in these remote reaches was provided by portable "schoolhouses" that consisted of a specially equipped and staffed rail car that would be towed into town by train, left on a siding for a few days, then moved on to the next village.

0:00 (0:55) Depart Laforest.

0:12 (0:43) On right, Key's Camp is just one of many hunting and fishing camps that dot CN's route through this lake country. Colorful canoes add charm to this woodland setting.

0:55 (0:00) Arrive Westree.

WESTREE, ON - This is one of the smaller stops, population 10 (more or less).

0:00 (0:30) Depart Westree.

0:18 (0:12) Cross Muskegoma River on 850-foot trestle.

0:29 (0:01) Minisinakwa Lake is on left.

0:30 (0:00) Cross Minisinakwa River and arrive Gogama.

GOGAMA, ON - This good-size town (over 600 population) has avoided isolation by situating just off the main highway between Timmins and Sudbury.

0:00 (1:26) Depart Gogama.

0:06 (1:20) Cross broad waters of Macaming River.

1:26 (0:00) Arrive Foleyet.

FOLEYET, ON - A lumbering community, located on the Timmins-White River highway and the Ivanhoe River, Foleyet is host to numerous moose hunters during the fall. Bear and other game are also found in the region.

0:00 (0:48) Depart Foleyet.

0:48 (0:00) Arrive Elsas.

ELSAS, ON - Elsas is a tiny, remote forest outpost, nicely ensconced on Kapuskasing (accent the first and third syllables) Lake. It seems half the town meets the baggage car to receive or send some sort of freight—boxes of french fries, furniture, a dog or two, the mail pouch.

0:00 (1:28) Depart Elsas along northern edge of immense Chapleau Game Preserve—one of world's largest.

0:02 (1:26) Nice view of Lake Kapuskasing is afforded on left.

0:50 (0:38) Cross Fire River.

1:00 (0:28) Cross Lower Minnipuka Lake.

1:28 (0:00) Merge momentarily with tracks of Algoma Central upon arrival Oba.

 OBA, ON - Oba's claim to fame is its location on the intersection of the Algoma Central Railway with the CN tracks. The Algoma Central connects Sault Ste. Marie, 245 miles to the south, with Hearst just 51 miles to the north. The line penetrates the spectacular Algoma Canyon, and excursion trains out of Sault Ste. Marie are extremely popular during the height of fall color.

0:00 (0:41) Depart Oba.

0:12 (0:29) Cross Kabinakagami River, another stream whose waters ultimately reach Hudson Bay.

0:27 (0:14) Cross Shekak River.

0:32 (0:09) Sawmill, at left, is one of but many along this stretch of right-of-way.

0:41 (0:00) Arrive Hornepayne.

 HORNEPAYNE, ON - This is the first town since Capreol that resembles a 20th-century community. The city has a city-center building, visible from the train, that houses schools, stores, athletic facilities and various city services.

0:00 (1:00) Depart Hornepayne.

1:00 (0:00) Arrive Hillsport.

 HILLSPORT, ON - This is another town devoted to lumbering.

0:00 (0:45) Depart Hillsport.

0:45 (0:00) Arrive Caramat.

 CARAMAT, ON - Caramat is nicely situated on a small lake by the same name.

0:00 (0:25) Depart Caramat.

0:24 (0:01) Large pole-producing mill is on immediate left.

0:25 (0:00) Arrive Longlac.

 LONGLAC, ON - This forest products oriented town anchors the northern tip of 44-mile-long Long Lake, once an important canoe route that was part of a thriving fur trade. Plywood plants are now the community's principal employers.

0:00 (0:39) Depart Longlac.

0:39 (0:00) Arrive Nakina.

NAKINA, ON - This is a major outfitting center for sportsmen who hunt and fish the region. Like the other communities along the route, Nakina was nurtured by the building of the railroad.

0:00 (1:34) Depart Nakina, as lakes grow more sparse.

1:15 (0:19) Note fire lookout tower off to left.

1:28 (0:06) Crossing Little Jackfish River on 798-foot-long, 74-foot-high trestle, look to left for view of northernmost waters of Lake Nipigon.

1:34 (0:00) Arrive Ferland.

FERLAND, ON - Just to the south of this lumbering hamlet is aforementioned Lake Nipigon, Ontario's largest body of water. It stretches 60 miles from north to south and bulges to 40 miles across at its widest point.

0:00 (0:46) Depart Ferland.

0:07 (0:39) Cross Mud River on 60-foot-high trestle.

0:46 (0:00) Arrive Armstrong.

ARMSTRONG, ON - This forest outpost is yet another community closely tied to both the railroad and the timber industry. However, unlike so many towns along the CN route, it is not reached solely by rail. It's possible to drive 150 miles straight south and reach the Great Lakes port city of Thunder Bay.

0:00 (1:39) Depart Armstrong.

Gain one hour as train passes from Eastern to Central Time. Set your watch back (forward if eastbound) one hour.

1:25 (0:14) At Flindt Landing, small footbridge leads to island with cluster of cabins. Body of water is Heathcote Lake.

1:39 (0:00) Arrive Savant Lake.

SAVANT LAKE - A few buildings and a small church at milepost 78.6 comprise village of Savant Lake. Lake itself is to the south.

0:00 (1:21) Depart Savant Lake.

1:21 (0:00) Arrive Sioux Lookout, where white mock-Tudor station with black trim reposes on right.

SIOUX LOOKOUT, ON - Approximately 2,000 people populate this major trading center of western Ontario. Bill Coo, in his *Scenic Rail Guide to Central and Atlantic Canada*, wrote that the town's unique name arose when Ojibway Indians used the nearby mountains to watch for American Sioux raiding parties.

0:00 (1:50) Depart Sioux Lookout.

0:22 (1:28) At Hudson, seaplanes are frequently berthed at lake's edge on right. Plaque commemorates bush pilots who, in 1926, airlifted supplies north to gold seekers at Red Lake.

1:50 (0:00) Arrive Red Lake Road.

RED LAKE ROAD - Trains frequently pass through this community of 100 (or less) when passengers neither board nor detrain.

0:00 (1:30) Depart Red Lake Road.

1:30 (0:00) Arrive Redditt.

REDDITT, ON - Redditt has the distinction of having this CN rail subdivision named for it.

0:00 (0:22) Depart Redditt.

0:22 (0:00) Cross Winnipeg River, then arrive Minaki.

MINAKI, ON - Scenic Gun Lake is just to the south of Minaki, where the Minaki Lodge once hosted weekenders that arrived here from Winnipeg by special excursion trains.

0:00 (2:15) Depart Minaki.

0:05 (2:10) Lakes abound and scenery becomes more attractive than ever.

0:21 (1:54) Through hamlet of Malachi as Lake Malachi, on left, routinely treats villagers to a stunning view.

0:30 (1:45) Note waterfall to right.

0:33 (1:42) Cross into Manitoba, boundary being readily identified by marker on right. We have just entered Whiteshell Provincial Park, a dreamland for canoe paddlers.

1:10 (1:05) Cross main line of CP Rail. In a moment, route runs straight as an arrow westward toward Winnipeg.

1:25 (0:50) Through Elma, as countryside turns more pastoral. Farms through here were originally 160-acre homesteads granted by government.

2:00 (0:15) Country is now all farming and flat as a pancake, as prairies take over.

2:15 (0:00) Cross Red River Floodway on 903-foot viaduct as train arrives at Transcona.

TRANSCONA, MB - This is an eastern Winnipeg suburban stop.

0:00 (0:17) Depart Transcona; Winnipeg's downtown skyline is directly ahead.

0:13 (0:04) Cross 55 feet above Seine River.

0:15 (0:02) Cross impressive Red River.

0:17 (0:00) Arrive Winnipeg's CN Station.

WINNIPEG, MB - In 1738 the French explorer Gaultier built Fort Route on the present site of Winnipeg. It wasn't until 1812, however, that a permanent settlement was established when Selkirk Settlors (led by Lord Selkirk) arrived and settled along the banks of the Red River, land which was granted to them by the

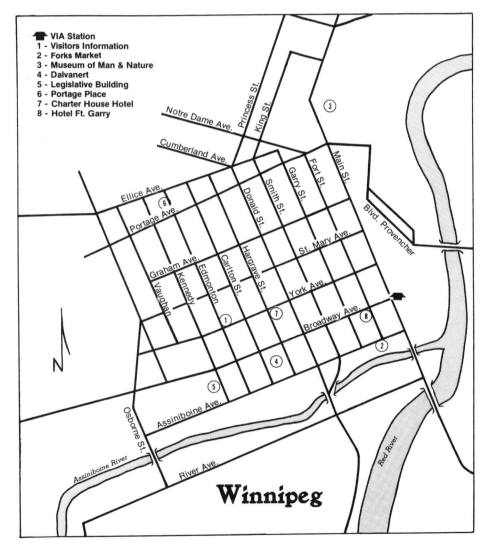

VIA Station
1 - Visitors Information
2 - Forks Market
3 - Museum of Man & Nature
4 - Dalvanert
5 - Legislative Building
6 - Portage Place
7 - Charter House Hotel
8 - Hotel Ft. Garry

Winnipeg

Hudson's Bay Company.

In 1835, the Hudson's Bay Company, whose home offices are now in Winnipeg, built Fort Garry to further protect its fur-trading activities. Then in 1881, with the arrival of the Canadian Pacific Railway, Winnipeg became a major center of railroad activity.

Agricultural lands attracted various immigrant nationalities in the early 1900s, which gave the town its first real growth and assured its permanence. Today, it is not only the oldest city in the prairie provinces of Manitoba and Saskatchewan, it is also the largest and is the capital of Manitoba.

VIA Station, 123 Main Street, on the edge of downtown, is a handsome structure designed by Warren and Wetmore, architects of New York's Grand Central Terminal. It has a sizable waiting room, snack bar, snack and beverage vending machines, gift shop, barbershop, numerous shopping stalls and storage lockers. There is pay-parking.

For reservations and information call 800-561-8630.

Unicity **Taxi**, 947-6611. There is a **cab phone** just inside the station entrance. **Local buses** stop in front of the station. For **rental cars**, call Avis, 989-7521, about a block from the station.

Tourism Winnipeg, 232-375 York Ave., R3C 3J3; (204) 943-1970.

Charter House Hotel, 330 York Ave., R3C 0N9; (204) 942-0101. Handsome rooms in a central location. Six blocks from the station. $53.

-**Hotel Fort Garry**, 222 Broadway, R3C 0R3; (204) 942-8251 or 800-665-8088. Historic hostelry, restored to its original luxurious state. Formal casino gambling. One block from the station. $79.

Some of Winnipeg's downtown points of interest, all walkable by the energetic, include: **The Forks Market**, behind the station at the junction of the Assiniboine and Red Rivers, a delightful river park setting for food, shops and galleries; the **Manitoba Museum of Man and Nature**, 190 Rupert Ave., has excellent sub-Arctic exhibits, including polar bears,

northern lights, the railroad to Churchill and Churchill itself (a planetarium and science hall are also here); and **Portage Place**, on N. Portage Ave., spans three blocks and contains 150 shops, restaurants, offices and movie theaters, including an IMAX large-screen movie system.

0:00 (0:57) Depart Winnipeg.

0:01 (0:56) Forks Market area and Forks National Historic Park come into view, below left.

0:03 (0:54) Cross Assiniboine River near its juncture with Red River. Waters will ultimately flow north into Lake Winnipeg.

0:06 (0:51) On right, ornate dome is distinctive feature of Winnipeg's Legislative Building.

0:34 (0:23) An interesting two-story depot on right and an old church on left are highlights through Elie. On western edge of town, cross Milk River, with neighborhoods of gracious homes lining its banks.

0:51 (0:06) At Nattress, cross Assiniboine River.

0:57 (0:00) Arrive Portage la Prairie.

PORTAGE LA PRAIRIE, MB - Literally translated as "prairie portage," the city is situated at the narrowest point between the Assiniboine River and Lake Manitoba. This spot once served as a resting point for both Indians and early settlers transporting their canoes between these two important waterways.

A fort was established at this strategic site in 1738, and from 1867 to 1868, the town held the distinction of being capital of the "Republic of Manitobah." Today, it remains a transportation hub of the prairies, with the CN and CP rail lines making an unusual prairie intersection, while the Trans-Canada and Yellowhead highways join here.

0:00 (1:04) Depart Portage la Prairie where our CN tracks gradually swing to right away from CP main line that continues on to Calgary.

0:12 (0:52) Landscape cannot get any flatter as CN tracks now reach across floor of ancient lake bed.

1:04 (0:00) Arrive Brandon North, where what has to be VIA's smallest station awaits

Cleaning of the Canadian — Jasper, AB
DORIS SWANSON

on left. Not much larger than a playhouse, depot is actually complete with benches.

 **BRANDON NORTH, MB** - This northern "suburb" stop serves the town of Brandon, a few miles off to left.

0:00 (0:14) Departing Brandon, someone has used old wagon on right to wish passengers a nice day.

0:04 (0:10) Indeed, you can ski Manitoba! On ridge in distance to left is winter sports area known as Glenorky Ski Resort.

0:13 (0:01) A 684-foot trestle carries us 90 feet over waters of Little Saskatchewan River. Look back to right to see spillway of dam momentarily delaying river's journey southward to its juncture with Assiniboine.

0:14 (0:00) Arrive Rivers.

RIVERS, MB - Named for the president of the Grand Trunk Railway, this town is but one of many wheat-oriented communities of Manitoba.

0:00 (2:12) Departing Rivers, watch for hangar-like buildings in several communities along this route which house both hockey and curling rinks.

0:39 (1:33) Cross Minnewashtack Creek on trestle over 1,500 feet in length.

0:43 (1:29) Trestle carries us high over Birdtail Creek.

1:11 (1:01) After milepost 213, watch for signs on both sides of track which pinpoint Manitoba-Saskatchewan border. From here on, landscape will begin to flatten more and more as we move westward.

1:14 (0:58) Large potash mine can be seen on left across valley. Mineral is used for manufacture of fertilizer.

1:29 (0:43) Rumble across trestle high above Cutarm River.

1:30 (0:42) Two more potash plants come into view, attesting to region's wealth of this mineral, one on left and another in distance right.

1:37 (0:35) Yet another potash plant can be seen off to right.

2:11 (0:01) Passing through extensive rail yards of Melville, note quaint onion-domed church to right.

2:12 (0:00) Arrive Melville.

 MELVILLE, SK - One of the larger towns along the route, Melville is a rail division point. Notice enclosed hockey rink just behind town's rather attractive, chalet-style depot.

0:00 (2:19) Depart Melville.

0:31 (1:48) Ukrainian influence is apparent in this part of Saskatchewan. Note Mosque-appearing church in Hubbard on right.

0:47 (1:32) Here is another church with Ukrainian flavor as we pass through town of Jasmine.

1:17 (1:02) Hills on either side of us are Touchwood Hills, named after dead poplar trees which make excellent firewood.

1:59 (0:20) Cross over Peter Lake at milepost 101.

2:10 (0:09) Now pass over much larger Boulder Lake.

2:19 (0:00) Arrive Watrous.

 WATROUS, SK - This is a resort community with hot mineral springs four miles north of here and which the Indians believed had unusual curing properties.

0:00 (0:59) Depart Watrous.

0:11 (0:48) Lake Manitou fills depression on right.

0:19 (0:40) Through Zelma where potash mine is visible on horizon right.

0:26 (0:33) At Alan, huge potash mine and what must be world's largest Quonset hut create impressive industrial scene off to right.

0:33 (0:26) Silver domed and shed-like buildings, on left, are distribution center for Engrow agricultural fertilizer.

0:50 (0:09) Crossing South Saskatchewan River, skyline of Saskatoon is prominent on horizon right, while three-stacked Queen Elizabeth Power Station is at left.

0:59 (0:00) Just before arriving Saskatoon, cross South Saskatchewan River.

 SASKATOON, SK - Located on the prairies of Saskatchewan, it is the second largest city in the province. Founded in 1882 as a temperance colony, it has grown to prominence as a center of one of the richest agricultural regions of Canada. It is sometimes referred to as the "City of Bridges" due to the large number that cross the South Saskatchewan River here.

 VIA Station, Chappell Dr., is located four miles west of downtown. An attractive, spacious facility with terrazzo floors. There are storage lockers and some vending machines. Free parking is adjacent to the station. For reservations and other information, call 800-665-8630.

 United **Cabs**, 652-2222.

Park Town Hotel, 924 Spandia Cr. E., S7K 3H5; (306) 244-5564. Renovated in 1990. Large, near-elegant rooms with river and university views available. Three or four blocks from downtown. Five miles from the station. $61.

-Senator Hotel, 243-21st St. E., S7K 0B7; (306) 244-6141. Built in early 1890s, but rooms very serviceable. Near the center of town. For the economy minded. $45.

 Western Development Museum, considerably south of downtown, has numerous frontier buildings moved here to represent an early-day town, including old cars, carriages, and a railway station.

Midtown Plaza is a delightfully executed downtown shopping mall, much of which is located in the old CNR station.

The **Ukrainian Museum of Canada**, 910 Spandia Cres. E., is one of Canada's finest ethnographic museums. Outstanding exhibits include ceramics, costumed dolls, Easter eggs (pysanky), a history of Ukrainian settlement in Canada and one of the finest textile collections in North America.

0:00 (1:10) Depart Saskatoon.

0:13 (0:57) On right, former station at Gandora now serves as a private home.

1:10 (0:00) Arrive Biggar, where sign at station platform proclaims "New York is big, but this is Biggar."

 BIGGAR, SK - Biggar is smaller than most towns with three museums. Biggar Museum and Gallery tells the story of the area's settlement. The Homestead Museum features a pioneer home, rural schoolhouse, general store and sod home, while five miles east, Kisser's Western Relics Museum indeed displays Western relics.

0:00 (1:14) Depart Biggar.

1:14 (0:00) Arrive Unity.

 UNITY, SK - This small prairie community has its own salt plant that offers tours allowing visitors to see how a variety of salt products are manufactured.

0:00 (1:15) Depart Unity.

0:30 (0:45) Large Manitou Lake off to right is notable for island in its middle.

0:40 (0:35) Leave Alberta and enter Saskatchewan. Provincial border is marked by sign at right.

Leave Central Standard Time and enter Mountain Time.

0:50 (0:09) Cross Ribstone Creek (three times).

1:15 (0:00) Arrive Wainwright.

 WAINWRIGHT, AB - Wainwright Canadian Forces base is just southwest of this Alberta community. Petroleum production has also been an economic mainstay.

0:00 (0:50) Depart Wainwright.

0:10 (0:40) Train now makes an airy crossing of impressive Battle River which lies some 200 feet below. Steel trestle is nearly 3,000 feet in length.

0:40 (0:10) Numerous sink holes throughout this area provide good habitat for migrating waterfowl, including Canadian geese. These small ponds now dot landscape on both sides of tracks.

0:50 (0:00) Arrive Viking.

 VIKING, AB - The name of this Alberta farming community reflects its Scandinavian heritage. Nearby quartzite rocks, carved by Cree Indians, are thought to relate to buffalo fertility rites.

0:00 (1:20) Depart Viking.

0:13 (1:07) Russian Orthodox Church, with its silver and white onion-shaped dome, is architectural jewel of Holden, across pond on right.

0:25 (0:55) Small red grain elevator on left serves as statement of sorts. Instead of "Alberta Pool," west side has been inscribed "Dirty Shorts."

0:32 (0:48) Huge Beaver Lake can be spotted in distance to right.

0:43 (0:37) Now, large Cooking Lake is on left.

1:06 (0:14) After passing through yards at Clover Bar, cross Saskatchewan River where refineries are most evident on fringe of Edmonton.

1:14 (0:06) Sizable coliseum on left is home to National Hockey League's Edmonton Oilers. Just to west of coliseum, with numerous flagpoles, is Edmonton Northland where numerous public events are held, including Klondike Days, trade shows, Farm Fair, etc. Even weddings are occasionally booked here.

1:16 (0:04) Edmonton's professional football team, the Eskimos, uses larger stadium on immediate right.

1:20 (0:00) Arrive Edmonton.

EDMONTON, AB - Edmonton has a shopping mall like Crocodile Dundee had a knife. Totally intimidating any would-be competitors, it's the largest in the world. It has twice the stores, half-again as many employees, nearly triple the number of parking spaces and it cost twice as much as the newer Mall of America in Minneapolis/St. Paul. A super-extravaganza that has to be seen to be believed, with stores and more stores (there are over 40 shoe stores alone); it has its own amusement-park attractions that include three roller coasters, a floating replica of the Mayflower (complete with submarine rides around its perimeter), a nifty theme hotel and a beach with surf—all under one immense roof. And some people even go to the Mall just to shop.

With such a dynamo on the west edge of town, it would seem Edmonton's downtown area might wither, even though the town is the provincial capital. This has not happened. The downtown has its own delightful shopping malls, a modern subway and enclosed pedestrian walkways that keep the city vibrant—both day and night, summer and winter.

VIA Station, 1004-104 Ave. in the CN Tower at 100 Street, constructed

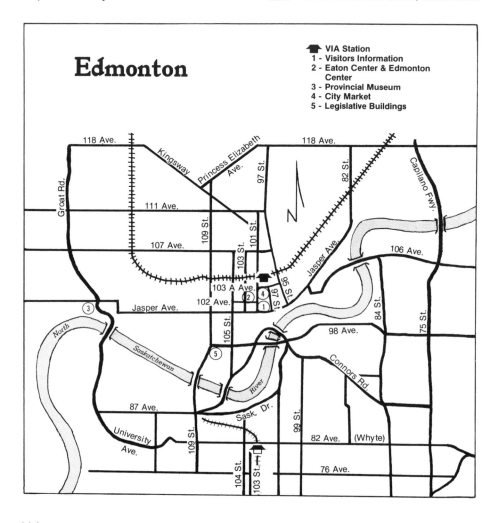

Edmonton, AB
JACK SWANSON

in the 1960s as part of an urban development project, has an unusual circular interior design with a gift shop, snack stand, storage lockers and pay-parking. For reservations and information, call 800-561-8630.

Yellow **Cab**, 462-3456. **Subway** is free within the downtown area and runs along Jasper Avenue and 99 Street. Nearest subway stop is Churchill Station, two blocks away on 99 Street. For **rental cars**, Thrifty has free city pick up and delivery during weekdays, 428-8555.

Visitor Information Center, Edmonton Convention & Tourism Authority, 9797 Jasper Ave., No. 104, T5J 1N9; (403) 496-8400.

Quality Inn Downtown, 10209 - 100 Ave., T5J 0A1; (403) 428-6442. Small motel in good location. Seven blocks from the station. $45.

-**Hotel Macdonald**, 10065 - 100 Street, T5J 0N6; (403) 424-5181 or 800-828-7447 (U.S.). A city landmark since 1915, this chateau-style structure was completely renovated by the Canadian Pacific Hotels at a cost of $20 million and reopened in 1991. Five blocks from the station. $130.

Within walking distance, shopping is available at the **Eaton Center**, including miniature golf and movies, just three blocks from the station, at 101 St. and 102 Ave. Across 101 St. is the **Edmonton Center** with still more shops and restaurants. The **Provincial Museum of Alberta**, 12845-102 Ave., has worthwhile nature and cultural exhibits.

The **Alberta Railroad Museum**, on northeast edge of town is western Canada's largest railroad museum. And, of course, for more shopping and sheer fun, there's the **West Edmonton Mall** described in the introduction above.

0:00 (1:42) Depart Edmonton, backing and retracing tracks eastbound for several minutes before backing onto main line at East Junction, then west through industrial scenes of Edmonton.

Station at Jasper
DORIS SWANSON

0:35 (1:07) Large cement plant and leading apparatus on right belongs to Inland Cement.

1:00 (0:42) "Onion-domed" church on right at Carvel is fine example of Byzantine architecture. This most distinctive design commonly characterizes churches of Russian, Greek and Ukrainian denominations.

1:09 (0:33) Cross into Wabamun via bridge spanning arm of Wabamun Lake.

1:11 (0:31) Huge power plant on right is Wabamun Generating Facility.

1:39 (0:03) With highway bridge paralleling on left, cross beautiful Pembina River approaching Evansburg.

1:42 (0:00) Arrive Evansburg.

EVANSBURG, AB - This stop serves the western fringe of Edmonton's widespread area. The town derives its name from a former mayor of this city.

0:00 (1:03) Depart Evansburg amidst rolling farmlands of western Alberta.

0:46 (0:16) High trestles across Wolf Creek and McLeod River provide sudden drama to this stretch.

1:03 (0:00) Arrive Edson.

EDSON, AB - Located approximately halfway between Edmonton and Jasper, Edson serves as a trading hub for its immediate area. It was named in honor of a vice-president of the Grand Trunk Pacific Railway, Edson Chamberlain.

0:00 (0:54) Depart Edson.

0:09 (0:45) Cross Sundance Creek atop another lofty bridge.

0:29 (0:25) With McLeod River bordering on left, peaks of Rocky Mountains can now be discerned, jutting above horizon in distance. Stands of tamarack trees are interspersed with spruce. Needles of this unique tree (also known as the larch) turn gold in fall and then drop off in preparation for winter.

0:33 (0:21) Train skirts shoreline of Obed Lake on right.

0:45 (0:09) Big white dome on right is coal-loading facility, supplied by conveyer belt extending to mine on far horizon. Trains are loaded as they pass through loader at two mph.

0:52 (0:02) Approaching Hinton, huge St. Regis pulp plant is on right.
0:54 (0:00) Arrive Hinton.

 HINTON, AB - This is the eastern gateway city to Jasper National Park. One of Alberta's two major pulp-processing plants, a St. Regis Pulp and Paper Mill, is located here.

0:00 (1:01) Depart Hinton.
0:05 (0:57) Climb atop bluffs overlooking Athabasca River Valley on right. Within several miles, train emerges in heart of Jasper National Park, with towering peaks and shimmering lakes an encompassing spectacle to behold. Park Gate is at milepost 206.
0:13 (0:48) Cross Athabasca River.
0:50 (0:11) Watch for bighorn sheep, elk and other wildlife that sometime graze rail right-of-way along this stretch of track.
0:59 (0:01) Large CN rail yards mark entrance to Jasper.
1:01 (0:00) Arrive Jasper where a steam locomotive, a totem pole and a "bear" all greet passengers at right.

JASPER, AB - Jasper National Park, named after Jasper Hawes, a fur trapper in this area in the early 1800s, is located in the midst of majestic mountain scenery. Like Banff, it is understandably one of the more popular vacation areas in the Canadian Rockies. Although crowded in the summer, it is not as frantic as Banff. September can be an ideal month to visit here.

VIA Station, 607 Connaught Drive, has a snack bar, a gift shop, storage lockers, luggage carts, a newsstand and redcaps. Free parking is adjacent to the station. For reservations and information, call 800-561-8630.

Jasper **Taxi**, 852-3146. **Greyhound/Brewster** bus terminal and **tour buses**, including icefield tours, are adjacent to the station. Tilden **rental cars** are located in the VIA station, 852-4972.

Information Center, 632 Connaught Drive (at Hazel). Call (403) 852-3858.

Whistler's Motor Hotel, Box 250, T0E 1E0; (403) 852-3361. Attractive rooms and nice restaurant. Across the street from the station. $109.

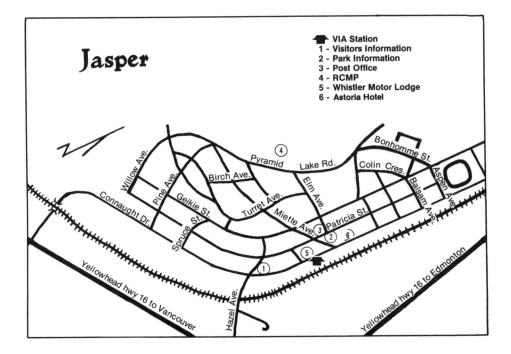

Jasper

VIA Station
1 - Visitors Information
2 - Park Information
3 - Post Office
4 - RCMP
5 - Whistler Motor Lodge
6 - Astoria Hotel

Canadian — Canadian Rockies
JACK SWANSON

-**Astoria Hotel**, 404 Connaught Dr., T0E 1E0; (403) 852-3351. Very attractive, smaller hotel, three long blocks from the station. $89.

-Numerous homes offer furnished **rooms** and moderate rates. Call **Central Reservations**, (403) 852-4242, for availability of these units as well as motels.

⭐ **Maligne Canyon, Medicine Lake and Maligne Lake** are located east of Jasper in the Maligne Valley. A spectacular gorge leads to the two lakes; Maligne Lake is in a breathtaking mountain setting.

Jasper Tramway carries passengers to an elevation of 7,380 feet on the Whistlers. A hike on to the summit provides an outstanding view of Mt. Robson.

0:00 1:53) Depart Jasper and head toward Yellowhead Pass and some of North America's most magnificent scenery! Trident Range will be on our left and Victoria Cross Range on our right as we make this ascent. Waterfalls, streams, snowfields and tunnels make this a railroading spectacular.

0:08 (1:45) Tramway to top of Whistlers Mountain is across valley to left.

0:24 (1:29) Those small wire fences that occasionally appear on uphill side of right-of-way are slide detectors which activate a red signal should there be a rockslide or snowslide blocking tracks. Propane tanks are for heaters that prevent switches from freezing.

🕐 Gain one hour as train passes from Mountain to Pacific Time. Set your watch back (forward if eastbound) one hour.

0:30 (1:10) Crest Yellowhead Pass at milepost 17.5. This is border between Alberta, just behind, and British Columbia, just entered. Tracks are only 3,718 feet above sea level; however, many of surrounding peaks soar to more than 11,000 feet. Yellowhead is one of lowest passes along entire North American Continental Divide. At this northerly point, waters flowing to east ultimately find their way into Arctic Ocean.

0:37 (1:01) Beautiful Yellowhead Lake stretches serenely beside tracks on left. Yellowhead Mountain is highest peak directly across lake.

0:58 (0:50) And now, Moose Lake is alongside of us at left, even larger than Yellowhead.

1:33 (0:22) Looking back, view is superb. One of dominant peaks is Mt. Robson at 3,954 meters—that's 12,972 feet—Canadian Rockies' highest.

1:38 (0:15) Through short tunnel.

1:40 (0:13) Rail lines divide, with our CN line heading to left (south) toward Kamloops and Vancouver, while the other (route of the *Skeena*) continues west to end of line at Prince Rupert.

1:44 (0:09) Rugged peaks to left comprise Selwyn Range.

1:53 (0:00) Arrive Valemount.

 VALEMOUNT,BC - This is a popular recreation area, particularly for fishermen. The town is situated at the very northern end of the Canoe Reach of skinny Kinbasket Lake.

0:00 (1:40) Depart Valemount.

0:05 (1:35) Excellent views are afforded in all directions; Premier Range is forward to right.

0:12 (1:24) To right, spectacular snowfields of Albreda Glacier create a perpetual blanket of white.

0:50 (0:50) Train now parallels N. Thompson River which will be followed into Kamloops.

1:06 (0:34) Note spectacular Pyramid Falls off to left.

1:38 (0:02) Mike Wiegele's heliskiing operation is in evidence on right where bevy of helicopters are parked.

1:40 (0:00) Arrive Blue River.

 BLUE RIVER, BC - This small way-stop is in a truly idyllic setting, popular with fishermen and attracting a worldwide clientele of heliskiers.

0:00 (1:50) Depart Blue River.

0:24 (1:26) Enormous rapids below, on left, make it clear we are headed downhill, as train traverses canyon sometimes referred to as Little Hell's Gate. Tunnel creates momen-

tary darkness.

0:25 (1:25) River now squeezes through Little Hell's Gate Gorge.

1:37 (0:13) Two large sawmills, on left, consume huge amount of local timber stands.

1:50 (0:00) Arrive Clearwater.

 CLEARWATER, BC - This is a lumbering and farming community. Countryside will evidence more agricultural qualities as we approach Kamloops.

0:00 (1:45) Depart Clearwater, where Clearwater River, on right, adds to already burgeoning North Thompson River.

0:24 (1:21) Note small aerial tram, to left, that offers forest rangers unique ride to fire lookout on Baldy Mountain.

1:10 (0:35) "Current Ferry," on right at McLure, uses force of stream to propel it across North Thompson.

1:45 (0:00) Arrive Kamloops CN station, situated on northern edge of city.

 KAMLOOPS, BC - The city is located at the confluence of the North and South Thompson Rivers. The first white men to reach the area were fur traders representing the Pacific Fur Trade Company. They arrived here in 1811 and found the Kamloops Indians (of the Shuswap Tribe) eager to trade. This led to the construction of outposts which were eventually taken over by the Hudson's Bay Company in 1821.

Gold was discovered near here in the early 1850s spurring further development. British Columbia became a province of Canada in 1871, permitting the Canadian Pacific Railway to be extended to Kamloops three years later.

Kamloops has a semi-arid climate with temperatures frequently soaring into the 90s during the summer months. Locals take to the beaches of the Thompson River in droves on warmer weekends. It is so warm that Kamloops has a surprising five-month,frost-free growing season.

0:00 (3:45) Depart Kamloops.

0:01 (3:44) Make first of many river crossings between here and Vancouver, as North Thompson is crossed with view of Kamloops to left. Soon cruise beside Kamloops Lake on left. After lake, route will first follow

Thompson River and then Fraser River into Vancouver.

CN and CP tracks parallel each other on opposite riverbanks, frequently exchanging sides. The *Canadian* uses the CN tracks.

0:55 (2:50) To right is Walhachin, now a mere grove of cottonwoods. In early 1900s, prior to WWI, settlers irrigated this arid land, hoping to create their own "Garden of Eden." However, men were called to arms leaving their beloved land to the elements. A devastating flood washed out their aqueduct, and Walhachin ultimately met its demise.

1:22 (2:23) Through arid flag stop of Ashcroft, and now swing southward, still following river. Ashcroft is one of driest spots in Canada, receiving less than ten inches of moisture per year.

1:23 (2:22) At milepost 50.3, watch for enormous osprey nest atop abandoned power pole on right (an old wood burner is just beyond). These large birds can sometimes be spotted gliding above river in search of fish, their favorite food.

1:31 (2:14) Here, at milepost 57, the last spike of what is now the CN was driven on January 23, 1915. At that time, it was the Canadian Northern Pacific Railway, and event marked completion of Canada's third transcontinental rail link.

2:02 (1:43) At Spence's Bridge it is still apparent, on slope to right, where landslide occurred August 13, 1905, when lower portion of mountain came rumbling across valley in matter of seconds, damming waters of Thompson River. Five people were buried alive and thirteen more were drowned when waters backed over nearby Indian village. Above to right, waterfall from Murray Creek literally shoots out from mountainside during springtime.

2:33 (1:10) Train enters "Jaws of Death," a particularly treacherous section of river, as canyon becomes narrow gorge. "Suicide Rapids" is term bestowed on frothy waters by intrepid white-water rafters who occasionally test their skills (and luck) along this stretch of river.

2:41 (1:04) Cross Fraser River, just across from Lytton, where muddy waters of Thompson merge into much clearer Fraser, on left. Simon Fraser, fur trader and explorer of British Columbia, put ashore at this point on June 18, 1808. Lytton, with its significant Indian population, lays claim to being longest continually occupied spot in North America.

2:55 (0:50) At Cisco Flats, both railroads now decide to exchange river banks in dramatic style. Original Canadian Pacific bridge was fabricated in Britain more than 100 years ago, arriving at Port Moody by ship, moved in sections by rail (of course) to present-day site, then erected by San Francisco Bridge Company. Bridge was eventually replaced.

3:42 (0:03) Beside new bridge, former auto aerial tram (discussed below), now rests on far side of river.

3:45 (0:00) Arrive Boston Bar.

BOSTON BAR, BC - This village was originally a gold-mining center. At one time, before highway bridge was installed, a unique cable tram, only large enough to hold one automobile, served as an aerial ferry between North Bend, immediately across the Fraser, and the Trans-Canada Highway here at Boston Bar.

0:00 (1:43) Depart Boston Bar.

0:10 (1:33) Across river, on right, creek cascades beneath CP's Skuzzy Creek rail bridge into Fraser River.

0:16 (1:27) Canyon narrows to mere 110 feet forming "Hell's Gate."

0:27 (1:16) Glimpse graceful structure of Alexandra Bridge spanning Fraser below on right.

The original Alexandra Bridge was built by Joseph Trutch in 1863 as part of the famed Cariboo Road. It was the first suspension bridge in British Columbia, and actually looked quite similar to its replacement (except the original sported wooden towers). It was destroyed by a flood in 1894, twenty years after its construction.

0:39 (1:05) Waterfall cascades directly overhead while train passes through tunnel.

0:50 (0:53) Obstruction at mouth of Fraser River Canyon is monolithic Lady Franklin

Hell's Gate

Two hundred million gallons of water per minute drain through Hell's Gate from 84,000 square miles of British Columbia. Each year, 2 million sockeye salmon swim upstream against this torrent to reach their spawning grounds. Simon Fraser reported it as "an awesome gorge."

The Pacific salmon industry was nearly ruined when rockslides in 1914, triggered by construction in the canyon, made passage so narrow that salmon-spawning was cut by 90 percent. Subsequently, Canadian/U.S.-built fishways slowed the stream flow enough to bring the salmon population back to normalcy. Now, a Swiss-built tramway swoops bright red gondolas to the bottom carrying 28 passengers per load for impressive views of the canyon. White-water rafters can often be seen challenging the rapids and a treacherous whirlpool called "Devil's Wash Basin."

Rock, named for widow of Sir John Franklin, arctic explorer who died in 1847 searching for Northwest Passage. Lady Franklin's efforts to find her husband led her here but she could not probe farther upriver because of this formidable barrier. Her courage, however, inspired numerous expeditions to search for Sir John, ultimately producing thorough exploration of Canadian Arctic region.

0:51 (0:52) Town of Yale is immediately across river.

In its day, Yale was one of the most important and exciting towns in the West. Founded in 1848 as a fur collection point for the Hudson's Bay Company, Yale's place in history was furthered when local gold discoveries occurred in 1858. Then with greater finds 400 miles farther north at Cariboo and Barkersville, construction of the legendary Cariboo Wagon Road started here in 1862.

Yale claims the first railway station west of the Rockies, the first town council in British Columbia and the first girls' finishing school on the B.C. mainland (once visited by the Duke and Duchess of York).

0:52 (0:51) Watch for Indian fish-drying racks, frequently draped with blue or orange plastic.

0:53 (0:50) Just after crossing Emory Creek, pass location where Onderdonk's first Yale construction locomotive was unloaded from ship to shore in 1880.

1:01 (0:42) Through flag stop of Hope.

1:29 (0:14) Up valley, to right across river, is Harrison Hot Springs, a fine resort in the mountains. As you might suspect, resort's hot springs are a major attraction. Beautiful Harrison Lake, as well as historic Harrison Hotel, add to area's appeal.

1:43 (0:00) Arrive Chilliwack.

CHILLIWACK, BC - This agricultural center is located in a broad, fertile valley, actually the delta of the Fraser River. The delta has taken several million years to form, and now covers bedrock with soil one mile deep. Steamboats once made port here during the gold rush days.

0:00 (0:24) Depart Chilliwack.

0:21 (0:03) On hill, in distance right, red-tiled roof and tower of Westminster Abbey are visible. This Benedictine Monastery was founded in 1954.

0:24 (0:00) Arrive Matsqui.

MATSQUI, BC - This is one more agrarian community, and the last stop before reaching Vancouver's densely populated suburbs.

0:00 (1:02) Depart Matsqui.

0:02 (1:00) Now, cross to north banks of Fraser at Page.

0:22 (0:40) Through Mission, a small community named for an Indian school established here in the 19th century, first and largest of its kind in the province. Attractive

Skytrain — Vancouver, BC
JACK SWANSON

station at left was proclaimed in 1909 by a local tabloid as "one of the swellest" along the line.

0:32 (0:30) Cross Stave River. It was near here that Billy Miner pulled off Canada's first train robbery in September, 1904—two years before his $15 holdup east of Kamloops. Miner was glamorized in the movie *The Grey Fox*.

0:33 (0:27) Literally pass through large lumber mill and yards.

0:39 (0:21) Fort Langley National Historic Park is immediately across river from ferry dock. Built in 1827 by Hudson's Bay Company, fort functioned as provisioning and administrative center for company and was to end American competition in Northwest. It was here that James Douglas declared British Columbia a crown colony in 1858 and fort became first capital.

0:54 (0:06) Cross Pitt River on 1,749-foot bridge with another center-pivot span.

1:00 (0:00) CP Rail repair shops and yards herald arrival at Port Coquitlam.

 PORT COQUITLAM, BC - Development of this area, including

nearby Port Moody, began with the 1858 gold rush. But the first major boom occurred 27 years later when the western terminus of the Canadian Pacific was planned for nearby Port Moody. Real estate skyrocketed in value, with some lots jumping from $15 to $1,000 each. The first shipment of rails arrived from England at Port Moody in May of 1883, and by August, 1885, the Marquis of Langsdowne, Governor General of Canada, was able to cross Canada for the first time without entering the United States (although not entirely by train since the track was not yet finished above Yale). In November, 1885, the trans-Canada route was complete, and the first transcontinental passenger train ceremoniously pulled into Port Moody at noon on July 4, 1886. The boom soon turned to bust, however, when the railroad was extended to a new Pacific terminal at Vancouver the very next year.

0:00 (0:55) Departing Port Coquitlam, cross river by same name before heading first south then west into megalopolis of Vancouver.

0:47 (0:08) At CN Junction, duck beneath

elevated tracks of Skytrain, Vancouver's modernistic, computer-operated commuter rail.

0:53 (0:02) Slip past VIA coach barn on left.
0:55 (0:00) Arrive at Vancouver's stately Central Pacific Station.

 VANCOUVER, BC - British explorer Captain George Vancouver discovered this area in 1792. It was a natural for becoming a seaport with its sheltered harbor and nearby forests as an important source of lumber. The arrival of the Canadian Pacific Railroad in 1884 and the development of the fishing industry spurred Vancouver to becoming one of Canada's great cities.

In a sparkling bay and mountain setting, offering relatively temperate weather year-round, the city has become a favorite western vacation spot.

Central Pacific Station, 1150 Station St., is a handsome facility built along classic lines. A huge four-faced clock (fashioned after a railroader's pocket watch) is the focal point of the lobby. The station has storage lockers, luggage carts, vending machines and a hotel phone board showing numerous accommodations. Besides station restaurant, fast food restaurants are within a block. The station is about a mile from the downtown business district.

For reservations and other information, call 800-561-8630.

Yellow **Cab**, 681-3311. **Local buses** and **Skytrain** (Vancouver's computer-run "elevated") stop in front of the station, 261-5100. Skytrain runs from downtown to eastern suburbs. **Greyhound** is located in the VIA station (Central Pacific). **Amtrak Thruway Bus** service is also available from this station to Seattle's King Street Station.

Greater Vancouver Infocenter, 200 Burrard St; (604) 683-2000.

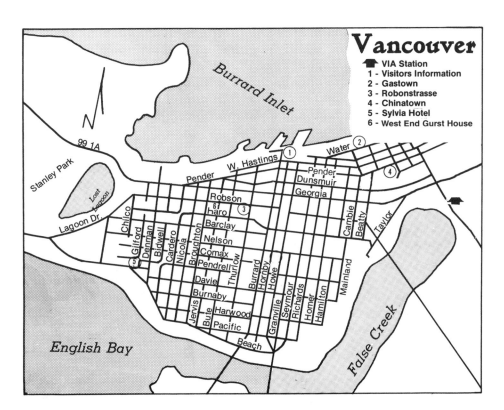

Vancouver

🚂 VIA Station
1 - Visitors Information
2 - Gastown
3 - Robonstrasse
4 - Chinatown
5 - Sylvia Hotel
6 - West End Gurst House

Sylvia Hotel, 1154 Gilford St., V6G 2P6; (604) 681-9321. Overlooks beach on English Bay, next to Stanley Park. Popular small vine-covered West-End hotel. Fine coffee shop and restaurant, both looking out at the Bay. About three miles from the station. $65.

-**West End Guest House**, 1362 Haro St., V6E 1G2; (604) 681-2889. Former residence, now an inn. Handy to Robson Street. Complimentary breakfast. $105.

Trolley Tours, much like Washington, DC's Tour Trains, are the slickest way to get around Vancouver's downtown area. A nicely planned route, complete with regularly scheduled stops, permits all-day sightseeing with unlimited boarding and reboarding for one round trip. Stops are made at Vancouver's major attractions. Maps and schedules are available at most hotels; 451-5581. **Stanley Park**, at the foot of Georgia St., is considered to be one of the finest parks in the world. On a beautiful peninsula, forming a bridged link to North Vancouver, the park contains a zoo featuring polar bears, penguins, gardens, trails, picnic sites and tennis courts. An aquarium, with 9,000 specimens of sealife, features killer and beluga whales.

Gastown, Water and Carroll Streets, is where Vancouver began. Now an historic site which permits shops to remain open on Sunday (a rarity in Canada), this restored area has fine restaurants, shops and night-clubs. Its zany, steam-spurting clock has become Gastown's trademark. Another downtown lure is a section of **Robson Street** (Robson Strasse) between Hornby and Bute. It's a shopping area with a charming European atmosphere.

Immediately across from the station is **Science World** where visitors experience hands-on science demonstrations. An **Omnimax** theater is also here.

And rail buffs will want to ride one of the area's biggest attractions, the **Royal Hudson Steam Train**. As its name implies, this is an excursion train pulled by one of the famous Royal Hudson engines, number 2860. The route begins at the British Columbia Railway Station in North Vancouver and makes a six-hour round-trip to Squamish in the summer. The scenery is spectacular. (See *British Columbia Railway* for route log and reservation information.)

Canadian — Canadian Rockies
JACK SWANSON

Hudson Bay

Two strands of silvery steel stretch endlessly toward the horizons both fore and aft of the *Hudson Bay* on its trip to Churchill. Indian village whistle stops help break the tedium, but soon these become redundant. No matter how monotonous (and certainly slow paced), this 1,055-mile trek from Winnipeg to Churchill is always an adventure and truly one of today's unique travel experiences.

The line was built to provide a shorter route to the world's grain markets, as well as direct access to Canada's interior for inbound goods and new emigrants. Although it has never become the epic transport that was once envisioned, it has indeed provided a means of exporting a portion of Canada's wealth of wheat and has had a profound influence on the development of the North's enormous resources. Unfortunately, the CN would like to abandon the line.

Two nights are spent on the train while making numerous stops to board and detrain local residents traveling from one flag stop to another. Sleeping car accommodations are definitely recommended.

Once there, the day can be spent seeing the sights and still start the return trip that evening. The major attraction is polar bear viewing which is best in late October and early November. It is worth noting that during the summer and fall, reservations should be made well in advance. Package tours are also offered by VIA Rail.

NORTHBOUND SCHEDULE (Condensed)
Winnipeg, MB - Late Evening Departure
The Pas, MB - Midmorning (2nd Day)
Thompson, MB - Early Evening (2nd Day)
Churchill, MB - Early Morning Arrival (3rd Day)

SOUTHBOUND SCHEDULE (Condensed)
Churchill, MB - Midevening Departure
Thompson, MB - Late Morning (2nd Day)
The Pas, MB - Early Evening (2nd Day)
Winnipeg, MB - Early Morning Arrival (3rd Day)

FREQUENCY - Departs Winnipeg Sunday, Tuesday and Thursday. Arrives in Churchill Tuesday, Thursday and Saturday. Departs Churchill same day of its arrival and arrives in Winnipeg Thursday, Saturday and Monday.
SEATING - Standard coaches.
DINING - Complete meal and beverage service.
SLEEPING - Berths, single and double bedrooms.
BAGGAGE - Checked baggage handled between major stops.
RESERVATIONS - Required for sleeping cars. Coach seats reserved when tickets are purchased.
LENGTH OF TRIP - 1,055 miles in 35 hours.

ROUTE LOG

 WINNIPEG, MB - See page 331.
0:00 (0:57) Depart Winnipeg.
0:01 (0:56) Forks Market area and Forks National Historic Park come into view, below left.
0:03 (0:54) Cross Assiniboine River near its juncture with Red River. Waters will ultimately flow north into Lake Winnipeg.
0:06 (0:51) On right, ornate dome is distinctive feature of Winnipeg's Legislative Building.
0:34 (0:23) An interesting two story depot on right and and old church on left are highlights through Elie. On western edge of town, cross Milk River, with neighborhoods of gracious homes lining its banks.
0:51 (0:06) At Nattress, cross Assiniboine River.
0:57 (0:00) Arrive Portage la Prairie.

 PORTAGE LA PRAIRIE, MB - Literally translated as "prairie portage," the city is situated at the narrowest point between the Assiniboine River and Lake Manitoba. This spot served as a resting point for both Indians and early settlers transporting their canoes between these two important waterways.

A fort was established at this strategic site in 1738, and from 1867 to 1868 the town held the distinction of being capital of the "Republic of Manitobah." Today, it remains a transportation hub of the prairies, with the CN and CP rail lines making an unusual prairie crossing, while the Trans-Canada and Yellowhead highways join here.
0:00 (2:40) Depart Portage la Prairie.

For the remainder of the evening, the *Hudson Bay* travels through southern Manitoba farming country that could easily pass for central Nebraska, flat and fertile lands interspersed only with patches of trees.
1:36 (1:04) One should not laugh at bumper stickers proclaiming "Ski Manitoba." A few miles west (left) is Mt. Agassiz Ski Resort in Riding Mountain National Park.
2:40 (0:00) Arrive Dauphin, where elegant three-story 1912 depot attests to town's for-

mer prominence as a CN division point.

 DAUPHIN, MB - A fort was constructed here as early as 1742 to help establish fur trading in the region, but it wasn't until the railroad arrived in 1896 that Europeans began to settle here, creating the community that now is a regional trade center.
0:00 (1:36) Depart Dauphin.
1:36 (0:00) Arrive Roblin.

 ROBLIN, MB - Another farming center.
0:00 (3:55) Depart Roblin.
0:22 (3:33) Enter Saskatchewan and leave Manitoba.

Between here and the town of Hudson Bay, Sask., the train stops at four small communities of east-central Saskatchewan: **KAMSAK, CANORA, STURGIS** and **ENDEAVOUR.**
4:04 (0:00) Arrive Hudson Bay.

 HUDSON BAY, SK - This eastern Saskatchewan trading center is the last stop on the *Hudson Bay's* brief westward arc through this province.
0:00 (1:55) Depart Hudson Bay.
0:20 (1:35) Dense forest consists mainly of black spruce, jack pine, aspen (white poplar), tamarack (they lose their needles in the winter) and some birch (similar in appearance to aspen but trunks often have bark peeling away).
1:05 (0:50) Re-enter Manitoba and leave Saskatchewan.
1:55 (0:00) Arrive The Pas.

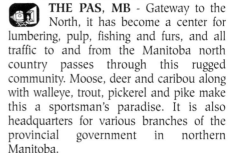 **THE PAS, MB** - Gateway to the North, it has become a center for lumbering, pulp, fishing and furs, and all traffic to and from the Manitoba north country passes through this rugged community. Moose, deer and caribou along with walleye, trout, pickerel and pike make this a sportsman's paradise. It is also headquarters for various branches of the provincial government in northern Manitoba.

In February, a renowned Trappers Festival is held for three days, when trappers, miners, lumbermen and First Nation people indulge in such competitive frolics as wood chopping, dog sledding, singing and dancing.

0:00 (1:12) Depart The Pas and immediately cross icy flow of Saskatchewan River which empties into nearby Cedar Lake—one of Lake Winnipeg's many adjuncts.

0:09 (1:03) Principal employer (along with government) of The Pas is off to right—a large paper mill.

0:11 (1:01) Flin Flon Jct. is where line divides, with a branch on left driving straight north to Lynn Lake.

0:32 (0:40) Clearwater Provincial Park, on left, is summer recreational area for residents of The Pas. Clearwater Lake is centerpiece of Park.

0:59 (0:13) Cormorant Lake sprawls in distance to left where myriad species of waterfowl take refuge. Locals claim lake is warm enough to swim in during "balmy" summer months.

1:09 (0:03) Little Cormorant Lake is on right.

1:12 (0:00) Arrive Cormorant at milepost 41.

CORMORANT, MB - This little community gets its appellation from the bird with the same name—an aquatic raven. Located on a narrow neck of land between portions of Cormorant Lake, it was the first large village on the Hudson Bay Railway. The early population was largely French and Scottish, many of whom intermarried with area natives.

0:00 (2:30) Depart Cormorant.

0:44 (1:47) Note outcroppings of pink marble. This area has provided marble for many of Canada's edifices.

1:03 (1:27) Flag stop of Wekusko (Cree for Herb Lake) where road leads to gold-mining activities at Snow Lake.

1:12 (1:18) Hargrave Lake is on right.

1:20 (1:10) Dense forests of spruce, tamarack and jack pine continue to border tracks, while tripod phone poles solve problem of unstable muskeg.

1:47 (0:43) At milepost 109, make rare highway crossing between The Pas and Churchill. This road leads from Winnipeg to Thompson.

2:30 (0:00) Arrive Wabowden at milepost 136.

WABOWDEN, MB - Perhaps the prettiest community along today's route, Wabowden acts as a transfer point for goods destined for more remote regions. The Brandon Experimental Farm is here and has had successful results with vegetables and small grains. Some small farms are operating nearby.

0:00 (1:12) Depart Wabowden, noting long wooden elevated sidewalk along left side of track to avoid muskeg. Immediately Bowden Lake appears on left. About two miles beyond (and out of view) is Setting Lake—an elongated body of water which serves as part of extensive Grass River canoe route, connecting Flin Flon with Nelson River.

1:12 (0:00) Native dogs anxiously await train at Thicket Portage (milepost 184) where train's cook usually drops off food scraps which are instantly snapped up by these voracious canines.

THICKET PORTAGE, MB - This is one of the oldest inhabited villages in the area. Besides its native Indian population, a number of Scandinavian and

Permafrost

Permafrost, that frozen ground just below the surface, is an engineering nightmare. It should be avoided first, kept frozen if it can't be avoided, or (the least practical) removed. It is particularly troublesome along this stretch of tracks and the railroad has implanted thermo-probes which can now be seen on either side of the track. Freon is used inside these probes to radiate heat from the ground to help keep the permafrost frozen.

Icelandic settlers have migrated here because of fishing opportunities. Sturgeon, as well as other commercial fish, are shipped from here to the U.S. A veritable maze of regional waterways focuses on Thicket Portage.

0:00 (1:40) Depart Thicket Portage and look left to see neat little church, complete with bell in belfry and white cross on top.

0:30 (1:10) At milepost 199.5, *Hudson Bay* begins a slow-grinding curl to left and away from main line starting a 30-mile side trip to mining city of Thompson.

1:07 (0:38) Cross Grass River.

1:28 (—) *Hudson Bay* slowly backs into wye, pulls out toward main line, and then slowly backs a mile into dead end at Thompson.

1:45 (0:00) Arrive Thompson's VIA station which is about a mile from downtown. A large Inco smelter, visible in distance, is working evidence of city's mining economy.

THOMPSON, MB - Like Sudbury, Thompson's reason for existing is nickel. Huge ore deposits are mined and processed by Inco Metals Company, which has created a surprisingly large and modern city in Manitoba's Northland (714 rail miles from Winnipeg). Train is normally here long enough to permit a quick trip into town, but first, be sure to verify train's departure time. The station is about a mile from town.

0:00 (1:33) Depart Thompson, retracing 30-mile route back to main line.

1:23 (0:00) Arrive Pikwitonei at milepost 213.

PIKWITONEI, MB - A Cree word meaning "broken mouth," Pikwitonei was once a major construction terminal for the railroad, with a roundhouse and other shop facilities. One of the more substantial-appearing villages along the route, it now survives largely on trapping activities. Canoe access to the region's waterways is also found here.

0:00 (3:10) Depart Pikwitonei, and work still deeper into very heart of Indian country where lifestyles have shown little change across time. Watch for mothers carrying their babies in moss bags and occasional Indian camps along right-of-way.

0:45 (2:25) At milepost 241, powerful Nelson River is crossed at Manitou Rapids. This 612-foot cantilevered span stretches a lofty 110 feet above river below. Waters of Assiniboine, Winnipeg, Red, English and Saskatchewan Rivers, after passing through Lake Winnipeg, all course through this impressive gorge, headed toward Hudson Bay. Whirlpools make these narrows particularly dangerous for canoers. Only significant rock cuts on rail line appear here on each side of chasm.

1:56 (1:14) Train usually stops at Ilford (milepost 285). As populous gathers to pick up mail it is obvious that train's arrival is the social event of the day.

2:18 (0:52) Cross under one of world's longest transmission lines carrying power to southern Manitoba from giant hydroelectric plants near Gillam.

2:58 (0:12) Pass through Luke, a flag stop named for mail carrier and trapper Luke Clemens. Some accounts relate that he was a brother of American author Mark Twain (Samuel Clemens), while others indicate he was a nephew.

3:10 (0:00) Arrive Gillam at milepost 326.

GILLAM, MB - Before construction was started on the nearby Kettle Generating Station in February 1966, Gillam was a village of only 356 people. With the construction and completion of this great hydroelectric facility (1,272,000-kilowatt capacity), Gillam became a thriving community with a population of more than 3,000. The power plant is situated about five miles from here on the Nelson River. Other hydroelectric projects are also located on the Nelson, just downstream from the Kettle plant. Heavily dependent on the railroad, Gillam has no highway link to the rest of Canada.

0:00 (6:55) Depart Gillam.

0:07 (6:48) At milepost 331, cross Nelson River at Kettle Rapids where lights of massive Kettle Generating Station can be seen two miles upstream, to left, while Long Spruce Generating Station is downstream.

Before long, the *Hudson Bay* begins to

traverse lowland coastal plains which are covered with frozen muskeg. Spruce and tamarack become sparse and stunted. This will be most apparent when dawn breaks, sometime before our arrival at Churchill in its bleak and barren setting. Additional nighttime stops are scheduled for villages of **WEIR RIVER** and **HERCHMER** at mileposts 373 and 412.

5:27 (1:28) At milepost 445, landscape becomes barren for some miles until "one-sided" trees reappear near Churchill River. Blowing ice crystals with prevailing northeast winds literally burn all growth off that side of trees.

6:43 (0:12) At milepost 503, first sight of Churchill is afforded on right where enormous grain elevator protrudes above horizon.

6:55 (0:00) Arrive Churchill at milepost 509.

CHURCHILL, MB - Churchill is situated almost 600 miles (approximately 1,100 rail miles) north of Winnipeg on the shores of Hudson Bay, a barren outpost where the modern world meets the Inuit frontier.

In 1688 the Hudson's Bay Company established a trading post near the current townsite, commencing trade with a shipment of eight casks of whale oil to England. In 1732, construction of Fort Prince of Wales was commenced by the British across Churchill Harbor from the present townsite and completed several years later. It was one of the most imposing fortresses in North America. In 1782 a French naval force sailed into the harbor and the fort surrendered without firing a shot. Today it is a National Historic Park which can be reached by boat in the summer when the park is open to visitors.

As western Canada developed its agricultural lands, demand increased for means of exporting grain, bringing about the eventual construction of the Hudson Bay Railroad (now part of the Canadian National system) in 1929, and the Port of Churchill in 1931 whose five-million-bushel grain elevators dominate the Churchill scene.

Perhaps the most unique feature of

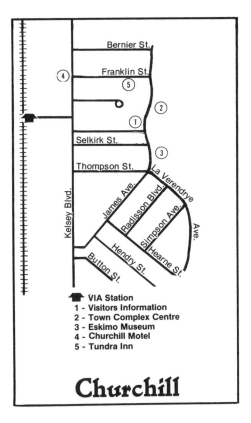

Churchill

- VIA Station
1 - Visitors Information
2 - Town Complex Centre
3 - Eskimo Museum
4 - Churchill Motel
5 - Tundra Inn

Churchill is the annual migration of polar bears through the town in the fall, an event that has been featured in a National Geographic TV documentary.

VIA Station is on the western edge of this compact community. There are no storage lockers, but the baggage room will hold your luggage if you wish. The station is not open the entire day, but is open at train times.

Churchill Taxi, 675-2345. **Rental cars** available at hotels. The **Airport** is near town, with less-than-daily scheduled air service.

Parks Canada has an information center at Bayport Plaza; (204) 675-8863.

There are several motels in Churchill in case you plan to stay overnight. Two of them are:

-Tundra Inn, 34 Franklin, P.O. Box 999,

ROB 0E0; (204) 675-8831 or 800-265-8563. Four blocks from the station. $83. (**Aurora Inn** is under the same management.)
-**Churchill Motel**, Box 218, ROB 0E0; (204) 675-8853. Good restaurant. Free shuttle services, three blocks from the station. $80.

All of the town is within easy walking distance of the station. The **Town Centre Complex** houses numerous facilities used by the residents and visitors alike. Under one gigantic roof are a health center, library, school, swimming pool, curling rink, cafeteria, theater, gymnasium, and other game rooms. Inuit and Indian art work are displayed throughout the complex. The **Eskimo Museum** has one of the finest exhibits of Eskimo art found anywhere.

Parks Canada Interpretive Center, located at Bayport Plaza, has slide shows and live performances in the months of July and August. Slide shows on request at other times. Ask to see their movie about building the railroad to Churchill.

Other points of interest in the Churchill area include **Fort Prince of Wales** (see text above) and **Cape Tatnam Wildlife Management Areas**, with 160 species of waterfowl and other birds.

Tundra Buggy Tours, (204) 675-2121 or 800-544-5049 and **Great White Bear Tours**, (204) 675-2781, have guided polar bear expeditions that last most of the day for approximately $160 Canadian, including lunch.

Station at Churchill, MB
JACK SWANSON

Other Manitoba Service

The following trains are only for the masochistic train buff. Neither has food service.

The Pas-Lynn Lake train makes a ten-hour trip from The Pas, departing late morning on Monday, Wednesday and Friday. The return departs Lynn Lake early morning on Tuesday, Thursday and Saturday.

Wabowden-Churchill has once-a-week service with the trip being interrupted by an extended layover of a day or more in Gillam.

Jasper
Calgary
Vancouver
Kamloops

Rocky Mountaineer

A very popular, private train, the *Rocky Mountaineer* follows the former *Canadian* route along the spectacular CP tracks through the heart of the Canadian Rockies as well as a leg that follows the CN route north of Kamloops to Jasper. The trip is designed as a sightseeing excursion and is scheduled so that travel occurs during daylight hours. At night, passengers enroute stay in hotels at Kamloops.

The western portion follows the Fraser and Thompson canyons between Vancouver and Kamloops. At Kamloops, the train divides into separate sections. One follows the route of the *Canadian* over Yellowhead Pass and past Mt. Robson (the Canadian Rockies' tallest peak) to Jasper, while the other takes the dramatic CP route to Banff/Calgary over Kicking Horse Pass and through the Spiral Tunnels.

Passengers can elect to take one-way trips to either Jasper or Banff/Calgary, or make a round trip which can cover both routes. Accommodations at those destinations are not included in the fare, although Kamloops accommodations are included.

The train carries coaches with high-backed reclining seats and a premium-fare, double-decked dome car. Coach passengers are served meals at their seats while dome-car passengers eat in their own dining room.

Excursions are seasonal only and run from late May through early October. Reservations should be made early: 800-665-7245 or (604) 984-3315.

ROUTE LOG

For route from Vancouver to Kamloops and from Kamloops to Jasper, see log of the *Canadian*, page 339.

Banff/Calgary to Kamloops is shown below with the log running from east to west. Certain towns are shown as stops only to give an easy reference point for the times shown in the log.

CALGARY, AB - Calgary is both the oil and cattle capitals of Canada. Even with its half-million-plus population, there is a cowtown image that Calgary has never really shaken off, an image that lends more than it detracts. This is Canada's Forth Worth.

The magnificent Canadian Rockies are but a stone's throw west of here, where Banff and Lake Louise attract summer throngs and winter skiers. And Calgary has its own annual summer event that draws thousands each July—the famed Calgary Stampede. This world-famous rodeo is the biggest production of its kind.

Station, 9th Ave. at Centre Street, is beneath the Calgary Tower in the heart of downtown.

Yellow **Cab**, 974-1111. Tilden has **rental car** pick up and drop off at the station, 262-6200. **C-Train**, Calgary's streetcar LRT system, which runs through downtown, is two blocks north.

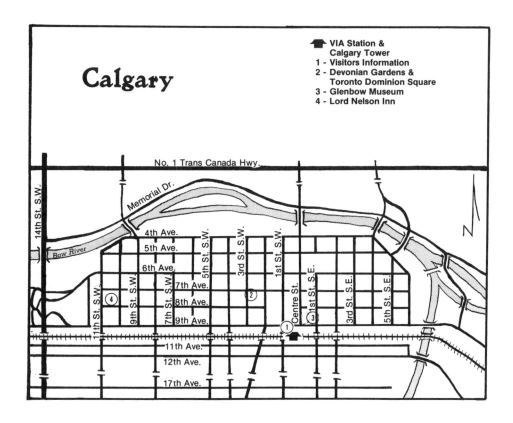

Calgary

VIA Station &
Calgary Tower
1 - Visitors Information
2 - Devonian Gardens &
    Toronto Dominion Square
3 - Glenbow Museum
4 - Lord Nelson Inn

No. 1 Trans Canada Hwy.
Memorial Dr.
14th St. S.W.
4th Ave.
5th Ave.
6th Ave.
Bow River
5th St. S.W.
3rd St. S.W.
1st St. S.W.
7th Ave.
8th Ave.
9th Ave.
11th St. S.W.
9th St. S.W.
7th St. S.W.
4
2
Centre St.
1st St. S.E.
3
1
3rd St. S.E.
5th St. S.E.
11th Ave.
12th Ave.
17th Ave.

Visitor Information Center, main level of Calgary Tower, (403) 263-8510 or 800-661-1678.

Lord Nelson Inn, 1020-8th Ave. SW, T2P 1J3; (403) 269-8262. About a mile from the station on the west edge of town, has large, attractive rooms with refrigerators, non-smoking floors, free underground parking, and, for rail fans, a view of the CP main line. Three blocks to C-Train. $65.

Several worthwhile attractions are within walking distance: the indoor **Devonian Gardens** and **Toronto Dominion Square**, 7th Ave. and 2nd St., with three levels of shopping; the **Glenbow Museum**, 1st St. and 9th Ave., housing beautifully exhibited displays of Western Canadian history and culture, one block from the station; and the **Calgary Tower**, directly above the station, offering a spectacular view of the city and a revolving restaurant.

The **Calgary Exhibition and Stampede** is a rodeo spectacular held each July at Stampede Park and can be easily reached from downtown by the C-Train.

0:00 (2:10) Depart Calgary.

0:34 (1:36) Bow River joins us on right, and will now escort *Canadian* to Lake Louise.

0:45 (1:25) Bearspaw Lake, on right, results from damming of Bow.

1:08 (1:02) View up river, on right, affords stunning panorama of Rockies.

1:13 (0:57) Ghost Lake, denying its appellation, is quite visible on right.

1:31 (0:39) Surprisingly glacial-green waters of Kananaskis River flow beneath us and into Bow. Some of Rockies' most awesome monarchs create formidable-looking barrier on left—but in moments, train will meet their challenge, starting a journey marked by spectacular scenery and some incredible feats of railroad engineering.

1:56 (0:14) Enter Banff National Park, one of most popular recreational areas in Canadian Rockies. Awesome Goat Range dominates scene on left. Keep sharp lookout for mountain goats and sheep, as well as elk, deer and other wildlife.

2:10 (0:00) Arrive Banff.

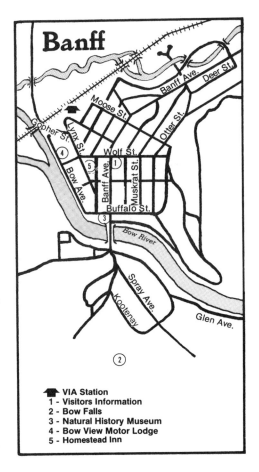

Banff

▲ VIA Station
1 - Visitors Information
2 - Bow Falls
3 - Natural History Museum
4 - Bow View Motor Lodge
5 - Homestead Inn

BANFF, AB - Banff National Park, named after Banff, Scotland, has long been one of the most popular resort areas in North America. Truly spectacular mountain scenery and heavy winter snows combine to attract thousands year-round to enjoy hiking, camping, auto touring, skiing and just plain relaxing.

Station, corner of Elk and Lynx Streets, is on the edge of Banff townsite.

Banff **Taxi**, 762-4444. **Avis** and **Tilden** are about four blocks from the station. The **Greyhound** and **Brewster Tours** bus terminal is a block from the station.

Visitor Information Center is at Wolf and Banff Ave., (403) 762-8421.

Bow View Motor Lodge, 228 Bow Ave., Box 339, T0L, 0C0; (403) 762-2261. Very spacious, bright rooms. Three blocks from the station. $105 (summer).

-**Homestead Inn**, 217 Lynx St., T0L 0C0; (403) 762-4471. Attractive rooms. Three blocks from the station. $109 (summer).

Outdoor activities are Banff's major attractions. Worthwhile museums include the **Natural History Museum**, 112 Banff Ave., the **Banff Park Museum**, 93 Banff Ave., and the Whyte Museum of the Canadian Rockies, 111 Bear St.

The **Banff Springs Hotel**, historic and expensive, is one of the most renowned resorts in the Canadian Rockies and is worth a visit just to see.

0:00 (0:42) Depart Banff.

0:05 (0:37) Looking back to left, whale-shaped mountain looming above Banff is Mt. Rundle.

0:19 (0:23) Massive shape of 9,393-foot Mt. Eisenhower slips by on right.

0:27 (0:15) Castle Mountain is dominant peak at right, just one of an array of spectacular summits that line each side of valley between Banff and Lake Louise.

0:35 (0:07) Famous Valley of Ten Peaks is now visible to left.

0:37 (0:05) At milepost 112, one of highest peaks to be seen on VIA's system is on horizon to left—11,640-foot Mount Temple.

0:41 (0:01) Approaching station for Lake Louise, beautiful Victoria Glacier which hangs directly above lake can be spotted to left.

0:42 (0:00) Arrive Lake Louise.

LAKE LOUISE, AB - This is the gem of the Rockies. The lake, together with its majestic Victoria Glacier, are overlooked by the famous Chateau Lake Louise, but cannot be seen from the tracks.

0:00 (0:47) Depart Lake Louise and commence climb toward Kicking Horse Pass, first of four mountain passes that line route through Rockies. (Rogers Pass, Eagle Pass and Notch Hill will follow in succession.)

0:10 (0:37) Train conquers summit of 5,403-foot Kicking Horse Pass, crest of Continental Divide, as we enter British Columbia and leave Alberta. Also, enter Yoho National Park and exit Banff National Park. Brown sign on left marks Great Divide.

0:16 (0:31) Beautiful Wapta Lake lies nestled on right. Patrons of lodge across lake have fine view of passing train as it glides along lake shore.

0:22 (0:25) Breathtaking view is afforded down valley of Kicking Horse River. Lower Spiral Tunnel can be seen down to right as we descend "The Big Hill."

0:24 (0:21) Enter Upper Spiral Tunnel which makes 288-degree curl to left under Cathedral Mountain. After traveling 3,255

Spiral Tunnels

The Spiral Tunnels were constructed in 1908 and reduced the grade of the track bed from a beleaguering 4.4% to an acceptable 2.2%. The Trans-Canada Highway now claims the former right-of-way. Before the tunnels were constructed, trains had to come to a complete stop at three safety switches that directed runaways to turnouts—like modern-day escape ramps for "eighteen wheelers."

feet in darkness, train will exit and be headed in opposite direction!

0:29 (0:18) Make one of several crossings of tumultuous Kicking Horse River.

0:30 (0:15) Enter 2,922-foot-long Lower Spiral Tunnel beneath Mount Ogden, while making astonishing 226-degree curve to right—coming almost two thirds of full circle.

0:41 (0:04) Pass through mixture of three tunnels and snowsheds.

0:47 (0:00) Arrive Field.

FIELD, BC - Railroading is the reason for Field's mountainside existence. Although the original survey would have placed the railroad above Field, this route was the final outcome. The roundhouse for helper engines no longer stands, but the turntable can still be seen off to the left. Field was named after Cyrus W. Field who promoted the first transatlantic telegraph cable.

0:00 (1:05) Depart Field and continue gradual descent into valley of Kicking Horse River.

0:20 (0:40) Mount Vaux, 10,892 feet, rules over valley on left.

0:28 (0:39) Jagged peak of Mt. Chancellor can be seen to rear on right.

0:32 (0:33) Although train now exits Yoho National Park, glorious mountain vistas continue.

0:38 (0:27) Momentary darkness prevails as train pierces first of several tunnels before arriving at Golden.

1:03 (0:02) Narrow path of Kicking Horse merges into broad Columbia River Valley, nicely backdropped by Dogtooth Mountain Range on left.

1:05 (0:00) Arrive Golden.

GOLDEN, BC - Although the forest industry provides Golden its primary source of income, tourism, for obvious reasons, is also a mainstay. Its central location between the peaks of Yoho and of the Selkirks affords easy access to innumerable hiking trails, fishing streams and lakes.

0:00 (2:54) Depart Golden and trace a course northward through gentle Columbia

Rocky Mountaineer route — Kicking Horse Pass, AB
JACK SWANSON

River Valley.

0:45 (2:09) Columbia River parts company as train swings southward along pretty Beaver River, green with glacial silt.

Gain one hour as train passes from Mountain to Pacific Time. Set your watch back (forward if eastbound) one hour.

1:00 (1:54) Enter Canada's Glacier National Park—one of western Canada's more rugged regions, dominated by Selkirk Range and perpetual ice.

1:06 (1:48) Crossing over Surprise Creek, long, straight cascade will be on right. Trestle is 416 feet across.

1:11 (1:44) Our train performs a "death-defying" crossing, 325 feet above Stoney Creek—Canadian Pacific's highest bridge! When completed in 1885, it was highest such structure in the world. Nice waterfall can be glimpsed up chasm to right, as train edges across bridge's 484-foot-long deck.

1:20 (1:27) Rather than struggle over Rogers Pass, trains go underground, traversing either the Connaught or the Macdonald Tunnel. The *Mountaineer* uses the shorter Connaught Tunnel both directions so passengers can cross the spectacular Stoney Creek Bridge.

1:27 (1:27) At west portal of Connaught Tunnel, note Illecillewaet Glacier clinging to mountainside, high above to left.

1:29 (1:25) Illecillewaet River escorts train in a steady descent from Rogers Pass.

1:34 (1:20) West portal of Mount Macdonald Tunnel is on immediate right.

1:52 (0:59) Three massive snowsheds protect tracks from devastating winter avalanches. At one time there were 31 such

Connaught & Mount Macdonald Tunnels

Eastbound freight trains use the five-mile-long Connaught Tunnel through Sir Donald Range of Selkirks—second longest rail tunnel in Canada. Construction of Connaught was started in 1913 after more than 200 persons were killed in avalanche tragedies on the route over the top between 1885 and 1911. The tunnel was completed in 1916.

Westbound freights use the recently constructed Mount Macdonald Tunnel, which is 9.1 miles long and surpasses the Burlington Northern's Cascade Tunnel (see route of the *Empire Builder* through Washington state) as the longest in North America. It is the seventh longest in the world and cost a whopping $24 million per mile to build, the world's most expensive nine miles of railroad track. This new tunnel reduces the 2.4% westbound grade to less than 1%, allowing CP Rail to avoid using up to 24 helper engines on their westbound freights. The tunnel is lined with concrete, not for structural reasons but to minimize resistance to the elaborate ventilation system's air flow.

sheds protecting descent through Selkirks, totaling five miles in length. Since mountain scenery was important in wooing passenger traffic, original builders installed "summer tracks" outside confining sheds.

2:20 (0:34) Exit Glacier National Park.
2:35 (0:19) Revelstoke National Park borders train on right.
2:44 (0:10) Cross impressive Illecillewaet River that has followed tracks for some time.

2:54 (0:00) Arrive Revelstoke.

REVELSTOKE, BC - In a postcard setting of lush forests, streams teeming with fish, towering mountain peaks on all sides, a ski hill and geothermal swimming, Revelstoke offers something for virtually every taste. The Revelstoke Railway Museum houses a collection of rolling stock and artifacts featuring the history of the CP Railroad.

0:00 (1:49) Depart Revelstoke, with fine view of Mount Begbie and Mt. Macpherson on left. Columbia River, which takes a northerly course around Selkirks rather than through them, is crossed one final time. Route now follows along Tonkawatla River toward Eagle Pass.

0:12 (1:37) Idyllic Wetask Lake on Eagle Pass rests beside tracks on left. CP line now accompanies Eagle River until Sicamous. Supposedly, in 1865, surveyor Walter Moberly discovered pass after sighting eagles flying through this small opening in Monashee Mountains.

0:24 (1:25) View of inviting Clanwilliam Lake is periodically interrupted as three short tunnels are encountered.

0:31 (1:18) Two sturdy snowsheds protect tracks from avalanches as train slips past beautiful Three Valley Lake cradled in Three Valley Gap.

0:32 (1:17) Cross Eagle River. In fall, watch for spawning salmon.

0:33 (1:16) Griffin (or Green) Lake is just to right of tracks.

0:38 (1:11) Castle facade of "Enchanted Forest" tourist stop, on left, makes rather bizarre scene in heart of Canadian Rockies.

0:41 (1:08) Very pretty Kay Falls can be seen cascading down valley side on left.

0:53 (0:56) Here, at Craigellachie, named after a valley in Scotland, final spike was driven into place for last section of trans-Canada railroad. Railroad financier Donald Smith performed honors at modest ceremony (last spike was iron, not gold) on November 7, 1885. Line had taken four and half years to complete. Monument off to right commemorates event at milepost 28.3.

1:09 (0:40) Valley widens in preparation of

Rocky Mountaineer
JACK SWANSON

entering land of Shuswap Lake.

1:14 (0:35) Enter Sicamous where splendid views of Shuswap Lake are first afforded. Here, a swinging span bridge permits boat passage through Sicamous Narrows connecting Shuswap and Mara Lakes. Shuswap has 750 miles of shoreline and is home to both Dolley Varden and Kamloops trout, attracting largest aggregation of houseboats anywhere in Canada, many of which are just to left.

1:16 (0:33) Tracks continue to border serene Salmon Arm of Shuswap Lake.

1:49 (0:00) Arrive town of Salmon Arm.

SALMON ARM, BC - This is the commercial hub of the Shuswap areas, as well as being an agricultural center featuring dairy cows, fruit (apples, strawberries and cherries), vegetables, sheep and poultry. An abundance of tourists in pursuit of water-oriented pastimes will be found during the summer months.

0:00 (1:45) Depart Salmon Arm.

0:02 (1:43) Cross 100 feet above Salmon River, as it nears journey's end at Shuswap Lake.

0:10 (1:35) Brief look is afforded down length of Salmon Arm.

0:38 (1:07) Water on right is westernmost reaches of Shuswap Lake.

0:40 (1:00) Lake briefly narrows into South Thompson from north. Adams is known for its enormous sockeye salmon runs every four years.

1:00 (0:45) Valley continues to widen as farm and ranchlands now blanket valley floor. Watch for occasional canoes plying through broad, still waters of South Thompson on right.

1:16 (0:29) Fields with awning-like shading across valley to left are ginseng farms. Ginseng is a medicinal herb, and the name comes from Chinese words meaning "likeness of a man" (because of the roots' appearance).

1:24 (0:21) At milepost 114, notorious American robber, Billy Miner, held up Canadian Pacific in 1906 and galloped off with only $15 of loot.

1:45 (0:00) Arrive Kamloops.

For route log from Kamloops to Vancouver, see route of *Canadian*, page 341.

Skeena

The superlative lakes and mountains of Jasper National Park and the pristine Coastal Range of British Columbia bedazzle *Skeena* travelers on a wilderness trip between Jasper and Prince Rupert. The ramble along the Skeena River Gorge into Prince Rupert is one of the loveliest excursions on the continent.

The *Skeena* is an all-daylight train during the summer months so that none of the scenery will be missed. This scheduling, however, calls for an overnight stop midroute at Prince George where passengers are responsible for their own lodging arrangements.

WESTBOUND SUMMER SCHEDULE (Condensed)
Jasper, AB - Early Afternoon Departure
Prince George, BC - Early Evening Arrival
Prince George, BC - Early Morning Departure (2nd Day)
Prince Rupert BC - Midevening Arrival (2nd Day)

EASTBOUND SUMMER SCHEDULE (Condensed)
Prince Rupert, BC - Early Morning Departure
Prince George, BC - Midevening Arrival
Prince George, BC - Early Morning Departure (2nd Day)
Jasper, AB - Late Afternoon Arrival (2nd Day)

FREQUENCY - Three times a week, departing both Jasper and Prince Rupert Sunday, Wednesday and Friday.
SEATING - Coach. Also Skyline Dome for First Class passengers.
DINING - Meals (at seats) for First Class passengers only.
BAGGAGE - No checked baggage.
RESERVATIONS - Required for First Class.
LENGTH OF TRIP - 721 miles in two days.

ROUTE LOG

 JASPER, AB - See page 339.

0:00 (3:40) Depart Jasper and head toward Yellowhead Pass.

Some of North America's most magnificent scenery will soon appear! The Trident Range will be on our left and the Victoria Cross Range on our right as we make this ascent. Waterfalls, streams, snowfields and tunnels make this a railroading spectacular.
0:27 (3:13) Those small wire fences, seen here on uphill side of right-of-way, are slide detectors which activate a red signal should there be a rockslide or snowslide.

Gain one hour as train passes from Mountain to Pacific Time. Set your watch back (forward if eastbound) one hour.
0:42 (2:59) Crest of Yellowhead Pass is reached at milepost 17.5. Enter province of British Columbia and leave Alberta. We are only 3,718 feet above sea level, however, many of surrounding peaks soar to more than 11,000 feet. Yellowhead is one of low-

est passes along entire North American Continental Divide. Waters flowing to east ultimately find their way to Arctic Ocean.

0:47 (2:53) Yellowhead Lake stretches serenely beside tracks on left. Yellowhead Mountain is highest peak directly across lake.

1:11 (2:29) Moose Lake now appears alongside at left, even larger than Yellowhead.

1:24 (2:16) Red Pass Junction at milepost 43.9 is where two rail lines divide. One CN line heads to left (south) down Blue River toward Kamloops and Vancouver, while *Skeena* will continue on due west, following route of Fraser River as far as Prince George. After that, Skeena River will be traced to train's final destination, Prince Rupert.

1:42 (1:58) Along this stretch, if sky is clear, passengers are treated to a fine view of Mt. Robson which bolts up at end of a valley on right. A dramatic scene indeed, with snow-fields clinging to its red, stratified face. It's Canadian Rockies' highest at 12,972 feet. Have your camera ready.

2:02 (1:38) Rearguard Falls in Fraser River are formidable obstacle for salmon that come all this way from Pacific Ocean. Falls, however, present a final and insurmountable barrier to salmons' journey. Mountains now start to become less rugged and somewhat softer as train continues westward.

3:21 (0:19) Pass high above Shuswap River.

3:40 (0:00) Arrive McBride.

MCBRIDE, BC - This is the first "city" west of Jasper, having been established during the construction of the Grand Trunk Pacific in 1912. A sportsman's delight, the area offers about any kind of quarry, from Dolly Varden trout to grizzly bear.

0:00 (4:45) Depart McBride.

0:05 (4:40) Below, on right, Oscar's Wildlife Museum makes a bizarre sight with various colored tractor tires for a fence, and a bear and a moose painted on building's side.

0:29 (4:16) Through a tunnel.

4:45 (0:00) Arrive Prince George.

PRINCE GEORGE, BC - Although many rail travelers stop here only to change trains (VIA to British Columbia

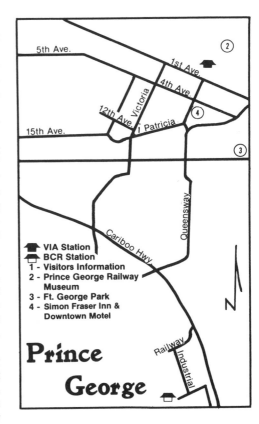

VIA Station
BCR Station
1 - **Visitors Information**
2 - **Prince George Railway Museum**
3 - **Ft. George Park**
4 - **Simon Fraser Inn & Downtown Motel**

Prince George

Railway or vice versa), there is reason to spend a little extra time in Prince George—especially for railfans. A growing rail museum, nurtured by an energetic group of local rail enthusiasts, has an excellent collection of rail cars and equipment, and there's even a small passenger train operation in the city's Fort George Park.

Prince George was little more than a spot on the map until the Grand Trunk Pacific reached this site in 1910. Lumbering and mining contributed to steady growth, and today Prince George is a city still largely dependent on those two industries.

There are two stations in Prince George: The VIA Station, which is on the edge of downtown; and the British Columbia Railway (BCR) Station located on the outskirts of the city, about four miles south of the VIA station.

-**VIA Station**, First Ave. and Quebec, serves VIA's east-west route through central British Columbia.

-**BCR Station**, 1108 Industrial Way. This is a small but very neat station in an industrial area of the city. For information, call 564-9081. There is very limited long-term free parking. The station also has a small gift counter. Write BC Rail Ltd., Passenger Sales & Service, Box 8770, Vancouver, BC V6B 4X6.

Cabs have a direct line at the VIA Station. Prince George **Taxi**, 564-4444. **Rental cars**: Tilden, 564-4847.

Prince George Visitors and Convention Bureau, 1198 Victoria St., V2L 2L2; (604) 562-3700.

Simon Fraser Inn, 600 Quebec St., V2L 1W7; (604) 562-3181. Very attractive rooms. Six blocks from the VIA station. $56.

-**Downtown Motel**, 650 Dominion, V2L 1T8; (604) 563-9241. Small economy motel, six blocks from the station. $52.

The Prince George Railway Museum, off of River Road and close to downtown, has a very fine assortment of rail cars, artifacts and other equipment, as well as a gift shop. The jewel is the Nechaco, a 1913 Pullman that was beautifully restored for EXPO 86. The **Fraser-Fort George Regional Museum**, located in Fort George Park, has a good number of well-displayed artifacts from the region's past. Also in Ft. George Park is the **Ft. George Railway**, offering rides in coaches pulled along a half-mile of track by a Grand Trunk Pacific six-ton work "dinkey," which has unusually small drive wheels that allowed it to operate on very steep grades.

0:00 (1:55) Departing Prince George, follow Nechaco River as it journeys westward toward Vanderhoof and British Columbia lakelands. Country is known for its timber and minerals.

0:55 (1:00) At Isle Pierre, "current ferry" (using stream's force as only source of power) transports vehicles across river.

1:55 (0:00) Arrive Vanderhoof.

VANDERHOOF, BC - This is the geographical center of British Columbia. It is also home to 50,000 geese that find refuge in the adjacent Nechaco Bird Sanctuary.

But each year, the third weekend in July, birds of an entirely different kind gather here when Vanderhoof holds Canada's largest "camp-in" air show. Canadian and U.S. military jets, aerobatics teams, antique fighters and numerous WWII aircraft entertain 20,000 spectators for two exciting days. If you're an airplane fanatic, you'll want to contact: Vanderhoof International Airshow, Box 1248, Vanderhoof, BC, V0J 3A0, or phone 604-567-3144.

0:00 (1:11) Depart Vanderhoof.

0:02 (1:09) Lumbering operations become more evident; Nechaco sawmills are on left.

0:05 (1:06) Huge Westar Timber Plateau operations sawmill is on left.

0:36 (0:35) Just north of Fort Fraser, "last spike" was driven on April 7,1914 to complete Grand Trunk Pacific line. After financial problems, railroad was absorbed into Canadian Pacific.

0:38 (0:33) Cross broad waters of Nechaco River.

0:45 (0:26) *Skeena* now skirts border of Fraser Lake on right. In July, fireweed along right-of-way and in nearby fields produces brilliant splashes of reddish purple.

0:53 (0:18) Lumbering industry remains quite evident as *Skeena* passes Fraser Lake Sawmills.

1:01 (0:10) Cross Stellako River. Its five-mile length reputedly makes it shortest river in province.

1:09 (0:02) Just before Endako, road to left leads to Endako Mine, world's largest open-pit molybdenum mine.

1:11 (0:00) Arrive Endako.

ENDAKO, BC - This is a service center, largely dependent on railroading (it's a division point) and, of course, the aforementioned Endako Mine.

0:00 (0:49) Depart Endako and follow Endako River.

0:37 (0:12) Tintagel Cairn, visible on right (through bushes), contains stone core which

Skeena — Kitwanga, BC
JACK SWANSON

was once part of Tintagel Castle in Cornwall, England. Castle was reputed birthplace of King Arthur (of Round Table fame), and stone was brought here during Canada's centennial in 1967 to help preserve community's heritage. Cairn also contains time capsule to be opened in 2067.

0:42 (0:07) Body of water, on left, is Burns Lake.

0:49 (0:00) Arrive Burns Lake.

BURNS LAKE, BC - Originally, Burns Lake was a mere telegraph relay cabin along the Collins Overland Telegraph Line. But when the railroad arrived in 1908, it gained civilized substance. Today Burns Lake is an important recreational outpost. Rockhounding is also popular, with large opal and agate deposits located nearby.

0:00 (1:07) Depart Burns Lake.

0:11 (0:56) Decker Lake now extends along tracks on left. Babine Lake, longest natural body of water in province, is just north of here, but too distant to see from train. With such a proliferation of lakes, moose are common to the area and can often be spotted

along right-of-way.

1:07 (0:00) Arriving Houston, "World's Largest Flyrod," on left, just east of visitors center, is obvious statement about region's most popular sport. Also, note sawmill display on west side of visitors center.

HOUSTON, BC - This community is the home of two giant lumbering companies, one of which, Northwood Pulp and Timber, has the largest enclosed sawmill in the world. Tours are available. Mining and tourism round out Houston's economy.

0:00 (1:02) Depart Houston through farm- and ranchlands, set scenically amidst Bulkley River Valley. Peaks of Coastal Range loom in distance, soon to escort *Skeena* on final leg into Prince Rupert.

0:01 (1:01) Stark, white-frame Christian Reformed Church faces tracks on left.

0:03 (0:59) Just west of Houston, tracks that veer off to left serve those two huge sawmills, mentioned just above. Here, Morice River flows into Bulkley.

0:45 (0:17) Pastoral splendor of Bulkley River Valley is epitomized by area surrounding Telkwa where dairy cows, green pastures

Route of the Skeena — Port Edward, BC
JEFF KARSH

and hay meadows are backdropped by towering Hazelton Mountains.

0:48 (0:14) Through Telkwa, one of oldest communities in valley, where Telkwa and Bulkley Rivers meet.

1:02 (0:00) Arriving Smithers, Hudson's Bay Mountain on left is regally graced with Kathlyn Glacier.

SMITHERS, BC - Established in 1913 as a division point on the Grand Trunk Pacific, Smithers was the first village to be incorporated in British Columbia. It is now the Valley's trading center. In 1979, most Main Street businesses were given a facelift and bear a resemblance to a Bavarian village—blending nicely with the town's alpine setting. Smithers' visitor center occupies what was once a buffet club car on the CN line between Toronto and Montréal.

0:00 (1:14) Departing Smithers, challenging golf course on right annually hosts prestigious Labor Day tournament.

0:08 (1:06) Handsome homes dot shoreline of Lake Kathlyn on right, with reflection of Skeena Mountains cast majestically across water. Skeenas are subclassification of Coastal Range. To left is impressive Kathlyn Glacier, cradled in Hudson Bay Mountains.

0:20 (0:54) High Bridge across frothy Trout Creek is first of several dramatic spans soon traversed.

0:30 (0:43) Pass through Moricetown, largest Indian village in Valley. East of here, Bulkley River squeezes through narrow gorge called Moricetown Canyon, where Carrier Indians still "subsistence fish" for salmon. Carriers once used fish traps (no longer legal); now, they fish with long gaffing poles, spearing these large fish with utmost skill.

0:40 (0:33) On right, Bulkley River descends into gorge—a preview of exciting canyons awaiting downstream.

0:42 (0:31) Rail buffs should seize opportunity to photograph train as it winds gracefully (to right) across towering Boulder Creek trestle. A short distance downline, bridge across Porphyry Creek affords similar possibilities.

0:59 (0:15) From high atop rocky ledges, train now embarks on inspiring four-mile adventure through cuts and tunnels of magnificent Bulkley Canyon. Below, cliffs compress Bulkley River into a surging torrent of white water. On opposite bank, waterfalls tumble down into river, further enhancing this spectacular stretch.

1:14 (0:00) Arrive New Hazelton.

NEW HAZELTON, BC - Three towns are clustered together here (New Town, Old Town and South Town) as well as myriad nearby Indian villages—all of which make up the area called "The Hazeltons." Indian lore pervades the region, and a reconstructed Indian village from the early 1900s can be explored. Numerous totem poles—one said to be the world's oldest—are found throughout the area. The area is famous for its stylized West Coast Indian art, sought after by international collectors.

0:00 (2:16) Depart New Hazelton. On left, imposing peaks are some of region's tallest, extending 8,000 feet above sea level. Mount Rocher Déboulé, with its 3,000-foot cliffs, dominates.

0:08 (2:08) Trestle across Sealy Gulch is not for faint-of-heart, perched nearly 200 feet above deep gorge.

0:10 (2:06) On right, Bulkley River has emerged from canyon and now carves swath through verdant pasturelands. In distance, Hazelton Mountains frame this most picturesque setting. Shortly downstream, Bulkley River flows into Skeena River, descending from north.

0:35 (1:41) Cross Skeena River which then borders route on left into Prince Rupert. On opposite bank, quaint little town of Nash makes enchanting centerpiece of scene seemingly plucked from travel poster.

0:48 (1:28) Kitwanga, A *Skeena* flag stop, is starting point for Stewart-Cassiar Highway which winds through wilderness north of here and traverses some of most spectacular scenery in British Columbia. Kitwanga is

Indian for "people of the place where there are rabbits." One of region's many totem poles is on left, immediately after passing burned-out rail station.

0:58 (1:18) Beautiful farmhouse adorns landscape on right at Woodcock. Jagged, dramatic Seven Sisters Range is at left, with seven very pronounced peaks.

1:06 (1:10) Old post office and general store are venerable structures seen on left at Cedarvale. An independent mission was established here in 1888. Its effectiveness earned town nickname "The Holy City," and for many years absolutely no work was performed on the Sabbath.

Descending gradually toward sea level, proceed along the scenic Skeena River Valley, with awesome glaciers stretched atop nearby peaks. At trackside, colorful mosses and ferns soften the terrain—a remarkable contrast to the rugged alpine climes looming just above.

1:41 (0:34) Old hotel is nostalgic relic on right at Pacific, now struggling to support its own weight.

1:59 (0:17) At Usk, note another "current ferry" that shuttles between homes on riverbanks. Flow of stream forces cable-guided craft from one side to other, while sign on far side instructs motorists to call for service by either ringing gong on pole or honking horn.

2:16 (0:00) Arrive Terrace.

TERRACE, BC - The largest community between Prince George and Prince Rupert is the center of large lumbering operations as well as government, transportation and service industries. Visitors will find much of interest in the region, including lava beds, fossils, hot springs—and as always throughout the province—fishing. A 92 1/2-pound salmon was taken by a rod and reel from the *Skeena* near here, a world record.

0:00 (2:10) Depart Terrace. Two more totem poles will appear at right.

0:04 (2:06) Cross Kitsumkaylus River, first of countless tributaries swelling Skeena River enroute to Pacific Ocean. Mountains of Kitimat Range now border route on both sides.

0:48 (1:22) Stretch between mileposts 39 and 50 features several sets of spectacular waterfalls, cascading down near trackside. (Mileposts are conspicuously tacked on adjacent poles.)

1:01 (1:09) All that remains of Kwinitsa are two small sheds. Lovely little station that once stood at trackside was moved to Prince Rupert where it now serves as railroad museum near Prince Rupert's VIA station.

1:27 (0:43) Rustic fishing piers on left are entrenched in general area where freshwater and saltwater begin to mix. At this point, river has widened to near half-mile breadth. Watch for harbor seals that sometimes frequent this segment of river.

1:37 (0:33) Fishing industry quickly takes center stage approaching Prince Rupert. Villages at Cassiar, Sunnyside and North Pacific are surrounded by colorful assemblage of boats, with daily harvests proudly displayed across docks. Waters now broaden into Chatham Sound, encircling Smith, Lelu and Ridley Islands.

1:47 (0:23) Cross bridge onto Kaien Island, home of Prince Rupert. Continue along docks, past terminals for Alaska and British Columbia ferries.

2:10 (0:00) Arrive Prince Rupert, its depot tucked neatly within rocky cove.

PRINCE RUPERT, BC - When you come to Prince Rupert, bring your raincoat. Its location on Kaien Island, where the Skeena River dumps into the Pacific, accounts for many misty days—some more misty than others. Even the Chamber of Commerce does not deny that the city gets more than its share of rainfall; they simply call it the "City of Rainbows."

But it's part of the atmosphere that makes Prince Rupert a bit like a miniature San Francisco—dazzling floral displays in the town parks, neat clapboard homes shelved on the hillsides, an interesting waterfront complete with fishing fleets and seafood eateries, and some gorgeous harbor sunsets. Yet more travelers are here to catch ferryboats: ferries to Seattle and Vancouver Island to the south; ferries up Alaska's Inside Passage to the north; ferries to the

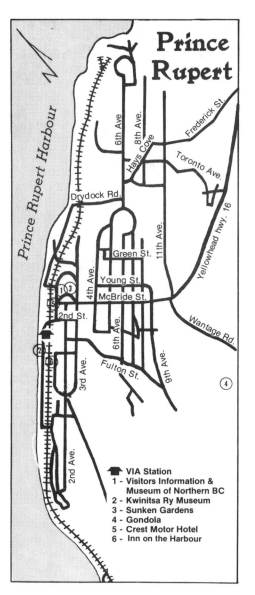

Prince Rupert

▲ VIA Station
1 - Visitors Information & Museum of Northern BC
2 - Kwinitsa Ry Museum
3 - Sunken Gardens
4 - Gondola
5 - Crest Motor Hotel
6 - Inn on the Harbour

Queen Charlotte Islands to the west.

VIA Station is situated on the harbor, directly below downtown. For reservations and other information, call 800-561-8630.

Skeena **Taxi**, 624-2185. Tilden and Budget **rental cars** are in the Rupert Square Mall next to the Inn on the Harbour. **Alaska State Ferries** sail

Current ferry — Skeena River
JACK SWANSON

northward up the scenic Inside Passage and southward to Seattle. **British Columbia Ferries** offer service south to Port Harvey on Vancouver Island, as well as the Queen Charlotte Islands.

Prince Rupert Visitors Bureau is located at 1st Avenue and McBride St. in the Museum Building. Call (604) 614-5637.

Those motels shown below are in the downtown area. If you plan to walk to any of these accommodations from the station, be prepared to climb. A cab is recommended.

-Crest Motel Hotel, 222 West 1st Ave., Box 277, V8J 3P6; (604) 624-6771 or 800-663-8150. An outstanding hostelry, complete with an elegant dining room, on a bluff overlooking the harbor. $95 to $105 (seaside).

-Inn on the Harbour, 1st Ave. and 6th St., Box 700, V8J 3V6; (604) 624-9107. Excellent downtown location, overlooking the harbor with adjoining restaurant. $60.

The following are in the downtown area. Be sure to visit the city's **Sunken Gardens**, small but immaculate; and **Service Park**, again small but colorful. **Sunsets** on the harbor, weather permitting, can be spectacular. The very fine **Museum of Northern British Columbia**, with exhibits of Indian and regional culture, is at the visitors center. And next to the VIA station is a small but wonderful **Railroad Museum** in the former Kwinitsa depot, depicting how life used to be for those who worked and lived in those remote outposts. It contains an excellent telegraph exhibit. For a commanding view of the town and the harbor, ride the **gondola** to the top of Mt. Hays, a few minutes by car from downtown.

Prince George
Lillooet
Vancouver

Cariboo Prospector

S omehow, Norway's rugged and spectacular fiords have been magically transported to Canada. Self-propelled Dayliners (rail diesel cars) of the incredible British Columbia Railway brush along the water's of Howe Sound as lofty peaks soar overhead. Traveling 461 miles from North Vancouver to Prince George, the railroad wends through ever-changing scenery, ranging from that just described to the more arid interior mountains of British Columbia.

Note that this train uses the BCR stations in North Vancouver and Prince George—not the VIA stations. See North Vancouver (below) for ticket information.

NORTHBOUND SCHEDULE (Condensed)
North Vancouver, BC - Early Morning Departure
Squamish, BC - Early Morning
Lillooet, BC - Early Afternoon
Williams Lake, BC - Late Afternoon
Prince George, BC - Late Evening Arrival

SOUTHBOUND SCHEDULE (Condensed)
Prince George, BC - Early Morning Departure
Williams Lake, BC - Late Morning
Lillooet, BC - Midafternoon
Squamish, BC - Early Evening
North Vancouver, BC - Midevening Arrival

FREQUENCY - Daily, each direction between Vancouver and Lillooet; Sunday, Wednesday and Friday, northbound contin-

ues on from Lillooet to Prince George; Monday, Thursday and Saturday, southbound from Prince George to Vancouver.
SEATING - Rail diesel car coaches, nonsmoking.
DINING - Tray meals included on all trains at no extra charge.
BAGGAGE - Checked baggage handled on all trains. Baggage for flag stops where agents are not on duty must be claimed from train baggageman before arrival.
RESERVATIONS - Reserved seats are required on all trains.
LENGTH OF TRIP - 461 miles in 13 1/2 hours.

ROUTE LOG

**NORTH VANCOUVER, BC** - North Vancouver, just across Burrard Inlet from Vancouver, is the southern terminus of the BCR.

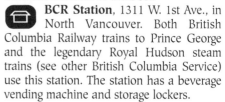**BCR Station**, 1311 W. 1st Ave., in North Vancouver. Both British Columbia Railway trains to Prince George and the legendary Royal Hudson steam trains (see other British Columbia Service) use this station. The station has a beverage vending machine and storage lockers.

Call (604) 631-3500 or 800-663-8238 for reservations and information. Inquire about bus service from Vancouver to station.
0:00 (1:16) Depart North Vancouver.
0:01 (1:15) On left is graceful Lions Gate Bridge. Look back on right where Royal

Hudson Steam Train can often be seen poking out from BCR shops.

0:06 (1:10) Cross Capilano River at confluence with English Bay on left.

0:10 (1:06) In late summer, bay frequently has dozen or more freighters waiting for berths to load Canadian grain for export.

0:12 (1:04) Dense, lush foliage contrasts nicely with modernistic high rises and beautiful homes of affluent West Vancouver. This is considered to be most expensive real estate in Canada.

0:23 (0:53) A long tunnel (1,700 feet) precedes first view of magnificent Howe Sound on left. Immediate waters are Horseshoe Bay. Area is renowned for its salmon fishing. Dock for ferries to Vancouver Island is below.

0:33 (0:43) Dome of 5,330-foot Mt. Wrottesley dominates opposite shore.

1:02 (0:14) Britannia Beach, at milepost 30, is where mining and smelting operations once stood at base of 6,645-foot Mt. Sheen. Barren top of 6,815-foot Mt. Sedgewick is forward on left, across bay.

1:08 (0:08) Forward on left is sharply defined Mt. Garibaldi, looming 8,786 feet above Squamish.

1:13 (0:03) On right, at milepost 39, is Stawamus Chief—reputed to be second largest rock in world. Monolith is a favorite with rock climbers who pit their skills (and luck) against its massive granite face, which rises 2,138 feet above the bay. Facility across bay is wood fiber plant.

1:16 (0:00) Arrive Squamish at milepost 40.

SQUAMISH, BC - Being situated at the northern tip of Howe Sound, near Garibaldi Provincial Park and the northern terminus of the Royal Hudson steam train, it is understandable why tourism is big business in Squamish. BCR locomotive shops are located here.

0:00 (1:05) Depart Squamish where rails follow route of Squamish River. Peak bolting up on right is Mt. Garibaldi.

0:09 (0:56) Commence through beautiful Cheakamus Canyon at milepost 47.

0:25 (0:40) Blue-green color of Cheakamus River on right is typical of mountain glacial streams. Cheakamus Canyon now becomes even more dramatic.

0:30 (0:35) Scenery is absolutely stunning, with Cheakamus Range sporting beautiful glaciers, back to left, and falls gracing canyon at right.

0:50 (0:15) Train will sometimes slow down at this point for better view over top of Brandywine Falls which plummet 280 feet to valley floor, below right.

1:05 (0:00) Arrive Whistler.

WHISTLER, BC - Quaint chalet architecture pervades this year-round resort, where skiing is the major attraction. The name Whistler comes from the marmot, a woodchuck which lives in the mountains and gives off a loud, shrill noise resembling a whistle.

0:00 (0:40) Depart Whistler.

0:02 (0:38) At Alta Lake, train crests summit of Coastal Range at 2,199-foot elevation (milepost 74). From here a gradual descent leads to fertile Pemberton Valley where root crops, such as potatoes and turnips, thrive.

0:04 (0:36) Blackcomb ski runs cut swaths down Blackcomb Mountain on right.

0:09 (0:31) At milepost 79, long and narrow Green Lake on left has 7,000-foot Rainbow Mountain for fine backdrop.

0:35 (0:03) Cascades of Green River rapids and then Nairn Falls add to charm of grand entrance to Pemberton.

0:40 (0:00) Arrive Pemberton at milepost 95.

PEMBERTON, BC - This is the major trading center for the lush Pemberton Valley. It was near here, along the Lillooet River, that early-day prospectors streamed by, seeking their fortunes during the gold-rush days. Massive Mount Currie towers above valley on right, at 8,364 feet.

0:00 (2:05) Depart Pemberton and cross Lillooet River.

0:06 (1:59) At milepost 99, pass through flag stop of Mt. Currie, serving one of British Columbia's largest Indian reservations.

0:10 (1:43) Train is now escorted by Birkenhead River until its arrival at Birken at top of Cascade Range.

0:24 (1:41) At milepost 109, Number Ten

Cariboo Prospector — Lillooet, BC
JACK SWANSON

Downing Street is curious location (and quarters) for British prime minister. House was built by war veteran who settled here and then worked as a mountain guide. Names of various battles in which he fought serve as exterior decor.

0:33 (1:32) At Birken, Birkenhead Provincial Park is in mountains just to left.

0:48 (1:17) At milepost 123, train begins journey along 15 miles of Anderson Lake shoreline, on right.

0:52 (1:11) Views are momentarily taken away as train cuts through a short tunnel.

0:58 (1:07) At milepost 129, McGillivray Falls can be glimpsed behind homes on left.

1:18 (0:47) Seton Portage, at milepost 139, lies between Anderson and Seton Lakes, and was site of first railway in province. Wooden rails were used to portage boats between lakes!

1:24 (0:40) Into darkness again, this time traveling through tunnel for 2,940 feet—a tunnel built to avoid landslides that once plagued this stretch of trackage. Emerge along banks of lovely Seton Lake, nestled between Mt. McLean on left and Cayoosh Range across lake. Penstocks, those giant tubes on left, bring water from higher elevations to power hydroelectric plant of B.C. Hydro and Power Authority. Seton Lake is darker than Anderson, due to glacial silt introduced through penstocks.

1:28 (0:35) At milepost 142, Shalalth was gateway to placer gold mining of Bridge River more than 100 years ago. (This type of hydraulic mining obtained gold from gravel deposits and is pronounced "plass-er.")

During school months, children board train here to be transported to Lillooet. Note colorful Indian murals on each end of shelter.

1:58 (0:07) At north end of Seton Lake, 9,200-foot Mt. Brew towers above valley on right.

1:59 (0:06) Dam, on right, has fish ladder for convenience of salmon heading upstream to spawn.

2:02 (0:03) Entry into Lillooet affords excellent view of BCR hopper cars being filled with woodchips from adjacent sawmill on right.

2:05 (0:00) Arrive Lillooet.

 LILLOOET, BC - Located at the confluence of the Fraser River and

Cayoosh Creek, placer mining during the last century made Lillooet, pronounced "Lil-loo-ET," a boom town of the gold-rush era. It was also an important provisioning point on the Cariboo Highway that led to the north. In spite of its mountain setting, temperatures frequently soar above 100 degrees during the summer, which partially accounts for the fine crops of watermelon, vegetables and fruit that are grown here.

0:00 (2:44) Depart Lillooet.

0:04 (2:38) Suspension bridge below right, built in 1903, is one of oldest of its kind in western Canada.

0:05 (2:37) Cross Fraser River, spanned by attractive silvery-steel bridge, and commence steep climb out of canyon for next 30 miles, gaining 3,000 feet in elevation before emerging on Cariboo Plateau at Kelly Lake.

0:11 (2:33) Below left, two fish ladders have been constructed in Fraser. Fish drying racks of natives are usually quite apparent through this area of canyon.

0:29 (2:11) Irrigated fields across valley are used to grow ginseng, a medicinal herb. Ginseng comes from Chinese words meaning "likeness of a man" because of the roots' appearance. It takes four years to produce a crop.

0:36 (2:04) After basic depot at Pavilion, a steady ascent is made, some of the most difficult and spectacular railroading in North America!

0:48 (1:42) At milepost 183, after passing through Moran, Fraser River snakes through canyon, a dizzying 2,678 feet below.

1:02 (1:32) Kelly Lake, at milepost 193, rests in a glorious setting, with Marble Range forming a most scenic backdrop on left. This is edge of great cattle country of the Cariboo.

1:20 (1:12) Through flag stop of Clinton, center of ranching, where renowned Clinton Ball is held each May during town's annual rodeo.

1:32 (1:00) At milepost 215, flag stop of Chasm is aptly named for a deep canyon nearby, formed at close of ice age when a stream from melting ice cut through lava-formed Fraser Plateau. Both rims of chasm will be visible in a moment on right.

2:07 (0:25) At milepost 243, Horse Lake is heart of guest ranch country and is highest point on British Columbia Railway, 3,864 feet above sea level. From here, train begins a gradual descent into cattle country of Williams Lake through forested, rolling countryside interspersed with open fields and meadows.

2:11 (0:21) Pride of Lone Butte is nicely restored railroad water tower, on right, at north edge of community.

2:22 (0:08) Exeter, our next stop, is below right.

2:28 (0:00) Arrive Exeter.

EXETER (100 Mile House), BC - This pretty little village is a trading and distribution hub for local ranching and lumbering activities.

0:00 (1:27) Depart Exeter.

0:16 (1:10) Herd of buffalo can sometimes be seen grazing on right.

0:20 (1:00) Peaceful waters of Lake LaHache stretch along tracks on right from milepost 274 to 281.

1:04 (0:12) Waters of Williams Lake are on right.

1:16 (0:00) Arrive Williams Lake at milepost 314.

WILLIAMS LAKE, BC - This is the "Cattle Capital of British Columbia," with thousands of critters being shipped, not only to Canada but also to the U.S. Lumber is also important, with large mills in and around the city.

0:00 (1:28) Depart Williams Lake.

0:23 (1:05) An airy crossing of Deep Creek takes place at milepost 331 on one of world's highest railway bridges—a 1,200-foot span, 312 feet above water.

0:30 (1:00) Soda Creek, at milepost 541, marks the point from which venerable river steamers plied Fraser River to Prince George and back—a 260-mile round trip.

1:29 (0:04) On outskirts of Quesnel, Western Plywood plant processes lumber into multi-layered wooden sheets of construction plywood.

1:33 (0:00) Cross Quesnel River on arrival Quesnel.

QUESNEL, BC - This city, pronounced kwah-NELL, serves as a regional trade center, and is home for several lumber-oriented industries.

0:00 (1:53) Depart Quesnel.

0:02 (1:49) String of lumber mills and pulp plant attest to Quesnel's claim to be one of largest lumber producing cities in world.

0:06 (1:47) Enormous gold pan, pick and shovel greet highway travelers, on left.

0:27 (1:33) At milepost 400, cross Cottonwood River Bridge which carries train a lofty 234 feet above that river. In 1921, Pacific Great Eastern Railroad (BCR's predecessor) hoped to cross farther downstream and form a link between Quesnel and Prince George. That attempt was thwarted by unstable soil, and it wasn't until 1952 that this spot was crossed at a cost exceeding one million dollars.

0:31 (1:22) At milepost 406, cross Ahbau Creek where silver spike ceremony at north end of bridge celebrated completion of Quesnel-Prince George section.

1:00 (0:53) Canyon Creek Bridge, at milepost 426, was once scene of feverish placer mining activities.

1:33 (0:20) From milepost 451 into Prince George, train is escorted by impressive Fraser River.

1:40 (0:13) Pull past lumber mills of Prince George on approach to that city. Then BC Rail yards appear at left.

1:53 (0:00) Arrive Prince George.

 PRINCE GEORGE, BC - See page 361.

Other British Columbia Service

Royal Hudson steam trains run from North Vancouver along Howe Sound to Squamish and return, Wednesday through Sunday, from early June through mid-September. 1-800-663-8238.

Whistler Express carries passengers in rail diesel cars from Whistler to Kelly Lake (just beyond Lillooet), Monday through Friday during the warmer months. 1-800-663-8238.

The *Malahat Dayliner* runs six days each week (no Saturday Service) northbound and seven days each week southbound between Victoria and Courtenay on Vancouver Island. Service is provided by rail diesel cars. Sandwiches and beverages can be purchased at Nanaimo and Courtenay during station stops. Be sure to purchase tickets early; summer weekends are particularly busy. Check with VIA for current schedule.

Mexico's Copper Canyon

TRAIN TRAVEL IN MEXICO has become so uncertain that extensive coverage of rail service in this country is no longer included in *Rail Ventures*. Discontinuance of dining cars and most sleepers, general deterioration of equipment and difficulty in obtaining reliable schedule information has made Mexican train travel impractical for all but the most venturesome.

Traveling by rail through Mexico's spectacular Copper Canyon region, however, still does remain a viable option. Certain travel agents can book Mexican train reservations, as well as accommodations, and at least one private American train offers first-class Canyon tours out of Tucson, Arizona.

Nearly 100 Years in the Making - The line was originally conceived in the late nineteenth century by private interests in the United States as a link between the Mexican port of Topolobampo on the Pacific Coast of Mexico and Midwestern U.S. markets. However, it was not until November 1961 that the final connection was made between Creel and San Pedro in the heart of the remote mountains of northwestern Mexico. This culminated a 50-year effort on this section alone, and was completed only after the Mexican government, with the expenditure of millions of dollars, took over the project. Although it has never become the major freight line envisioned (tying Kansas City with the Pacific), it does provide important access to marvelous scenery and a place where nearly 50,000 Tarahumara Indians live, a people who are recognized for their unusual running abilities.

What's in Store - The route (Chihuahua to Los Mochis) offers what is often cited as the most scenic train trip in North America (and occasionally called the most scenic in the world). Passage stirs the emotions of even the most galvanized traveler. Numerous waterfalls, multi-colored cliffs and canyons, tropical fruit trees, 37 bridges and 86 tunnels highlight this journey. The rails follow a tortuous 300-mile route from mile-high Chihuahua, crossing over the Sierra Madre Occidental Mountains while reaching an altitude of 8,071 feet, and finally descending to Los Mochis at sea level. The highlight is the canyon itself, which is four times the size of the Grand Canyon!

When traveling from Chihuahua to Los Mochis, the trip starts out on a serene note, passing through farmland, much of which was settled in the early part of this century by Mennonites from Canada. Scenes are quintessential Mexico, with antiquated farm machinery pulled by oxen or burros here and there. But later, the character of the land changes, with lumbering activities in evidence and tropical orchards and wildflowers enhancing the countryside. Soon the train enters Creel, the major trading center for the Tarahumara Indians. After Creel, the terrain is quite rugged, and shortly before reaching Divisadero Barrancas, the journey's midpoint, the tracks actually cross over themselves while making a complete loop to gain elevation.

Copper Canyon
DORIS SWANSON

At Divisadero passengers get one of the best views of the Barranca del Cobre—the Copper Canyon. (It obtained its name from the copper mines that operated in the canyon, not from its color.) Forested, sloping sides descend to more tropical areas near the bottom where one can make out the Urique River. If you look carefully, you may be able to see some of the cliff dwellings of the Tarahumara. Baskets, drums, violins and other hand-made objects are sold by the Tarahumara at trackside.

Farther downline, the deepest part of the canyon can be seen from the train, turning thoughts to track maintenance (fortunately, it *is* well-maintained). Then, a bit later, the train passes next to a spectacular waterfall above Temoris. And the view looking down at Temoris, two hairpin curves below, is startling. Tunnels and trestles abound as the final descent is made to Sufragio, the intersection with the Pacific Railroad and just 40 minutes from the end of the line at Los Mochis.

If You Go - Since the altitude is quite high for long segments of the trip, warm clothing is advisable, especially during the cooler months of the year. Also, if booking on the Mexican train, keep in mind that more spectacular scenery viewing occurs during daylight hours when going from Los Mochis to Chihuahua rather than the reverse. This is particularly true during the shorter days of winter.

Several options are available when making arrangements to go, two of which are described here. For those who would prefer a first-class (bordering on deluxe) tour, contact Sierra Madre Express of Tucson, 800-666-0346. This company offers eight-day tours by private train, using sleeping cars, specially designed "patio" cars and a dome-diner. (Please note that your editor has a small equity interest in this company.) If you prefer taking the Mexican train, Town & Country Tours (Phoenix, AZ) can arrange either independent or six-day escorted tours of the Canyon, 800-528-0421.

Equipment

IN THE UNITED STATES

Virtually all of Amtrak's rolling stock has been designed and built within the last several years. Long-distance trains west of the Mississippi River are equipped with bi-level Superliner cars giving passengers the ultimate in roominess, comfort and unobstructed, high-level viewing of the landscape. It is their height, however, that prevents this equipment from being used in parts of the East where clearances pose a problem. The East is served by Amfleet and Superliner equipment, depending on the routes. Also, newly designed and built Viewliner equipment is being phased into service.

Amfleet - This was the first new equipment to go into service in the Amtrak era. These cars use a strong tubular-shell body and produce a reasonably smooth and quiet ride—with a sleek, almost futuristic appearance. Designed for shorter and medium distance trips, Amtrak has, on occasion, also had to press them into service for longer hauls on some eastern routes. The newer Amfleet II design has larger windows and more spacious seating for those longer runs. Amfleet includes coaches, diners and cafe cars but no sleepers.

Standard Amfleet coaches have reclining seats but no leg rests on the shorter hauls. Overhead luggage storage, reading lights, attractive appointments and rather small windows create an airliner atmosphere. Longer haul Amfleet cars use reclining seats with leg rests and allow more leg room by installing fewer seats per coach.

Club seating has only three seats to a row, two on one side of the aisle and one on the other, giving a special luxurious effect. Attendants furnish food and beverage service at your seat with more elaborate menus than those available at the cafe counter. Of course, club fares are higher than coach.

Amdinettes have a cafe counter and tables for light, hot meals and snacks. Trays can be taken to the tables or to coach seats, and some trains offer food service at the tables. Amcafes are coaches with a food and beverage counter in the middle, also offering light meals, sandwiches and other snacks.

Superliners - Coaches are roomy and attractively designed with tasteful appointments. Reclining seats are wide, offer plenty of leg room and have both leg rests and footrests. Large windows provide excellent viewing and individual overhead reading lights add to the luxury. Folding trays, ala the airlines, are also provided. Luggage can be stored overhead as well as beneath the seats, and extra luggage storage compartments are on the lower level just as you enter. Besides upper-level seating, several seats are on the lower level and are available to handicapped travelers who would find the circular climb to the upper level an obstacle. Rest rooms are also on the lower level.

Most sleeping cars have five deluxe bedrooms, 14 economy bedrooms, a family bedroom and a special handicapped bedroom. Each sleeper has one unisex bathroom upstairs and several downstairs. There is also a shower on the lower level.

Deluxe bedrooms extend almost the entire width of the car, are on the upper level, have two beds for sleeping two to three people, and include an enclosed bathroom that even has a shower. During the daytime there is a sofa and swivel chair for seating. These bedrooms are lettered A through E, with A at the end and E near the middle.

Economy bedrooms sleep two and are extremely compact, but aisle windows give them a more roomy appearance. These have two berths sleeping a total of two and having facing couches during the day. There is also a very thin closet, a fold-down table and individual comfort controls. Luggage storage is virtually nil. There are no in-room toilet facilities. Economy bedrooms one through ten are on the upper level with the lower numbers toward the center of the car while 11 through 14 are downstairs, again with the lower numbers toward the center.

If you choose an Economy Bedroom, viewing is pretty much limited to one side of the train only, unless the compartment occupants across the aisle cooperate by leaving their drapes open. With a Deluxe Bedroom, there is no compartment across the aisle, only an outside window, and viewing in both directions is fairly good.

The family bedroom is quite spacious, is on the lower level and has room for up to three adults and two children but no toilet facilities. The handicapped "special" bedroom is on the lower level, can accommodate a wheelchair, will sleep two adults and has a specially equipped rest room. Meals will be delivered to these special rooms.

Bedrooms, particularly for summer or holiday travel, should be reserved well in advance.

Lounge cars offer splendid viewing from swivel, upper-level chairs through windows that extend from almost floor level upward and wrap into the ceiling overhead. Downstairs there are tables and a snack bar. The viewing from the upper level of these cars is superb.

Diners have seating for 72 persons at 18 tables, all on the upper level. The kitchen is on the lower level with an elevator arrangement for delivering food to the dining area.

Viewliners - A long testing and development phase has ended for Amtrak's newest rail cars, a period which saw prototype sleepers that combined the best of Superliner technology and comfort. These are single-level cars (to allow for Eastern clearances) with two rows of windows that give upper berth occupants their own viewing portals. Sleepers have 14 compartments (double or single), two deluxe bedrooms (with showers) and a handicapped bedroom. Every room has a sink and a toilet as well as luggage storage space under the seats and over the aisles. Aisle-side windows give both the room and aisles a more spacious feeling. Besides sleepers, there are also coaches and diners.

Horizonliners - These coaches and diners were initially put into service on the busy shorter routes out of Chicago (including to Detroit) and *San Joaquin* service in California. The windows are small, like Amfleet I, but instead of Amfleet's confining tubular construction, the sides are flat with a brushed aluminum exterior.

Turboliners - Certain service in New York state is supplied by racy Turboliners. These sleek beauties provide streamlined service between New York City and upper New York State. Designed to run in a five-car consist, power is supplied by diesel-electric "power

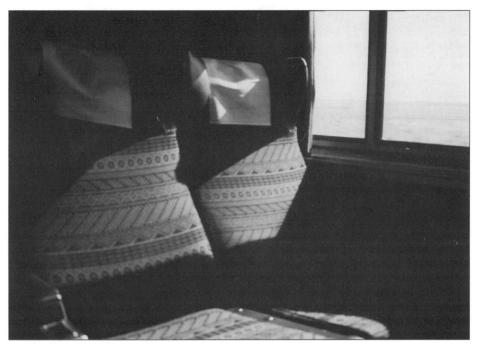

Superliner coach
JACK SWANSON

coaches" at both the front and rear of the train. The center car offers food service and the last car usually has a 2-1 seating configuration, draped windows and Custom Class service. This section is reserved seating and, although more expensive, would be the best choice during the busier holiday seasons. Regular coaches are unreserved and are in standard rows of four.

California Cars - As their name implies, these cars were built and developed for use in the state of California. They are in operation on the Bay Area *Capitol* trains, some of the *San Jouquin* trains and some may be used in San Diego service. These are bi-level coaches with rather narrow seats that recline only slightly, while seat backs are low enough to allow good viewing. Upper-level luggage storage is in airline-style bins above the seats. Larger luggage can be stored downstairs at boarding level.

Metroliners - Metroliner Service, Amtrak's high-speed Northeast Corridor service, is provided by specially equipped Amfleet cars pulled by Swedish-designed (but U.S. built) electric locomotives.

Heritage Fleet - Fortunately, nearly all of this older equipment, which Amtrak inherited and then refurbished, has been retired. The few sleepers left in operation are due to be discontinued as soon as replacements are available.

IN CANADA

Sleeping Cars - Canadian sleeping cars offer bedrooms sized to accommodate one, two or three persons and also "sections" with upper and lower berths using only drapes between the aisle and berths for privacy. During the daytime, all sleeping accommodations become seating areas for their nighttime occupants.

Single bedrooms (formerly called roomettes) have rest room facilities which, unfortunately, cannot be used once the bed is lowered. Additional rest room facilities are available at the end of the car.

Double and triple (formerly known as drawing room) bedrooms use upper and lower berth arrangements and have a wash basin and a toilet that can be used regardless of the position of the beds. There are overhead storage spaces for luggage and small closets with rather limited space for hanging clothes. Adjoining double bedrooms can be used as a four-person room by opening a common wall between the two bedrooms.

Sections, during the daytime, are two facing couches open on the aisle side and make into upper and lower berths at night with heavy drapes between the berths and the aisle. Rest rooms are located at the end of the cars.

Coaches - Traditional Canadian coaches are equipped with reclining seats which have leg and footrests. Luggage can be stored overhead and often at one end of the car. Rest rooms are located at one end of the car, generally with ample room for changing clothes. Their heavy construction gives them an extremely smooth ride.

Dome cars - VIA Canada dome cars are especially equipped coaches and observation cars with a separate raised seating area in the center of the car. Here, passengers look out of a second-story greenhouse, so to speak, with an unobstructed view of the landscape as well as the entire train.

On VIA's transcontinental trains, rear-end observation domes are called Park cars, each named for a national park, while mid-train domes are known as Skyline cars.

LRC Trains - Canada is using these trains in their Corridor service. LRC's (Light, Rapid, Comfortable) are designed for high-speed service in heavily populated areas, and have an innovative "power-banking" system that allows a higher speed on curves as the train automatically tilts to the inside. Besides their speed, extreme smoothness of ride is a characteristic.

Rail Diesel Cars - These are in limited use in Canada. As their name implies, they are self-propelled, diesel-powered coaches, each having the capability of traveling in either direction. Seats are reclining, but no leg rests, and there are folding trays similar to the airlines. The British Columbia Railway uses these RDC's exclusively, and VIA uses them for service between Sudbury and White River. (Some limited use of these cars is also made by the Alaska Railroad.)

Appendix

Telephone Numbers for Reservations and Information*

AMTRAK

Boston, MA	(617) 482-3660
New York City, NY	
(all 5 boroughs)	(212) 582-6875
Philadelphia, PA	(215) 824-1600
Washington, DC	(202) 484-7540
All other U. S. locations	1-800-USA-RAIL
	1-800-872-7245
From Canada	1-800-872-7545
For Metroliner Service only	1-800-523-8720
For Group Travel	
(minimum 15)	1-800-872-1477
Hearing impaired persons	
with access to a	
teletypewriter can call	1-800-523-6590

VIA RAIL CANADA

Newfoundland:
St. John's, Gander, Grand Falls,
   Corner Brook, Stephenville,
   Bishops Falls. Call your Travel Agent
   or nearest CN Roadcruiser office.

All Other Locations	1-800-561-3926

Prince Edward Island:

All Locations	1-800-561-3952

Nova Scotia:

Halifax	429-8421
All Other Locations	1-800-561-3952

New Brunswick:

Moncton	857-9830
Saint John	642-2916
All Other Locations	1-800-561-3952

Québec:

Montréal	989-2626
Québec City	692-3940
All Other Locations	1-800-361-5390

Ontario:

Hamilton	522-7533
Kingston	544-5600
London	672-5722
Ottawa	244-8289
Toronto	366-8411
Windsor	256-5511
Other Area 519, 613, 705	
and 905 Calls	1-800-361-1235
All Area 807 Calls	1-800-561-8830

Manitoba, Saskatchewan, Alberta,
   British Columbia,
Yukon and Northwest

Territories:	1-800-561-8630

People with speech or hearing problems
   may communicate through
   telecommunication devices for the
   hearing impaired.

The access numbers are:

Toronto Area	368-6405
All Other Locations	1-800-268-9503

USA: For VIA train information or
   reservations in the USA, contact your
   Travel Agent or call l-800-561-3949.

* **Use the telephone number appearing**
   opposite the city, state or province
   from which you are calling.

Index